The Challenge of Truth

Reflections on *Fides et Ratio*

EDITED BY JAMES McEVOY

PREFACE BY CARDINAL CAHAL DALY

VERITAS

First published 2002 by
Veritas Publications
7/8 Lower Abbey Street
Dublin 1
Ireland
Email publications@veritas.ie
Website www.veritas.ie

ISBN 1 85390 695 6

Cover design by Bill Bolger
Printed in the Republic of Ireland by Betaprint Ltd, Dublin

*Veritas books are printed on paper made from the wood pulp of
managed forests. For every tree felled, at least one tree is planted, thereby
renewing natural resources.*

*To the Rector, priests and students
of the Down and Connor Seminary
at St Malachy's College, Belfast*

When people cease to believe in God,
they do not believe in nothing
but in anything at all.

G. K. Chesterton

CONTENTS

CONTRIBUTORS

Cahal Brendan Daly was born in Antrim in 1917. He was a *peritus* at the Second Vatican Council and has been a bishop since 1967. He was made Cardinal by Pope John Paul II in 1991. He is Archbishop Emeritus of Armagh and has published and broadcast widely.

Thomas Kelly is a Doctor of Philosophy of the Université de Fribourg and a lecturer in Philosophy at NUIM. He is president of the Irish Philosophical Society.

Francesca Murphy is a Reader in Divinity and Religious Studies at Aberdeen University. She has published specialised studies in theology and literature.

Timothy Mooney holds a PhD from the University of Essex and lectures in Philosophy at UCD.

Thomas Norris, a priest of the Diocese of Ossory, lectures in Dogmatic Theology at the Pontifical University, Maynooth, and is a member of the International Theological Commission.

James McEvoy is a priest of the Diocese of Down and Connor and Dean of the Faculty of Philosophy at NUIM. He is Director of the Irish Centre for Faith and Culture.

Patrick Gorevan is a PhD of the Pontifical Athenaeum Santa Croce and author of several published studies in philosophy. He is a chaplain to third-level students in Dublin.

Mette Lebech studied at the University of Copenhagen and the Université Catholique de Louvain. She lectures in Philosophy at NUIM.

Kevin Doran is a PhD of the Gregorian University and an expert on the philosophy of Karol Wojtyla. He holds pastoral appointments in Dublin Archdiocese.

Bruno Forte is Professor of Dogmatic Theology at the Catholic Faculty of Naples and a member of the International Theological Commission.

Brendan Purcell lectures in Philosophy at UCD. He is a priest of the Archdiocese of Dublin and is the author of books and journal articles on philosophical anthropology and politics.

PREFACE

Cardinal Cahal Daly
Archbishop Emeritus of Armagh

The Irish Centre for Faith and Culture was formally opened by Bishop Donal Murray on 1 December 1997. It is one of a number of such Centres set up across the world in recent years. Each of them is autonomous, but all are engaged in activities similar to those of the Pontifical Council for Culture in Rome. That in turn results from the fusion of two Pontifical Councils instituted by the Pope in 1982, namely the Council for Culture and the Council for Dialogue with Unbelievers. These were merged in 1993 into a single Council for Culture whose President is Cardinal Paul Poupard.

The term 'Faith and Culture' was used by the Second Vatican Council in its Pastoral Constitution on the Church in the Modern World *(Gaudium et spes;* see Chapter II, §§ 57-62). The Council acknowledged the positive values present in modern culture, such as

> scientific study and strict fidelity towards truth in scientific research, the necessity of working together with others in technical groups, a sense of international solidarity, an ever clearer awareness of the responsibility of experts to aid people and even to protect them, the desire to make the conditions of life more favourable for all, especially for those who are deprived

of the opportunity to exercise responsibility or who are culturally poor.

It declared that 'these values can provide some preparation for the acceptance of the message of the Gospel'. At the same time the Council pointed to the defects of modern culture, including a tendency to regard science and its methods as the criterion for all truth and to foster a spirit of agnosticism about all other knowledge, and particularly about religious and moral truth. The Council called for new efforts to cultivate the human spirit 'in such a way that there results a growth in its ability to wonder, to understand, to contemplate, to make personal judgements and to develop a religious, moral and social sense'. The Council called upon the members of the Church to strive for a new relationship with the people of their own generation who are not members of the Church, and try to have a balanced understanding of their ways of thinking and feeling. It asked the faithful to 'blend modern science and its theories and the understanding of the most recent discoveries with Christian morality and doctrine'. It urged them thereby to ensure that 'their religious practice and morality can keep pace with their scientific knowledge and with an ever-advancing technology', and thereby be able to 'test and interpret all things in a truly Christian spirit'. Much of the agenda of the Irish Centre for Faith and Culture is contained in these words of the Council.

Pope Paul VI called 'the split between Gospel and Culture without doubt the drama of our time'. He concluded that 'therefore every effort must be made to ensure a full evangelisation of culture, or more correctly of cultures'. 'They have to be regenerated', he said, 'by an encounter with the Gospel'.

Pope John Paul II has made the evangelisation of culture one of his favourite themes. It is interesting in this regard to recall that Archbishop Wojtyla was closely involved, at an important stage, in the drafting of *Gaudium et spes,* and also that he has frequently expressed his admiration for his predecessor Pope Paul VI. He has himself, however, further developed the notion of the evangelisation of culture in new directions. He has stressed that it demands not only the proclamation of the Gospel in all cultures, but also dialogue between faith and all the many expressions of culture as well as all the agencies that help to shape and form culture. The new evangelisation so often called for by Pope John Paul II is to be addressed not just to individuals and communities, but to cultures and to the culture-forming institutions and agencies, such as universities, the sciences and technologies, the media, the cinema, drama, the arts, poetry and literature generally. In modern society, particularly in the West, these institutions are often either indifferent to religion or hostile to it, and their indifference or hostility helps to shape public attitudes, making them either uninterested in or resistant to religious thinking. This is the context in which the Christian faith has to be lived and transmitted.

Evangelisation and dialogue with culture are, therefore, closely linked. The Christian faith has itself, as a matter of historical record, been, ever since its first proclamation, a creator and shaper of culture. It has had a role in laying the moral foundations for democratic societies. It has helped to create and sustain the corpus of moral values and the principles of justice, fraternity and solidarity that underpin civil society and that lead to true human flourishing, even in such areas as trade, business and international relations. The Christian faith has inspired much of the world's greatest architecture, art and literature. It has left its imprint on the languages and literature of much of the world. Many of the great classics of world literature cannot be understood without knowledge of the Christian faith and of the Bible. The Christian faith has influenced the development of philosophy and has had an important role in the origins and development of science and medicine. For all those who share that faith and who seek to share it with others and to transmit it to future generations, the questions of faith and culture in today's post-modern society are therefore of vital importance. The Pontifical Council for Culture and the various national Centres for Faith and Culture seek to be a resource in this whole field. They seek to be open to all who work in the culture-forming institutions, or in the culture-related fields of art and literature, or in the world of media, politics or business.

The Irish Centre is one of the more active of such centres. It originated from an initiative of the Irish Episcopal Conference. Its Director is Father James McEvoy, Professor of Philosophy at the Pontifical University of Maynooth and at the National University of Ireland, Maynooth. Its Secretary is Reverend Dr Eoin Cassidy, Professor of Philosophy and Registrar at Mater Dei Institute, Dublin. A short list of its achievements to date gives some idea of the breadth of view with which it interprets its remit, and of the range of its interests. The Centre has published a report commissioned by the Irish Catholic Bishops Drugs Initiative, with the title, *A Faith Response to the Street Drug Culture*, edited by Dr Eoin Cassidy (Irish Centre for Faith and Culture, 2000). The same Centre organised a conference on *Prosperity with a Purpose: What Purpose?*, whose papers were collected and edited by Eoin Cassidy and published in a book with that title (Veritas, 2000). Dr Cassidy has also co-edited (with Donal McKeown and John Morrow) *Belfast: Faith in the City* (Veritas, 2001), and published 'Religion in the Inner City' (*The Furrow*, Feb 2001, pp. 101-109).

The present volume is a collection of the papers delivered at a Colloquium on Pope John Paul II's Encyclical, *Fides et Ratio*, held at Maynooth on 19 and 20 May 2000. The papers cover many aspects of the relationships between revelation and reason, philosophy and theology, philosophy and reason as doorways to faith, faith as a spur to rational exploration; and the influence of Edith Stein and of Max Scheler on Karol Wojtyla's philosophical and spiritual journey and the challenges and problems of Christian mission today, and on the bearing of the encyclical *Fides et Ratio* upon the future of Europe.

The volume is an indication of the relevance of the Irish Centre for Faith and Culture to contemporary problems and interests in Ireland and internationally. Its publication will, it is hoped, generate wider interest in the Centre and its work. Doubtless, it will be followed by further conferences and publications on other aspects of the multiple relations between faith and culture. It is essential that the voice of the Church and of Christian faith be heard in contemporary debates about moral and religious issues in the Irish, European and globalised worlds of today. The Irish Centre is well situated to give expression to that voice.

I am pleased to have been asked to write a preface for the volume. I believe that readers will find here inspiration for that sense of opportunity and of urgency for which the present Pope has called in his Encyclical on the Church's missionary mandate in today's world, *Redemptoris Missio*. After pointing out that the number of those who do not know Christ and do not belong to the Church has doubled since the end of the Second Vatican Council, the Pope goes on to say that, 'on the other hand, our own times offer the Church new opportunities in this field'. He goes on:

> God is opening before the Church the horizons of a humanity more fully prepared for the sowing of the Gospel. I sense that the moment has come to commit all of the Church's energies to a new evangelisation and to the mission *Ad Gentes*.

The response to the Pope's call demands intellectual reflection as well as faith and hope and love. The 'seeds of the Gospel' in cultures and in human reason and the human heart and its aspirations, in the human search for meaning and for hope, in art and literature, and in scientific and philosophical enquiry, need to be identified and need to be given a favourable environment in which to grow. This volume will help to inspire new responses to the appeal of the Pope in his most recent encyclical at the beginning of the new millennium, *Novo Millennio Ineunte,* for 'pastoral initiatives adapted to circumstances [e.g. of Ireland today] so as to bring Gospel values to bear on society and culture'.

INTRODUCTION

James McEvoy

The Encyclical Letter of Pope John Paul II concerning Faith and Reason was first published on the internet (a sign of the times) on 14 September 1998, the Feast of the Exaltation of the Holy Cross. Because it discusses issues such as faith and culture, the nature of truth, philosophy and seminary education, and the purpose of theology, this encyclical has been studied more by intellectuals and in specialist journals than in newspapers and pastoral magazines. Yet it serves in many ways as a key to the thought of the Holy Father, and a clue to his method and procedure in the twelve other encyclicals he has previously issued, such as *Evangelium Vitae* and *Veritatis Splendor.* That in itself would justify its study and examination, even if no regard were to be paid to the future and what the latter may hold in store. In reality this encyclical may be expected to retain its worth for generations to come, such is the basis it lays for the intellectual life of the Catholic Church.

Fides et Ratio (*F&R*) is a very personal encyclical: that is something on which most commentators agree. The Pope's own lifelong interest in philosophy marks the letter as a whole and stamps itself upon its every chapter. Is it the Pope's own work? Many are consulted, both in Rome and throughout the Catholic Church in the course of the preparation of a major document, but there is evidence to suggest that John Paul II took an active and major part in shaping the final document. This letter had a very lengthy gestation, going back to the early years of the pontificate. The addressees of the letter are (as always) principally the bishops of the Catholic Church in communion with Rome. They are reminded in this case of the practical encouragement they are required to lend to teaching and research institutions that may be present in their dioceses and provinces.

Of the thirteen encyclicals issued up to now in the course of the present pontificate, the letter on Faith and Reason has the most direct impact on faith and culture, and hence on the work of the Irish Centre for Faith and Culture, which is located in St Patrick's College, Maynooth. The claim is made in the encyclical that divine Revelation has been granted as a universal message destined for every culture on earth. Each culture expresses in its own way the universal human search for meaning and for truth. The absolute claim to truth that is made by Christianity on the basis of Revelation does not level cultures downwards or deny them their diversity, but through evangelisation places instead a novelty at the heart of each of them, a novelty that is able to go to the roots of each culture and become the source of new growth and new life, in short of cultural vitality. The novelty in question is, of course, Jesus Christ.

* * *

Under the auspices of the ICFC and the Pontifical University Faculty of Philosophy a colloquium was held at St Patrick's College, Maynooth entitled 'The Diakonia of Truth: An Exploration of *Fides et Ratio*' (20-21 May, 2000). The expression 'Diakonia of Truth' appears in the encyclical itself. (*Diakonia* is the Greek word for 'service'). The papers delivered there form the core of the present book, whose editor wishes to express his thanks to each of the conference speakers, especially those who came from outside of Ireland, namely Monsignor Bruno Forte (Naples) and Dr Francesca Murphy (Aberdeen). Additional

authors have since been recruited in order to complete the picture
regarding the encyclical, and equal thanks are due to each of these.
Cardinal Cahal Daly, Archbishop Emeritus of Armagh, merits the
thanks of the editor in particular degree for agreeing to write a preface
to the book, as well as for the chapter he has contributed to it, despite
all the pressures upon his time which travel and many engagements
create. The organisers of the colloquium would like to express their
appreciation to Archbishop (now Cardinal) Desmond Connell for
graciously agreeing to preside over the opening of the event, and also
to Mgr Dermot Farrell, President of St Patrick's College and of the
Pontifical University, for lending encouragement to their efforts and
for chairing the closing session. The Maynooth Scholastic Trust and
the ICFC both made grants to defray the expenses of the conference
and help with the costs of publication, and deserve the sincere thanks
of the editor. Ms Ann Gleason lent help with the preparation of the
contributions for publication, and is gratefully acknowledged.[1]

* * *

This collective work follows a plan in three parts. In the first of these,
four professionals from the fields of philosophy and theology get to
grips with the central perspectives of the encyclical and endeavour to
explain its message, which may be summarised in brief terms, as
follows. Both disciplines, philosophy and theology, make their best
contribution to wisdom when they are integrated in the mind of the
Christian believer. There they are not schizophrenically separated.
Each retains its specific character, neither disfiguring the other, neither
borrowing the other's clothes. Each is what it is. Neither ever replaces
faith, which is based beyond rational discovery, upon God's self-
revelation. Provided that the two disciplines are integrated (and not
simply mixed) in such a mind, then they cease to be simply two
unrelated disciplines and two methods. They become dynamically-
interacting partners in the search for truth, and also in its exploration
and expression.

What role has philosophy in particular played in the life and thought of the man who became Pope in 1978? The second part of the book consists of four explorations of the intellectual journey which the young Karol Wojtyla made as a worker, a seminarian and a young priest at Lublin and Rome. One contribution is journalistically biographical, telling the story of his early acquaintance with philosophy, while the others explore his intellectual indebtedness to phenomenological philosophy and the relationship of his thought to it, in the critical discernment he made of that movement, and the features of personalism which mark his thinking in notable ways, as Pope and author of encyclical letters.

The intellectual effect of *F&R* will be with the Church for a very long time; in all probability it will not be overhauled for several generations to come. Even when it is, it will continue to influence its successor documents probably in much the same way as *Aeterni Patris* (1879) and the Second Vatican Council have influenced *F&R* itself. The third section of this book recommends certain perspectives opened by the letter, regarding European culture, world cultures and religions, and the strengthening of dialogue among people of good will regarding human dignity and development. In an epilogue, some gleanings from the reception of the encyclical are quoted (in translation where necessary) and considered, to show in what specific ways it has evoked comment and even provoked some criticism.

* * *

Much thought has gone into the composition of *F&R*, with the result that the encyclical repays slow reading. If read at a gallop it might appear difficult, even confusing. Nietzsche, by the way, gave a valuable injunction about the art of reading when he remarked, 'Die Philologie ist die Kunst, langsam zu lesen; die wahre Goldwiegekunst': Philology is the art of reading – slowly; it is the true art of weighing gold!

Words of St Bonaventure (chosen from *The Journey of the Soul to God*) are quoted at the close of *F&R* (Conclusion, #105). The

Franciscan invited his own reader to recognise the inadequacy of 'reading without repentance, knowledge without devotion, research without the impulse of wonder, prudence without the ability to surrender to joy, action divorced from religion, learning sundered from love, intelligence without humility, study unsustained by divine grace, thought without the wisdom inspired by God.'[2] The same invitation is extended to every reader of *F&R*.

The usefulness of this collective work will be judged by its authors in terms of the appetite it arouses in its readers for the serious study of *F&R*, which is a seminal writing comprising a series of challenges that go in intent far beyond the confines of the Catholic Church, and indeed of Christianity.

Notes

1. Sincere thanks are returned to Dr Thomas Kelly for his revision of the translation of Mgr Forte's paper, and to Mr Hugh O'Neill for helping with the proof-reading of the entire volume.
2. Saint Bonaventure's *Itinerarium Mentis in Deum*. With an Introduction, translation and commentary by Philotheus Boehner OFM, NY, 1956; Prologue #4, p. 33.

PART I

Reason and Faith, Philosophy and Theology in
Fides et Ratio

INTELLEGO UT CREDAM: REASON AND PHILOSOPHY IN RELATION TO FAITH

Thomas Kelly

Introduction

In this paper, I shall concentrate on the third chapter of *Fides et Ratio* (*F&R*), which takes as its title *intellego ut credam,* and shall examine the coming together of faith and reason from the perspective both of reason, and of that vital expression of the life of reason that is philosophy. My treatment will attempt to identify and amplify some of the major themes of this rich work, and will be divided into four parts: firstly, I begin with the conception of human transcendence which is mediated in this chapter of the encyclical; secondly, I continue via an analysis of the nature of truth, the goal of all rationality; thirdly, I consider those existential tensions and issues which are inherent in the life of human reason, and in our aspiration to truth; and in the fourth place, I consider faith as the natural completion of philosophy. Together, I suggest, these themes from *F&R* constitute the portrait of a rationality that is inherently philosophical, and also coevally God-centred and authentically human. I trust that it will also become clear in the course of my presentation what direction I think the encyclical indicates for any philosophical investigation to take if that investigation is genuinely to deserve the title 'love of wisdom'.

The Restless Heart

Though nowhere quoted explicitly, Augustine's cry, in the first chapter
of the first book of the *Confessions,* 'Thou hast made us for Thyself,
and our hearts are restless until they rest in Thee',[1] echoes throughout
this chapter of the encyclical. To say that the human heart is restless in
this way is to say that the very nature of the human person contains,
indeed *is,* an impetus beyond the flux of immediate experience and the
transient satisfactions which the resources of its world and itself can
provide, towards something that can assuage an existential longing.

Even when we attain all we ever wanted, we are aware that the
passage of time deprives us of what we have. To awaken philosophically
is to be aware of our vulnerability and of the inevitability of death, our
own and that of those we love. To have this awareness – and it may only
be forced on us by bereavement or by some other 'limit experience' – is
to know the unawakened state for a fool's paradise.[2] We are forced to face
the possibility that only vacuity lies ahead of us, that our life is lived in
suspension over the void, and that all we cherish and all we long for is
ours, if at all, for but a little moment, and even when ours, may bring
us only disillusionment and disappointment. Our small needs and
longings must seem futile and absurd before this emptiness, and our
delights and solaces are disrupted by the very possibility of their
disruption. In the face of the awful reality of suffering and despair, can
our brief and threatened existence have a meaning, or is it but 'a tale told
by an idiot, full of sound and fury, signifying nothing', as Macbeth feels
it to be? We are constantly threatened by the possible absence of
meaning, by a descent into futility, and thence into despair.

Must we accept this vision as unalterable, and can we only resolve
to brave the shocks existence deals us until, eventually, we cease to be?
Should detachment and endurance be our key, indeed our only,
virtues? It is only on an absolute foundation that life can achieve
meaning and coherence, that is, only on a foundation that does not
share our vulnerability and contingency. And it is here that our
greatest vulnerability is revealed, for our search for such a foundation
is capable of being interrupted and tragically misdirected.

This is an awareness that all at some time find to be theirs, and some always. It is this paradoxical, or better, metaxic, situation that gives birth to the search that is philosophy: a search for what, if anything, can still the restless yearning that is the human heart. And this idea of rest, of a place wherein desire is assuaged, and where there is a final end to striving and to pain, is a dominant note in this chapter, in the encyclical as a whole, and indeed in the entire teaching of John Paul II. To use the Pope's own words:

> ... people seek an absolute which might give to all their searching a meaning and an answer – something ultimate, which might serve as the ground for all things ... a final explanation, a supreme value, which refers to nothing beyond itself and which puts an end to all questioning. ... there comes for everyone the moment when personal existence must be anchored to a truth recognised as final ... which confers a certitude no longer open to doubt. ... What inspires all these [that is, philosophers and non-philosophers alike] is the desire to reach the certitude of truth and the certitude of its absolute value.[3]

The martyrs, we are likewise told, found the truth about life in the encounter with Jesus Christ, and 'nothing and no-one could ever take this certainty from them.'[4] It would be worth dying for such a still point, for if we could attain it, any loss could be braved, and with equanimity. Ultimately, such a still point must be the truth of what it is to be human: the kind of truth that led the Greek philosopher to survey the wreck of his fortunes and the calamity that overtook his city and his family, and to say with serenity, 'I have lost nothing'. Yet what is this truth? To ask, to live, that question is, at last, to do philosophy, and the examined life, the only life worth living, is to live in, to live out, that question. As Camus famously remarks, the only serious question is that of suicide.

Yet this truth, though we do not possess it, is not distant from us: it is the truth of what we are, of what the human 'between' is. To move towards it is not to traverse a vast, foreign distance, which could be travelled without our finding it: it is to know the place that we already inhabit for the first time. This place, this between, is, precisely, between the truth and the void, and it is this suspension that constitutes the transcendence proper to the human person, if by transcendence is meant the overcoming of existential ignorance, our stretching-out towards this unknown, but not alien, truth. This is a fundamental point, not only for our consideration of this text, but also for our philosophical understanding in general. Let us therefore keep the metaphor embodied in the word 'transcendence' before us during what follows. Transcendence comes from the Latin *transcandere*, which means 'to step over'. The metaphor then, is one of surpassing, of stepping beyond a limit, and that in a given direction, and as a continuing process. Or perhaps, and more profoundly, as an always being-beyond, being ever beyond this, or any, limit.

The reality of human transcendence is a *leitmotiv* of this encyclical, but so also is the finitude that is coeval with transcendence, which is the fundamental tension of our situation: we transcend but can do so only as limited. We go beyond, we are not already beyond, our limit. We are lovers, desirers, seekers, and not possessors of wisdom, a point brought out by the diverse yet similar origins in Greek of the words 'philosopher' and 'sophist'. Unlike the sophist, the expert, the spin-doctor, we don't have all the answers, which we can pass on for a fat fee. The serenity that we experience in friendship with wisdom is one that can only accompany the labour of the search. Truth, the truth of the person, attracts us precisely in and through its absence, an absence that is not a sheer privation, but a hope and a promise given in and as the very capacity to know, which is rationality. As the encyclical, to my mind elegantly, puts it:

> Human beings would not even begin to search for something of which they knew nothing or for something they thought was wholly beyond them. Only the sense that they can arrive at an answer leads them to take the first step.[5]

And further:

> Everyday life shows well enough how each one of us is preoccupied by the pressure of a few fundamental questions and how in the soul of each of us there is at least an outline of the answers.[6]

There is something of which a radical and profound ignorance is impossible. There are inklings, there are hints, there are traces to be followed. Here there is no equivalent of tone deafness and colour blindness, or the blank incomprehension when we find our selves face-to-face with the truly alien, with the non-human, with what Heidegger might call the merely present at hand. Existential questions are bridges that lead, not into the gulf of nescience, but into what is already dimly and obscurely glimpsed from where we now stand, however clouded this apprehension may be by ignorance and error, and crossing these question-bridges to the territory that both the content and the structure of the question intend, is the core of what transcendence means.

Human existence, it is not too far-fetched to say, is this question, is this bridge: to be is to ask what it means to be, to ask, what our ultimate fate is, and what we may hope for. These are what Pope John Paul calls the serious questions, which make human beings truly what they are, and he tells us that 'they are questions which express the urgency of finding a reason for existence, in every moment, at life's most important and decisive times as well as more ordinary times'.[7]
The Pope emphasises the dignity and responsibility inherent in this existential situation. The dignity is honoured by him in the claim, traditional in Catholicism and rendering the Faith hospitable to philosophical inquiry, that human reason is capable, in and of itself, of knowing something of God, that is, of establishing the existence and reality of that absolute goal of human longing and striving. Though we are, of course, incapable by ourselves of establishing ourselves in the divine life of grace, or of knowing transcendent divine truths without

revelation, we can at least espy, however dimly, what the Pontiff calls that ulterior truth that would explain the meaning of life. The responsibility as well as the dignity inherent in our situation is also honoured by the Pope in the recognition that our search is an expression of our most profound liberty. In this way, the search is truly ours, and belongs to us as free and sovereign persons, even while it arises from the deepest tendencies of our nature. The Pope addresses this human depth as the deep reasonableness of our existence, since this free and rational search as he puts it, 'summon[s] human intelligence and will to search freely for a solution which can reveal the full meaning of life.'[8]

In a passage in the *De Vera Religione*, which speaks profoundly to us of this human between, Augustine advises us *noli foras ire, in teipsum redi*,[9] go not outside, return into thyself. In this extraordinary and, for philosophical enquiry, I would suggest, programmatic, passage,[10] Augustine bids us rise above the mutable, rise even above ourselves, and strive by reason to go beyond reason, to attain to that place where the light of reason itself is lit. For the heart of rationality is Being, and rationality is no more, but certainly no less, than our ability to know and love Being, in short, our ability to *be* in Being.

I find this transcending movement that Augustine describes to be identical to the rational and existential movement portrayed in the encyclical in the following terms:

> when *the why of things* is explored in full harmony with the search for the ultimate answer, then human reason reaches its zenith and opens to the religious impulse. The religious impulse is the highest expression of the human person, because it is the highpoint of his rational nature. It springs from the profound human aspiration for the truth and it is the basis of the human being's free and personal search for the divine.[11]

It is in this fruitful and deeply suggestive passage that the Pope approaches an issue that is dear to the hearts of metaphysicians, and is, if I may say it, a preoccupation of my own. The issue is this: a person is essentially a metaphysical animal. Metaphysics is not the name of a philosophical discipline merely, but the word for the most fundamental and constitutive movement of the human spirit, one that takes us beyond, *meta*, mutable and temporal reality, *ta physika*, and leaves us face to face with Being itself, which is coevally existence and person. This is good news in the truest sense of *Euaggelion*, which anticipates and makes possible the hospitable reception of a deeper Good News. It is untrue that what is not built on the foundation of radical despair is without foundation of any kind, and is thus the most stupid form that dishonesty can take, namely self-deception.

It is this movement beyond the temporal, I argue, which constitutes human transcendence. I shall not defend or elaborate this view here and now,[12] but I find it to be one of the motivating themes of *F&R*; though I find it throughout the encyclical, I find it most succinctly and clearly expressed as follows:

> There is therefore a path which the human being may *choose* to take, a path which begins with reason's capacity to rise beyond what is contingent and set out towards the infinite.[13]

Here freedom and intellect emerge co-ordinately within the same constitutive movement and stretch out towards that place where the light of reason is lit, and personhood and rationality reveal the secret of their nature. Again as the encyclical puts it: 'What is sought is *the truth of the person* – what the person is and what the person reveals from deep within.'[14] And we may read the phrase 'truth of the person' to mean the revelation of what at once transcends – *is* beyond – and yet constitutes, the person.

There are two complementary, and, like the supports of an arch that come together at the keystone, mutually supporting, ways in which this truth may be attained. One way is the outer way, the cosmological way, classically represented by the thought of Saint Thomas, which considers the nature of the world, and finds the evidence of the existence of God, as giver of existence, and thus as self-supporting existence, in the insufficient existence of mundane entities. This way has come under attack by Kant and Hume; I will not venture here, for lack of space, to defend the view that this way can be vindicated as valid, but I will venture the comment that my own work has convinced me that Hume and Kant were misguided and that the cosmological way remains open to the searching philosophical mind.[15]

The second way, best represented perhaps by Augustine, considers the person from within, and tries to decipher the ultimate meaning of personhood and its constitutive elements. This is the way, not only of Augustine, but also of such comparatively recent thinkers as N.J.J. Balthasar of Louvain. In his work published in 1946, *Mon moi dans l'être*, Balthasar discovers the self as the culmination of all existence, in which a previously mute world finds voice, consciousness, and value:

> Le monde devient intelligible en acte d'intelligibilité, par l'agir humain. ... La raison d'être métaphysique du monde est dans les moi. L'opération cosmique tend vers l'homme. Le monde tend à se faire connaître, à se faire utiliser par les moi. Un monde sans un moi émergeant du monde comme animal raisonnable, est une contradiction dans l'être.[16]

God, for Balthasar, is my last end, and through the mediation of selves, God is also the last end of the prehuman world that is incapable of reflection. If this approach is correct, it means both that the self reveals something essential about the nature of existence – existence ultimately *is* selfhood – and that the third-personal, Thomistic approach can reveal anticipations of the self, and of ultimate selfhood, in the prepersonal: for example, to be an entity is to be a quasi-self. A more profound example might be provided by freedom as a, or even the, foundational transcendental property of Being. In that case, each level of entity is represented by an ever more perfect degree of freedom, and human, moral freedom is a freedom that exists *within* the freedom proper to all entities as such, and yet is a particularising enrichment of that general freedom, standing to it, perhaps, as 'living' stands to 'body' in 'animal'.

But there was another thinker, just a little earlier than Balthasar, who looked, as Augustine bade, from the self upward, or better, inward. In *Finite and Eternal Being*, Edith Stein writes:

> What is the ego that is aware of its being? ... If I turn towards its being, it shows in itself a two-fold aspect: that of being and that of non-being. The 'I am' cannot sustain the glance ... The being of which I am aware as my being cannot be separated from transitoriness. Since it is 'actual' being – that is, present and real – it is 'punctual' in the sense 'of a point' that is a 'now' between a 'no longer' and a 'not yet'. But while fluctuating, it is split into being and non-being, [and] the idea of pure being is revealed to us, the being that has no 'non-being' in itself, in which there is neither a 'no longer' nor a 'not yet', [a being] which is not temporal but eternal.[17]

How strikingly close to Augustine's vision that passage is. Yet the cosmological, or better, third-personal, perspective is still very much in evidence; what is said here might be said of any temporal entity, be that entity of personal nature or not, be it conscious or not – what we have here is a conscious temporal entity, a person, speaking third-personally of her self.[18]

Nevertheless it is in this second way, in this first- and second-personal way especially, that God is revealed as person; not simply as He Who Is, but, as Buber would have it, in commenting on the name of God as revealed in Exodus, as He Who Is There, namely *for* us, as loving, liberating and ultimately salvific Other.[19] To affirm the existence of God is both to affirm at last the existence of the truth on which we can rely, and also that that truth has a face. And it is here precisely that the significance of the self becomes apparent, along with the contribution that is proper to the personal, Augustinian way, the insight that can be gleaned nowhere else. For in this way selfhood is revealed as image par excellence of the Divinity, while the self's non-alien Other, and the self's orbit about this Other, are thereby also made manifest.

Both ways in concert, then, can come to an intellectual vision of the One who transcends all things, Who – not Which – is beyond all temporal entities, and grants existence to all insofar as, and for as long as, they are, and Who is at the same time, my self's absolute Thou, in conversation with Whom alone am I an I.

The Hallmarks of Truth

These broader, programmatic issues need to be, and in this encyclical, are, accompanied by more minute philosophical reflection. The leading concept of the analysis that we have been up to now examining is truth, and so, this concept must come under scrutiny and its dimensions be mapped. The Pope stresses the architectonic nature of truth – without this notion that dimension of human existence, namely the intentional, which makes anything like thought and language possible, would be done away with. This is why scepticism, as the denial of truth, cannot be stated coherently, and any plausible attempt to do so must, like a good conjuring trick, misdirect the audience's attention if the jiggery-pokery is to go on undetected.[20] We might remark here that, although this has been known at least since Plato wrote the *Protagoras*, it is the business of the sophist to prevent you from seeing it.

To speak or think is to rely on there being truth, on our speech being able to present what is as it is; and when we attain knowledge, we do so in the form of true propositions. If I can be said to know something, represented by proposition p, then p is true, and moreover, my knowing that p is true is tantamount to my knowing that I know p. In this way, the notion of truth carries with it the reflexivity whereby my own psychic states and mental operations are open and available to me. More profoundly, truth has the self as proximal pole. Part of what it is to be a self is to be capable of knowing the truth. Since what I perceive as truth is nothing other than what is as manifest, as true, truth is coterminous with what is, and so has existence as distal pole. Truth is thus the axis that connects my self as capable of truth to all that is insofar as it is.

The foundational feature of Aquinas's teaching on truth is that it is existence that is intended and revealed in and through truth, and that it is all existence – as true – that is the proper object of intellect. *Esse* is not mere brute occurrence, but a light by which entities are illuminated as they are, insofar as they are. Thus, in considering things as true I am not led away from them to something else – idea or representation or the like – rather, I am brought in truth to the revelation of things as they are in themselves. We may add here in passing that it is the disjunction of things as they are revealed and as they are in themselves that is the scandal of modern philosophy.[21]

Moreover, truth serves as regulative idea. What is true settles disputes and is what is to be preferred above all opinions, which themselves are only intelligible as attempts at reaching the truth, i.e., as truth claims. This idea is reinforced in our encyclical by means of the principle that no one can be genuinely indifferent as to whether or not what they claim to know is true. Such an indifference in effect amounts to radical scepticism, in that, only if there are no real propositions, no truths, can there be nothing to choose between propositions. Likewise, it is an abuse of language, and indeed, of one's partners in conversation, to talk about 'what is true for you, or me', or worse still, to talk about 'my reality' or 'my truth' as though one could own truth. This again is a piece of incoherence, because whoever says that truth is relative is claiming this as an absolute truth, or otherwise that it is only true for him that truth is relative. It is because this is so that truth has its characteristic hard-edged, whether-you-like-it-or-not, quality.

If all this is so, then, further, truth is the good of the intellect, what the intellect, in effect, exists for, where intellect may thus be defined as a person's capacity to know the truth. In this way, truth is in effect a value, and not only partakes in the nature of value by being object of desire, but is morally imperative in the way that values are. And further, truth enjoys a unique relation with the good: in that the good is the truth to be done, there is no good without truth, just as, in that truth is ineluctably a value, there can be no truth without the good.[22]

This love-knot, if we may so call it, which unifies truth and the good is traced in the encyclical in two major ways. In the first of these ways, the nature of the truth as value, as good, is revealed in its relation to our desire for it. The good is, precisely, that which calls forth our loyalty, fidelity and obedience, which are, nonetheless, freely bestowed. Such summoning of freedom and freedom's response defines the very nature of value, and of the structures of our moral life. An absolute value is one that calls forth an absolute adherence; it is in the nature of the good to be absolute and the supervenience of the claims of one good over another are not evidence to the contrary: the more perfectly good something is, the more valuable it is, and the more absolute its claim on us. The kinds of scepticism that we have mentioned are not only intellectually disastrous but are morally repugnant also. In the end, if the good and the true are coterminous, so are the irrational and the evil. The claim of truth is the claim of the real, of Being itself as true, and fidelity to this claim constitutes the moral aspect of the rational life, or rather the essence of the rational life viewed as moral. One cannot be a knower without at the same time being conscientious and principled. To be faithful to truth is to search for truth, to live in expectation of the truth, and to do all in one's power to attain it, beyond all mere opinion, error, or sophistry. It is this vision that motivates the present encyclical, and when we have grasped this, we have, I suggest, come to the work's moral core.

The encyclical thus shows its nearness to the thought of John Henry Newman, who in the following noble words from the *Grammar of Assent*, tells us what it is to be faithful to truth:

> We have arrived at these conclusions – not *ex opere operato*, by a scientific necessity independent of ourselves – but by the action of our own minds, by our own individual perception of the truth in question, under a sense of duty to those conclusions and with an intellectual conscientiousness.[23]

The encyclical is permeated in more than one way by something very like Newman's preference for the concrete and personal over the systematic and abstract. In this quotation we find ourselves in the skin, as it were, of one who lives in fidelity to truth. I must use logical tools to arrive at my conclusions, but ultimately, since life is finite and evidence often imperfect, my work results in a claim to truth, and this claim emanates from an existentially situated and finite person who loves the truth – a philosopher in the best sense – and from the conscientious and informed judgement of that person as engaged in the search for truth. Indeed it is this aspect of the person as conscientious knower, I believe, that is intended in the encyclical when the Pope tells us that it is a mark of adulthood to be able, independently, and, we may add, therefore responsibly, to distinguish the true from the false. It is here also that we encounter the true meaning of philosophy. Philosophy is not a discipline so much as a way of being. Neither need it be 'about' such philosophical topics as the nature of the good or the categorial framework of language. Philosophy is lived fidelity to truth, whatever that truth may be, and as such, philosophy is the essential structure of the rational, intellectual life.

The second way in which truth and the good are related is traced in the encyclical in the following manner: truth is not something merely to be known and rested in, but to be done. The Augustinian rest we have mentioned is neither passivity nor inertness. To know the truth is to act in accordance with it, and the good is the truth that guides action. Truth in this sense is the vision of the good. I quote:

> In acting ethically, according to a free and rightly tuned will, the human person sets foot upon the path to happiness and moves towards perfection. Here too it is a question of truth.[24]

Truth in this sense is not merely propositional or transcendental. Truth is meant here as authenticity, namely as what is revealed as genuinely good and fulfilling for the person, over and against what militates against our living up to what we are. Again I quote a seminal passage in the chapter under consideration:

> It is essential, therefore, that the values chosen and pursued in one's life be true, because only true values can lead people to realise themselves fully, allowing them to be true to their nature. The truth of these values is to be found not by turning in on oneself but by opening oneself to apprehend that truth even at levels which transcend the person. This is an essential condition for us to become ourselves and to grow as mature, adult persons.[25]

'True' in the first sentence of that quotation is used in two senses. First, a value may be said to be true if, and indeed, only if, it can lead people to realise themselves fully, and allow them to be true to what they are, as persons. But what is truth in this second sense of being true to what one is as a person? Clearly, what is meant is again faithfulness. Faithfulness, that is, to what the person is capable of becoming in fulfilment and maturity, faithfulness to nature as good. Once again, faithfulness to the good is presented as a loving and free submission to the call of the good.

But there is more in that quoted passage. Again we encounter the truth of human transcendence which is restless until it finds a place where it can genuinely rest and be truly at peace. Again we encounter the call to rise above ourselves to the place where the light of reason itself is lit. This is the progressive opening of oneself, through fidelity, to ever wider and deeper, more humanly significant truth. Yet in counselling us against turning in on ourselves, the Pontiff does not want us to forget the person and to neglect the constitutive truth at the heart of the person; rather we are being warned, I think, against the fundamental error that permeates modern philosophy from Descartes onwards, namely that danger that I elsewhere call solipsism.[26] This is the idea that the only thing one can encounter is the self, one's own ideas or projections, and that in consequence, all meaning must be generated in, and by the resources of, the finite self. This is the claim that I can know the truth, as Descartes puts it, *me solum alloquendo*. In that phrase one can hear the first sound of the *solus ipse* which becomes an overwhelming roar in the epistemology of Kant and in idealism. One might say without oversimplification that the difficulty that besets philosophy from Descartes onward is the increasing inability of philosophers to contextualise the self in Being, and the consequent increasing danger of the interruption of meaning, of absurdity, and of nihilism. It is no wonder that philosophy tends from the eighteenth century onward to be anti-metaphysical, and if our interpretation of metaphysics is correct, then philosophy runs a risk amounting to a certainty that the isolated self gets increasingly cut off from the only possibility whereby meaning can be given it, for meaning is possible for us only on condition that we can make that turn into Being which is metaphysics.

To close this section of our paper, then, we summarise those dimensions of truth adumbrated by the Pope: there is truth as 'the truth proper to propositions'; truth as transcendental, as coterminous with, and as revelation of, what is insofar as it is, and therewith truth as proper goal and defining value of intellect and the intellectual life; there is truth as the authentically good, and truth in the sense of 'being true *to*', that is, fidelity to the good; and finally truth as transcendence, as free and willed growth towards Being and towards the Divine.

Existential Tensions
Persons are beings of the *metaxu*, of the between, and much of human life is lived in the space generated in the tension of opposites. The life of the intellect is no different in this respect, and in this section of our paper we shall follow the Pope's analysis of some of these.
In the first place, human transcendence is by no means an inexorable march towards truth. Our search for truth is open to the distortions caused by what are referred to in the encyclical as the limitation of reason and the inconstancy of the heart. We are free, and infidelity as well as fidelity are real possibilities for us. It is possible, we are

reminded, to turn away from the truth out of fear of its demands. We may add that this very tendency can become articulate, and find expression in the various forms of sophistry and ideology, and become what Newman would call sins against the light. In any human undertaking that is meant to accomplish anything it is necessary to take account of our fallibility and weakness. Yet this need not lead us to despair, for, in a sentence that contains the whole philosophical anthropology inherent in this encyclical, the Pope tells us that: 'One may define the human being, therefore, as *the one who seeks the truth*'.[27]

As we shall see, this now familiar central claim yields a complementary one which shows that the life of faith is not alien to the philosophical life of reason. Let us follow this process.

Even though rationality is sufficient for the grasping of natural truth, this is not to say that *my* reason alone is sufficient for the task. Thus, truth is gained only by means of an intersubjective process. It is *we* who alone can hope to come to a knowledge of the truth, not I. The Pope here underlines that it is the community and never an isolated individual that can succeed in looking reality in the face. *We* advance in knowledge gradually, by means of the finite increments and additions, the conjectures and the verifications (or better, falsifications) contributed by individuals to the common patrimony of wisdom and knowledge; but individuals come to learn and to know only by participating in this essentially communal and historical process. The isolated individual can know nothing, can learn nothing; in this as in all human things, we need each other, and can accomplish little or nothing alone. To learn and to know, we rely one upon another.[28]

This theme of the ineluctably social and communal nature of knowledge has been taken up by various contemporary philosophers, such as Habermas and Apel. But the Pope's analysis bears an emphasis, again reminiscent of the thinking of Newman, upon the fact that such communities are made up of individual persons, and that the best kind of relation that can exist between them is one of love and respect.

Let us now briefly limn in the communal dimension of the search for truth. At bottom I am born into a language, a culture and a tradition, at a certain point in history. This is analogous to occupying a station-point in space, which gives a perspective within a horizon. From this station-point, some things are revealed, some are hidden, some things loom, others recede. Nothing is seen at once from all sides, and I must move if I am to correct the inevitable distortion that this situation naturally brings with it. Every tradition is a patrimony of truth. Every tradition enables me in my search for truth. As we are told, such historico-cultural factors mediate a range of truths, which I believe 'almost instinctively'. Yet what is handed down to me and to us can and must be evaluated through critical inquiry. But whether as receiver of what is handed down or as engaged in research or critical evaluation, I must rely upon others. Who could personally verify the flow of information that comes day after day from all parts of the world? The answer is no one, or at least, no *one*. It is this that makes it possible for the determined sceptic to make such an assertion as, say, the war in the Gulf never happened, and thereby of course to trivialise the reality of the human suffering that that war caused. Likewise, who could assess critically the countless scientific findings upon which modern life is based? No *one* could, for such findings are the products of a range of communities of scientific practitioners. If I visit a medical specialist, I have to trust that he or she is an expert on the condition from which I am suffering, and can correctly prescribe appropriate treatment. Philosophy and the other disciplines exist to make me able to receive this patrimony; but equally, and sometimes more vitally, they exist to unmask the fraudulent, the bogus, and the sophistical.

It is clear where these questions take us: my intellectual life is one that requires me to trust other persons, but if that is so, I must myself be trustworthy, and neither a fool nor a knave. This is an irrefrangible reciprocity: it is only because I am trustworthy that I can trust others, and there is a promise, an act of good faith, more or less explicit, in the very fact of my participation in any discipline. Where this fails, the discipline ceases to be, since we are then thrown back on our own slender individual resources, and are at the mercy of the predatory sophist. Epistemic canons such as the repeatability of experiment are the guarantees of this good faith. The underpinning of all intellectual disciplines is coevally ethical and logical, and we cannot have a value-free logic any more than we can have an illogical ethics. There is no such thing as a value-free discipline, and it is a great mistake to think that disciplines are value-free simply because they don't happen to be about values. A scientist who cooks the books is not a scientist: but more, he is not simply 'not a scientist' in the sense of being a layman: he is, in fact, a bad man.

In sum, it is one thing to believe *that* x is the case, but it is another to believe *in* something or someone. What the Pontiff is saying here is that 'belief that' requires 'belief in' if 'belief that' is to be possible. This truth is voiced in the encyclical in the following way: the human being, namely, the one who lives for truth, is also the one who lives by belief.

Belief in the sense of 'belief in' has the nature of trust, for in believing we entrust ourselves to the knowledge acquired by other people, and hence to them as possessing reliable judgement and the competence and conscientiousness that make them credible. I quote:

> belief is often *humanly* richer than mere evidence, because it involves an interpersonal relationship and brings into play not only a person's capacity to know but also the deeper capacity to entrust oneself to others, to enter into a relationship with them which is intimate and enduring.
>
> Human perfection ... consists not simply in acquiring an abstract knowledge of the truth, but in a dynamic relationship of faithful self-giving with others. ... in the act of believing, men and women entrust themselves to the truth which the other declares to them.[29]

Such thoughts might have been – indeed were – expressed by Newman. Here the reciprocity of trust and trustworthiness is brought out, and the ethical imperative of truthfulness is incarnated in and as a loving relationship of mutual self-giving and mutual reliance. Theories of the ethics of communicative action are no longer strange on the continental philosophical scene, and have been put forward by such authors as Lorenzen and Apel, and most notably by Habermas, whom we have mentioned. But the emphasis on the individual that we find in this encyclical is not merely a stylistic difference with these thinkers; the Pope's teaching shows that rationality is essentially incarnate, and is not an inevitable and disembodied dialectical process, which may even be at odds with the contingency and diversity of the concrete. Indeed the Pope's teaching has the advantage of being at home in the concrete.

It is just such an apparent disjunction between the rational and the real that is exploited by Rorty and others, who are interested, for sophistical reasons, in banishing the idea of truth and of the process of its attainment to a twilit, fictional realm, never to be reached in real life. I suggest that it is precisely this hospitality to the concrete to be found in the Pope's teaching that is the antidote to that kind of falsely disjunctive sophistry.

Moreover, going further in the same direction, the Pope brings out from the background the part played by the informal in the search after truth.

> Truth ... is attained not only by way of reason but also through trusting acquiescence to other persons who can guarantee the authenticity and certainty of the truth itself. There is no doubt that the capacity to entrust oneself and one's life to another person and the decision to do so are among the most significant and expressive human acts.[30]

Even though my ideas may ultimately take the form of published truth-claims backed up by evidence, and offered for testing to the whole community of investigators in my discipline, it is in and through my recourse to a select group of people whom I implicitly trust that I formulate my ideas and develop them to the point where they are worth presenting to the community of investigators. My first laboratory is my dialogue with my friend, who in generosity not only makes available his acumen and advice, but also gives me the support and interest that make me confident in using my own gifts and in developing my own thoughts.

> It must not be forgotten that reason too needs to be sustained in all its searching by trusting dialogue and sincere friendship. A climate of suspicion and distrust ... ignores the teaching of the ancient philosophers who proposed friendship as one of the most appropriate contexts for sound philosophical inquiry.[31]

One is forcibly reminded here of the Platonic Socrates for whom philosophical engagement and friendship were inseparable. As Socrates himself says in the *Gorgias*:

> The very reason why we acquire friends and children is that, when we ourselves grow old and make slips, you younger people may set us right both in actions and in words.[32]

This passage strongly evokes love and friendship as the only genuine context of ongoing inquiry, although it contains a double irony. The main opponents – we cannot really call them dialogue-partners – of Socrates in that dialogue are Callicles and Polus, the would-be tyrant and the born follower, respectively. They are motivated by anything but a love of wisdom, and still less by friendship for Socrates; we might read these words of Socrates as ironic, in view of the war and battle that occupy especially the later pages of the dialogue, but – and here is where the irony turns around on itself – Socrates is entirely serious in his offer of a friendship that can act as a true therapy of soul for both men but especially for Callicles, who, in a chillingly effective dramatic moment of the dialogue, rejects that offer of friendship, together with the search for truth, because they call upon him to renounce those devisings of his own heart, which he prefers to truth, and also to friendship and justice. Though Plato seems to have believed that we cannot intentionally sin, he gives us in Callicles the portrait of a man who commits intellectual and spiritual suicide, who sins against the light. It is precisely this classical picture, I suggest, which vindicates the Pontiff's teaching regarding the connection between the search for truth and friendship.

The Call of the Divine
This then is the Pope's portrayal of the life of reason, the *intellego* in *intellego ut credam*. What then of the *ut credam*? It is a truth, in but not exclusively of, religion that we are able to love God because God loved us first. To advance in the intellectual life, to follow the path of transcendence through fidelity to the truth that is good, and the good that is true, is to discover, not an impersonal good, as Plato conceived it, but something that excels even that noble conception. The meaning for which my life has been a search is a person, and one who has, all along, been searching for me.

> Ah, fondest, blindest, weakest,
> I am He whom thou seekest!
> Thou dravest love from thee, who dravest Me.

The words are Francis Thompson's and they form the end of his mystical poem, *The Hound of Heaven*. They embody the insight which is the true Augustinian rest of which we have spoken and with which this encyclical is filled. For 'love' in that last line, read not only love but also completion, peace, and heart's content. It is here that the disparate elements revealed in our analysis come together. That search for the truth, that fidelity, that transcendence now take the form of friendship – 'I call you friends for I have revealed to you everything I have learned from my Father' – and with it the form of Sonship. What was abstract and theoretical now attains the concreteness proper to that friendship as lived. Faith is indeed trust, not finally in fallible men

and women, but in the one and unshakeable foundation, which
cannot deceive or be found wanting: and thereby it is trust in what
that One says of Himself. As Aquinas puts it in the hymn *Pange
Lingua*, which I quote here in the translation of Gerard Manley
Hopkins:

> What God's Son has told me, take for truth I do;
> Truth Himself speaks truly, or there's nothing true.

The words of St Thomas are spoken in the context of the Eucharist,
but are equally to be applied to revelation as a whole. Truth emerges
as 'He', better, as 'Thou', not 'it'. Moreover, His speaking is a doing.
Revelation is not just a 'theoretical' account of what the Godhead is
like, beyond our power to know, but an unveiling of love as ultimate
meaning of existence and as alive and active, reaching out to each
individual person to work their salvation. Revelation is the Good
News of the salvific nature of God's creativity, and is to be understood
only as active, as integral to that Divine activity.

I understand in order to believe not only because my search for
truth leads me to know something of God, but because Divine
revelation is possible only to a hearer capable of hearing it. To reveal
himself to us, God must use our language, our rationality. This means
that revelation is the completion of rationality. Too often, faith is
presented as something supernumerary and decisionistic, to be
accepted fideistically. Such an attitude undermines both faith and
reason, and deprives each of the mutual support of the other.

Here then, is a task to be performed both by philosophers and
theologians, working in harmony. The vindication of faith in a non-
fideistic way must show that the nature of the rational life that
philosophy both is and uncovers – the truth of the person – is not only
preserved by faith but is deepened and extended by faith. Such a
vindication, in short, must show that reason is not lost or derailed in
faith, but that in faith reason becomes even more itself than it could
ever have hoped to be without faith. This is what it means to say that

faith is the fulfilment of reason. Indeed, this completion is only a particular instance of what grace always achieves – we become more ourselves by loving God, not less. We become more ourselves in accepting the love of God than we ever could hope to have been otherwise. Losing our lives is, we are assured, saving our lives.

This interdisciplinary task, then, is one of the practical results of Pope John Paul's teaching, and it cannot be accomplished without a certain shifting and rebuilding. It involves me as a philosopher taking the faith seriously, and theologians taking philosophy seriously, as the Pontiff recommends elsewhere in the encyclical. It means that both philosophers and theologians must unite not only to unmask the evil that fideism is, but also to question certain common assumptions that currently go unchallenged, such for example as the widely held belief that there is no successful argument for the existence of God.

In this context, another task awaits both philosophers and theologians. Let me phrase it thus: philosophy did not occupy the classical stage alone and was conditioned in its development not only as search for truth but partly also as response to its rival, sophistry, as virtually all Plato's works bear witness. Even logic, which many view as a morally neutral calculus, was born as a distinct discipline out of the clash between philosophy and sophistry. Aristotle's earliest logical work is found in the *De Sophisticis Elenchis*, which is an attempt to show the sophists' tricks for what they were. It was, I think, Aristotle's quasi-biological, taxonomic analysis of sophistic arguments that led him to the discovery of logical form, a discovery that constitutes the beginning of logic as a distinct branch of study. Far from being morally neutral, logic's original home was in the attempt not only to find truth but to rescue it from sophistic concealment. Sophists work like stage magicians, in that their whole business is to misdirect the audience's attention, so as to prevent them from seeing what the trick really is. As it was then, so it is now, and the need to unmask sophistic reasoning is, if anything, greater now than then, for sophistry is nothing if not adaptable.

However, before we finish let us return to that place where faith and reason meet. Wisdom, we are told, enters holy souls in all ages, making them friends of God and prophets. Reason's finding its true self in faith, which is friendship with, and trust in, God, leads to a deepening of our philosophical understanding of human existence. The only way I can express this faith-deepened understanding is by saying that in it, human existence is revealed as eucharistic. A properly philosophical understanding of the relation between God and world shows, as I have said, what it means to say that God is creator, namely that everything that exists, at every moment of its existence, receives that existence directly from God, as gift. To say that God is creator is to say that God is the personal giver of the gift of existence from moment to moment, as long as I exist. To say God does anything else is to say that God does something less. Thus it follows that God's salvific action, which is at the same time a self-revelation, is part of God's creation of the world. Moreover, to say that God gives existence is to say that, since God *is* existence, his creation is to be understood already in philosophy as the gift of participation in his life, in his reality, which can only be reciprocated as eucharistic return of our being, and indeed that of the presubjective and ontologically mute world – which, as Balthasar holds, we represent – to God in faith.

Now, I hope I shall be forgiven that last paragraph, particularly by theologians. I would like to assure them that it does not represent any attempt to poach on their territory, to do theology in an amateur way. Rather, it represents the attempt of a philosopher to think within that area in which reason finds itself in faith, and limited though any such attempt must be, it needs to be carried out; it can, I venture to hint, only be improved by the benevolent aid of theology.

In conclusion then, God cannot reveal himself to the ontologically deaf, but only to persons who can hear and respond, that is to say, to all persons as persons. I understand in order to believe means, I open myself to the truth of Being in order to be able to entrust myself to that friendship in which alone my yearning heart finds rest. The best part of the great wisdom contained in this encyclical is the recognition that the Good News that I receive in faith is other but not alien: for I recognise, from its dimly reflected image in and as my personal nature, the loving face that is revealed to me in faith, but which, even there, is still seen through a glass darkly.

Notes

1. Though there is a quotation, in # 24, from the Good Friday Liturgy of the Roman Missal that is thoroughly Augustinian: *ut te semper desiderando quaererent et inveniendo quiescerent.*
2. As scripture has it, 'Thou fool! This night I require thy soul of thee.' Luke 12, 20.
3. *Fides et Ratio,* # 27. (Referred to below as *F&R*)
4. *ibid.,* # 32.
5. *ibid.,* # 29.
6. *ibid.,* # 29.
7. *ibid.,* n. 28
8. *ibid.,* n. 28
9. Quoted in *F&R,* # 15.
10. See my paper 'God, Man, and Metaphysics', delivered at the Rome conference *Metaphysics for the Third Millennium,* in September 2000, and which is to be published in the *Proceedings*; see also my analysis of the Augustine passage in my study *God and Time: A Suite of Essays in Metaphysics* (forthcoming).
11. *F&R,* n. 28.
12. See my forthcoming book *God and Time: A Suite of Essays in Metaphysics.*
13. *F&R,* # 24. Emphasis added.
14. *ibid.,* # 32.
15. Again see *God and Time.*
16. *Mon moi dans l'être* (Louvain, Éditions de l'Institut Supérieur de Philosophie, 1946), p. 152. 'The world becomes actually intelligible through the action of man [in knowing] ... The world's metaphysical reason for existing is to be found in selves. The working of the cosmos tends towards man. The world tends to make itself known, to allow itself to be used by selves. A world without a self emerging within it as rational animal is a contradiction in Being.'
17. Quoted in Writings of Edith Stein, edited and translated by Hilda Graef (London, Peter Owen Ltd, 1956), p. 198.
18. Indeed, even Heidegger, who treats 'who'-talk as more profound than 'what'-talk, describes the who of Dasein from the outside vantage provided by third-personal talk. Perhaps it is only in Augustine that 'I and Thou'

language truly predominates, in that such language is performative (of dialogue), and Augustine writes, at least in the *Confessions*, as a partner actually engaged in the Dialogue which for him human existence, in particular his own, is.

19. For a discussion of Buber on this point see Pamela Vermes, *Buber on God and the Perfect Man* (London, Washington, Littman Library of Jewish Civilization, 1994), chapter 8.

20. This is a position that I must leave for the moment undefended: but I hereby overtly issue the challenge implicit in it.

21. See my study *Language and Transcendence* (Bern, Lang, 1994), Introduction.

22. See my treatment of the Good, the True, and their interwovenness in *Language, World, and God*, chapters 10 and 11.

23. *An Essay in Aid of a Grammar of Assent* (London, Longmans, 1895), chapter VIII, section 2, p. 318.

24. *F&R*, # 25.

25. *ibid.*, # 25.

26. *Language and Transcendence*, Introduction

27. *F&R*, # 28.

28. See my treatment of the thought of K.-O. Apel in *Language and Transcendence*.

29. *F&R*, # 32. My emphasis.

30. *ibid.*, # 33.

31. *ibid.*

32. 461e

CREDO UT INTELLEGAM: THE RELATIONSHIP BETWEEN PHILOSOPHY AND THEOLOGY IN THE CATHOLIC TRADITION

Francesca Murphy

This paper interprets the relationship between philosophy and theology in *Fides et Ratio* (*F&R*) in relation to Étienne Gilson and Henri de Lubac's understanding of the relationship of natural or anthropological desire and its supernatural fulfillment. I will begin with two images, one relating to islands, and the other to gardens. Sometimes, when I have read one thesis too many that makes the discovery that Barth, or T.F. Torrance, or Aquinas, were non-foundationalists, I feel that some theologians are treating non-foundationalism as a rescue boat, which can tow them away from the mainland, where their colleagues are horrid to them for making such absurd claims as that God became man, to an island all of their own, where they can speak a language that is incommensurable with the secular languages. Were a Christian dissident to tire of island life and send out a message in a bottle, his theological monoglotism would preclude the secular monoglots on the mainland from accurately decoding his plea for help. The discovery that one interpretation of *F&R* that is doing the rounds proposes that it promotes non-foundationalism put me in that mood, of feeling that some people are simply too embarrassed to say in public that the Christian language corresponds with reality.

Sometimes, even when we give notional assent to the unity of reason and faith, there still linger in our minds some rather strong images of their division. And then we think we have to chose between two positions, one of which pictures faith as a gardener who uproots reason and replaces it with artificial orange trees, specially parachuted down from heaven for the purpose, and another that imagines faith as a promiscuous gardener who dumps manure all over the rude wild fruit-trees of reason, in order to make them flourish all the more. In the post-Reformation debates, Catholics have on occasion described Protestants as saying the first, and both Catholics and Protestants have envisaged the second as the Catholic position. The Protestants have added, as Alvin Plantinga does in relation to *F&R*, that 'the Catholic view neglects ... the fact that non-Christian philosophy is not merely handicapped by the "inherent weakness of human reason" (*F&R* # 75); it is rather that philosophers, like humanity generally, are *fallen*, and in need of *conversion*.'[1] One of the flaws in the 'wild-fruit trees of reason' image is that, once one has accepted it, one has, probably inadvertently, redefined human nature and human reason from an entirely anthropological perspective, as if these trees just happened to be growing where they are, without having been planted there in the first place by the very same Manure Dumper.

A more charitable interpretation of the non-foundationalist reading of *F&R* than the one I began with is that it is a salutary reminder that the encyclical is steeped in theology from beginning to end; the encyclical sees the relationship of philosophy to theology in the light of faith. One obvious rejoinder to that is 'what else could you expect the Pope to do?', but, within the Pope's own lifetime, the official Curial practice looked a little different to this. Many of the neo-Thomists who taught at Rome in the first half of the twentieth century saw the modernist crisis as emerging out of the swampy depths of Hegelian metaphysics and Kantian epistemology, and they seemed to believe that as a condition of keeping theology orthodox, we must straighten out our philosophy. Although their clear aim was to protect theology and doctrine from modernist contamination, still, their philosophy was made to appear in a context neutral disguise, as if it just happened to be leading up to the right sort of theology. They passed off their own version of Thomism as *the* only viable philosophy with which Catholic theology can make fruitful contact. What they were doing, unconsciously, perhaps, was to make theology reliant upon a philosophy; to make the trees produce the soil, as it were. In those neo-Thomist days, philosophy produced demonstrations of the existence of God, on the ground of pure reason, and it was felt that the theology that was superadded to these demonstrations could not float without them. The Pope came to intellectual maturity at a time when this way of going about things was still rather influential. *F&R* emphasises, therefore, that there is no 'official philosophy of the Church, since the faith as such is not a philosophy'.[2] The 'background' philosophy to the encyclical is, nonetheless, broadly Thomistic. The author might agree with Étienne Gilson's observation that 'A Thomist is a free spirit. This liberty assuredly does not consist in having neither God nor man for a master, but rather in having no other master than God, who enfranchises all the others.' Just as Saint Augustine pronounced, '*Dilige, et quod vis fac*', 'love and do what you like', so 'in identically the same spirit and in the same profound meaning ... the disciple of saint Thomas can say: "believe and think what you like." Like charity, faith is liberating.'[3] The encyclical's idea of the 'autonomy' of philosophy finds its roots in some such conception as this, and not in an idea of a 'separated', neutral philosophy. *F&R* mentions that the 'fruitful relationship between philosophy and the word of God' can be seen in 'John Henry Newman, Antonio Rosmini, Jacques Maritain, Étienne Gilson and Edith Stein'.[4] I intend to bring out the 'Gilsonian' element in the encyclical in this paper, but not to treat it as a manifesto for 'Gilson Thomism.'

One drawback in explaining *F&R* with reference to one or more academically recognisable philosophers is that the encyclical does not always use the term *philosophy* in the *official* sense of the term, where the officials in question work in Philosophy Departments. *F&R* says that: 'To be consonant with the word of God, philosophy needs first of all to recover its *sapiential dimension* as a search for the ultimate and overarching meaning of life.'[5] The word 'sapiential' has the connotation of a concrete and complete human being grasping after reality, rather than simply an intellect in search of abstract truths. The encyclical seems in this way to direct us to biography as a mode of apologetics. The human appetite for biography is a hook upon which a philosophical theology can be threaded.

Pius X, Pius XI, and Pius XII made numerous official pronouncements about the relation of faith and reason, many of them concerned with the promotion of Thomism in seminary education. It is difficult to imagine any of them remarking in such an encyclical, that 'Modern philosophy has the great merit of focusing attention upon man.'[6] Everyone knows that Karol Wojtyla was precisely such a modern philosopher; he wrote his doctoral thesis on Max Scheler, and followed that up with a near-impenetrable work of phenomenological philosophy, *The Acting Person*. Rocco Buttiglione said that the use of phenomenology suggested itself to Wojtyla because here '*the starting point is man*.'[7] It has been more common, in the history of Christian thought, to take *being* as one's first principle, and Buttiglione notes that 'From a methodological point of view, perhaps, it is not quite the same thing to begin from being ... as to begin from personal experience.'[8] Where St Thomas defines the person *objectively*, phenomenology enabled Wojtyla to throw some light upon the person as *subject*. In those days when he was Wojtyla, the author of *F&R* wrote that 'in St Thomas we can see very well the person in his objective existence and action, but it is difficult to catch sight of the living experience of the person.'[9] What Wojtyla was striving to get at, philosophically, was the moral experience of the person. He is not discarding either Thomism or being as a first principle, but rather approaching the *Summa Theologiae* through the section on human behaviour, that is, ethics.[10] The neo-scholastic philosophy of the nineteenth and early twentieth centuries was written in conscious opposition to Descartes, and to German Idealism; Descartes with his bifurcation of human nature into a *cogito* and the body juxtaposed to it, and Fichte or Hegel, with their deduction of the categories of being out of an all powerful and yet 'empty' Subject. Wojtyla takes the morally responsible person, the ethical human being, as his starting point, in order to attack the same question from another angle: for the ethical human being is a *concrete reality*, whose living acts cannot be divorced from his thoughts.[11] For Wojtyla, ethics concerns the world of living human activity as it is related to the good. He knew, as a pupil of Aquinas, that being and the good are convertible. Whereas we know the true, we love the good. Sometimes imaginative problems can be genuine ones, for Christian apologetics. A real problem for contemporary Christian apologetics is that knowledge of truth tends to be conceived statically, as the reproduction of an eternal formula in the knower's mind. This is a travesty, of course, but one may best circumvent it by conceiving the true in terms of the good; for the words 'love of the good' immediately suggest a journey and an adventure, an active process. In *Love and Responsibility*, Wojtyla explains the love of two persons as the sharing in a common good, which they find in one another, and which they give to one another. There is a passage in that book that I don't fully understand, but which always captures my attention: 'The external concreteness and uniqueness of the situation which we call love is closely connected with its internal aspect, with what it is in each of the persons, who are as it were actors in the drama of their own love. Love is … a drama in … that it is made up of happenings and of action (to do, to act is the meaning of the Greek *drao* …). Thus the "*dramatis personae*" discover the plot of this drama in themselves, perceive their love as … one of great and absorbing importance in their inner lives.'[12] Drama is concerned with the building of a self, in relation to other actors, within the horizon of the good. The subject of philosophy in *F&R* is not entirely dealt with in *metaphysical* terms. Rather, *F&R* is in some way an encyclical about ethics. So far as the writer of *F&R* is concerned, every human being, philosopher or not, and Christian or not, is engaged in the drama of the search for meaning. The dramatic analogy entails that both seekers, and the sought, are conceived as persons.

The question of whether philosophical reason and revealed truth have any serious, fruitful overlap was thoroughly ploughed over in France during the 1930s. One historical source of *F&R* is the debate about 'Christian philosophy' that took place, quite literally, in a crowded lecture theatre, at the Sorbonne, in February, 1931. The philosopher Émile Bréhier had claimed that *Christianity*, which is a mystery, and *philosophy*, which is a purely rational pursuit, have never genuinely been combined in one head. The Société Française de Philosophie recruited Étienne Gilson and Jacques Maritain to argue in favour of the possibility of Christian philosophy, against Bréhier and Léon Brunschvicg. The opponents of Christian philosophy had many clerical allies. They were a group of neo-Thomists who believed that the very *truth* of Aquinas' rational arguments requires that these arguments be defined as being autonomous of his theology. One of the most active of the clerical opponents of Christian philosophy was Canon Fernand van Steenberghen. He said that there are no Christian philosophies, only true philosophies. The very opposite of a non-foundationalist, Canon van Steenberghen steered so clear of fideism that he began by separating reason and faith, in principle. Gilson was throughout his life an increasingly stout opponent of the neo-Thomistic positions, to the extent that scholars have interpreted his defence of *Christian* philosophy as a rejection of *philosophy* as such. Avery Dulles has stated that, 'Against Gilson', the Pope in *F&R* 'holds that there can be a valid philosophy which is not influenced by revelation'.[13] If we study the transcript of the debate, we can see that Gilson defended the thesis that God's self-definition in Exodus, as 'I am that I am', gave philosophy a new ground to explore. Without the notion of necessary being, contained in that definition, philosophers would not have noticed the *philosophical* truth that the ground upon which they stand is contingent, and asked 'Why is there something rather than nothing?' Bréhier's response to this argument was that it is a wide open question 'whether the Exodus could have been used philosophically without Aristotle.' Gilson replied, 'I freely agree with you ... I do not think there would have been a Christian philosophy without Greek philosophy, but that does not prove there was no Christian philosophy.'[14] Bréhier's definitions of Christianity, as a mystery, and of philosophy, as an exercise of reason, was intended to show that the two are logically repugnant. Gilson's reply to Bréhier was that, whilst it is true that Christianity and philosophy are distinct concepts, nonetheless, the pair have never existed purely as *concepts*, for 'the only things which exist are religious men and philosophers.' And it may simply be a fact, paradoxical but inescapably real, that that funny animal, the living conjunction of Christianity and philosophy, has existed. Gilson had returned to Paris for this debate from Aberdeen, where he was giving the Gifford lectures, published as *The Spirit of Mediaeval Philosophy*. The argument that he gave there for the existence of Christian philosophy is *historical*. With reference to the ideas of contingent being and personalism, for example, Gilson claimed that thinkers have developed new philosophical ideas on the ground of believing themselves to be living in the world described by the Scriptures. They had noticed elements of reality that had never been articulated before. In the Sorbonne debate, he came back over and again to the novelty, the fresh invention, which belief in revelation had supplied to human reason. Gilson took it as *experientially* fundamental that the Christian philosopher is not a schizophrenic, whose thoughts and beliefs inhabit different personae. Gilson was not afraid to turn to common sense, psychological arguments. But these were not his trump cards. After making the psychological or experiential point, Gilson went on to explain by reference to the *facts* that revelation had actually engendered reasonable ideas: and this he did, for example, by reference to the philosophical use of the Biblical notion of the 'radical origin of things.'[15]

Gilson's ally in the debate was Jacques Maritain. Maritain's argument was essentially a psychological one, that a person's philosophy is linked to their moral condition, or status. He pointed to the 'subjective reinforcements' that assist the Christian philosopher. For Maritain, the virtue of faith, in relation to philosophy, is primarily moral. He said that philosophy requires, not just clear thinking, but 'rectifications and purifications of the individual, an ascesis not only of the reason, but of the heart, for one philosophises with one's whole soul, just as one runs with one's heart and one's lungs.'[16] And, with reference to the infused or theological virtues, Maritain claimed that the '*habitus* of contemplation' synergetically 'spiritualises the *habitus* of philosophy.[17] With clear reference to these slightly different orientations, of Maritain and Gilson, *F&R* states that:

> Christian philosophy has two aspects. The first is subjective, in the sense that faith purifies reason. As a theological virtue, faith liberates reason from presumption, the typical temptation of the philosopher. The second aspect of Christian philosophy is objective, in the sense that it concerns content. Revelation clearly proposes certain truths which might never have been discovered by reason unaided, although they are not of themselves inaccessible to reason. Among these truths is the notion of a free and personal God who is the Creator of the world ... The notion of the person as a spiritual being is another of faith's specific contributions.[18]

Maurice Blondel skipped the Sorbonne debate, and published his critique of the various positions advocated there as an appendix to the transcript; Gilson did not forgive him for this *esprit d'escalier* until 1962. Blondel argued that Christianity and philosophy do not come together as easily as its advocates think, because philosophy is governed by the spirit of 'closure', whereas Christianity is infinitely open: 'can that which is *not* conceivable be philosophical?' he asked.[19] Blondel denied the possibility of Christian philosophy, on a definition of philosophy as an exercise in which a philosopher looks at problems from the outside, and puts them in a box when he has done with them. He calls philosophy a 'self-sufficient and exclusive system'. He was, perhaps, stating philosophically the imaginative obstacle to philosophical apologetics that I mentioned earlier: the Christian Gospel is too much alive to be confined in the boxes of philosophical *answers.* Christian philosophy does not exist in the shape of a manual of 'Great Answers to Tough Atheistic Questions'; what has existed, according to Blondel, is the Christian mind, as dynamically activated from within, by Christ. For Blondel, Christian philosophy is the continuous exercise of the Christian mind, taken as a whole, perpetually probing the problem of human existence. The author of *F&R* is inclined to include the insights of the philosopher of *action*. He states that 'philosophical *enquiry*' must be given primacy over the 'philosophical system.'[20]

This ecumenical Pope goes on to mention that 'seminal insights' are found 'even in the philosophical thinking of those who helped drive faith and reason further apart'. Such 'insights', he says, are found in 'penetrating analyses of perception and experience, of the imaginary and the unconscious, of personhood and intersubjectivity'. Our broad-minded writer is naturally opening his arms to the existentialist phenomenologists, such as Merleau-Ponty, with his *Phenomenology of Perception*, and Sartre, with his writings on imagination. It may seem to be a *reductio ad absurdum* of foundationalism to include atheists amongst the co-workers in the formation of Christian philosophy.

A genuine, non-Catholic non-foundationalist has criticised *F&R* on precisely those grounds, and since Alvin Plantinga's remarks are so incisive, it seems worthwhile to quote them:

> Much of philosophy is a categorical renunciation of Christian belief, and an attempt to work out a view of the world wholly incompatible with that of Christian theism. Contemporary philosophy doesn't look at all like an incomplete approximation to Christian truth; nor is it the case that contemporary philosophers, if they heard the gospel, would see that this is really what they were looking for all along. Instead (so it seems to me), much contemporary philosophy is a development and elaboration of a view of the world (and indeed, a view of the world that is at bottom *religious*) that is antithetical to Christianity. Thus it is less a deliverance of reason than the

articulation of a rival faith. ... naturalists and relativists, philosophers like Quine or Dennett or Derrida or Rorty, are not confused Catholics. ... Nor is it the case that if they heard the gospel, they would see it as the fulfillment of what they were looking for all along. Indeed, nearly all of them have heard the gospel; most, I suppose, were brought up as Christians of one sort or another, and have rejected it. Instead, they are working out the implications of a way of looking at the world, a way wholly incompatible with Christian theism.[21]

One could suggest that the consciously non-Christian 'religions' that Plantinga says are found in most modern philosophical systems are equivalent to myths. *F&R* teaches that the great achievement of Greek philosophy was to uproot the ancient myths, replacing them with universal truths. '*Superstitions* were recognised for what they were, and religion was, at least in part, purified by rational analysis.'[22] Precisely because it is founded in a theological personalism, *F&R* scarcely neglects the need for conversion, and that includes conversion from imprisonment in myth.

It seems to me that Plantinga's criticism of the understanding of the relation between philosophy and theology in *F&R* would be entirely accurate *if* the encyclical were actually based in the image that I mentioned at the beginning, those wild fruit trees of reason that are doing quite well on their own accord, and, quite coincidentally, happen to flourish to their finest when the Gardener comes along to put the manure of faith on them. Plantinga is right on target, if faith is objectively extrinsic to our search for meaning. But he may be looking at the wrong map altogether, an old map one might say, so ancient as to derive from the baroque era. Basing itself on a yet more antique, Patristic and mediaeval schema, one that sets out from theology, and not anthropology, the encyclical envisages the shape of human biography as being naturally related to faith. As we have seen, the Pope stresses that it is not philosophical *systems* but the activity of philosophical *enquiry* that is fulfilled by faith, and he seems to picture the root of enquiry as having a moral dimension; in the old language, it is rooted in desire. Philosophical enquiry is the concrete activity of a concrete moral subject. In this sense, the question of the 'relateability' of theology and philosophy comes back to one of *context*. Those who want philosophy and theology to keep their distance want philosophy and theology to be, respectively, the contextless exercise of rationality or of faith. Against this, Gilson argued that he had never met any 'pure philosopher … whose reason never frequents its irrational neighbours.'[23] The philosopher who consciously binds his reason to the unreason of faith, is not only doing what all men do, inadvertently, but actually connecting his reason with its *source*. Newman put the definitive statement of the contexuality of reason and belief in *The Grammar of Assent*. For Newman, the broader context in which thinking takes places is *action*, and action cannot wait on logical proofs: 'to act you must assume, and that assumption is faith.'[24] The demand for an a-contextuality of philosophical reason is born of the wish that it be technical and impersonal. Once we make reason a neighbour to belief, we may find, with Newman, that 'Instead of trusting logical science, we must trust persons.'[25] What we learn, when we entrust ourselves to persons, has, of course, a personal stamp; it is something unique, and to that extent a wayward curve in the straight grooves of rationality. It is creative because it is completely out of logical sequence. As we read in *F&R*, 'reason which is unrelated to an adult faith is not prompted to turn its gaze to the newness and radicality of being.'[26] Whereas the Cartesian mathematicism begins by doubting everything, Newman prefers that we 'begin with believing everything … offered to our acceptance', because that 'is the true way of learning.'[27] Apprenticing oneself to a teacher may not be an especially *melodramatic* act, but the choice of a master in the craft one would be taught is a dramatic act, in the sense of a public expression of who we are and whom we would make ourselves. As the Pope says in *F&R*, 'the capacity to entrust oneself and one's life to another person and the decision to do so are among the most significant and expressive human acts.'[28] As Gilson so often noted, God told Moses his name; what we have to teach others is what we ourselves are: 'the truths sought in this interpersonal relationship are not primarily ... philosophical. Rather, what is sought is the *truth of the person* – what the person is and what the person reveals from deep within.'[29]

Now, suppose that it is not just a hypothesis that reason and belief lean on one another. Suppose reason is naturally turned to belief, or 'real assent', in order to root itself in actuality, and belief really does need reason for its intelligent articulation. What would happen if the philosophers denied any connection with irrational mystery, and the theologians hived off into their own private foundations? Replacing its roots in actuality with a drive to explain everything, reason would produce its own set of *trompe l'oeil* mysteries. Its rational formulas would congeal into a mythology. Determined to hang on to its autonomy, philosophy would create a Theology out of itself. The most difficult point for the technically minded philosopher to figure is that philosophy will not be submerged into theology, if the two share a common context. But, when it denies the relationship of reason to belief, philosophy creates a shadow-counterpart to belief. On the other hand, the most problematic idea for the twenty-first century punter to grasp is that theology is not simply an extension of philosophy. The man on the Clapham omnibus is most likely an unconscious Hegelian, who thinks of theology as the storybook philosophy of life, with pictures. In Augustine's time, as in our own, a decadent metaphysics had begun to tell stories. Augustine got from the Manicheans and the Gnostics that total explanation of everything that ordinary folk today have found in the *Celestine Prophecy*. The first 'personal conversion' of Augustine was his slow escape from pantheism, achieved by slowly removing from God every trace of the materiality in which the Manichean myths clothed Him. *F&R* describes the second, and perhaps more difficult 'conversion' of this great intellectual figure. The encyclical recalls Augustine's realization that Manicheanism, founded on reason, compelled him to believe 'absurd myths'; it was refreshing to be told, by the Christians, that he had simply to believe some things that cannot be demonstrated. Christianity thus offers a moral appeal to be true to the innermost desires of one's nature. As a young philosopher, the Pope was drawn to phenomenology because it speaks about the concrete, bodily and spiritual, subject. A bodily subject has to face the inevitability of death. In concluding his list of philosophical subjects that are open to theological meaning, John Paul II observes that the 'theme of death ... can become for all thinkers an incisive appeal to seek within themselves the true meaning of their own life.'[30]

In his contribution to the Christian philosophy debate, Maurice Blondel commented that Christ 'liberates the philosopher from systematic pretensions' by making philosophy face dynamically toward the discovery of the supernatural.[31] The debate went on for several years. In 1936, after it had petered out into a quarrel amongst the Catholics about the autonomy of Aquinas' philosophy, Henri de Lubac published a description of the overall argument, in which he said it had all been about the natural desire for the supernatural vision. That phrase refers to the human search for a goodness perfect enough to requite an infinite love. The Baroque Thomists, from Cajetan to Réginald Garrigou-Lagrange, had resolutely denied that Augustine, or Aquinas, taught any such thing. Well before 1946, when de Lubac published *Le Surnaturel,* this had become a sort of unofficial, official orthodoxy. The Officials considered that if one said that human nature is naturally oriented to seeing God, and if a natural orientation cannot be denied, then God is required to fulfill a human desire. They thought that this makes God less than perfectly free. And so they invented the hypothesis of a 'state of pure nature', which is impermeable to grace. But then, de Lubac says in *Surnaturel,* they forgot that the pure nature was hypothetical, and defined the whole order of nature in terms of it. One of the side effects of the scholastic idea that human nature is oriented to a purely human end, is the clear cut division of philosophy and theology. De Lubac claims that it was not just philosophers like Descartes who brought about the division of faith and reason, but also theologians, by way of their concept of a pure nature, which is satisfied with human ends, and is not driven by a yearning for a perfect Good.

De Lubac showed that the denial of a natural yearning for God begins in the fifteenth century with Cajetan. After the Jesuit was silenced, Gilson wrote a series of frontal attacks on Cajetan; for he himself had claimed since 1922 that Thomas teaches the natural desire for the supernatural. He argued that Cardinal Cajetan over-interprets Aquinas, in making him divide philosophical demonstrations from revealed faith. For instance, in reading the first question of the *Summa*, Cajetan envisages God as neatly distinguishing between those things that are unknowable to the human mind, which he revealed, and those things about Himself that are potentially knowable, which he left for philosophers to find out by themselves. Gilson saw this logical distinction between unknowable and knowable 'revelabilia' as creating a separated philosophy. He argued, to the contrary, that in the first article of the *Summa*, Aquinas is picturing God as having before him a *concrete* end, the salvation of the human race, and so, He went ahead and revealed the whole lot, in order to achieve the *practical* aim of human salvation.[32]

Some people wonder whether, if you take away the merely historical fact of their author's having been influenced by revelation, the Christian philosophers' arguments still work, and if they do, whether they are really founded on grace, as Gilson said they are. If the arguments work in theory, how can the historical facts matter to them? They may be forgetting that we are *actually* living in a world that has been changed by grace. Both Gilson and de Lubac take the question down, from its elevated hypothetical plane, to lived *reality*. In *Surnaturel* de Lubac claimed that Augustine never theorised in the abstract about what prelapsarian Adam might have known, but rather, always spoke about a concrete fact, 'the present role of grace', which the Bishop of Hippo assessed by reference to Scripture, tradition, and his own 'personal experience'.[33] *F&R* is most obviously characterised by such down to earth, or concrete thinking; here philosophy simply means human questioning, the thread that runs through all human lives, and which runs up against death as a threat, not only to one's survival, but to that as yet unrequited love that drives us all. The neo-scholastics feared that if we posit a natural desire for God, God then has no free choice about fulfilling that desire. De Lubac responds to this by indicating that God freely created human beings in the knowledge that they would desire him. The natural desire for the supernatural is 'the permanent action in us of the God who created the moral order', it is 'nothing other than his call'.[34] Thomas distinguished two types of movement toward God. One is the natural return to the source, shared by all animate creatures, angels and human beings. But the other is that truly human thing, a gratuitous love.[35] So the natural desire for the supernatural is not, as it were, biological or mechanical, but free, and therefore moral. What we desire is not that God is automatically programmed to face us; what we need is the 'gratuitous communication of an eternal person.'[36] The Baroque scholastics had defined the summit of divine and human freedom in *indifference* towards its choice. If freedom is the highest good, then it must be entirely neutral as to its objects, or else they make some demand upon it, and the chooser is *not entirely free*. Wojtyla was deliberately overturning this way of thinking when he wrote, in *Love and Responsibility*, that '*Freedom exists for the sake of love*. ... Love commits freedom and imbues it with that to which the will is naturally attracted – goodness. The will aspires to the good, and freedom belongs to the will, hence freedom exists for the sake of love, because it is by way of love that human beings share most fully in the good. ... man longs for love more than for freedom – freedom is the means and love the end.'[37] This means that freedom always operates in a context. And so too, human questioning about death has a given and concrete context. Created human beings ask about death *because* grace calls them to do so; both Gilson and de Lubac emphasised, from the very beginning, that the giver of the one is the giver of the other. Thus conceived, philosophical questioning by human beings and God's search for humanity in history are freely inter-related. Philosophy and theology do not follow one after another, in a straight line, but, in the image that the Holy Father uses in *F&R*, pursue one another in a 'circle.'[38]

It is true to say, relating the encyclical to the debate of the 1930s, that 'the Pope's positions coincide ... closely with those of de Lubac.'[39] But the work of *contemporary* theology that the encyclical seems to me most clearly to echo is Hans Urs von Balthasar's *Theo-Drama*, the ethical portion of the writer's trilogy. The *Theo-Drama* begins from the premise that one needs to find a way of founding each person's uniqueness, travels through modern philosophy, psychology and sociology, and concludes that the only way of founding personal uniqueness is in the divine call to each human being; this call is in its turn founded in the ontological vocation of Christ, the Son. One of the most endearing features of the *Theo-Drama*, to me, is the way in which it reactivates the old image of the atoning work of Christ as a defeat of death, darkness and the devil. That notion had fallen fallow, in modern theology since the seventeenth century. Von Balthasar translates the ancient imaginative idea of a descent into Hell, to do battle with the devil, into the philosophical terms of the human problem of death. He has been criticised for giving a merely anthropological view of atonement, of beginning from the merely human problem of death. But this is to ignore the fact that, from the first page of the first volume, von Balthasar's anthropology is Christological, that his theology encircles his philosophy. The teaching of the encyclical is likewise that there are no merely 'anthropological' problems, that the shape of human biography can only be fully understood through Christ.

Notes

1. Alvin Plantinga's discussion of *Fides et Ratio* was published in the Internet journal, *Books and Culture*, 'Special Section on Faith and Reason: Philosophers Respond to *Fides et Ratio*', July/August 1999, available at www.Christianity.net.
2. John Paul II, *Fides et Ratio* (Catholic Truth Society, 1998), # 76. (Referred to below as *F&R*)
3. Étienne Gilson, *Le Philosophe et la Théologie* (Librarie Arthème Fayard, Paris, 1960), p. 221.
4. *F&R*, # 74.

5. *ibid.*, # 81.
6. *ibid.*, # 5.
7. Rocco Buttiglione, *Karol Wojtyla: The Thought of the Man Who Became John Paul II*, translated by Paolo Guietti and Francesca Murphy (Grand Rapids, William B. Eerdmans, 1997), p. 61.
8. *ibid.*, p. 73.
9. Karol Wojtyla, 'Il personalismo Tomista', pp. 146-147, cited in *ibid.*, p. 82.
10. *ibid.*, p. 73.
11. *ibid.*, pp. 61, 81.
12. Karol Wojtyla, *Love and Responsibility*, translated by H.J. Willetts, revised edn (London, Fount/Harper Collins, 1982), p. 114.
13. Avery Dulles, 'Can Philosophy be Christian?', *First Things*, April 2000.
14. Gilson speaking in Maurice Blondel, Émile Bréhier, Léon Brunschvicg, Étienne Gilson, Xavier Leon, Jacques Maritain, Édouard Le Roy, transcript of the debate about Christian philosophy, held on 21 March 1931, 'La Notion de Philosophie Chrétienne', *Bulletin de la Société française de Philosophie*, vol. 31: 37-93 (1931), 57.
15. *ibid.*, p. 57.
16. Maritain speaking in 'La Notion de Philosophie Chrétienne', p. 63.
17. *ibid.*, p. 66.
18. *F&R*, #76.
19. *Bulletin de la Société de Philosophie*, Séance du 21 Mars, 1931, Appendice, lettre de Maurice Blondel, 'La Philosophie Chrétienne existe-t-elle comme Philosophie?', p. 88.
20. *F&R*, # 4.
21. Alvin Plantinga, 'Faith and Reason: Philosophers Respond to *Fides et Ratio*'.
22. *F&R*, # 36, my italics.
23. Gilson speaking in 'La Notion de Philosophie Chrétienne', p. 47.
24. Newman, *Grammar of Assent* (Notre Dame, University of Notre Dame Press, 1979), p. 91.
25. *ibid.*, p. 269.
26. *F&R*, # 48
27. Newman, *Grammar of Assent*, p. 294.
28. *F&R*, # 33.
29. *ibid.*, #32.
30. *ibid.*, # 48.
31. Maurice Blondel, 'La Philosophie Chrétienne existe-t-elle comme Philosophie?', p. 91.
32. Étienne Gilson, 'Note sur le Revelabile selon Cajetan', *Medieval Studies*, vol. 15: 199-206 (1953), 200-202.

33. Henri De Lubac, *Surnaturel: Études Historiques*, (first published 1946, reprinted Desclée de Brouwer, 1991), p. 47.

34. *ibid.*, p. 487.

35. *ibid.*, pp. 247-249.

36. *ibid.*, p. 483.

37. Karol Wojtyla, *Love and Responsibility*, pp. 135-136.

38. *F&R*, # 73.

39. Avery Dulles, 'Can Philosophy be Christian?', *First Things*, April 2000.

A PHILOSOPHICAL RESPONSE TO THE ENCYCLICAL

Timothy Mooney

Writing about his experiences of Catholic Missionaries in the South Seas, Robert Louis Stevenson remarked that they were distinguished by their sensitivity to local cultures and traditions. They not only taught the truths of faith, but sought to preserve what was good in these cultures and traditions. In short, they did not seek to destroy the latter, rather to reconcile with revelation and church teaching what is universal and yet uniquely expressed in them.[1] It could well strike the student of philosophy reading *Fides et Ratio* (*F&R*) that an analogous process is at work in this encyclical. Pope John Paul II is informed not only by the perennial philosophy of St Thomas Aquinas, but also – and very notably – by the work of one of the twentieth century's greatest philosophers, Edmund Husserl (himself a teacher of the recently canonised Edith Stein). Whilst Aquinas and Husserl have many common concerns, my major interest in this essay is with the influence of Husserl, since reference to the latter facilitates the clarification of many of the arguments to which the Pope has recourse.

Husserl's influence is particularly evident in ## 80-99 of *F&R*, which are concerned with the status of theology in contemporary intellectual life. Like all sciences, human and natural, theology begins with a number of givens: it accepts a transcendent and supernatural reality, and more specifically a loving God who has created an initially ordered world populated by persons who can come to know and love Him, not just through natural reason, but subsequently and most fully through revelation. Most of these givens for theological clarification are specific articles of faith, and faith brings us in turn to the question of reason, for we would not wish to see faith as something unreasonable or irrational. For mediaeval philosophers like St Thomas Aquinas, faith and reason can and should run together. What he means by faith in something or someone is a belief in or about that thing or person that is warranted by reason. Even if one cannot prove the existence of the thing or person or of some property belonging to them, it is more rational than not to affirm it. Faith has to be less than absolutely certain knowledge in order to be faith, but more than bare belief to escape the arbitrary and irrational. Husserl would add that a rational belief must involve at least an implicit appeal to actual or possible evidence; even if it cannot be verified (as opposed to being justified) in the present, it must be capable of this in the future.[2]

The very title of the recent encyclical bears witness to a difficulty, and perhaps even a crisis, in contemporary thought, namely its inability to see the connection between faith and reason. When many contemporary thinkers talk about faith, what they really mean is blind faith, that is, unwarranted belief or superstition. And if the faith that underpins theology is unwarranted, then theology itself will be devoid of justification. Rational justification is part of the essence of philosophy. Hence philosophers will typically state that the best philosophical position is the one that, whilst maintaining internal coherence, is capable of giving the most adequate explanation of the widest range of phenomena. In *F&R*, therefore, the Pope has amongst his chief concerns the following questions: What kind of philosophical position will be coherent, open to faith and able to support it, thus serving as part of the prelude to theology? By the same token, what kind of philosophical positions will involve incoherence and closure, being destructive of faith and of the possibility of theology?

In the sections already mentioned, the Pope observes that a philosophical position that leads on to faith and theology will have a sapiential dimension – it will be a love of wisdom searching for the overarching and ultimate meaning of life. This philosophy will also verify the human capacity to know the truth, and will have a genuinely metaphysical range going from phenomenon to foundation. Put another way, it will go beyond appearances towards an absolute and ultimate ground.[3] The philosophical positions destructive of faith and theology, on the other hand, will invariably show either one or more of the following attitudes: phenomenalism; scepticism; relativism; subjectivism; historicism; nihilism; scientism; pragmatism, and utilitarianism.[4] The attitudes from this list that are of particular concern in the present essay are those of scepticism, relativism and scientism.

I

Of all thinkers recent and contemporary, it is Husserl who is foremost in his rejection of scepticism. He attacks it most famously in 'Prolegomena to Pure Logic', the preliminary essay to his *Logical Investigations* (1900/01). A distinction is drawn between total scepticism about the notions of truth and knowledge, and partial scepticism about the reliability of our sensory knowledge of the world. The total sceptic, of which there are not very many, will say that there is no truth, or that there is no knowledge. Husserl notes that the proposition 'There is no truth' amounts in its sense to the proposition 'There is a truth that there is no truth'. This is self-referentially inconsistent or absurd, since the consequent content of the proposition denies what the antecedent proposition affirms.[5] The same holds true of the claim that there is no knowledge – it amounts in sense to the claim that one knows there is no knowledge.

For Husserl, the violation of logical laws is at its grossest in such cases, for the sense of the theses rejects those laws on which the rational possibility and proof of any thesis depends.[6] It may of course turn out to be the case that the total sceptic is unable to understand the basic laws of logic, or even that he rejects them. Thus he might say that his theory is only true for him; that only he can really understand it; that the laws of logic do not apply to him, and so on. Husserl comments that in these cases one quite simply cannot persuade the sceptic of his error. More importantly, however, there is no need to persuade him, even if one would like to do so – all that is necessary is to have refuted him in an objectively valid manner. On such trivial insights, adds Husserl, every scepticism must come to grief.[7] This follows very closely on Aristotle, who remarked that the man who refuses to accept the principle of non-contradiction is little better than a vegetable, for rational discourse with him is impossible.[8]

The other form of scepticism is partial scepticism, instantiated in the claim that our sensory knowledge of the world is unreliable. What is really antifreeze can smell like lemon juice, what is really a straight stick can look bent in water, and so on – we are constantly prey to illusion. Husserl replies that if everything coming through the senses were illusion, then I would never be able to know this. I can only grasp that something is an illusion in the first instance if I have something that I can set against it, have a further sensory experience that reveals its falsity (tasting the antifreeze or touching the stick). Husserl thus invokes the counterfeit objection – we can only know that a coin is false if we have experience of a genuine one. Even the sceptic must operate with some standard of sensory truth, and even he can surmount illusion – to discover that something is false is to be capable of leaving it behind.[9] A further argument employed by Husserl against such a sceptic is the existential one: whether one be a total or a partial sceptic, it is impossible to live according to one's theory, to put it to the test of practice. To hold a thesis that one cannot live is an abrogation of rational responsibility, and in point of fact, to be able to live at all one must live in certainty of the world.[10]

II

Relativism is another position rejected by the Pope, and so too by Husserl, who describes it as specific scepticism or species scepticism. Relativism is a mode of scepticism; it denies the existence, not of truth or of morality, but of truths or moral laws that are universal, that apply or can apply to all peoples in all cultures. Husserl makes the point that the denial of universal truth means that a proposition can be true for one group of people or one species, but false for another people or species. But this is plainly absurd – one and the same content of a proposition cannot be both true and false. This is the principle of excluded middle: a proposition is either true or false, it cannot be both true and false. What is true is absolutely and intrinsically true, whether it is different people, or even angels or God, who apprehend it. This does not mean, on the other hand, that every truth must be understood in exactly the same way. The proposition 'mammals cannot breath through water' is true for men and for angels, but we understand it as creatures to whom it is far more relevant. For Husserl, there is one single truth in every case, but sometimes equivocal uses.[11]

Relativism about truth also runs up against the problem already seen with scepticism, that of failing to achieve self-referential consistency. David Detmer has recently attacked relativism on just this ground, using arguments that are once again drawn from Husserl. If truth exists, but is merely relative to a particular culture, then surely this truth will itself be merely relative to the culture in which it is asserted. But how then should we understood it, since it seems to be a universal, transcultural claim? On the other hand, this truth may be an exception to a general rule that all truths are merely relative to a particular culture. But one could then enquire why, if we are able to admit one exception, we cannot then admit other exceptions.[12]

The other main form of relativism is moral relativism. On this account, there are no universally valid standards of right and wrong.

The latter are merely feelings or preferences of individuals or groups, and what we call right is merely enforced for practical purposes, to protect life and property. But if this were the case, there would be strictly speaking no morality, and no possibility of convincingly criticising the actions of this or that person or group (say of Charles Manson or of the Bolsheviks). Respect for persons could only be defended on the grounds of being likeable or practical or useful (which raises the question of who defines what is likeable or practical or useful in the absence of universal, rational standards). In practice, whenever we invoke notions of respect, we almost always appeal to a universal standard (which is why it can be amusing to observe the performative inconsistency of apparent relativists or nihilists describing as fascists others with whom they happen to disagree). Immanuel Kant made the point that moral actions cannot be relative; a truly moral action must be able to pass the test of being universalised with consistency into a principle, for otherwise it will be self-destructive, ultimately undoing its own very possibility. The example he gives is that of lying. It might be argued that telling lies is alright if it gets one out of trouble. But the problem with this is that it cannot be universalised with consistency, for if we all began to tell lies to avoid difficulties, people would soon disbelieve that anyone could tell the truth, and lies would be of no use whatsoever.[13]

One strategy of the defender of relativism might be to maintain, that for all of its apparent inconsistencies, relativism at least encourages respect for the other. The problem here, however, is that it brings us back to the question of universality. Why should respect for the other be taken as anything more than a value relative to one particular culture? But if we accept that respect for the other is a universal value, it is still hard to see how relativism can encourage it. Detmer has noted that relativists are quick to insist that the beliefs of others are not to be seen as inferior to ours, only as different. But by the same token, these different beliefs cannot be seen as superior to ours, and relativists are not too quick to make this second observation. Relativism thus removes one of the most powerful motives to study the views of the other – the idea that the other may be right and that I myself may be wrong.[14] As the Pope remarks in a remarkably similar vein, the belief that one can know a universally valid truth is the essential condition for sincere, authentic dialogue. On this basis alone is it possible to overcome division and to journey together towards the full truth.[15]

III

The final target of the Pope that I will consider in some detail is scientism. Scientism refuses to admit the validity of forms of knowledge other than those of the natural sciences, relegating religious, ethical and aesthetic knowledge to the realm of mere fantasy. Scientific knowledge is all that there is, and it can in principle, and some day in fact, explain everything. Of all closed attitudes, scientism is the most difficult to combat, for its proponents can point to the enormous success of the natural sciences. But it is nonetheless open to criticism. Science is usually described as systematic and formulated knowledge, and in the case of natural science it aims at the understanding, prediction and control of natural processes first revealed through the senses, unaided and aided. The theories of science, however, cannot be fully or finally proven. According to Husserl, they can best be seen as functional models whose worth lies in their range of explanation and prediction.[16] They are also open to replacement by other theories with a wider explanatory and predictive range. The later theories can falsify the earlier ones and show them up as limited, but these once again cannot be finally proven, which is why practising scientists more usually talk of the best available theory.[17]

The lack of finality in science means that the idea of what constitutes a scientific explanation is open to change. At the end of the nineteenth century it was believed that all things could be reduced to universal mechanical laws of matter and motion. But this belief was destroyed by the work of Max Planck and Albert Einstein, amongst others. It is of little use stating that one can give a mechanistic explanation if one does not know what one means by mechanics.[18] The project of complete scientific explanation has also run into trouble at the level of subatomic physics. Werner Heisenberg showed that the very instruments that we use to measure the velocity and position of subatomic realities actually distort the behaviour of these actualities – we cannot get to them as they are in themselves. Hence some scientific knowledge is – both in fact and in principle – indirect and inferential for human beings. It may be rationally warranted, but it is not for this reason a first-hand or non-perspectival apprehension of reality.[19]

A crucial realm of existence that natural science is unable to explain (despite the enormous advances in cognitive studies) is mind or consciousness in general, up to and including self-awareness. Consciousness is already distinct in that it is not a thing, but a function or state, as recognised by Aristotle.[20] It is also distinct in virtue of being not only within the world, but being an irreducible perspective on the world. Husserl describes this as the paradox of human subjectivity.[21] Consciousness is not hidden in the sense of lacking 'outer' criteria, for it is expressed in our various forms of movement or comportment, in a jaunty walk or a smile. The conscious state of confidence or of amusement, however, is not a potential object of perception. Colin McGinn calls this the problem of cognitive closure. We know – with respect to our world at least – that conscious states depend on parts of the brain, but they cannot be observed by directing the senses onto the brain. We can trace electrochemical processes in neural pathways, but these show us only brain states, not conscious ones.[22]

Some scientists and philosophers claim that the inability to 'see' consciousness will not stop us explaining it in terms of natural science. Once we manage to build a computer programme that can answer all the questions and perform all the theoretical tasks expected of a human, we will have explained consciousness because we will know how to create it. This is the famous 'Turing Test' formulated by Alan Turing.[23] But there is then the problem of how we could, without first-person authority, know we have created it. In Husserl's account, conscious states are irreducible – to properly know 'what it is like' to be conscious in various ways, as Thomas Nagel will later put it, one must actually live through these states. Nagel has gone on to contend that such states manifest 'qualia' that cannot be set out in propositional form.[24]

The Turing test cannot show that what is crucial to consciousness has been achieved, namely, the fact of understanding things or knowing their meaning. In his 'Chinese Room' experiment, John Searle asks us to imagine a computer program that is given questions in Chinese and can give back answers to these questions in Chinese. A computer program is purely formal or syntactical. It can only be given rules of sentence-construction, and lists of other words that any one word can represent. And a program with an exhaustive list of words that other ones stand for and of sentence-construction could give answers that are so good as to be indistinguishable from a real Chinese speaker. But dealing purely with rules of combination, it could not be said to understand what the words actually mean – it could satisfy the Turing Test without grasping the semantic contents constitutive of consciousness.[25]

Only beings with consciousness can have morality and art and religion, for each of these presupposes a certain type of conscious knowledge. Morality presupposes an appreciation of universal norms of right and wrong. Art presupposes an appreciation of harmony and proportion and clarity. And religion presupposes an appreciation that we are not our own origin, any more than natural being in general is its own origin. It is precisely these dimensions – which natural science cannot explain adequately – that are covered by ethics and aesthetics and theology. All of these disciplines bring us beyond the natural world. They represent, not so much a failure of natural science as the fact that its mathematical approach is of restricted range. Husserl noted that this approach only became problematic when it was posited as the solution to every question.[26] Furthermore, mathematically based natural science from the sixteenth century onwards has always been concerned with *how* the universe is and *how* it has developed. Even though natural science can point to order and design in the universe, its concern is not with the fact *that* the universe is – that fact provoking the question of the reason for spatiotemporal actuality from its first moments.[27]

IV

If the points set out above hold up, the way is left open for a philosophy that affirms wisdom and truth and has a genuine metaphysical range going from phenomenon to foundation. It will involve a rational openness to transcendence, to that which goes beyond each of us individually and beyond humanity collectively. In this regard I would like to conclude by noting that three major forms of transcendence are identified by Husserl – of things, of persons, and of the ground of order in general. The simplest of worldly things are already characterised by transcendence. We are only given aspects of them, and can never see all of their aspects at the blow. When we gain new aspects, furthermore, we lose others. Hence there is always the possibility of being surprised by things – they can reveal completely new aspects that surprise us, or even show themselves as other or illusory. The meaning of the transcendence of things and of the world is always more than I can be given in the present. Here we discern a rational incorporation of scepticism and finitude into philosophy: we have certainty about things and the wider world, but it is a warranted certainty, contingent on new experiences continually confirming it.[28]

Transcendence also characterises persons, described as objects in the world and subjects with a point of view on the world. But this transcendence should not be seen in a dualist fashion, after Descartes. As mentioned above, conscious states are expressed in a person's movements and comportment. Husserl puts this very well: the human body is through and through a conscious body: every movement is full of mind – coming and going, standing still, laughing and dancing and speaking.[29] The point is that the body is full of mind, rather than being its container. This being the case, the transcendence of consciousness is not of something behind the body, but of something beyond the body. I can never live the other's states from his perspective, such as he lives them. Distance is not to be regarded as a tragedy that befalls otherness, but a very condition of otherness, of genuinely other persons.[30]

The third type of transcendence alluded to by Husserl is the transcendence of an intelligent creator and conserver, and this is indicated by the order of the natural world. Prior to the constructions of scientific theory, he argues, we experience in our lives a harmonious flow of experiences that are not recalcitrant to ready comprehension. But for consciousness, this world-order is contingent: it is entirely possible logically that it could break down and leave us with utter chaos, like a television set completely out of tune. Just such a hypothetical breakdown is outlined in Husserl's thought-experiment of 'The Annihilation of the World'.[31] This order cannot be due to us, since we do not control the ingress of harmonious experiences, and it cannot be explained by science, which once again deals with how the ordered world is, but not with its origin. Order therefore provides us with rational grounds for believing in the existence of an extra-worldly divinity. The transcendence of this Being transcends not just the world but human consciousness, and hence is quite unique.[32] In Husserl's phenomenology, therefore, faith can be understood as warranted by reason, that same reason whose explanatory limits and urge towards ultimate truth give faith a due place.

Notes

1. 'An Open Letter to the Rev Dr Hyde of Honolulu' in *The Works of Robert Louis Stevenson*, (London: Heinemann, 1924), Tusitala Edition vol. XXI, pp. 30-41. It should be observed that Stevenson also had great admiration for many of the Presbyterian missionaries whom he encountered.

2. *Summa Theologiae*, IIaIIae, 2,10, *Summa Contra Gentiles* I, 3-8. See also
    Husserl's *Cartesian Meditations*, trans. Dorion Cairns (The Hague,
    Martinus Nijhoff, 1960), pp. 59-60. (Referred to below as *CM*)
3. *Faith and Reason*, ##81-83. (Referred to below as *F&R*)
4. *ibid.*, ##80, 82, 87-90, 98.
5. *Logical Investigations*, trans. J.N. Findlay (London, Routledge and Kegan
    Paul, 1970), vol. I, p.142. (Referred to below as *LI*)
6. *ibid.*, pp. 135-136.
7. *ibid.*, p. 139.
8. *Metaphysics*, 1006a, 12-17.
9. *CM*, pp. 57-59.
10. *The Crisis of European Sciences and Transcendental Phenomenology*, trans.
    David Carr (Evanston,Northwestern University Press, 1970), pp. 142-143.
    (Referred to below as *CES*)
11. *LI*, pp. 140-141.
12. David Detmer, 'Husserl's Critique of Relativism' in B.R. Wachterhauser
    (ed.), *Phenomenology and Skepticism* (Evanston, Northwestern University
    Press, 1996), pp. 103-105. To be abbreviated as *PS*.
13. *The Moral Law: Kant's Groundwork of the Metaphysics of Morals*, trans. H.J.
    Paton (London, Hutchinson, 1948), p. 85.
14. *PS*, p. 107.
15. *F&R*, # 92.
16. *CES*, p. 43. For Husserl, these models are ultimately the products of
    conscious subjects. Veering away from scientific realism, he criticises those
    theorists who project the realm of mathematical idealities into the actual
    world itself and reduce the latter to the former, mistaking for true being that
    which is only a method. *ibid.*, pp. 51-52. However, the scientific realist
    could reject Husserl's first point and accept his second, retorting that there
    is no difficulty with this method's being taken as a provisional account of
    things in themselves so long as it is not taken as all-encompassing. On my
    understanding, *F&R* would implicitly involve some such version of
    scientific realism, following as it does in the tradition of Thomistic (and
    early Husserlian) realism.
17. On the notion of falsification in the progression of the sciences see Karl
    Popper's *The Logic of Scientific Discovery* (London, Hutchinson, 1959).
18. cf. Alfred North Whitehead, *Science and the Modern World* (London, Free
    Association Books, 1985), p. 21.
19. This idea also underlines Heisenberg's popular *Physics and Beyond* (New
    York, Harper and Row, 1971). See also his *Physics and Philosophy* (New
    York, Harper and Row, 1971).

20. *De Anima*, 412b-413a.
21. *CES*, p. 178ff. Such a characterisation is made in the process of Husserl's final explication of his transcendental idealism, but does not of itself commit one to such a position.
22. Colin McGinn, *The Problem of Consciousness* (Oxford, Blackwell, 1991), p. 3.
23. Alan Turing, 'Computing Machinery and Intelligence', *Mind*, 59 (1950), 433-460.
24. *LI*, pp. 277-278; *CES*, p. 233ff. See also Thomas Nagel, 'What is it Like to Be a Bat?', *The Philosophical Review*, 83 (1974), pp. 435-450.
25. John Searle, 'Minds, Brains, and Programs', *Behavioural and Brain Sciences*, 3 (1980), pp. 417-424.
26. *CES*, pp. 21-67.
27. Here I am of course making use of Ludwig Wittgenstein's remark that 'It is not *how* things are in the world that is mystical, but *that* it exists.' *Tractatus Logico Philosophicus*, 6.44, trans. D.F. Pears and B.F. McGuinness (London, Routledge and Kegan Paul, 1961), p. 73.
28. *CM*, pp. 57-58, 61-62.
29. *Ideas Pertaining to a Pure Phenomenology and to a Phenomenological Philosophy. Second Book: Studies in the Phenomenology of Constitution*, trans. R. Rojcewicz and A. Schuwer (Dordrecht, Kluwer Academic Publishers, 1989), p. 252.
30. *CM*, p. 109.
31. *Ideas Pertaining to a Pure Phenomenology and to a Phenomenological Philosophy. First Book: General Introduction to a Pure Phenomenology*, trans. Frank Kersten (The Hague, Martinus Nijhoff, 1982), p. 109ff.
32. *ibid.*, pp. 133-134. A crucial difference between *F&R* and these pages of Husserl is that, in the latter, God is a Being whose existence must be 'bracketed' in the course of a methodologically idealist programme of explanation. In this programme, Husserl neither affirms nor denies the thesis of the independent actuality of the external world. He converts the world of both the ordinary person and the scientist into phenomenon only, and in so doing places the thesis in parenthesis. This parenthesis or bracketing brings the thesis into relief so that its meaning can be explicated, or rather that component of its meaning that is 'transcendental', i.e. due to the synthetic activities of the conscious subject. The very strength of the evidence for God's existence is in Husserl's view an obstacle to uncovering the meaning contributed by the finite subject. Because faith posits the actuality of a Creator behind the world (itself to be bracketed as phenomenon), the thesis of a Creator would complete an external or third-

person account including the natural and human sciences but neglecting the finite subject. Hence the thesis of a Creator must itself be bracketed for the purposes of meaning-explication. It is of course questionable whether a Christian could reconcile this position (even if merely methodological) with faith in our radical dependence on God in every facet of our Being.

REVELATION IN RELATIONSHIP TO THEOLOGY AND PHILOSOPHY

Thomas Norris

At the beginning of St Luke's Gospel there is an episode that sets in dynamic relationship revelation, theology and philosophy. As such it provides a paradigm for the subject of Chapter 4 of the encyclical. The episode is that of the annunciation to Our Lady. St Luke (1:26-38) underlines the dramatic dialogue at the core of the encounter as well as the significance of the event for the history of salvation.[1] The angel Gabriel makes known to Mary that God has an eternal Son and that she has been chosen by the Father to welcome that Son into the world on behalf of Israel and of humanity. Furthermore, the enfleshment of the Son of the Most High in Mary's flesh will occur through the agency of the Holy Spirit. Here one has a clear statement of the fact of the revelation that both fulfils Old Testament revelation and provides the content and substance of the new and eternal Covenant. That content is nothing less than the very 'Son of the Most High' (1:32) now offered to Mary to become her Son also, and the gift of the Holy Spirit who 'will come upon Mary' (1:35). The two arms of the Father, to use the language of St Irenaeus[2], are extended to Mary as the sign of the Father's election and of his eternal merciful love that would embrace the world through Mary at this summit moment of revelation. And Mary says, 'I am the handmaid of the Lord, let it be done to me according to your word' (1:38). Mary's faith, by which she 'gave God's infinity dwindled to infancy welcome' (G.M. Hopkins)[3], is the perfect correlative of the revelation now culminating at this vital stage of the dialogue of the God of 'the House of Jacob' (1:33) with Israel and with humanity as represented by and personified in Mary.

Now what is truly fascinating in Luke's account is that 'Mary's faith did not end in a mere acquiescence in divine ... revelations'.[4] Luke highlights the fact that Mary 'treasured all these things and pondered them in her heart' (2:19), and concludes that she 'stored up all these things in her heart' (2:52). 'She does not think it enough to accept, she dwells upon it; not enough to possess, she uses it; not enough to assent, she develops it; not enough to submit the Reason, she reasons upon it' (Newman, *ibid.*). Revelation and faith had led immediately into theology and, by implication, into the activity of reasoning that we call philosophy. 'And thus she symbolises to us, not only the faith of the unlearned, but of the doctors of the Church also, who have to investigate, and weigh, and define ... to anticipate or remedy the various aberrations of wrong reason'. Mary, then, is 'an example [of] the use of Reason, in investigating the doctrines of faith'.[5] And by implication she is also an 'example' in philosophy that is the product of reason, being reason in its orderly and investigative operation. And so at the very beginning of the New Testament as event we find a living paradigm for the subject matter of Pope John Paul's encyclical, *F&R.*

Humankind is an enigma.[6] The fact stands out the moment one looks at the story of the search of *homo sapiens* for the meaning of human existence. This is where the encyclical begins: 'In both East and West, we may trace a journey that has led humanity down the centuries to meet and engage truth more and more deeply ... A cursory glance at ancient history shows clearly how in different parts of the world, with their different cultures, there arise at the same time the fundamental questions that pervade human life: *Who am I? Where have I come from and where am I going? Why is there evil? What is there after this life?*[7]

Now this strongly suggests that it is legitimate to see in the religious story of humankind a kaleidoscope of responses to this quest which largely defines the human being. These responses are also capable of classification, according to a hermeneutic of orientation based on the essential structure of each one. Such a classification might then enable us to grasp, by way of comparison and contrast, the divine freshness and originality that live deep down in Christian Revelation.

First, there is the way of the primitive religions. Under the double impact of death and evil, on the one hand, and the luminosity of the cosmos, on the other, these religions sought communion with the divine as perceived in the more lasting strata of the cosmos. There are certain key elements in these religions. First, they are polytheistic, since their gods 'always represent some aspect of human need, the need for protection from the perils of nature, the need for defence in battle, the need for love. The gods are always gods in service of man'.[8] A second aspect of these religions is that of mythology. Mythology is important for its view of time as primeval time and for its use of imagery taken from our spatio-temporal world.

Next, there is the way of the great religions and of philosophy. The moment man became aware of the inadequacy of the religions was a moment of breakthrough to a new and better way towards the Divine. God is not any part of the cosmos. In fact, he is beyond the cosmos. The greatness of this tradition and breakthrough is that it purified man's age-old quest and desire, and pointed out the way to succeed in the quest for the Beyond or the Beginning. There cannot be many gods, in fact only one, and this One is unlike all of the things around us. This transcendent God of the philosophers is 'the God who can be sought only by the way of radical negation, in which the self in an ultimate act of abandonment cuts itself loose from everything finite and loses itself in the infinite abyss of the nameless one'.[9]

Unquestionably, such abandonment enjoys a great nobility as is obvious both in the great religions of Asia and in classical philosophy. According to many theologians and philosophers, such as Eric Voegelin[10] and von Balthasar,[11] however, these religions founder for two reasons. First, the individual person has to abandon his original intuition of his own worthwhileness and lovableness. Secondly, the

One discovered by philosophy and the great religions is impersonal and faceless. 'It is not possible to love a faceless Infinite. Here once again the original intuition of love is denied. And so it would seem that man's original search ends in an *aporia*.[12]

Is there any way beyond this dilemma in which the search for the Divine requires the negation of the 'I', as well as the rejection of the world and of the many, since all are incompatible with the One, the Divine? The nation of Israel made the breathtaking discovery that it is not we who seek God primarily, but it is God who seeks us out. In the tension between the human and divine poles of existence, the divine pole is the prime mover. This is the germ idea in the election of Abraham and in the unfolding of his mission: 'in you I will bless all the nations of the earth' (Gen 12:3).[13] The history of the children of Abraham introduces a movement that is the complete reverse of the basic impulse of the primitive religions, the great religions, and philosophy. 'For here, it is no longer the man Abraham who starts out in search of God. It is God himself who speaks to man, who leads him, not to religious meditation on the Absolute but to a way of simple obedience to the divine will'.[14] They discover his love for them both collectively and individually in the saga and the vicissitudes of their history as the Chosen People to whom the God of Abraham gives the gift of covenants, the blessing of the Law, and the guidance of the Prophets.

The Way of Judaism, however, is the way of God seeking an ever deeper communion with his people, a communion that they find increasingly difficult and beyond their capacities. Their traumatic discovery is that they are not capable of living in the divine-human *Lebensraum* opened up for them by the God of Abraham, Isaac and Jacob.[15] Accordingly, the God of Israel promises a fulfilment within history at a time to be decided by God in the future. Thus Israel looks towards an historical future, 'a vanishing point, an *omega*, when the ever imperfect, again-and-again broken covenant becomes finalised, the messianic time arrives, the lines of God and people cross each other in a final event'.[16] The notion of the future time, the messianic time, is thus central in Israel.

These two religious approaches, that of Israel towards a future where God will bring his fullness in a way that will inaugurate 'the fullness of time', and that of the great religions, philosophy and the primitive religions where the divine is in the Beyond, are irreconcilable. They are 'like the vertical and the horizontal. One cannot be a Zen Buddhist and a Communist at the same time. One cannot devote one's life to the furtherance of world progress and at the same time withdraw from the world'.[17] Here, then, we are faced with a deepening of the dilemma. Can this vertical as it were of the primitive and the non-Christian religions, with their impersonal faceless Divinity together with the negation of the world and our humanity as the only way to the Divine, ever be reconciled with the horizontal of Judaic futurism and hope? That is the question.

'But what is irreconcilable in the world (the vertical and the horizontal) forms a cross, an empty cross that cannot be occupied by anyone. Jesus Christ alone can fill this empty space, because he is the fulfilment both of pagan human longing *and* of Jewish hopeful faith. He is the Word of God for all mankind'.[18] For in Christ the divine search of the God of Abraham, Isaac and Jacob for all humankind expressed through his instrument, Israel, has intersected with the age-old search of humankind for the Beyond and the meaning of human and historical existence. His cross in fact effectively symbolises this synthesis. In the elegant words of T.S. Eliot, 'Here the impossible union of spheres of existence is actual'.[19]

Christ effectively overcomes the dilemma in the search from below where the divinity is faceless and so not the love fulfilling humankind's primordial intuition that reality is love. He also overcomes the rejection of the other and of the world, since his Incarnation and cross affirm both the infinite value of each person as 'the brother for whom Christ died' (I Cor 8:11), and the preciousness of each moment of time because the moment the Timeless entered time, every moment of time has entered Eternity. 'We saw his glory, the glory that is his as the only Son of God, full of loving kindness and rocklike fidelity'(Jn 1:14). The very Ground of Being smiles on us in the Incarnation and on the cross as a parent smiles on a child.

Brief Overview of the Faith–Reason Relationship in the Time of the Church

The Marian paradigm with which we began powerfully indicated that the fullness of revelation and the faith that is correlative to it, far from rendering obsolete the philosophical and theological quests, only served to heighten their liveliness. The woman who 'let all God's glory through'[20] is the very model of that devout and searching reasoning that faith presupposes, stimulates and guides. Now indeed there was an unending abundance of life and light in the eternal Word made flesh, for the good reason that in him 'all the fullness of God was pleased to dwell' (Col 1:19 RSV). The Marian 'pondering', 'storing' and 'treasuring' would perpetuate itself in the time of the Church, and issue in the form of theology and philosophy mutually refining each other yet balancing delicately in the harmony of revealed Faith and searching Reason.

The drama of that perpetuation during the Christian centuries deserves some little attention at this juncture. Joseph Ratzinger describes the interaction of revelation and philosophy and theology in a temporal sequence of unity, distinction, opposition, and new relationship.[21] It is not the only reading of the interfacing of faith and reason that is possible. It is, however, appropriate for our immediate concerns.

In the earliest times the unity of theology and philosophy is the norm. A vivid instance is Justin Martyr, a professional philosopher who in the middle of the second century became a Christian for the reason that he found in revelation not an alternative to philosophy but its fulfilment. Christianity for Justin was 'the only true and profitable philosophy'.[22] According to Eric Voegelin, Justin was convinced that 'gospel and philosophy do not face the believer with a choice of alternatives, nor are they complementary aspects of truth which the thinker would have to weld into the complete truth; in his conception, the Logos of the gospel is rather the same Word of the same God as the *logos spermatikos* of philosophy, but at a later stage of its manifestation in history'.[23] It was precisely this unity that allowed the

Fathers of the Church to detect in the cultures of the nations the 'seeds of the Word'. This allowed for an inculturation of the Gospel that led to a new flowering of the culture being evangelised, as its particular *logoi spermatikoi* germinated in the encounter with revelation.

A fascinating corroboration of this fact is to be found in the earliest Christian art. Original research shows that 'in its earliest beginnings Christian art arose out of the quest for the true philosophy', a finding that dashes the idea that the relationship between faith and philosophy is quite abstract. 'It was philosophy which enabled the first plastic expressions of the faith ... the shepherd, the *orans* and the philosopher'. The philosopher image represents the true person of wisdom, the one who is the 'prototype of the *homo christianus* who has received the revelation of the true paradise through the Gospel'. Besides, 'the figure of the philosopher now becomes the image of Christ himself'. For Christ alone holds the answer to the universal problem of death. And the most penetrating question, the question stinging and piercing the side of each and every man and woman, is the question of death. 'Philosophy, the search for meaning in the face of death, is now represented as the search for Christ': he is the 'one philosopher who gives an effectual answer by changing death and, therefore, changing life itself'.[24]

The earlier phase of unity between faith and philosophy was to be followed by their distinction. This distinguishing was in a unique way the work of St Thomas. 'In his thinking, the demands of reason and the power of faith found the most elevated synthesis ever attained by human thought, for he could defend the radical newness introduced by Revelation without ever demeaning the venture proper to reason' (#78). The lines of demarcation between them were drawn in the following manner. 'Philosophy is the search of unaided reason for answers to the ultimate questions about reality. Philosophical knowledge comprises exclusively that sort of knowledge which reason as such can gain by itself, without the guidance of revelation ... Theology, in contrast, is rational reflection upon God's revelation; it is faith seeking understanding. It does not, therefore, discover its contents by itself but rather receives them from revelation, in order then to understand them in their inner coherence and intelligibility'.[25] It was an easy step from this to the insight that the domains of inquiry belonging to philosophy and theology could be distinguished as the natural and supernatural orders, respectively. This distinction effectively distinguished revelation and philosophy, faith and reason, grace and nature.

Distinction, however, quickly led to separation and even opposition: '… since the late Middle Ages, philosophy has been paired with pure reason while theology has been coupled with faith and this distinction has moulded the image of the one as well as the other'(#17). Mutuality now leads to mutual rejection or at least mutual distrust. As *F&R* puts it, 'what for Patristic and Medieval thought was in both theory and practice a profound unity, producing knowledge capable of reaching the highest forms of speculation, was destroyed by systems which espoused the cause of rational knowledge sundered from faith and meant to take the place of faith' (#45). Thus today the world of philosophy is often suspicious of any kind of dialogue between revelation and reason, faith and philosophy. Philosophers such as Heidegger and Jaspers, to mention just two instances of recent philosophers, stress that philosophy is by its very nature questioning. It follows that whoever believes he already knows the answers is no longer capable of philosophising. For Jaspers, whoever supposes himself in possession of the answers has failed as a philosopher: the open movement of transcendence is interrupted in favour of an imagined ultimate certainty. Of course, Jaspers is categorically opposed to the very idea of revelation. The reason is that 'God for him is not a personal being but a mere cipher of transcendence, and thus God cannot be expected to speak and act in history except in a mythological sense'.[26] In that instance one would have to speak of the rejection of revelation and faith, and not only the separation of them from philosophy and reason.

But if philosophy separated from, and then opposed, revelation, the reverse also happened: revelation and theology entered into the

REVELATION, THEOLOGY AND PHILOSOPHY

rejection of, and opposition to, philosophy. The first seeds of this opposition go back to Tertullian, who is famous for the adage, 'Credo quia absurdum!' But it flamed up again and again in the Middle Ages. The opposition of Luther is famous, and was reactivated again in the last century by Karl Barth who saw the idea of *analogia entis* as a kind of Trojan horse welcomed into the household of faith. Here he saw the ontological option of Catholic Theology condensed in a formula that bonded the *philosophical idea of being and the biblical notion of God.* Famously, Barth set his face totally against any kind of continuity or unity between revelation and philosophy, and proposed paradox instead.

This brings matters, it seems, to an impasse. 'On the one hand, philosophy defends itself against the prior given which faith implies for thinking; it feels that such a given inhibits the purity and freedom of its reflection. Theology, on the other hand, defends itself against the prior given of philosophical knowledge as a threat to the purity and novelty of faith'.[27]

A Context for Understanding the Church's Interventions

Now this sequence sets up the context for understanding the Church's interventions in the great debate. These interventions are described in the happy phrase 'the diakonia of the truth' (#2). The impasse arrived at shows the need for intervention, not because the 'Church has a philosophy of her own' (#49), but because she is convinced that Faith and Reason are in harmony since both are gifts of the one God of truth. They are after all 'the two wings on which the human spirit rises to the contemplation of the truth' (#33). Furthermore, she is convinced of the multiple injuries that the antithesis of faith and reason causes to both. These injuries affect the true meaning of reason and philosophy, as well as, logically, of revelation and theology. 'The censures were delivered even-handedly: on the one hand, *fideism* and *radical traditionalism,* for their distrust of reason's natural capacities, and, on the other, *rationalism* and *ontologism* because they attributed to natural reason a knowledge which only the light of faith could confer' (#52). Eventually the impasse was picked up at the First Vatican Council where 'for the first time an Ecumenical Council ... pronounced solemnly on the relationship between reason and faith' (#52). What was the core of that teaching? *Dei Filius* provides an epitome, as follows, 'There are two orders of knowledge, distinct not only in their point of departure, but also in their object'.[28]

The Situation Today

The encyclical is most forthright in its assessment of the situation at the end of the second millennium. 'Surveying the situation today, we see that the problems of other times have returned, but in a new key'. The most striking aspect here is the phenomenon of 'the deep seated distrust of reason which has surfaced in the most recent developments of much of philosophical research'. Here we are face to face with what has come to be aptly called 'weak reason'.[29]

The *significance* of this phenomenon should not be missed. The result of reason's opposition to and rejection of faith was initially autonomous reason. From the French Enlightenment onwards philosophy tried to eclipse faith altogether. The bitter fruits of that experiment over the past two centuries are obvious in the apocalyptic ideologies that have traversed the globe. And now a Pope has to plead with the modern world to believe in reason, its dignity, and its power to reach the truth in its own domain! The irony arising from the need for that plea should not be overlooked.

Philosophy must believe in the capacity of reason to reach truth. Failure to undertake that project leads to a crisis of the truth itself: it cannot be known. A defeatist attitude in this vital area means that philosophy must rest content 'with more modest tasks such as the simple interpretation of facts or an enquiry into restricted fields of human knowing or its structures' (#55). And there is talk at times of 'the end of metaphysics'.[30]

Theology, too, is being revisited by 'the temptations of other times'. They appear in the guise of 'a certain *rationalism*' (#55) where an uncritical acceptance is offered to certain philosophical opinions. This allows them the scope of being norms that either approve or reject areas of revealed truth! Philosophy becomes the measure of revelation! Corresponding to this rationalism, 'there are also signs of a resurgence of *fideism*' (#55). The encyclical mentions a number of symptoms of such a malaise. First, there is the failure to recognise the 'importance of rational knowledge and philosophical discourse for the understanding of faith, indeed for the very possibility of belief in God'. Such a failure of course departs from the explicit teaching of *Dei Filius*[31] that highlighted the unity in distinction of philosophy and theology as the perfect antidote to both rationalism and fideism, a point reiterated strongly in *F&R* when it claims that 'the relationship between theology and philosophy is best construed as a circle' (#73).

A further sign of fideism is a 'biblicism' that 'tends to make the reading and exegesis of Sacred Scripture the sole criterion of truth' (#55). This view and practice is in direct conflict with the balanced teaching of *Dei Verbum* where it is a case of Scripture and Tradition combining to 'comprise a single sacred deposit of the Word of God entrusted to the Church'.[32] The truth is that 'the supreme rule of her faith'[33] 'derives from the unity which the Spirit has created between Sacred Tradition, Sacred Scripture and the Magisterium of the Church in a reciprocity which means that none of the three can survive without the others' (#55).

Finally, there is the symptom of fideism that is apparent in 'the scant consideration accorded to speculative theology, and in the disdain for the classical philosophy from which the terms of both the understanding of faith and the actual formulation of dogma have been drawn' (#55). These specific complaints of the encyclical constitute a challenging examination of conscience for Catholic theologians, and also for all theologians who would wish to relate dynamically divine revelation and the unceasing quest for answers to the questions that are ineradicable from the human spirit.

The Wisdom of the Cross or the Wisdom of the World? A Proposal
According to the New Testament, Jesus Christ crucified and risen is
the summit of divine revelation. He is therefore the Word of God fully
unfolded and communicated to humankind. Perhaps Nicholas of
Cusa puts it most vividly: 'This one voice [of Jesus] proclaims that
there is no other life except life in the Word, and that the world,
proceeding from the Word, is sustained in its existence by the Word
and guided back to its origin ... After this mighty voice had grown
continually louder through centuries up to John, the voice of one
crying in the wilderness, it finally assumed human form and after a
long succession of modulations of teachings and miracles which were
to show us that of all frightful things the most frightful had to be
chosen by love, namely death, it gave out a great cry and died'.[34] What
is the relation between this revelation and that universal search for
truth that is expressed in philosophy? What is the relation between 'the
wisdom of the Cross' and the philosophy of being? This question is of
central and abiding significance. For the truth is that 'the preaching of
Christ crucified and risen is the reef upon which the link between faith
and philosophy can break up, but it is also the reef beyond which the
two can set forth upon the boundless ocean of truth' (#23).

   In one of the earliest texts of the New Testament, the First Letter
of Paul to the Corinthians, these great questions are addressed. For
Paul saw clearly that 'the depth of revealed wisdom disrupts the cycle
of our habitual patterns of thought, which are in no way able to
express that wisdom in its fullness ... The crucified Son of God is the
historic event upon which every attempt of the mind to construct an
adequate explanation of the meaning of existence upon merely human
argumentation comes to grief. The true key-point, which challenges
every philosophy, is Jesus Christ's death on the Cross' (#23).

   Paul saw the crucified Christ as the way in which God chose to
reveal himself, *to say who he is*, and *to tell us who we are*. The cross is
not the way in which we would travel in order to find the truth, but
it *is* the way in which God travels towards us in order to communicate
the final truth of his being and also the truth of our being.

Furthermore and most importantly, it is 'the word of the Cross' (1:18) that shows us the wisdom of God.

Paul, however, notices how this revealed wisdom of the cross is under attack from the wisdom of the world of his time. In fact, he names two versions of that wisdom. '... while the Jews demand miracles and the Greeks look for wisdom, here are we preaching a crucified Christ; to the Jews an obstacle that they cannot get over, to the pagans madness, but to those who have been called, whether they are Jews or Greeks, a Christ who is the power and the wisdom of God' (1:22-4). Paul identifies here two standard attitudes that the German exegete, Ernst Käsemann, describes as 'egocentrisms'.[35] The one is a religious 'egocentrism'. It is typified by certain followers who demand of God a manner of acting and of speaking in conformity with what they adjudicate to be appropriate. They look for a God who will show his *dynamis* by the way of miracles, and not through the mercy and the seeming weakness of the cross. Their mindset is truly set against any other way for the God of the Old Covenant to act. In a word, they think and act in such a manner as to tell God how to be God, and so claim for themselves the role of being the measure of the truth of God, of his interventions and even of his very nature!

The other 'egocentrism' is the specifically intellectual or philosophical one, being that of the Greeks who are bold enough to presume that by the energy and the light of speculative thought they can plumb the depths of God. Little wonder that they would dismiss the claimed wisdom of a crucified Christ: it is 'madness'! No true philosophy could accept this message for its sheer irrationality! Both 'egocentrisms' set up horizons that are absolutely closed to what God can and has done, and to the manner in which he has done it, a manner that shows 'a Christ who is the power and the wisdom of God' (1:25). The encyclical points out that for both 'egocentrisms' 'what is required is a decisive step towards welcoming something radically new', since 'in order to express the gratuitous nature of the love revealed in the Cross of Christ, the Apostle is not afraid to use the most radical language of the philosophers in their thinking about

God', for 'Christ is the power and the wisdom of God'! What is necessary is to enter into 'the logic of the Cross' (1:18). In that way the crucified Christ acts as the 'demystifier' of the man or woman who is falsely religious or intellectual and who wishes to set himself or herself up as the measure of the depths of God himself. At this point *F&R* makes a comment that is most insightful and germane to the central theme of the encyclical: 'Reason cannot eliminate the mystery of love which the Cross represents, while the Cross can give to reason the ultimate answer which it seeks' (#23).

The fact is that the core of Christian revelation as manifest in the shock of the cross, 'the un-Word at the core of the Word',[36] far from being the enemy of reason and of philosophy, is their authentic friend and ally. However, for philosophy to reap this great benefit, it must go through a deep *metanoia*. It is necessary, in fact, that human intelligence should take on the very form of the Crucified in its activity and in the dynamism of searching. In *F&R* 76 the theme is approached where the issue of a so-called 'Christian philosophy' is broached. The term indicates 'a way of philosophising, a philosophical speculation conceived in dynamic union with faith'.[37]

It involves two aspects that determine its identity. The first is subjective and consists in the fact that faith purifies reason. 'If faith, as we have seen, consists essentially in accepting the wisdom of the cross revealed in the event of the Crucified and Risen Lord, it is obvious that reason itself will be profoundly touched by the grafting of this event on to the heart of the person. Reason itself will be redeemed by the Pasch of Christ'.[38] This means that reason must plunge into the death and the resurrection of Christ in order to rise with Christ (see Rom 6:3-11).

The Pope mentions two ways by which this purification of human reason and so of philosophy can be done. The first consists in the fact that 'faith liberates reason from presumption, the typical temptation of the philosopher'. It is this presumption that is the object of St Paul's vigorous inveighing against philosophy in I Corinthians, as well as the censures of the Fathers, while closer to our own times 'philosophers such as Pascal and Kierkegaard reproached such presumption'. The second way of purification consists in the courage to tackle questions that are difficult to resolve if the data of revelation are ignored. Revelation 'stirs philosophy to explore unexpected paths and warns it against false trails'.[39] Among these questions are 'the problem of evil and suffering, the personal nature of God and the question of the meaning of life or, more directly, the radical metaphysical question of Leibniz, "Why is there something rather than nothing?"' (#76).

The second aspect of the influence of faith on reason is objective, since it has to do with content. The central truths of divine Revelation could never have been known by unaided reason. As well as these core truths, however, 'Revelation clearly proposes certain truths which might never have been discovered by reason unaided, although they are not of themselves inaccessible to reason' (#76). Among these truths is the notion of a free and personal God who is the Creator of the world, the notion of sin as it appears in the light of faith, which helps to shape an adequate philosophical formulation of the problem of evil; the dignity, freedom and equality of human beings; and the meaning of history as event.

When one combines these two aspects, namely, the purification of reason and the thrust of reason towards the ultimate depth of the truth revealed by God, we could say that human intelligence is not only called to open itself to the abyss of the wisdom of the cross, welcoming it into itself, but also to make its own the dynamism of dying to itself and of rising with Christ. Here is reason's very law of life! 'Human knowing, in other words, is freely called to accept a certain 'crucifixion' in order to be redeemed and recreated by the Spirit of the Risen Lord who freely leads it to penetrate into the mystery of God that is fully revealed in Christ. In this dynamism, reason is not denatured but becomes progressively and fully itself according to the full stature of the plan of God for the human creature'.

Some Concluding Comments

1 The relationship between revelation, theology and philosophy is seen by *F&R* against the horizon of history. This means that it looks at this key relationship on the broad canvas of the human story of *homo sapiens* and the incoming history of divine revelation which makes its own specific, though not separate, history, the history of 'God with us', what one might call 'the Immanuel History'. The encyclical begins with the assertion that 'in both East and West, we may trace a journey which has led humanity down the centuries to meet and engage truth more and more deeply'. However, it also highlights the fact that 'the Church is no stranger to this journey of discovery – she has made her pilgrim way along the paths of the world' (#1).

2 If *F&R* looks at its theme along an historical horizon, it still concentrates principally on the situation of faith and reason today. In fact this is its focus. Broadly speaking, it notices both a decrease of faith in Divine Revelation, as well as a decrease of faith in reason, 'faith' in the second instance denoting confidence in the capacity of reason to find the truth in the vital areas of the meaning of human existence, the existence of God, the problem of evil, the way to happiness, the truths of the moral order, and the immortality of the soul. This is the phenomenon described today as 'weak reason'.

3 For our world this is like a drama where the plot has been tragically lost, so that we live in a civilisation bursting with energy and activity, but without any idea whatsoever of the goal or the purpose of such activity.[40] This is, in fact, the insinuation of the poetic opening words of *F&R*, 'Faith and reason are like two wings on which the human spirit rises to the contemplation of truth: and God has placed in the human heart the desire to know the truth – in a word, to know himself'. It is logical, in the light of this drama, that the encyclical should address the vital issue of the re-integration of revelation and philosophy. Its theme, therefore, is

not faith on its own, nor philosophy on its own, but faith and philosophy in dynamic tension with each other. The encyclical is a pressing appeal for philosophy and faith to 'recover their profound unity which allows them to stand in harmony with their nature without compromising their mutual autonomy' (#48).

4 A measure of the seriousness of this breakdown in relationship is to be seen in the fact of an Ecumenical Council picking up the subject in the nineteenth century in a particularly formal and extensive fashion. An historical analogy suggests itself at once and perhaps provides a view. The great debates of the fourth to the eighth centuries on the truth of Christ and of the mystery of God, debates entirely driven by the sting of the various heresies, were the context and cause of the first Ecumenical Councils where the foundational dogmas of the faith were struck off one by one. I do not think that fact is without significance for the intervention of the First Vatican Council in the context of the struggle then raging in the wake of the French Revolution between the faith and the claims of enlightened reason. The First Vatican Council, in giving such central importance to the issue as to put it high up on its agenda, bears witness to the seriousness of the issue and to the ripeness of discussion and insight necessary to make an adequate statement on the unity in distinction of faith and reason.

5 Perhaps the best analogy of all for the relationship between faith and reason is that of the relationship between the two natures of Christ. As Chalcedon teaches, these two are related 'without confusion and without separation' in the one Person of the eternal Word of the Father. In a similar way, Christian wisdom involves a synthesis of philosophy and theology, which is not a mixing of the two nor a situation where theology denies philosophy its proper autonomy in relation to methods and field, and philosophy denies theology its distinct source and methods.

6   We began this paper with the event of the Annunciation where we detected a paradigm for the interrelating of revelation, faith and reason. The Pope concludes his encyclical with a Marian analogy: 'Just as the Virgin was called to offer herself entirely as human being and as woman that God's Word might take flesh and come among us, so too philosophy is called to offer its rational and critical resources that theology, as the understanding of faith, may be fruitful and creative. And just as in giving her assent to Gabriel's word, Mary lost nothing of her true humanity and her freedom, so too when philosophy heeds the summons of the Gospel's truth its autonomy is in no way impaired' (#108). The encyclical ends with the delightful quotation that Mary is 'the table at which faith sits in thought'.[41]

7   The Encyclical avoids staying on the high plateau of principles: it descends in fact to the plane of particulars and the demands of detail. In the course of this chapter I highlighted one such particular, namely, that of the historical event that is the summit of the whole of divine revelation, the Event of Christ Crucified (#23, #76, #97). I did so for two purposes: first, to focus attention on the final bonding of God's self-revelation with the philosophical search for the ultimate answer to the mystery of human existence as this mystery is made acute in the mystery of death, 'a metaphysical thorn lodged in man's being'.[42] The second reason was to highlight the propensity of faith and reason to register mutual disdain, philosophy accusing revelation of foolishness or fancifulness, and revelation refusing to give the apostolic account of the hope that is provided by revelation, a hope that precisely because it is universal in its claim, must give an account of itself at the bar of reason. In this way the Pope's desire that 'the *parrhesia* of faith must be matched by the boldness of reason' (#48) can be attained. 'Indeed, there is almost nowhere that we need a more courageous faith and a bolder reason than in the opposition between 'the wisdom of the world' and 'the wisdom of God', which St Paul sets before the Corinthians in his first letter'.[43]

8 The encyclical not only addresses particular issues, but also throws down very specific challenges to theology and to philosophy. For example, in #93 there is the challenge to consider the *kenosis* of God, 'a grand and mysterious truth for the human mind'. The challenge here is to think out the true meaning of this wonder of the faith in the light of the mysteries of the Incarnation and the Blessed Trinity. This means that the *kenosis* of God in Christ is the revelation of the inner life of God who is the Holy Trinity. This leads furthermore to the challenge to think out a new understanding of created being in the light of the revealed nature of Uncreated Being. Thus there comes into view what Klaus Hemmerle calls a 'trinitarian ontology'.[44] Perhaps here one could locate concretely an aspect of 'the reef beyond which faith and philosophy can set forth on the boundless ocean of truth. Here we see not only the border between reason and faith, but also the space where the two may meet' (#23).

Notes

1. See Feargus Ó Fearghail, 'The Literary Forms of Lk 1,5-25 and 1,26-38', *Marianum* (Rome), xliii (1981), 321-344; Robert J. Karris, 'The Gospel According to Luke', in *The New Jerome Biblical Commentary* (London 1993), pp. 680-1 for useful exegetical comments; and Hans Urs von Balthasar, 'Mary – Exemplar of the Church', from *Pneuma und Institution*, as translated in Medard Kehl and Werner Loser (eds), *The von Balthasar Reader* (Edinburgh 1982), pp. 218-20 for helpful theological comments.

2. See St Irenaeus, *Adversus Haereses*, IV, pr. 4; IV, 7, 4; IV, 20, 1; V, 1, 3; V, 5, 1; V, 6, 1; V, 28, 4; *Demonstratio Apostolica*, 11.

3. In the poem 'The Blessed Virgin compared to the Air we Breathe', in Gerard Manley Hopkins, *Poems and Prose Poems*, selected and edited by W. H. Gardner (London, 1986), p. 55.

4. John Henry Newman, *Oxford University Sermons* (London, 1900), p. 313.

5. *ibid.*, pp. 313, 314.

6. See the perceptive treatment of this subject in Walter Kasper, *An Introduction to Christian Faith* (London, 1980), pp. 13-35; Angelo Scola, *Questioni di Antroplogia Teologica* (Roma, 1997), pp. 33-6.

7. *Fides et Ratio*, #1. (Dublin, Veritas Publications, 1998). (Referred to below as *F&R*)

8. John O'Donnell, 'Hans Urs von Balthasar: The Form of his Theology', *Communio*, 3 (1989), 459.

9. *ibid.*, 460.

10. Eric Voegelin, 'The Gospel and Culture', chapter in *Published Essays 1966-1985*, volume 12 of *The Collected Works* (Baton Rouge and London, 1989), pp. 172-212; for an exposition of the key themes of Voegelin's thinking see Maurice P. Hogan, *The Biblical Vision of the Human Person. Implications for a Philosophical Anthropology* (Frankfurt am Main, 1994).

11. See Hans Urs von Balthasar, *Spirius Creator. Skizzen zur Theologie III* (Einsiedeln, 1967), pp. 20-25; an English translation of this text is available in Medard Kehl and Werner Loeser, eds, *The von Balthasar Reader* (Edinburgh, 1982), pp. 99-102.

12. John O'Donnell, *ibid.*, p. 460.

13. In the Septuagint, 'In you all the nations shall be blessed', repeated in Sir 44:21 and in Gen 18:18; 22:18; 26:4; 28:14.

14. Hans Urs von Balthasar, 'Catholicism and the Religions', *Communio*, I (1978), 8.

15. idem, *Herrlichkeit. Eine theologische Aesthetik. Alter Bund* (Einsiedeln, 1967), 'Die Geschichte des Bundes aber erwies, dass das erwæhlte Volk nicht fæhig war, im Bereich der absoluten Liebe zu existieren', p. 383.

16. 'Theology and the Aesthetic', *Communio*, I (1981), 69.

17. *ibid.*, 69-70.

18. *ibid.*, 70.

19. T. S. Eliot, *Four Quartets: The Dry Salvages*, V.

20. Gerard Manley Hopkins, *op. cit.*, p. 55.

21. Joseph Ratzinger, *The Nature and Mission of Theology* (San Francisco, 1995). The title of the German original is *Wesen und Auftrag der Theologie: Versuch zu ihrer Ortsbestimmung im Disput der Gegenwart* (Einsiedeln, 1993).

22. Justin Martyr, *Dialogue with Trypho, 8, 1*.

23. Eric Voegelin, 'The Gospel and Culture', in *Published Essays 1966-1985* (Baton Rouge and London, 1989), p. 173.

24. J. Ratzinger, *op. cit.*, pp. 13-14.

25. *ibid.*, 16.

26. A. Dulles, *Models of Revelation* (Dublin, 1983), p. 10.

27. J. Ratzinger, *op. cit.*, p. 19.

28. DS 3015; The Pastoral Constitution on the Church in the Modern World *Gaudium et Spes*, # 59 quotes the text.

29. The Anglican Newman writing about Faith and Reason during the Oxford Movement portrays the common perceptions at the time in these terms,

'According to ... popular sense, Faith is the judging on weak grounds in religious matters, and Reason on strong grounds. Faith involves easiness, and Reason slowness in accepting the claims of Religion': *Oxford University Sermons* (London, 1900), x. And so Reason has weakened drastically through losing contact with theology and revelation.

30. Klaus Hemmerle, *Thesen zu einer trinitarischen Ontologie* (Einsiedeln, 1976), 7f.

31. See B. J. Lonergan, *Method in Theology* (London, 1972), pp. 337-8, '... the separation [of philosophy and theology] weakened both natural theology and systematic theology. It weakened natural theology for abstruse philosophic concepts lose nothing of their validity and can gain enormously in acceptability when they are associated with their equivalents. It weakened systematic theology for the separation prevents the presentation of systematics as the Christian prolongation of what man can begin to know by his native powers'.

32. Dogmatic Constitution on Divine Revelation, *Dei Verbum*, # 10. 32. *ibid.*, # 21.

33. The radical reciprocity of Scripture and Tradition and Magisterium has clear trinitarian overtones. It also provides an interesting hermeneutic of the different positions generally associated with the Churches and Ecclesial Communities emanating from the Reformation, as well as the reductionism inevitably visited upon the written Word of God when unaccompanied by the witness of Tradition and the *diakonia* of Magisterium.

34. Nicholas of Cusa, *Excitationes*, I, 3, *Opera*, Basel 1565, 411-2.

35. Ernst Kæsemann, 'Il valore salvifico della morte di Gesú in Paolo', *passim*, in *Prospettive paoline*, Italian translation (Brescia, 1972); see also Piero Coda, *Evento pasquale, Trinità e storia* (Roma, 1984), for an extended treatment of the Paschal Mystery and the Trinity.

36. See Hans Urs von Balthasar, *The Glory of the Lord*, (Edinburgh, 1989), vol. I, pp. 77-89.

37. For an interesting treatment of this topic see A. Dulles, 'Can Philosophy be Christian?', *First Things*, 102 (April 2000), 24-30.

38. Piero Coda, 'Sapienza della croce, e astuzia della ragione', Conference paper given at the Pontifical Lateran University, Rome, 3rd March 1999.

39. A. Dulles, 'Can Philosophy be Christian?', *First Things*, 102 (April 2000), 29.

40. See Eric Voegelin, 'The Gospel and Culture', 172-212, *passim*.

41. Pseudo-Epiphanius, *Homily in Praise of Holy Mary Mother of God*, PG 43, 493.

42. J. Ratzinger, *The Nature and Mission of Theology*, 23.

43. Bernhard Koerner, 'Thinking beyond the Reef: the Cross, Faith, and
    Reason in the Trinitarian Ontology of Klaus Hemmerle', *Communio*
    3(1999), 666.
44. See note 29.

THE PARTICULARITY OF CULTURES AND THE UNIVERSALITY OF TRUTH

James McEvoy

Fides et Ratio (*F&R*) contains much more than the teaching on faith and reason, though that is indeed its central message, and on philosophy and theology which is annexed to the former. Culture is referred to in seventeen of its one hundred and seven paragraphs and is thematised in ##70-71. Culture is placed in relationship to other realities such as tradition and language, religions and philosophy, revelation, faith and the mission of the Church. The rich nature of the term, its interrelatedness with others, and the significance assigned to it in *F&R* make it a worthwhile exercise to examine the encyclical letter from the perspective of culture.

'Culture': Etymology and Meaning

Consultation of the original Latin text reveals that *cultura* and (more rarely) *humanus cultus* are both employed. Both are rendered in English by the term 'culture', and the two Latin terms are probably synonymous; at any rate they will be treated as such in what follows. *Cultura* derives from the Latin verb *colo*, which means 'to cultivate'. Modern Western languages (both Romance and Germanic) employ derivatives of *cultura*, and it is a noteworthy fact that modern Greek does likewise, since the ancient and medieval forms of that language did not possess any equivalent term. *Cultura* becomes a compound term, e.g. in *agricultura* (Latin *agricola*, a farmer, cultivator of the field, *ager*), and French *viticulture* (the tending of the vine). In its original sense then the term *cultura* designated the relationship of work-activities (such as tilling, sowing, caring for growth, harvesting) to nature (climate, soil, seed, growth, fruit, flower, ripening.). A notable metaphorical employment of the word *cultura* refers primarily to the capacities of human nature (energy, emotions, intelligence, memory, will, etc.) and to the order placed upon these by society and tradition, which confer some particular shapes upon the human material, and bring about form.

Contrasting senses may be given to the terms culture and civilisation (especially in German: *Kultur/Zivilisation*), though for the most part the English (and indeed the French) usages remain confused and the meanings somewhat indistinct. Yet the two are so sharply separate in etymology that a difference between their meanings can be suggested. 'Civilisation' comes from the Latin *civis, civitas* and designates the typical, visible achievements of city dwellers who draw upon technology to build, to produce goods, to establish and maintain communications, and to prosecute war or defend the peace. What we may think of as the values associated with each of these terms, 'culture' and 'civilisation', differ sharply enough to be distinguishable along the following lines.

It is through our culture that we are enabled to shape the energies within us, whereas civilisation gives us mastery of our environment – through technology – turning natural energy into an instrument that can be used productively. Culture is more internal than that; it comes from tradition and relates us to our past. It is allied to education, which formally hands on and develops the values handed down. Civilisation can be transplanted from one place to another whereas culture is grown on the spot, and develops by osmosis with neighbouring cultures, as well as through the freedom and initiative of individuals. But culture always has some means of self-renewal also, through the retrieval of forgotten achievements and their reinterpretation. Many definitions of culture have been attempted, emphasising some of the attributes just mentioned. Perhaps the most accessible of all passes through the nature and finality of culture: it is there to express what it means for a given community to be human; it is that people's unique way of sharing in human nature, with all the ambivalence which that implies; a culture will have both light and dark sides.

Culture in *Fides et Ratio*

Of the thirteen encyclicals issued up to now in the course of the present pontificate, *F&R* has the most direct impact on faith and culture.[2] The claim is made in the encyclical that divine Revelation has been made as a universal message destined for every culture on earth. Now cultures are usually viewed (by anthropologists in particular) under the heading of difference and plurality, sometimes with an implication of relativism. In the more philosophical perspective adopted in *F&R*, by contrast, each culture has quite specific characteristics, yet each, when considered in its depth, is an expression of the one human nature. Every culture therefore expresses in its own way the universal human search for meaning and for truth. The cultures of the world are a unity-in-diversity or a diversity-in-unity, depending upon the angle of viewing. The absolute claim to truth that is made by Christianity on the basis of revelation does not level cultures downwards or deny them their diversity, but places instead a new, vital element at the heart of each of them, a novelty that is able to go to the roots of each culture and become the source of new growth and new life, in short of cultural renewal and growth. 'Catholic' means universal. It means not levelling down, but linking up and unifying in depth.

Cultures and the Understanding of Faith

The encyclical places its central reflection on human culture within the wide scope of its ch. VI, 'The Interaction between Theology and Philosophy', which is the culmination of the document. It is in this

chapter that lessons are drawn from the series of surveys that fill the
earlier parts – lessons that are then distilled into a number of
challenges to Catholic theologians and to philosophers regarding their
professional practice (in the final ch. VII). Ch. VI, including the
doctrine of culture that it proposes, has been carefully prepared from
the beginning, for the document, though long (over 30,000 words)
unfolds according to a plan and has an inner logic that is impressive
(though one finds that it takes repeated readings to learn to relate the
different parts and the various themes to the whole).

   F&R falls into two parts: a foundational one (Introduction and chs
I-III) that might be headed 'The human relationship to truth',
followed by what one may call the message section, which addresses
the relationship between philosophy and faith, and philosophy and
theology. Culture is mentioned in some way in every chapter, but is
thematised only in the context of how philosophy and theology should
be interrelated. Why this precise location for the thematic of culture?
The argument is developed (#65) that theology is required for the
hearing of faith (*auditus fidei*) and the understanding of faith
(*intellectus fidei*).[3] By the former is meant the reception of revelation
throughout the centuries of the Church's history. Understanding the
faith (*intellectus fidei*) is the more speculative theological task, meant
as it is to meet the demands of reason. Now theology in each of these
modes has need of philosophy. That need is spelt out in systematic
detail. Dogmatic theology (#66) should be able to draw upon a well-
defined body of truths concerning the universe and mankind, and
indeed Being itself (i.e. metaphysics, and philosophical anthropology).
Fundamental theology (#67) seeks to give an account of faith (cf. I Pet
3:15); faith and reason are both required in this basic service of truth.
Moral theology (#68) explicates the New Covenant and how it should
be lived, and to fulfil its task it 'must employ a correct philosophical
standpoint, whether with regard to human nature and society or to the
universal principles of ethical discourse.'

   But where and how does culture enter this account? It is first
introduced as part of a contemporary challenge to the message which

the encyclical seeks to renew and impart. The letter notes that traditional appeals to philosophy as the uniquely privileged partner of theology in the elaboration of a Christian wisdom is not taken for granted at present. Why should theologians not strike off on new paths of understanding? Why not explore partnerships with natural science, for example, or with history (#69)? Why on the other hand canonise an élite practice of philosophy at the expense of ethnic, traditional and local wisdoms? Could not faith inculturate itself better in the latter than in philosophy, which is, after all, Greek in origin and largely European in its development? Why should the entire Church be tied in a Eurocentric way to particularities of its tradition and past? These questions have been in the air for some time. They invite a response and they deserve one. It is from them, and from the consideration given them and the discernment entered into in their regard, that the encyclical's teaching about culture directly derives.

Cultural Diversity and the One Universal Truth of Salvation (##70-71)

Views such as those just mentioned that favour the natural and hermeneutical sciences as partners of theology, or foster a positive relationship between faith and regional cultures, contain an obvious and uncontroversial truth, and they turned up of course at the Second Vatican Council.[4] In what follows *F&R* undertakes a dialectical discernment, of a particularly Catholic kind, one feels, which aims at a *both ... and* outcome rather than an *either ... or* one. The stricter logic of the latter requires that one of the disjunctive terms be rejected in favour of the other in which the whole truth is from then on held to reside. By contrast the former position seeks to assemble the parts of a single truth, by trying to discern where each one should fit in, at what level it holds true, and what it can do for and within the organic whole. This operation begins from a resounding *No!* ('the role of philosophy must not be forgotten!' – #69) but enjoins a larger *Yes!*: philosophy is required if the different cultures are to talk to each other and their exchanges are to bear fruit .

This piece of reasoning, which may be regarded as a good example of Catholic dialectic at work, is nothing other than the methodological translation of the Catholicity of the Church, in which universality and particularity are both present, while neither excludes the other, each requires the presence of the other, and the one Church subsists in the whole multitude of races, peoples, tongues and traditions: it is Pentecost ever renewed in history.

Culture and the diversity of peoples (to paraphrase #70) are not new and unheralded experiences for the Church, for ever since the Gospel was first preached she has been meeting different cultures and contending with them:

> Christ gave his disciples the command to go out to all places, 'even to the ends of the earth' (Acts 1:8) in order that the truth revealed by him be passed on; he gave the means simultaneously for the Christian community to recognise the universality of the message and the obstacles arising from the diversity of cultures. (#70)

It is to St Paul that *F&R* goes in search of a New Testament thematisation of the drama of the one faith and its reception in many cultures. The Apostle of the Gentiles reminded the Ephesians, 'But now in Christ Jesus, you who once were far off have been brought near in the blood of Christ' (Eph 2:13). One may regard Judaism as a particular culture, even though it was more than that at the time of Paul, since it was the bearer of a relationship to the one and only God, and it carried within itself from the beginning an implicitly universal message of salvation. Nevertheless since it had its own language, law and customs the Apostle, who of course belonged to it, was entitled in truth to present it as being surrounded by 'a wall', meaning that what is most particular within a culture presents a barrier to others and makes them outsiders to it, foreigners, gentiles – proselytes at best. Particularity in language and customs, in other words, hinders access from outside of a given culture. Such a metaphorical wall of protection and of exclusiveness surrounded Israel. Paul proclaims that with the coming of Christ as saviour of all, those who were 'far off' and 'foreigners' (Eph 2:19) have been brought near, made 'fellow-citizens', as it were, and members of a single family or 'household of God'. The wall has come down, the hindrances have been removed and the barriers have been broken, because Christ brings peace and unity:

> In Christ the promise of God becomes a universal gift: no longer circumscribed with the particular characteristics of one nation with its own language and customs, but destined for all, as a birthright from which each may freely draw. From the diversity of places and customs, in Christ all are called to participation in the unity of the family of the children of God ... Jesus breaks down the walls of division and in a unique and perfect manner creates a unity through participation in his mystery. (#70)

St Paul reflected unremittingly upon the opening up of the original Judaeo-Christian community to the 'nations' – to the different cultures, in modern parlance. He must have done so, to have been able to express the kernel of the experience in such a simple metaphor as the breaching of a wall and the creation of peaceful unity. The generation that has witnessed the tearing down of the Berlin Wall in 1989 and the reunification of Germany can feel a powerful echo of the Pauline image, the more so as the Berlin event came about not through war but as an effect of the human mind and spirit defeating a materialistic, state-imposed ideology.

The meeting of Christian faith with the diversity of cultures brings a new reality into being. In each culture the deepest impulses of human nature find expression – the universal in the particular. Yet the particular way in which the human is expressed is unique to each. Taken together, therefore, the cultures of the world constitute a variety of approaches to the truth of what we are as human beings. Each one humanises its group in a unique way, and at the same time it gives its members an openness to universality and transcendence, and passes on through tradition some notions of the divine as active in nature and the universe. Everyone is the child of a particular culture and may in turn make a contribution to its enrichment. Considered in relationship to each other, cultures exchange goods and also ideas; to seek enrichment and fulfillment is one of their most basic characteristics. *F&R* argues on these grounds that every 'culture contains within itself the capacity for recognizing the divine revelation.' (#71)

Pentecost: Many Languages, but One Message Proclaimed and Heard

How is one to envisage the result of introducing the Christian message into the diversity of cultures? *F&R* is ready once again with a New Testament answer, Pentecost (quoting Acts 2:7-11): the pilgrims gathered together for the feast at Jerusalem ('Parthians, Medes, Elamites … ') wondered at the experience of receiving a message ('the mighty works of God') that came through the mouths of Galileans, but which each of the visitors heard and understood in his or her own tongue; each one could understand that that message of salvation had the same meaning for himself or herself as it had for the Galileans, and brought with it the same promise, the same fulfilment, the same experience of the Spirit of God, the same belonging to the community. The quasi-miracle of translation between natural languages ('the same meaning but in two different tongues'⁵) is expressed by the author of Acts, St Luke; for it is supposed by the narrative that those pilgrims, though Jewish by family descent, had lost Aramaic and spoke as their native language the tongues of the countries in which they lived. But there is more meaning here than the wonder of the translateability of discourse. The Apostolic Church is making at Pentecost the experiential discovery that, filled with the Spirit of God, it is enabled to preach the word of salvation outside of the historical Israel, and thus providentially to overcome the barriers of culture first erected in punishment of the hubristic sin of the people of Babel (Gen 11:1-9), viz. the division of humanity into language groups.

Culture, in the eyes of the Church, is neither an incidental nor a normative reality. But a reality it is and it must be taken account of and properly evaluated.[6] No culture constitutes a norm for judging the truth of divine revelation; it would be a misjudgement if someone were to reject God's revelation in whole or part because it appeared to run counter to that person's native culture. On the other hand the novelty that the Christian message brings to every culture is the call to truth whole and entire ('vocatio ad plenam veritatem'), and the true form of liberation from the effects of sin. This truth, and this setting free, are not something external or alien to any given culture; they are not yet another, different cultural form that must win or lose in rivalry and conflict with the others. Christian faith will not spell the ruin of a culture, but will implant a new source of life in it that will stimulate spiritual and human growth.

The experience of the earliest Church at Pentecost has been repeated many times over. It serves as the model for the meeting between Christian truth and cultures, or what is usually designated by Roman documents 'the inculturation of the Christian faith'.

But first let us complete the depiction of culture in F&R.

Cultural Diversity and Truth

Besides ##70-71, which focus upon culture, other references to it are found throughout the encyclical. Some of these are largely incidental, others add something to the central thematisation. It is worthwhile to refer here to those that fill out the picture.

Every cultural and religious form of life, it is claimed (#1), offers essential ways to self-knowledge ('Know Yourself' is the starting point of F&R). The primordial questions about human life and its value, questions that express the uniqueness of humans within the universe, arise at all times and places:

> Who am I? Where do I come from? Where am I going? Why do evils appear? What remains to us after this life?[7]

In illustration, reference is made to Israel, India, China (Confucius and Lao-Tze), the Buddha, Homer and the Greek tragedians, and the philosophers Plato and Aristotle. The opening of the encyclical makes a panoramic effect. It also conveys a message that will recur: cultures are diverse and each is quite particular, yet each one expresses what it is to be human. Something universally human comes out in the questions that are asked, and these are everywhere similar. A later thesis (#3) continues this line of thought: the human mind is very enquiring; it wonders what lies at the bottom of things, it looks for truth; and this innate philosophical propensity links all cultures in a deep pattern of complementarity, despite all their differences. There is a spiritual heritage, something like an implicit philosophy, that surfaces again and again (#4). Philosophy as it is practised must remain in contact with this pre-academic heritage, if it is to become once again a formative force in culture – a position that contemparary academic philosophy has lost (#6).

How can the central event in Christian faith, the Incarnation, life and death of Jesus Christ, escape circumscription within the boundaries of time and place and the particularity of Israelite culture? The question is raised (#12), and is met by the response that 'only in the mystery of the Incarnate Word is the mystery of man revealed.'[8] It recurs in reference to the combat between the cross of Jesus Christ and the pride of human reason (#23): the wisdom of the cross (cf. I Cor 1:20 ff.) and the love revealed in it cannot be denied or overcome by philosophy, or absorbed into it, or emptied out by it, since this wisdom 'breaks through every cultural border' to challenge each and every human being in their humanity, the philosopher included.

The meeting of the early Church with pagan culture is brought into focus in the context of the Church Fathers' meeting with philosophy, in ch. IV where the history of the meeting of faith and reason is passed in review (##36-48). Early representatives of the new faith voiced criticism of the pagan intellectual culture ('What has Athens to do with Jerusalem – the Academy with the Church?', asked Tertullian, #41) and of gnosticism in particular (St Irenaeus of Lyons).

Believing wholeheartedly as they did, they were fully alive to the dangers of syncretism and apprised of the harm that the uncritical assimilation of pagan belief and practice would certainly do to the Church. The Fathers exercised a critical discernment, with Christian belief as the touchstone of truth, regarding Neoplatonism (the Cappadocian Fathers and St Augustine, #40). Their syntheses in varying degrees incorporated philosophical truths into theology in order to penetrate the faith with understanding – not to dilute it or alter its content, or reduce it to philosophical categories. They recognised that pagan culture, and philosophy in a particular way, could be viewed in providential terms as a *praeparatio evangelica*, and they endeavoured to bring to light all that was implicit and preparatory in the pagan devotion to wisdom (Gk *philo-sophia*). These thoughts evidently occupy an importance place in *F&R*'s programme regarding culture. They are based solidly on the patristic scholarship of the past fifty years, especially that touching Neoplatonism and the Church.[9] At a later stage in the document the hope is expressed that philosophy (in the noble sense of the word) 'will be the place where human culture and Christian faith come together, and will provide the place of agreement between believers and non-believers (#79).

The diversity of cultures has down the ages demanded an adequate response from theology (#92). The Church's teachings admittedly do reflect the culture of the age in which they were formulated, for historical and cultural conditioning is unavoidable for language users (#95). However, the truth of dogma is not relativised by these factors nor confined within the setting of its historical emergence, but as truth it goes beyond historical time and the particularity of circumstances.

In the concluding section (##100-108) philosophy is again drawn into the space of cross-cultural dialogue, and the hope is expressed that the Christian philosopher can help to discover areas of mutual understanding where dialogue may be pursued concerning the peaceful co-existence of the different races and cultures present on the world scene.

But how does *F&R* ally its world-wide perspective on the different peoples and cultures with the deliberate promotion of philosophy, which originated in Greece, and developed in Europe in its Christian form? Are these two stances not to be contrasted or opposed, as universalist and particularist; and if not how can they be reconciled?

Eurocentrism?

The decades following the Second Vatican council have witnessed numerous efforts on the part of Catholics in various parts of the world (notably in Asian and African countries) to make a new *rapprochement* between their faith and their native cultures and traditions. The faith and culture movement in the Church, which has developed rapidly under the encouragement of Rome with the Pontifical Council for Faith and Culture as its umbrella, is in part a product of these efforts at a deeper inculturation of the faith and a more receptive attitude to particular cultures in all their density of meaning and tradition. Christians from the Indian sub-continent and some foreigners working there as missionaries have sought to make a Christian adaptation of certain categories and attitudes deriving from the long history of Hindu philosophical thought. African theologians have endeavoured of recent decades to identify elements of tradition and proverbial wisdom within their tribal cultures, and to highlight values coming from their people's traditions, such as the wider family, the strong sense of community and the traditional consciousness of the spirits of the dead.

F&R extends positive support to this search, in particular to those in India who seek to 'unlock the treasures from their inheritance which can be joined to their faith and so enhance the richness of Christian teaching' (#72). The echoing of the language used earlier in the document regarding the early Church and non-Christian culture is doubless deliberate. The reminder that the Council with its declaration *Nostra Aetate* gave encouragement to this process of discernment is positive and encouraging.[10] The three norms or guidelines proposed in the encyclical should not be seen as restrictive, but as giving shape and lending some clarity to the undertaking. The first of these concerns the universality of the human spirit, which is essentially the same in all cultures. The third concerns the distinctiveness of Indian thought (a quality that is not in question), and counsels against regarding every cultural tradition as being purely and simply enclosed in its own particularity, for to do so would run counter to the first norm. It is with the second of the three that the question regarding Eurocentrism may and should be raised:

> When the Church deals for the first time with cultures of great importance, but previously unexamined, it must even so never place them before the Greek and Latin inculturation already acquired. Were this inheritance to be repudiated the providential plan of God would be opposed, who guides his Church down the paths of time and history.[11]

This insistence that the philosophical heritage the Church received early in its history cannot be renounced, might look like the canonisation of a Eurocentric thought, in a way that might endanger the inculturation of Christian and Catholic faith in an Indian, oriental or African setting. (In fact, it is probably aimed critically at the 'de-Hellenisation of Dogma/Christianity' movement, which, originating with Adolf von Harnack around 1900, has found some Catholic defenders ever since the sixties). The question can be put in these terms: can truth speak beyond the limits of the cultural form(s) from which it has sprung; can it speak in such a way as to engage all, and to be for each human being a truth that concerns that person, irrespective of cultural setting?

How Greek or how Latin must the Church be in its thought? Its roots, after all, are neither. The Jewish wisdom literature and its continuing value for Christian faith is the theme of the second chapter of *F&R*, which notes that Egyptian, ancient Near-Eastern and Hellenistic cultures conditioned the scene in which the Wisdom Literature of Israel originated, so that the latter grew up in contact and in dialogue with ancient wisdom and with Greek philosophy. Moreover, the fourth chapter focuses on the meeting of the faith with Greek *philosophia* in the patristic, Scholastic and contemporary ages. While these chapters will not be examined here, some considerations directly relevant to the question about Eurocentrism must be mentioned, even though none of them can be developed here.

Cultural loss, or the loss of values (including religious ones) inculturated and inherited from the past, is a feature of life in Europe that has prompted Pope John Paul II to appeal to Europeans: 'We must never tire of saying and repeating to Europe: rediscover yourself! Rediscover your soul!'[12] But that is a quite different thing from urging cultural colonialism.

The Self-transcendent Dynamic of Cultures

In the biblical record a constantly-renewed struggle is revealed between particularity and universality, or the desire of Israel to be just itself and be for itself alone, isolated in its nationhood and ethnicity; and on the other hand the recognition that God is not only the God of Israel but the God of all mankind, the maker of heaven and earth, the beginning and end of all, the 'wholly other'. God struggles with the people (through the words of the prophets, notably) to draw them out of their own particular cultural identity (for example, the golden calf at Sinai; the early sanctuaries and associated rites, and the later ambition for monarchical power and glory), and lead then towards self-transcendence, so that Israel may become 'a sign for the nations', the bearer of a truth that is quite simply the truth for all, whatever their origin or race or tongue. Abraham may fittingly be selected to stand for the surpassing of what was particular: 'Leave your country and family and your father's house and go to the land I will show you'. (Gen 12:1)

St Paul, the Apostle of the Gentiles, was following this basic tendency of the Bible when he required that the law should not be imposed on gentiles. If faith in Christ and becoming one with him is sufficient to save sinners then the law, including circumcision, means nothing any more, save possibly a hindrance to accepting salvation on God's terms. In short, 'there is now neither Jew nor Greek, male or female, slave or free' (Gal 3:28). What was culturally and religiously proper or reserved to Israel must not made obligatory for non-Jews who will believe in the same Messias/Christ, still less must it be made a handicap or a barrier to their finding their way to an equal faith. The cultural property of Israel, in language (Hebrew and Aramaic), norms of social existence (the Torah) and relationship to the land (*Eretz Israel*), must in Paul's eyes be regarded as particularities, ethnic features that were meant, as part of divine providence, to educate the people in view of the coming of the Messiah. Paul put his weight along with the Apostles (Gal 2) behind the option for the universal that became the overwhelming insight and consensus of the Christian Church: that Christ is unique, and the truth of salvation through his death and resurrection belongs to all peoples, as also does the universal, moral part of the Torah (as distinct from the ritual and dietary injunctions).

A similar spiritual dynamic governed the encounter of the Fathers of the Church with Greek philosophy.[13] They were far from taking over Hellenistic culture for its own sake, for the inner meaning it had for itself meant little to these Christian thinkers: what interested them was not Greek religion, or the syncretistic cults of Isis or Serapis, or the mystery religions; the notion that Christ could be presented as the true Dionyos or Hercules or Asclepius had only a passing attraction for Christians, while the sacred sites and the oracles of Greece and Egypt meant nothing at all to them. The philosophical impulse of Greece and its achievements through Plato, Aristotle, the Stoa and Plotinus, on the contrary, exercised the Fathers repeatedly. In philosophy the latter appreciated the purifying critique of polytheism. They saw that the philosophical standpoint had made possible for its adepts a critical distance regarding their own Greek or Latin culture. They realised that this standpoint resulted from the philosophical search for the transcendent, unique divinity, or Logos, or One. The Christian mind met Greek and Hellenistic culture, not in the purely particular features of the latter but at the point where it was moving beyond itself in the direction of universality. The culture was never canonised by the Church, but the most universal results of philosophical thought were sifted through and integrated into what was from the start, and what remained all through, a Christian theology and anthropology.

The Church of today has no interest in initiating the Christians of Asia or Africa into Greek or Latin culture as such, but it continues to place value upon following paths towards the universal openness of truth: truth that is the same for all and is thus able to create a common awareness – a communion. Where the Church finds philosophy of this kind in the future its attitude will be similarly disposed, whatever the geographical or linguistic origin of the thought; with the proviso that the latter is not of the kind that rules out the question of truth or wishes to promote relativism or scepticism, but is working through reason to search for truth in the way that responds to the very core of being human. The encyclical maintains that the longing for truth and the desire for God have the same origin in the deepest needs of every person; they are near neighbours within the human spirit.

Courage for the Truth: the True Encouragement

'Plato is indeed a friend, but the truth is even more so' (Aristotle). Truth has always needed good friends, and has hitherto found them when most in need. At present relativism is widespread, making the defence of truth an urgent call. Relativistic attitudes come from more than one direction.[14] The fall of communism in 1988-1990 has contributed to their growth. The events of those dramatic years in Eastern Europe meant the crumbling of a system of thought, even more than that of walls and of the Party. Marxism-Leninism made a resounding claim to scientific status. Its aim was to replace Christian hope based on faith with a rationally-grounded, materialistic dialectic holding the key to a better future for all mankind. The collapse of the communist system discredited the theory and has left a vacuum, not only in the countries immediately affected but among intellectuals of the left, who, in Western Europe and elsewhere, had subscribed to the ideology, and who found themselves, following 1989, wearing (and sharing) the Emperor's new clothes. Some of the disappointed have rallied to the notion of communicative thinking and acting (developed by Jürgen Habermas, the last representative of the Marxist Frankfurt School). This tries to elevate relativism into a political philosophy, in which tradition and religious faith are sidelined as the enemies of free thought, and also of democracy. In the growing public awareness of Europe the new relativism is being portrayed as the basic principle of democracy. How can there be tolerance in the public sphere so long as one or more contributors to what should be debates feel(s) entitled to indicate the right path, the true way in this or that regard? Community, communication, communicative thinking: the values indicated by these expressions depend vitally (it is claimed) upon the open competition of views that represent possible fragments to be assembled into a better future, but none of which can claim to be simply true. Relativity and the free, open society, within this outlook (which unites liberals and ex-Marxists), are the same thing.[15] In theology also a pluralistic theory of religions (John Hick), hard though it is to define in a formula, comes out as relativistic and in tune with some intuitions of Eastern (and especially Indian) origin that attract a good deal of sympathy in Western minds at the present time. Post-metaphysical philosophy and apophatic or negative theology of Asiatic origin have proved to blend easily together. In New Age writings relativism comes from the mastery attributed to the subject of experience, who is encouraged to overcome both the objectivising reason typical of science and the Absolute of traditional faith, by using the intoxication of music, rhythm and dance to achieve a sort of ecstasy of unity with the non-personal, spiritual energy of the universe. Postmodern thought has contributed its mead to the constellation of relativism, by a deconstructive practice that leaves only fragmentary and provisional meanings.

In promoting the dialogue between faith and philosophy, even the philosophies commonly practised in academic settings, *F&R* urges philosophers to take seriously once again what it calls 'the sapiential dimension' of philosophy, meaning by that the search for the truth about existence in its entire setting. The origins of *philo-sophia*, devotion to wisdom, should be allowed to inspire minds once again with the love of truth. The invitation stands open to philosophers to seek enrichment and stimulus in the search for wisdom by listening to the religious message of the Christian faith. No notable philosophical movement has remained quite apart from the springs of religious belief, either in Greece, Rome, India, European Scholasticism or German Idealism. To rule out in principle all contact with religion would mean that somewhere down the line the question of truth, the very essence of philosophy, would be sacrificed and silenced. Philosophy that has given up on asking who we are, where we come from, why we suffer, what life is worth and what we may hope for, in other words a decadent philosophical style that meets the deepest questions only with sceptical resignation, has abdicated from the role of reason and withdrawn from the most human claims of truth.

The firm conviction that truth is what counts most in human life, and that it is present in the world and accessible to people today, is perhaps the central affirmation of *F&R*. Despite what is referred to as 'the crisis of truth' this letter has no condemnations to pronounce but much encouragement to offer, to members of the Catholic Church, to its thinkers, and to philosophers outside it. To have the courage to seek the truth about human life in all its facets and to follow it wherever it may lead, is the challenge which the encyclical places before philosophers. Truth is not something that human minds have constructed and that is indifferent to the shape of social life, and even of peace and understanding among the peoples and cultures of the world. Truth is greater than we are. It carries us. It overpowers no-one, it convinces and enlightens by being precisely what it is. It would be a false humility on the part of human beings to deny we have a capacity for truth, or no longer to admit that we are made for truth and it is our highest reward, the food of the mind.

Courage for the truth is what the Pope wishes to restore to people. He does so in the evangelical conviction that (only) the truth can and shall make us free (cf. Jn 8:32). He firmly believes that the questions

about truth that arise concerning our human existence include the
question of God and the affirmation of his existence. He shares also
his conviction that there can be a communion of cultures in the truth
that unites them. The divine revelation, he insists, is not an alien and
alienating force; far from being foreign to the cultures of the world it
answers an inner expectation that is present in each of them, since each
culture expresses what is deepest in the human person, including the
desire for self-knowledge, the longing for healing and forgiveness, and
the hope for the overcoming of injustice, and for life beyond death.

Notes

1.   The two classic twentieth-century European/Western statements on culture
     are T.S. Eliot, *Notes Towards a Definition of Culture* (1948) and Joseph
     Pieper, *Leisure as the Basis of Culture* (1955). Another influential work is
     Christopher Dawson's *Religion and Culture* (London, 1948).
2.   And hence upon the work of the Irish Centre for Faith and Culture at
     Maynooth. The text of the speech delivered at the opening of the centre by
     the Bishop of Limerick, Donal Murray, has been printed: 'The Soul of
     Europe', *The Furrow* (January 1998), 3-7.
3.   St Ambrose of Milan wisely reminded himself (as well as his readership) that
     'It is not through philosophy (*dialectica*) that it has pleased God to save His
     people.'
4.   *F&R* itself refers in footnotes to the Pastoral Constitution on the Church in
     the Modern World *Gaudium et Spes*, # 15, and also the Decree on the
     Church's Missionary Activity *Ad Gentes* # 22; in Flannery (ed.), *Vatican
     Council II*, p. 915 f.; 839 f.
5.   Translation between natural languages could be called a theoretical
     impossibility but a practical necessity!
6.   *Nostra Aetate*, # 2: 'Let Christians, while witnessing to their own faith
     and way of life, acknowledge, preserve and encourage the spiritual and
     moral truths found among non-Christians, also their social life and
     culture'. (*Vatican Council II*, ed. Flannery, p. 739). Two recent, general
     accounts of the interrelationship of Christian faith with contemporary
     culture are: Michael Paul Gallagher, *Clashing Symbols: An Introduction to
     Faith and Culture* (London, 1997); Aidan Nichols, OP, *Christendom
     Awake: On Re-Energising the Church in Culture* (Edinburgh, 1999). Also
     worth reading is David Braine, 'The Relationship between Philosophy

and Cultures', in *L'Osservatore Romano*, weekly edition, N. 31 (4 August 1999) 5-6.

7. These questions echo the opening paragraph of *Nostra Aetate*, which detects their presence in all the religions of the world.

8. A quotation in *F&R* from *Gaudium et Spes*, # 2, in Flannery, *Vatican Council II*, p. 922. Pope John Paul II developed this idea in his first encyclical, *Redemptor Hominis*, and it has remained central to all his major writings.

9. This scholarship is reflected in *The Relationship between Neoplatonism and Christianity*, ed. T. Finan and V. Twomey (Dublin, 1992), p. 170.

10. Declaration on the Relation of the Church to Non-Christian Religions, *Nostra Aetate*, 28 October 1965, in *Vatican Council II*, ed. Flannery, pp. 738-742.

11. The letter continues: 'This is a law appropriate to the Church of all the ages, even of that which is to come. She will perceive herself enriched from the daily access of treasures acquired from oriental cultures and in this new inheritance she will discover indicators for showing how a fruitful dialogue with these cultures may be entered upon, one which will help humanity in its journey to a new future.'

12. Pope John Paul II to CCEE, 11 October 1997.

13. J. Ratzinger, 'Die Einheit des Glaubens und die Vielfalt der Kulturen. Reflexionen im Anschluß an die Enzyklika *Fides et ratio*', in *Theologie und Glaube*, 89 (1999), 141-152.

14. See the reflections of J. Ratzinger, 'Zur Lage von Glaube und Theologie heute', in *Internazionale katholische Zeitschrift Communio*, 250 (1996), 359-372, to which we are indebted.

15. 'Nowadays there is a tendency to claim that agnosticism and sceptical relativism are the philosophy and the basic attitude which correspond to democratic forms of political life. Those who are convinced that they know the truth and firmly adhere to it are considered unreliable from a democratic point of view, since they do not accept that truth is determined by the majority', Pope John Paul II, *Centesimus Annus*, # 46

PART 2

The Student Karol Wojtyla and the Philosopher Pope

THE SINGULAR SHAPE OF KAROL WOJTYLA'S STUDIES

James McEvoy

Among those who have written on *Fides et Ratio* (*F&R*) it is a commonplace to observe that only the present Pope could have issued this particular encyclical. *F&R* expresses a definite commitment to philosophy, and it fixes for the Church the objective of a Christian humanism strongly marked by philosophy. Theology, of course, is not omitted from its view; it would in any case be contrary to the spirit, and naturally to the text, of the letter to consider philosophy without reference to theology, or vice versa. That is the whole point of it: these two disciplines contextualise each other. Granted his exceptional presence in this letter, it is interesting to enquire what role philosophy has played in the life and thought of the man who became Pope in 1978.

Writing about the encyclical letter the distinguished North American philosopher W. Norris Clarke SJ (Emeritus of Fordham University) has described it as

> [A] remarkable one in many ways. Athough he never talks about himself in it, it is actually the distillation, worked out over some eight to ten years, of his own personal experience of what it means to be a fully alive Catholic intellectual, reflecting at the

same time the authentic Catholic tradition of what it means to be a fully developed *Christian mind,* with its two complementary dimensions, *faith* and *reason.*[1]

It might, I think, be said that the Holy Father exemplifies his own thesis about philosophy and theology and that he does so with considerable distinction: both disciplines make their best contribution to wisdom when they are integrated in the mind of the Christian believer.

A Wartime Seminarian

In what ways does the earlier intellectual history of Karol Wojtyla (b. 18 May 1920) leave a stamp upon *F&R*? We are fortunate to possess an account of his youthful studies by George Weigel that is both rounded and readable.[2] As a seminarian, Karol Wojtyla naturally studied philosophy. However, the circumstances in which he did so were those of war-torn, Nazi-occupied Poland and the city of Kraków. On February 18, 1941, at a time when Karol was working as a quarryman at a mine, he returned home one evening to find his father dead. His mother had died already in 1929 and his elder brother in 1932, so that at the age of twenty he found himself alone in the world. The young man began to work at the nearby Solvay chemical plant in October of that same year. Up until that time his interests had centered on Polish national-romantic literature, the stage (both as a budding actor and as a writer), and poetry. He lived a fervent life of prayer, searching for a life calling. A year later he was accepted by the Archdiocese of Kraków as a candidate for the priesthood. The external features of his life changed but little in consequence of this decision, for he continued his work – there was at that time no seminary to live in. For the next two years he studied as best he could, until on 6 August 1944 the Archbishop, Adam Stephan Sapieha, initiated an underground seminary in his own residence. The end of bitter warfare came to Poland in January 1945; in the following year, after only four years of this rather extemporised preparation, Karol was ordained priest (1 November 1946). Two weeks later he left Poland for postgraduate formation at Rome, where he completed his doctoral studies in theology at the Angelicum University in June 1948. Such, then, is the bare outline of his student career.

The reason for clandestinity at Kraków was of course the severe difficulties that the occupying power, and in particular the Gestapo, had created for the diocesan seminary in an attempt to control all of its activities. The reception of new seminarians was *verboten*. The Archbishop responded by taking on aspirants as so-called parish secretaries and having them attend classes at the seminary. However, this institution was subjected to frequent Gestapo raids. On one occasion five students were arrested, and either executed or despatched to Auschwitz. The Archbishop responded to this outrage by creating an underground seminary. Candidates, secretly accepted, were instructed to continue to work at their jobs, to keep their candidature strictly confidential, to study in their own time and to take examinations individually by ad hoc arrangements with individual professors.

Karol Wojtyla was among the first ten seminarians chosen for this extraordinary kind of formation. He did much of his reading during his regular night shift at the plant. This included books representative of neo-Scholasticism. In particular he digested a book on metaphysics that had been published in Polish in 1926 by Kasimierz Weiss. Wojtyla had never encountered anything like it, his reading interests up to then having been confined to religion, literature, poetry and above all drama. However, he persevered, and as he later said,

> After two months of hacking my way through this vegetation I came to a clearing, to the discovery of the deep reasons for what until then I had only lived and felt ... What intuition and sensibility had until then taught me about the world found solid confirmation.[3]

In other words (as George Weigel justifiably remarks), through his early philosophical reading Wojtyla was inoculated against the infection of radical scepticism, and he imbibed the realist conviction, fundamental to the thought of Aristotle and St Thomas, that the world is intelligible and that the human mind is equipped to reach knowledge of things as they are. Despite his later exposure to phenomenology he was never to diverge from this strictly realist path. Nothing much is known about his part-time reading course in philosophy. No doubt it had the Scholastic and neo-Thomistic character that was universal in seminaries, with attention falling centrally upon logic, ethics, metaphysics (including philosophical psychology and cosmology), and natural theology. His course cannot have lasted very long since he was ordained after only four years of study, most of it presumably being devoted to scripture and theology.

Postgraduate in Rome

Let us make a jump to Rome, where, between 1946 and 1948 Wojtyla completed his studies for the licence in theology and the DD. His supervisor was Père Réginald Garrigou-Lagrange, who was an acknowledged master of neo-Thomistic thought, in both philosophy and theology. Wojtyla wrote his dissertation in Latin: *Doctrina de fide apud S. Ioannem a Cruce* (The Doctrine of Faith According to St John of the Cross). His choice of topic is indicative of two things: firstly, of the interest he had developed several years beforehand in Carmelite spirituality and mysticism, and, secondly, of the freedom that his supervisor accorded him in the choice of research area. He performed excellently at the oral examination, but he did not formally receive the DD from the Angelicum, since he had not sufficient resources to submit the thesis as a printed book and so was unable to fulfil the requirement for the formal awarding of the degree. He returned to Poland and submitted the same work to the Faculty of Theology of the ancient Jagiellonian University (where he had begun studies in literature shortly before the war, in 1938-39), which conferred the degree of DD on him in December 1948. Following two years as a parish-based university chaplain he began (in September 1951) a further two-year period of study, as required by his bishop. Polish universities have a structure similar to those of Germany, and Karol was to take the *Habilitation,* or higher doctorate, with a fresh thesis. Although his degree was to be theological in character, the context of his work was in fact to be philosophical ethics, by virtue of his own choice: he undertook the examination of the *Wertethik* (value-ethics) of Max Scheler. Fr Wojtyla's thesis represented a critical turn in his intellectual life.

Through reading Scheler he encountered phenomenology, the new philosophical current that had been brought before the war from Husserl's circle at Freiburg-im-Breisgau to Poland (Lwów), by Roman Ingarden. Husserl undertook the rigorous ('scientific') description of all the phenomena of consciousness in their differentiated intentional structures (the relationship of the different kinds of mental act to 'things', or objects). He aimed at renewing what the Enlightenment had called the science of man, by means of an exhaustive, rigorous and universal descriptive analysis of the experience of the subject. Wojtyla did not agree with the Husserlian approach to the phenomena of consciousness in its entirety however, because the founder of the school had drifted back towards idealism, against the clear tendency of his own earlier thought, against the very slogan of the movement ('*Zu den Sachen selbst*': 'to the things themselves', i.e. the immediate phenomena of conscious experience), and in spite of the respectful admonitions of leading pupils of his own such as Dietrich von Hildebrand and Edith Stein. Wojtyla came to regard phenomenology as an important instrument for probing the inner dimensions of experience, both moral and spiritual. However, his thought was thoroughly anchored in realism, in particular moral realism, and hence in the search for moral norms grounded in the reality of human nature.[4] Far from being itself a doctrine, or an 'end to metaphysics', phenomenology was, and is, for Karol Wojtyla a method of philosophical anthropology, a complement to tradition rather than its overturning. Phenomenology was to teach him sensitivity to human experience, especially moral experience, the experience, that is to say, of attractions and love, of moral reflection, conscientious evaluation

and judgement, the exercise of freedom, and growth as a person –
topics that have been at the centre of his interests during all his later
life.[5] Scheler's analysis of such states as sympathy and resentment
helped Wojtyla to approach the inner spiritual realities of moral choice
in a personalist way. An influence of Emmanuel Mounier's Christian
personalism may also be present. The title of his thesis was *An
Evaluation of the Possibility of Constructing a Christian Ethics on the
Basis of the System of Max Scheler.*[6]

The Young Professor at Lublin

The Jagiellonian Faculty of Theology was suppressed by the
Communist regime early in 1954. Dr Wojtyla received a junior
academic appointment at the Catholic University of Lublin (KUL), in
the Faculty of Philosophy, where he lectured on ethics. From then
until he became bishop he was to commute by train (a journey of
between three and four hours), from Kraków to Lublin. Unfortunately
only a little can be said here about Lublin (founded in 1918), that
heroic institution which survived all the forms of discouragement and
discrimination that officialdom could devise, while managing to keep
a high standard of intellectual life. It was at that time the only Catholic
academic institution in the whole of Eastern Europe.

A small group of professors, including the young Wojtyla, set
themselves to meet regularly in order to coordinate their philosophical
teaching in such a way as to meet the challenge of the surrounding
Communist ideology. The convictions of this group have been
summarised in the following four strategic philosophical principles that
they worked out and refined in the course of their discussions.[7] The first
was *realism*, the conviction that we can know at least some things as they
are and that our capacities of knowing are basically attuned to reality.
They believed, in other words, that the further one moves as a
philosopher away from realism in, say, a Kantian or a Hegelian or a
Husserlian direction, the more trouble one gets into. Secondly, they
determined to begin philosophy by reflecting upon *human experience,*
starting from the capacity for wonder and the search for truth as the

defining characteristics of the human condition. Thirdly, they made a fundamental *commitment to reason* and concomitantly to the rational critique of irrationalism and political ideology. These men had after all lived through foreign, National Socialist occupation, propaganda and terror, and their country and Church had emerged from that, only to be ruled by the omnipresent communist state (Poles sometimes refer to themselves, rather wryly, as the nation that lost the Second World War – twice!). The philosophical search for rationally justifiable positions in ethics and politics, as well as in philosophy generally, was meant to give the lie to the forces of ideology and persecution by which the life of Europe had been shadowed. They committed themselves, finally, to the interrogative study of the *history of philosophy*. They regarded the history of philosophy not as the mere shell of the nut, or as a sort of booster rocket that launched thought before being dropped completely, but as the potential teacher of the present day, and as a source of wisdom that had not been simply rendered redundant by modernity, the Anglo-French Enlightenment and the cultural impact of the natural sciences. In short, these members of the Lublin Faculty of Philosophy sought to work out an approach that would be distinctively modern and at home with the language of the human subject, while at the same time remaining deeply grounded in the philosophical tradition of the West and not forgetful of its ancient roots and its striking medieval, scholastic developments. Over the years of their shared intellectual life the group became bound together in affection and friendship. Here we may no doubt locate the existential origin of a passage in *F&R* that sees friendship as the ideal setting for the flourishing of the search for truth (#33).

The reader of *F&R* can easily trace the presence of these four strategic emphases in the document.

Wojtyla's personal situation was to change dramatically when, on 4 July 1958, he was appointed auxiliary bishop of Kraków by Pope Pius XII. In fact he decided to continue his teaching career by travelling back and forth to Lublin. Even as cardinal (from 1965 on) he held on to his university teaching. Out of a fund he had established much earlier from his own earnings he brought the research assistants and the advanced students of ethics by train from Lublin to Kraków, to his residence where his seminars were held, since he no longer had time to commute across the county. Only when he left Poland to become Pope did his career as a lecturer finally cease. He remained always in the lower academic grades (as a *dozent* or lecturer), but was given the title of Honorary Professor of the KUL – one that he still holds. It is a plausible assumption that by continuing to lecture while already bishop and archbishop he wished to demonstrate publicly the strength of the Church's commitment to education, in the first place, but even more fundamentally to philosophical research, especially in anthropology and ethics.

The Philosopher-Pope

It is not commonly known that Castel Gandolfo was the scene, each summer for a number of years, of a week of philosophical reflection and exchange organised on the initiative of the Pontiff. He addressed invitations to selected prominent figures in philosophical faculties from various countries to come and take part in the discussion of topics that he himself proposed. The philosophers in question were, it is believed, drawn from a wide variety of currents; they were not selected for their religious affiliation. He also brought young philosophers from his native country to assist at the week's exchanges, as an encouragement to them to broaden their horizons through these international contacts. The Pope himself, on holiday from Rome, attended the daily sessions, listening to the views expressed while no doubt considering the points of view underlying the expressed opinions, weighing analytic interventions against French or German hermeneutical or phenomenological approaches. John Paul II is a skilled listener. He did not intervene in the discussions; he was there to observe, to inform himself, to learn and discern, to evaluate silently – and also perhaps to prepare *F&R*.

This Pope has an exceptionally wide cultural range of reference. He learns from listening as well as from reading. His own university writings are not learned in the usual academic sense (he used few bibliographical references, preferring to go straight to arguments and to perform those repeated circlings of his around issues, until these are clarified – a sort of peripateticism belongs to his method). He wanted to go on learning as Pope, and he had the means (in every sense of the word) to do it! What a good use of money and influence! Among the modern Popes, it is no denigration of the others to affirm that he is the only one who could have written the encyclical *F&R*.

From this recital of facts several things emerge. John Paul II is sometimes described as an amateur in philosophy on the grounds that he does not hold any degree in the subject. On the other hand, his *Habilitation* thesis could just as easily have been presented to a philosophical faculty as to a theological one. However, the philosophical faculty at the Jagiellonian University had fallen under the influence of the official atheistic and communistic ideology, so that a thesis of the kind Wojtyla wrote simply could not have been presented there for examination.

Secondly, the mark of his strongly phenomenological interest is to be found in his two books, *Love and Responsibility* (1960), and *Person and Act* (1969).[8] Wojtyla, however, saw in phenomenology the complement to the great tradition of metaphysics, not its replacement; a method for exploring subjectivity in a modern way, an implement for personalist thinking, but not in any case the abandonment of realism and of the normativity of truly personal existence. Several commentators on *F&R* have drawn attention to the Thomistic doctrine of truth that underlies the letter. The same could be said of the Pope's more personal thought, namely that it is raised upon the Christian tradition with the wisdom of St Thomas Aquinas as a distinctively strong element. Recourse is had to contemporary streams of thought (phenomenology and personalism) in order to rejuvenate the tradition through exploration of the human subject in all its dimenions of experiencing, knowing, willing and acting. The somewhat abstract Thomistic account of human agency and moral causality is worked through from the point of view of the experiencing, acting subject.

Thirdly, the fact that the name of Edith Stein appears in the encyclical no doubt indicates the kinship of spirit the Pope feels in her regard, his own fascination with her life and his deep admiration for her as a saint of our times.[9] He has described her as 'a paradigmatic figure'. His reverence for her is reflected in his sermon for her beatification preached in Cologne on 1 May 1987 – in the city where she had entered the Carmel and in the country whose political authorities had martyred her. Teresa Benedicta a Cruce was proclaimed a saint on Sunday, 11 October 1998; later in the same week (15 October) the encyclical letter on Faith and Reason was released to the world at a press conference. The proclamation must have been a personally moving event for the Pope, in virtue of the kinship of spirit he has with the new saint.

Notes

1.   W. Norris Clarke, SJ, 'John Paul II: The Complementarity of Faith and Philosophy in the Seach for Truth', *Communio: International Catholic Review*, 26:3 (1999), 557.

2.   George Weigel, *Witness to Hope: The Biography of Pope John Paul II* (New York, 1999). This comprehensive life surpasses and replaces previous biographies, including the much-read but perhaps overrated and politically tendentious book by Carl Bernstein and Marco Politi: *His Holiness: John Paul II and the Hidden History of our Time* (London/New York, 1996).

3.   Quoted by Weigel, p. 70.

4.   For the relationship between Thomism and phenomenology in his discussion of freedom, choice and decision, see the contribution by Kevin Doran in this book.

5.   The mature fruit of his university teaching on the person and in particular on love, sexuality and chastity is to be found in his first book: Karol Wojtyla (Pope John Paul II), *Love and Responsibility*, trans. H.T. Willetts (London, 1981), p. 319 (first published in Polish in 1960).

6.   Regarding his debt to Scheler, in particular for the critique of Kantian formalism, and also his criticism of the decidedly subjectivist tendency of the value-ethics, see the contribution by Patrick Gorevan in the present volume.

7.   Weigel, pp. 130-135. See also J. Seifert, 'Karol Wojtyla and the Cracow/Lublin School of Philosophy', *Aletheia*, 1981.

WOJTYLA'S STUDIES   133

8. Translated into English by Anna-Teresa Tymieniecka. Apparently it is a
    difficult work to translate; the quality of English version has not gone
    uncontested.
9. The parallels in their thought are explored by Mette Lebech in her
    contribution to the present volume.

KAROL WOJTYLA IN PHILOSOPHICAL DIALOGUE WITH MAX SCHELER

Patrick Gorevan

Fr Karol Wojtyla was asked in 1951 by his Archbishop in Kraków to take a two-year sabbatical in order to write a *Habilitation* thesis that would qualify him to teach at university level. In turning to Max Scheler's work as the topic of his dissertation Wojtyla's intention was to develop a personalist approach to ethical matters, which would echo the approach he had been taking in his pastoral apostolate with young marrieds and soon-to-be marrieds, in which he had been 'confronting doctrine with life'.[1] In Scheler's personalism he also hoped, more broadly, to find a grounding for Christian ethics, as the title of his dissertation suggests.[2] In the latter hope he was to be disappointed, for he came to the conclusion that Scheler's phenomenological approach, for all its interesting themes, was not able to do justice to many central aspects of revealed Christian morality. His exposure to Scheler did, however, fulfil his first wish, and a number of Schelerian themes and approaches were to influence him in his apostolate of the pen. This essay will touch on:

- a brief introduction to Max Scheler;
- Karol Wojtyla's critical engagement with Scheler;
- some areas where Scheler's work proved a positive influence on Wojtyla.

Max Scheler

Max Scheler was born in Munich in 1874 and studied at Munich (1894-95) and Berlin (1895-96). In 1896 he moved to Jena, and chose to write his doctoral thesis there under the direction of Rudolf Eucken. In Jena, Scheler completed his first major works, establishing an independence from the ruling Kantian ideas.[3]

Scheler as phenomenologist (1906-1922)
Scheler's philosophical development was given encouragement by a meeting with Husserl in 1901. Scheler recounts the meeting as follows:

> When the present writer made the acquaintance of Husserl ... in Halle in 1901, a philosophical discussion ensued regarding the concepts of intuition (*Anschauung*) and perception. The writer, dissatisfied with Kantian philosophy ... had come to the conviction that what was given to intuition was originally much richer in content than what could be accounted for by sensuous elements, by their derivatives, and by logical patterns of unification. When he expressed this opinion to Husserl and remarked that this insight seemed to him a new and fruitful principle for the development of theoretical philosophy, Husserl pointed out at once that in a new book of logic, to appear presently, [i.e. *Logische Untersuchungen*, Volume II] he had worked out an analogous enlargement of the concept of intuition (*kategoriale Anschauung*). The intellectual bond between Husserl and the writer, which has become so extraordinarily fruitful for him, dates back to this moment.[4]

The impact made on Scheler's philosophical method and views by Husserl's approach was both deep and thoroughgoing. He found this method very congenial and of great benefit in the development of his own work. It represented a mode of access to the objective world of essences, and as such served as an ideal vehicle for his interest in rehabilitating the objective, *a priori* hierarchy of values and feelings, in a criticism of Kant's formalism.

It soon became clear, however, that Scheler had his own approach to the ideal essences of phenomenology, and in particular to the central place of value in this realm:

> One of his students reported that when Scheler asked the rhetorical question 'How is reality given?' his immediate response to his own question was 'Through feelings!' Prior to the act of knowing or willing, the person anticipates the object to be known or willed through feelings.[5]

For Scheler values have a central place in phenomenology, for they give nature and unity to the object. Husserl considered that values are founded on the individual things of nature by way of having a contingent predicative relation to them.[6] For Scheler 'all value-free or value-indifferent things are such only by means of a more or less artificial abstraction, through which we leave out of consideration values that are not only always given along with it, but also constantly pre-given'.[7] There is a stage in the grasping of values wherein the value of an object is clearly and evidentially given *apart from* the givenness of the bearer of the value. Thus, for example, a man can be distressing or repugnant, agreeable or sympathetic to us without our being able to indicate how this comes about.[8] This is in marked contrast to Husserl's notion of valuation as a 'dependent phase which stratifies itself over and above a concrete presentation, or, conversely, falls away again.'[9] Scheler's *personal* rapport with Husserl was also difficult. He never wished to be known as a disciple or follower of Husserl, even though he took some part in the editing of the phenomenological *Jahrbuch*, along with Reinach, Pfänder and Geiger. Scheler was reluctant to consider phenomenology a 'school' of philosophy. There was no fixed body of knowledge, attributable to the founder, which could be passed on and taught. The only way of finding out how fruitful phenomenology is and of making progress in it is the '*practice* of this attitude of consciousness'.[10] So it would not be possible for one man to lead the way in such a wide-ranging task. Consequently, Scheler remarks, it would be incorrect to ascribe to Husserl the type of guiding role played by Kant, Fichte or Hegel in regard to their followers.[11]

Husserl, for his part, did not hold Scheler in any great esteem, indeed he resented his sparkling and ebullient personality, which, during his years in the phenomenological movement in Munich, threatened to eclipse Husserl's own authority in the group. 'One needs brilliant ideas', he is supposed to have said in regard to Scheler, 'but one must not publish them.'[12] But publish them, or publicise them, Scheler did, thereby winning himself a rapid notoriety. Between 1912 and 1921 he had written almost all of his main works: *Formalism*, on ethics, *The Nature of Sympathy*, on intersubjectivity, empathy and love, and *On the Eternal in Man*, on the philosophy of religion, as well as a plethora of minor essays and propaganda material during the war years. He was soon regarded as the 'number two' phenomenologist. Husserl, however, regarded the 'fruits' of the phenomenology practised by Scheler and his devotees as 'fool's gold'.[13] After Scheler's death in 1928, Husserl was to refer to Heidegger and Scheler as his 'two "antipodes"'.[14]

Scheler's later thought

Perhaps Husserl's reservations were proved correct by later developments in Scheler's thought, after his 'turning-point' (*Wende*) in 1923 and up to his untimely death in 1928. From Catholic theist, he became a 'panentheist', a believer in God-in-the-making, a powerless spirit (*Ohnmacht des Geistes*) sublimating the vital energy of the world. There are, roughly, three groups of explanations for this surprising development: some, including Heidegger and von Hildebrand, are convinced that personal matters and psychological factors threw Scheler into new commitments and reactions;[15] others felt that Scheler was merely responding to the inherently paradoxical nature of the real;[16] others still, that the changes had much to do with inherently unstable elements already contained within his thought.[17] Whichever explanation is correct, Scheler's later thought (much of which is in an unfinished state), did not exercise influence on the wide circle of Catholic philosophers, later to include Karol Wojtyla, who saw his phenomenological works as an inspiring way to renew Catholic philosophy.

Scheler and Catholicism

Scheler's role as a Catholic in the German philosophical world in the years from 1915 to 1923 is well described in the anecdotes told of him by Husserl's then research assistant, Edith Stein. Around the year 1935 she wrote that she owed her first encouragement in the direction of Catholicism to Scheler. He had influenced her 'far beyond the sphere of philosophy':

> He was quite full of Catholic ideas at the time and employed all the brilliance of his spirit and his eloquence to plead them ... the rationalist prejudices with which I had unwittingly grown up fell, and the world of faith unfolded before me.[18]

Many other converts had received the impulse of Scheler's insights and intuitions: Peter Wust, Otto Klemperer and Dietrich von Hildebrand are the more obvious examples. Victor Frankl, the Jewish psychologist, speaks of carrying *Formalism* around with him like a copy of the Bible.[19] When *On the Eternal in Man*, Scheler's main work in the area of religious philosophy, appeared in 1921, the Jesuit scholar Erich Przywara remarked that 'Max Scheler's laying of the foundations of religion would constitute a turning point in German philosophy comparable with Husserl's works in the areas of epistemology and logic.'[20]

A number of Catholic philosophers of religion of the time were indeed profoundly influenced by Scheler, including Karl Adam, Karl Rahner, Romano Guardini and Arnold Rademacher.[21] They saw Scheler's theory of religion, based on the phenomenology of religious experience, as a new and refreshing personalist departure for Catholic thought: the God of religion 'is' and lives only in the religious act, not in metaphysical thought-processes. In his phenomenology of religious acts and experience, Scheler discovers man as the being who searches for God. Man must love God or idols (*Gott oder Götzen*).[22] While some would claim that religion is anthropomorphism, Scheler replies, in a phrase that also describes Karol Wojtyla's approach to anthropology, that one can only do justice to *man* by explaining him in a 'theomorphic' way, as the image and likeness of God.[23]

Wojtyla himself, in the introduction to his dissertation, explains why he thinks that Catholic thinkers were drawn to Scheler's work. In the first place, he points out that Scheler's phenomenology offers a link between human acts and their objects, and finds moral value within these objects, challenging the empty formalism of the time. Secondly, Scheler's ethics gives particular attention to the role of love for the *person*, and the ethical significance of imitation and discipleship of ethical models, both of which are congenial with themes of Christian morality.[24]

Karol Wojtyla on Scheler

Karol Wojtyla's *Habilitationsschrift* (*Habilitation* thesis) engages centrally with Scheler's main work in value theory, *Formalism in Ethics*. Despite the title, this is in fact an *attack* on formalism (particularly that of Kant) in which Scheler defends the strictly *a priori* character of values, concluding that it is possible to raise an absolute and *a priori* system of ethics on the basis of the values intentionally perceived by feeling. There is no need to remain at the level of formal mental structures, as Kant believed, in order to achieve an objective and non-empirical basis for morality. Scheler takes on many of the principles of Kantian moral formalism, the 'colossus of steel and bronze' which had to be removed from the path if progress were to be made in ethics.[25]

In *Formalism* Scheler applies phenomenology to affective feeling in order to show that emotional life and the values which it intuits cannot be relegated to the realm of sense-data, since these values are 'given', intentionally, to the acts of emotional feeling, whereas sense-data are not. Emotional life is content-laden (*material*) but it is not necessarily *a posteriori* and empirical and certainly not chaotic, as Kant held. Values are in fact hierarchically ordered, from those of the absolute, relating us to God, through spiritual and vital values to those of sense and pleasure.[26] Moral goodness is to be found in actions and attitudes that respect this hierarchy (*Rangordnung*).

Scheler also held that as we enter into the lives of other persons our moral life draws inspiration from them. Love, the key to the world of person and value, enables us to discover and imitate personal models (*Vorbilder*) whose *ordo amoris* and world of values we find ourselves wishing to imitate and that transform us after their pattern. Religious figures like Jesus Christ, sages like Socrates, artistic and heroic figures – all offer us entry into this sphere of values.

Despite his strong defence of ethical personalism and his concern to base ethical life on personal assimilation of personal models, Scheler warns against a notion of person based on substance, or of an objective 'thing which executes acts'. The person is, experiences himself and is known only in the execution of such acts. We may not borrow spatial metaphors to arrive at or search for some kind of substance 'behind' or beneath the activity, for persons cannot become an object. The only way we can reach knowledge of a person is by co-execution of his acts.[27] 'Whoever has the *ordo amoris* of a man, has the man himself.'[28] Love alone, reaching to this order of the heart, permits people to *be* and be known.[29]

Wojtyla's 'Auseinandersetzung' with Scheler

Wojtyla's dialogue with Scheler in his *Habilitationsschrift* was thorough and painstaking. Miecyslaw Malinski reports that his friend remarked to him that he had decided to translate Scheler's *Formalism* into Polish, since his German was simply not up to reading it.[30]

Wojtyla's criticisms of Scheler center on the question of perfectionism. In an essay on Scheler written in 1956, he explains that ethics, for him, is a *personal* thing, for moral actions reflect and perfect the person performing them. Ethics is always about the human being, the material object of ethics. This is the ultimate question that he will ask about Scheler: whether his ethics allows for people to become better human beings through their actions.[31]

This gives rise to Wojtyla's major difficulty with Scheler's value-ethics. Moral values, for Scheler, are not sought directly: they are the fruit of a correct achievement of other values, according to their hierarchical ranks. It is 'better' to prefer spiritual values, for example, to sensual ones. The values of the holy are more elevated than those of life, the values of the spirit are to be preferred to those of the senses. Morality ('good' and 'evil') emerges in this comparison and preference (or rejection). Wojtyla finds this rather remote from real life. If we ask 'Is prayer a good act here and now?', this question cannot be answered simply by saying that it incarnates the highest values, those of the absolute. There are situations when spiritual demands should be postponed in the face of pressing material concerns. Wojtyla also sees in this the risk of a kind of Manichaeanism, in which sensory values are seen as morally evil simply because they are felt as lower.[32]

He strongly attacks Scheler's view that it would be 'pharisaical' to strive directly for one's own moral perfection, and that moral values are only given 'on the back of' (*am Rücken*) or on the occasion of one's taking the hierarchically-correct attitude to the other values. Wojtyla's argument is that while Jesus accused the Pharisees of acting in order that their virtue be seen, Scheler's whole ethical theory is likely to end in a similar cul-de-sac: it is geared to affective perception of one's own values, one's *ordo amoris*. Having that as supreme end would be no less pharisaical. For Wojtyla, Scheler has not so much unmasked pharisaism as provided a devastating critique of the basic premise of his own system.[33]

Limits of personal imitation in Scheler
It is in his passages on following Christ as a moral pattern that Wojtyla feels that Scheler comes closest to a Christian approach to ethics. The love of an ideal person, a saint, a hero, someone who incarnates

particular values, draws us into that moral goodness, for we make their ethos our own. This seems close to the Gospel ethic of following Christ, and also to the Aristotelian view that the good man is the model and measure for others, but there are crucial differences to be noted.

For a Christian ethic, the good man (as for Aristotle) was a good *human being*, someone who realised inwardly the perfection proper to a rational human being and incarnated the good qualities that this implies. Imitation of such a person meant a real effort to live one's life according to the model represented by him. For Scheler, on the other hand, the perfection of moral value is simply an intentional emotional identification on the ethical agent's part with the values which he or she loves 'along with' Christ, or with any other ethical model chosen. Its significance is fundamentally psychological, and it is hard to see how it could impinge on morality, understand as making one a better person.[34]

Drama of human freedom

This autonomy and supremacy of value in Scheler's theory also leaves the whole question of freedom in doubt. The pattern for behaviour or *ordo amoris* is handed down in advance. A motivated human will is determined by the values that it receives from the emotive and value-intuitive faculties.

This means that the genuine drama of freedom is not played out. The will is in direct dependence on the *Wertfühlen* (value-feelings) and merely *executes* their vision. The person, Wojtyla concludes, 'is not the efficient cause of the values achieved by the will.'[35] We can say nothing about how ethical values emerge from human action. Values are part of the personal world of the person but they are not the object or fruit of his actions in any way. They make his willed actions of rather little account. 'Scheler reduces the essence of personal life to emotion, and reduces moral life to the emotional grasping of values. This is a total distortion of human action'.[36]

Wojtyla's conclusions

The root of Scheler's partial approach to ethics is not his phenomenology, but the bias towards the emotions that distorted some of his phenomenological analyses:

> Scheler ... has decisively cancelled out the normative character of ethical values, and this is the consequence of the distancing of values from the actions of the person. This is rather surprising, because the act of conscience as a personal experience linking the individual to ethical values is actually an object of phenomenological experience. If Scheler, as a phenomenologist, does not discover the active rapport between the person and ethical values through his analysis of the act of conscience this is due not so much to his phenomenology as to his emotionalist premises.[37]

Wojtyla's conclusions are thus negative but not dismissive. Scheler's thought can be of 'collateral' assistance in developing a Christian ethics, in particular when it comes to analysing ethical situations, for phenomenology is more of a pedagogy than a fully-fledged philosophy.[38] It can help us to discover moral good and evil, and see how these are part of human experience. It cannot, however, define objectively what makes an action good or evil, for this demands that we go beyond phenomenology. But even that moment of 'going beyond' is itself the fruit of a phenomenological experience, in that our conscience brings us to search for the reasons, and the basis, for the moral values and norms that arise in a fully ethical life. This is why Wojtyla insisted that the problem with Scheler was that he did not use the phenomenological method to the full in examining moral experience. He asked not so much 'What is given in experience?' as 'What *can* be given?' Emotionalism had defined both the question and the answers.

Scheler's Influence on Karol Wojtyla

Karol Wojtyla's thought remained marked by his brush with phenomenology. He claimed in his thesis on Scheler that it can serve as a pedagogical help in approaching experience, even when it needs to go beyond itself for a metaphysical foundation.[39] His writings as Pope sometimes offer flashes of analysis that suggest that phenomenological influences are still to be found. In 1992, for example, in an exhortation on the formation of priests, he talks about Gospel discernment of the 'signs of our time'. This discernment is not provided by knowledge of a situation, important though that is. The situation must also be *interpreted*, so that the good be distinguished from the evil, the signs of hope from the threats:

> Gospel discernment gathers from the historical situation – from its events and circumstances – not just a simple 'fact' to be precisely recorded yet capable of leaving a person indifferent or passive, but a 'task', a challenge to responsible freedom – both of the individual person and of the community.[40]

While this interpretation is inspired by faith in Christ and by the challenge of his words it is also resonant of a phenomenological turning to 'the things themselves', and, in Schelerian terms, to the value-essences that are to be found in experiences, situations and facts of everyday life.

We now trace the influence exerted by Scheler's phenomenology of value on Karol Wojtyla's approach to the following themes:

- Resentment;
- The notion of shame;
- The person.

Resentment

In 1912, Scheler published his essay on Resentment.[41] It is his view that modern man has developed a resentful spiritual attitude to virtue, found especially in utilitarian approaches to morality and to love. The concept of virtue, he felt, needed a 'rehabilitation'.[42] We are tempted to reject, as 'value-less', what we are not able to achieve. This is what happens to technical society, which confines itself to merely material progress, as though spiritual betterment had no worth.

Wojtyla's chapter 'The Rehabilitation of Chastity' in *Love and Responsibility* is a conscious tribute to Scheler's theory, from whom he also borrowed the title of the first section, 'Chastity and Resentment'.[43] If virtue needs 'rehabilitation', he claims, following Scheler, that this is because of *resentment* in its regard. It is resented precisely by those who, realising that a higher value needs a greater effort of will, deliberately minimise its significance. In this sense he compares it to St Thomas' definition of *acedia* (sloth), a 'sadness arising from the fact that the good is difficult.' Resentment goes farther: it actually distorts the features of the good so that it no longer receives the respect it deserves. This distortion serves as an inner satisfaction for the powerless and resentful person.

Chastity is the virtue that has most been outlawed from the soul by resentment. For Wojtyla, chastity should be the integration of love within the lives of the persons as well as between them. Failure to achieve this integration means that love does not ripen into a feeling at the personal level, so that the moral, virtuous component of love does not develop – and for Wojtyla it is only the profound realism of virtue that is able to offer complete security against the sensual and emotional reaction to another. If this is taken to be love, chastity seems to be a hindrance or an obstacle to it, and this is where resentment towards it often emerges, regarding chastity as an impossible (and thus resented and denigrated) ideal.[44]

Wojtyla's rebuttal of resentment takes the form of a question: can we actually hope to integrate sensual emotion within the personal level of love? Can the emotions connected with sexual reactions become part of a personal attitude in which the value of the other person is paramount? Love in a world of persons, he answers, must possess its ethical wholeness and fullness (*integritas*). Psychological factors are not

enough, but need to be taken up into the personal attitudes. Chastity
is another name for this integration, and without it love cannot ripen
and mature.[45]

Shame and humility

In *Love and Responsibility*, Wojtyla refers directly to Scheler's attention
to the phenomenon of *shame*, and of sexual shame in particular.

The feeling of shame, for both thinkers, is always built on and protects
positive self-value. Scheler evokes shame as a promise of beauty. It
allows us to discern depths of value and beauty that a shame-less,
'objective' view of things and people would not be able to. Shame is
able instinctively to conceal and reveal the depth of beauty to be found
within the person.[46] True love and shame are correlative to one
another.

For Wojtyla 'the experience of shame is a natural reflection of the
essential nature of the person.'[47] Shame, or sexual modesty, is not a
flight from love, but on the contrary the opening of a way towards it.
'The spontaneous need to conceal mere sexual values bound up with
the person is the natural way to the discovery of the value of the person
as such', for the value of the person is closely connected with its
inviolability, its status as 'something more than an object of use.'[48]
Shame is a natural form of self-defence for the person against the
danger of descending or being pushed into the position of an object
for sexual use. Wojtyla goes further than Scheler into the workings of
shame in sexual love by affirming that it is, or can be, absorbed by
love. Love precludes treatment of the person as an object for use, and
so it is able to generate a relationship where this is no longer a risk, and
thus shame, that protection of personal values, is absorbed into a
rapport in which these values are safe from attack.[49]

Since becoming Pope, Karol Wojtyla has engaged in further
analyses of the experience of shame, drawing on the early chapters of
Genesis. In a series of profound meditations on the testimony of 'the
beginning', he explores the question of shame in a manner that goes
even farther beyond the Schelerian approach, including as it does the

question of shame as a boundary situation between innocence and sin.[50]

Both Wojtyla and Scheler analyse the phenomenon of shame without reduction. They examine the contrast between shame and prudery, and display the link between shame and the values that it permits to emerge. Finally, both are at pains to point out the difference between shame and a sort of Manicheanism that would regard that which ought to be hidden as evil. The fact that an action should best be carried out privately does not suggest that it is wrong.[51]

For Scheler, shame also goes beyond this individual emotion, for it enables us, at a *cosmic* level, to be aware of the mysterious depths to be found within the world. He links shame, at a spiritual level, with reverence. It is shame and reverence that offer us the world as a mysterious profundity and give our perspective a breadth and a fullness that beggar our understanding and make us aware of the narrowness and limitation of our perspective. He adds that scientific and even artistic conquering of the world have made such emotions less straightforward for us.[52]

Karol Wojtyla has often evoked this attitude to the world in his writings, particularly since becoming Pope:

> we need ... to *foster*, in ourselves and in others, *a contemplative outlook.*[53] Such an outlook arises from faith in the God of life, who has created every individual as a 'wonder' (cf. Ps 139:14). It is the outlook of those who see life in its deeper meaning, who grasp its utter gratuitousness, its beauty and its invitation to freedom and responsibility. It is the outlook of those who do not presume to take possession of reality but instead accept it as a gift, discovering in all things the reflection of the Creator and seeing in every person his living image (cf. Gen 1:27; Ps 8:5).[54]

If we learn the lesson of humble mastery and dominion aright, we will be left not with a domineering and aggressive approach to the environment, both human and ecological, but 'the priority of ethics over technology, in the primacy of the person over things, and in the superiority of spirit over matter.'[55] This is Pope John Paul's definition of the kingly function of dominion over the world, a 'reverent' dominion that does not take possession of, much less manipulate the world around us.

The person

In *Crossing the Threshold of Hope*, the Pope referred to the genesis of his personalism:

> In *Love and Responsibility*, I formulated the concept of a *personalist principle*. This principle is an attempt to translate the commandment of love into the language of philosophical ethics. *The person is a being for whom the only suitable dimension is love.* We are just to a person if we love him. This is as true for God as it is for man. Love for a person *excludes the possibility of treating him as an object of pleasure.*[56]

While this principle has drawn upon a number of philosophers, including Kant, there is little doubt that the formulation owes something to Scheler's repeated claim that knowledge of the person is not detached or 'objective' but must always pass through love. In a central passage from *The Nature of Sympathy*, Scheler had revisited the approach to the person that was characteristic of his ethics:

> It is characteristic ... of individual personality that we only become acquainted with it *in* and *through* the act of loving, and that its value as an individual is likewise only disclosed in the course of this act. Being an 'object' of love represents, as it were, the only objective status wherein personality has existence and can therefore be manifested. Hence the utterly misguided 'rationalism' of seeking to account for one's love for an individual person ... the element of the personal in man can *never be disclosed to us as an 'object'.* Persons cannot be

objectified, in love or any other genuine act, not even in cognition.'[57]

Precisely in the context of human love, this time in marriage, Pope John Paul has applied this insight on many occasions: apropos of the question of 'trial marriages', he remarks:

> reason leads one to see that they are unacceptable, by showing the unconvincing nature of carrying out an 'experiment' with human beings, whose dignity demands that they should be always and solely the term of a self-giving love without limitations of time or of any other circumstance.[58]

Karol Wojtyla's philosophy of the person had already been summed up in the title and the working out of *The Acting Person*, published in 1969 as the summary of a long process of phenomenological investigation, which came to the conclusion that the person is most truly revealed in action, and morality is the truth of human action. If we were to detach human action from moral values we would have engaged in an artificial operation that would turn our attention away from its full dynamism.[59] This could also sum up Wojtyla's perception of the greatness and limitations of Scheler's thought: his ability to open unsuspected depths of human personality and feeling, limited by his inability to come to terms with the power of freedom and with the moral *agency* at work in actions, reflecting – and constructing – the person in his deepest value, the *bonum honestum*.

Conclusion

Ten years later, in a preface to the English edition of the same work, written weeks before his election, Wojtyla paid tribute to Scheler, a 'major influence' upon his reflection. But, he added, if we want to reach to the source and unity of man, the Aristotelian conception of 'human act' is a necessary starting point. Phenomenology has failed to uncover it.[60]

In an earlier essay on Scheler, written in 1959, Karol Wojtyla refers
to Fr Jacek Woroniecki, another Polish academic priest who had felt
drawn to Scheler.[61] Woroniecki had often referred to the ethics of
values, in particular to Scheler, and had sensed 'in an intuitive way'
that there were points of contact or similarities with St Thomas and
with Christian ethics. He, however, never had the opportunity to test
these intuitions. Karol Wojtyla spent much time and effort doing so,
and his conclusion was that while Scheler's and other
phenomenological analyses could *complement* traditional thinking
about man, the intuited *similarities* with Aquinas and with the central
principles of Christian ethics did not in fact survive a more extensive
treatment. Like Woroniecki, perhaps at his suggestion, he had
expected more in Scheler's philosophy than he was actually to find.

Notes

1. This early apostolate is reflected in Karol Wojtyla, *Love and Responsibility*,
   trans. H.T. Willetts (London, Collins, 1981), p. 15.
2. Karol Wojtyla, *Valutazioni sulla possibilità di construire l'etica cristiana sulle
   basi del sistema di Max Scheler*, trans. S. Bucciarelli (Rome, Logos, 1980).
   (Referred to below as *Max Scheler.*)
3. His doctoral thesis (*On the Relations between Logical and Ethical Principles*)
   and his *Habilitationsschrift* (*On Transcendental and Psychological Method*).
   These are both published in volume I of Scheler's collected works,
   Gesammelte Werke (referred to below as *GW*), ed. by Maria Scheler and
   Manfred Frings (Volumes I-XI, Berne, Francke Verlag, 1954-79); (Volume
   XII-XV, Bonn, Bouvier, 1987-97)
4. Max Scheler, 'Die deutsche Philosophie der Gegenwart', in GW VII, p. 308
   (translation from H. Spiegelberg, *The Phenomenological Movement*, The
   Hague, Nijhoff, 1960) vol. I, p. 229).
5. Quoted in Rainier Ibana, 'The Stratification of Emotional Life',
   International Philosophical Quarterly, 31 (1991), 461-471 (p. 461).
6. cf. Husserl, *Ideas*, trans. by W.R. Boyce Gibson (London, Allen & Unwin,
   1931), sections 116, 117.
7. *On the Eternal in Man*, trans. by B. Noble (London, SCM Press, 1960), p. 86.
8. cf. *Formalism in Ethics and Non-Formal Ethics of Values*, trans. by Manfred
   S. Frings and Roger Funk (Evanston, Northwestern University Press, 1973),
   p. 17. (Referred to below as *Formalism*).

9. *Ideas*, section 95.
10. Max Scheler, 'Die deutsche Philosophie der Gegenwart', *GW*, VII, p. 309.
11. cf. *ibid.*, p. 327.
12. H. Spiegelberg, *Doing Phenomenology* (The Hague, Nijhoff, 1975), pp. 280-1.
13. H. Spiegelberg, *The Phenomenological Movement*, vol. I, p. 230.
14. E. Husserl, 'Letter to Ingarden', quoted in H. Spiegelberg, *The Phenomenological Movement*, vol. I, p. 230.
15. cf. M. Heidegger, 'In Memory of Max Scheler', oration pronounced in 1928 and trans. by T. Sheehan in *Heidegger, the Man and the Thinker* (Chicago, Precedent, 1975), pp. 159-60; Dietrich von Hildebrand, 'Max Scheler als Persönlichkeit', *Hochland*, 26 (1928-29), pp. 70-80 and H. Lützeler, *Der Philosoph Max Scheler* (Bonn, 1947), pp. 8-11.
16. cf. N. Hartmann, 'Max Scheler', *Kantstudien*, 33 (1928), ix-xvi (xv).
17. cf. J. Collins, 'Roots of Scheler's Evolutionary Pantheism', *Cross-roads in Philosophy* (Chicago, Regnery, 1969), pp. 106-31 (p. 108).
18. Edith Stein, *Life in a Jewish Family*, trans. by D. Koeppels, (Washington, I.C.S., 1986), p. 260.
19. cf. W. Mader, *Max Scheler* (Hamburg, Rowohlt, 1980), p. 46 and V. Frankl, 'Uno psicologo si racconta', *Studi Cattolici*, 34 (1990), 196-207 (p. 200).
20. E. Przywara, *Religionsbegründung Max Scheler-J.H. Newman* (Freiburg, 1923), p. 1.
21. Heinrich Fries, *Die katholische Religionsphilosophie der Gegenwart* (Heidelberg, Kerle, 1949), pp. 176-84, 253-83.
22. Max Scheler, *On the Eternal in Man*, trans. by B. Noble (London, SCM Press, 1960), p. 267.
23. cf. John Paul II, 'The Image and Likeness of God', Apostolic Letter *Mulieris Dignitatem*, 15 August 1988 (Dublin, Veritas, 1988), #8, and General Audience of 9 April 1986, published in *Catechesis on the Creed* vol. I, *God, Father and Creator* (Boston, Pauline Books & Media, 1996) pp. 221-25.
24. K. Wojtyla, *Max Scheler*, p. 22.
25. *Formalism*, pp. 6-7.
26. *ibid.*, pp. 253-254.
27. cf. *ibid.*, p. 387.
28. Max Scheler, '*Ordo Amoris*', trans. by David Lachtermann, in *Max Scheler: Selected Philosophical Essays* (Evanston: Northwestern University Press, 1973), p. 100.
29. cf. *The Nature of Sympathy*, trans. by Peter Heath (New Haven: Yale University Press, 1954), pp. 152-161.
30. Quoted in George Weigel, *Witness to Hope* (New York, Harper Collins,

1999), p. 128. Weigel adds that in a conversation in 1996 Pope John Paul confirmed that this was his approach to the project.

31. cf. Karol Wojtyla, 'In Search of the Basis of Perfectionism in Ethics', *Person and Community* (New York,Peter Lang, 1993), pp. 45-56 (p. 53).

32. cf. Karol Wojtyla, 'On the Metaphysical and Phenomenological Basis of the Moral Norm', *Person and Community* (New York, Peter Lang, 1993), pp. 73-94 (p. 85).

33. cf. Karol Wojtyla, *Max Scheler*, p. 133.

34. cf. Karol Wojtyla, 'On the Metaphysical and Phenomenological Basis of the Moral Norm', pp. 87-89.

35. Karol Wojtyla, *Max Scheler*, p. 144 and cf. p. 233.

36. *ibid.*, p. 160.

37. *Max Scheler*, p. 234 (my translation).

38. cf. Rocco Buttiglione, *Il Pensiero di Karol Wojtyla* (Milan, Jaca Book, 1982), pp. 73-78.

39. cf. Pope John Paul II, Encyclical Letter, *Fides et Ratio*, 14 September 1998 (Dublin, Veritas, 1998), # 83.

40. Pope John Paul II, Post-Synodal Exhortation *Pastores dabo vobis*, 25 March 1992 (Catholic Truth Society, London, 1992), # 10.

41. An extended version is available in *Ressentiment,* translated by W.H. Holdheim, edited with an introduction by Lewis A. Coser (New York, Free Press of Glencoe, 1961).

42. The essay 'Zur Rehabilitierung der Tugend' (The Rehabilitation of Virtue) was first published by Scheler in 1915 (GW III).

43. Karol Wojtyla, *Love and Responsibility*, trans. by H.T. Willetts (London, Collins, 1981), pp. 143-47. This work was originally written in 1960.

44. cf. *ibid.*, p. 147.

45. *ibid.*, pp. 167-72.

46. cf. *Über Scham und Schamgefühl,* first published in 1933, in GW X, pp. 100-02.

47. Karol Wojtyla, *Love and Responsibility*, p. 178.

48. *ibid.*, p. 179.

49. cf. *Love and Responsibility*, pp. 181-82.

50. cf. Pope John Paul II, General Audiences of 19 December 1979 and 28 May 1980, published in *The Theology of the Body* (Boston, Pauline Books & Media, 1997), pp. 55-58 and 114-17.

51. For an interesting discussion of this point, cf. Michael Nolan, 'Aquinas and the Act of Love' in *At the Heart of the Real* (Dublin, Irish Academic Press, 1992), pp. 172-73.

52. *Über Scham und Schamgefühl*, p. 89.

53. cf. Pope John Paul II, Encyclical Letter *Centesimus Annus*, 1 May 1991 (London, Catholic Truth Society, 1991), # 37.

54. Pope John Paul II, Encyclical Letter *Evangelium Vitae*, 25 March 1995 (Dublin, Veritas, 1995), # 83.

55. Pope John Paul II, Encyclical Letter *Redemptor Hominis*, 4 March 1979, (London, Catholic Truth Society, 1979), # 16.

56. *Crossing the Threshold of Hope*, trans. by J. & M. McPhee (London, Jonathan Cape, 1994), pp. 200-01.

57. Max Scheler, *The Nature of Sympathy*, pp. 166-67.

58. Pope John Paul II, Post-Synodal Exhortation *Familiaris Consortio*, 22 November 1981 (London, Catholic Truth Society, 1981), # 80.

59. cf. Karol Wojtyla, *The Acting Person*, trans. by A. Potocki (Dordrecht, Reidel, 1979), pp. 10-11.

60. *ibid.*, viii.

61. Karol Wojtyla, 'On the Metaphysical and Phenomenological Basis of the Moral Norm', *Person and Community*, p. 73.

WHY DOES JOHN PAUL II REFER TO EDITH STEIN IN *FIDES ET RATIO*?

Mette Lebech

Sister Teresa Benedicta of the Cross, better known by her name in the world as Edith Stein, was beatified on 1 May 1987. The process for her beatification was introduced in the early sixties by the then Archbishop of Cologne, and it proceeded as that of a martyr. She was canonised on 11 October 1998, and was further honoured by Pope John Paul II when she was made Patroness of Europe, along with Catherine of Siena and Birgitta of Sweden, on 1 October 1999 – in a gesture to complement the existing patronage of Sts Benedict, Cyril and Methodius.[1]

In the encyclical *Fides et Ratio* (*F&R*) she is pointed out as one of those thinkers who in recent times illustrate the fruitful relationship between philosophy and the Word of God (#74), the others mentioned being John Henry Newman, Antonio Rosmini, Jacques Maritain and Étienne Gilson.[2] Among these, she is the only martyr.

The association of martyrdom with philosophy is rare, but it is not entirely unprecedented. In fact, both patron saints of philosophy died as martyrs. St Justin Martyr (*c.* 103-165) was a pagan philosopher who after his conversion to Christianity instituted a school of Christian philosophy at Rome, and who wrote (among other things) two apologies and *The Dialogue with Trypho*. He was beheaded at the command of the Prefect Rusticus of Rome for being a Christian. St Catherine of Alexandria (*c.* 307) was known as a Christian philosopher who was imprisoned for objecting to sacrifice to the Emperor. She converted fifty scholars to Christianity while she was awaiting her execution. She was tortured on a wheel and beheaded.

Edith Stein, however, is our contemporary. John Paul II has called her a 'paradigmatic figure'[3] and a 'symbol embodying the deepest tragedy and the deepest hopes of Europe'.[4] There is a special link between John Paul II and Edith Stein. His reasons for pointing her out provide the framework for this study.[5] I suggest that these reasons can be divided into three categories: the personal, the practical and the objective, which will be treated under the following headings: 1. Edith Stein as mirror; 2. Edith Stein as symbol; 3. Edith Stein as philosopher.

Edith Stein as Mirror

In the *Magna Moralia,* a Greek philosophical work attributed to Aristotle, the mirror is used as an analogue of the friend: friends are alike and have much in common – they 'explain' one another by intimate illustration. Stein and Wojtyla have much in common: they have places, masters, pursuits and problems in common, but each relates to these in slightly different ways. Because of these slight differences they 'illustrate' one another, in the same way that family members shed a curious light upon one another.

Common places

Both Stein and Wojtyla were born in what is today Poland. Stein was born in Breslau (today Wroclaw), in the province of Silesia, 150 miles northwest of Kraków. Stein's family on both sides came from the little town of Lubliniz (Lubliniec), half way between Breslau and Kraków, and about twenty miles west of Czestochowa.

Wadowice, Wojtyla's birthplace, is some twenty miles southwest of Kraków, in the province of Galicia. It is situated only about ten miles southeast of Auschwitz (Oswiecim), which still lies within the boundaries of Upper Silesia. It was in Kraków that Wojtyla would enter the clandestine seminary in the autumn of 1942. It was in Auschwitz that Stein was to die around 9 August 1942: Wojtyla was then twenty-two years of age, and Stein fifty-one. The few days or hours Stein spent in the extermination camp of Auschwitz, Wojtyla is likely to have spent working in the Solvay chemical factory, some thirty miles away.

Breslau was Prussian when Stein was a child, and she identified herself as German, not as Polish. When Lublinitz became Polish after the First World War her mother's family sold their property and some moved to Oppeln (which remained German), only thirty miles to the west, whereas other relations went to Berlin to establish themselves there. They were all German speakers and pro-German. However, to Stein's mother Lublinitz remained 'home', and Stein herself would often visit the place as a child, together with her siblings. As they were allowed to please themselves and were not over-supervised in Lublinitz, the place was like a haven.

Wojtyla is of course Polish and of Polish origin. His parents came from Bielsko-Biala, forty miles southwest of Kraków. His father spoke German and taught it to Karol, but Karol's native language was Polish. The father also introduced him to the Polish romanticism of Sienkiewicz, Mickiewicz, Slowacki and Norwid, all singing the glory of the 'non-country' Poland. Galicia being as close to Silesia as Derry is to Donegal, it may be justified to say that our two personages were from the same country, but of different nationalities.

In Wadowice around 20% of the population was Jewish. Wojtyla remembers the father of his Jewish childhood friend as a Polish patriot, who fought with the Poles in the battle of the Vistula that won the Poles their precarious restoration of nationhood after the First World War. Stein's active involvement in the First World War as a nurse at the Russian front testifies to her patriotism also, this time on the side of the Germans.[6] The Jews of Central Europe were very much part of the life of the nations in which they lived, but with the rise of Nazism, and especially with the invasion of Poland, Jews and Poles came to have something in common: they both had their 'living' space converted into National-Socialist *Lebensraum*.

However, Germany meant not only Nazism but also Göttingen: 'Dear Gottingen! [Stein exclaims] I do believe only someone who studied there between 1905 and 1914, in the brief flowering time of the Göttingen School of Phenomenology, can appreciate all that the name evokes in us'.[7] Wojtyla, of course, did not study in Göttingen, indeed he was not yet born at the time when its school of phenomenology was flourishing. Yet the life of the Göttingen Circle and its vivid discussions would become familiar to him through his studies of Scheler, who, like Stein and Wojtyla, had come to Göttingen drawn by phenomenology.

Analecta Husserliana tried, in 1971, under the leadership of Anna-Teresa Tymieniecka, to rekindle the spirit of Husserl's *Jahrbuch für Philosophie und phänomenologische Forschung*. Stein and Wojtyla 'met' three times in this new forum, the *Analecta*. The theme of Volume V is phenomenological anthropology.

In it are reproduced texts from the Third International Conference of the International Husserl and Phenomenological Research Society (March 1974). Philibert Secretan's paper is called 'Personne, individualité et responsibilité chez Edith Stein', whereas Wojtyla addresses himself to 'The Intentional Act and the Human Act'. In Volume VI (covering the *Fourth International Conference* of the said society, held in January 1975), Wojtyla addresses 'Participation or Alienation', whereas Philibert Secretan again talks about Edith Stein: 'The Self and the Other in the Thought of Edith Stein'. The discussion is still about phenomenological anthropology, and the two contributions of Wojtyla lie in direct prolongation of his book *Person and Act*, which was later to be published in English as the first monograph in the series of the *Analecta*. In Volume XI (covering the same society's conference in March 1976) Secretan, for the third time, writes about 'Edith Stein on the "Order and Chain of Being"', and Wojtyla addresses this time the same topic: 'The Degrees of Being from the Point of View of the Phenomenology of Action'. This time the discussion is about metaphysics, but still viewed from the standpoint of anthropology. Even if Wojtyla was only actually present on the last occasion, while Secretan spoke only at the first two, Wojtyla must have been struck at this stage by a similarity of approach between himself and Stein, and above all by their common interest in the human person. It is probably in the course these meetings of minds that Wojtyla came to 'know' Stein.[8]

Common masters

Both 'came' to Göttingen to work, Stein primarily with Husserl, Wojtyla primarily with Scheler. Wojtyla 'came' (even though not in person) after having completed a full education in theology, his primary degree not being in philosophy. He was, so to speak, a 'mature student' at Göttingen. Stein, on the contrary, was attracted by phenomenology from her earliest youth. Theology would be acquired (not without struggle) with the help of Thomas Aquinas, much later on in her career.

Husserl (1859-1938) is credited with being the 'Father of phenomenology'. He became known to Stein through Breslau seminars on the psychology of thought. In the course of these, she kept coming across references to Husserl's 1900-01 work, *Logische Untersuchungen* (Logical Investigations), and became convinced that Husserl was, as she later put it, 'the philosopher of our age'.[9] In the *Logical Investigations* Husserl rejected what he had come to understand as his own earlier psychologism, and proposed in its stead a new science that was to investigate the phenomena in their very act of appearance, and distill their eidetic structures, without any theoretical prejudgement. This was the science of phenomenology, and pure logic as well as the whole edifice of science was to be founded on it. Its motto was *Zu den Sachen Selbst!* (To the things themselves!) By discarding psychologism, subjective idealism and naturalism, Husserl intended to analyse logical phenomena in their purity. Transforming Brentano's descriptive phenomenology, conscious acts were to be scrutinised according to their intentionality, i.e. in their structure of being a mental act (*intentio*) directed towards something (*intentum*). But intentional acts were also to be investigated according to their varying degrees of fulfillment, the highest degree being certain evidence. From around 1905 Husserl began practising what he called the 'reduction'. It implied a concern to focus on the intentional act in which the object was given, to the point of reducing the intentional object to it. Husserl would from then on talk about 'transcendental phenomenology'. Already the 1913 work *Ideen zu einer reinen Phänomenologie und phänomenologischen Philosophie* (Ideas Pertaining to a Pure Phenomenology and to Phenomenological Philosophy) bears the mark of this crucial change. Subsequent works would confirm this direction.

Stein met Husserl for the first time in 1913, and found a man who had come to think that the philosophical programme she had first been attracted by should be taken forward in a somewhat different direction. This direction would disappoint Stein, just as it disappointed Scheler, Conrad Martius, Von Hildebrand and many others of the early phenomenologists, because they felt it departed from experience. Much as they revered the one whom they called 'The Master', they responded to this new direction by endeavouring to develop the philosophical programme in the direction that they thought it ought to take. For Stein, the disappointment would be the first step in the direction of an intersubjective metaphysics – a path that would later lead her on to Christianity and Christian mysticism. Max Scheler (1874-1928) claimed to have developed the phenomenological method independently of Husserl. Feeling on this account less indebted than did the young phenomenologists, he was even more critical than they of Husserl's transcendental turn. Scheler had never in fact been at any of Husserl's classes, and thus was not, in any strict sense, a pupil of Husserl. However, he had known Husserl since 1901 and had often corresponded with him. When Scheler had his licence to teach withdrawn (as a consequence of the scandals surrounding his two divorces), Husserl invited him to Göttingen, where he lectured privately with much success. His aim was to construct an ethics on a phenomenological foundation, distinct on the one hand from the dominant Kantian formalism, and, on the other, from consequentialist utilitarianism. Ethics, according to Scheler, does not depend either on a single formal principle, such as the categorical imperative, or on the factual consequences of the act, but rather on the values the acting person seeks to realise. Values, he believed, are neither abstract principles nor particular material things. They are the importance given to particular things, and are therefore detectable in emotions. As such they can be analysed phenomenologically, and they form a hierarchy – the spiritual and the personal ones taking precedence over the sensible and the vital ones.

To Stein, Scheler embodied 'the phenomenon of genius'.[10] To Wojtyla, on the other hand, Husserl was the unquestioned founder of phenomenology. Stein knew Scheler, and debated with him, but she considered Husserl alone to be her teacher. Wojtyla studied Scheler with the intention of developing the foundations of a Christian ethics from the latter's premises, but in the end found his theories wanting. Phenomenology, however, retained Wojtyla's respect right into his pontificate.

Historically speaking, Phenomenology derived from Scholasticism (through Husserl's teacher, Brentano [1838 – 1917]), not only its basic concept of intentionality, but also some elements of its analysis pertaining to the concepts of object and subject. This is why neither Stein, as she discovered Thomas Aquinas, nor Wojtyla, when he decided to investigate Scheler, came unprepared to the task.

Thomas Aquinas (1225-1274) taught at Paris, Orvieto, Rome, Viterbo and Naples, at the time when the idea of the university was still young. He conceived it as his vocation to confront (and to synthesise in writing) Christian thought with the philosophical heritage of Greece and Rome. At the centre of his philosophical system was Being, considered as substance in the wake of Aristotle, but also as participated Idea, as Plato had held. Already the orchestration of this philosophical synthesis, and its blending with the Christian thought of the Church Fathers (and of Augustine in particular), demonstrates the ease with which Thomas conducted his thinking. His success, however, was gradually magnified over the centuries, as his writings became standard study for clerics and philosophers alike. The Reformation condemned his kind of synthesis, declaring it offensive to the purity of the Faith, whereas Catholics by way of reaction clung even tighter to what they considered to be both reasonable and worthy of God. This controversy conditioned the development of Thomism. Wojtyla knew Aquinas through his seminary formation in Kraków, as well as through Père Garrigou-Lagrange OP at the Angelicum in Rome. Thomism became for him a foundation to build on or a starting point for personal reflection,[11] and it was as such that he transmitted it to his students.[12] He studied with them in seminar form the entire *Summa Theologiae*. Stein came to study Aquinas when, at the request of Father Erich Przywara, in 1925, she started to translate *De Veritate* into German. She made the effort to understand Aquinas from her phenomenological point of view, and to translate his terms into its idiom. The result was a fresh understanding of the presuppositions of Thomistic thought, an appreciation of a kind that could hardly be gained by anyone whose first formation it was.

St John of the Cross was the common master in mysticism of Stein and Wojtyla: Wojtyla wrote his first doctorate, and Stein her last book, on the thought of the Carmelite mystic. The tradition of adopting masters in philosophy, mysticism, art or in any other spiritual discipline is in fact not unlike the rabbinic tradition known to Jesus of Nazareth. The Academy, of course, was a Greek invention, and the university a medieval one, but the very idea of a teacher teaching in a tradition recurs in intellectual as well as in practical disciplines and arts. In this sense Jesus of Nazareth is of course *the* common Master of Stein and Wojtyla.

Common pursuits

Stein had gone to Göttingen out of an irresistible drive: 'I could not proceed with anything except on the basis of some inner drive. My decisions emerged from a level of depth that I myself was unable to grasp clearly. But once something had emerged into consciousness and taken a definite shape in my mind, then nothing could hold me back.'[13] This drive was on more than one occasion to bring her close to total exhaustion: as she finished her doctorate; and as she decided to give up her academic career in order to teach with the Dominican nuns in Speyer. She first understood this 'drive' as a vocation to philosophy. It led her to phenomenology, and afterwards through the parting with Husserl, into the utter uncertainty of an academic world closed in the first instance to women, and in the course of time also to Jews. As no satisfactory outcome lay immediately ahead, the pursuit was bound either to broaden out or to dry up. The years of frustration before she accepted the teaching-post in Speyer were probably the most fruitful, for it was during this time that she wrote her three phenomenological treatises: *Psychic Causality, Individual and Community,* and *On the State.* During this period she also requested to be baptised. The pursuit deepened.

In the outlook of John Paul II, the desire for God commands a double commitment – to the person, and to truth.[14] In reading about the life of Stein while preparing for her canonisation, he must have been touched by the evidence that she was someone who was dedicated to truth and to individual persons also, and who, through this double commitment, discovered the unity of both in God.

Common problems

At the centre of the philosophical preoccupations of both Stein and Wojtyla there lies, as has already been said, the human person. Their different orbits around this common theme, however, take them into different regions of the sky. Stein, the phenomenologist, would study psychology and politics; and finally theology because the study of the person could not reach completion without it. Wojtyla, the theologian, would describe the role of the free act in the formation of personality in order to construct a Christian ethics.

Their focus on the person would also be for both thinkers the point of intersection between philosophy and theology. Stein experiences the purely philosophical investigation of the person as incomplete, and is pushed into theological anthropology when she endeavours fully to comprehend the person. Wojtyla likewise uncovers the openness of the acting person towards the transcendent. To him the acting person is fulfilled only in the act of love, and the commandment of love of neighbour therefore completes philosophical anthropology perfectly 'from above'.

Wojtyla's personal reasons for pointing towards Stein (the places, masters, pursuits and problems they had in common) are all concerned with the similarity between himself and her. This similarity, however, is intelligible and open because it reflects the universality of the experience they shared.

Edith Stein as Symbol

Wojtyla also has a practical reason to point towards Edith Stein in *F&R*. Her symbolic character communicates quite clearly both the harmony of faith and reason reflected in a human life, and the ultimate wisdom of God that is the Cross.

The word 'symbol' comes from the Greek *sumbolon*, which refers to the ancient practice of cutting a token in two, so that the two people in possession of the bits can recognise each other for the purpose of some transaction. In modern language a symbol is a sign which, by synthesising a complexity of meaning, evokes or represents it – as the cross symbolises Christianity, the queen her country and the child a hope for the future. A symbol can rarely be confined to one particular significance to the exclusion of all others, however. The child, for example, symbolises not only hope for the future but also vulnerability, and work related to its protection.

The Pope also is a symbol, even a sign, of contradiction – a title he chose for one of his books.[15] The symbolic quality of his person renders his actions significant to people around the globe, and makes his task very delicate and demanding.

Edith Stein is, like the Pope, symbolic in her roles as reformer, disciple and leader. She is a reformer in her roles as a professional woman and a philosopher. In her day these were still very difficult roles to interpret in an acceptable way, but Stein combined massive intellectual power with sacrificial tenderness, in a manner that seems to have appeared to her own public as beautiful. Indeed her graciousness is still refreshing, being generally agreeable to feminists and conservatives alike:[16] her philosophy of woman is discussed widely.

As a disciple her martyrdom is symbolic. Born on the Feast of Yom Kippur (the Atonement), she came to have a singular understanding of the power of expiation. A premonition of her death made her choose for her name in religion Teresa Benedicta of the Cross, because she accepted the saving power of the death of the Messiah for herself also. She died a Jew, of course, like Christ.

As a leader she was the symbol of the Jews trapped in the heart of Europe: outcast and idolised, accomplished and sacrificed, she reckoned herself a scapegoat, a holocaust for Europe. Because she accepted this destiny for the sake of 'her people' – Jews, Christians, Germans alike – she makes much sense as a Patroness of Europe.

The symbol Edith Stein has also been 'a sign of contradiction'. Her philosophical achievements were denigrated, but also assimilated by philosophers close to her;[17] her Christian monasticism was resented, as well as admired by her family;[18] and her canonisation was applauded by Jews, but also regretted as an assault against the memory of the Holocaust.[19] Symbols may be helpful to us because they do not restrict our thinking, or even confine it to a particular direction. They glow with meaning and puzzle us, like fire. John Paul II's practical reason for referring to Stein is that her symbolic quality makes her visible from afar like a torch, even if a multiplicity of interpretations of her life remains possible.

Edith Stein as Philosopher

At the centre of Stein's life and symbolic character stands her vocation as a philosopher. Wojtyla's personal and practical reasons for pointing towards her are therefore rooted in this objective reason: she was an outstanding Christian philosopher, indeed among the greatest of the twentieth century.

We are fortunate today to have even more of Stein's philosophical writings than those she herself planned for publication. This is due to the Carmelites, to the Stein-Archives, and to the Herder-editors of *Edith Steins Werke (ESW)*[20] who now in addition have planned a critical *Edith Stein Gesamt Ausgabe (ESGA)* in 24 volumes.[21] The translation and publication of the *Collected Works of Edith Stein (CWES)* in English is due to the ICS-publications of Washington DC.[22]

Stein's life and work can be divided into four periods, each marking a definite step in her philosophical development:[23]

1. The phenomenological works of her youthful prime comprise *On Empathy* (her doctoral thesis, 1917); *Philosophy of Psychology and the Humanities* (with its two parts: *Sentient Causality* and *Individual and Community,* 1922) and *On the State* (1925). All of these are phenomenological investigations in dialogue with (as well as in reaction to) Husserl's philosophy. We can broadly characterise this period as phenomenological.

2. After she decided to teach with the Dominican Sisters in Speyer she translated Newman's *Letters and Diary 1801 – 1845,* and Aquinas' *De Veritate.* She wrote a famous article on the relationship between Husserl's phenomenology and the philosophy of Aquinas, to commemorate Husserl's seventieth birthday,[24] and she also held the lectures on the vocation of woman that made her famous in Germany. These lectures are collected in one volume under the title *Die Frau.*[25] In this period she absorbed and came to grips with Thomism.

3. When she gave up her teaching at Speyer she did so in order to dedicate herself full-time to academic work. The writings of these years mark Stein's maturity as a philosopher, lecturer and writer,

and include her *Introduction to Philosophy* (1931), *Act and Potency* (1931, later expanded into the first part of *Finite and Eternal Being*), and the two essays in anthropology, *Aufbau der menschlichen Person* (1932) and *Was ist der Mensch?* (1933), which both result from her lectures in educational theory given at the Münster Marianum. The engagement with the Münster Marianum was interrupted by the Nazi prohibition against Jewish professionals, and this was the event that prompted her to write her unfinished autobiography *Life in a Jewish Family* (1933-35), and also gave her the time to do it. This period is dominated by her interest in anthropology.

4. From her Carmel days come *Finite and Eternal Being* (1935-36) and the unfinished *Science of the Cross* (1942). Both were written at the request of her superiors. In addition, she composed a series of minor hagiographical writings for the edification of the sisters.[26] The two major works were both intended for publication, but the publishing of works by Jews had become practically impossible in the years following 1939. They were published after the war as the first volumes in the series of *Edith Steins Werke*. The composition of the work *Finite and Eternal Being* leads us to characterise this period as ontological.

There is a clear development in Stein's thought. In her youthful writings she was concerned with filling the lacunas she saw in Husserl's thinking, while elaborating and expanding on the phenomenological method, which she found to be the only one that could meet her own scientific standards. Around the time of her baptism, in 1922, Christian mysticism became something she felt compelled to explore. In and through this meeting with a new discipline, her thought was first confronted with, and was later to thrive on, Scholasticism together with its inherent Aristotelianism. Whereas in the works of her youth she acknowledged the reality of an experience of faith, and treated of it among other conscious experiences, by the time we come to her later writings that very experience has penetrated her own personality and thought completely. The mature works are no longer so much preoccupied with phenomena as they are centred on being. They do, however, still find their point of departure in conscious experience, and conscious experience is never far away from the ontological analysis.

The theme that underlies this development is the human person. It is Stein's efforts to understand the complexity of inner experience, and its anchorage in personality as well as in bodily expression, which leads her on to see that the person cannot be understood in isolation, either from the physical forces that surround it and by which it lives (the energy-levels of consciousness are causally related to the body), or from the community of which it is part (our habits of thinking are shaped in a community). These factors, which have an impact on consciousness, lead her to presuppose a plurality of persons (in contradistinction to Husserl's transcendental ego), constitutive of the world in which they live. It also leads her to a more confident approach to reality, which is alive and real with all the power that I lend to the personal perspective of the others.

It is still the individual human person who constitutes the centre and summit of her later philosophy of being, and therefore brings the phenomenological method into her ontology, as its foundation 'in relation to us'. Its foundation in relation to itself, i.e. the foundation it has outside of all reference to any particular human perspective, is Being, which to the believer is also accessible as personal in God.

The development of her thought from phenomenology through Thomism to anthropology and ontology is organic: the elements are present throughout, but they are not always equally in the foreground. To get a clearer grasp of her philosophy, let us take a closer look at each of these elements.

Phenomenology

Stein understood phenomenology to be a method of investigation and an attitude of dedication to the meticulous and scientific description of the phenomena as they appear.[27] To suspend our judgement of reality (by the *epoché*), and to reduce experience to what is experienced (by the *phenomenological reduction*) form part of the phenomenological discipline required by the fact that the phenomena stand in a (for us) uncertain relationship with what is. These methodological precautions leave us with the stream of consciousness of which the 'pure I' is the underlying unity. Stein endorsed Husserl's descriptive phenomenology of the *Logical Investigations*, as well as the transcendental phenomenology put forward in the *Ideen I*. She maintained, however, that phenomenology was in need of a thorough investigation of just that kind of act through which we appreciate the consciousness of other people: empathy. Without such an investigation it would remain unclear by what means the foreign subject was constituted, and therefore what intersubjectivity could possibly mean. Her findings in *On Empathy* were therefore intended as a contribution to the phenomenological enterprise. It was only later, when working as Husserl's assistant, that Stein realised the distance between herself and Husserl. To her, empathy provided a means of obtaining knowledge about the world as another sees it. Empathy yielded within consciousness the very objectivity of the world as constituted between subjects perceiving it. Here was what would provide science with a secure foundation, here was, as she says, true *próté philosophia*.[28] For Husserl, empathy (though he, like Stein, understood it to be the means of constituting the other as other) could not distract him from the race towards transcendental solipsism. To him the ego is not constituted in reiterated empathy as a psycho-physical individual person, it is self-constituted. The insertion of the 'I' in the world and the understanding of persons therefore becomes more problematic. This is why Stein's doctoral thesis on empathy simultaneously marks Stein's adherence to, and her departure from, Husserl's transcendental phenomenology.

The parting evolved into a crisis when Stein, having obtained her degree, was engaged as Husserl's assistant for thirteen months. During this period she put in order and prepared for publication notes made by Husserl over a number of years, the manuscripts finally published after Husserl's death as *Ideen II* and *III*. She also prepared for publication the *Notes on Time Consciousness,* which were later to be published by Martin Heidegger. It became clearer for Stein during these months that Husserl was not prepared to heed the insights gained from Stein's analysis of empathy and the constitution of the individual person. Stein regarded this as a failure, because it left the idea of constitution, in particular intersubjective constitution, hanging in the air. Unable to convince him of the need to explore inter-subjectivity anew, she asked to be relieved of her duties in order to be able to devote more time to her own work. It was against this background that she used her theory of empathy as a basis for constructing a *Philosophy of Psychology and the Humanities.*[29] In this work she explored how the realms of the soul and of the spirit are constituted. She intended in this way to make a contribution to the understanding of the foundations of psychology and of the 'sciences of the spirit' (*Geisteswissenschaften*).

In its first part this work analyses the phenomena of causality within the sentient soul, i.e. how necessitation, contrary to motivation, occurs and is experienced. The purpose is to determine the causal relations between the body and consciousness, and to describe the contours of this necessitation, which is radically different from that of logical necessitation or spiritual motivation. Psychology, she claims, depends on this distinction, and without having a clear understanding of how causation and motivation interact, psychology as a science would be unable to determine its own object precisely.

The second part of *Philosophy of Psychology and the Humanities* investigates the impact of the community on the individual. It seeks to ascertain the extent to which the individual is influenced by the community, as well as to determine the mechanisms through which the community is constituted by individuals. The work relies on an analysis of common consciousness in which and through which explanations of events and the events themselves make sense. The discipline of history and the other branches of the humanities have their objectivity from and in this common consciousness. The analysis of its nature therefore constitutes the foundation of the humanities.

The two parts taken together seek to determine what constitutes persons: nature – the metabolism of life that penetrates all psychic life; and society – the cultural presuppositions that determine the conscious life of the individual.

Thomism

After her baptism Stein was encouraged by her spiritual director to take up her academic studies anew through the study of Thomas Aquinas. The meticulous work of translation, commentary and systematisation was not unfamiliar to her. As Husserl's assistant she was accustomed to bring into a coherent whole piles and piles of stenographed manuscripts, and as a teacher of Latin and German at the Dominicans in Speyer she had command of both languages. Above all, translation afforded her a way to become familiar with the thought of Thomas himself.[30]

As a student of Husserl Stein had conceived a distaste for mistaking the history of philosophy for philosophy itself. In consequence of this, her purpose in translating the *De Veritate* was not philological but systematic: she wanted to translate Aquinas, not only into German but into modern German philosophical idiom, and thus to bring Thomas' thought into dialogue with phenomenology. She did this by succinctly rendering the meaning, and establishing the relevance, of each article in relation to the whole, thus producing a very readable text, one that is closer to Thomas' own work than many modern day translations, which incorporate his students' work in the form of objections. It appears at first glance to be a translation, but in fact the genre is that of a scholastic commentary, where translation and commentary are marked carefully by signs in the 'lay-out' and where the author's interpretation illuminates both the text commented on and the commentator's point of view.

The choice of *De Veritate* among all the works of Aquinas was dictated by circumstance and interest alike. However, among Aquinas' works, *De Veritate* is not the writing with the most impressive structure. It is Saint Thomas' earliest series of publicly disputed questions, and it consists of twenty-nine such, stitched loosely together around the theme of truth. The content, however, testifies to the synthesis of Aristotelianism and Christianity that would later be systematically developed in the *Summa Theologiae*, and it highlights Thomas' metaphysics of knowledge as precisely that: a metaphysics of knowledge. Stein comments:

> The teaching on knowledge (*Erkenntnislehre*) given [...] is rather different from modern epistemology ('*Erkenntnistheorie*'), as it has developed since the Renaissance. It has no claim to be the foundation of all other philosophical disciplines, and does not pretend to be a science without presuppositions: it is part of a great metaphysics. Knowledge is here a real event which presupposes a threefold world of realities: the uncreated and eternal Spirit of God, the world of things created by Him, and the finite spirits created by Him. This differentiation in the real world prompts a differentiation of knowledge. So that not even a common definition of 'knowledge-as-such' is possible.[31]

In the passage quoted Stein looks in vain for a transcendental analysis of knowledge. She finds in its stead knowledge understood in relation to being, the first concept of the mind. In her later article on the relationship between Husserl and Aquinas,[32] she states that even if we could give an account of knowledge as such, it would not be sufficient to account for the limits of human knowledge. This is in fact the point where Husserl and Aquinas part ways:

> Phenomenology proceeds as though our reason had no limits in principle. Certainly, it grants that its task is endless and knowledge is an unending process. But it heads straight for its goal: that is, the full truth, which as a regulative idea sets the course it is to take. From the perspective of this philosophy there is no other way to the goal. St Thomas' view is also that

this is the way of natural reason. Its way is endless, and this implies that it can never reach its goal but only approach it step by step. Another consequence is that all human philosophy is bound to be fragmentary.

Thomas, however,

> would never admit that this is the only way of knowledge, nor that truth is but an idea that must be actualised in an unending process – and hence never fully. Full Truth *is*; there is a knowledge that embraces truth completely, a knowledge that, rather than unending process, is unending, infinite, fullness at rest. Such is the *divine knowledge*.

The sheer temporality of our knowledge proves to us the existence of such Eternal Being, as Stein will show in the beginning of *Finite and Eternal Being*. The distinction between natural and supernatural knowledge is therefore not, as Husserl would have it, an empirical distinction. It is a transcendental one, based on the nature of our knowing as temporal and finite. Faith, the basis of supernatural knowledge, is a way to go further along the naturally desired way of knowledge, by relying in trust upon an infinite Intellect making itself known through Revelation.

Anthropology

It was Stein's phenomenological anthropology, in particular her understanding of the temporality of the ego, which determined her development as a phenomenologist and her acceptance of the philosophy of Saint Thomas. She investigated the phenomenon of empathy, both in its essence and in its power to constitute the psycho-physical individual as well as the person. She founded psychology on the constitution of the psycho-physical individual understood in its causal and motivational structures, and she founded the humanities on the constitution of the person caused and motivated by the society of which the latter is constituted as an individual and as a member. Thus Stein's phenomenology of intersubjectivity is developed into her mature philosophy of the person, which, she now contends, cannot be completed without a theological foundation.

Her two most substantial contributions to anthropology, *The Structure of the Human Person* and *What is the Human Being?*, are complementary; both stem from her brief period as a lecturer in 'scientific pedagogy' at Münster. The Marianum had embarked on the considerable adventure of developing a new Catholic education theory, of which Stein's twin work attempted to lay the anthropological foundations. In *The Structure of the Human Person* she discussed the ability of various anthropological theories to meet the requirement of providing a foundation for education. The anthropology of German idealism, of depth-psychology and of existentialism, all fall short of justifying the fundamental attitudes to be transmitted by any Catholic education: respect for nature as a given and for its laws of development; mutual trust and attention as a precondition for understanding; and responsibility towards, as well as trust in, God. Having defined the *telos* of Catholic education, she proceeded to develop an anthropology that takes into account the human being in all its dimensions: as a material thing, an organism, an animal, a soul and a social person. She discussed the origin of the human species in the light of Darwinism, and the influence and claims of race and nationality on the identity of the human person. Finally, she addressed the relationship between philosophical and theological anthropology. She claimed that the human, finite being cannot be understood in isolation from the Infinite upon which it depends. Moreover, experience does not give us conclusive results as to the origin or goal, either of the individual or of the whole of humanity, but Revelation, on the other hand, is 'given to humans, so that they may know what they are and what they must do'[33]. And thus, in so far as anthropology is incomplete without knowledge of the beginning and the end of the 'story' about the human person, it must be completed by a theological anthropology. However, had we had other kinds of privileged access to these realities (through communication with a greater spirit, for example), that would perhaps suffice. But given that Revelation is precisely such a public communication, it seems satisfactory to accept it as such, after some personal probing of its genuine character.

What is a Human Being? was planned as the continuation of the lecture series, but was never delivered as such. When Stein could no longer teach she worked up the already prepared material into a scientific study, which, however, has reached us in an unfinished state. Its subtitle: *A Theological Anthropology*, reveals that it was thought to constitute both the prolongation and the foundation of the *Structure of the Human Person*, in accordance with the expectations raised by the last part of this work. It treats of the common nature of human individuals, of the creation of the human being and of the Fall, of the Saviour and the state of the saved. It reaches from the direct creation of the soul by God to the sacraments, and examines the value and dignity of the human person. The questions of origin and end, indispensable for the educator, are thus addressed fully in this work.

Ontology

Stein attributed to the fleeting nature of human experience (its temporality and finitude), the finding that purely philosophical knowledge of the beginning or the end is beyond our reach. Even so, the I of my experience seems pointless if it is confined within the narrow limits of my own experience. In thinking, moreover, the I is brought into contact with what lies beyond the fleeting now, because it implies identification, which, even as it is coming into being and passing away in the stream of consciousness, nevertheless transcends time into the realm of the ideal. Yet thinking is unmistakably a capacity of the human intellect, and in it we have access to what transcends time: the eternal. Stein's great attempt at an ascent to the meaning of Being, *Finite and Eternal Being*, opens with these reflections.

Developed out of her second attempt at the *Habilitation*, (namely *Act and Potency*), the work, which she called her 'spiritual testament', centres on the question of being. 'The confrontation of Thomistic and phenomenological thought follows in the objective treatment of this question'.[34] Stein first clarifies that conscious experience depends upon being, as the latter would be unthinkable without the former: being is first understood simply as what is identifiable by and in thought. She thereafter proceeds through an analysis of the various forms of being (temporal, finite, infinite and eternal, on the one hand; essential, real, actual and potential, on the other), to a specific analysis of substance (form and matter). She then approaches the characteristics of being (*Seiendes*) as such (the transcendentals), before she enters into the domain of the meaning of being (*Sinn des Seins*). This she grounds in the mysterious, personal individuality of a substantial I.

In the section entitled 'On the meaning and possibility of a Christian philosophy' Stein reflects specifically on the relationship between faith and reason. She initially poses the problem in terms of the relationship between medieval and modern philosophy. The medieval philosophers saw in Revelation the measure of all truth, even as they regarded philosophy as an enterprise with its own distinct identity. Maritain, Stein argues, sees this distinctiveness as a distinctiveness of object. This, according to Stein, is incorrect, firstly because the object of philosophy is not distinct from any of the other sciences, but instead founds them and defines their respective objects. Secondly because philosophy as wisdom is the perfect *opus rationis*, the last rational explanation obtainable of the meaning of being.

Maritain had said that Christian philosophy was a special way of being (Stein writes *Zustand*) of philosophy. He held that the spiritual ability to search and hold truth was strengthened through grace, and that philosophy was enriched by the concepts developed within theology (e.g. the concept of the person). Moreover he stated that the world itself changes as it is seen through the eyes of faith. This means that the believer, in performing the perfect *opus rationis*, would be irrational if he relied only on natural reason, through having at his or her disposal a superior source of truth. Maritain was ready to admit that moral philosophy could not be conducted as pure philosophy. He did not, however, as Stein does, admit this for the remainder of philosophy: 'The fundamental truths of our faith – concerning Creation, the Fall, Redemption and fulfilment – shed a light after which it is impossible that a pure philosophy, i.e. a philosophy relying exclusively on natural reason, could fulfil its task of accomplishing a *perfectum opus rationis.*'[35]

This may imply that philosophy is accomplished through theology, but not that it is accomplished as theology. Christian philosophy is a seeing-together, a *Zusammenschau*, of Reason and Revelation. But because faith is a 'dark light', even if it is the closest we come to God's vision, every ray of light such philosophy can cast is very precious.

As the Pope points towards Edith Stein in *F&R*, he points towards a philosopher who dedicated her life to philosophy, and who centered her contribution on the human person. By seeing both together (the person and philosophy) she saw more than the sum of the parts. What she saw is what makes her an outstanding Christian philosopher.

Conclusion

I have tried to show the reasons that the Pope could have had for mentioning Edith Stein in the encyclical *F&R*. They have been divided into three kinds: the personal, the practical and the objective. Among the the personal reasons I have mentioned the places, masters, pursuits and problems they have in common. As a practical reason I have alluded to Stein's symbolic character, which makes her appealing to very different people. As the objective reason I have listed her philosophy, and briefly developed its main elements: phenomenology, Thomism, anthropology and ontology. I hope that against this background it has become more clear why *F&R* refers explicitly to the work of Edith Stein, and why John Paul II points her out among the thinkers who have reconciled belief in the Word of God with philosophy and scientific method. I have not seen it as my task to compare the respective philosophies of Karol Wojtyla and Edith Stein, either concerning the relationship between faith and reason or anything else; this would be a very worthwhile task, but of another order. I have simply sought to shed light on the reasons John Paul II had to point out Edith Stein as a Christian thinker, and I hope at the same time to have introduced the interested reader to some of the thoughts of her rich and inspiring work.

Notes

1. For a detailed account of the process, see J. Sullivan, 'The Path to Beatification' in W. Herbstrith OCD, *Never Forget*, Carmelite Studies 7 (Washington, ICS Publications, 1998).

2. Vladimir S. Soloviev, Pavel A. Florensky, Petr Chaadaev and Vladimir Lossky are mentioned from the Eastern context.

3. G. Weigel, *Witness to Hope: The Biography of Pope John Paul II* (Harper Collins, 1999), p. 540.

4. Pope John Paul II, Apostolic letter issued *motu proprio* proclaiming Saint Bridget of Sweden, Saint Catherine of Siena and Saint Teresa Benedicta of the Cross co-patronesses of Europe, 1 October 1999 (3).

5. Other studies have compared their philosophies or their lives, see for example G. Kalinowski, 'Edith Stein et Karol Wojtyla sur la personne', *Revue Philosophique de Louvain*, 82:4 (1984), pp. 545-561. Reprinted in *Autour de 'Personne et Acte' de Karol Wojtyla: Articles et Conferences sur une rencontre du thomisme avec la phenomenologie* (Aix en Provence, Presses Universitaires d'Aix en Marseille, 1987); K. Haarlammert, 'Johannes vom Kreuz stand am Anfang. Zwischen Leben und Wirken Edith Steins und Johannes Paulus II, gibt es zahlreiche und überraschende Verbindungen', in *Edith Stein – Leben im Zeichen des Kreuzes*, ed. by Klaus Haarlammert (Pilger Verlag, Speyer, 1987), pp. 45-52; M. Cecilia, 'Edith Stein e il magistero di Giovanni Paolo II nella *Redemptoris Mater*' in *Rivista di Vita Spirituale* 49:2 (1995), pp. 62-70; Maria Cecilia del Volto Santo: 'Edith Stein e il magistero di Giovanni Paolo II nella "Mulieris dignitatem"', in *Rivista di Vita Spirituale*, 50 (1996), p. pp. 23-37; L. Garcia, 'The Primacy of Persons: Edith Stein and Pope John Paul II', in *Logos: A Journal of Catholic Thought and Culture*, 1:2 (Summer 1997), pp. 90-99; E. Sakowicz, 'Jan Pawel II o Edycie Stein', in *Szukajac prawdy: Edyta Stein w kulturze polskiej*, ed. Anita Czarniecka-Stefanska, Wydawnictwo Uniwersytetu Wroclawskiego (Wroclaw, 1998), pp. 9-14.

6. The correspondence with Roman Ingarden is particularly interesting in this regard. Ingarden was a Polish nationalist, and he and Stein often discussed issues relating to nationality and the state. See Band XIV of *Edith Steins Werke*.

7. Edith Stein, *Life in a Jewish Family* (Washington, ICS-publications, 1986), Chap. VII, p. 239.

8. Wojtyla seems to have encouraged Ingarden, whom he knew in Krakow, to give his appreciation of Stein's philosophical contribution, resulting in his 'Die philosophischen Forschungen Edith Steins' in Waltraud Herbstrith (ed.), *Edith Stein – eine grosse Glaubenszeugerin* (Ploger Verlag, Anweiler, 1986). This, however, testifies only to the fact that Wojtyla did not know her work at the time, and George Kalinowsky therefore rightly underlines that his position was reached independently of Stein ('E. Stein et K. Wojtyla sur la personne', pp. 545-561). The comparison Kalinowski attempts to make regarding the human person suffers, however, by the lack of sources available to him at the time: *Aufbau der menschlichen Person* and *Was ist der Mensch?* were published only later. Wojtyla's philosophical formation is described, e.g., in R. Buttiglione, *La pensée de Karol Wojtyla* (Communio, Fayard, 1982).

9. Stein, *Life in a Jewish Family*, Chap. V.5, p. 219.

10. *ibid.* Chap. V.5, p. 218.

11. Weigel, *Witness to Hope*, p. 87.

12. *ibid.*, p. 95.

13. Stein, *Life in a Jewish Family*, p. 94.

14. *Canonisation homily.*

15. *Sign of Contradiction*, St Paul's Publications (Slough, Middlegreen, 1979)

16. L.L. McAlister, 'Essential differences', *Philosophy Today*, 37 (Spring 1993), pp. 70-77.

17. See M. Sawicki, *Body, Text and Science: The Literacy of Investigative Practices and the Phenomenology of Edith Stein* (Boston, Kluwer, 1997), where a detailed investigation of Stein's works for others under their name is undertaken.

18. Several of Edith's family-members have collaborated in editions of her philosophy, e,g. the nieces Susanne Batzdorf and Waltraut Stein.

19. Concerning Stein's relationship with Judaism much has been written by both Jews and Christians. For an introduction to the problem see W. Herbstrith, *Erinnere dich – vergiss es nicht: Edith Stein – christlich-*

JOHN PAUL II AND EDITH STEIN

jüdische Perspectiven (Plöger, Annweiler und Essen, 1990); trans. by Susanne Batzdoff as *Never Forget: Christian and Jewish Perspectives on Edith Stein* (Washington, ICS-publications, 1998).

20. *Edith Steins Werke* (Referred to below as *ESW*), Herausgegeben von Dr Lucy Gelber and Michael Linssen OCD, *Archivum Carmelitanum Edith Stein, in Zusammenarbeit mit der niederlændsichen und der deutschen Ordensprovinz der unbeschuhten Karmeliten* (Freiburg-Basel-Wien, Herder, 1962).

21. The *Edith Stein Gesamt Ausgabe* (Referred to below as *ESGA*), is edited by the 'Edith Stein Institut' in Würzburg under the direction of Michael Linssen OCD, in collaboration with Prof. H.-B. Gerl-Falkovitz (Dresden) and others. It is planned that 4 volumes will appear every year until the end of 2010, beginning in Autumn 2000. The 24 volumes will be published under 5 headings: Biographische Schriften (Bd. 1-4); Philosophische Schriften (bd. 5-12); Schriften zur Anthropologie und Pädagogik (bd. 13-16); Schrifen zur Spiritualität (bd. 17-19) and Übersetzungen (bd. 20- 24). So far six volumes have appeared.

22. *Collected Works of Edith Stein* (Referred to below as *CWES*), (Washington D.C., ICS-publications), vol. 1: *Life in a Jewish Family*; vol. 2: *Essays on Woman*; vol. 3: *On the Problem of Empathy*; vol. 4: *The Hidden Life*; vol. 5: *Selfportrait in Letters* (to appear: vol. 6:); vol. 7: *Philosophy of Psychology and the Humanities*; vol. 8: *Knowledge and Faith*.

23. Sawicki's 'Chronology of Writings of Edith Stein (1891-1942)', available at the Baltimore Carmel website, is a helpful reconstruction of the chronology of the Works of Edith Stein, in particular as this chronology is not observed by either of the editions of her Collected Works.

24. 'Husserls Phänomenologie und die Philosophie des hl. Thomas v. Aquino: Versuch einer Gegenüberstellung.' in *Jahrbuch für Philosophie und Phänomenologische Forschung*, Ergänzungsband, p. 315-338, translated in M.C. Baseheart, *Person in the World* (Kluwer, Dordrecht, 1997) and, alongside the original dialogue-version rejected by Martin Heidegger, in E. Stein, *Knowledge and Faith* (*CWES*) vol. 8.

25. *CWES*, vol. 2.

26. *Das Verborgene Leben*, *ESW*, vol. XI, *The Hidden Life*, *CWES*, vol. 4.

27. See for example *On Empathy* (*CWES*, vol. 3), Chapter II, 1. pp. 3-6 (1-4 in the German) and 5. (a), pp. 21-22 (22-23 in the German).

28. *On Empathy* (*CWES* vol. 3), Chapter II, 5. (a), p. 21 (22).

29. *CWES*, vol. 7.
30. 'The translation of the *Questiones Disputatae de Veritate* constituted for me a necessary way towards penetrating the thought of Saint Thomas'. *Des Hl. Thomas von Aquino Untersuchungen über die Wahrheit*, in Deutscher Übertragung von Edith Stein, (1. Band, Otto Borgmeyer, Breslau, Vorwort). My translation. A note to the Husserl and Aquinas article reads 'I purposely avoid the term "Thomism" since I base my comparison not on any traditional scholastic system but on an overview drawn from Thomas' writings.' *CWES*, vol. 8, pp. 137-8, trans. by Walter Redmond.
31. *ibid.*, p. 32 – Commentary on q. 1. My translation.
32. *Husserl and Aquinas: A Comparison* in *CWES*, 8, pp. 1-63.
33. *Der Aufbau der menschlichen Person, ESW* bd. XVI, p. 194.
34. *Endliches und Ewiges Sein, ESW* vol. II, p. XIII.
35. *ibid.*, p. 24.

FAITH AND FREEDOM IN THE PERSONALISM OF KAROL WOJTYLA

Kevin Doran

The Experience of Efficacy

One thing that both phenomenology and personalism have in common is the tendency to make some kind of notional distinction between 'human being' and 'person'. We find this in Scheler's distinction between *Life* and *Spirit.*[1] We find it again in the bipolarity that Mounier sees between the *individual* and the *person.* He describes the individual as the 'diffusion of the person on the surface of his life, and his readiness to lose himself there.'[2] It should not be surprising, therefore, that we find something similar in the thought of Karol Wojtyla.

From an ontological point of view it is quite clear that Wojtyla regards every human being as a person, and every human person as a human being. In his study of the human person, however, Wojtyla approaches the person from the perspective of phenomenological experience, and specifically the experience of personal action. The person is not just someone in whom or to whom events merely 'happen'. Through the reflexive function of consciousness, a person experiences himself as the actor (i.e., the one who is the cause of what is happening). This is what Wojtyla calls the experience of *efficacy.* While efficacy is a term that could be applied to non-human causality also, Seifert points out that it is used by Wojtyla as a *terminus technicus,* to describe the experience that a person has that a particular act is of his own making.[3]

The importance of the experience of efficacy in the specifically personal act is that it is through his own efficacy that the potentiality of the person is brought to act. The experience of efficacy links the person immediately with his action, and is closely related to the experience of responsibility. 'We attribute the act to this self as its conscious author. In such agency there appears the factor of will and therefore of liberty and hence that of moral responsibility. This brings us to what is essential in man's subjectivity.'[4]

In this short article I intend:

• to outline how, in Wojtyla's thought, the self-transcendence of the person is inextricably linked to the fundamental freedom that underlies the experience of efficacy

• to suggest that this same personal efficacy underpins many of the central themes in the social teaching of Pope John Paul and

• to discuss how revealed truth might be said to enhance rather than to inhibit human efficacy.

Efficacy and Self-transcendence

Without denying the need for definitions, Wojtyla saw that definitions tend to focus our attention on what is static. He felt that no definition is capable of adequately expressing the dynamism of the human person. For this reason, he has reservations about what he describes as St Thomas's 'objectivistic view' of the person.

> He shows us the particular faculties, both spiritual and sensory, thanks to which the whole of human consciousness and self-consciousness ... takes shape, but that is also where he stops. Thus St Thomas gives us an excellent view of the objective existence and activity of the person, but it would be difficult to speak in his view of the lived experience of the person.[5]

From self-knowledge to self-determination
Wojtyla also expresses some concern about how St Thomas' definition of the will as 'rational appetite' is to be undestood.[6] The term 'appetite' seems to imply something that only happens in man. But St Thomas clearly saw the personal will as having the capacity to act in a way that is independent of external causality, other than the original creative causality of God in giving the will its inclination toward everything that is good.[7] For Wojtyla, the will is the free expression of the personal dynamism of man.

> Every voluntary action is, of its nature, intentional. In other words, it is directed towards some object of the will. The will which is manifested in action is not, however, exclusively directed towards intentional objects. In a very real sense the person is himself the primary object of his own action. In virtue of his self-knowledge, he is also *self-possessing*.[8]

This is so precisely because the person experiences himself, and no one else, as the actor who is at the origin of his own actions. His will is an expression of who he is and is primarily engaged in the bringing to act of his own potency. It can be truly said, therefore, that the person, through the actions that he performs, and through his choice of intentional objects, determines who he becomes. A game of football or basket-ball may be a helpful image here. In any ball game, goals follow on possession. It is the same when it comes to achieving personal goals. Self-possession is an essential condition of self-determination. In saying this Wojtyla is not denying the objective reality of human being. There is no question of the person's determining himself *essentially*, because action is consequent on being. The first act of every person is the act of being itself. To say that a person is *self-determining* is simply to say that this first act of *being* is in turn a potency to further or *conjugate act* by means of which the person determines himself accidentally, through the exercise of his own freedom.

There is one other aspect of the experience of efficacy that is worth noting before we go on, and this is the fact that the person is *self-governing*. Children frequently complain: 'Now look what you made me do!' But my experience of efficacy tells me that, while other people can make things happen that have consequences for me, *nobody can make me do anything*. Similar insights are expressed by both Gabriel Marcel and Victor Frankl.[9]

The point of all this is that when we approach the person through the experience of personal action, we discover this rich dynamic stretching from the experience of efficacy, through self-possession, to self-determination and self-governance. These are the stages on the journey of personal self-transcendence.

The transcendence of the person in the act

For Kant, the term 'transcendence' refers to what is *a priori* and therefore 'beyond' in the sense that it is outside the scope of empirical experience. When Wojtyla uses the term 'transcendence' he uses it in a double sense. Man transcends himself in knowledge by possessing objects that are outside himself, and this is what Wojtyla refers to as 'horizontal transcendence'. When Wojtyla refers to the transcendence of the person in the action, however, he means that the person, as it were, steps beyond the boundaries of his fixed nature. This transcendence is what Wojtyla calls 'vertical transcendence', because it involves the person's possession of himself as object. He sometimes refers to this as 'the immanent profile of human action', so that it is a kind of immanent transcendence, or a transcendence within.[10]

When he talks about the transcendence of the person in this way, Wojtyla is not suggesting that the person ceases to be what he was and becomes something else. Even when, in a moment of discouragement, I wish I was someone else, what I really want is to be myself being someone else. Otherwise, all that would happen is the annihilation of myself, which is of no advantage whatever to me.[11]

It is in the exercise of his freedom, or self-determination, i.e. in action rather than in occurrence, that a person transcends himself.[12]

The very core of personal action is decision, and Wojtyla offers us an analysis of what happens when we make a decision. In the first instance, I become aware of some object that captures my interest. My initial response to this object presented in my experience is to examine it more closely on an ontological level. 'Is this real?' 'What is it?', etc. These questions lead to the making of a cognitive judgement. The object, as well as presenting itself to my intellect, also presents itself to my will and attracts its attention. This attraction is what Wojtyla calls motivation. It is in the nature of man to be attracted by what is good. Of fundamental importance is the fact that, while motivation attracts the will, it leaves the will free. There could be no action, and therefore no self-transcendence, in the absence of this freedom.

Before the will responds to motivation (either by accepting or rejecting it), the object is referred once again by the will to the judgement of truth. This time it is a question of establishing whether or not the object is a positive value, worthy of the attention of the will. (Is it compatible with the truth about the human person, and about myself as a person?). This is the *value* judgement. Wojtyla, like St Thomas believes that moral goodness is objective; what *is* is directly related to what *ought* to be done. It is this reference to truth that guarantees the freedom of the will. In some situations, there may be two or more objects each of which is recognised as a positive value, and each of which motivates me. It may not be possible to realise them all. In most cases, when I browse through a holiday brochure, it is with a view to selecting only one of the holidays on offer. For Wojtyla, there is no real choice between a positive and a negative value. Authentic choice is always between two goods. Of itself, choice is purely hypothetical or theoretical. It does not commit me to anything. It is decision that transforms choice into action. Once the object that motivates the will has been recognised as a positive value, the will makes a free decision that commits a person to seeking the realisation of that good. It is this moment of decision that constitutes the basis of personal action. It is in decision that I transcend myself (or bring my potency to act). It is in decision also that morality has its roots. While there is a real difference between choice and decision, the difficulty that people experience in deciding sometimes seems to have its roots in the fact that the choice of one good implies the rejection of others. At times we feel oppressed by the freedom to choose, rather than by the lack of choice.

The act of decision may have effects and consequences outside the person who acts, but it also has its efficacy with regard to the acting person himself. This is precisely because in the act of will I move *myself* towards realising the objective good (or evil) by which I have been motivated. In the course of action, according to Wojtyla, I experience myself as both the subject of the action and the object towards which the action is directed. When I perform an action, 'the consequence is external with regard to the person, but it is also internal to, or immanent in, the person.'[13] Something of the sense of vertical transcendence is captured in the reflexive verbs that we find in many European languages. In French, for example, when we mean 'I have decided to…' we don't say 'J'ai décidé', but rather 'Je me suis décidé(e).' In the act of decision, as in all truly personal acts, I am both the subject who acts and the primary object of the action. It is also possible to illustrate this by using a physical example. If I decide to run from Sutton Cross to the Summit of Howth, there is a sense in which *arriving at the Summit* is the object of my action. In another sense, however, *I* am the object of the action, because it is *I* who become moved from here to there; it is *I* who gain exercise, or who become relaxed.

By virtue of the very fact that it is performed by a person, every truly personal action has what Wojtyla describes as 'personalistic value'. This is the value that is realised in the person himself or herself, as opposed to the external or objective value.

Self-transcendence and personal integration:
Parallel to the goal of self-transcendence, and closely related to it, is the task of achieving the 'integration of the person in action'. Wojtyla explores the bodily dimension of man (the *soma*) and points out that

it has its own dynamism, which he calls *reactivity.* Similarly the *psyche* has a dynamism of its own, which Wojtyla calls *emotivity.* The *soma* and the *psyche* are integral elements of every human being, and any discussion of the person that sought to exclude these two dimensions would be meaningless, for Wojtyla. The reactivity of the body and the emotivity of the *psyche,* however, simply happen in man. In isolation from the act of the will, they have no personalistic or moral value. In any truly personal action, the reactivity of the body and the emotivity of the psyche are brought under the guidance of the rational will, and are placed at the service of the whole person. Through integration, man's reactivity and his emotivity are joined to the efficacy of the the person who acts.

Personal Efficacy in the Magisterium of John Paul II

In the course of his writings, Pope John Paul II frequently refers to the essential link between freedom and truth that is so characteristic of personal action. Much of what he has to say about personal action in *The Acting Person* is reflected in the encyclical *Veritatis Splendor.* The Pope recognises that, in our time:

> the situation of the world of the senses within space and time, physico-chemical constants, bodily processes, psychological impulses and forms of social conditioning seem to many people to be the only really decisive factors of human reality.[14]

He points out that this has the effect of undermining the dignity of human freedom. In opposition to this view he argues that:

> human acts are moral acts because they express and determine the goodness or evil of the individual who performs them. They do not produce a change merely in the state of affairs outside of man but, to the extent that they are deliberate choices, they give moral definition to the very person who performs them.[15]

It is important to note that, while they are not identical, there is a close relationship between the personalistic value of an action and its moral value. The personalistic value is that which is attributed to the action precisely because it is carried out by a person, as an expression of his or her free decision. The moral value of the action is defined by 'the relationship of man's freedom with the authentic good. ... Acting is morally good when the choices of freedom are in conformity with man's true good, and thus express the voluntary ordering of the person towards his ultimate end: God himself'[16] While objective moral goodness is independent of the personalistic value of the action, the moral responsibility of the acting person is intimately linked to his efficacy.

The worker as personal subject

One of the central themes of the magisterium of Pope John Paul II is that of human work. It is the subject matter of one of his earliest encyclicals, *Laborem Exercens*. The Pope acknowledges that 'work has an ethical value of its own, which clearly and directly remains linked to the fact that the one who carries it out is a person, a conscious and free subject; that is to say, a subject that decides about himself.'[17] This personalistic value of human work is rooted not only in human freedom, but in the truth about the human person.

> Man has to subdue the earth and dominate it, because as the 'image of God' he is a person, that is to say a subjective being capable of acting in a planned and rational way, capable of deciding about himself, and with a tendency to self-realisation. As a person, man is therefore a subject of work. As a person he works, he performs various actions belonging to the work process; independently of their objective content, these actions must all serve to realise his humanity, to fulfil the calling to be a person that is his by reason of his very humanity.[18]

The Pope acknowledges on numerous occasions that the world of work is a context in which man, the subject of work, can become depersonalised and degraded. This happens when the other person or group is seen as 'just an instrument with a work capacity and physical strength to be exploited at low cost and then discarded when no longer useful.'[19] The worker can cease to experience himself as free and responsible and can be made to feel instead that 'he is just a cog in a huge machine moved from above, that he is for more reasons than one a mere production instrument rather than a true subject of work with an initiative of his own.[20] Even in the very exercise of his freedom, man can experience a loss of control, when it seems that the fruit of his own work may well turn against him and destroy him. This happens when technology or the environment is used in a manner that is not consistent with the truth about the human person; when the ultimate goal of human existence is obscured by more immediate and more pragmatic objectives. Instead of transcending himself through his work, the worker is often in danger of being absorbed into the work, or even destroyed by its fruits.[21]

Social structures and personal action
There is probably no other theme that so pervades the magisterium of John Paul as that of human solidarity.[22] He describes the attitude of solidarity as the appropriate moral response to the reality of intersubjectivity. He repeatedly reminds his listeners that solidarity is something active, which engages our freedom. It is not a feeling of vague compassion or shallow distress at the misfortunes of so many people, both near and far. On the contrary, it is a firm and persevering determination to commit oneself to the common good; that is to say to the good of all and of each individual, because we are all really responsible for all.[23]

Neither is solidarity an attitude that reduces the other person to the level of a passive recipient to whom some good is done. Rather is the attitude by which, in effect, we acknowledge and affirm the other as an acting person, with whom we can participate in common action, which is oriented to the achievement of the common good, in accordance with reason.

> Solidarity helps us to see the 'other' – whether a person, people or nation – not just as some kind of instrument, with a work capacity and physical strength to be exploited at low cost and then discarded when no longer useful, but as our 'neighbour', a 'helper' (cf. Gen 2:18-20), to be made a sharer, on a par with ourselves, in the banquet of life to which all are equally invited by God.[24]

In attempting to address the problem of underdevelopment, and the widening gap between rich and poor in the world, the Pope argues that we must again face the fact that much of what passes for disaster and misfortune is in fact the fruit of personal efficacy that has been directed towards sectional interest rather than towards the attainment of the common good.

The Pope specifically identifies two related attitudes that are at variance with a proper understanding of the truth about the human person, namely the 'all-consuming desire for profit', and 'the thirst for power, with the intention of imposing one's will upon others.'[25] It is not out of place he says, to speak of *structures of sin,* which are the outcome of these attitudes. These structures are rooted in personal sin, and thus always linked to the concrete acts of individuals who introduce these structures, consolidate them and make them difficult to remove. One can certainly speak of 'selfishness' and of 'shortsightedness', of 'mistaken political calculations' and 'imprudent economic decisions.' And in each of these evaluations one hears an echo of an ethical and moral nature. Man's condition is such that a more profound analysis of individuals' actions and omissions cannot be achieved without implying, in one way or another, judgments or references of an ethical nature.[26]

The Pope's conviction that responsibility for action always belongs to the individual person is rooted in his insight, in which he disagrees with Scheler, that while people may act in common, the subjectivity of the group is never anything more than a quasi-subjectivity.[27] The person only retains his integrity and his transcendence when he retains the responsibility for his own actions. Likewise, the experience of responsibility or duty is reflexive as well as reflective. It is related to the person's experience of himself as the actor, rather than simply as someone to whom something is happening. Acting together with others, therefore, is not so much a question of a plurality of persons doing one action, but of a plurality of personal actions all of which are oriented to the same end. One criticism of socialism that Pope John Paul makes is that 'it maintains that the good of the individual can be realised without reference to his free choice, to the unique and exclusive responsibility which he exercises in the face of good or evil.'[28] This, he says, involves a mistaken understanding of the person. It is in fact 'by responding to the call of God contained in the being of things that man becomes aware of his transcendent dignity. Every individual must give this response, which constitutes the apex of his humanity, and no social or collective subject can substitute for it.'[29]

Family
In his writing about the family too, Pope John Paul explains that the human person gradually transcends himself or herself, through decisions that are made in freedom.

> But man, who has been called to live God's wise and loving design in a responsible manner, is a historical being who day by day builds himself up through his many free decisions; and so he knows, loves and accomplishes moral good by stages of growth.[30]

This moral good, which the couple seek in their marriage, has its roots in the truth about the human person. With specific reference to the relationship between conjugal love and the transmission of life, the Pope explains that the goodness of any procedure 'must be determined by objective standards' that are 'based on the nature of the human person and his or her acts.'[31]

When it comes to the education of children, particularly spiritual and moral education, there are so many influences in play that parents often seem to experience their role as a reactive one rather than a proactive one. It can sometimes seem that the attitudes of the young 'happen', rather than being formed. Once again, of course, many of the quasi-cultural influences to which children are exposed, especially in advertising and in entertainment, are not accidental but come about as a result of personal decisions that are taken by individuals in industry and in the communications media. Against that background, Pope John Paul emphasises the need for parents to engage actively in the education of their children, both for the good of the children themselves, and for the good of society.[32] It is in carrying out this activity, he suggests, that parents achieve their own self-transcendence.

> By virtue of their ministry of educating, parents are, through the witness of their lives, the first heralds of the Gospel for their children. Furthermore, by praying with their children, by reading the word of God with them and by introducing them deeply through Christian initiation into the Body of Christ – both the Eucharistic and the ecclesial body – they become fully parents, in that they are begetters not only of bodily life but also of the life that through the Spirit's renewal flows from the cross and resurrection of Christ.[33]

Personal Freedom and Revealed Truth in *Fides et Ratio*

Personal freedom (experienced as efficacy or self-possession) is fundamental to self-transcendence. The demands of truth can sometimes be experienced as a limitation imposed on freedom. Pope John Paul recognises, however, that the desire for truth is deeply rooted in human nature.

> People can even run from the truth as soon as they glimpse it because they are afraid of its demands. Yet, for all that they may evade it, the truth still influences life. Life in fact can never be grounded upon doubt, uncertainty or deceit; such an existence

would be threatened constantly by fear and anxiety. One may define the human being, therefore, as the one who seeks the truth.[34]

In all of what has gone before, we have spoken about truth as something that people can discover through the use of reason, and which is objective rather than subjective. It has a direct relationship to reality, and is not simply a matter of opinion.[35] We discover, or 'arrive at' the truth, but it is not our own creation. We can accept the truth or reject it, we can come to understand it differently, but we cannot stop it from being true. We can make choices and decisions, enlightened by the truth, both the truth about the human person and the truth about the world around us. Far from being an obstacle to our freedom, this objectivity of truth is actually the guarantee of our freedom. It gives us a sound basis for the choices and decisions we make, without which we would simply be pulled in different directions by the objects that attract or motivate us.

Participating in the quest for truth
One of the characteristics of our human nature is that, in our search for truth, none of us is capable of absorbing the whole truth. Much of what we accept as true is taken on trust. It is the fruit of the research and the reflection of others. This is increasingly the case in a world in which knowledge is becoming more and more specialised. For this reason, Pope John Paul suggests that 'the one who seeks the truth is also the one who lives by belief.'[36] In the act of belief a person transcends himself or herself and enters into an interpersonal relationship in which the issue is no longer simply the person's capacity to know, 'but also the deeper capacity to entrust oneself to others, to enter into a relationship with them which is intimate and enduring.'[37] What we gain in the process, according to Pope John Paul, is an insight into the truth of the human person.

It should be stressed that the truths sought in this interpersonal relationship are not primarily empirical or philosophical. Rather, what is sought is the truth of the person – what the person is and – what the person reveals from deep within. Human perfection, then, consists not simply in acquiring an abstract knowledge of the truth, but in a dynamic relationship of faithful self-giving with others. It is in this faithful self-giving that a person finds a fullness of certainty and security. At the same time, however, knowledge through belief, grounded as it is on trust between persons, is linked to truth; in the act of believing men and women entrust themselves to the truth which the other declares to them.[38]

The important point to bear in mind is that while another person may be the source of some knowledge or information that I have, the decision to accept this information as truthful is inextricably linked with my own judgement as to the truthfulness or reliability of the other person as a witness or as a source of knowledge. To the extent that the decision to trust is my decision, I remain free in the face of the truth declared by the other person, and indeed in the relationship of trust itself

Reason is liberated by faith

Reason is 'oriented to truth and is equipped moreover with the means necessary to arrive at truth.' It is clear from even a cursory reading of *F&R* that Pope John Paul does not see any conflict between divine revelation and the rational quest for truth. On the contrary, he frequently asserts that faith complements and perfects the insights towards which reason has already pointed. 'In studying revelation and its credibility, as well as the corresponding act of faith, fundamental theology should show how, in the light of the knowledge conferred by faith, there emerge certain truths which reason, from its own independent enquiry, already perceives.'[39]

Notwithstanding the achievements of philosophy, the Pope points out that, on its own, reason inevitably falls short of an adequate understanding of the truth about the human person. Modern philosophy has placed the focus on man but 'the positive results achieved must not obscure the fact that reason, in its one-sided concern to investigate human subjectivity, seems to have forgotten that men and women are always called to direct their steps towards a truth which transcends them.'[40] The ultimate truth about the human person can only be understood in the light of faith. The Pope reiterates the teaching of the Second Vatican Council, that 'only in the mystery of the Incarnate Word does the mystery of man take on light. For Adam, the first man, was the type of him who was to come, Christ the Lord. Christ the new Adam, in the very revelation of the mystery of the Father and of his love, fully reveals man to himself, and brings to light his most high calling.'[41]

In this way, while reason ensures that faith can be expressed coherently and consistently, faith liberates reason, and allows it to reach its ultimate goal.[42] Indeed it is possible to read *F&R* in a way that suggests that the content of faith is the final cause of reason, and that – as such – revelation confers its ultimate dignity on human reason. 'The desire for truth, therefore, spurs reason always to go further; indeed, it is as if reason were overwhelmed to see that it can always go beyond what it has already achieved.'[43]

The freedom of the children of God

In the opening paragraph of *Veritatis Splendor*, Pope John Paul reminds us that truth is attractive.[44] Our reason is naturally drawn to the truth, including that truth which it is unable to penetrate without the assistance of faith. There is, according to the Pope, an obligation on every person, deriving from his or her personal nature, to seek the truth and to adhere to it. This includes the practical truth about what is to be done. It includes opening oneself to apprehend that truth even at levels that transcend the person. This is an essential condition for us to become ourselves, and to grow as mature, adult persons.[45] The question that arises is the extent to which, in the face of this obligation, we can be said to remain free. Does faith happen to us, or is the believer in some sense the cause of his own faith?

To the extent that God's revelation is self-gift, it is something that happens to us. St Augustine is just one of many Christian philosophers and mystics who have expressed the experience of being sought out, or touched by God, notwithstanding their own smallness and sinfulness.

> Late have I loved you, O beauty so ancient and so new: late have I loved you: You were always within me, and I abroad, seeking you there. I rushed madly about in the midst of forms beautiful which you had made. You were always with me, but I was not with you. The very things which had not been, unless they were in you, kept me from you. You called me by name, You cried aloud to me, and your voice pierced my deafness.[46]

As we have already seen, when we decide to accept the truth that is declared to us by others, the most important truth we reach is the truth of the other person. It seems that this must also be the case where revealed truth is concerned. Faith allows us to enter into the mysteries of the Incarnation, the Trinity, the Resurrection, in a way that would be impossible by the use of reason alone. In each of these mysteries, however, we are ultimately led into intimacy with God, and into a deeper understanding of the meaning of our own personal existence. In the final analysis, the content of faith is a *who* rather than just a *what*; it is faith *in*, rather than simply faith *that*.

But faith is not something that is done to us, so much as it is someone who comes to us. God, who is the ultimate good, motivates us to seek him. Like all the other goods that motivate us, however, God leaves us free. It is left to us to refer that motivation to the judgement of truth, and to make our act of faith in response to his gift of faith. The reference to truth, in this case, has to do with the truthfulness of God. The seeker after truth must, in effect, decide whether or not God can be accepted as a reliable witness. This is why, as Pope John Paul explains:

the Church has always considered the act of entrusting oneself to God to be a moment of fundamental decision which engages the whole person. In that act, the intellect and the will display their spiritual nature, enabling the subject to act in a way which realises personal freedom to the full. It is not just that freedom is part of the act of faith: it is absolutely required. Indeed, it is faith that allows individuals to give consummate expression to their own freedom.[47]

While the content of faith transcends reason, it does not conflict with reason. The function of reason is to find meaning, and to 'discover explanations which might allow everyone to come to a certain understanding of the contents of faith.'[48] With this in mind, Pope John Paul encourages a close relationship between philosophy and theology.

Indeed to argue according to rigorous rational criteria is to guarantee that the results attained are universally valid. This also confirms the principle that grace does not destroy nature but perfects it: the assent of faith, engaging the intellect and will, does not destroy but perfects the free will of each believer who deep within welcomes what has been revealed.[49]

The essential characteristic of the gift of faith is that the One who gives is Himself the gift. The gift of faith is, therefore, deeply personal. It seems appropriate, therefore, that the response to that gift should also be deeply personal. Of all possible acts, the act of faith is the one in which the efficacy of the human person is most perfectly expressed and in which the self-transcendence of the person is most perfectly achieved. This is because the act of faith, and all the other acts that flow from it, require a free decision to trust, and because the act of faith, above all acts, is the one most intimately directed towards the ultimate end of the human person.

Notes

1. cf. Ernest W. Ranly, *Scheler's Phenomenology of Community* (The Hague, Martinus Nijhoff, 1966), pp. 20-21.
2. Emmanuel Mounier, *Révolution Personnaliste et Communautaire*, in *Oeuvres de Mounier* (Paris: Editions du Seuil, 1960), vol. 1, pp.176, 177.
3. cf. Josef Seifert, 'Karol Cardinal Wojtyla and the Cracow/Lublin School of Philosophy', *Aletheia* (1981), 159
4. Karol Wojtyla, 'The Person: Subject and Community', *The Review of Metaphysics*, 33 (1979/80), 280.
5. Karol Wojtyla, 'Thomistic Personalism', in *Person and Community: Selected Essays*, Catholic Thought from Lublin, 4, trans. by Theresa Sandok, OSM (New York, Peter Lang, 1993), pp. 170, 1.
6. cf. e.g., Saint Thomas Aquinas. *Summa Theologiae*, I IIae, Q.18, Art.2., ans.
7. cf. *ibid.*, I IIæ, Q. 9, Art. 6.; cf. also Karol Wojtyla, 'The Will in the Analysis of the Ethical Act', in *Person and Community: Selected Essays*, Catholic Thought from Lublin, 4, translated by Theresa Sandok, OSM, (New York, Peter Lang, 1993), pp. 3-21 .
8. Karol Wojtyla, *The Acting Person*, in *The Yearbook of Phenomenological Research: Analecta Husserliana* (Dordrecht: D. Reidel, 1979), vol. 10, pp. 3-367 (p. 108).
9. cf. Gabriel Marcel, *II Mistero del'Essere*, (Roma: Borla, 1987), p. 289; Victor Frankl, *Man's Search for Meaning: An Introduction to Logotherapy.* Preface by Gordon W. Allport (New York: Pocket Books-Washington Square Press), 1984).
10. Karol Wojtyla, 'Teoria-Prassi: Uno Tema Umano e Cristiano', *Incontri Culturali* (Rome), 10 (1977), 36.
11. Desmond Connell, 'Substance and the Interiority of Being', *Neue Zeitschrift für Systematische Theologie und Religionsphilosophie*, 25:1 (1983), 68-65.
12. cf. Karol Wojtyla, *The Acting Person*, Ill.
13. *ibid.*, 150.
14. Pope John Paul, *Veritatis Splendor*, # 46
15. *ibid.*, # 71
16. *ibid*, # 72
17. Pope John Paul, *Laborem Exercens*, # 6
18. *ibid.*
19. Pope John Paul, *Sollicitudo rei Socialis*, # 39
20. *ibid*, # 15
21. cf. Pope John Paul II, *Redemptor Hominis*, # 15; cf. also Pope John Paul II, *Fides et Ratio*, # 47

22. Kevin P. Doran, *Solidarity: A Synthesis of Personalism and Communalism in the Thought of Karol Wojtyla/Pope John Paul II* (New York: Lang, 1996).

23. Pope John Paul II, *Sollicitudo Rei Socialis* # 38; cf. also idem, Homily at Maputo, Mozambique, *18/9/88*, § *12,AAS* 81 (1989): 358; idem, Address to U.S. President George Bush, *27/5/89,AAS,* 81 (1989): 1315/6; idem; Address to the Civic Authorities, Rome, 20/11/90, § *2,AAS* 82 (1990): 885; idem, Address to Youth, Naples, Italy, 10/11/90, § 5, *IGP2* XIII-2 (1990): 1078.

24. Pope John Paul II, *Solicitudo Rei Socialis,* # 39

25. cf. *ibid.,* # 37

26. *ibid,* # 39

27. cf. Karol Wojtyla, *The Acting Person,* 277; cf. also Max Scheler, *On The Eternal in Man* (London: SCM Press, 1960), p. 125.

28. Pope John Paul II, *Centesimus Annus,* # 13

29. *ibid.*

30. Pope John Paul II, *Familiaris Consortio,* # 34

31. *ibid,* # 32

32. *ibid,* # 36

33. *ibid,* # 39

34. Pope John Paul II, *Fides et Ratio,* # 28 (Referred to below as *F&R*)

35. cf. *ibid.,* # 44 & # 56

36. *ibid.,* #31

37. *ibid.,* #32

38. *ibid.*

39. *ibid.,* # 67; cf. also *ibid.,* # 80

40. *ibid.,* # 5 and cf. *ibid.,* # 46

41. Second Vatican Council, *Gaudium et Spes,* # 22; cf. also Pope John Paul II, *Redemptor Hominis,* # 8, & *F&R,* # 60

42. *F&R,* # 20

43. ibid, # 42; cf. also # 48

44. cf. Pope John Paul II, *Veritatis Splendor,* # 44;

45. Pope John Paul, *F&R,* # 41

46. St Augustine, *Confessions,* Book x, Ch. XXVII

47. *F&R,* # 13

48. *ibid.,* # 42

49. *ibid.,* # 75; cf. also *ibid.,* # 43, and # 108

PART III

Perspectives Opened Up
by the Encyclical

FAITH AND REASON: THE INTERPRETATIVE KEY TO THE PRINCIPAL ENCYCLICALS OF POPE JOHN PAUL II

Bruno Forte

'Faith' and 'Reason' are the two terms around which John Paul II builds his reflections on human being and the highest vocation of persons. This is true not only for the encyclical on 'Faith and Reason' but for the entirety of his magisterium as both thinker and pastor. In order to understand better the meaning of this affirmation it will be necessary to understand the meaning of the two terms '*fides*' and '*ratio*' in the light of two backgrounds: the time in which Karol Wojtyla worked, and that of his heart. Together these two constitute the very core of his 'theological biography'. It is only in this way that the full meaning of these two terms, and the reason for which John Paul II speaks of them as the 'two wings on which the human spirit rises to the contemplation of the truth',[1] can be fully understood.

What Reason? The Events of the Time

In the events of the twentieth century, 'reason' stands out as the singular and decisive protagonist: lying at the very heart of the story of the modern era, it sees its apex and its decline in this century. Opening with the triumph of 'strong reason', which was characteristic of the Enlightenment, modernity has led to the widespread dissemination of an experience of fragmentation and non-sense typical of 'weak reason', one that has flourished since the fall of the ideologies. Succeeding what may be referred to as the 'lengthy' century, which began with the French Revolution and ended with the outbreak of the Great War (World War I), is the so-called 'short twentieth century' (E. Hobsbawm), which is marked by the affirmation of the extremes of totalitarian and ideological models, which were to lead ultimately, in 1989, to their own collapse. Max Horkheimer and Theodor W. Adorno described the process in a powerful metaphor at the beginning of their work on the dialectic of Enlightenment: 'The fully enlightened earth radiates disaster triumphant'.[2] The Enlightenment – taken in the broadest philosophical sense as a continuous process – pursued the objective of ridding men and women of all fear so as to give them absolute and complete control of their destiny, thanks to a boundless faith in the power of reason: the Enlightenment's extreme outcome – the outcome which we can see in the drama of two world wars and the high costs of totalitarianism – can be recognised in the condition of renunciation, in the denial of questions of meaning and the search for a foundation, all of which can be viewed as being part of the so-called 'weak reason' condition. Three stages can be identified in this process, stages that lie at the origin of the crisis in European consciousness as it reaches the threshold of the third millennium. These stages can be represented through the metaphors of light, darkness and dawn respectively.

a) *The light of strong reason and its decline*
The first stage is characterised by the metaphor of light, which expresses the principle inspiring modernity, the claim that mature reason can understand and illuminate everything. In accordance with this claim the ability to embrace the world rationally means making the human person master of his/her own identity. Emancipation is the dream that pervades all of the great processes undertaken to allow this transformation into the modern era to take place. This belief in being able to triumph over every obscurity through the use of reason is expressed in absolute visions of the world, that is, in ideologies.

Ideology tries to impose the order of reason on the whole of reality to the point of establishing a complete identification between the ideal and the real. Ideology excludes any form of diversity, and is by its very nature violent. Thus, the dream of totality becomes inexorably totalitarian. It is not by chance, nor is it an accident of history, that all forms of modern ideology have resulted in totalitarianism and violence. Indeed, it is precisely this historical experience of the violence of totalitarian ideologies that has produced the crisis surrounding the absolute pretensions of 'enlightened' reason.

b) *The night of weak reason*
If mature reason sought to give a sense to everything, then the 'weak reason' of the post-modern condition sees meaning in nothing, and purports to recognise the possibility of there not being any meaning whatsoever. This condition is expressed in the metaphor of darkness: it is a period of ruin and of failure, of confusion and uncertainty; a period that is, above all, marked by indifference. For many people, the rejection of the strong and total horizons offered by ideologies further reveals an inability on their part to seek any form of meaning, and this has in its turn led to the extremity of a loss of all belief in seeking out the ultimate reasons for human life and death. This epochal crisis in European consciousness can be seen clearly in the face of 'decadence' – ultimately a loss of value and an inability to measure itself against anything. In this way, passion for the truth has become less evident. The 'strong culture' of ideology shatters into the several shards of 'weak culture', within which lies a 'sea of solitary figures', and in which the 'immense' loss of hope folds in on itself and is reduced to the narrow horizon of the individual's own particular interest. In this way, the end of ideologies appears more truly as the pale avatar of a coming idol, namely a total relativism, which is characteristic of those who no longer have any faith in the power of the truth, and as a result seem destitute of any capacity to move from phenomenon to foundation. This is the extreme face of the crisis surrounding European consciousness at the close of the 'short twentieth century'.

c) *The dawn of an open and questioning reason*

In analysing this process, which takes us from the triumph of modern reason to decadence, we cannot ignore the presence of some signs of change and of hope, with which we associate the metaphor of the dawn. There is a 'nostalgia for a perfect and consummate justice' (Max Horkheimer), which allows us to see some possibility of a search for occluded meaning. We are not talking of '*une recherche du temps perdu*', of a nostalgic indulgence confined to the past, but rather of a systematic attempt to rediscover a meaning that goes beyond that of ruin and failure, one that enables people to discern a horizon that inspires and moves them towards embarking on a journey. Among the many expressions used in relation to this search we should note the use of the phrase 'rediscovery of the other'. We are witnesses to a growing awareness of the need for solidarity, at interpersonal, social, and international levels. We discern the emergence of a 'nostalgia for the Totally Other' (Max Horkheimer), that is, for a rediscovery of the ultimate questions and of the ultimate horizon. This emergence outlines the need for a new consensus about ethics in order to motivate moral involvement, not in light of the benefits that arise from such involvement, but rather in light of the good in itself that such involvement engages. The nostalgia evident in the crisis of our present time bears the face of the other, not only the face of our neighbour, but also of the Other, that is, the transcendent foundation of life and of living together. So we can say that there are some signs of a return to a reason that is open to transcending itself and to seeking out the Other.

What Faith? A Theological Biography

It is in the historical events – as described above – that Karol Wojtyla's intellectual and spiritual life is lived. His 'theological biography' develops from within the historical context in which it has grown and over which it has had considerable influence. His most proper identity as thinker and as pastor finds its essence in a strong faith. Every aspect of his existence and of his work is characterised by a living and fruitful relationship with the Christian God. If Wojtyla develops a strong sense of the Transcendent as an alternative to the rationalistic pretences of ideology, and as characterised by a true and pure mystical experience in response to the renunciation of its own foundation by 'weak reason', he does not hesitate to propose a thoughtful faith that does not flee the challenges of searching intelligence. In both of these attitudes the faith of John Paul II is highly responsible, never calling on one to step outside of history, but rather to insert one's faith into history, and this with a precise ethical consciousness. In this way the parameters of the faith to which his magisterium bears testimony are clearly outlined: a mystical faith, a thoughtful faith, a responsible faith.

a) *A mystical faith*

A constant and characteristic motive present in the word and life of John Paul II's magisterium is a sense of the absolute primacy of God. We are not dealing here with one element among others, but with a dominant note: we are referring to the horizon and dwelling-place within which, and from which, everything else is born. The design of the living God is the motive behind the life and work of Karol Wojtyla: a precious indication of this is given in the very structure of his magisterium as expressed in his encyclicals. This structure is radically theological and deeply trinitarian. The fundamental cycle is represented by the three encyclicals *Redemptor Hominis* (1979), dedicated to the Son, *Dives in Misericordia* (1980), consecrated to God the Father, and *Dominum et Vivificantem* (1986), on the Person and work of the Holy Spirit. This trinitarian structure resounds significantly also within the proposed itinerary for the great jubilee year 2000 in the *Tertio Millennio Adveniente* (1994). Everything else is built upon this foundation: the reflection on anthropology presented in the three encyclicals already mentioned is built on it; it is present in *Laborem exercens* of 1981 on the dignity of human work, in the apostolic letter on women, *Mulieris Dignitatem* of 1988, in the encyclical on ethics proposed in *Veritatis Splendor* of 1993, in *Evangelium Vitae* of 1995, and in the encyclicals on the social question, *Sollicitudo Rei Socialis* of 1988 and *Centesimus Annus* of

1991, and finally in the encyclical dedicated to ecclesiology, which is worked out in light of the absolute uniqueness of the Redeemer and of the Trinitarian Communion, that is, *Redemptoris Missio* of 1991, in *Slavorum Apostoli* of 1985 on Eastern Christianity, and in *Ut Unum Sint* of 1995 on ecumenism. Significant attention is dedicated to a reflection on Mary, offered in *Redemptoris Mater* of 1987, wherein the various aspects of the Christian mystery are gathered together in the rich icon of the Mother of the Redeemer, in which everything returns to the work of the Trinity and to the glory of God.

Right from the very beginning, Karol Wojtyla's research has, among other things, borne witness to the strong impact of mystical experience on thought about the truth. Proof of this is evident in his doctoral thesis, which was dedicated to the Doctrine of the Faith according to St John of the Cross (1948), and defended within an academic context – the Angelicum University – an institution marked by the predominance of the neo-Scholasticism, and therefore by not a few reservations regarding a theology that finds its essence in the mystical. It was to remain the profound conviction of Wojtyla, as both man and as thinker, that the light necessary for a clear understanding, one capable of discerning the Divine design for life and history, shines from an experience of God, as the following words from a great mystic poet much loved by Wojtyla, say with the greatest intensity:

> ¡O lámpadas de fuego,
> en cuyos resplandores
> las profundas cavernas del sentido,
> que estaba oscuro y ciego,
> con extraños primores
> calor y luz dan junto a su Querido![3]

Truly – and as an important witness from the '*Orientalis*' affirms – 'it is not conscience that illuminates the mystery, but the mystery that illuminates conscience. We can only give thanks for that which we can never know.'[4]

b) *A thoughtful faith*

This strong emphasis on the mystical dimension does not in any way detract from the questioning and searching character of faith: the faith of John Paul II is, and will always remain, thoughtful! '*Fides nisi cogitetur nulla est*' – 'if faith does not think it is nothing'. These words of Saint Augustine[5] – quoted in *Fides et Ratio*[6] – express the profound conviction behind Karol Wojtyla's entire existential and intellectual itinerary, for whom to think means both to move continually from phenomenon to foundation, and to take these two poles of this transcendent movement with the utmost seriousness. In the encyclical *F&R* the Pope writes: 'We face a great challenge at the end of this millennium to move from phenomenon to foundation, a step as necessary as it is urgent. We cannot stop short at experience alone; even if experience does reveal the human being's interiority and spirituality, speculative thinking must penetrate to the spiritual core and the ground from which it rises.'[7] This concept of thought – which faith can never renounce, if faith really wants to be as it should be, namely a faith of historical beings open to Mystery and entrusting themselves to it – matures in Wojtyla as a result of an encounter with two great authors to whom he owes his intellectual formation. On the one hand we have Thomas Aquinas, with whom he became fully familiar during his years studying at the Angelicum, and, on the other hand, we have Edmund Husserl, the father of phenomenology, to whom the future Pope was to dedicate much research. Wojtyla draws on St Thomas's metaphysical demand to lead the phenomenon back to the foundation in order to avoid falling into that inconsistency which characterises much pragmatic and purely functional thought. From Husserl he learns to give full value and attention to the phenomenon, which is itself the key to gaining access to the metaphysical depths of all that exists. The sobriety of Husserl's phenomenology and the attention that it focuses on others and on things, precisely as they appear to us – an attention which is another peculiar characteristic of Karol Wojtyla – is expressed, for example, in the words which follow, taken from Husserl's *Ideas:* 'everything that is offered to us in "intuition" is to be accepted simply as it is offered, but also only within the limits within which it is presented.'⁸

To stop short at phenomenological observation would, however, reduce reality to the all-too-narrow horizon of only that which can be experienced. This is why true phenomenological intuition points to the essence, that is, to a transcendence of the phenomenon, in the direction of that which profoundly constitutes it, both in its identity and in its relatedness. It is at this point that St Thomas's lesson completes the study of Husserl: the world of beings is constituted by Being's intimacy to, and immanence in, each being; here we have the true and ultimate foundation of reality. In a formulation of great speculative audacity Thomas affirms that: '*Esse autem est illud quod est magis intimum cuilibet, et quod profundius omnibus inest*'.⁹ To summarise, the ontological level coincides with the profundity of reality: it is that which gives stability and dignity to that which exists, and avoids everything being reduced to a fugitive moment that is inconsistent and empty. However, though the phenomenon is transcended in the direction of its foundation, so as to draw on the profound source and hidden root of the phenomenon, the foundation in its turn is attainable only by means of the phenomenon, and that means through history, so that no devaluation of worldly reality is therefore admissible. Thus, thoughtful faith will live in a twofold and unique fidelity: in faithfulness to the eternal, and in equal faithfulness to the earthly, thereby uniting heaven and earth in one unique movement: transcending towards the ultimate Mystery, yet returning to things in their concrete particularity.

c) *A responsible faith*

The third characteristic attributed to faith in the theological biography of Karol Wojtyla is his sense of being responsible: by this adjective we want to indicate the ethical relevance of the experience of believing. The polemic of the Reform against 'works', when taken to be a means of merit and salvation, has favoured a certain separation between the life of faith and the active life. Thereby, we arrive, on the one hand, either at a kind of spiritualism, which is characterised by an evasion of history, or, on the other hand, at pragmatism, which has, above all, exiled God from the sphere of worldly responsibilities. However, the presence in history of Wojtyla the believer, has always been acute. He has always been involved in history, from the years of his resistance to Nazism to that period when he faced the daily struggle against militant ideological atheism and communist totalitarianism, to the battle against that ethical emptying which is characteristic of consumerist capitalism. Even in this area there was a thinker in whose school the future Pope was formed. Here we are speaking about Max Scheler. In response to the 'formalism' of Kantian ethics that ran the risk of reducing moral behaviour to good intentions, Scheler emphasised the value of a 'material ethics', one which would be attentive to the actual contents of actions, and would not simply be limited to the purely intentional or formal aspect. The ethics of values moves in this direction because it recognises a real criterion in values and not just some abstract and theoretical reference. It recognises a criterion that takes on a visible form in the actual living out of historical choices and responsibilities. John Paul II has always demonstrated a great interest in the ethical dimensions of choice, even those that are apparently more speculative. His own fundamental theoretical work, *The Acting Person,* is rigorous and speculative, and is founded on the indissolubility of the relationship between personal being and moral action within the tangibility of decision-making. Through faith, ethics draws on the ultimate horizon, in which the actual value of penultimate choices is located and qualified. Through ethics, faith inhabits that real space from within which it can itself translate into history, and within which it dwells alongside the living questions which inspire the investigation of fundamental positions in the light of the Absolute, in whose horizon the weight and the value of every act is ultimately qualified.

What Kind of Encounter Between Faith and Reason?

Beyond the '*aut-aut*' the challenge of an '*et-et*'.

'Faith' and 'Reason' – understood from within the context of the particular historical period in which John Paul II grew up and has lived, and in the light of the figures who played such an influential role in determining his theological biography – are tightly woven together in a vital relationship by a reciprocal stimulus and enrichment. In the encyclical *F&R* the Polish Pope affirms above all what he has experienced in his intellectual adventure and in his own spiritual experience as a protagonist of our time. If the presumptions of enlightened reason excluded all elements linking the world of faith with the dominion of rationality, thus opposing reason and faith in an '*aut-aut*' without any remission, then the history of modernity has shown how this exclusion has been lethal for reason, which has thereby become inexorably totalitarian and violent. This is why Karol Wojtyla has emphasised that the recovery of the correct relationship between faith and reason is of vital urgency, not only for those at the service of the proclamation of the faith, but also so as to promote the dignity of the human person. The '*et-et*' that the Pope proposes – and which is to be found '*in actu exercito*' in all of the works that he has produced as thinker and as pastor – moves in three directions: the first could be defined as a sort of apologetic for 'open reason'; the second refers to faith as something truly involved in search: '*fides quaerens intellectum*'; while the third relates more directly to the actual encounter between these two terms (faith and reason), in an open and reciprocally fecund dialogue.

a) *A reason aware of its limits, and open to transcending them.*
F&R is, in the first place, an apology for reason.[10] In an era marked by a crisis of trust in the possibility of reason, the direct result of ideological adventures, such an apologetics is indeed far from insignificant! Reason is not defended in terms of an absolute knowledge that is presumptuously closed in on itself, but rather is seen as the fundamental instrument by which human beings set out to live

in the service of the truth to which reason is originarily called by the very fact that it exists. What is at play here is the idea of truth itself.[11] If truth is a possession to be manipulated, as ideological reason was inclined to maintain, then the person is, and remains, closed within their own horizon of the truth, closed in, indeed, to the point of suffocation, as the historical career of ideology demonstrates. If, instead, truth is not a possession to be captured and held within the confines of reason, but rather is the objective and transcendent Other that also includes us, then it is not possible to open oneself to the truth without posing the ultimate questions and without allowing oneself the possibility of listening to the various ways in which the transcendent and sovereign truth also reaches us. To summarise then, the truth is not circumscribable on the basis of '*cogito ergo sum*', of the axiom 'I think, therefore I am', but rather has to be grasped from within the experience of '*cogitor ergo sum*', of 'I have been thought of, therefore I am'. Truth is the custodian of existence, and only it can open up a flight beyond oneself toward the Other in transcendence.

What the Pope emphasises is faith in the capacity of reason to open itself up to the truth, and thus of being an 'open reason'. A refusal of this is not the full exercise of reason, but rather a weak exercising of it, one that renounces the possibility of opening up to the horizon, towards the Transcendent. Looking at the metaphysical question again, taken in its etymological sense as that which lies 'beyond physical things', and as that which moves beyond the phenomenon to arrive at the foundation, we can see that this proposal is the one true issue worthy of philosophy, and to which human beings are predisposed by the radical nostalgia that they bear within them from the very first moment of their existence. It is at this point that philosophy appears truly not to be in competition with theology. Instead it appears to be united with it by a thought that searches for horizons and listens to the various ways by which the Other speaks to us: this, precisely, is the thinking of faith.

b) *A faith which seeks*

The encyclical clearly affirms that there is no one Christian philosophy, even if it supports the full legitimacy of a 'Christian Philosopher', that is, of 'a philosophical speculation conceived in dynamic union with faith'.[12] Two thousand years of Christianity bear witness to this speculation. Indeed, even the inculturation of faith in new contexts would be superficial if it were to omit this two thousand year history, which has produced extraordinary fruit in the Western consciousness and beyond. This history of the thinking of the faith shows how it is possible to exercise philosophical interrogation rigorously, and to be, at the same time, open to the gift of revelation. From this point of view one can understand how philosophy is the ground of the possibility of mutual understanding and of dialogue with those who do not share the faith: reason is not limited, but rather, empowered by faith; neither, on the other hand, is faith dominated by or subjected to, reason. Reason and faith are two sources of knowledge that are neither identical nor in competition: one is the pure exercise of our intelligence, the other is the reception of the light that comes from on high through the gift of revelation. These two sources do not annul or suppress one another, but rather converge. It is this encounter of human transcendence with the advent of the Divine that constitutes the thought of faith, a faith that makes philosophical questioning its own and enriches it through the word of revelation to which faith listens.

In this way, dialogue is made possible between theologian and philosopher, between reason and faith, in the degree to which each one is open to the possibility of its own transcendence. A philosopher who poses radical questions does not exclude the possibility of hearing the advent of the Other; a thinker of the faith who recognises the pronunciation of the Divine Name in revelation integrates philosophical questions with the understanding he has been given. In the light of these premises it is possible to point out from among contemporary philosophies three great spirits that animate this searching faith ('*fides quaerens intellectum*'). The first one is that of a philosophical thinker who is open not only to transcendence but also to the recognition of it through revelation. We are dealing here with so-called 'Christian philosophy' that involves the full use of reason within the horizon that is disclosed to it through belief in the Divine's self-communication in history. Then there is a second model that can be characterised as that philosophy that poses radical questions and is open to ultimate questions, but it is not joined in obedience to faith. There are various thinkers who move in this direction, including some of the greatest of the nineteenth century. For this form of thought the encyclical constitutes an invitation to enter into a dialogue with faith in revelation and with theology, in the belief that the truth of revelation neither competes with, nor is adverse to, philosophical research, but rather is open to the wonder of transcendence. A third possibility refers to so called 'weak reason', that is, to the thought that prejudicially closes itself off from the possibility of transcendence and from the questions that surround transcendence, not recognising any power in human reason to transcend itself in its movement toward the objective truth. Certainly, in the face of such thought the encyclical presents itself as critical, and rightfully so, since a thinking that, from its very beginnings, denies the possibility of an objective truth and of a transcendent movement toward it, condemns the person to a sort of 'solipsism', a solitude that makes of human society nothing other than a 'sea of solitary figures'. In reality, the encyclical challenges the 'weak' or 'nihilist' thinkers to measure themselves against their own philosophies. In this way, it presents itself as a challenge and as a testimony to the highest dignity of human reason and the possibilities inherent in reason to arrive at the truth, even before any concrete decision is made about how to arrive at it. In this sense then, the entire anthropological magisterium of John Paul II is summarised in the most concise possible way.

c) *Faith and reason listening to the Other*
The terms in which the encyclical articulates the dialogue between philosophy and theology, between faith and reason, are profoundly

respectful of the reciprocal dignity and autonomy of these two worlds, and at the same time, of their necessary and fecund relationship. In the spirit of his entire magisterium as thinker and pastor, the Pope affirms that the recognition of a truth that is universally valid – that is, the truth of revelation – does not lead to any intolerance, since it brings one to recognise the value that exists in every human person, in his/her questioning and possible responses, and offers a criterion in relation to which everyone, beginning with the believer, can measure his/her own affirmations and acquisition of the truth. Dialogue is possible, then, and is useful, where the interlocutors accept being measured by the truth that transcends them and that, to some degree, embraces them. This would not be possible where one of the two dialogue-partners holds him- or herself to be the exclusive guardian of the truth, or, even goes so far as to identify him- or herself with it. The Pope affirms the transcendence proper to the truth in relation to thinking through faith, a thinking that lives, that is, through obedience and through profound attention to revealed truth, and not in a stance of domination towards it. Even dogma should not be interpreted as a limit to the progress of human thought, but as the bulwark against its regression, that is, as a factor which resists any refusal on the part of reason regarding the profundity of revealed Mystery.

The custody of the message and the freedom of the question do not cancel each other out, but instead meet each other. We are not talking about imposing limits on philosophy: if philosophy is understood as the exercise of radical questioning, philosophy cannot but recognise its own limits, which constitute the reason why it questions in the first place. If the highest task of reason is to understand reason, then reason cannot but recognise that it is limited by its own incapacity to give a reason for everything, especially for the ultimate mystery of existence. The fundamental philosophical question, 'Why is there something and not nothing?', a question which has turned up again and again, even within great contemporary philosophy, coincides with the radical impossibility of giving a reason why everything exists. Thus, one can say that philosophy is only really philosophical when it recognises rather than denies its true limit. In this encyclical, and indeed throughout his entire magisterium, the Pope reminds us that revelation is the gift by which God helps reason to open up to that which lies beyond the inherent limit it has already recognised. At the threshold of 'the wonder of Being', acknowledging the paradox of existence, and unable to find an explanation for existence in reason alone, reason disposes itself to listen for an Other, to hear His speech in words and in events. This does not make reason any the less reason, but rather renders it more thoughtful. Faith in revelation is not a competitor of reason. Instead, it is what stimulates reason towards transcendence, nurturing and strengthening it, opening it up to horizons that would otherwise remain unknown and impenetrable to it.

It is here that the history of Western philosophy, even in the modern era, affirms the fecundity of the encounter that is possible between faith and reason. How much light has the Christian revelation shed on human beings to make them more intense searchers, opening them up to horizons that alone can truly answer their thirst for meaning and their nostalgia for peace! God is not in competition with man: He is man's friend. He is the Creator that came down and drew near to us in order to draw us closer to him, in a Covenant that is celebrated fully in the person of the Redeemer. This encounter, fulfilled in Christ, is the true reason for Christ's absolute singularity in the salvation of the world, and of it John Paul II has been called to act as the herald through his entire itinerary as thinker and pastor. He has entrusted this task to the Church through the encyclical *Fides et Ratio*. It is precisely for this reason that the encyclical should be taken as the concisest possible compendium of all the fundamental themes which this Pope, who came from the East, has desired to announce, and has announced, to the Church, to the world, for the glory of God and the salvation of human beings. *Fides et Ratio* is the interpretative key to his encyclicals and embodies wholly the entire message of his teaching and of his life.

Notes

1. John Paul II, Encyclical Letter *Fides et Ratio,* Preface (Dublin: Veritas Publications, 1998), p. 3. (Referred to below as *F&R*).
2. Max Horkheimer and Theodor W. Adorno, *Dialectics of Enlightenment* (NY, 1969), p.3
3. St John of the Cross, *Flama de Amor Vivo,* translated: *The Living Flame of Love'.* 3rd Stanza; 'O Lamps of fire! / In whose splendours / The deep caverns of feeling, / Once obscured and blind, / Now give forth, so rarely, so exquisitely, / Both warmth and light to their Beloved.' Trans. by Kieran Kavanagh, *The Collected Works of St. John of the Cross* (London: Nelson, 1966), p. 579.
4. P. Evdokimov, *La Donna e la Salvezza del Mondo* (Milano: Jaca Book, 1980), p. 13.
5. St. Augustine, *De Praedestinatione Sanctorum,* 2,5:PL 44, 963.
6. *F&R,* p. 79.
7. *F&R,* p. 83.
8. E. Husserl, *Ideen zu einer Reinen Phänomenologie und Phänomenologischen Philosophie,* trans. F. Kersten, *Ideas Pertaining to a Pure Phenomenology and to a Phenomenological Philosophy* (The Hague: Nijhoff, 1982), vol. I, 24. p.44.
9. Thomas Aquinas, *Summa Theologiae* I q. 8 a. 1 c.
10. *F&R,* p. 56: 'Faith thus becomes the convinced and convincing advocate of reason'.
11. The word 'truth' appears 208 times in the text of the encyclical.
12. *F&R,* pp. 110, 76.

FAITH AND REASON: DIATRIBE OR DIALOGUE? A REFLECTION ON *FIDES ET RATIO*

Cahal B. Daly

Pope John Paul's latest encyclical, *Fides et Ratio* (*F&R*), 'Faith and Reason', opens on an almost lyrical note:

> Faith and reason are like two wings on which the human spirit rises to the contemplation of truth.

This is the thirteenth encyclical of the present pontificate, and it is the work not only of a pastor, committed to living and proclaiming the truth of God in love, but also of a philosopher. The Pope is a philosopher in his own right, one who studied Husserl and Scheler and other modern philosophers in the phenomenological school, and who is also steeped in the great philosophical tradition extending from Plato and Aristotle through Augustine and Thomas Aquinas to modern philosophers, among whom he names Maritain, Gilson and Edith Stein.

The Pope's mention in this document of Edith Stein, or St Teresa Benedicta of the Cross, is significant, because Karol Wojtyla followed a philosophical route similar to that of Edith. She was the favourite disciple of Edmund Husserl and could have had a distinguished academic career in philosophy in Germany but for the discrimination

against women in the German university system until after the second
World War, and also the persecution of Jews under Hitler, which led
eventually to her martyr's death. She had owed her conversion, under
God, to the reading of the autobiography of St Teresa of Avila; after
reading the whole of the 'Life' at one sitting during one entire night,
she put the book down, saying: 'That is the truth'. Edith later turned
her attention to St Thomas Aquinas, whose great but less well known
De Veritate she translated into German.

After his studies in philosophy, Karol Wojtyla did his doctoral
thesis in theology on St John of the Cross. The future Pope was a lifelong admirer of St Thomas Aquinas, whom in this encyclical he calls
'a master of thought and a model of the right way to do theology' (#
66), and 'an authentic model for all who seek the truth' (# 114). Pope
John Paul II, therefore, came to phenomenology by way of Aquinas,
while Edith Stein came to Aquinas by way of Husserl's
phenomenology. Both were devotees of St John of the Cross and of
Carmelite spirituality.

Quite apart from his authority as inheritor of St Peter's role and
responsibility in the Church, Pope John Paul is a thinker of great
stature and originality, deep reflection and wide-ranging culture. If he
were not Pope, he would still be one of the great theologians and
philosophers of our time. In his many writings and addresses, both
before he became Pope and since, he has made important
contributions to theology and to philosophy. He will certainly rank
among the great Popes of all time. In *F&R* there is a sureness of touch
that points to a writer at home in a domain that through a life of
reading and reflection he has made his own.

F&R can be called the third part of a trilogy, of which the two
earlier parts were *Veritatis splendor*, 'The Splendour of Truth' (1993),
on 'certain fundamental questions of the Church's moral teaching',
and *Evangelium vitae*, 'The Gospel of Life' (1995), on 'the value and
inviolability of human life'. While *Veritatis splendor* and *Evangelium
vitae* deal with what the Pope calls the contemporary crisis in moral
philosophy and moral theology, *F&R* addresses what he identifies as

the crisis of truth and of meaning in modern philosophy and in modern culture generally. The latest document, therefore, deals with the deeper and wider problems of which the problems of moral and ethical truth are part. The three texts form a coherent whole, in which each part sheds light on the others. The questions dealt with in the three encyclicals are as follows:

> Who am I? Where have I come from and where am I going? Why is there evil? What is there after this life? (*F&R*, # 1). What must I do? How do I distinguish good from evil? (*Veritatis splendor*, # 4) What is man? What is the worth of the human person? (cf. *Evangelium vitae*, # 2)'

One of Pope John Paul's themes is that of the recurrence of the same fundamental questions across the whole history of philosophy, and the consistency of the answers given to these questions by the thinkers of the 'great tradition' that spans the centuries and the cultures of humanity. He speaks of the 'implicit philosophy' of humanity and of the universality of basic truths and values agreed across the ages and the empires and republics of history. It is interesting in this connection to compare the questions that the Pope is asking with those that set Immanuel Kant off on his quest for truth in science, philosophy and morals. Kant's questions were:

> What can I know?
> What must I do?
> What can I hope for?

Importance of Philosophy

F&R is a sustained affirmation of the importance of philosophy in finding responses to the questions of today's world, in confronting the contemporary crises of truth and meaning, and in engaging in the necessary dialogue between Christianity and modern non-Christian systems of belief and unbelief, and also in responding to the questions and challenges posed to human reason by divine revelation itself. The encyclical is overwhelmingly positive in its intent. It is not a list of errors to be condemned, but a call for philosophical reflection and research as a basic medium in mankind's search for truth and as a necessary aid for the believer and the theologian in exploring the meaning and intelligibility of the content of the truth revealed by God in Jesus Christ. It is a call to move beyond diatribe to mutually beneficial dialogue.

The encyclical returns again and again to the two-fold affirmation; firstly, that truth is ultimately one and that truth cannot contradict truth (something already declared by the First Vatican Council), and secondly, that all truth has its source in God. The Pope quotes the striking sentence of St Thomas Aquinas that 'every truth, by whomsoever it is spoken, comes from the Holy Spirit.' This wonderful act of trust in the universality and timelessness of truth is found in Christian writing since the earliest times. We find it more than fifty years ago in G.K. Chesterton, especially in books like *Orthodoxy* (1908) and *The Everlasting Man* (1925); or in C.S. Lewis, in many of his writings – we need only cite his 1943 Riddell Lectures, published as *The Abolition of Man* (1944). In the second Christian century, St Justin the Martyr pointed to analogies between ancient Greek thought and the truths of the Christian faith, and claimed that all truth had God for its author: 'Whatever was truly said by any person anywhere' he declared, 'is the property of us Christians' (*Apologia II* 13). This might be held by some to be an early exercise in Christian arrogance and triumphalism; instead, it is an early assertion of the position from which Christianity has never wavered, namely that all truth is ultimately one, that truth cannot contradict truth, that faith cannot contradict reason, though it transcends it, nor right reason contradict faith, and that all human truth finds its home and its completion in the plenitude of the truth revealed by God in Jesus Christ. St Justin's was not a universally held view in the earliest days of the Church. There were those who, like Tertullian, would have exclaimed: 'What is there is in common between Athens and Jerusalem?' This however was a minority view, reflecting the beginning of Tertullian's descent into fundamentalism and rigorism. The great Christian tradition agreed with Justin and, of course, Justin's thought was only an echo of the Prologue of St John's Gospel:

> The Word was the true light
> that enlightens all men and women
> coming into this world (*John* 1:9)

This conviction of the existence of universal truths, accessible to all men and women of good will, and of basic truths shared by thinkers of all traditions, leads the Pope to exhort teachers and students of philosophy to 'develop their thought in organic continuity with the great tradition', which runs from the Greeks through the ancient Christian writers and the great medieval masters, and includes 'the fundamental achievements of modern and contemporary thought' (# 85). The Pope emphasises the autonomy of philosophy, insisting that faith and Christian teaching do not infringe on this autonomy but rather reinforce it. He stresses that philosophy cannot be of service to theology or to faith unless it is faithful to its own principles and methods. If and when philosophy conflicts with divine revelation, it is bad philosophy and should be corrected from within the resources of philosophy itself.

Openness to the Transcendent

On the other hand, revelation and theology free philosophy from restrictions wrongly placed upon human reason by false philosophical preconceptions. Again and again the Pope deplores the excessive modesty of much of contemporary philosophy and its reluctance to address ultimate questions. This is particularly found in doctrinaire atheism, which rejects *a priori* the possibility of metaphysics and the capacity of human reason to know anything beyond empirical data and the material world. Positivism in its various forms claimed to have demonstrated that metaphysics is not just impossible, but is literally nonsense. A.J. Ayer's *Language, Truth and Logic* was the most brash and self-confident assertion of this view in English in modern times, and this book featured on best-sellers' lists in the non-fiction category in the 1940s and the 1950s. Language about God, in this view, is merely an expression of subjective attitude, personal feelings and individual wish, or wish-fulfillment. To the neo-Darwinian, Richard Dawkins, is attributed the remark that religion is a form of mental illness. For such thinkers, religion has and, of its nature, can have, no factual content and no objective reference.

Apart from the fact that an *a priori* rejection of metaphysics is itself a metaphysical statement and can by its own presuppositions be only an expression of subjective feelings, Ayer's conclusions have been systematically and comprehensively disproved. Ayer himself in later life referred to this book as the work of a brash and an angry young man, even pronouncing it to be quite simply false. Nevertheless, as often happens, the conclusions of a book or a system of philosophy can continue to be influential factors or *idées-force* in generalised culture long after its arguments have been refuted. A kind of diffused positivism or vague agnosticism is a pervading presence in modern culture. It is reinforced by the dominant place of science in modern society, and by the tendency to regard science as the norm of all knowledge and truth.

Pope John Paul uses the term 'scientism' to describe a resultant trend in modern thought that in principle 'refuses to admit the validity of forms of knowledge other than those of the positive sciences' (#85). Thus, questions about the ultimate meaning of human life, about human origins and destiny, about God and the afterlife, and about moral truths, are held to be unanswerable, and perhaps even nonsensical. This can lead to a form of nihilism that 'is at once the denial of all foundations and the negation of all objective truth' (#90). Inevitably, this leads to a rejection of the notion of the sacredness of human life and of the absoluteness and universality of moral values. In a telling phrase, the Pope concludes that such trends in modern culture can lead 'little by little either to a destructive will to power or to a solitude without hope' (#90).

Relativism

Another thought-pattern that has found its way from contemporary philosophy into the mainstream of popular culture, or into what the Germans call the *Zeitgeist*, the spirit of the age, is relativism. It is widely assumed that truth is relative to the time and culture in which it is believed, relative to the community or group by whom it is believed, relative to the person who believes it or to the context in which it is uttered, but does not have universal validity. The attention paid in some forms of moral philosophy to the emotive as distinct from the descriptive use of language conduces to the view that religious or theological statements, or moral or ethical statements, are expressions of feeling or attitude, 'pro' attitudes or 'anti' attitudes, towards certain statements or towards certain actions, but are not descriptions of anything that is or could be objectively real or true, or could have reference to 'how the world is'. Judgements about right or wrong are simply expressions of emotion, and are in no way factual. Moral argument thus becomes a 'dialogue of the deaf', because what I call 'good' is what I personally like or approve, and what I call 'evil' is what I personally dislike or disapprove, and can have no truth value for those of different emotional orientation, or personality profile, or cultural conditioning. The influence of this thesis, stemming from positivism and a positivistic philosophy of language, is widespread in contemporary debate. It leads to an uncritical and unargued, and almost unconscious, abandonment of the notion of universal and absolute moral truths. Criticism of this trend was one of the principal aims of *Veritatis splendor* and *Evangelium vitae*, and is one of the themes of the present encyclical also. The Pope notes 'a widespread distrust of universal and absolute statements' in any domain (#56); although, one can add, particularly in the domain of moral judgement.

Relativism in Mass Culture

One of the features of our age of mass communications is the development of what we can call a mass culture. This can diffuse itself widely across whole populations' ways of thinking and speaking and become the standard language of communication. Ideas and phrases can break loose from the philosophical propositions and systems of philosophy in which they had their origin and can seep into the mainstream of mass culture. They can continue to influence people's ways of speaking and reacting long after the original propositions may have been refuted and the original system discredited. I deliberately say 'ways of speaking and reacting', and not 'ways of thinking'; because these ideas and phrases are repeated unthinkingly and are not critiqued or challenged. The late Elizabeth Anscombe, the favourite pupil and the literary editor of Wittgenstein, said, 'This is the kind of thing that constantly keeps being said, and the only reason why it is said is because it keeps being said'. Plato stated the business of philosophy as being to 'challenge the hypotheses', or to 'challenge the assumptions' of contemporary culture; he remarked that 'the unexamined life is not worth living'. Plato's dialogues remain to this day a classic reference point for challenging popular assumptions. One of the regrettable aspects of today's mass popular culture is that its assumptions are not being challenged, its preferred and admired life-styles are not being examined. Everything else is challenged on the basis of these contemporary assumptions, but they themselves remain unchallenged. That is one of the reasons why *F&R* is so timely; for this encyclical is in part a call to philosophers, and indeed to people in general, to challenge these assumptions by the criteria of sound and rigorous philosophy.

The Pope touches on several of these unchallenged assumptions. One of the commonest is the claim that moral judgements are relative. Few statements are more common than that a person's moral values are his or her own personal opinions, and that no person has the right to impose his or her values on others. It should be clear that the statement itself is self-contradictory, for the speaker is implicitly assuming that it is *true*, objectively and independently of his personal opinion, that his moral values are relative to and dependent on his own personal opinion. But furthermore, there clearly are many moral values that such speakers do regard as universally and absolutely true: one could list for example the moral evil of genocide and ethnic cleansing, of rape, of domestic violence, of racial intolerance, of discrimination on grounds of gender or race, of child sex abuse, child prostitution, torture, fraud, et cetera. So-called moral relativists are, of course, quite right to regard such moral judgements as I have listed as being universally and absolutely true and binding on all others as well as on themselves; but this is a flat contradiction of their stated principle that moral values are as such personal and not objective or universal or absolute.

It is worth noting that one set of moral values that is particularly held to be personal and private is that which has to do with sexual morality. One of the paramount principles of the prevailing mass culture is that sexual freedom, at least in relationships between 'consenting adults' of either sex, must be vigorously protected from all constraints and restrictions; and it is quite impressive to note to what lengths, under the influence of that culture, society will go to defend and uphold so-called sexual freedom. Contraception and even abortion for school-children, abortion on demand, new definitions of marriage and the family – all these are required in the cause of sexual freedom. One could well call this one of the new dogmas of the post-modernist age. It is paradoxical to see this new 'dogma' dominant in a culture that prides itself on being anti-dogmatic.

Moral Judgement and Tolerance

Another of these diffuse ideas of vaguely philosophical origin is the feeling that moral judgement of the actions of others shows intolerance and lack of compassion. This idea is not universally applied, but there are many areas, particularly the area of sexual morality, where it is held to be axiomatic. The old adage, however, holds good, namely that it is possible and right to condemn sin but to love the sinner. Nobody should be more ready than the Christian to love and forgive the sinner, while condemning the sin. Condemning the sin of another includes the realisation that, if I were to do what that other has done, I would myself be guilty of sin. But this is accompanied by the awareness that I cannot read another's conscience, I cannot know the state of another's mind, the degree of awareness of this action that he or she possessed, the pressure to which he or she was subject. Moral theology and philosophers of the great tradition always held that grave sin required full knowledge and full and free consent, as well as grave matter. If I condemn another's sin, it is always on the assumption that he or she did act with full knowledge and full consent of the will; but this only God can know. As a Christian, I remember the Lord's words: 'Judge not and you will not be judged'. Gabriel Marcel once remarked that these words were the foundation of the metaphysics of the human being. A person should be more concerned to condemn his or her own sins than the sins of others. This truth has never been better expressed than in the parable of the Pharisee and the Publican. But it remains true that moral decline can only accelerate if we refrain from moral judgement and remain silent about moral truth. As the Apostolic Exhortation, *Familiaris Consortio*, reminded us, quoting Pope Paul VI, to proclaim the moral truth 'constitutes an eminent form of charity for souls' (#33); the quotation is from *Humanae Vitae* (#29).

Furthermore, as the Pope points out, moral judgements are based upon the existence of moral truths. People can be convinced by moral reasons and by reasoned argument that what they once held to be right is morally wrong. The very existence of philosophical reasoning about morals presupposes the possibility of universal moral truth. Only belief in the possibility of knowing a universally valid truth can make possible, as the Pope says, 'sincere and authentic dialogue between persons.'

Even the welcome emphasis, in contemporary philosophical and political discussion, on forgiveness in conflict resolution presupposes objective and universal moral truth. If others are not bound by my moral condemnation of murder and terrorist violence, there is nothing to forgive. If the terrorists do not share the victim's moral values they will neither ask for nor accept forgiveness. The Nuremberg trials of Nazi war criminals presupposed an absolute and universal moral code. Explicitly or implicitly the trials were predicated on the existence of a universal natural law, binding on all peoples and transcending all reasons of state or appeal to 'superior orders'.

Human Rights

Universal moral values are the foundation of the existence of universal human rights. Human rights is another area that greatly needs rigorous philosophical scrutiny. Real progress was made in the second decade of the last century in the recognition and legal classification of human rights, and considerable progress also in their practical implementation. The Universal Declaration on Human Rights was one of the greatest achievements of the United Nations Organisation, and celebration of it in 1998, on the fiftieth anniversary of its promulgation, has been well merited. Nevertheless, the international community and national communities remain in a state of great confusion about human rights. Questions about the basis of human rights are difficult to answer in societies that are turning their back on religion, and which lack consensus on moral issues and lack agreement about the very possibility of universal moral truths. Lord Denning declared that 'if religion perishes in the land, truth and justice will also'. Questions about reconciling individual rights with individual and social responsibilities do not find coherent answers in contemporary societies. Questions about harmonising the rights of minorities with the common good are usually avoided as too difficult, and all too often are resolved in terms of political expediency. Philosophical analysis is needed but is very rarely attempted. This is perhaps one of the reasons why debate, in Ireland and elsewhere, on human rights all too often degenerates into reciprocal trading of insults.

No contemporary has made a greater contribution than Pope John Paul II both to the philosophy and theology of human rights and to their advocacy, often in the face of powerful despots and tyrannical regimes. We have only to recall his public statements in Poland, in Cuba and in Nigeria. His teaching and action on human rights are in part inspired by his personalist philosophy, which in turn has traces of the influence of philosophers like Husserl, Scheler, Paul Ricoeur and Emmanuel Levinas, all of whom he has studied. But it owes much more to Christian revelation. Pope John Paul's anthropology is God-oriented and Christ-centred. It rests on the truth that the human being is created in the image of God and is re-made in the image of Jesus Christ. This is the most solid foundation for man's inviolable dignity as a person and for his inalienable human rights, and it accords profoundly with what philosophy tells us about the uniqueness of the human person.

This teaching of Pope John Paul has deepened and strengthened the whole doctrine of human rights. It is a clear example of how philosophy can assist theology, and how it can itself be enriched by divine revelation and by theology, while retaining its integrity as an autonomous rational discipline.

Connected with confused ideas about moral values is, inevitably, a confused concept of conscience, though this can sometimes be traced back to theological as well as to philosophical aberrations. In the case of conscience, as well as in that of moral values, what is overlooked is that moral judgement, as well as conscience, is a grasp of moral truth. One's own moral experience and the exercise of examining one's own conscience surely convinces one that moral truth is not something that I create, but something that is independent of me, judges me, challenges me, humbles me and often condemns me. The adage that 'conscience makes cowards of us all', is verified in one's own experience.

Much more could be said on all these topics; but what I have said may perhaps offer some indications of the role that philosophy can play in challenging unchallenged assumptions in modern culture. *F&R* calls on philosophers to undertake that task as a matter of urgency.

Theology and Philosophy

Pope John Paul II speaks of the contribution that faith makes to reason and theology to philosophy. He declares that faith pushes reason to its limits, and constantly encourages it to be bold in exploring the mysteries within the created world, and especially within the human being, which point to the great mystery beyond the limits of reason. He points to the new concepts, hitherto undiscovered by reason, which divine revelation brought within the ambit of philosophy, such as: the concepts of a free and personal God; of the creation of the world in freedom and love by God; of sin; the notion of the human person as a spiritual being, made in God's image; the conviction of the absolute sacredness of human life and the absolute moral wrongness of murder and suicide; the recognition of the inviolable dignity of the human person. These are the truths that are the foundation of human dignity, equality and freedom. They are Christianity's great legacy to liberal and democratic societies. They are the unacknowledged foundation of the American Declaration of Independence and of the democratic principles formulated by the first Dáil Éireann. Paradoxically, the truth of many of these principles was presupposed by the French Revolution. They underpin much of the Common Law of Britain and of Ireland. Right reason could in principle have discovered these truths, but in fact very rarely did so; but, once they are revealed, they become part, not just of philosophy, but of the civilised heritage of mankind. The Pope also stresses the support that philosophy can give to theology and even to faith, in exploring divinely revealed truths more deeply, in showing their interconnectedness, and in developing a higher synthesis or synergy between revealed truth and rational knowledge.

Dialogue with Modern Culture

Pope John Paul speaks of 'postmodernism'. This, he says, is a name given by some commentators to an age in which, they claim, the time of certainties is irrevocably past, and the human being must now learn to live in a horizon of total absence of meaning, where everything is provisional and ephemeral (#91).

The Pope calls, however, for dialogue with this modern culture, and even with philosophical thinkers who deny the existence of God or the possibility of divine revelation; even in these, he says, 'there can be found precious and seminal insights'. He says that even philosophy completely independent of the Gospel's revelation is 'always open – at least implicitly – to the supernatural' (#75).

There is an urgent need at this time, and specifically in our country, for this kind of dialogue with modern culture. The Pope stressed the importance of philosophy as 'often the only ground for understanding and dialogue with those who do not share our faith'. He goes on to say:

> Such a ground for understanding and dialogue is all the more vital nowadays since the most pressing issues facing humanity – ecology, peace and the coexistence of different races and cultures, for instance – may possibly find a solution if there is clear and honest collaboration between Christians and the followers of other religions and all those who, while not sharing a religious belief, have at heart the renewal of humanity (#104).

He quotes the Second Vatican Council, which called for this dialogue, even with those who 'are hostile to the Church and persecute her in various ways' (#148).

Dialogue between Christians and atheists or humanists, however, has too often been aimed at polemical refutation rather than reciprocal understanding – aimed at 'putting down' the other, rather than listening to the other, consisting sometimes in verbal abuse of the other rather than alertness to the truth of the other. This is not the kind of dialogue called for by Pope John Paul.

Pope Paul VI wrote a classic analysis of dialogue as a guide for exchanges between Catholics and unbelievers in modern society. This was in his first encyclical, *Ecclesiam Suam,* published in 1964. As Pope John Paul was to do later, he called for a dialogue of mutual openness to learning from the other, a dialogue of charity. He wrote:

> The Church should enter into dialogue with the world in which it exists and labours. The Church has something to say. The Church has a message to deliver, the Church has a communication to offer. ... Before converting the world, indeed, in order to convert it, we must meet the world and talk to it ... and before speaking it is necessary to listen, not only to a person's voice but to his or her heart. A person must first be understood, and when he or she merits it, agreed with. ... Let us stress what we have in common, rather than what divides us. (## 65, 68, 87, 109)

As examples of the possibility of such a dialogue, and as indications of its potential fruitfulness, I wish to select two modern thinkers and writers. I hope to suggest that they support the Christian claim, reiterated by the popes whom I have quoted, that no truth spoken by any philosopher, no insight of any creative writer, no experience of the human search for truth and goodness, is alien to Christian experience or untranslatable into Christian terms. When we Christians think, as St Paul enjoined us to think, of 'everything that is true, everything that is noble, everything that is good and pure, everything that we love and honour, and everything that can be thought virtuous and worthy of praise' (Philippians 4:8), we are thinking with people of good will everywhere. It is a remarkable feature of Christianity that it can accommodate into itself all that is positive and good and true in other religions and philosophical traditions without betraying its own integrity. The classical dramatist Terence wrote: 'I am human, and I regard nothing that is human as alien to me'. The Christian can say: 'I am a Christian and I count nothing that is true and good in other traditions as alien to me.'

To illustrate this theme I choose two unbelievers, Albert Camus and Samuel Beckett. Camus remained to the end a convinced atheist, but he could perhaps be said to belong to the more humanist side of the atheist spectrum. He certainly was what Pope John Paul calls a 'searcher for truth', always ready to follow wherever truth might lead. Beckett was a non-believer too, but never a militant or crusading atheist, never a cynical one, but always ready to smile at the follies and foibles of the human predicament. Beckett's writings frequently contain religious and biblical allusions.

Albert Camus

Perhaps Albert Camus's most famous, and certainly his most frequently quoted, saying is the opening sentence of his book, *Le Mythe de Sisyphye* (Paris, 1942):

> There is only one really serious philosophical problem: and it is the problem of suicide. To judge whether life is or is not worth living is to respond to the fundamental question of philosophy.

Le Mythe de Sisyphe has been called 'the breviary of an unbeliever'. In it Camus concludes that life does not make sense. However, it is the human being alone who asks that life should make sense, and he can ultimately live in the world only by confronting its absurdity with 'clear-sighted indifference', accepting all the consequences of its tragic nature, and living it defiantly in spite of its senselessness. This is a dramatic way, enhanced by splendid Camusian rhetoric, of suggesting that suicide is an inauthentic choice. Camus' own answer to his opening question is that, at a certain level, life is not 'worth living', but that the true response to this conclusion is to live heroically in permanent revolt against the brute senselessness of life. Revolt, he says, is 'one of the only coherent philosophical positions'. One 'lives better' by living with meaninglessness, without illusions, without hope, without consolation; but also without submission, without complicity and without resignation. Suicide, by contrast, is capitulation to absurdity and resignation to senselessness, not conquest of it.

Camus, however, moved beyond the positions of *Le Mythe de Sisyphe* and of *L'Homme Révolté*. In the latter book already he wrote that 'the individual acquires and increases his meaning in moving towards ... renouncement of self for the benefit of others'. This intimation of meaning and value was accentuated by his involvement in the French Resistance against Nazi occupation. This became a watershed in his life. Some men whom he admired as persons of high moral integrity were executed by the SS. Camus felt that more than verbal indignation was called for and that moral protest must take the form also of militant protest. He did not cease to be a man of reflection, and he saw that the human being does not merely demand meaning in life, but also is a source of moral value; and that this gives human life a value that transcends, and somehow transforms, its meaninglessness.

In his remarkable *Lettres à un ami allemand* (the 'German friend' is fictional), he rejects the moral nihilism implicit in his earlier writing. He says that 'something in the world has meaning, and that is the human being'. He says:

> This world has no other reasons except the human being, and it is the human being which we must save if one wishes to save one's idea of life.

As if conscious of being accused of 'softening' his earlier views, Camus goes on:

> You will ask me: 'What does it mean to save man?'; but I cry out to you with my whole being: it means not to mutilate him, to give him some opportunities for the justice of which man and man alone has the conception.

There is a definite movement here towards the objective reality of moral value. There is even a sense of universal moral values. There emerges a demand for love and respect for human life and human dignity. There is a sense of human solidarity. There is a readiness to forgive. To the 'German friend', in his fourth letter, Camus says:

> In spite of you, I want to call you a brother. To be faithful to our own faith (in humanity) we want to respect in you what you do not respect in others. ... In spite of our mutilated dead and our villages of orphans ... we remain without hatred towards you. We want to destroy your power, but without mutilating you in your soul.

In a lecture delivered in Paris in 1944, Camus declared:

> The most difficult victory which we have to win over the enemy is a victory over ourselves; it consists in this still greater struggle to transform our desire for hatred into a desire for justice. ... The enemy is still the brother enemy. We must denounce his crimes but we cannot either hate him or despise him.

There is no need to say how Christian these words are, though spoken by an avowed unbeliever. Nor is there need to point out the relevance for our situation in Northern Ireland of these words, spoken in Paris in the midst of war and cruelty and holocaust.

We are a considerable way here from the total absence of meaning or of hope in *Le Mythe de Sisyphe*. Camus has rediscovered moral absolutes in his more profound reflection on the transcendent within the human being; and now he can live with hope in human dignity and human solidarity, and in the ultimate triumph of justice. Indeed one could interestingly set statements of Camus in parallel with statements of Pope John Paul II on issues of universal human rights and human dignity.

Camus's philosophical evolution owed something to dialogue with Catholic philosophers and theologians, and, paradoxically, to a rather bitter controversy that he had with François Mauriac. Camus believed in the value and the necessity of dialogue. In a talk that he gave in 1948 at the Dominican Monastery at Latour-Maubourg in Paris, he said:

> The world needs real dialogue; falsehood is just as much the opposite of dialogue as is silence, and the only possible dialogue is between people who remain what they are and speak their minds. This is tantamount to saying that the world of today needs Christians who remain Christians. The other day at the Sorbonne, speaking to a Marxist lecturer, a Catholic priest said in public that he too was anti-clerical. Well, I don't like priests who are anti-clerical any more than philosophers that are ashamed of themselves.

Samuel Beckett

Samuel Beckett certainly did not write *Waiting for Godot* in order to explore the great metaphysical themes of human origins and destiny and the search for the transcendent. He may well have intended instead to show human beings as condemned to futility, but vainly endeavouring to console themselves by the illusion of waiting for some divine intervention to bring meaning into their lives and salvation into their condition. There is nevertheless a Christian reading or viewing of *Waiting for Godot*. The Christian can find in it echoes of St Augustine's famous restlessness: 'You have made us for Yourself, O God, and our hearts are restless until they rest in Thee'. The Christian finds, in Pozzo's words, echoes of the tragedy of life and of death without God: 'They give birth astride of a grave, the light gleams an instant, then it's night once more'; or in Vladimir's words: 'Astride of a grave and a difficult birth. Down in the hole, lingeringly, the grave-digger puts on the forceps. We have time to grow old. The air is full of our cries'. 'Living we Die' seems to be the cry of the walking dead in Beckett's play, where the birth canal and the grave become one. This, in striking contrast, was the name given to a collection of testimonies of faith in life with God, beyond the grave or beyond the Nazi crematoria, by Christians in Nazi death camps, namely, *Dying we Live* (ed. by Helmut Gollwitzer *et al*, Fontana Books, 1958)

But this is not all that Beckett has to say about the human condition. In another of his works, entitled *The Lost Ones*, Beckett spoke of the human being's inescapable urge and need to climb, to search for the 'way out' towards the light. He knows that 'all has not been told and never shall be', yet he knows that to abandon the climb and the search is to cease to be human. 'The need to climb,' he said, 'is subject to strange resurrections'. And so, as long as the human race endures, there is what he calls 'this little people of searchers'. Beckett's view has overtones of the myth of Sisyphus, a story from Greek mythology about a person doomed forever to push a heavy boulder laboriously to the top of a steep mountain only to find, each time he reaches the summit, that the boulder slips out of his hands and rolls down the mountainside again. Beckett remains in a state of austere and steadfast hopelessness about arrival at final Truth, but remains resolutely convinced that the search itself is a part of the human condition.

The Christian belongs to this 'little people of searchers'. How unexpectedly similar the phrase is to Our Lord's words about the *pusillus grex*, the 'little flock': 'Fear not, little flock, for it has pleased your Father to give you a Kingdom' (Luke 12:32). The Christian knows that Jesus Christ is the Word, and all that is true and good in all the world's philosophies and traditions and cultures comes from Him and can point the way back to Him. The Christian believes that this Word is God's final revelation to the world of the mystery of His own eternal being and of His infinite truth, and that nothing more remains to be said or to be known than Jesus Christ, to know whom is to have eternal life. But the Christian knows also that not all has yet been told, or ever in this world shall be told about the truth contained in that one Word. The Christian knows that the one who has found must still search, the one who has arrived must still climb.

That great Christian gentleman, bishop and scholar, the late Archbishop George Otto Simms, would not have disowned fellowship with the same fraternity of searchers as Samuel Beckett. In a Response to Bishop Donal Murray's Bedell – Boyle lecture, held under the auspices of the National Bible Society of Ireland, in 1991, Archbishop Simms spoke of 'the human search for truth, and the hope that keeps us alive and active'. He spoke of 'the hiddenness of God as well as the revelation of God in the Scripture'. He said:

> There is a story that runs like a thread through the Bible: the theme of seeking and finding.

He found this theme in the Greek and New Testament word for truth, '*aletheia*': meaning something hidden that is now revealed. He saw this word as, more profoundly, meaning something hidden that cannot be left hidden but must be brought into the open. The truth of God, the word *aletheia* hints, will out.

Beckett's 'lost ones' are for the Christian the 'found ones', the ones who, through no merit of their own, have been sought and found by the God of Truth and Love. Archbishop Simms quoted St Augustine's prayer:

> Help us, Lord, so to seek you whom our souls desire to love, that we might both find you and be found by you.

St Augustine elsewhere said:

> [God] lifted me up high enough to see that there was something to see, but that I was not yet fit to see it.

People who are sincerely searching for truth, even when we radically disagree with them, are our friends and allies, not our enemies. Their search for truth can inspire and help our own search for deeper understanding of the Truth, which has been revealed to us in Jesus Christ, but of which we are so unworthy and to whose challenge we respond so hesitantly and so lukewarmly. Faith and grace, transcending, but never conflicting with, the truth of reason, can make us fit to see the face of Him who is Truth in Person.

FIDES ET RATIO: CHARTER FOR THE THIRD MILLENNIUM

Brendan Purcell

Let me begin with a few introductory remarks on the cultural context for *Fides et Ratio* (*F&R*) before developing what I think are two central aspects of the encyclical.

It is obvious that *F&R* addresses the crisis of contemporary Western culture, a crisis marked by a yawning emptiness that still idolises individual reason and individual autonomy. It's a disillusioned, deconstructed culture, where many, 'distracted from distraction by distraction',[1] get lost in various *divertissements* to kill the time.

But that's not all there is to it. Alongside this loss of confidence in autonomy, whether of the individual, of science, of legal and political rights, even of art, there's also the excitement of the widening of horizons in space and time, with the result that now we're able to be in contact with every contemporary culture, along with all those in human history back to the paleolithic, some 50,000 years ago.

And both of these factors – (i) the consciousness that we belong to a world-wide civilization of reason that has lost the plot, and (ii) that there's the possibility and challenge of growing enormously if we can find a way to re-awaken the common humanity we feel we share with people of every other background, culture, and religion, or moral conviction – are part of the cultural background to *F&R*. Written at the end of the second millennium, with other works of the Pope, it's a proposed intellectual foundation for the third. How? Let's go back to the beginnings of the first and the second Christian millennia.

The Incarnation of the Word, who founded the Church, and the struggle to enter into the public life of humanity, marked the first millennium of Christ. If the Roman Empire was an imperial husk without spiritual substance, for that very reason huge numbers of its members welcomed Christianity as providing that substance. Of course Christianity aimed at more than the mere temporary stabilisation of a world empire. It was aiming at a transformation of our life in time by focusing on our life beyond time. In what Eric Voegelin sees as the basis for a theology of history, this focus was expressed in Augustine's phrase, '*Incipit exire qui incipit amare*': 'he begins to leave [the City of Man], who begins to love' (which is the passport to the City of God).[2]

Early in the second millennium, mystic philosophers and theologians like Anselm, Thomas and Bonaventure, among others, developed an intellectual synthesis of nature and grace, of reason and faith, of created and uncreated being. Aquinas differentiated the activity of human reason from that of a reason enlightened by revelation. In the context of his *History of Political Ideas*, Voegelin remarks:

> It is no exaggeration to say that the authority of Thomas and his superb personal skill in achieving the harmonization [between the spheres of reason and of faith] for his time have decisively influenced the fate of scholarship in the Western world. He has shown in practice that philosophy can function in the Christian system and that revealed truth is compatible with philosophy; and he has formulated the metaphysical principle that gives philosophy its legitimate status in Christianity.[3]

That philosophical and theological synthesis entered into the intellectual fabric of what we know as Christendom, extending into the high Middle Ages.

At the threshold of the third millennium, I would suggest that *F&R* is the intellectual expression of John Paul II's attempt to mark out a path towards a new, spiritually grounded, world-wide civilisation. He is doing this at a time of even greater need, and also of more fully universal challenge, than existed at the beginning of either the first or the second millennium. Already in the prophetic sign of the 1986 Assisi World Day of Prayer for Peace he convoked leaders of all faiths. That convocation indicated how he saw this new era of dialogue between representatives of most of the world's religions. As George Weigel remarks, this event 'was the most visible expression of John Paul's conviction that all truth is related to the one Truth, who is God.'[4]

There has been a precedent for *F&R*. Weigel, in his biography of John Paul II, notes that *F&R*

> was the first major statement on the relationship between faith and reason in almost 120 years. The First Vatican Council had taught in 1869–1870 that human beings could know the existence of God through reason, and Leo XIII's encyclical, *Aeterni Patris*, had proposed the philosophy and theology of Thomas Aquinas as the model for a synthesis of faith and reason. But much had happened in world civilization since the late nineteenth century – not least, philosophy's drastically diminished confidence in its capacity to know the truth of things.[5]

Rino Fisichella has suggested that *F&R* (on the truth of human existence) and *Veritatis Splendor* (on the moral life to be led in imitation of Christ) are the two side-panels of a triptych, with *Redemptor Hominis* – where the icon of Christ has been painted – at the centre.[6] In a talk on the encyclical he gave in California, Cardinal Ratzinger quoted C.S. Lewis' *The Screwtape Letters*, where Screwtape pointed out to the junior demon how educated people can become anaesthetised from the truth by 'the historical point of view':

The historical point of view, put briefly, means that when a learned man is presented with any statement in an ancient author, the one question he never asks is whether it is true. He asks who influenced the ancient writer, and how far the statement is consistent with what he said in other books and what phase in the writer's development or in the general history of thought it illustrates ...[7]

In comments he made at the presentation of *F&R* Cardinal Ratzinger pointed out that the central matter of the encyclical is 'the question of truth ... the basic question ... which spans all eras and seasons of life and of the history of humanity.' And the Pope, in a homily on the Sunday after *F&R* was presented, said: 'Woe to humanity which loses the sense of truth, the courage to seek it, and the trust to find it. Not only faith would be compromised by this, but also the very meaning of life.'

In *F&R*, it seems to me that the theme of Christ as Truth for all of humanity is developed more than in any previous Church document. John Paul II noted in his Apostolic Letter, *Tertio Millennio Adveniente* that 'In Jesus Christ, the Word made flesh, time becomes a dimension of God, who is himself eternal.' (# 10) *F&R* will help us appreciate better how the third millennium of Christ too can become 'a dimension of God', a deeper expansion of the Incarnation into the history of universal humanity at this moment of apparent tragic emptiness and exciting challenge.

What I'd like to focus on now are two of the principal themes of the encyclical: firstly, the need to bring together faith and reason, the defining and ongoing dialogue between Jerusalem and Athens; secondly, the reaching out to every cultural matrix throughout the world as an expansion of that first cultural dialogue. Could we draw those two strands together – firstly, that of faith and reason, and secondly, that of reaching out in dialogue with the entire human family – so that we have a single Christian perspective on the problems, a perspective that could also be appreciated by our billions of brothers and sisters on earth motivated by the same quest for truth as we are, without sharing our faith? Perhaps – if we read *F&R* in terms of the kind of *kenotic* and *trinitarian hermeneutic* developed in the spiritual writings of Chiara Lubich, or theologically by, among others, Piero Coda.[8]

A Christological Context for the Dialogue between Faith and Reason

How can a Christian unite faith and reason? The opening words of *F&R* – which have become those most quoted – already suggest an answer:

> Faith and reason are like two wings on which the human spirit rises to the contemplation of truth; and God has placed in the human heart a desire to know the truth – in a word, to know himself – so that, by knowing and loving God, men and women may also come to the fullness of truth about themselves.

The encyclical is saying with unparalleled emphasis that what our culture needs is not faith alone, not reason alone, in the separation that has marked and marred modern culture, but a re-integration of both. One way of understanding philosophy (which stands for the 'reason' aspect of our existence) is as *man's search for God*. And, drawing on a famous title by Heschel, we can see revelation as an expression of *God's search for man*.[9] So the task of integrating reason and faith may be understood in terms of the intersection of these two quests.

The first search, of man for God, can be seen at its most profound and most anguished, in Christ. Because, if we try to understand the Why of the Incarnate Word at the moment of his most extreme suffering on earth, when he cried out to the Father, 'My God, my God, why have you forsaken me?', we are perhaps touching at its fullest the quest for truth hidden in the heart of each human being. In the darkest of dark nights, more than a Nietzsche or a Sartre, Jesus experienced the anguish of a Why? without an ultimate answer – an anguish that characterises what elsewhere the Pope has spoken of as the collective dark night of Western culture.

What of the second search? *F&R* explicitly refers to the *kenosis* of God in #93. Because he is Incarnate Word, Jesus is also, in his mission as Second Person of the Trinity, God in search of each human being. And that search involves what poor human words have expressed as the dark night of God, in which the Divine Word, plunging towards the abyss of human weakness, in some fashion appears to 'lose' his own divinity.

Of course, since there is only the one Person, divine and human, we can say that in Jesus, both quests, of man for God, and of God for man, coincide.[10] And that is perhaps the most profound basis for the unity and complementarity of faith and reason, revelation and philosophy, and the ground for the successful interaction and expansion of both quests. For us, reliving by grace those two Whys of Jesus, the task is to ensure that the civilisation of reason (and the twentieth century showed amply the unlimited cruelty of reason without mercy) is grounded in a civilisation of love.

Where can we see these Whys meeting in contemporary culture? David Walsh, in his *The Third Millennium: Reflections on Faith and Reason* (Georgetown University Press, 1999) develops *F&R's* discussion of this necessary intersection of contemporary culture with Christianity. The Dublin-born Professor of Politics at Washington's Catholic University of America takes an unusual, but powerful approach towards the modern world. Essential to its identity are, for example, the importance of science and of human rights. If Stanley Jaki, building on the writings of the great French historian of science, Pierre Duhem, has done most to uncover the medieval Christian origins of modern natural science, authors like Harold Berman and Brian Tierney have pointed to the basis of modern rights theory in the medieval canonists.

For Walsh, the big question is whether what emerges from that medieval past can survive outside a Christian context. Most moderns would answer that with a resounding yes. So that, for most moderns, natural science and legal and political rights not only can exist in a secular world, but their very claim to legitimacy as the basis for a pluralist culture derives from a denial of their Christian parenthood in the past.

Still, as *The Third Millennium* notes, that certainty of autonomy from any religious context is wearing thin for science and rights just now. Science has run into all sorts of problems whenever the various sciences try to go beyond their partial view of reality to speak about the whole. Astronomy and physics are unable to deal with the mystery of creation, biology has its controversies about evolution, neurology runs into the difficulties of consciousness. Because scientists are also human beings, they can't help peering over the boundaries of their sciences, and wondering where what they're studying comes from. But the methods of the natural sciences cannot deal with the bigger question of existence. They have to take for granted the mysterious origin of what they can only deal with as given, as data.

There's a related boundary-problem connected with human rights too. All the legal discussion regarding genetic engineering, the right to be born in a certain way, the right to die – these discussions aren't just the beginning of a 'slippery slope' on the way to who knows what barbaric practice. Rather, they open up an abyss: the abyss of 'creating' something that will have rights of a certain kind. But that's an incoherent use of the language of rights that presupposes human beings, and ultimately makes no sense without them. Human beings are of infinite dignity, and any discourse about human rights flows from that dignity, never the other way round.

In the concluding section of his recent *Guarded by Mystery*,[11] Walsh explores the boundary problem posed by modern artists and their art. Often in their experience of the anguish of the cry without an answer, these artists are far closer to the radical intersection at the heart of the experience of Jesus than they are aware. It's an experience well expressed by Walker Percy:

> If a novelist has a secret, it is not that he has a special something but that he has a special nothing. In this day and age, I think, a serious writer has to be an ex-suicide, a cipher, a nought, zero.

Being a naught is the very condition of making anything. That's the secret. People don't know that writing well is simply a matter of giving up, of surrendering, of letting go. You say, 'All is lost. The jig is up. I surrender. I'll never write another word again. I admit total defeat. I'm washed up.' What I'm telling you is, I don't know anything. It's a question of being so pitiful God takes pity on you, looks down and says, 'He's done for. Let's let him have a couple of good sentences.'[12]

For David Walsh, Christianity has the most unblinking clarity about the world we're in. It's far less likely to think that the various reforms human beings think up to eliminate corruption, crime, family breakdown, will succeed. Not that there shouldn't be developed whatever legal and political safeguards may be possible, just that we shouldn't lose too much sleep over the periodic failures either. The point is that the world only yields finite satisfactions. Christianity points out that our true fulfilment is in unity with God after death, a fulfilment we work towards seriously but serenely in this vale of tears, enduring all its failures as Christ did.

Walsh's conclusion is that Christianity is indispensable not only for our eternal salvation but also for our fulfilment in this life. It's the most viable sustaining influence in modern civilisation, correcting the false absolutes of the latter's understanding of science and human rights. Through the Church, the Christian revelation is the vehicle for divine redemption's entering time and redeeming human civilisation for eternity. Only by means of the continuing presence of the Divine Word in the third millennium of His Incarnation can human history be guaranteed genuine human progress. *The Third Millennium* expands that argument of *F&R* that the faith of Christianity is essential to reason and the culture of our time, if it is to remain fully human. And, I would add, that interplay between human imperfection seeking perfection, and divine perfection reaching out to human imperfection – at its highest in the Incarnate Word – is also the reality which constitutes human history since the Incarnation.

A Trinitarian Context for Dialogue between Christian and all other Cultures

Just after its opening words on faith and reason as the two wings by which the human spirit rises to the contemplation of truth, *F&R* widens out the dialogue to the new cultural context within which the Church finds herself at the dawn of the third millennium. This may be seen, perhaps, as the other major focus of the encyclical:

> In both East and West, we may trace a journey which has led humanity down the centuries to meet and engage truth more and more deeply... Moreover, a cursory glance at ancient history shows clearly how in different parts of the world, with their different cultures, there arise at the same time the fundamental questions which pervade human life: *Who am I? Where have I come from and where am I going? Why is there evil? What is there after this life?* These are the questions which we find in the sacred writings of Israel, as also in the Veda [the foundational Hindu writings] and the Avesta [the Zoroastrian texts]; we find them in the writings of Confucius and Lao-Tze, and in the preaching of Tirthankara [=Jainism] and Buddha; they appear in the poetry of Homer and in the tragedies of Euripides and Sophocles, as they do in the philosophical writings of Plato and Aristotle. They are questions which have their common source in the quest for meaning which has always compelled the human heart. (#1)

The Pope now indicates how the Church both belongs to this common quest of humanity, and has a providential role to play within it:

> The Church is no stranger to this journey of discovery – the Church has made her pilgrim way along the paths of the world to proclaim that Jesus Christ is 'the way, and the truth, and the life.' It is her duty to serve humanity in different ways, but one way in particular imposes a responsibility of a quite special kind: the *diakonia* [service] *of the truth*. (#3)

This second aspect of *F&R* poses the question of the underlying framework required for developing our dialogue, not only with the culture of reason, as it emerged in Greek philosophy and Roman law and politics, but with all the other great cultures of human history. The almost two millennia of dialogue with that Graeco-Roman world, which continues in terms of the dialogue with non-religious secularism, has for the last few centuries required the enormous expansion mentioned in #1 of *F&R*.

The experience of Jesus is rooted in its trinitarian context. We've suggested that the integration of the dialogue between faith and reason can be found at its most profound in Christological anthropology with the intersection of the two Whys? of the Crucified Christ. Now, further, the expansion of that dialogue to universal humanity will be understood at its deepest in terms of a Trinitarian anthropology.

The being of each of the persons of the Trinity is eternal dialogue with the other, a dialogue requiring each to become 'nothing' in order to allow the other to be. So the radical openness of the Gospel to the dialogue with every culture, in which the Church is reconfiguring herself as the sustaining horizon of the postmodern world,[13] is already mirrored for us in the inner life of God, One and Three. That Trinity functions as the model and goal of all our dialogues, as the Russian film director, Andrei Tarkovsky, noted in his commentary on his film, *Andrey Rubleev*. He remarks on the culminating appearance of the painter Rubleev's vision of three mysterious beings who appeared to Abraham, united in an unmoving movement of love in his masterpiece, 'Troitsa':

> At last, here is the 'Trinity', great, serene, penetrated completely by a thrilling joy, the source of human brotherhood. The concrete division of one alone into three and the triple union in one alone opens out a wonderful perspective on the future yet to unfold throughout the ages.[14]

In these dialogues, we'll understand that each of the cultural matrices – whether mythic, philosophic, revelational, or the various forms of secularity from modernity to postmodernity – is enriched by the others, even with the need to be purified by the at times immoderate critique of the others. And we'll understand that unless we're prepared to reach out to the genuine quest for truth underlying the matrices different from, if not necessarily opposed to ours, we will be impoverished by the disappearance of any of them.[15]

The capacity of Christianity for uniting different cultures in a common civilisation has already 'unfolded throughout the ages.' In its first millennium, the experience of the Irish missionaries living, as St Patrick did, in deep communion with the Trinity, and who were able to reach out in love to every other culture as their own, was not an exception. This was how a common Christendom developed that was not a world empire of hollowed-out subject peoples. Even today, the Byzantine and Slavic peoples (Russians, Bulgarians, Czechs, Slovaks, Poles, Serbs and Croats), the Germans, French, Italians, Spanish and Portuguese, the Celtic peoples and the Hungarians, all of them have inherited national cultures, which, if not founded by Christian saints, were at least profoundly renewed and re-invigorated by their moments of historic Christian conversion. Jean Daniélou has well caught the mutual giving and receiving between the Church and the various cultures, when he wrote:

> First ... the Church is not to be identified with any single race, culture or society; just as Christianity, whose original idiom was Aramaic, absorbed in time the culture of the Hellenes and finally the social structure of Rome, so now the Church must grow to be Chinese in China and Indian in India – all things to all men ... But secondly, the Church, in its freedom from any permanent attachment to a particular civilization, derives an imperishable enrichment from each of the cultures with which it is united: and equally – to take a particular example – China can welcome Catholicism, and allow it to take root in Chinese culture, without repudiating the capital value of its existing investment in Latin forms ... The true Church is no more Greek

or Latin than Chinese or Indian. The Church of the future will have passed through all history and incorporated every variety of human civilization, in order to wear that wedding dress, 'a robe of rich embroidery' (Ps. 44,15), for the eternal union with the Bridegroom.[16]

And in this moment of intersection of every culture of humanity, a moment that cannot be filled by mere economic or political or entertainment internationalisms, we can offer as a genuine 'DNA' for a universal humanity, a trinitarian vision and life – but only if, like Jesus, God and man, we make our painful exodus from our own cultures.

It's our task to find a way to share our Christian vision at the full height of *F&R*'s exciting agenda to be the world-culture for a universal humanity, with our non-Christian sisters and brothers, along with those of non-religious convictions. If we do so, then the dynamism and enormous sweep in space and time of trinitarian spirituality will capture not just the imagination, but the heart of younger generations – often longing for a united world – as it captured the hearts of those living in the empty husk of a world-empire without a spiritual substance at the dawn of the first millennium of Christ.

Is it really possible for us to 'lose' ourselves again and again in order to reach out to those of other cultures, particularly those in our own society who have partly or entirely renounced their Christian background? Well, there is one human being who did that so completely that she even won us over! Since the Annunciation, it could be said that she belonged in a special way to the trinitarian culture, with a deep inner relation to the Father, the Holy Spirit, and her Son. Yet, more than anyone, she went 'outside the camp' and shared in her Son's annihilation. By accepting his last request of her, and his own forsakenness, the Desolated One united her will with the Forsaken One, standing by him on the cross. With him, she too underwent a double exodus: by 'losing' being the mother of the Messiah, she lost her human role as Flower of Israel. But also, in consenting to 'lose' her motherhood of God, she shared her Son's awful experience of 'exodus' from the Trinity, and through that loss became Mother of all humanity. So she can help us to live the Why, of human quest intersecting with the Why of divine search, that alone fulfils the human spirit. And, by being ready to lose all that's most human and most divine for the sake of the other, she encourages us to expand our quest to the entire human family. This is why *F&R* concludes with the reminder that we too should *philosophari in Maria*, praying that our journey into wisdom, the 'sure and final goal of all true knowing',

> be freed of every hindrance by the intercession of the one who, in giving birth to the Truth and treasuring it in her heart, has shared it forever with all the world. (#108)

Notes

1. cf. 'Burnt Norton', in T. S. Eliot, *Collected Poems 1909–1962* (London: Faber and Faber, 1980), p. 192.
2. The reference to Augustine's commentary on Psalm 64.2 concludes Eric Voegelin's essay, 'Eternal Being in Time' in his *Anamnesis*, trans. and ed. by Gerhart Niemeyer (Columbia: University of Missouri Press, 1978), p. 140.
3. Eric Voegelin, *History of Political Ideas, vol. II: The Middle Ages to Aquinas*, ed. by Peter von Sivers (Columbia: University of Missiouri Press, 1997), pp. 209-10.
4. George Weigel, *Witness to Hope*, p. 848.
5. George Weigel, *Witness to Hope: The Biography of Pope John Paul II* (New York: HarperCollins, 1999), p. 841.
6. Rino Fisichella, 'Introduzione', *Fides et Ratio: I rapporti tra fede e ragione* (Casale Monferrato: Piemme, 1998), p. 16.
7. Cardinal Joseph Ratzinger, 'Culture and Truth: Reflections on the Encyclical', *Origins*, 28:36 (February 25, 1999), p. 627.
8. cf. Chiara Lubich, *Il Grido* (Rome: Città Nuova, 2000); Piero Coda, *Evento Pasquale: Trinità e Storia* (Rome: Città Nuova, 1984).
9. Abraham Joshua Heschel, *God in Search of Man: A Philosophy of Judaism* (New York: Noonday, 1976).

10. Fisichella reminds us that *Fides et Ratio*'s official date of publication was the Feast of the Exaltation of the Cross, a day which celebrates the great Why of Jesus (*Fides et Ratio: I rapporti*, p. 13)11. David Walsh, *Guarded by Mystery* (Washington DC: Catholic University of America Press, 1998). For a recent discussion of the quest for the divine in some modern artists, see John Golding, *Paths to the Absolute* (London: Thames & Hudson, 2000).

12. Percy Walker, 'Writing in the Ruins', Interview with Robert Cubbage, *Notre Dame Magazine*, Autumn 1987, p. 31.

13. cf. Walsh, *The Third Millennium*, p. 151.

14. Quoted in Olivier Clément, *L'esprit de Soljénistsyne* (Paris: Stock, 1974), p. 299.

15. cf. Chapter 4 of Walsh, *The Third Millennium*.

16. *The Lord of History: Reflections on the Inner Meaning of History* (London: Longmans, 1958), p. 40f.

EPILOGUE: GLEANINGS FROM THE RECEPTION OF *FIDES ET RATIO*

James McEvoy

In the following pages a selection of readers' reactions to *Fides et Ratio* (*F&R*) is reproduced, to illustrate some motifs in the reception of the letter. 'Reception' is used to designate intellectual contact and influence of one author on another, especially the impact of an authority of some kind whose views are 'received' by others and given currency. Most of the quotations have been chosen because they are thoughtful summaries of some theme or other of the encyclical, but the last one has been included deliberately to represent a widespread and influential point of view that raises an objection to it.

We begin with Cardinal Lustiger of Paris, who wrote an appreciation of *F&R* in a collective publication that followed the encyclical swiftly into print. He employs a gospel simile to illustrate the benefit that faith can bring to the human reason, in line with the reflections of the papal letter:

> Like the Good Samaritan of the Gospel, faith is able to become the neighbour of the human reason, not to make the latter the slave of a divine light which would blind it, but in order to heal the reason and restore it to its proper autonomy, in putting it back up on its feet, and on the authentic road on which it can

move forward to truth. By faith, revelation is like the neighbour of reason, holding it back from despair. How many of our contemporaries, whether they acknowledge this or whether they refuse to do so, stop half way on the road .... [1]

André-Mutien Léonard, Bishop of Namur (Belgium), was for many years professor of Metaphysics at the *Université catholique de Louvain*. He published extensively on German idealism and wrote books on Christian faith and contemporary philosophies, and also on the foundations of ethics. Since becoming bishop he has completed a trilogy on the Blessed Trinity, keeping pace with the papal encyclicals on the three Divine Persons that appeared in the three years prior to the Jubilee Year of 2000. In his writings the faith/reason problematic parallels the encyclical quite closely.[2] From his commentary on *F&R* comes the following thought about 'perennial philosophy':

> Philosophical reflection has given rise to systems of thought, each system being the limited expression of an *élan* of thinking which no particular doctrine can claim to enclose within it. Born of this immense effort is, notably, a treasury of questions, of principles, of fundamental theses, of distinctions and concepts, which make up the stock-in-trade of what is sometimes called *philosophia perennis*, that implicit philosophy of people and of cultures which is the eternal philosophy of humanity.[3]

Philosophy has been reduced to a marginal function within education and culture, through taking no longer the whole but the particular as its object:

> In our times philosophy is becoming less and less a wisdom throwing light on the ultimate destiny of man. With some notable exceptions (e.g. Bergson, Maritain, Blondel, Bruaire) it has become a 'marginal' reflection in the etymological meaning

of the word, i.e. a reflection on the margin of the multiple expressions of culture, more and more drowned in the disparate forms of particular rationality which, being prisoners of a narrowly functional and utilitarian conception of truth, end by turning against man himself.[4]

On the Christian philosopher in dialogue the same author writes,

The Christian philosopher as a Christian will be particularly attentive to the extra light which Revelation brings, but as a philosopher he will share with all the "friends of wisdom" an attention to rational argumentation. That will be a terrain favourable to fruitful meetings.[5]

Père Georges Cottier is a Dominican theologian, at present the theological adviser to the Pope ('Theologian of the Pontifical Household', or 'of the Sacred Palace'). For many years a professor of philosophy at Dominican third-level institutions, he has published widely on numerous themes relevant to this encyclical. He underlines thus the positive nature of the challenge that the document throws down to philosophers:

The Pope can only encourage philosophers to have confidence in the capacities of the human reason with regard to that search for the full and ultimate sense of life which was traditionally the object of philosophy.[6]

Leo Scheffczyk, born in Poland but German speaking, is an Emeritus Professor of dogmatic theology of the University of Munich, and the co-author of a multi-volume work of Catholic dogmatic theology. He was made a cardinal in 2001, in acknowledgement of his outstanding contribution to contemporary theology. He has always practised the philosophical development of theological problematics, e.g. on creation and evolution, and he continues to advocate this distinctively Catholic method:

The reproach [of mistrust of reason] refers to the absence of any relation to transcendence on the part of philosophy, and to the sacrifice of metaphysics; [the same reproach] is also conceptualised under the notion of 'forgetfulness of being' (not of course in the way Martin Heidegger means); the latter has as its consequence the loss of contact with the objective truth which lays the foundation for the dignity of man.[7]

A North American Jesuit priest, himself a convert to Catholicism, who was slso made a cardinal in 2001, Avery Dulles (son of the late John Foster Dulles, erstwhile US Secretary of State), has written widely on Catholic apologetics and ecclesiology, as a member of the Faculty of Theology of Fordham University, NY. He makes the following striking analogy:

Faith and reason, as described by John Paul II, are united like the two natures of Christ, which coexisted without confusion or alteration in a single person. Christian wisdom, similarly, involves a synthesis of theology and philosophy, each supporting and benefiting the other ... The entire encyclical is an inspiring summons to the pursuit of a wisdom in which theology and philosophy are harmoniously integrated to the advantage of both and the detriment of neither.[8]

Jorge L.A. Garcia is a Professor of Philosophy at Rutgers University, New Brunswick. He has published widely on ethics, including questions about race, social division and public policy. Regarding the interrelationship of faith and philosophy in the encyclical he comments:

The more interesting passages offer John Paul II's suggestions on how faith can help philosophy remain true to its vocation by remaining on the trail of the answers it seeks and drawing closer to them. The very suggestion that religious faith might actually assist philosophy is shocking to those who see philosophy only as religion's enemy ... As many philosophers today view religious faith with contempt, so many religious people view philosophy with suspicion.[9]

Alasdair MacIntyre is one of the foremost moralists at the present time. One of his books, *After Virtue*, has been widely acclaimed for its re-statement of virtue ethics in the style of Aristotle and Aquinas, and he is a communitarian thinker deeply convinced of the inherent sociability of mankind. A convert to the Catholic Church, he regards the encyclical highly as a contribution to philosophy, in particular because it advocates epistemological realism in the wake of St Thomas:

> *Fides et Ratio* not only is an encyclical about philosophy, as was *Aeterni Patris*, but is also, as *Aeterni Patris* was not, itself a contribution to philosophy, inviting philosophical scrutiny of its arguments and assertions in a way that is rare, perhaps unique, among encyclicals. It does so just because the questions which are central to it are in part philosophical questions and the encyclical insists that in pursuing them 'philosophy must remain faithful to its own principles and methods' (#49).[10]

Jan Ross may seem to be out of place in this selection of voices, for he writes as a correspondent on cultural issues in the German weekly, *Die Zeit*, which is not known for any particularly favourable leaning towards the Church and its message. Covering the encyclical shortly after its appearance Ross summarised his reflections as follows:

> In turning away from the final questions reason has become freer but also narrower, and made itself indifferent, bored with itself, no longer the agency responsible for the life-riddles of good and evil, of death and immortality. The voice of the Pope has lent courage to many people and to whole peoples; it has

also sounded hard and cutting in the ears of many; but if it goes quiet, that will be a moment of terrible silence.

* * *

The letter has been acclaimed in a very widespread way. However, that is not to say that every aspect of it has met with universal approval. In particular, attention will be drawn to a criticism levelled against it by a prominent English philosopher.

Anthony Kenny received his philosophical education at Rome (Gregorian University) and Oxford. A former president of the British Academy, he has received a knighthood for his contributions to philosophy. Although no longer a believing Catholic he has a lively admiration for the philosophical achievements of St Thomas Aquinas, and never tires of reminding the English-speaking philosophical public of the value of the latter's philosophy of mind, in particular.

The Tablet commissioned several authors to review *F&R*, Kenny among them (his article 'The Pope as Philosopher' appeared on 26 June 1999, pp. 874-6). Some of these contributions tended to adopt that recognisably *Tablet* tone regarding Roman publications generally, which consists in taking note, condescending to award some good marks here and there, but giving the overall impression that *The Tablet's* own correspondent could have done a much better job than the anonymous functionaries of the Roman dicasteries, or even the Pope himself. Kenny naturally avoids any such tone, placing on record in fact his respect for the Pope's intelligence and intellectual ability.

Kenny makes reference to the implications of the letter for seminary training in philosophy (more and better is to be expected there) and regarding theologians ('Those who refuse to learn from philosophy find themselves philosophising unwittingly and badly'), but naturally enough it is the message for philosophers that chiefly interests him: 'What will philosophers outside the Pope's domain make of *Fides et Ratio*?' Kenny believes they will find that the autonomy of their discipline is not respected by the Pope.

It is not easy to reconcile the claim that philosophy is autonomous with two others of the Pope's theses: that the task of philosophy is to discover the meaning of life, and that the meaning of life is something settled once for all by Christianity. If these three theses are all true, then philosophy's task is already done before it begins. (p. 876)

Now the encyclical taken at face value repeatedly asserts the autonomy of philosophy, arguing that the starting-point, method and argumentation used in philosophy must be those developed within the historic discipline. Kenny, on the one hand, acknowledges the respect accorded to philosophy's autonomy of method in *F&R*, but, on the other hand, he insists that the encyclical does not leave the philosopher free to reach conclusions contrary to the truths of Christianity:

Philosophy [as *F&R* envisages it] enjoys autonomy with regard to premises, but not with regard to conclusions. Its freedom is not the freedom to journey to different destinations, but freedom to reach the one possible destination by different routes. (876).

This was so obviously the criticism that would be made, that the stress on the autonomy of philosophy is repeated throughout the letter, in at least five contexts. Philosophy should be respected by the theologian as an autonomous method and content. Even when employed by the theologian philosophy should not lose its nature, its methods, its style of argumentation, etc. Most tellingly perhaps, it is stated that 'A philosophy which did not proceed in the light of reason according to its own principles and methods would serve little purpose' (# 49). In other words, the Pope values philosophy so much *as an access to objective truth*, that *it would serve literally no purpose* to accept an adulterated or attenuated simulacrum of philosophical wisdom.

Kenny's view appears to coincide with the commonly-made assertion that philosophers must be free to think what they like, or as they like, or according to their individual lights. If this is part of what he means, it is already part of what is meant by living in a democracy and is surely uncontroversial in all quarters. Some who, like John Paul II, lived under totalitarianism would be the strongest defenders of the civil freedom of thought and speech, both of philosophers and of every member of society.

From the viewpoint of a liberal, agnostic or secular philosopher, an unfriendly caricature of the Pope's position could be drawn as follows: *The Pope first reassures us that we are all free to enquire and to reach any conclusions our arguments lead us to, but then he presents us with a series of conclusions as truths to which our arguments must lead.*

A caricature may, after all, serve a useful purpose by sharpening a view or position until it comes into focus. It may be the case that the position about faith and reason enunciated in the encyclical is not fully intelligible to those who do not share it, or who cannot even imagine themselves as dwelling momentarily within it. But there is surely nothing in itself wrong or irrational about considering reason, or philosophy, and faith in the same context and under the heading of truth; if there were, then the entire tradition of Catholic thought since St Augustine would have to be pronounced irrational and misguided, in ways that all its leading exponents somehow failed to discern – the present Pontiff being on this supposition merely the latest in the long line of the deluded.

Implied in the ultimate unity of truth is a relationship of some kind between faith and reason/philosophy. Some of the truths of revelation are not compatible in logical terms with certain philosophical positions or conclusions. One example is determinism, the thesis that denies freedom of the will. The example most insisted on by *F&R* concerns truth: scepticism and relativism regarding truth (#82) are incompatible with truths of faith. Now these two sets of truth claims cannot both be asserted, on pain of contradiction, and the truths of faith must be upheld. In positive terms, Aquinas's realistic account of truth is commended (#44). What becomes, in the light of this, of *F&R*'s commitment to the autonomy of philosophy?

Philosophy, in the view of the encyclical, begins in wonderment and questioning concerning the meaning of life, suffering, death and what may follow it. Every human being is a philosopher, and by our nature we desire to know and understand. In pursuing such enquiry we are realising the good of the mind, which aims at truth. The autonomy of philosophy is the same thing as the autonomy of the human enquirer. External constraints upon this deeply rational pursuit always endanger the freedom of the enquirer's assent to the answers that his or her reason proposes as true. The caricature outlined above results from a misreading of the encyclical. It is the view of human nature and of truth that underlie the letter (and that owe their essentials to Aquinas), which strictly requires that the autonomy of philosophical enquiry and research be fully recognised. To repeat the words of the Pontiff, 'it would serve little purpose' to prevent philosophy from working in accordance with its own principles and methods, when one is profoundly commmited to the philosophical view that truth is the specific good and fulfilment of the human mind, and that enquiry into it is of central importance in each human life and in every culture.[11]

The same point has been put more eloquently by Cardinal Joseph Ratzinger, writing before the publication of *F&R*, in 1993: 'Faith does not menace philosopy ... it defends philosophy because it needs it; faith needs philosophy because it needs man who questions and seeks. It is not questioning, in fact, which places obstacles to faith but that closure that no longer wants to question and holds truth to be unreachable or not worth striving for. Faith does not destroy philosophy, it champions it. Only when it takes up the cause of philosophy does it remain true to itself.'[12]

The claim advanced by the encyclical about the mutual enrichment of philosophy and faith emerges from the centuries-old Catholic tradition regarding reason and faith, philosophy and theology. Kenny's criticism appears to bypass that stance through an assertion rather than meeting it on its own grounds. *F&R*, when all is said and done, is not about *The Path from Rome* but the road from Athens to Jerusalem!

From the viewpoint of John Paul II, theology should be able to work alongside and in collaboration with philosophy, each aiming at the kind of wisdom it is capable of achieving, and both together being expected to magnify the light that wisdom can throw on the human scene. The philosophical approach that is able to deliver such fruitful collaboration is not of the kind that is pursued in a secular or agnostic framework of thought and living. Philosophers who take the view that some version of this framework is best for them, and moreover that the whole set of such approaches exhausts the range and capacity of philosophy as such, have no choice but to deny validity to the enterprise sketched out by *F&R* and to offer arguments of roughly the kind advanced by Kenny. That denial may be made even more strongly, if it invokes the strictures of Heidegger upon the 'impossible enterprise' of Christian philosophy. But stronger or weaker as the case may be, it amounts to the assertion that the 'reason' in the phrase 'faith and reason' is not philosophical reason in its pure state, but a hybrid of faith and reason, or even a graft of philosophy onto theology, something therefore that lacks autonomy and the freedom to move where it will. From the perspective of *F&R*, on the other hand, the Catholic achievement in philosophy has a character that is not repeatable on any other terrain but its own. It is specific; it has a long history going back to the early centuries; it can count a number of thinkers to whom the title 'philosopher' could not credibly be refused; and it is capable of entering into dialogue with other philosophical perspectives. If it were to be lost the resulting impoverishment would have negative repercussions not only upon the Church but upon Christian rationality.

The profession of Christian faith should not be thought of as vitiating the believer's philosophical activity, provided that the due autonomy of thought is respected and not violated. *F&R* argues that the holding of faith is capable of radicalising the strictly philosophical questions by giving rise to a creative tension in the mind. Kenny even doubts whether the office of papacy and the pursuit of philosophy are compatible; John Paul II's answer would probably be that 'faith and reason seem to be like two wings by which the human spirit is raised up toward the contemplation of truth' (*F&R* #1). Many Catholics, and perhaps even some others, would feel that the admirable vigour of the Pope's own mind owes much to his practice of philosophy as well as theology. Can it not truly be said of him that he has managed (in the words of Cardinal Avery Dulles already quoted), to integrate both disciplines in his mind 'to the advantage of both and the detriment of neither'?

Notes

1. Cardinal Lustiger, 'Un encouragement. Un devoir', in *Foi et Raison: Lectures de l'encyclique Fides et ratio* (Paris, 1988), p. 11.
2. This is notably the case in his *Foi et philosophies: Guide pour un discernement chrétien* (Namur, Culture et Vérité, 1991).
3. *ibid.*, p. 33.
4. *ibid.*, p. 47.
5. *ibid.*, p. 71.
6. *ibid.*, p. 112. This article ('Les philosophes et la philosophie interpellés') was reproduced in *Nova et Vetera* (Fribourg), 73 (1998.4), in a special number on *Fides et ratio*.
7. Leo Scheffczyk, in *Forum Katholische Theologie* 15 (1999) 48-59.
8. Avery Dulles, 'Can Philosophy be Christian?', *First Things*, 102 (2000), p. 27.
9. J.L. Garcia, 'Death of the (Hand)maiden: Contemporary Philosophy in Faith and Reason', *Logos: A Journal of Catholic Thought and Culture*, 2:3 (1999), p. 15.
10. A. MacIntyre, 'Truth as a Good', in *Thomas Aquinas: Approaches to Truth*, (The Annual Aquinas Lectures at Maynooth), ed. by J. McEvoy and M. Dunne (Dublin, 2001).
11. I have summarised here the argument put forward by MacIntyre in the article referred to above.
12. Joseph Cardinal Ratzinger, *The Nature and Mission of Theology: Essays to Orient Theology in Today's Debates*, trans. by A. Walker (San Francisco, 1995), p. 29.

READING ABOUT
FIDES ET RATIO:
A SHORT INTERNATIONAL
GUIDE

The Latin original and vernacular versions
The original Latin text
Litterae Encyclicae Fides et Ratio, Vatican, Libreria Editrice Vaticana, 1998. Available on the Vatican internet web-site, along with translations into English, German, Italian, Spanish, Portuguese and Polish.

In English
Faith and Reason. Encyclical Letter of Pope John Paul II, CTS, 1998. Printed also by Veritas, Dublin, 1999, and various other Catholic publishers.

A parallel Latin/English text of the encyclical will appear, in a new translation by Anthony Meredith SJ and Laurence Paul Hemming, in a volume entitled *Restoring Faith in Reason,* ed. by Susan Frank Parsons and Laurence Paul Hemming (Series: Faith in Reason: Philosophical Enquiries), London, SCM Press, 2002. The volume will include a commentary on *Fides et Ratio* by James McEvoy and a number of ecumenical explorations of it.

Collective explorations

L'Osservatore Romano published between November 1998 and July 1999, in its various language editions, a series of seventeen contributions on aspects of the encyclical, written by Catholic theologians and philosophers from various parts of the world.

The authors were G. Cottier OP, E. Berti, R. Fisichella, M. Gilbert SJ, A. Vanhoye SJ, A.-M. Léonard, P. Henrici SJ, E. dal Covolo SDB, Paul Gilbert SJ, G.B. Sala SJ, W. Kasper, J. McDermott SJ, S. Pinckaers OP, D. Braine, F. Viola, M. Sancho Sorondo, V. Possenti.

These articles, taken all together, are the most thematically comprehensive analysis available up to the present of the themes of *Fides et Ratio.*

The Tablet (London) carried in issues between May and July 1999 several assessments of the encyclical made by British and North American authors.

Blackfriars magazine carried four articles relative to *Fides et Ratio,* 81:955, September 2000.

Foi et Raison: Lectures de l'encyclique 'Fides et ratio', Paris, Cahiers de l'École cathédrale, 1988. Includes contributions by Cardinal Lustiger, Mgr André Léonard, A. Chapelle SJ, G. Cottier OP, and several others.

Fides et Ratio: Lettera Enciclica di Giovanni Paolo II, Testo e commento teologico-pastorale a cura di Rino Fisichella, San Paolo, Milan, 1999. (Articles by J. Ratzinger, G. Reale, R. Lucas Lucas, G. Cottier, R. Fisichella, L. Clavell, F. Botturi, A. Scola, L. Alici, C. Dotolo, A. Stagliano).

Communio: International Catholic Review (Twenty-fifth Anniversary Issue), 26:3 (1999). A Symposium on Pope John Paul II's *Fides et*

Ratio. Contributions include essays by W. Norris Clarke SJ, Kenneth L. Schmitz, Martin Bieler, Angelo Scola, Robert F. Slesinski, etc.

Logos: A Journal of Catholic Thought and Culture, 2:3 (1999). This number contains essays relating to themes of *Fides et Ratio* by J.L.A. Garcia ('Death of the [Hand]maiden') and the late G.E.M. Anscombe ('Practical Truth').

Nova et Vetera (Fribourg), 1999 n. 4. Contains the French version of *Fides et Ratio* together with studies bearing on its themes, by Dominican theologians J.-M. Garrigues, J.-M. Poffet, Ch. Morerod and G. Cottier.

Faith and Reason, ed. Timothy L. Smith, introduction by Ralph McInerny, Chicago, St Augustine's Press, 2001. Papers on relevant topics by J. Dougherty, S.Th. Pinckaers, W. Hoye, M. E. Sacchi, B. Ashley, G. Goodell, L. Chammings, P. Hodgson, J. Haldane, S. Baldner, V. Possenti, J. Hittinger, C. Martin, R. Brague, M. Sherwin, A. Llano, etc.

Individual assessments

Avery Dulles SJ, 'Can Philosophy be Christian?', *First Things*, 102 (April 2000) 24-29.

Anthony Kenny, 'The Pope as Philosopher', *The Tablet* (26 June 1999) 874-876 (part of series, 'Faith and Reason').

Alasdair MacIntyre, 'Truth as a Good', in *Thomas Aquinas, Approaches to Truth*, ed. by James McEvoy and Michael Dunne, Dublin, 2002.

Richard John Neuhaus, 'A Passion for Truth: The Way of Faith and Reason', *First Things* 88 (December 1998) 65-73.

Joseph Ratzinger, 'Die Einheit des Glaubens und die Vielfalt der

Kulturen. Reflexionen im Anschluß an die Enzyklika *Fides et Ratio*', *Theologie und Glaube* 89 (1999) 141-152. English translation: 'Culture and Truth: Reflections on the Encyclical', in *Origins* 28:36 (25 February 1999).

Leo Scheffzyck, 'Theologisches Plädoyer für die Vernunft: Zur Enzyklika *Fides et Ratio* Johannes Pauls II', *Forum Katholische Theologie* 15:1 (1999) 48-59.

James Swindal, 'Ought there to be a Catholic Philosophy?', *American Catholic Philosophical Quarterly* 73:3 (1999) 449-475.

INDICES

Index of Names

Kenny, A., 259-64
Kierkegaard, S., 93

L
Lao-Tze, 110, 248
Léonard, A.-M., 255
Lévinas, E., 230
Lewis, C.S., 222, 242
Lubich, C., 244
Luke the Evangelist, St,
  79-80, 108
Lustiger, J.-M., 254
Luther, M., 87

M
Malinski, M., 140
McEvoy, J., 12
McGinn, C., 72
MacIntyre, A., 258
Marcel, G., 184, 228
Maritain, J., 49, 52-4, 154,
  175, 219
Mary, 79-80, 84, 96, 251-2
Merleau-Ponty, M., 55
Mounier, E., 128, 181
Murray, D., 9, 119, 238

N
Nagel, T., 72-3
Newman, J.H., 32-3, 36,
  39, 49, 57, 154
Nicholas of Cusa, 90
Nichols, A., OP 119
Nietzsche, Fr., 17
Norris Clarke, W., SJ 123

P
Patrick, St, 250
Paul, St, 90, 92, 96, 106-7,
  114-5, 233
Paul VI, Pope, 10, 228, 232
Pascal, Bl., 93
Percy, W., 246
Pieper, J., 119
Plantinga, A., 48, 56
Plato, 30, 40, 43, 110,
  115-6, 160, 226, 248

R
Rademacher, A.,138
Rahner, K., 138
Ratzinger, J., 84, 120, 242-
  3, 262
Ricoeur, P., 230
Rorty, R., 39
Rosmini, A., 49, 154
Ross, J., 258

S
Sartre, J.-P., 55
Sawicki, M., 178-9
Scheffzyck, L., 256
Scheler, M., 12, 50, 127,
  134-53, 158-60, 181,
  190, 219, 230
Searle, J., 73
Secretan, Ph., 157
Seifert, J., 182
Simms, G.O., 238-9
Socrates, 40,140
Sophocles, 248
Stein, E., St (Sister Teresa
  Benedicta of the Cross),
  12, 29, 49, 65, 127, 132,
  138, and John Paul II
  154-80, 219-20

T
Terence, 233
Tarkovsky, A., 249
Tertullian, 87, 110, 222
Thomas Aquinas, St, 27,
  31, 42, 49-50, 60-1, 65-
  6, 85, 126, 131, 145,
  158, 161, 165, 170-2,
  179, 182-3, 185, 209-10,
  219-20, 222, 230-2,
  261-2
Thomson, F., 41
Tierney, B., 245
Tirthankara 248
Turing, A., 72
Tymieniecka, A.T., 157

V
Van Steenberghen, F., 52
Voegelin, E., 81, 84, 241
Von Hildebrand, D., 127,
  137-8, 159
Von Balthasar, H.U., 62, 81
Von Harnack, A., 113

W
Walsh, D., 245-7
Weigel, G., 124-5, 151, 242
Wittgenstein, L. ,77
Wojtyla, K.: see John Paul
  II, Pope
Wust, P., 138
Woroniecki, J., 150

Index of Themes

A
Action, 57, 142-3
Anthropology,
  philosophical, 173-4
Art, 85, 246

B
Being, 50-1, 160, 167, 175,
  183, 210, 217

C
Catholicity, 106
Chastity, 145-6
Conscience, 230
Councils, Ecumenical,
  Chalcedon 95
  Vatican I, 88; *Dei Filius*
  88-9, 95
Vatican II, 105, 232; *Dei
  Verbum* 89, *Gaudium et
  Spes* 9-10, *Nostra Aetate*
  112
Cross, of Jesus Christ, 83,
  90-3, 110
Cultura ,101-2

Culture, 101-22
–and civilisation 102-3
–and dialogue 111
–and diversity, 107-8
–and dogma, 111
—evangelisation of, 10-13
–and faith, 109
–mass, 226
–and particularity, 106-8
–and transcendence, 114
–and truth, 15, 101-22
–and universality, 115

D
Desire, natural, 47, 59-61
Dialectic, Catholic, 105-6
Dialogue,40, 216, 232-3
–Christological context of, 244-7
–between faith and philosophy, 117, 214-5
–Trinitarian context of, 248-52

E
Education, Catholic, 173
–moral, 191
Empathy, 168-9
Encyclicals, Papal,
–*Aeterni Patris* (1879) 242, 258
–*Ecclesiam suam* (1964) 233
–*Humanae Vitae* (1968) 228
—of Pope John Paul II:
–*Redemptor Hominis* (1979) 207, 242
–*Dives in Misericordia* (1980) 207
–*Laborem Exercens* (1981) 188, 207
–*Slavorum Apostoli* (1985) 208
–*Dominum et Vivifiantem* (1986) 207
–*Redemptoris Mater* (1987) 208

–*Sollicitudo Rei Socialis* (1987) 208
–*Redemptoris Missio* (1990) 13, 208
–*Centesimus Annus* (1991) 208
–*Veritatis Splendor* (1993) 14, 187, 207, 220, 225, 242
–*Evangelium Vitae* (1995)14, 207, 220, 225
–*Ut Unum Sint* (1995) 208
–*Fides et Ratio* (1998) *passim*
—Other Apostolic Letters of Pope John Paul II:
–*Tertio Millennio Adveniente*, 207, 243
–*Mulieris Dignitatem*, 207
Enlightenment, 88, 129, 203-4
Eurocentrism, 105, 112-4
Europe, 114

F
Faith *passim*
–and culture ,103-19
–and philosophy, 95, 257
–and reason, 66, 84-7, 175, 195; harmony of, 87, 241
–seeking understanding, 111, 212
Family, 191
Fideism, 87
Freedom: see 'Liberty'

G
God, existence of, 28, 118-9
Göttingen Circle, 157

H
Hope, 83, 96, 205
Human Rights, 229-30, 246
Humanism, Christian, 123

I
Inculturation, 85, 105, 113, 214

Irish Centre for Faith and Culture (Maynooth) 9-12, 15

K
'Know Yourself.' 109,119

L
Liberty, 26, 32, 49, 61, 93, 142, 187-8, 191-2, 195
–and responsibility, 147, 182
Love and Responsibility, 61, 131, 145, 148

M
Manicheanism, 58, 141, 147
Metaphysics, 27, 35, 74, 125, 171

P
Pentecost, 108-9
Person, 58, 140, 148-9, 158, 162-3, 168-70, 174-6
–*The Acting Person,* 131, 133, 149, 157, 187, 211
Personalism, 56, 128, 131, 134, 140, 148, 181-97
Phenomenology, 59, 65-75, 131, 135-150, 157
–and Husserl, 65-75, 127, 158, 162, 171
–and Scheler, 127, 135-50, 159-60
–and Stein, 127, 138, 154-80, 209
–transcendental, 159, 167
–of intersubjectivity, 172
Pontifical Council for Faith and Culture, 9, 112
Philosophy in *F&R*, 33, 49, 51, 110
–autonomy of, 223, 254, 259-64
–and culture, 110
–Christian, 52-5, 59-60, 92, 175-6, 214
–Greek, 114-5

–marginalised, 255-6
–perennial, 255
–and phenomenology, 143
–sapiential dimension of, 50, 67
–and theology, 16, 47-64
–of woman, 164
Polytheism, 81
Positivism, 223
Postmodernism, 117, 231

Q
Questioning, fundamental questions, 60, 93, 109, 118, 206, 216, 221, 248, 258, 261

R
Rationalism, 88
Rationality, 26, 42
Realism, 127-8
Reason, 42, 129
–and faith, 43,48, 57-8
–and modernity, 212
–and philosophy, 21
–weak reason, 88, 94, 207, 215
Reception of F&R, 254-64
Relativism, 69-71, 116, 205, 225-7, 261

Resentment, 144-6
Revelation, 53-4, 119
–and faith, 80
–and theology, 79-100
–and philosophy, 79-100

S
Scepticism, 67-8, 116-7, 261
Scholasticism (and neo-Scholasticism), 50, 126, 160, 166
Scientism, 71-4, 224
Search for meaning, 23, 51, 80, 103, 217
Search for truth, 35-9, 42, 118, 192-5, 222, 239
Self, 28-30
Sin, 228
Solidarity, 189-90
Solipsism, 34-5, 215
Sophist, 30, 43

T
Theology, 65
–and philosophy, 62, 89, 104
Thomism (and neo-Thomism), 48-9, 52, 126, 161, 165, 167, 170-2, 175

Totalitarianism, 129, 204-5
Tradition, philosophical, 219, 221, 223
Transcendence, 24-6, 74-5, 184, 186, 195, 210
–self-transcendence, 182, 185-6, 192, 197, 206, 214-5, 236
Trinity, Divine, 97
Trust, 37-9, 44, 193-4, 197, 212
Truth, 30-35, 118, 172, 193, 213
–and good, 31-2, 51, 88, 262
–call to, 109
–De Veritate, 171
–unity of, 222, 261

V
Value, 136, 142, 144, 160, 185-6
Value theory/ethics, 139, 141-2, 211

W
Will, 183, 185
Wisdom, Christian, 257, 262
Work, 188-9

£7.50

The First
INDIAN

Making Waves

The real lives of sporting heroes on, in & under the water

Also in this series...

Golden Lily
by Lijia Xu

The fascinating autobiography from Asia's first
dinghy sailing gold medallist

more to follow

The First
INDIAN

Dilip Donde

FERNHURST
BOOKS

Published in 2016 by Fernhurst Books Limited
62 Brandon Parade, Holly Walk, Leamington Spa, Warwickshire, CV32 4JE, UK
Tel: +44 (0) 1926 337488 | www.fernhurstbooks.com

Published in India in 2014 by Maritime History Society

A catalogue record for this book is available from the British Library
ISBN 978-1-909911-49-9

Photography
All photographs supplied by Dilip Donde

Designed by Rachel Atkins
Printed in the UK by Clays Ltd, St Ives plc

Contents

Foreword

by Sir Robin Knox-Johnston

The Indian sub-continent has a seafaring heritage that goes back at least five millennia. Its long seaboard provided a cradle for seamen that still exists today. In my own time with the British India Steam Navigation Company, we relied on this plentiful source of people accustomed to the sea to provide the seamen for our vessels.

Since Independence in 1947, the Indian Merchant Navy and the Indian Navy have expanded hugely, but yachting has remained the sport of a few. One organisation that has appreciated the value of boat handling skills, and the effect of wind and tide on a vessel, is the Indian Navy. So it was not a total surprise when I received a message from Retired Vice Admiral Manohar Awati, asking for advice on how he could send a young officer around the world solo as an encouragement to the sport, and also to put India on the solo circumnavigating map. Both seemed excellent objectives and I responded quickly.

I had served with Indian crews for nearly 14 years during my time at sea. India had been my home for five years, living in Bombay, now Mumbai, and it was where I built my 32 foot Bermudian Ketch *Suhaili* which became the first boat to ever circumnavigate the world non stop and solo. So I had a knowledge

7

and love of India and its people.

At the time I was preparing my 60 footer to participate in the Velux 5 Oceans solo around the world race and felt that if the young officer joined me for the preparation period, he would pick up an awareness of what was involved in taking a boat into the watery Himalayas of the Southern Ocean for a month or more, and that is how I came to meet with Dilip.

The rest of the story is about Dilip Donde. A solo sailor is solo, cut off from the world and outside assistance and dependent upon their own character and resourcefulness. This book is a tribute to Dilip's determination to achieve the objective and become the first Indian to ever sail solo around the planet.

Sir Robin Knox-Johnston, 2016

Preface

He who would go to sea for pleasure, would go to hell for a pastime.
   – Old French Proverb

On 27 Apr 2006, I volunteered for what then appeared to be an absolutely crazy project. 'Project Sagar Parikrama', as it would soon be christened, involved building a sailboat in India and then undertaking a solo circumnavigation of the earth in the boat. I volunteered for the project without really thinking and with absolutely no idea of what I was getting myself into. Till then I did not know that people sailed solo in big yachts nor had I ever set foot on a large yacht. I had been a recreational sailor since joining the Navy, content with sailing dinghies on weekends and enjoying my time outdoors whenever I could. I did do a short tenure on the Navy's sail training ship INS *Tarangini* as the first mate but there, with a crew of over 70, solo sailing was the last thing on my mind! I wasn't alone in my ignorance; it was shared by over a billion Indians. In a way, by volunteering for the project without a second thought, I had thrown myself in the deep end of the pool without bothering to enquire about swimming lessons.

   I did manage to keep my head above the water eventually and

that is what this book is about. Some 170 people had already completed a solo circumnavigation before I volunteered for the project. So in a way, I was treading a somewhat beaten path. The crucial difference was that I was trying to do it in India, with an almost total ignorance of the subject, an inherent inertia against anything new and an intransigent and quixotic bureaucracy.

When I finished my voyage, most people I talked to wanted to hear about the experiences I had at sea, not realising that the hard work put in for over three years, before starting, was responsible for my safe return. The story of Sagar Parikrama would be incomplete without talking about those three years. For me they were as exciting as, and often more unpredictable than, sailing the Southern Ocean. When I look back at my journey from volunteering for the project to finishing the circumnavigation, I realise that there were a number of plots and subplots in the story with me being the only constant. This book, thus, is an attempt to tell the whole story as I lived through it.

The challenge of Project Sagar Parikrama when looked at in its entirety was not just about building a boat and sailing her solo around the world. The single biggest hurdle was neither the boatbuilding nor sailing solo through the Southern Ocean. It was to keep believing in myself that the project would happen notwithstanding the odds stacked against it. I was not the first person who was given the opportunity to do the project by the Navy. But I was definitely the first to grab it. Had I not done so, I am sure someone else would have. But then every time I looked at myself in the mirror, for the rest of my life, I would have thought, "I had the opportunity and I could have done it, but I didn't!" What a horrible feeling that would have been! Not having to live with something like that is perhaps the biggest reward I got from the project – it was well worth the effort and risks.

In India, a government project that meets all deadlines, exceeds its aims, manages to stay under budget while leaving a proud legacy and a million dollars worth of hardware for future generations would be an anomaly – but that is exactly what has been achieved by this project. It is thus an Indian success story in more ways than one.

Commander Dilip Donde

Acknowledgements

While a single person undertakes a solo unassisted circumnavigation, the project cannot be completed without the wholehearted support of a number of people who contribute in its planning, preparation and execution. Without them, the sailor would not be able to go to sea in the first place. The success of the project, thus, is the success of the team with the solo sailor being the representative to receive the kudos on their behalf. It is thus important to acknowledge the contribution of the team members; some of whom were actively involved with the project at various stages while others helped without being directly involved.

Solo circumnavigations in modern boats are expensive affairs. Inevitably, the first and the biggest hurdle is to get the necessary funds. In my case, this hurdle was easy to surmount thanks to the generous funding provided by the Indian Navy and, by implication, the Indian taxpayer. While making sure the necessary funds were made available, the Navy gave me a free hand to use them as I deemed fit. This is all the more remarkable considering my lack of experience and the odds stacked against the project at every stage.

The Navy and the Indian taxpayer are faceless entities made up of well meaning people but there are many I can name who went out of their way to make this project happen. In a project lasting almost four years, the list can go on for a couple of pages. I will thus try to prune the list by naming a few and asking the others to excuse me for not including their names – this does not reduce my gratitude towards them in any way.

First and foremost, I must thank the mentor of the project, VAdm Manohar Awati (Retd), for conceiving the idea of a solo circumnavigation by an Indian in an Indian built boat. It was a big idea that only someone like him could have conceived and pursued so relentlessly. Thanks also to Adm Arun Prakash (Retd), then Chief of Naval Staff, for accepting the idea and handpicking me for the task, Adm Sureesh Mehta (Retd), his successor, for keeping up the momentum, VAdm Sunil Damle (Retd), VAdm Shekhar Sinha (Retd), RAdm N K Misra (Retd), Cmde R S Dhankhar, Cmde Sukhdev Virk (Retd), Capt Subir Sengupta, their successors and officers from Naval Headquarters who steered the project; Capt S J Contractor (Retd) for selecting the boat design and getting us in touch with Sir Robin Knox-Johnston, the first person to sail solo and non-stop around the world; and Sir Robin Knox-Johnston for putting us on the right track and mentoring me. In fact, in 2006, when everyone at home doubted me, he confidently ordered the first copy of the book that I would write on completion of my solo circumnavigation. And three years after completion of the project, when I was still struggling with the book, he put me in 'voluntary solitary confinement' at his lovely house in the UK to ensure that I completed the book you are about to read!

I am quite convinced that anyone can do a circumnavigation in a well-built boat while the best of sailors would falter in a badly built one. My debt of gratitude, therefore, is to the boat-builder Mr Ratnakar Dandekar and his team at Aquarius Fibreglas Pvt Ltd, Goa. It was as much a pioneering project for them as it was for me and they exceeded all expectations while standing up to the challenge. Ratnakar is the face of his company but he had a large team with him, all of whom put in their best to produce the fine boat *Mhadei* is. Some of them may read this book while many others will not get the opportunity to; nevertheless, my gratitude towards them remains the same.

I thank Mr Johan Vels from the Netherlands for teaching us the nuances of building a boat like *Mhadei*, Mr Alan Koh of International Paints for showing us how to make the boat pretty, boat designer Van de Stadt Design Bureau and all the equipment suppliers for providing us a good design and equipment that could withstand the Southern Ocean as well as our inexperience, and Mr Nigel Rowe for suggesting we install a wind vane steering, which perhaps saved my life in the Pacific.

While successful completion of such a voyage is important, it is equally important for the story to reach a wide readership to enable them to be a part of the adventure. The blog I wrote from sea achieved this to a large extent. This was thanks to the efforts of my close friend Cdr Anshuman Chatterjee, who designed my blog, and Mr Mandar Karmarkar who regularly plotted my positions while I was at sea and eventually prepared a track chart of the entire voyage. Many of the photographs in the book and those in my blog were clicked from the excellent camera I received days before departure thanks to the efforts of Cmde Amar Mahadevan.

Many thanks to my one-man shore support crew and training partner Cdr Abhilash Tomy who joined me a few months before departure and became indispensable. I couldn't have asked for anyone better! A special thanks to my mother and the rest of the family for getting totally involved with the project, never showing their apprehensions, and lending a helping hand whenever required.

Finally, I express my gratitude to the Maritime History Society and its Curator, Cdr Mohan Narayan (Retd), for readily offering to publish this book in India, Mrs Arati Rajan Menon for editing the draft, pro bono, and the team of Manu and Madhuri Naik for designing and printing the Indian edition. I am delighted that this international edition is being published by Fernhurst Books, UK – I am grateful to Jeremy Atkins for offering to publish this.

Commander Dilip Donde

Chapter 1

A Path Less Travelled

"Dilip, are you in some sort of trouble with the Navy?" asked my mother one evening as we finished dinner at home in Port Blair. I had pushed away the empty dinner plate absentmindedly and was back to working on my laptop.

"What makes you think so?" I asked, trying to sound as nonchalant as possible while my brain was busy trying to word a suitable reply. The moment I had been apprehensive about for the past two months seemed to have arrived.

"Why have you suddenly started getting so many calls from Naval Headquarters, including the office of the Naval Chief? I think it is all very unusual so will you please tell me?" She had been staying with me for the past nine years and must have noticed the change in my routine since I got back from a sailing trip to Mumbai two months back. Through the years I had made it a point never to take any work home, howsoever busy the schedule. Since my return, however, I had been sitting almost every evening with a laptop borrowed from the office, reading up and writing well past midnight.

"I won't call it trouble but, yes, there is something I got myself into when I visited Mumbai for the sailing trip. I didn't tell you earlier as the whole thing still appears a bit harebrained and

17

unrealistic to me," I mumbled, trying to find the right words to break the news and minimise any possible resistance.

"You can tell me whatever it is," persisted my mother.

"The Navy has been looking for someone to undertake a solo circumnavigation in a sailboat and I volunteered, though I am not exactly sure what it involves." I decided to play it straight, acutely aware of my terrible diplomatic skills, and waited for her reaction. The reaction was surprisingly positive, though not too unexpected. "That is very good. Give it your best shot, opportunities like this don't come every day, but remember it is a one-way street!" she responded after a pause. "Don't ever think of backing out."

I decided to test her further by telling her that there was a good possibility that I may not come back alive from the trip. No Indian had undertaken such a trip, less than 200 in the world had been successful, and no one kept count of the unsuccessful attempts. That didn't deter her much as she calmly replied that I had to go some day like everyone else and it would be far better if I went trying to do something worthwhile! All she asked, in return of her full support, was to be able to read up as much as she could on the subject.

With her full support assured, I decided to fill her in on the events so far...

On 27 Apr 2006, before the start of the Mumbai to Kochi J 24 sailing rally that I was participating in, I met Capt Dhankhar, the Navy's Principal Director of Sports and Adventure Activities. Since he had flown down to flag off the rally along with the Chief of the Naval Staff, or CNS, the conversation was about ocean sailing in the Navy. As I escorted him to the Sailing Club moorings, he almost casually mentioned that the Navy was toying with the idea of sponsoring a solo circumnavigation by a naval officer.

"Can I be a part of it in some way?" I blurted out, stopping him in midsentence, throwing naval protocol to the winds. I just couldn't help it, the whole idea sounded so exciting though I had no clue what exactly was involved.

"Would you like to take it on? Should I tell the CNS that you have volunteered or do you need a little time to think about it?" he asked in his characteristic measured tone, with a hint of scepticism.

"Yes sir, please do tell the CNS that I want to volunteer, I don't need any time to think!" I replied, my brain in overdrive. Less than a minute back I was ready to play any part, howsoever small, in this unknown project because it sounded interesting and suddenly the entire project seemed to be falling in my lap. I didn't bother to ask what exactly the Navy had in mind, all my fuzzy brain could sense was that this was something exciting and I shouldn't let go of the opportunity.

"Okay, now that you have volunteered, can you make a project report and send it to me by next month?"

In less than five minutes of what seemed like casual talk, I had gotten myself into the biggest soup in my life with a very vague idea about what exactly it was!

The Captain had been my instructor during my Clearance Diving course and had observed me closely during those stressful days. That, along with my declared enthusiasm for ocean sailing and my past experience as the Executive Officer of INS Tarangini during her first round the world voyage in 2002-2003, probably prompted him to check if I was interested in this project. Apparently I wasn't the first person he had asked but was definitely the first to fall for the idea, thus ending his search.

Later in the day, the CNS, Adm Arun Prakash, flagged off the rally. In his speech he declared that the Navy was ready to sponsor a solo circumnavigation under sail provided someone volunteered to take on the challenge. As we lined up for a group photograph, he approached and said, "Dilip, I heard *you have volunteered!" I just nodded my head and murmured, "Yes sir. Let us see."*

"So that is the story so far. Now I am required to make a detailed project report and send it to Naval Headquarters as of last month, which explains the frequent calls from Delhi. Honestly, I don't have a clue about the subject and have been trying to read about it on the Internet, which seems to be the only source of information here." I promised my mother that I would pass on whatever I read on the subject to her and got back to finalising my report. Her unstinting support was a burden off my head. I didn't realise it then, but I had just conscripted the first member of the team for 'Sagar Parikrama', as the project would be called.

More than a month went by and I still hadn't submitted my project report. One reason was a fairly busy work schedule that allowed me to read up on the subject only after dinner at home; the other, a total lack of knowledge about the subject. It would be an understatement to say that I was groping in the dark. The more I started reading, the more I started realising that this was not something romantic and poetic as I had initially thought but would involve a lot of hard work and would be far more difficult than what I had imagined. Surprisingly, though, that increased my excitement and determination to make it happen.

By Jul 2006, I managed to submit my project report to Naval Headquarters (NHQ) and decided that if I had to do a circumnavigation it had to be a proper circumnavigation under sail, going through the Southern Ocean, round the three Great Capes, Cape Leeuwin, Cape Horn and the Cape of Good Hope. I could have proposed following the route taken by the previous Indian sailing expeditions in *Trishna*, *Samudra* and INS *Tarangini* through the Suez and Panama canals, called it a circumnavigation and no one would have been wiser, in the country at least! In fact, on hindsight, things would have turned out to be much simpler as I could always have pointed at 'precedence', something that opens many a door when dealing with the bureaucracy. I could have had a whale of a time stopping at 40 to 50 ports over a period of a year or two with a smooth sail through the Trade Winds! But then that wouldn't have been the real thing. Even if the Navy, and the taxpayer who was essentially funding my trip, didn't realise it, I would, and it just would not be right!

A month went by after I submitted the report. I was still clueless about what exactly to do. While I continued reading on the subject and sending the odd email enquiring about suitable second-hand boats, the whole idea had started getting a bit fuzzy and unrealistic as I got caught up in day-to-day activities.

For probably the first time ever, I had planned a nice holiday in Aug 2006; I had invited a close friend to the Andamans to explore the islands, booked my tickets to go to the mainland after that, handed over my duties at work in time and was all set to have a good time! My friend arrived as planned – and so did the calls from NHQ and a certain Vice Admiral Manohar Awati (Retd)! I was told that I was to go and work with Sir Robin Knox-Johnston, who apparently was the first person to have sailed solo and non-stop around the world. I had no idea who he was or what his achievements were. I did download information about him from the Internet but didn't get much time to read with a house full of guests. All I knew was that he was trying to get ready to take part in a solo round-the-world race called the Velux 5 Oceans Race and had resigned from the chairmanship of his company as the company was conducting the race. When asked for his advice on my project, his response had been simple and characteristic: "Send him to work with me and he will know all there is to learn!"

The frequency of calls and the things I was supposed to do 'as of yesterday' increased so much that I was sitting in my office almost as much as on any working day. I finally got myself recalled from leave, little realising that that was the last, albeit short, holiday I would get for the next five years!

I left the Andamans before my friend – still at my home and now exploring the islands alone – and headed for the mainland. I was to go and meet the ever enthusiastic Vice Admiral Awati before heading for Delhi to complete my deputation formalities. The 80-year-old admiral had been egging on the Navy for years to undertake a solo circumnavigation. He lives with his wife in a remote village called Vinchurni, about 320 km from Mumbai, which with a population of 500 is small even by Indian standards! I landed in Mumbai, borrowed a friend's car and went searching for the village few had heard of, finally making it by afternoon. I had interacted with the Admiral in passing some 10 years ago and he obviously didn't remember me. We talked about the project, which wasn't much really as it was more of an idea at that stage. He and his gracious wife made me feel at home instantly and when they insisted I spend the night with them instead of heading back to Mumbai and driving past midnight, I agreed without much fuss. As I was to stay for the night, I went for a nice long walk with the Admiral in the evening and had a sundowner with his wife while he retired to bed at 1900 h. The conversation was both interesting and varied. I enjoyed their company and left for Mumbai early the next morning. Much later and I am not sure how, I started getting a feeling that I had been under some sort of a probation and under observation during my stay!

Two years into the project, when I had developed a good rapport with him, I finally asked him if what I suspected was true. He very calmly told me that I was indeed under observation and that after I had gone to bed he woke up and discussed me with his wife! While he had formed a favourable opinion about me, he wanted to take a second opinion from his better half as he relies on her gut feeling more than his own. Apparently, she told him that I seemed alright and should be able to take on the project!

"What if either of you had thought that I was not the right person for the job?" I asked.

"I would have asked the Navy to send me another guy!"

The next day, I drove up to Mumbai and met Capt Soli Contractor (Retd), then Commodore of the Royal Bombay Yacht Club. He had represented India at the Munich Olympics in 1972 and was to be the technical advisor for the project. While talking to him, I realised that not only was I to be the first Indian to undertake this project but that the trip was to be undertaken in an Indian built boat. Never mind that India has virtually no yacht building industry to speak of! The whole idea was sounding crazier by the day and thus more exciting.

The next stop on what was fast becoming a voyage of discovery was Delhi. I was quite unfamiliar with the city in general and NHQ in particular, having steered clear of any appointment there so far. It was a whirlwind visit getting the paperwork ready for my deputation and for the project that was to follow. The Chief of the Naval Staff wanted to meet me before I left.

The first question he asked me, in humour and with a smile on his face, when I walked into his office was, "Dilip, have you gone completely mad?" I grinned, "Looks like that, Sir!" I had served on his staff 11 years back when he was commanding the

Eastern Fleet and he knew me well. He wanted to know if I was under any sort of pressure and understood what I was getting into. Once he was satisfied, we got talking about the project. He was retiring within a month and promised to get the 'Approval in Principle' from the Defence Minister before retiring. He also insisted that I draft out a letter giving an outline of the project, addressed to all the naval formations. I was a little sceptical; we knew what we wanted to achieve but had no firm idea as to how we were planning to achieve it. When I naively pointed this out to him, he explained that he wanted the project to happen and the best way to ensure that it did not get scuttled after he retired was to leave his successors no option! He had already thought of an appropriate name for the project, 'Sagar Parikrama', literally meaning circumnavigation of the oceans in Hindi. No other name could have summed up the nature of the project so well and in simpler words.

While doing the rounds of NHQ and within an hour of the government approving my deputation to go and work with Sir Robin, I landed up at the personnel directorate. The 'Sea Board' for my course to decide the list of eligible officers to go to sea had been held the previous day. Not making it in the Board means the end of your career as you have virtually no chance of making it to the next rank. I bumped into an old friend who worked there. "I have made it in the Board, but unfortunately you haven't," he informed me, pulling a long face. "Cheer up mate, I'm quite glad!" was my reply. "Now I can concentrate on my project full time!"

Chapter 2

An Invaluable Apprenticeship

Once my paperwork was done, I began writing to Sir Robin asking him if he wanted anything from India, what sort of clothing to carry, his exact location, what I was to do once I got there, and so on.

There were so many questions and with no one to answer them at home, I kept shooting out mails as and when something popped up in my head. After a while, I started feeling a bit sheepish and started one of my mails with, "Here is another silly question..." His reply was prompt and something I will remember all my life. "There is nothing like a silly question! A question is a question and I would rather have you ask as many of them as you want rather than come here and be lost at sea!" I have followed his advice ever since and in a project where we were trying to learn everything from scratch, it was valuable advice indeed. When he asked me to get an audio CD of the 1960s Bollywood epic *Mughal-e-Azam* for him I was mighty amused. A few days later when I got to know him better, I realised the reason.

I landed in London and was received by the assistant to the Indian Naval Advisor who promptly transported me to Waterloo station and despatched me to Portsmouth by the next available train. Once in Portsmouth, I called up Sir Robin who asked me to come over to Gosport, a short ferry ride away. I was to call him once I reached Gosport and we were to go to an Indian restaurant for dinner with some friends. I reached Gosport alright, only to discover that I had left Sir Robin's telephone number at my hotel in Portsmouth. I tried looking for him for a while, which wasn't easy as we had never met before. I gave up after a while and headed back to Portsmouth feeling like a real idiot. What a wonderful way to start an apprenticeship!

The next morning, I reached Gosport and called up Sir Robin. He appeared within minutes and took me to the boatyard right next to the ferry point. I had never met a knight before and naturally addressed him as 'Sir'. He sorted that out within the first two minutes by telling me to drop the 'Sir' and address him as Robin. He had an overall ready for me, and told me that his ulterior motive in allowing me to come and work with him was to brush up his Hindustani which he had picked up while working with the British India Steam Navigation Company in the 1960s.

Thus began my most valuable apprenticeship. The first task was to sand the boat's boom and get it ready for painting, something that I had never done in my life. Robin's boat, *Grey Power*, a carbon fibre 'Open 60', had been entirely stripped down and was being reassembled to get her ready for the race. The pace of work over the next three weeks was hectic. I would reach the boatyard by ferry around 0830 h everyday and start doing whatever work came my way. Robin would always be around to answer any questions, allocate work and help out while working the hardest among us all. His enthusiasm and stamina were amazing and extremely infectious. We would work through the day, often skipping lunch, till about 1900 h daily and then muster up at a bar outside the boatyard to unwind and go over the day's work.

By the time I reached my hotel at Portsmouth after a ferry ride and a 15 minute brisk walk I would be in danger of falling asleep under the shower!

We were quite an interesting bunch, mostly volunteers, of varied backgrounds and ages. Charlotte (Charlie), the youngest member of the team, had just finished college and was spending her summer holiday working on the boat. Timothy Ethridge (Tim), an American in his 50s, had applied to sail round the world in the Clipper Round The World Race later that year. Most of us didn't have much technical knowledge but were willing workers, enjoying the experience and determined to do our best. That seemed fine with Robin who would always be at hand to guide us, never getting upset if we committed any mistakes, as we often did.

There were also some technicians, painters and specialists who would come and do the work while we assisted them and kept learning. I slowly graduated from sanding the boom to helping fit out equipment on the boat. Every day was a new learning experience. I was seeing a large yacht being fitted out for a round-the-world ocean race for the first time. Having been an executive officer in the Navy all my working life, I was not too conversant at working with tools; in the Navy, there is always some technical manpower available. As I worked, I became increasingly confident about using various tools and working with my hands, something that would hold me in good stead later.

I managed to get a day off in the three weeks in the UK and used half a day to catch up on my sleep and the rest of it to visit the old Portsmouth Dockyard where Nelson's flagship *Victory* is berthed as part of a museum. Meanwhile, *Grey Power* was renamed *Saga Insurance* after Robin's main sponsors at the

Portsmouth waterfront. After a few more days of work we set out amid fanfare for Bilbao, Spain, to be on the start line for the race. As we started setting the mainsail, everything seemed to be going wrong. The mast seemed to be snaking up instead of standing upright and the swing keel wouldn't swing! I was assigned the simplest job, that of holding the boat on course while Robin and others tried to sort the problems out. There was no alternative but to turn back. The mast and rigging needed to be tuned but the problem with the keel still foxed everyone. As Robin came to the tiller and sat down, mulling over the problem, visibly upset, I asked him if he had turned the swing keel switch to the 'on' position. "What switch?" he asked. I asked him to hold the tiller, ran down and put on the switch – the swing keel started working! He had been busy while we were working on the swing keel and was not aware of the switch. One more important lesson learnt: Know your boat like the back of your hand!

We finally set sail for Bilbao with a crew of six. Robin, Tim, Charlie (missing her freshers' week for the sail), Richard, a friend of Robin and a barrister by profession, Juan, a South African sailor who had recently earned his RYA Yacht Master's ticket, and me. At sunset and after crossing the Solent, Robin divided us into two watches for the rest of the trip. He was to head one watch and I, the other. I had never sailed a large yacht before and told him so. Cool as a cucumber, he asked, "You have a naval watch-keeping ticket, haven't you?" "Yes", I replied. "Well that's more than enough. Wake me up if you feel there is a problem." With that, he got inside the boat and went off to sleep. He did ensure that I had Juan and Richard with me on my watch, both of whom had been crewing large yachts. The boat was still far from ready; only the basic instrumentation like the compass was working as we hadn't had the time to wire up the rest. She had to be hand steered as the autopilot was yet to be wired.

An Open 60 is quite a beast to sail; designed for speed and to withstand the extreme punishment of the Southern Ocean, there is very little thought given to crew comfort. Even a basic fitting like a toilet is missing as that would add more weight and one more opening in the hull. 'Buck it and chuck it' is the only solution to relieve oneself! As we crossed the shipping lanes around the UK and France and entered the Bay of Biscay, often called the Bitch of Biscay or Beast of Biscay, I realised the reason for the expletives. Strong head winds, whipping up big seas, and a boat sailing upwind at over 15 kts, heeling at an impossible angle, slamming on every wave while making noises as if she was possessed and wanted to break herself! While on watch we would get splashed every few seconds by the sea spray and the resultant cold would permeate right down to the marrow of my 'tropical' bones!

One night as I was lying in my bunk, having woken up to go and relieve the watch on deck, my body just refused to obey me. "How the hell did I get myself in this situation? This is not even close to the Southern Ocean, which I am expected to cross alone." I just kept lying there for a couple of minutes, frozen in more than one way! "Misery is being on an Open 60 in the middle of a Bay of Biscay gale. Nice definition. But do I seriously want to go through with this endless madness, trying to go round the world alone?" I thought to myself. But then the incorrigible alter ego piped up, "Well, would you rather be pushing files at NHQ for the rest of your life?" I was at the tiller, fully dressed and tethered to the boat to do my watch, in the next five minutes. "Good God, what a horrible alternative that was!" Sometimes inspiration comes in strange ways.

We reached Bilbao after four days and were warmly received by the late Jose Ugarte, the legendary Spanish solo circumnavigator, among others. With only three weeks to start the race, the work on the boat continued at the same blistering pace as before. Meet at the hotel's restaurant at 0700 h all groggy eyed and achy for a big breakfast and be on the boat by 0830 h after negotiating the traffic in an alien city with signage in an alien language. Work till about 1900 h, go over the day's work at a bar on the Marina and get back to our hotel by 2130 h, again negotiating the unfamiliar Bilbao roads. Our tiredness and inability to read Spanish sometimes led to really funny situations. Once, hopelessly lost and finding our way back, we crossed the toll booth for a tunnel en route twice in a span of 30 minutes, from the same side!

My last name 'Donde', which means 'where' in Spanish, was a source of amusement to the Spaniards. Once Robin joked, "Hell of a prospective circumnavigator you are with a name that means 'where'!" I told him that it actually stands for "where next", the next having been abbreviated and that I shall sail around the world! "Well said!" said Robin with a big grin.

They were exciting times. Apart from work there were plenty of discussions with Robin about India, history and a host of subjects. He was still trying to brush up his Hindustani, which was a source of much amusement to everyone. Once, leaving for the hotel at about 2100 h, with a car full of dog-tired occupants, Robin was adamant on stopping for a haircut on the way as he was worried about not being able to get any free time later. There was almost a mutiny in the car at his suggestion. I muttered quietly to Robin in Hindi, "Robin *sahib, seedhe ghar chalo warna joote padenge,* haircut *baadme lena!*" (Let us head home straight, else we will get thrashed; have a haircut later.) Robin just said, "*Achha,*" and headed straight back to the hotel with everyone wondering what exactly transpired between the two of us for Robin to abandon the plan.

I remained in touch with people back home, including Admiral Awati, Capt Contractor and the folks at NHQ who would keep airing their apprehensions which, having no knowledge on the subject, I would often pass on to Robin. One day, he couldn't take it anymore and told me, "Indians are among the most capable people I have seen, but then why are you guys so under confident of yourselves?" His question shook me and I often mull over it, especially after the successful completion of the project, when people still cast aspersions about the ability of an Indian to undertake similar ventures. His advice for the project was really simple and to the point. In the order of priority and difficulty: "Get the funding, get a good boat and then it's just sailing!" He couldn't understand why we were making such a big fuss over the whole thing considering that the first time he ever sailed solo was when he started his non-stop circumnavigation way back in 1968. "Just go and sail, you will do it," he told me. Encouraging words, when everyone at home doubted the whole idea.

On the morning of 22 Oct 2006, as we were heading for the start of the Velux 5 Oceans Race, Robin asked me if he owed me anything. He was, of course, asking if he owed me any money for the sundry items bought for the boat. Embarking on a solo circumnavigation, one likes to ensure that there are no IOUs for obvious reasons. My first response was, "No, nothing. All accounts have been settled." As he turned his attention to something else, I blurted out, "Robin, come to think of it, you do owe me something." Surprised, he turned back and asked, "What?" I replied, "You owe me my project!" He just smiled and told me, "Absolutely! Just let me get back."

I saw Robin off at the start of the Velux 5 Oceans Race and headed back home. My head was full of the new things I had seen and worked on. My so-called 'training' was over and it was time to get things moving.

By the time I got back, Admiral Arun Prakash, a few days short of retirement, had managed to get 'Approval in Principle' from the Defence Minister for spending Rs 6 crore (about $ 1.25 million) for project Sagar Parikrama. I called on him in his office and he introduced me to the next Chief of the Naval Staff, Admiral Sureesh Mehta, who assured all support for the project.

I got back to Port Blair basically to pack my bags and shift base. It would have been next to impossible to run a project like this from Port Blair so I was being transferred to Mumbai, to work on it full time. I called on the Commander-in-Chief, a Vice Admiral, before leaving as I had been on his staff. When I explained to him the reasons for my transfer and what I was planning to do, the conversation became rather interesting.

"We can't do it, it is impossible!" said the Admiral with an air of finality.

"But others have done it in the past, so why can't we?" I replied, totally taken aback with such a response.

"Oh, they are born sailors; they have sea water in their veins," explained the Admiral.

"Sir, I think everyone is born the same way and everyone has to learn. I think it is just a matter of working towards it. As we are attempting this for the first time in the country, we will need to work harder than others but it cannot be impossible. At worst we will fail but at least we would have the satisfaction of having given it our best shot," I replied, trying to keep the growing anger in my head out of my voice.

I was making every effort to keep a straight face and a civil voice while thinking, "You son of a gun, so far I was just thinking of sailing solo around the world, now I shall sail solo around the world, just wait and watch!"

"Then you go and do what you want, what have you come here for!" said the Admiral, dismissing me rather rudely.

"I just came to bid farewell as I have been transferred out and won't be meeting you again. Thanks for everything, Sir."

I walked out of the office with steam coming out of my ears, barely suppressing the impulse to slam the door on my way out. If this was the sort of encouragement I was going to get, there was only one way to go! I had to complete the trip successfully, no shortcuts, no excuses.

Chapter 3

A Suitable Boat

We still weren't very clear about the choice of a boat. Robin had suggested purchasing an old proven boat instead of trying to build one from scratch. That way we would have a reliable boat for an untested skipper at considerably less cost. Considering the almost total absence of a yacht-building industry in the country, it made sense. But then Admiral Awati, whose idea it was in the first place, was insistent that we build the boat in India. He had a bigger vision, that of kick-starting a yacht-building industry in the country as a spinoff of the project.

So do we just build the boat in the country or do we design it too? The latter would have meant stretching things a bit too far and I would have been the obvious guinea pig, trying to sail the boat alone. What material did we want the boat built from: wood, steel, aluminium, fibreglass or carbon fibre? Robin's boat, the only yacht I had worked on and sailed briefly, was made of carbon fibre. But then she was a thoroughbred racing boat, fast but at the same time very unforgiving and expensive. Did I, with my limited experience, want to zip around the world on the very first trip and at considerably more cost and risk? Or should I choose a slower but more forgiving boat with more chance of success? Also what did we plan to do with the boat once the trip was over? A large yacht is a big investment and you cannot just discard it after one trip. The most logical option was to use the boat for training the next generation of ocean sailors for the Navy. In that case, the boat would need to be able to give a few decades of service while being used by people with very little experience. What about ease of maintenance, quality of finish, availability of material in the country, the statement such a boat should make to the rest of the world about the Indian yacht-building industry, selection of a suitable designer... So many factors to be considered, so many opinions! I had never felt so inadequate about my lack of knowledge on a subject.

Capt Soli Contractor (Retd) suggested buying a Colin Mudie design, whom he represented in India, and building the boat in steel. The Navy already had the tall ship *Tarangini* designed by Colin Mudie. We needed a yacht that could be sailed solo, not a tall ship! Also having served on *Tarangini* I was apprehensive about the finish of the boat if built in steel. I was not too keen on aluminium, having seen the maintenance problems faced by some of the naval ships with aluminium superstructures. Robin added another angle to the discussion. His opinion was that the whole idea of Sagar Parikrama and doing it in an indigenously built boat was to make a statement to the world about the ability of Indians in seafaring as well as boat-building. Building the boat in steel would not make that statement as it would hardly be a novelty. So the boat should be built from a more modern material and design. Someone even suggested a steel-hulled 'Chinese junk rig' for its supposed ease of handling. Except for Robin, none of the advisors had any experience of sailing solo in the Southern Ocean. The discussions would almost always end with, "She is your boat, you have to sail her so you take the final decision." Unfortunately I had virtually no experience of building boats or sailing them solo. The best I could do was to listen patiently, do my research and use a lot of common sense. We finally decided on building a fibreglass boat and Capt Contractor suggested the 56-ft *Tonga* design from the Van de Stadt Design Bureau, Netherlands. The boat was to be built as a one-off construction by using the method of 'wood core fibreglass' suggested by the designer.

Chapter 4

Apprenticeship Again

I went back to work on Robin's boat in Jan 2007 during his first stopover at Fremantle, Australia. I had worked on the boat for six weeks before the start of the race and was keen to see the results of my handiwork. It was nice getting back to the boat and meeting Robin. This time he had a professional shore support team and some rookie volunteers like me. I was hoping to be at Fremantle to receive Robin when he arrived and see for myself the punishment inflicted by the sea upon the crew and the boat. Unfortunately the mandarins at NHQ took their time and I landed up a week before Robin was to depart!

It was an interesting trip right from the word go. I was to fly out of Delhi by a flight departing at 2030 h. At 1900 h I was still sorting out my paperwork at NHQ. Realising that I would miss the flight if I delayed any further, I requested a friend to finish the rest of the paperwork and rushed to the naval mess on a scooter. By the time I arrived at the mess, my fingers were numb with cold and I could barely tie my shoelaces. Luckily, I managed to get an auto-rickshaw, the only means of transport that could be summoned at short notice, put myself in it, promised the driver more than double the fare if he drove like a maniac, and reached the airport by 2015 h. I was never so relieved to see a flight delayed by a couple of hours!

As a naval officer I had to fly Air India, which also acted as my agent for the routes where the airline did not fly. On reaching the airport, I realised my flight was to have a good six-hour stopover in Mumbai. It was tempting to drop by at home, about 15 minutes from the airport, instead of waiting the whole night. But when I checked out the possibility, I was told I couldn't do that as I had already 'emigrated' out of India in Delhi and flown part of the sector, from Delhi to Mumbai, on an international flight. That left no choice but to hang around at the airport through the night, with home just a stone's throw away! I promised myself that I would catch up on my sleep once the flight took off, as the legs of my flight seemed fairly long. My ticket mentioned that my entire journey would be completed in two legs; from Mumbai to Singapore and then to Perth with a four-hour stopover in between. The airline had obviously forgotten to mention the fine print as the flight finally went hopping via Hyderabad, Singapore, Bali and then to Perth, landing me at my destination after over 36 hours!

In Bali, all the passengers were required to get off the plane in the middle of the night and go through security, only to get back in the same plane on the same seat. While killing time at the airport, I bought some duty-free cigarettes for Robin, including some Indonesian clove ones that for some strange reason have 12 cigarettes in a packet instead of the usual 10 or 20. When I landed in Perth and was waiting to clear Customs, I noticed plenty of signs urging passengers to truthfully declare whatever they had or face stiff penalties. Having heard a lot about how strict the Australian Customs were, I mentally counted the number of cigarettes in my baggage and realised that I had two cigarettes extra! The immigration officer, a tired lady at the end of her night shift, couldn't find the details of my passport or visa when she tried to scan it. She asked me for my details, trying to buy time while she decided my future. I gave her the story of being an Indian naval officer dropping by to work on a yacht as a volunteer on an official passport and visa, which further confused her. Still nowhere close to a solution, she asked if I had anything to declare. I told her I had two cigarettes extra in my baggage and if she had issues with that I was ready to dump the entire lot. "You mean you have two cartons of cigarettes extra?" "No, I am saying two cigarettes extra. Two sticks, you see!" That was the last straw. She just led me through a back door that opened outside the airport, wished me luck with whatever I was up to and vanished. I think she had had enough for the shift!

Thankfully, there was a taxi waiting for me at the airport that took me to my hotel. "Your booking is from today Sir, so your room will only be ready by 1400 h." What a wonderful thing to hear after travelling for 36 hours! "There are, however, two letters for you." One was from the Indian Defence Advisor in Canberra welcoming me to Australia and wishing me a pleasant stay while the other was from Robin, also welcoming me and intimating that he would pick me up at 0900 h and head straight for the boat. It was already 0700 h. The hotel informed me that I would be required to pay a crazy sum of AUD 65 if I wanted to have my breakfast at their restaurant as the free breakfast with the accommodation would only be available from the next day. I finally opened up my suitcase in the hotel lobby, used their restroom, asked the reception to shift my baggage whenever my room was ready, made a dash to a small diner at the end of the street for a nice breakfast at one tenth of the cost, and just about made it back by 0900 h to greet Robin, who was all charged up as usual. He had lost a lot of weight, not unexpected after having raced across the better part of the Atlantic, solo. We headed for the boat and started pottering around immediately. I finally stumbled back to my hotel room past 2200 h! The routine for the trip had been set and so it remained till I left Fremantle a week later.

I got back from Fremantle on 15 Jan 2007. A day after starting the second leg of his race from Fremantle, Robin had turned back because of problems on his autopilot. I heard the news while waiting at Singapore airport. The last time too when he started his race from Bilbao, he had been forced to enter La Coruna when his boat was battered in a storm. Both times I would have liked to go back and help with the repairs to the boat but I was on government deputation and changing schedules would have been next to impossible. He was keen that I visit him during the next stopover at Norfolk, USA, but I realised I would be wasting a lot of time and energy getting approvals for that trip and even then with a very slim chance of success. I decided instead to get back home and start making the specifications for a boat for Sagar Parikrama, which was to be the first step before shortlisting a boatyard followed by floating tenders, finalising a contract and, finally, boat construction.

Chapter 5

Finding a Boatyard

Capt Contractor had obtained study plans for the Tonga 56 boat he had recommended. While the study plans cost € 45, the boat designs would cost € 19,000 including royalty to the designer to build one boat off his drawings. The design plans were for a charter version of the boat in aluminium though the boat designer assured us that the same could be built in wood core fibreglass as we had planned. While the design showed the sail plan, an internal layout for a charter version and the basic fittings; the exact fit-out of the boat, the make and specifications of the fittings and equipment and any modifications we required had to be decided by us. Selecting a good boat builder was crucial. As I had never heard of a boat builder in the country who had built a sailboat, I wrote to Goa Shipyard Ltd who had built the Navy's tall ship INS *Tarangini*. This was also in accordance with the naval policy of giving preference to a public-sector yard. Goa Shipyard promptly indicated their unwillingness to have anything to do with the project as they were busy with larger orders!

Capt Contractor suggested a small privately owned yard in Goa, Aquarius Fibreglas. No one seemed to have heard about the yard or its owner, Mr Ratnakar Dandekar. Meanwhile Naval Headquarters, in an effort to keep everything above board, appointed a team to undertake a capacity assessment study of various boatyards in the country. The team visited Aquarius Fibreglas and three other yards; one in Billimora, Gujarat, and the others in Kochi. Once the yards had been shortlisted, necessary tenders would be sent to them. The yards would then be shortlisted again based on a technical evaluation of their bids. That completed, the qualified bidder who had quoted the lowest price would be called for the final contract negotiation. It was going to be a long process just to get the boat construction started.

I had, meanwhile, started shortlisting the equipment I thought should be fitted on the boat while concurrently doing a rough costing. It was interesting work, something I had never done before. As there was virtually no one to ask in the country, I would often send emails to Robin, asking for suggestions on some equipment or other. Despite racing through the Southern Ocean and later through the Atlantic, he would always reply and help me move ahead.

In Feb 2007, I met Nigel Rowe, chairman of Sail Training International and an accomplished solo sailor, in Mumbai. I had earlier met him in Spain while working with Robin. While discussing equipment for the boat, he suggested that I fit wind vane self-steering on the boat. I was a bit sceptical initially as I had already planned to fit two electronic autopilots. Nevertheless I included it in the specifications and later got it fitted. Two years later, sailing in the middle of the Pacific with New Zealand 2,000 nm behind me and Chile 3,000 nm ahead, I couldn't thank Nigel enough for making that suggestion, when both my electronic auto pilots gave up in a span of 30 minutes and I was left with no other self-steering gear except the wind vane!

My rough budgetary estimates were ready by Feb 2007 and I sent them off to NHQ. The problem was, as no one had an idea about the cost and specifications of the boat, we had no reference to check the reasonability of the bids received from the boatyards. I had been promised Rs 6 crore for the project. I decided to keep Rs 4 crore for the boat and the balance for the rest of the project.

Chapter 6

Training on Old Sameer

While I was doing the paperwork for building the boat, my lack of time spent at sea on a yacht, solo or otherwise, was weighing heavily on my mind. The first time I met Capt Contractor, my supposed coach for the project, he suggested training with an old 34-ft boat, INSV *Sameer*, which belonged to the Navy and was lying almost unused in Kochi. He seemed very confident about it then, which I later realised wasn't too surprising, as he hadn't seen the boat properly! Once he saw how poorly maintained she was, he started developing cold feet and told me the boat wasn't seaworthy and couldn't be sailed to Mumbai for my training. I had not kept any money aside in the budget for a training boat as I was banking on *Sameer* and now I was being told that she wasn't seaworthy! I finally put my foot down and decided to sail the boat from Kochi irrespective of her material state. I planned to get her repaired as best as I could at the Naval Dockyard in Mumbai. That way, I could get experience in sailing as well as repairing the boat.

It was an interesting sail from the word go. The first job was to get a crew. Having found no volunteers, the Western Naval Command nominated three officers to sail with me and we met in Kochi for the first time. One of them tried to board the boat and suddenly developed severe backache, almost on cue! That left me with the two other guys. I asked them about their experience and realised they were greener than I thought. The youngest, Lt Reddy, had recently been appointed to a ship to earn his watch-keeping ticket. Both had sailed dinghies at the Naval Academy as part of their basic training and that was it.

The boat was indeed in a mess; heavily loaded with all sorts of junk, painted with over nine layers of paint, more than 10 years old, ill-fitting sails and a cranky engine, that more often than not needed to be cranked by two people. Looking back, an email I sent to a friend listing out the howlers we faced while getting her ready, and my reaction to them (in italics), makes for interesting reading.

a. Sir, you asked me to make the slack guard rails taut. I have tightened them a bit but don't want to go any further as they may break!

I thought they are supposed to be strong enough to prevent me from getting washed overboard! (Finally made them taut at sea on my own!)

b. Please carry a 40 kg portable diesel generator along with 100 litres of fuel for charging the two batteries onboard and charging your mobile and laptop!

But the batteries can be charged by an alternator fitted on the engine!

What if the engine does not work and in any case there is no inverter onboard (weighing 500 gm and costing Rs 500) to give a 230-V supply to charge your mobile?

Eventually I left the generator ashore on the threat of cancelling my trip, the alternator stopped working as the fan belt connecting it to the engine broke after six hours of running (the spare fan belts were about twice the size required!), and I was without power for a couple of days with hardly any worry. As for charging the mobile phone, I used it whenever required and just switched it off the rest of the time!

c. On the same issue as above, "If you don't have power, even your GPS won't work; how will you know where to go after that?"

When I joined the Navy, no one had heard of GPS and things ran pretty much okay, so thank you very much for your concern.

d. Some of the food items expected to be taken on the trip, in addition to ready-to-eat meals, for three persons, with each leg not expected to be more than four days:
   i)   Pickle – 01 kg
   ii) Sugar – 05 kg
   iii) Coffee – 01 kg

e. How many days victuals can *Sameer* carry?

Depends on what you want to eat and how much space you are ready to sacrifice for it! I can stock her up with a year's supply of freeze-dried food if you want.

f. Amount of fuel, oil and water expected to be carried:
   i)   Diesel – 210 ltrs in the main tank, 200 ltrs in jerry cans (fuel consumption not more than 2 ltrs/hr, approx speed 4 kts)
   ii) Engine oil in jerry cans – 20 ltrs (sump capacity 3 ltrs)
   iii) Petrol and kerosene – 20 ltrs and 100 ltrs respectively (consumption – petrol only to start the generator and 2 ltr kerosene/hr)

iv) Water – 400 ltrs in fitted tanks with potable water and 100 ltrs of drinking water in jerry cans.

g. How can you start the engine without an ERA or ME (a technical sailor)?

By turning the key or cranking it by hand, you dummy!

h. Why can't a genoa or spinnaker be smaller than a jib?

I better ask the guy who created these names!

i. Where are the reefing lines on the mainsail? What are reefing lines?

You are expected to be teaching seamanship to the entire Navy, for crying out loud.

j. Please learn to handle the boat in the Kochi channel, then go out and practise the same at sea.

Won't it be easier and safer to do both together at sea?

k. The skipper of *Sameer* is to submit a tracing of the detailed passage plan, showing the route he will be taking, ETAs and ETDs from Kochi to Mumbai 48 hrs before departure.

Would someone please give me the exact winds and currents (accurate to four decimal places in strength and direction) I will be facing during the entire trip to make this plan?

l. Please ensure continuous communication with the shore. Do you need an escort ship? Do you want an aircraft to fly over you every day?

I am touched by your concern!

I suppose that is all for now. More will follow.
Dilip

We eventually managed to reach Mumbai with a jury rigged forestay, a barely functional engine, no electricity, on emergency steering and with only mobile phones for communication! It was still something to feel good about. We had proved everyone wrong about our ability to sail her and completed the trip without raising an alarm.

En route, during the pit stop at Goa, I met Ratnakar for the first time. At that time he was just another shortlisted boat builder I was trying to assess, whereas for him I was just another naval officer who had come to check him out. He had never done a naval contract before and I had no clue about boat building. He showed me his facility where he built small rescue craft used by merchant ships, primarily out of fibreglass. I didn't understand much of it. The boats he showed were very different from what I was hoping to sail in. The question that kept nagging me was, "Will this guy be able to build a boat that I can trust my life with, in the Southern Ocean, all alone?" I finally decided to put all my cards on the table and told him bluntly, "Let us get one thing straight. All I am asking for is a top quality boat that will take me around the world. My life depends on her. If I come back alive, I will forever praise you and be your brand ambassador for life. If the boat does not survive, I will ensure you will never build another boat ever!" He just smiled in his usual unassuming way and said, "Don't worry, you will come back alive!"

I took him to *Sameer*, to show what I didn't want in a boat. I wanted the boat to be as strong and uncomplicated as possible. I think he got the general idea. Somehow I developed a gut feeling that this unassuming and straight-talking guy, of all the other boat builders I had met, would do the best job and build a reliable boat that I could trust my life with. In the end, he more than lived up to that confidence.

Back in Mumbai, I now was stuck with two jobs: push the paper work required for the project and get *Sameer* repaired with the help of the Naval Dockyard.

Chapter 7

Humour in Uniform

While I was sailing *Sameer*, there was another crisis brewing in the project at Naval Headquarters. The cost of the boat design, which was to be bought from Van de Stadt Design Bureau, Netherlands, was working out to about Rs 10.5 lakh. As per government regulations, the designer was required to provide a bank guarantee amounting to 10 per cent of the amount, sign a 30 page standard contract, despatch the drawings and then wait for his payment to be cleared by the Navy. The designer flatly refused to accept such lopsided conditions and instead sent a two-page contract printed on plain paper and signed by him. That was unacceptable to NHQ. The whole thing was stuck in a bureaucratic mess.

I volunteered to go to Delhi to help sort out the mess, only to realise on arrival that there were many more issues that needed to be sorted out. The next 10 days or so proved to be a test of my patience, diplomatic skills and sense of humour.

One of my first visits was to a bureaucrat who had been refusing to move the file sanctioning funds for the project. Apparently, he wanted a day-to-day programme for the entire voyage, which was likely to start two years later. It is difficult enough to give the ETA of a sailboat two days in advance. How does one give the day-to-day programme two years in advance when the boat construction hasn't even started?

The night before the meeting, I jotted down all the possible questions he could ask and the answers that would help him understand the project and clear the file. When I met him the next day, I gave him the 'sales pitch' of the project in language as simple as I could manage. I told him what exactly sailing entailed, what a sailing yacht was, how I was planning to sail around the world solo, how this was the first time an Indian was attempting it, etc. Feeling mighty impressed about how smoothly I had 'sold' my project and fully prepared to answer any questions, I asked him if he had any. He looked at me with a deadpan expression and uttered a single word that totally stumped me:

"Why?"

"What do you mean, why?"

"Why do you want to do this?"

"Because no Indian has done it so far."

"But why does it need to be done? And why won't you use the engine on the boat when it is there?"

I suddenly started feeling as if I was taking part in an episode of *Yes Minister* with an Indian twist! It took all my patience and diplomatic skills to keep a straight face, answer all the queries and get an assurance that he would clear the file.

While in Delhi, I met a friend posted at NHQ who told me that a file about my project had landed up on his desk and he was required to give his professional opinion on it. As he had no clue about sailboats, he asked me to drop by at his office and explain things over a cup of coffee. When I saw the file the next day, my eyes popped out! It was at once amazing and hilarious. It had been started for listing out the specifications required for a boat for project Sagar Parikrama and this was the first time I was having a look at it. The recommendations were real gems, too good not to share with a naval friend who understood sailing...

*

Hi! Came to Delhi yesterday to push my files as the case seems to have got stuck in the red tape here! Planning to have a meeting on 18 Apr with COP and CNS. Let us see where this leads.

The type of questions I am being asked:

a. What provisions does your boat have to pass under bridges during the circumnavigation?

Actually I am planning to circumnavigate the earth and not Willingdon Island in Kochi.

b. The boat should have a foldable mast for reason at (a) above.

Brilliant! The mast is almost 27 m in height and supposed to withstand forces you can't even dream of! You don't want it folding itself in the Southern Ocean, do you?

c. What performance guarantees would the suppliers of equipment fitted onboard be giving? The stuff you have recommended is exorbitant! Why import it? Why not buy a cheaper design?

Hello, we are talking about my life here! Don't think anything is too exorbitant for that.

d. You have to pay € 19,000 for a design! That much for a bunch of papers and that too with a stipulation that you can use them only once?

The bunch of papers is a result of years of R&D. Go tell Bill Gates that the CD of his software should cost only Rs 10, the same as that in Palika Bazar for a blank one!

e. Why can't you sail through straits and canals? *Tarangini* sailed through the Red Sea.

Red Sea, a strait!

f. Why can't you carry a spare set of sails onboard? Just fold them up and put them in a bag.

We are talking about carbon fibre and Kevlar sails here. I will buy a round of drinks to the four people who can lift the mainsail together and carry it around! Anyway, a set of sails would cost Rs 30-40 lakh each.

g. Why do you want to import a 15 ltr/hour reverse osmosis plant (the smallest available) when a 3 ton/hour plant is available in India and is being fitted on ships? You should be happier with more fresh water.

Ever wondered about comparing the weights, sizes and power consumption of the two? I can go round the world with 3 ton of water and still have enough to drown myself in at the end!

h. Why don't you have motorised sails?

Why don't I motor down the route keeping the sails ashore?

i. (This is an old one from a hydrographer no less!) Why can't the Navy give you an escort ship? Don't tell me the Navy can't do it. The ship can keep following you.

Wonder if you ever stopped and reflected how big the sea was.

j. The boat should have a draft of 5-8 ft.

We are talking about a mast of about 27-m height! Imagine a 5-ft keel balancing that.

k. The keel should not be in the centre but should be longitudinal along the hull.

That's really revolutionary; not that I quite understand what it means!

l. The mast should be hollow to allow wiring through the mast.

Haven't heard of any solid aluminium masts so far.

m. The boat should be equipped with an air compressor and air storage banks.

Brilliant! I will direct the stored air on to the sails in nil wind conditions.

n. The boat should have a package A/C.

For sailing in the roaring 40s?

o. The windshield should have a heating arrangement and window wipers.

Windshield of a sailboat? I am planning to go in a boat not a car or aircraft.

p. All NBCD items and fire extinguishers should be available onboard.

Haven't we heard that before, "You are all sunk if you don't have the proper NBCD protection!"

q. The engine room, bridge, etc., should have a fixed fire-fighting system. There should be flooding alarms fitted in the bilges and all important compartments.

Wow, never knew my poor boat was supposed to have all these compartments.

r. The boat should be fitted with a refrigerator, deep freezer and microwave oven.

How did this guy know about my weakness for chilled beer and gourmet food? Wonder how I power these and what do I do with the additional weight?

s. The boat should be capable of anchoring every night during the circumnavigation.

I am expecting to have a couple of kilometres of water under the keel for the better part of the voyage. How am I supposed to anchor every night and for what?

As it is not fair to take pot shots only at naval officers, here is a nice one from an undersecretary who has returned my file a couple of times.

"Why should different boats travel at different speeds? They all should be able to travel at the same speed and the time taken between ports should be the same for all of them."

Do your files do that? Then why should boats be any different? After all, they are steered by humans too!

The list goes on and on. I am not sure whether to be amused or appalled at the level of ignorance. I suppose I should start listing these out and publish them once I am out of the Navy!

Life is really looking up!

Dilip

*

I could see my yet-to-be constructed boat getting buried under a pile of files with not a fighting chance of recovery. I went to the officer, a senior Captain, whose directorate had initiated the file. We were old shipmates and he was very keen to help me.

"Sir, do me a favour, let the file remain in circulation. I have already made my specifications and sent them to NHQ. Trust me, using those we will get a better boat."

"Don't worry, leave that to me. You go ahead and do what you feel is right," he replied with a smile, sizing up the problem instantly.

Six months later when I visited NHQ again for finalising the boat building contract, I met an officer who told me that he was really pushing my file as he wanted to help me and that the specifications would be ready in a few weeks.

Well, one crisis averted! For the moment at least. The problem of getting the design was still hanging fire. It was quite a ridiculous situation really. The Navy was ready to pay for the design, the designer wanted to sell his design but the two couldn't agree on the modalities of payment. At one point I offered to pay the money for the bank guarantee out of my pocket and get moving but that was not acceptable either. In every office I would hear the same rhetoric, "It is not possible to get the design under the present rules and with the designer's attitude. So just drop the idea." My standard answer was, "Look guys, I am planning to sail round the world, you think I can't find a way to get a design?"

Finally, a meeting was arranged at Delhi between the Chief of the Naval Staff, his deputies and Admiral Awati, the mentor of the project. The Admiral and Capt Soli Contractor arrived in

Delhi for the meeting and very unexpectedly started having cold feet just two hours before the meeting. "Look", said the Admiral, "I am a very impatient man and tend to lose my cool in a meeting very fast. All these admirals of today have been my youngsters and it won't look nice if I lose my cool in front of them. So it will be better that I don't attend!" I had had just about enough by then. I looked him and Soli Contractor straight in the eye and gave my ultimatum, "Sir, I have staked everything for this project. While I will appreciate your help in making it happen, I will go ahead and pull it through even if you are not around. It is your call, either you are with me or you are not!" A series of meetings followed that day and by the end of them we had worked out a solution acceptable to everyone.

I got back from Delhi and started working to repair *Sameer* and get some sailing experience. I soon realised that before facing the sea in a boat I had to first learn to repair and maintain her on my own.

I had been sailing the boat around the harbour whenever I could get a breather from submitting paperwork to NHQ and repairing the breakages that occurred at the end of each sail. The monsoons were less than a month away and I had started worrying about a safe berth for the boat as the present mooring off the Naval Sailing Club would soon become unsafe. The Naval Dockyard was filled to capacity with big steel hulled warships with hardly any space left for a fragile yacht like *Sameer*. Everyone agreed that the boat needed a safe berth but no one could provide a good solution to the problem. I eventually gave up the idea of sailing the boat during the monsoons and decided instead to concentrate on keeping her safe. That way I would be able to learn to repair her at my pace without losing sleep over her safety. The situation was becoming desperate with the onset of the monsoons and it was time to do something unorthodox.

The dockyard has a well-sheltered tidal basin that I thought was ideal for keeping the boat safe for a few months. The problem was that everyone seemed to be taking priority over us. I checked the tides and found that the tidal basin would be opened during the spring tide and then remain closed for the next two to three months till the tide rose to that height again. If I could somehow sneak the boat inside the basin before it was closed, the dockyard would have no option but to keep her there. On a Friday evening, a few hours before the basin was to be closed, I sneaked *Sameer* in, tied her alongside a pontoon inside and vanished. I went back to my office and made a signal informing everyone that I had tied the boat in the tidal basin, fully aware that no one would notice the signal till Monday morning. The trick worked! By Monday morning, there was a lot of hue and cry but no one could open the tidal basin till the next spring tide. The boat was safe and I told the complainers, tongue in cheek, that I had informed all of them about the movement of the boat before the basin closed. What a wonderful feeling getting back at the bureaucracy using its own tricks!

I managed to get some work done on the boat in the next few months but, more often than not, it was just bailing out water a couple of times a week whenever she flooded with the monsoon rains. While it seemed hard work then, it did help me get more and more independent and innovative. The boat was in a bad shape anyway and I couldn't have made her any worse even if I tried. I would often start trying to repair something on my own using borrowed tools from ships around, instead of waiting for qualified dockyard workers and wasting time. Sometimes I would manage to repair things, sometimes not, but there was always the satisfaction of having tried my best, having learned what it takes to do a particular task and test my capabilities.

Chapter 8

Training Boat

Right at the beginning of the project, it was clear that building a suitable boat was a time-consuming process. My lack of experience was always hanging over me like a sword. I needed a boat to train myself. My advisors came up with the idea of purchasing a smaller ocean-going yacht to enable me to get some much-needed 'sea time'. I was told to make the specifications for such a boat and initiate the process for procuring it. Needless to say, that became a sub-project in the main project. Even then it looked like a bit of a nonstarter but I was clutching at straws and desperate to try anything. My lack of experience also meant that few would take me seriously. 'Too many advisors and too few workers' had been the bane of my project and it would continue till the end. I spent considerable time going through the procurement process, learning in the bargain the complexities of government procurement, escrow accounts, 'High Sea sales' and a host of other things that a trained diver like me had never heard of. At one point, I joked to a friend that in the end I may or may not become the first Indian solo circumnavigator but would definitely become a good logistic officer in the Navy!

We shortlisted a 43-ft Beneteau to be procured off the shelf from France. I was to go to La Rochelle, France, to pick up the boat and sail her home through the Suez Canal. If that didn't make it spooky enough, what with my total lack of experience, I was supposed to do it in the next five days because after that the financial year would end and the funds would evaporate! The whole thing sounded like my mother telling me to go buy some vegetables from the market down the street and do it quickly before the market closed. Thankfully some sense prevailed and the whole venture was scrapped at the last minute. Personally, I heaved a sigh of relief, well justified on hindsight.

The inertia of our system is such that it takes much effort to get things moving and then almost as much to stop them. I discovered this in the next couple of months when I was ordered to start the procurement process afresh despite protesting that the boat for my circumnavigation would almost be ready by the time we could get a 'training boat'. I would rather sail the boat I was to do the circumnavigation in than waste time learning to sail a training boat.

"You asked for a training boat, now go and get it, we are funding it, and this time we will ensure that you get it!"

"But I don't need it. My boat will almost be ready by the time we manage to go through the procurement process."

"But you asked for it!"

"Yes, that was last year and in different circumstances. A lot has happened since then."

"Not our problem. You better get cracking on it and get the training boat."

I started getting a feeling of déjà vu and started wondering seriously if the Navy wanted me to sail around the world or procure boats for them that may or may not turn up. Luckily, I had grown wiser with experience and managed to brush the whole thing under the carpet rather diplomatically.

Chapter 9

The Eldemer Episode

Sometime in Sep 2007, I got a call from the Officer-in-Charge of the Navy's Seamanship School in Kochi telling me about a Prof Radhakrishnan who owned a catamaran called *Eldemer* and was looking for crew to sail it to Southeast Asia. He thought it would be a good training opportunity for me. I was so desperate for sea time that I readily agreed without having seen the boat. I got in touch with the Professor, a 78-year-old astrophysicist and son of nobel laureate Dr C V Raman, who insisted I called him Rad. Rad wanted to make one stop at Galle in Sri Lanka and then head for Malaysia and Thailand. He said that I better hurry up if I didn't want to miss the trip as the boat was almost ready. I managed to convince NHQ to allow me to sail on the boat for sea experience and rushed to Delhi to sort out the necessary paperwork.

It was back to running around from office to office with my files. I am not sure if Edwin Lutyens, the architect of South Block, realised the effects the imposing corridors of his edifice would have on harried naval officers trying to push their cases against the intransigence of the Indian bureaucracy. I would often start suffering symptoms of vertigo, running around from office to office with my files!

I finally managed to get all my clearances through and reached Kochi, all ready to set sail. Rad didn't seem to be in much of a hurry and we set sail a few days later. There were four of us on the boat, all volunteers like me and none of us with any experience of sailing the *Eldemer*. Even before we were out of the harbour and had set all the sails, things started falling apart! The mast spreaders landed on the deck one after another and the mast, only supported at the top and bottom, started whipping around, threatening to snap. Within an hour, Rad realised the futility of continuing with the trip and we turned back, motoring our way back to harbour.

Everyone was disappointed. Rad didn't seem too worried though. He was sure that things could be repaired in a few days. In my enthusiasm to sail, I had not paid much attention to the design and construction of the boat. The disastrous start forced me to pay more attention to these aspects and I started noticing the shortcomings in the boat. There appeared to be basic design issues in the rigging. When I pointed them out to Rad, he countered with a series of calculations that went over my head. In an effort to figure out the issues, I was applying basic seaman's logic with no calculations to support me; on the other hand, he, the scientist, believed everything could be calculated. I finally backed out by asking for an overnight trial sail before we tried to embark on a longer trip, complex calculations notwithstanding.

The repairs and modifications took longer than expected. By the time we were ready for a trial sail, our file for the boat's construction had made progress in Delhi and I thought it prudent to follow that up instead of spending my time at sea. We did go for an overnight trial sortie before I left, but there was not much wind and we really couldn't test the boat properly. I wished good luck to a rather disappointed Rad, explaining the need for me to be back in Delhi or Mumbai to move my project along. It was small consolation that I was the last of the crew members to leave.

While working with Rad one morning, I got a call from NHQ asking for the date I would start my circumnavigation.

"Date for commencing circumnavigation? I haven't thought about it yet. Shouldn't we be thinking about the date to start the boat's construction first?"

"The boat construction will start and finish. That is being looked after by another directorate; we want to start your file for the circumnavigation and need the date you plan to start."

"But we don't even have a boat yet; the construction contract is yet to be finalised, this is the first time we will be building a boat like this in the country; we have no idea when the construction will finish or what speeds she will sail at. How do you expect me to give you a firm date?"

"Do you want to do the circumnavigation or not?"

"Of course I want to!"

"Then tell me when you want to start!"

"Okay, if all goes well we should be able to get the boat ready by 2009 and then it will make sense starting in Aug or Sep." I reasoned trying to work back from a summer crossing of the Cape Horn in Jan and assuming that the boat would be capable of doing at least 100 nm a day.

"Fine, whatever you say, so what date do you plan to start?" I realised that the person at the other end of the phone was not going to take no for an answer till I came out with a date.

"Okay, 15 Aug 2009! I will start the circumnavigation on that day."

"Why that day, how are you sure you will be ready?" pat came the next question.

"I am not sure about anything right now. You wanted a firm date, so I am giving you one," I replied, fast losing patience and feeling like a character

out of Catch-22!

"You better tell me the reason you want to leave on that day, because I will need to put that in my file noting."

"Because it is a very good day, you see. No better day than Independence Day to start such a path-breaking voyage," I blurted out, desperate to get out of the situation while muttering under my breath, "And I will be independent of all this stupid red tape!"

"Okay, you better leave that day because it will be a pain to change the date later."

"Of course I will leave, Sir. You have my word."

So was decided the date of my departure, standing on a jetty in Kochi, under the blazing sun, over a mobile phone, with not even a calendar for reference. I got back to Rad's boat and started rummaging through the weather maps and publications to see if I had made any blunders with regard to the weather routing. I slowly realised, to my relief, that the date selected by me actually made a lot of sense.

Chapter 10

Training Sortie That Wasn't

Sometime in the afternoon of 07 Nov 2007 I got a surprise call from Commander Bram Weller of the South African Navy. I had met him a month ago during the World Military Games in Mumbai and he had promised to do whatever he could to help me.

"Dilip, would you like to do a delivery trip from Cape Town to the US on a catamaran?" he asked, getting straight to the point. "You will need to be in Cape Town by next week. I know it is very short notice but it may be worth it. See if you can manage."

Bram had kept the promise he made when we talked about my project over a drink at the Naval Sailing Club during the World Military Games. He had spoken to some of his friends in Cape Town and managed a berth for me on a brand new, 46 ft catamaran that was to be delivered in Florida. It would be a 7,000 nm trip with one stop, a chance to get the necessary sea time I had been trying so hard for. It was a win-win situation for everyone. I would get my sea time, the catamaran manufacturer would get a free crew, and the Navy would only need to pay for my air ticket, instead of spending a fortune on buying a training boat. The tight timeframe was the only concern.

"That is great news Bram! I will be there for the trip; let me start working on NHQ right away," I said, barely containing my excitement.

By the end of the day, I had managed to convince people at NHQ, pre-empted possible delays owing to bureaucratic inertia by emailing the necessary file notings that would be needed to process my case, and finalised my plans to head to Delhi. I had less than a week to sort out my paperwork with the government, arrange the necessary funding, get visas for South Africa and the US, and reach Cape Town. It was an ambitious timeline but this was an excellent opportunity and I was desperate.

I rushed to Delhi the next day and started running around, yet again, getting my clearances and visas. I was trying to finish a job in a day or less that would otherwise have taken a week. Richard, the skipper with whom I was to sail, had started getting anxious as his company was asking him to leave as soon as possible to enable delivery of the boat to the client before Christmas. The drama that unfolded can best be captured by the emails we exchanged over the next few days.

Tue, 13 Nov 2007
Hi Dilip,

How are things going your side? Hope you are managing okay. Please let me know. The people in the office are getting a bit nervous if you can make it. They want me to leave Monday or Tuesday latest. If you think the time is too short I will have to find other crew. Hope to hear from you soon.

Richard

Wed, 14 Nov 2007
Dear Richard,

Going full steam ahead and trying my best to hasten things up. Will let

you know by Fri.
   Dilip

Wed, 14 Nov 2007
Hi Dilip,

   Good to hear from you. Hope things are going to plan. Please tell me you can be in Cape Town Monday latest. I took over the yacht and the factory and Stewart Marine want me to leave ASAP. I could hold them till Monday latest, but if you are being delayed they want me to find other crew so I can leave soon.

   Really sorry for the pressure, but it is up to the 'powers that be' who call the shots. Let me know if you can meet the deadline. If you get here on Monday we will clear the yacht straightaway and leave ASAP. Unfortunately you won't get to see much of our beautiful city. Once again sorry for the short notice.

   Richard

Thu, 15 Nov 2007
Dear Richard,

   I am trying to get all the paperwork done before the weekend, which includes the two visas. Definitely should get one of them by tomorrow. Trying to put pressure through NHQ and Military Attaches to get the other one too. If that does not work, can only leave by Mon night and be there by Tue afternoon. The government has approved my visit already and is paying for the air tickets.

   No problems about hopping on the boat straight from the aircraft and sailing off. Sightseeing can happen later at leisure.

   Will keep you posted on a daily basis. Sorry for keeping you hanging like this but as you said, the powers that be call the shots!

   Dilip

Fri, 16 Nov 2007
Hi Dilip,

Good to hear you are making progress. If you manage to get all the visas will you be able to fly earlier? Will tell the office you will be here on Monday to keep them happy. If you arrive later, I will make some excuses. Good luck for tomorrow. Keep me informed.

Richard

Fri, 16 Nov 2007
Dear Richard,

Got the South African visa. Running for US visa. Unlikely to get it over the weekend. Trying my best for Mon. Will let you know.

Dilip

Sat, 17 Nov 2007
Dear Richard,

Booked my air ticket today. Will leave Delhi 2030 h on 19 Nov and arrive Cape Town 1410 h by SA 333 on 20 Nov via Dubai and Jo'burg. This is if I get my US visa by 1800 h on 19 Nov. If not, should definitely get the visa by 20 Nov and I arrive on 21 Nov by the same flight. I have a full fare ticket so changing dates at short notice is not an issue. We can sail the evening I arrive. Hope you can sweet-talk your office till then! You need to give me the directions for reaching the boat or, if possible, we can meet at the airport and head for the boat.

Buying an open ticket from Fort Lauderdale to New Delhi for the return trip.

Dilip

Sun, 18 Nov 2007
Hi Dilip,

Good to hear you are making progress. When you know which flight you are on let me know. You will have to book a flight from Jo'burg to Cape Town. I will need to know what time you will land so either me or Kirsty will meet you at the airport. Really hope you leave on Monday as we must get going to keep everyone happy. I must order some meat for the trip. Do you eat chicken and steak? Must it be halaal? The fish we will eat we have to catch, so some fun coming up.

    Richard

Sun, 18 Nov 2007
Dear Richard,

My flight from Jo'burg to Cape Town is SA 333 arriving Cape Town 1410 h. Will confirm the day tomorrow depending upon the progress at the US Embassy.

I have no problems about any food or meat except that I avoid drinking milk as it gives me a stomach upset. As far as I am concerned the only categories of food are edible or non-edible! So feel free to get whatever you like.

    Dilip

Mon, 19 Nov 2007
Hi Dilip,

Hope you got it all together. Good luck, enjoy the passage.

    Bram

Mon, 19 Nov 2007
Dear Bram, Richard,

Not quite yet, I am afraid. Unlike the SA High Commission, the US Embassy wasn't so cooperative. When I went to collect my visa at 1630 h today, they told me it was not ready yet and will be ready by 1630 h on 20 Nov. Had to postpone my ticket three hours before departure. So I start from

Delhi at 2030 h on 20 Nov and reach Cape Town 1410 on 21 Nov by SA 333 via Dubai and Jo'burg.

Really sorry for all this chaos.

Richard, I will call you before boarding the flight tomorrow.

Dilip

Tue, 20 Nov 2007

Hi Dilip,

Sorry to hear about your visa. Good luck for tomorrow. Give me a call when you land in Jo'burg. We will meet you at the airport. My no. is 0824725942.

Richard

Tue, 20 Nov 2007

Dear Richard,

After all this running around, the US Embassy seems to have put a spoke in the wheel. They asked me to send my CV, list of publications, itinerary, etc., to them by today evening and will give clarifications only by tomorrow afternoon. This is really unusual for an official visa which is processed within 24 hrs. Regrettably, that means I am stuck and not even able to give a reasonable assurance to you.

It may be a good idea to start looking for a standby crew as you must be finding it difficult to hold your company too long. Let me know when you will be leaving if you get another crew. If the Yanks give me a visa and I can make it before that, well and good, otherwise I miss the trip. I feel really embarrassed to keep you hanging like this but I really don't know what more to do or what's bugging the US Embassy.

Dilip

I was at my wits' end by now. It was clear that there was some bureaucratic mix up at the Embassy. Why else would someone ask for a list of publications and itinerary from a sailor on a boat delivery trip? All I wanted was to be allowed to get off the boat in an US port and catch the next flight home. I decided to keep trying nevertheless, becoming quite a pest in the bargain, bugging anyone and everyone who could talk to someone at the US Embassy and sort out this mess.

Wed, 21 Nov 2007
Hi Dilip,

Really bad news. I will see if I can get other crew in the meantime. See what you can do and let me know if there are new developments. Hope you can sort it out today. Good luck.

Richard

Wed, 21 Nov 2007
Richard,

Thanks for the encouragement. Should come to know in a couple of hrs.
Dilip

My South African friends had been so considerate, I decided not to give up and keep trying. At 1630 h, the US Embassy handed me my visa instead of the clarifications they had promised to give me! They probably figured out that I actually was a harmless sailor and not some scientist in disguise hiding state secrets. In less than an hour, I was sitting in the Air India office, trying to book myself on the first available flight to Cape Town. The lady doing the booking didn't seem too convinced about my plans, not surprising given my record of changing plans at the last minute!

"Are you really ready to go?"

"Yes, this time I am, and in a tearing hurry!"

"Okay, be at the airport in six hours; unfortunately you will have to spend a night at Johannesburg airport and we cannot give you a hotel booking."

"No problem, as long as it is the earliest I can make it." "You can't make it any faster."

"Okay, give me the ticket, don't worry, this time there won't be any cancellation," I assured her confidently.

With the ticket in hand and a sense of relief I walked out of the office, mentally ticking off my checklist for departure. Okay, two tasks left before departure, call up Richard at Cape Town and confirm arrival details, then run to the mess, pack up my stuff and head for the airport!

More relieved than excited, I called up Richard from a public phone right next to the airline office.

"Hi Richard, this is Dilip from India, I will be catching a flight in the next couple of hours and reaching Cape Town tomorrow. I can hop on the boat straight from the airport and we can sail out."

"I am sorry Dilip, but I will be sailing out tonight. I have managed another crew and cannot hold on any longer."

"One more day, please! Can't you take an extra crew, look I am ready to sleep on the deck and don't even need a bunk!"

"I am really sorry but I can't wait any longer. I will ask the company to let you know if there are more such trips in the pipeline."

"Well, okay, have a safe trip and thanks a lot for being so patient."

Richard had been more than patient with me. He had gone

out of his way to help an unknown sailor from a different country even if it meant sticking out his own neck and putting his reputation on the line.

Within 30 minutes of assuring Air India about my intention to board their flight, I was running after them to cancel my ticket, this time for good. My trans-Atlantic training trip was over even before setting foot on the boat. I was in a state of shock.

"So, what next?" I asked myself.

"Nothing! Let us get back to the mess, have a nice stiff drink and call it a day. Tomorrow, we sort out the paperwork for cancelling the trip and head home the day after. Let us forget about training for a while and concentrate on building a boat," replied my exasperatingly stoic alter ego.

Chapter 11

A Womb for the Boat

While running after training boats that had little chance of becoming available or trying to sail old boats to get some 'sea time' was fine, the core activity of the project was to build a suitable boat and it was important to maintain focus. As mentioned earlier, the paperwork for the process had commenced at NHQ in 2007 once my rough specifications were ready and a capacity assessment team had been appointed to shortlist boatyards from across the country.

The team shortlisted four boatyards they thought had the potential to build the boat we wanted. I was not a member of the team but was told to render any assistance they required as none of the team members had any experience of yacht building or sailing. I was naturally very curious about their results. The success of the project and, to an extent, my life depended on the quality of the boat. I had already visited Aquarius Fibreglas at Goa and formed a favourable opinion of the boat builder Ratnakar Dandekar. The yard did not have a shed large enough to build a boat of the size we wanted but Ratnakar had promised to set up the necessary infrastructure if he got the contract. He, of course, did not have any experience of sailing, building a sailboat or building anything for the Navy!

The second prospective boat builder came to visit me in my office at the Naval Sailing Club in Mumbai. I briefed him about the project and started showing him all the material I had, including the design plan, specifications and budgetary quotes. He cut me short soon enough with the information that his family had been boat builders for the past 150 years and he was confident about building whatever we wanted.

"So what can I do for you?" asked the builder, looking a bit disinterested with my lists of specifications and design plans.

"Like I told you, build a strong boat that will get me back alive!"

"You need not worry about that, sir! My family has been building boats for so long and it is no big deal building another one for you. So tell me, what more can I do for you?"

"Well, give me a good price!"

"Sir, the boat will get built and you will get a good price, which is no big deal! But what more can I do for you?"

I just didn't understand what he was getting at and blurted out, "Make sure you deliver the boat in time, or earlier if possible."

How dumb, the guy must have thought! "Sir, don't worry, boats get built eventually. But what can I do for you?

And then the penny dropped, 'You' being the operative word! I suddenly realised what he was getting at and wasn't sure whether to get angry at his audacity or laugh at my dumbness! I needed to get out of the situation diplomatically.

Trying to look as nonplussed as possible I told him, "Look, my life depends on the quality of the boat you build. If you build a bad boat, I won't be able to get back to enjoy whatever you are trying to offer me. The Navy pays me well and I am quite content with what I get. Now if you would like go through the specifications in detail..."

I happened to be in Kochi, where two of the four yards were located, when the assessment team decided to pay a visit. I tagged along to have a look. We visited Praga Marine Pvt Ltd, who had been making fibre glass dinghies for the Navy for many years. The boat builder liked the idea of the project but seemed reluctant to undertake the boat building owing to an overflowing order book. Out of the four yards, he was the only one who understood sailing and it was a bit disappointing to get an outright 'no' from him.

A visit to another yard nearby was interesting. The yard had previous experience in building and supplying power yachts, used as Admirals' barges, to the Navy. They seemed to be well equipped to build fibre glass boats and had perhaps the most impressive facility amongst the four shortlisted yards. The manager, who came to take us around, didn't seem too interested in us nor have any idea about a sailboat. We were carrying the study plans received from the designer and some photos of sailboats to explain our requirements. The total lack of interest shown by the manager was a bit unnerving. I told him that the boat may cost well over a million dollars, which warmed him up a bit and he finally agreed to have a look at what we wanted to build! As I was showing him the photos, he pointed his finger at the boom of a sailboat and asked, "What is that horizontal white line in the picture?"

"Why, it's the boom!"

"Oh, okay! What is that for?"

Eventually, the capacity assessment team recommended all the four yards for issue of a tender. No one was perfect but we didn't have a choice. I was worried by what I had seen of the yards and the experience or rather inexperience of the boat builders. There wasn't much I could do about it. The Navy was going to stick to the government procurement procedure, which meant all four yards would be asked to submit their offers and the lowest bidder would eventually bag the contract. I wanted a top quality boat but I did not have any say in selecting the yard. Even if I had, I could not find any particular reason to be partial to one over the other. On a personal level, I had developed the most favourable impression about Ratnakar. It was just a gut feeling that this straight talking guy would deliver whatever he promised, but gut feelings are not acceptable in government procurement procedures.

While drafting the terms and conditions of the contract, I insisted on at least three visits by the boat designer's representative to the yard during various stages of construction. This was my attempt at ensuring quality of construction in the absence of any expertise in the country. On hindsight, this turned out to be the most important and beneficial clause in the contract, both for the project and Ratnakar.

The draft tenders did their rounds on the files at NHQ and were eventually despatched to the four boatyards. Only two yards responded and the bid submitted by Aquarius Fibreglas was substantially lower. I went to Delhi to finalise the contract. A few minutes into the meeting, Ratnakar was asked to give a discount on the price quoted by him. This is an archaic and, at times, absurd way of working in the Indian Government where the establishment is only worried about bringing down the price once the technical conditions have been finalised, often at the cost of quality. Ratnakar, working with the Navy for the first time, was taken by surprise.

"You asked me to give my lowest quote, which I have given. How can you ask me to go lower than the lowest quote? I am sorry but I can't go any lower!"

"But we have to bring down the price," insisted the representative of the financial advisor, secure in the knowledge that he would never need to step on the boat.

The Commodore chairing the meeting saw a standoff developing and asked Ratnakar to step out of the room and wait. Once Ratnakar went out, the Commodore asked me what I thought of the pricing.

"Sir, the pricing is very reasonable. At this price, he can forget about any profits and should consider himself lucky if he manages to break even. I think we should instead concentrate on ensuring that we get a quality product and not fight over small change."

"How can you be so certain?" asked the Commodore, aware of my inexperience in these matters.

"Well, I did the costing for the boat while making the specifications and have a fairly good idea how much it would cost. Ratnakar's quote is as close to rock bottom as one can get."

Ratnakar was eventually called back in the room and the deal was sealed with the financial advisor's representative extracting a 1 per cent discount for the construction of a 'yacht' for the Indian Navy. It would have been so much better for everyone if that person had instead advised us on the wording to be used in the contract. As we were to discover over a year later, under Indian excise laws, a yacht is categorised as a luxury item and attracts considerable duty.

It took another two months for NHQ to draft the boat construction contract. Admiral Awati and I had started getting rest-less with the delay. There wasn't much time left if I were to start on 15 Aug 2009. Ratnakar was being given a year to complete the boat construction. All of us were aware of the tight deadlines we had set for ourselves. Ratnakar finally decided to start the construction on Christmas of 2007, a day before he was to go to Delhi to sign the contract.

I had not taken any leave for the past two years and decided to use this opportunity to have a few days' break before I got too busy with the boat construction. The plan was to drive down to Goa a few days before Christmas, stopping for a day or two at one of the many scenic places en route before finally arriving for the so called 'keel laying' ceremony of the boat. As I was sitting in my car at a toll booth on the outskirts of Mumbai, waiting for my turn to move ahead, my car was rammed from behind by a trailer that made the car jump and wedge itself under a trailer ahead. I managed to escape unhurt but the car was badly damaged and there ended all my plans for one last, albeit short, holiday. I towed the car back to Mumbai and flew down to Goa barely in time to attend the ceremony. It is only natural for peo-ple to get a bit superstitious on occasions such as these. While everyone was glad I had escaped unhurt, I could see lines of worry and 'bad omen' written on many a face. I laughed off the worries by saying, "Good we had the accident! The quota of bad luck has been expended there and the boat we are about to start building is going to be extremely lucky!"

I tried my best to look composed and confident to everyone but personally I was extremely apprehensive. This boat was going to be my sole companion on a voyage of discovery, her strength and quality would make the difference between disappearing at sea and coming back alive. She better be a good boat, strong to withstand the punishing Southern Ocean and large hearted to forgive my inexperienced handling. I think that was when I started talking to the boat – and I have never stopped since. She didn't have a name yet, I just called her 'boat' or 'girl'.

"Let us go on the biggest adventure of our lives sweetheart, let us sail around the world, just the two of us and let us come back to tell the stories. Be strong; be good, we are going to learn to look after each other, there isn't going to be anyone else!" I kept talking to the soon-to-be-constructed boat while going through the motions of the blessing ceremony (*puja*) and meeting people, most of them for the first time.

Admiral Awati, Capt Soli Contractor and his family were present. So was Ratnakar's family, including his parents, sisters and their families. Everyone seemed excited about the project. It felt good. The boat we were going to build had already started gathering a fan following. She was not going to be a just another piece of hardware, she had already started developing a personality and a group of people who cared for her. She was going to be the best boat in the world! She was going to be my boat.

Chapter 12

Finally, Some Sailing

I returned home to Mumbai from the keel laying ceremony and sailed out to Kochi within a week on a J 24 boat. The aim was to participate in an offshore sailing rally from Kochi to Kavaratti, the administrative capital of the Lakshadweep group of islands 200 nm west of the Indian mainland. Usually, a couple of J 24 boats would be carted by road from Mumbai to Kochi for the rally, sailed and then again carted back. Now, I was desperate for all possible offshore sailing I could do, so I suggested sailing the boats to Kochi some 600 nm away to participate in a 200 nm rally. The J 24 boat is essentially a day sailing boat used more for keel boat racing inside harbours than for ocean cruising. Being a harbour racing boat, it did not have any amenities to live on-board nor any provision to shorten sail if the wind picked up. Getting a crew to sail the three boats proved more difficult than expected. While many were keen on participating in the rally, few were interested in delivering the boats to the start line and none in getting the boats back after the rally. Finally, after a fair bit of coaxing, cajoling and coercing we managed to get two sets of crew, one to take the boats to Kochi and participate in the rally and another to get the boats back. It was an interesting trip for more than one reason.

The Navy, wary of any possible mishap, insisted on deputing a ship to escort us and drew up plans to make us sail in a proper naval formation with elaborate communication plans and reporting procedures. However, within hours of setting sail, the poor escort ship saw her herd break ranks and disperse, each trying to follow their own course at varying speeds. By next morning, all the boats were out of sight and radio communication range, with the hapless escort trying out all possible search patterns to locate them. The winds were very light and we were mainly relying on the land and sea breezes, often drifting over a windless sea. The escort would get restless during such calms and try to take us in tow, at times creating some excitement in an otherwise dull sail, as noted in my diary entries.

08 Jan 2008

0730 h – *About 40 nm from Kochi, nil winds. Towing rope of escort snagged in the first boat's keel while being taken in tow. The boat was dragged athwartship and almost capsized while the other two piled up on the first one. Tow cut off by the first boat. The ship had had enough and sailed off in a huff.*

0900 h – *All three boats sailing in over 20 kts of winds and squally weather.*

1800 h – *Alongside at Kochi.*

The organisers of the rally had mentioned Sagar Parikrama to the local press and there was a fair amount of interest in the local media. Kochi was also getting ready to host the Volvo Ocean Race, so offshore sailing was the talk of the town. I answered whatever questions the media posed, trying to look as calm as possible but the apprehensions in my mind were growing. Now that the project had started developing some degree of hype, would we be able to produce the results expected from us? I was talking to Ratnakar regularly and knew he had started cutting the strip planking that would form the core of the boat. Simultaneously, we had started finalising the equipment to be fitted and their sources of supply.

The rally passed off peacefully without a major incident with the winds remaining light for the entire duration. The brief stay at Kavaratti was probably the best part. The Lakshadweep group of islands are small pristine coral islands with turquoise blue lagoons, white sand and undoubtedly the best diving sites in the country. I had fond memories of doing some excellent diving in the area and it was wonderful to revisit these places again after almost 10 years.

We sailed the boats back from Kochi to Mumbai, often getting towed by impatient escorts thanks to frequent light or head winds, reaching Mumbai in the first week of Feb 2008. I started getting a feeling that I had learned what I could from offshore sailing on J 24s and it was time I started paying more attention to the boat we were building. While sea time and training were important, it was even more important that the boat we were building was well built and that I knew her well.

Chapter 13

Robin's First Visit

On 08 Feb 2008, I picked up Robin from Mumbai airport. I had extended an invitation to him to come down to India two years ago and he had kept his promise to help me with my project once his race was over. He was making a longish detour in Mumbai on his way from the UK to China. The boat construction was yet to gather momentum. If we wanted to make any major changes to the boat design, this was our last chance; it would be too late once the boat started taking shape. I was well aware of our lack of experience in building and sailing a yacht while Robin had a lifetime of experience doing just that.

We got down to poring over the drawings and making lists of modifications right away. The idea was to make the boat more forgiving, reliable and efficient. "I want the boat to be idiot proof," I would often say loud and clear, "because I am going to be sailing her!"

As mentioned earlier, Robin had started his merchant navy career in Mumbai. We visited the ship-breaking yards of Mumbai and the adjacent shops selling stuff from the stripped ships. Robin had stories galore about how he bought cheap equipment from the area while building the *Suhaili* well before I was born. A lot had changed in the city since then and we didn't find too many useful things in the shops but it was nice to move around in areas I would otherwise never bother to visit, listening to stories of a different era.

Listening to Robin talk about how he built the *Suhaili* from his own funds really bolstered my confidence. Compared to what he had to go through, my project looked like a 'five star' project with everything laid out on a platter! I didn't really need to struggle for funds as long as I could tolerate and find my way through the idiosyncrasies of the bureaucracy. Unlike Robin, who had to find time from his job to build a boat, I was working full time on my project, which essentially meant that I was getting paid to do my project. If he could build his boat in Mumbai over 40 years ago with so many obstacles, and sail her around the world non-stop, there was no reason why I should not be able to do it with far better resources and technology at my disposal.

It was an interesting way to work. Once we had gone over the drawings, we kept discussing the boat and project while moving around in Mumbai. We visited an old fort on Cross Island, just off the Mumbai docks, discovering over 200-year-old fortifications and guns in ruins. Took a quick drive through the National Defence Academy, my alma mater in Pune, for no particular reason except to go for a long drive and have a look at the countryside. Ate all sorts of Indian food and even arranged Indian cookery classes for Robin at home. Between discussions about British Indian history, traditions in the Armed Forces and the intricacies of Indian epicurean delights, the focus was always on the boat and the subsequent solo circumnavigation.

Chapter 14

The First Hurdle

Right from the beginning, we were conscious of the extremely tight timeframe we had set for building the boat. This meant very little spare time to accommodate delays and a steep penalty clause if the delays did occur. Sometime in mid Feb 2008, just when I thought the construction would start picking up pace, Ratnakar gave me a call.

"Dilip, we have a problem. The seasoned red cedar wood we bought for making the boat's core isn't seasoned well enough. The designer has recommended less than 14 per cent moisture in the wood, we have 20 per cent. I have stopped construction and can only begin when we get seasoned wood."

"What? Didn't you give the specifications to the saw mill and check the moisture when you ordered the wood?" I blurted out, trying to keep a calm voice while fighting feelings of anger, despair and shock.

Apparently Ratnakar had bought the red cedar wood, grown in the highlands of North Kerala, from a well-recommended saw mill in Mangalore with the assurance that it met all the specifications laid down by the boat designer. There was no reason to double check the moisture content after having paid a hefty premium for quality seasoned wood. Once the logs were cut into strip planking of the required shape and size for making the boat's core, he had done his last check and stumbled upon a potential disaster. No one would have realised if he had used the wood in that condition, certainly not me who, as the Navy's official overseer responsible for ensuring quality construction, didn't even know what the gauge for measuring the moisture looked like! The effects would perhaps have started showing after a year or so, well after the boat's warranty was over and I was in the middle of the Southern Ocean! Unseasoned wood, that is wood with high moisture content, tends to start warping as the moisture evaporates slowly. It would only be a matter of time before a boat constructed out of such wood would start distorting and develop leaks.

"So, can we get seasoned wood at such short notice? How long does it take to season the quantity of wood we need and what do you do with all the wood you have invested in?" I asked even as I was getting the feeling that the answers would not be what I wanted to hear.

"I don't think anyone would season the wood we have cut at short notice. We will need to search if someone has a stock of seasoned wood, which I am afraid is quite unlikely, but let us try our best," replied Ratnakar without much conviction.

Over the next two weeks, I tried to contact anyone and everyone I knew in the boat building and construction industry, drawing consistent blanks, while Ratnakar travelled around the country experiencing similar results. When I broke the news to Admiral Awati, he was furious. "If this is the way we are going to be constructing the boat, I am not sure where all this is leading. What sort of boat builder have we landed up with?" thundered the octogenarian. We had spent over a year arranging the funds, finalising the boat building contract, importing the design and finally getting the go ahead from the Navy to start construction and now were sitting pretty because we didn't have wood to build the boat!

Time was running out, and fast. In the end, Ratnakar lost patience. He decided to stop searching for wood or kilns around the country and take matters in his own hand or rather, to his own yard. He built a makeshift shed in the yard, lined it from inside with thick tarpaulin to create as much insulation as possible before finally installing 10 electric room heaters and a heavy duty dehumidifier to create a hot and dry environment. The strip planks, already cut, were laid out on the floor with small wooden vices holding them to prevent them from warping as they dried. The wood seasoning kiln was up and running! In his characteristic way, Ratnakar had simplified the whole process of wood seasoning and found a workable solution. Regular measurements of the humidity in the wood indicated that the process was working well and by the end of another two weeks he had enough wood to start making the boat's core. *Mhadei* had started taking shape.

Chapter 15

Our Boat Building Guru

As mentioned earlier, I had insisted on at least three visits by the boat designer's representative at the boat builder's expense as a quality control measure. As the boat designer didn't have anyone he could spare for the job, he asked Mr Johan Vels, a retired boat builder, to represent him. None of us realised it then, but in asking Johan to represent him, the designer had unwittingly given us the biggest leg up for building the boat.

Johan, a six-and-a-half-feet Dutch giant in his mid 60s, is a retired boat builder with experience of building over 250 boats of all possible types and sizes. He had set up his boatyard in Holland some 40 years back, seen it flourish and then gutted in a fire. He eventually resurrected the yard before finally selling it to lead a more relaxed life as a consultant. He had worked in Southeast Asia earlier but this was his first experience working in India.

We met over dinner the day he landed in Goa and I briefed him about the project. In the next few days, there were endless discussions on every aspect of boat building, including the various modifications suggested by Robin. As we got to know Johan better, we realised that he was much more than just a boat designer's representative. He had tremendous experience in every aspect of yacht construction and was ready to share it as long as we were ready to listen. It wouldn't be an exaggeration to say that during his first visit, we didn't even know what to ask him! He couldn't believe that Ratnakar had agreed to a timeframe of one year to build the boat.

"I wouldn't agree to anything less than 18 months for a boat this size, and that only after I have discussed every modification and fitting on the boat with the boat owner for at least a week," he told us.

He had an odd bunch of people before him. Ratnakar was the boat builder but didn't have any experience of building sailing yachts. Ottavio, Ratnakar's Italian carpenter, had hands on experience working in a yard and sailing but not much of running a boatyard. I had no experience of building anything but knew how to sail and was the obvious guinea pig of the entire venture!

"If you guys really want to build this boat well and in time, you better work together as a team," was Johan's simple advice. His first impression about the whole venture was far from favourable. Our lack of knowledge and the chaotic way things tend to work in India probably convinced him that we were trying to bite far more than we could chew and were doomed to fail. Nevertheless, he kept his apprehensions to himself, patiently answered all the questions we posed to him, and many that we should have posed but didn't. As we progressed with the boat building, Johan became our main boat building consultant and Ratnakar's mentor, teaching him the finer points of building a boat as well as running an efficient boatyard. We had been lucky yet again! Right at the beginning we had met Robin whose guidance had proved invaluable and now we had bumped into Johan to guide us on constructing a top quality boat. A year later when the boat was almost ready, Johan confessed that he was very happy to have been proven wrong about his first impression.

Chapter 16

Adieu Sameer

Between constructing and finalising equipment for the new boat and doing the paperwork for a training boat I was reluctant to waste time on, I couldn't lose sight of good old *Sameer*, the 34-ft dilapidated sloop I had sailed to Mumbai against all advice. The boat was still lying in Mumbai and my grand plans of sailing her around the Indian coast to train myself had been watered down considerably by the reticence of the technocracy. I realised that I was wasting too much time and energy just looking after her and trying to get her refitted without getting any real training or experience. It was time I got her sailworthy enough to undertake the 600 nm passage to Kochi and get her off my hands. I managed to convince the Naval Dockyard to take her up on a slipway at its boat repair shop and started working on her whenever I could get the time. I managed to get some work done on her hull and get a shaft seal fabricated at the dockyard to ensure that she would not leak and sink alongside. I also managed to get rid of over nine layers of paint off her hull. While training as a cadet many years ago, our training chief had quipped that in the Navy you grease everything that moves and paint everything that does not. The boat's maintainers before me seemed to have taken this joke rather seriously!

The progress of work on *Sameer* eventually came to a standstill owing to a shortage of funds. This may sound implausible for a naval boat but the funds were buried deep under layers of red tape and I had no more patience to dig them out. I got the boat ready as best as I could, politely refused the Navy's offer for an escort, and kept mum about the non-functional engine, unreliable steering and almost everything else in the boat. A couple of cruising boats were sailing out from Mumbai to Goa as part of the Vasco da Gama Rally and I decided to tag along. I reasoned that we would have boats around us for the first half of the trip if we needed assistance and if the boat could sail the first 200 nm without a problem, she should be able to sail the next 400 nm too. I was more apprehensive about the reluctance of Headquarters to let us sail if they came to know the boat's material state. To avoid taking any chances, the Captain responsible for adventure activities at Command Headquarters was included as part of the two-member novice crew till Goa. He was keen on doing a short sailing passage and was happy to let me be the skipper because of his lack of sailing experience. I readily agreed and told him to just hop on and leave everything to me. The actual material state of the boat was divulged to him only after we crossed the start line along with other boats. He was horrified with the actual state of the boat but it was too late to turn back; the skipper would never agree to it!

We eventually made it to Kochi without much ado. The experience taught me an important lesson: In a sailboat, as long as you can put up some sail and have some means of steering, you can keep going. Having done just that over a 600-nm passage with a novice crew boosted my confidence considerably. *Sameer* had served her purpose; it was time to let her go while I concentrated on the new boat construction. I handed over *Sameer* at Kochi with a long list of recommendations for her refit and upkeep; my little parting gift to the boat.

Chapter 17

Mhadei

Naming a boat can be tricky business, probably as tricky as naming one's child. The name has to be feminine, it must be unique and it should mean something; even better, have a story to it. If you are convinced the boat is on her way to finding a place in a nation's maritime history, things become even more complicated. All of us involved with the project had been giving it a thought but had not been able to come up with anything interesting. While taking *Sameer* back to Kochi in Apr 2008, I had managed a brief stopover at Goa, to check on the boat's construction. Admiral Awati was also in town. A self-confessed history buff, he had been visiting the interiors of Goa checking out sculptures from the Kadamba period 2,000 years ago. On the morning of 18 Apr 2008, I was waiting with the Admiral and Ratnakar to catch a ferry to go to the boatyard. We were stand-ing under the shade of an ancient mango tree laden with fruit; a cool breeze was blowing. The Admiral was telling us about his trip in the interiors of Goa where he had seen sculptures of the sailors' goddess, Mhadei, standing on a boat complete with a mast, the outline of a sail and a crow's nest. He mentioned that the river flowing close to the area was named after the goddess.

"But sir, this is Mhadei, the parent stream of the Mandovi

river in Goa," said Ratnakar, pointing at the river flowing next to us, on whose opposite bank our boat was taking shape.

"How would that name be for the boat?" the three of us said, almost in unison.

"Well she is Dilip's boat, he has to have the final word," decreed the Admiral.

"Sounds good! Mhadei, it is!"

Thus was decided the name for our boat, standing under a mango tree with one of the greatest sailors in history, Vasco da Gama, staring down on us from the Viceroy's Arch close by. The name met all possible criteria; it was feminine, I had never seen a boat by that name before and it definitely had a story. Our ferry arrived shortly and we reached the boatyard. The boat was still in the form of an un-laminated wooden core. In India, when a child is named, it is usual to have a small ceremony where the baby's name is whispered in its ear for the first time. While we never got down to a ceremony, I did manage to steal a quiet moment in the boat shed; I touched *Mhadei* and whispered her name to her. The Admiral, as the mentor of the project, took on the responsibility of informing everyone and dashed out an email a day later, which perhaps best explains the origin of her name.

Dear All,

The Sagar Parikrama team has, for some time, been considering a name for our boat. A number of suggestions were considered but rejected as not being either evocative or apposite. I was in Goa recently to look at the progress of construction and took the opportunity to visit the interior near the Ghats to look at the recent historical and archaeological finds, which throw interesting light on the Boat Devi cult prevalent among the people here. In numerous temples in and around the towns of Valpoi, Sanvardem and others, the Boat/ Nau Devi is carved in the local black volcanic stone, depicting her seated in a boat which is shown in some detail with mast, crow's nest, sails, oarsmen, etc. These carvings belong to the Rashtrakuta and Kadamba periods of history of Gomantaka/Goa. The source of the Mandovi is not far from here in the Ghats.

The infant Mandovi is the Mhadei hereabouts. She is worshipped along with the Devi which is the presiding deity here. Professor Pratima Kamat, Professor and Head of History at Goa University, was my guide. She explained to me the fascinating Boat Devi culture of Goa and its historical-cultural connection with the maritime cultural traditions of the faraway Orissa coast around the great temple of Konark. Here was a wonderful example of the cultural unity of India.

The Mhadei flows towards the sea. She becomes the Mandodari as she approaches her destination near the ancient Kadamba port city of Gopakapattan, which was near today's Goa Velha. It was the Kadamba capital. The Portuguese had some difficulty with the word Mandodari. They conveniently converted the name to Mandovi, the river on which our boat is being built. The Mhadei is the parent stream. The Parikrama team is of the view that the name Mhadei for the boat will be both evocative and appropriate. It honours the Boat Devi of Goa and seeks her blessings for a successful circumnavigation in the name of both Gomantak and India.

Best wishes in the name of the Mhadei,
Manohar Awati

The boat's core, made from planks of seasoned red cedar glued together, was slowly taking shape in Goa. Once the core was ready and rubbed down to a smooth finish, it was to be laminated with layers of glass fibre and epoxy resin. The wood would give the necessary shape and stiffness to the boat while the glass fibre epoxy laminate would protect the wood and provide strength to the boat. Thus, the wood core was like the skeleton of the boat, providing shape, while the laminate was the muscle, protecting the skeleton and providing strength. This would be covered by epoxy filler and, finally, by paint, which would be like the skin of the boat, protecting everything inside and making the boat look good.

The lamination process is basically a chemical reaction between the glass fibre and epoxy resin. Like many chemical reactions, this one is susceptible to environmental conditions like the ambient temperature and humidity. In order to ensure the right ambient conditions, Ratnakar had planned to enclose the boat in a big plastic tent equipped with air-conditioners and dehumidifiers. He was confident of commencing the lamination by end Apr 2008 and had prepared sample laminates using the fibreglass mat and epoxy resin in the presence of the surveyors. The samples were to be sent for testing to a laboratory approved by the surveyors. Everything seemed to be going as planned when I got one of those dreaded calls from Ratnakar in the last week of Apr 2008.

"Dilip, bad news, we may have to delay the lamination."

"Oh no, not again! What now?"

"We did an in-house test on one of the laminate samples before sending it to the lab approved by the surveyor. The sample failed the test. Obviously, the epoxy we bought from the Indian supplier isn't good enough. I have ordered a new stock from the UK by air freight and hope to receive it in a week or so. It is costing double the amount but I don't see any alternative."

Even if the epoxy arrived within a week as promised, we would need to make fresh laminate samples in the presence of the surveyor and get them tested before going ahead with the lamination. I could see a setback of another month at least.

Three weeks later, I was in Goa with the surveyor, witnessing fresh laminate samples being prepared. The wooden core was looking impressive and I had started getting an idea about the size of the boat. There were rolls of fibreglass mat piled till the roof, each one cut to size and numbered to ensure ready availability once we started the lamination. The temperature outside the boat's air-conditioned tent was touching 40°C with over 80 per cent humidity while inside, the boat was sitting in a comfortable 25°C with less than 50 per cent humidity. Unfortunately, the lab test reports on the test laminates were likely to take a couple of weeks. I took Ratnakar out of the surveyor's earshot and asked, "So when do you plan to start the lamination?"

"Tonight," came the nonchalant reply.

"But shouldn't we get the laminate test results first? What happens if the test fails again?"

"Don't worry, it won't fail this time, we are using the best material available in the market."

"Well, what happens if the test fails for some reason? Would we then need to remove the bad laminate and go through the process again?" I asked, trying to play devil's advocate.

"In that case, we will need to build a new core; the old one cannot be used. But trust me, that won't be required. I have done my homework, consulted Johan and am confident. We really don't have the luxury of wasting any more time."

"Okay, you are the boss, you know best," I said, trying my best to silence the sceptic within me. That night, a little past midnight, Ottavio quietly went to the boatyard and applied the first layer of epoxy on the boat, starting the lamination process that would continue non-stop for the next 36 hours, keeping everyone on their toes. We did eventually get better than expected test results for the laminate tests, putting all doubts to rest. Ratnakar's gamble had paid off.

The laminated core took a week to cure itself and was now looking like a boat's hull kept upside down. The next step was to turn the hull over and laminate the inner part before starting to build the boat from inside. This was easier said than done as the hull was over 17 m long, 5 m wide and weighed almost 6 ton. It also didn't have any stiffeners inside, making it susceptible to crumpling up from uneven stresses. Everyone was apprehensive about the operation but no one had the perfect solution. The Navy, used to doing everything systematically and not willing to take chances, wanted Ratnakar to submit the procedure he was planning to follow along with a set of calculations justifying the procedure.

Poor Ratnakar was at his wits' end. He has a hands-on approach to things and is used to taking risks. That does not mean he is reckless. He does his homework well, gets on with the job and makes things happen, dealing with problems as and when they arise rather than getting bogged down thinking about them. Having always been the boss of his own yard, he is not used to justifying his actions to too many people. His approach, thus, was exactly opposite to that of the hierarchical naval bureaucracy he was dealing with. The two seemed to be heading for a standoff. Admiral Awati called me to hear my two pennies' worth.

"Sir, I think the best thing the Navy can do to ensure things happen smoothly is to leave Ratnakar alone. We have to trust him. He is well aware of the repercussions of a mishap at this stage. If anything goes wrong, our project will be delayed but

Ratnakar will surely be heading for bankruptcy. He has far more at stake than all of us put together!"

With the Navy refusing to budge, Ratnakar had no option but to submit a detailed procedure and calculations. The date of the operation was to be intimated separately.

"Do you want to see the calculations too?" asked Ratnakar, sounding rather doleful on the phone.

"No, I won't understand them nor do I really care as long as you know what you are doing. I trust you and am sure you will do the best. If things don't work out for whatever reason, we will see how to salvage the situation. If you want me to come down to Goa or do anything else, just let me know."

"Don't waste your time coming to Goa, I will manage. I definitely don't want any of the people who have been gunning for the calculations to be present. I will already be on the edge and they will really stress me out, which may lead to mistakes. I am planning to do the uprighting operation on Saturday morning and will be informing the Navy about it on Friday evening. There is no way anyone will make it to the yard at such short notice."

"Perfect! If anyone from the Navy has issues about you not informing them earlier, direct them to me, I will look after them. Do give me a call when you finish. Good luck!"

I spent that Saturday morning sitting with my mobile phone in hand, avoiding the urge to call Ratnakar. We had already spent half the time allocated for building the boat and a mishap at this juncture would probably have ended the project. Finally, close to noon, when the waiting had almost got the better of me, I was relieved to receive a call from Ratnakar, "We have finished. It was much easier than expected. A bit of an anticlimax really. The boat is in her cradle; we start working on Monday."

The boat building progressed at a fast pace. The empty hull started getting filled with stiffeners, tanks and bulkheads. The deck was 'vacuum bagged' in place, which involved using the weight of the atmosphere to glue the entire deck in place. *Mhadei* had started looking like a boat with a shapely transom; it was time to paint her and finish the hull. One morning as I was leaving home for work, Ratnakar called. "Have you laid down any specifications in the contract for the quality of finish for the boat?"

"No. Actually I didn't know such specifications exist. I was only focused on the strength of the boat and never bothered how she would look," I replied, wearing my ignorance on my sleeve.

Ratnakar had received a fairly large quantity of paint free from a manufacturer. He was now being offered better quality paint at a hefty price that promised a mirror finish.

"Yes, I would like the boat to look good. Who wouldn't? But as I have not mentioned anything about her looks in the contract, it would be wrong on my part to insist on anything now, especially when it is costing so much and I cannot ask the Navy to pay you for it. But do remember that she is your boat too, your name, as her builder, is forever going to be associated with her. I leave the decision to you."

By evening, Ratnakar confirmed that he would be paying the extra amount to get the good quality paint and the equipment required to apply it.

The paints and special equipment that arrived from Singapore were soon followed by Alan Koh, our painting expert. Alan had agreed to come down to India to teach us the right techniques and make our boat look pretty. He insisted on making the boat's surface 'smooth as a baby's bottom' before applying any paint.

This was easier said than done as our 'baby' was 17 m long, 5 m wide, 2 m tall and had a very curvy bottom that reflected light and magnified imperfections. She also had fairly strong sides that needed to be rubbed down painstakingly with sandpaper to make them smooth. It used to be maddening to see Ratnakar's workers rubbing down the boat through the day to remove the imperfections. In the evening, we would try and have a look at the hull as critically as possible, marking out the imperfections we noticed with pencils. "No, not good enough, we can't start painting tomorrow. Let us try the day after," Alan would say before shutting shop and heading for a late dinner. Finally, after almost a week's postponement, Alan decided to start painting. Three days later, when he had finished and was ready to leave, I could see my face reflecting off a gleaming *Mhadei*!

While *Mhadei's* hull was taking shape in her special shed, her keel was being fabricated outside. The designer had specified a 9-ton iron keel filled with lead and Ratnakar had been trying to figure out the best way to fabricate it for some time. Making the outer iron jacket in the shape specified by the designer was not a problem but pouring 8 ton of lead in it was something he had never done before. After checking out and discarding a number of expensive options, he came up with a simple and cost effective solution that only a desperate Indian boat builder could have thought of!

He bought a very large flat pan and gas burner, commonly used for making jaggery in the sugarcane growing areas close to Goa. Two of his workers would put some lead ingots in the pan as it heated up. "Lead melts at 200°C and by 300°C it can flow like water," explained Ratnakar. Once the lead was watery enough, his workers would simply scoop up a small portion using a ladle and pour it into the keel.

"We need to adjust the position of the keel often, sometimes heat up a small portion, to ensure the lead is evenly distributed inside. I am also building up one side of the jacket as we keep filling the lower portions to ensure no gaps are left in between," he explained. Bit by bit, pouring about 2 kgs at a time, the entire 8,000 kgs of lead was emptied into the keel jacket. This was then shaped with epoxy filler to remove imperfections and painted in time for the fitment.

We now had the 17 m-long and 2 m-tall hull required to be fitted with a 1.8 m-tall keel. Both weighed about 9 ton each, the difference was that the weight of the hull was distributed over a large area while that of the keel was concentrated in a very small area. The keel was to be bolted to the hull with 11 thick stainless steel bolts for which the hull would need to be raised by at least 4 m. But we didn't have 4 m of working space between the hull and the roof of the shed. Nor had the floor of the shed been re-inforced to take on the 9 ton of concentrated weight of the keel. Clearly, the proverbial camel had outgrown its stable!

To get over this rather 'weighty' problem, a pit was dug close to the river next to the yard. A concrete platform was created in the centre of the pit to take on the weight of the keel. The keel was now loaded onto a trolley, brought over the pit and lowered into the pit. It was now time to fix the boat to the keel, as against the conventional way of fixing the keel to the boat! It was a tricky operation, trying to align all the 11 bolts of the keel with the holes drilled for them through the hull. The hull itself was suspended over the pit with two cranes that kept lowering and adjusting it slowly. Any misalignment would lead to uneven stresses on the hull and cause serious damage. Luckily, to everyone's relief, the whole operation got over without an incident and the boat was bolted to the keel.

That night, I made an entry in my diary: *"Keel fixed by bolts to become a part of her forever. A case of someone gaining 9 ton in a day!"*

Once the keel was fitted, things had to move fast. The plan was to break the dam between the river and the pit in which the boat was now standing, float the boat, and pull her out in the river. The operation could only be done during spring tides taking advantage of the highest tide. At any other time there wouldn't be enough water under the boat's keel to float over the broken dam. This meant a three-day window around the full moon in December or a month's wait for the next full moon. The dam had already started leaking and the pit had to be kept dry by running a heavy duty pump regularly. It didn't look like the dam would hold for another month. We decided to float the boat on the midnight of 12 Dec which was a full moon and the tide was the highest around midnight.

On the morning of 12 Dec, around 0700 h in the morning, I reached the boatyard with Ratnakar. We had been working late at night and he had spent the night on the island instead of going home. We were the first to arrive and there was no one else in the yard. The boat seemed to be standing at a peculiar angle and the pit was full of water. The pump used for pumping the water out of the pit was not working and the person responsible for it was nowhere to be seen.

"Ratnakar, do you think she is floating?" I asked, wondering if I had closed all the watertight openings the previous night.

"Yes, I think she is," replied Ratnakar, already running towards the boat.

We jumped onto the boat and started checking for leaks.

There was some water inside the boat but Ratnakar soon identified it as coming from the opening for the boat's log and closed it. As we were checking the boat for any other leakages, I joked to Ratnakar that the boat seemed to be in a hurry to float. And now that she had decided to float herself, we should do the ceremony for floating her then and there. Traditionally, in India, one would break a coconut and offer flowers on such an occasion.

"I agree, I think we should. Why don't you go get a coconut and some flowers," he replied, busy with his inspection.

"Are you serious?"

"Of course I am; see if you can get some in the village."

"Okay, I will be back shortly," I said, getting off the boat and heading for the car.

I managed to get a coconut from one of the few shops on the island that had just opened but getting flowers didn't seem that easy. As I was driving around the island looking for some wildflowers, I came across a temple. Most temples have a flower shop outside as people like to buy them for offering to the deity. The shop hadn't yet opened though and there wasn't anyone in sight. I barged into the temple and bumped into the priest, going through his morning chores. He seemed a little surprised to see me, wearing a pair of old shorts and T-shirt with a few days' stubble on my face. I probably looked more like a burglar than a devotee.

"Look, my boat has decided to deliver herself prematurely. Can you give me some flowers to do the ceremony? The flower shop outside hasn't opened yet and I can't seem to get any on the island," I pleaded, eyeing the few fresh flowers in front of the deity. He didn't seem to understand me but when I repeated myself, joining both hands and looking suitably pious, he picked a few and gave them to me.

I ran back to the boat floating in the still water. Ratnakar had finished his inspection by then and was relieved to find no leakages. The two of us went to the bow, broke the coconut, offered the flowers and said a silent prayer, standing there with folded hands. One had staked his life's work on building her, the other was going to stake his life on sailing her!

By afternoon, the tide receded and the boat sat back in the pit, waiting to be floated again and taken out. We had an early dinner at the only restaurant on the island and headed for the yard. It was a cool, clear night with a glorious full moon, the brightest in the past 15 years. As the boat was about to float, Ratnakar and his wife Mona did a small *puja* on the bow of the boat, breaking another coconut, this time for the formal ceremony. A couple of hours later, close to midnight, we pulled her out with ropes tied at the bow and stern and tied her alongside a pontoon in the river. *Mhadei* was finally in her medium, two weeks before the deadline given by the Navy!

We started fitting out *Mhadei* the day after she was floated out. The equipment required to be fitted on her had been arriving from all over the world for the past few months and I had started referring to the shed it was stowed in as 'Aladdin's cave'. We had to import almost everything thanks to a near total absence of market for yachting equipment in the country. Johan, realising our problems, had helped in sourcing the bulk of the equipment using the services of a specialised company in Europe. A large part of it, especially the bigger items, had been sourced directly by us. It was an interesting insight into today's globalised world where a company registered in one country would be manufacturing an item in another and selling it to us through a dealer in a third country. The mast and rigging came from South Africa, the engine, manufactured by a Swedish company, was shipped out of Spain, the sails from New Zealand, steering from Denmark... the list was endless. Ratnakar's fixed price contract with the Navy meant that any cost-cutting on buying the equipment would add to his profit while any extra costs would go out of his pocket. Right from the beginning, he insisted we get the best equipment for the boat, irrespective of the costs involved.

Very early in the project, while planning to source the equipment, he told me, "Dilip, I don't understand much of the stuff, nor do I have the time to spare on doing the research. She is your boat; you decide what you want to fit and whom to buy it from. Just let me know how much money is required to be paid and to whom. We will worry about the costs later; for now let us get the best available."

Unlike a power boat or ship, a sailboat has to have everything precisely fitted on her. The ultimate aim is for her to be able to sail on her own with a little help from the crew. Even slight misalignments or mistakes can become major irritants at a later stage. Johan's three visits as per the contract were already over by the time we floated *Mhadei*. After having a look at the equipment required, we didn't have any doubt left in our minds that we needed him for at least one more visit to ensure everything was fitted perfectly. Johan came down to Goa for his last visit in Jan 2009. He helped us fit out the boat precisely by making mockups of almost everything before actually installing the equipment. Before leaving, he complimented Ratnakar on building a fine boat saying, "If you come and visit us in Holland with the boat, we will be proud to say that you are one of us." It was quite a compliment from someone with his experience.

By the second week of Jan 2009, it was time for *Mhadei* to say adieu to her birthplace on Divar Island. She would never return there again. The presence of three bridges on the river, between the yard and the sea, would make it impossible for her get to the yard once the mast was stepped in. We moved her to a naval jetty on the Zuari River, further south, for stepping the mast that had already arrived from Cape Town. The day after we moved *Mhadei* to her new location, Chris, our rigger, arrived to fit the mast and rigging. This was his first visit to India and he was a bit bewildered by the heat and chaos of Goa as well as the spicy food! To our delight, we discovered he was a passionate sailor in addition to being the most experienced rigger of our mast maker. The mast was stepped in a day and it was time to start sailing.

We sailed *Mhadei* for the first time on 23 Jan 2009, which happened to be Ratnakar's birthday and his first experience of being on a sailboat. It was a wonderful feeling, finally sailing her after dreaming about her for over two years! We had a nice and easy sail under Chris's guidance followed by a celebratory dinner in the evening. During the dinner, Ratnakar's birthday was almost forgotten as everyone was excited with the sail and wanted to talk about it. Any hopes Chris had about finishing the job quickly and heading home were dashed when he discovered that the forestay was almost a meter short! There was no other option but to wait for an extension piece from Cape Town that would take a week or two to arrive. On hindsight, this proved to be a blessing in disguise as we could learn to sail the boat and fit new equipment with Chris's help. He was averse to sitting idle and was happy to sail with us, putting us through our paces. Often we would be accompanied by friends, family and the workers who built the boat – the *Mhadei* fan club as I started calling them.

The deadline of 25 Feb 2009 for handing over the boat to the Navy was fast approaching and we still had a lot of equipment to fit and trials to conduct. The Navy constituted a team to conduct the boat's trials off Goa. Most of the team members were good friends who had been following the project since it started. That helped as they concentrated on improving things rather than point fingers at the shortcomings.

The date for handing over *Mhadei* to the Navy was fixed for 12 Feb 2009 to suit the Chief of Naval Staff's convenience. The handing over ceremony was to take place at the INS *Mandovi* Boat Pool in North Goa, where we had been fitting her out. I had asked the Navy to commission the boat as a naval ship with a white ensign and call her INS *Mhadei*. However, that was not agreed to and we were, instead, allowed to fly a blue ensign as a 'Fleet Auxiliary'. As the mentor of the project, Admiral Awati took on the responsibility of extending invitations for the ceremony. His charisma is such that, apart from the CNS, we had two serving and two retired Commanders-in-Chief, and a host of other dignitaries and well-wishers attending the function. I don't think any Fleet Auxiliary has managed to attract so much brass while being inducted in the service.

The ceremony itself was quite simple. The Navy has an elaborate procedure for commissioning ships. As I couldn't find anything for Fleet Auxiliaries, I decided to devise my own, which was to let Admiral Awati introduce the boat to all present before letting Ratnakar hand over the keys to the CNS and take him onboard for a visit. Realising that she was a sailboat and could be sailed out without using the keys, we decided to hand over a winch handle with the keys for good measure. I was so preoccupied with the boat's fitting out that I totally forgot to nominate anyone as the Master of Ceremonies for the function. Not that I had anyone I could nominate with any authority!

"Sir, can you also double up as the Master of Ceremonies for the function? Ratnakar will be handing over the boat to the CNS and you will be introducing me, so it may look odd if either of us is the MC. I can't think of anyone else I can ask," I asked, feeling very sheepish as I went to pick up Admiral Awati for the ceremony.

"Don't worry, leave that to me; you just look after the boat," said the nonplussed Admiral on his way to becoming the most senior Master of Ceremonies in Indian naval history.

A few days after *Mhadei* was handed over to the Navy, the Central Excise Department of the Indian Government issued a notice to Ratnakar, raided his office and impounded his account books. The reason: non-payment of excise duty for *Mhadei*! Ratnakar had signed the contract with the Navy in good faith, without reading the fine print of the excise manual. The Navy had assured him that no duties would be required to be paid as *Mhadei* was a naval boat. The excise officials however pointed out that as per their rules, all types of boats except a yacht were exempt from paying duty as they considered a yacht to be a luxury item. *Mhadei* was a functional boat, nowhere close to being a luxury yacht, but we had made the mistake of calling her a yacht while drafting the contract. The excise officials read about a yacht being handed over to the Navy in the newspapers and took action against the boat builder! Had we called her anything else, they wouldn't have bothered.

Obviously, Shakespeare had no experience with the great Indian bureaucracy when he uttered his famous words, "What's in a name!" A lot of money, headaches and paperwork, as we were soon to discover. If that were not enough, the Customs Department sharing offices with the Excise Department decided to be one up on their cousins and slapped a steeper duty, declaring all the exemptions given by them null and void. It was a ridiculous situation with one arm of the government, the Revenue Service, trying to extract money from another arm, the Defence Ministry, with the boat builder getting caught in the crossfire for no fault of his.

We could ill afford such nonsense at this time when we required the boat builder's full attention on the boat. To his credit, Ratnakar didn't let the mess affect the work on the boat and took things in his stride. He had, almost four months ago, asked his deputy to look after his business and had been concentrating full time on building *Mhadei*. Eventually, it would take him over a year to sort out the issue, get the notices cancelled and recover all his money as per the contract from the Government.

Chapter 18

Mhadei's Baby Steps

A day after *Mhadei* was handed over to the Navy, Robin arrived in Goa. We had invited him for the ceremony the previous day but he couldn't make it owing to a busy schedule. He had agreed to give *Mhadei* a look over, fine tune her and teach me a few tricks of the trade. He also needed some sun and warm weather having spent the previous week in the Arctic with temperatures of 43°C below freezing. It was an immensely fruitful and enjoyable visit. Robin stayed at the Wardroom of the Indian Naval Academy where the boat was berthed and we would go out sailing almost every day with Ratnakar, Ottavio and anyone else who cared to join us. Each day was a learning experience, with Robin suggesting a whole lot of small but significant improvements to the boat that could only come from someone with a lifetime of sailing experience. By the end of his visit, we had a long list of things that needed to be done on the boat, but she had passed Robin's scrutiny. "A nice strong boat to sail around the world," he wrote in the visitor's book before leaving. Quite a compliment considering the state we had been in, less than a year back.

Thus far the maximum I had sailed *Mhadei* was for an overnight trip with Robin, Ratnakar and Ottavio. It was time to take her someplace now, show her off a bit and gather some sea miles under the keel. Mumbai was the obvious choice. She had been registered at Mumbai, so officially that was her home port. I had planned to sail alone, having had my share of crew searches during my training voyages on other boats earlier. It would have been difficult to sail those boats alone so I didn't have an option. Now I finally had a boat that was rigged to be sailed alone and I had every intention of making the best of it. When I told Admiral Awati about my plan, he asked if he could sail with me. It was impossible to refuse him though I was a little worried about his age.

"I have no problem sir as long as your wife allows you. Can you ask her first?" I said, knowing well that his wife would be worried about her 82-year-old husband sailing out with an untested boat and skipper. I am not sure how he managed it but a couple of hours later he called me, all excited, to tell me that his wife was okay with him sailing on *Mhadei* as long as I was onboard.

We sailed out of Goa on the morning of 03 Mar 2009, and planned to be ready with the sails up as the sea breeze picked up by noon. We were expected to reach Mumbai by noon on 05 Mar 2009 to be in time for a welcome planned by the Western Naval Command. The work on the boat had continued till the day I left and more was still required to be done. Though I had been involved in fitting the equipment, things were still new to me. During the sailings so far, Ratnakar and Ottavio had always been onboard to sort out problems. I didn't have that luxury anymore.

We motored out of the Mandovi River and I set sail with the Admiral taking the wheel. The sea breeze was yet to pick up so I decided to continue motoring for a while longer and started filling up the fuel day tank to enable the engine to continue running. The engine, however, didn't seem to like that idea, spluttered a bit in protest and died. As I was moving around, alternating between setting up the boat to sail towards safe waters and trying to figure out what had gone wrong with the engine, the Admiral started telling me to head back to harbour.

"What happened?" asked the worried Admiral.

"I am not sure, I am trying to figure out," I replied absentmindedly, trying to think.

"I think we should get back to the harbour, get the problem rectified and then head for Mumbai. Don't worry about the ETA at Mumbai; I will handle it with the C-in-C. Just ask Ratnakar to send a boat to tow us in," he urged, looking worried. I mumbled something, still trying to figure out the problem. Returning back to harbour was the last thing on my mind.

"I said, let us head back now!" said the Admiral, raising his voice and getting impatient.

Realising that it was time to assert the skipper's authority, I stood before him, looked squarely in his face and told him as evenly as I could, "Sir, she is a sailboat and as long as the sails are up she can keep moving. We have sufficient food and water to reach Mumbai even with the worst of winds so enjoy the sail while I try to figure out the problem. We are not turning back."

I managed to zero down the problem to airlocks in the fuel line of the engine and with a little help from the Admiral got it running again. A few days later, after we had finished the trip safely, I got a letter from the Admiral confessing what he had been up to that day. "Would my probation ever end!" I thought as I read his letter with a smile,

"........*Your determination came through loud and clear on the very first morning out of Goa when the engine decided to stall. I tried a bait. You did not bite it. You got the engine going. I was happy to see your determined approach to your task. Well done! I also appreciated your rather matter of fact manner in dealing with me. I do not like sycophants! You are not one of them, thankfully."*

The rest of the trip turned out to be as interesting. By the next morning, trying to look for a decent breeze and in an effort to avoid fishing traffic close to the coast, we had opened out over 50 nm from land. Our satellite communication set had stopped working and the Navy had lost track of us, which in itself wouldn't have been so bad. Unfortunately, a worried Mrs Awati rang up the Commander-in-Chief of the Western Naval Command in the morning, asking about her husband's whereabouts and all hell broke loose! On the boat, we were blissfully unaware of this and were enjoying a nice, hot breakfast. The Admiral, far more experienced in naval matters, asked me if I had heard anything from the Navy since the night before. I told him about our communication problem and assured him that I was trying to close coast to get within mobile phone range to enable me to pass our position to the Navy.

"I think we should hear something from them in an hour; I will be surprised if we don't," he said confidently. Sure enough, in less than an hour, I heard a naval reconnaissance aircraft calling us on the VHF communication set, trying to establish contact and ascertain our position. The aircraft flew over us in a couple of minutes and was followed by a string of visitors in the form of Navy and Coast Guard ships in the vicinity, all of whom had been told to keep an eye out for us.

We reached Mumbai on 05 Mar 2009, with a stiff 18 kts breeze behind us. It was great to romp about in Mumbai harbour for a while before finally motoring inside the Naval Dockyard and being received ceremonially by the C-in-C. It was a special day for me, full of mixed emotions. It would have been my Dad's 67th birthday had he been alive. He loved working with his hands and would have enjoyed helping me build and sail *Mhadei*. Also, at the other end of the pier, my first and only naval command INSDB T–55 was getting decommissioned. Life did seem to have moved on!

A press conference followed the reception, my first about the project and quite an introduction to what I would be facing in the future. As I reached home after telling the same story to half a dozen reporters, I got a call from a reporter from a Hindi TV channel. He had interviewed me a while ago and wanted some clarifications urgently before airing the interview. I have deliberately written the interview in 'Roman Hindi' to allow people who understand Hindi to better appreciate the humour.

Reporter: *Hame bataya gaya ki aap ki boat hawa se chalti hai; kya yeh such hai?* (We have been told your boat moves by wind power; is it true?)

Me: *Ji.* (Yes.)

Reporter: *Par hame pata chala hai ki is usme electricity hai.* (But I have come to know that you have electricity onboard.)

(Obviously thinking, "I caught you! You have been hoodwinking everyone, using electricity to run the boat and telling the world that it runs on thin air! Here is my scoop!")

Me: Electricity boat *ke* instruments or light *chalati hai par* boat *hawa se chalti hai.* (The electricity is used for the boat's instruments and lights, but the boat is powered by wind.)

(Sorry, no scoop here so the next one...)

Reporter: *Is* trip *me aap kis jagah par rukenge?* (Which places will you stop at during the trip?)

Me: Australia, New Zealand, Falklands and South Africa.

Reporter: *Achha* (Okay), A........., New........., Scotland, South.......

Me: Not Scotland, Falklands.

(I gave up after spelling it out to him twice and hearing Scotland again and again! So now I had to add another 15,000 miles to my trip!)

And then came the best part...

Reporter: *Hamne suna ki aap ke* boat *main 900* ton *ke keel lage hai.* (I have heard that you have 900 ton nails fitted in your boat.)

(An image of a nail the size of a bridge's girder flashed before me!)

Me: *900 nahin, 'keel' 9* ton *ka hai, Puri* boat *ka vajan 23* ton *hai.* (Not 900, the keel weighs 9 ton, the entire boat weighs 23 ton.)

Reporter: *To aise 900* ton *ke kitne keel* boat *me lage hai?* (So how many such 900 ton nails are fitted?)

"Boat *main kitne keel*"? (How many nails in a boat?) I was wondering whether to tell him that there are hundreds or thousands and that one cannot keep track of the number of nails fitted on a wooden boat, till I realised what the problem was!

Me: *Yeh* keel *Hindi wala keel nahin,* boat *ke ek part ko angrezi main* keel *kehete hai jiska vajan 9* ton *hai.* (This keel is not the keel you are referring to in Hindi, which means a nail. The boat has a part that is called a keel in English and it weighs 9 ton.)

Thankfully the interview ended there!

Chapter 19

Colombo Calling

I had been asking the Navy to appoint someone to help me with the project for almost two years now. The folks at NHQ had taken the word 'solo' a bit too literally and had expected me to do everything on my own so far. It had started becoming increasingly difficult to balance the requirements of sailing while keeping up with the ever growing paperwork. Finally, in late Mar 2009, Lt Cdr Abhilash Tomy was deputed as my shore support crew. Abhilash, a maritime reconnaissance pilot, had started his sailing career as a dinghy sailor. He had worked as the shore facilities manager for the Volvo Ocean Race stopover at Kochi a few months earlier and had then been sailing with Prof Radhakrishnan in the Gulf of Aden. He was one of the three naval officers who had volunteered to be my shore support cum standby crew. By the time the Navy issued orders for him to join me, I was ready to sail *Mhadei* from Mumbai to Goa. I left a list of things for him to do in Mumbai before heading for Goa with Pramod, our newly hired handyman or *tindal* as he was called in the local lingo.

It was nice to have someone I could delegate work to and head to sea, assured it would be done by the time I reached the next destination. The trip from Mumbai to Goa was fairly fast and uneventful with a good north-westerly wind behind us. Unlike the earlier trip, there was no celebrity crew onboard, so everyone left us alone. I had also managed to get work done on the satellite communication set during the stay in Mumbai, so I was available on the phone at all times.

We reached Goa and Abhilash joined us in a few days. There was a peculiar problem we had landed up with that needed to be sorted before doing any serious sailing. The luffs of our sails were a little longer than desired and needed to be shortened. There was no facility in India to do the work so the sail maker had advised sending them to Hong Kong or New Zealand. While the work on the sails would be done free, the substantial costs of air-freight would need to be borne by Ratnakar. The boat would be without sails for almost a month, which would upset our schedule. More important, with the Customs Department already at loggerheads with the Navy and Ratnakar, exporting the sails for repairs and then re-importing them seemed rather risky. As we were trying to find a solution, I found a 'Made in Sri Lanka' label on one of the snuffers supplied with the sails. The sail maker confirmed that there indeed was a large production facility in Sri Lanka and if we could take the sails there, he would instruct them to do the needful.

This was excellent news. We decided that it would be simpler and cheaper to sail the boat to Sri Lanka, 300 nm from the nearest naval port of Kochi, instead of packing the sails and air-freighting them. We wanted to sail the boat as much as possible anyway, so why not sail her to Sri Lanka! This would also enable us to keep clear of Customs, save on the freight costs and monitor the work done on the sails in person.

We sailed out of Goa on 08 Apr 2009 and headed for

Kochi. The plan was to stay there for a few days and finish the Immigration formalities before finally setting sail for Colombo. Since arriving from Mumbai, we had been sailing *Mhadei* for short day trips whenever we could. However, this was the first overnight trip for Abhilash and me. We reached Kochi close to midnight with plenty of thunder, lightning and gusty winds for company. As we got more conversant with sailing we would recognise these as equatorial squalls, shorten the sail and think nothing of them. But that night, experiencing it for the first time on *Mhadei*, the whole thing felt rather dramatic. After a brief stay in Kochi, we headed for Colombo on *Mhadei's* first foreign trip.

The Sri Lankan war against the LTTE was at its peak and the port of Colombo was like a fortress with a total ban on small boats, including fishing boats in the vicinity. It was only because we were a naval boat that we managed to get the necessary permissions to enter. We left Kochi on a Thursday morning telling everyone that we would reach Colombo by Sunday morning. A tropical cyclone was brewing in the Bay of Bengal, causing some sort of funnelling effect for the wind through the Gulf of Mannar. This was the first time we had to reef the mainsail as the wind started crossing 20 kts and there was a swell of about 2 m. There was plenty of excitement on the boat and a bit of anxiety too as this was the first time we were sailing *Mhadei* through such weather. In a couple of months, both Abhilash and I would get seasoned enough to sleep peacefully through such conditions, confident that the boat would look after herself.

Thanks to the excellent winds, by Friday evening we were less than 30 nm from Colombo, trying to reduce speed by shortening sail. I decided to call up Naval Headquarters to ask them if we could enter a day earlier. To my surprise, my request was turned down with some silly bureaucratic excuse and we were told to stay put at sea till Sunday morning, our original ETA. This didn't make any sense to me and I was trying to ask them to reconsider their decision.

"Sir, the winds are gusting beyond 25 kts and there is a cyclone raging in the Bay of Bengal. Why do you want us to stay out in such conditions when we can be safely in the harbour by first light tomorrow? The Indian Defence Advisor has already intimated that the Sri Lankan Navy has no issues if we get in a day early," I pleaded.

"Okay, let me get back to you," said the voice at the other end of the phone before hanging up.

I got a little impatient after waiting for two hours. When I checked the satellite phone I realised it had stopped working. Brilliant! Now we had no means of communicating with the powers that be in Delhi and our last instructions were to remain at sea till Sunday morning. I broke the news to Abhilash, my trusty crew. "Sunday routine [holiday in naval parlance] shall be observed on *Mhadei* tomorrow. Enjoy the forced holiday at sea! For now let us divide the sea watches and get some sleep."

By morning, the winds almost died and the temperature hovered close to 40°C. We sailed close to the harbour and requested port control to convey our welfare to our Defence Advisor over the phone. The rest of the day and the following night were spent aimlessly pacing outside Colombo harbour before finally entering on Sunday morning as planned.

I later came to know that while we took turns sleeping peacefully on the boat; things became rather excitable at the War Room, the operations centre of the Navy in Delhi that was responsible for tracking us. The last news received from us, before the phone played up, had been that the weather was getting worse and we weren't exactly comfortable. With no communication after that, people at the War Room started creating their own doomsday scenarios and spent a sleepless night making contingency plans and planning aircraft searches to be launched at first light the next morning. The incident did have a positive fallout, especially when the cause of the problem was identified to be something as silly as lack of sufficient balance in the telephone account. From then on, *Mhadei* started getting the same attention and organisational support received by a naval unit at sea. We also got an iridium satellite phone on loan as a backup for the Fleet Broadband set we had.

We got to work almost as soon as we tied up alongside, taking off the sails and packing them to take to the factory the next day. It was quite an eye-opener, seeing hundreds of workers at the factory, mostly women, making sails of all sorts for different boats, from dinghies to super yachts. Interestingly, most of them, despite having worked there for many years, didn't know how the sails were used on boats but were keen to find out. We promised to send them photos of our boat with the sails up once we got back. As soon as the sails were ready, we hauled them back to the boat and started fitting them, ably assisted by volunteers from the Sri Lankan Navy and pepped up by hot cups of tea sent by their ships berthed in the vicinity. In less than a week, we had finished our work and it was time to head back home.

The return trip took longer with either headwinds or no winds throughout. I was planning to keep well clear of the coast throughout the trip but *Mhadei* seemed to be keen on having a look at Cape Comorin (Kanyakumari), the southern tip of the Indian mainland. She conspired with the wind gods and we landed up passing a couple of miles from the Cape, getting a good view of the windswept beaches and mountains beyond. After a very brief stopover in Kochi, we headed for Goa, already planning the next trip.

The morning after we left Kochi, we had our first close shave with a merchant ship and realised how vulnerable a sailboat could be. I had been sleeping below deck for some time, Abhilash was on deck and *Mhadei* was sailing on autopilot in a light breeze. For no particular reason I woke up with a start and stumbled on deck to see if everything was okay. Abhilash had dozed off and there was a huge red tanker with '*Dauntless*' written in bold capitals across its bows, looming less than 200 m astern and heading straight for us. A couple of minutes more and the giant would have run over us, undaunted and unaware! I tacked the boat in panic, swinging her by over 90° and out of the tanker's path, getting nicely buffeted by its wake as it slithered past us.

We reached Goa without any further incident. I left the boat with Abhilash and Ratnakar, with a list of minor issues that needed to be looked at and was off to Delhi. It was necessary to debrief NHQ about the last trip, learn from the mistakes and fine tune the planning of the next trip to Mauritius, which would be the last trial and training voyage for *Mhadei* and me, respectively.

Chapter 20

The Mauritius Adventure

The timing of the Mauritius trip was important. The idea was to sail back with the strong south-westerly monsoon winds that usually set close to the equator by mid May and advance north over the Arabian Sea. This would give me some experience of sailing in conditions similar to the Southern Ocean where I would be sailing with following winds and seas. Well, at least that is what I thought then, discovering a couple of months later that the southwest monsoons are not a patch on what one encounters in the Southern Ocean. The initial plan was for four of us, Robin, Ratnakar, Abhilash and I, to sail from Goa to Mauritius. I was to drop them off at Mauritius and sail back alone. Unfortunately, both Robin and Ratnakar couldn't make it, leaving Abhilash and me to do the trip.

We set sail late in the afternoon of 15 May 2009 from Goa and were seen off by a naval helicopter that flew around for a while clicking photos. A north-westerly sea breeze helped us open out from the coast and by sunset we were out of sight of land. As I went around the boat checking out things, I discovered that the thrust block, a part of the boat that held the propeller shaft bearing, had almost uprooted itself. This meant that we would not be in a position to use the engine for too long if needed. Turning back for repairs or entering Kochi on the way to carry out repairs would have meant delaying the trip by a couple of days and disrupting the entire schedule. I was more worried about the explanations I would have to give to NHQ. It had been hard enough getting the approvals for the trip, convincing many that the boat and her crew could actually undertake the trip safely. I didn't mention the problem to anyone, including Abhilash, my sole crew member. "Why stress him out now?" I thought, watching him lounge on the deck enjoying the sunset and breeze. We had an excellent run till the Equator, almost 1,000 nm to the south, over the next week. The sea was calm with a steady following wind, allowing *Mhadei* to charge south with the gennaker up most of the time. It was an idyllic sail with *Mhadei* virtually sailing on her own, without the need to put in a reef or alter course. We crossed the Indian peninsula and the Island of Sri Lanka 200 nm to our east and were moving southeast of the Maldives group of islands. The aim was to continue heading south till about 8° South latitude, leave the Chagos Archipelago to our west and then head southwest towards Mauritius. That would enable us to make a fast 'reach' using the south-easterly Trade Winds we were expecting to encounter as we sailed into the Southern Hemisphere. This was all in theory, planned after going through various navigational publications, routeing charts and weather reports. As we would soon discover, the wind gods have a plan and mind of their own!

Two days short of the equator, we encountered Neptune's sentinels in the form of thick dark clouds with pelting rain, strong erratic winds and big grey seas. *Mhadei*, sailing serenely so far, started getting thrashed around in the squalls. The novelty of having a refreshing shower in the rain soon wore off when we didn't see the sun for a whole day. The three of us did our first equatorial crossing under sail at 0400 h on 20 May 09 with *Mhadei* thumping on a 2 m swell. A day later, close to sunset, as *Mhadei* was getting tossed around in the swell and I was pottering inside getting ready to cook dinner, all electrical gadgets switched themselves off. Abhilash, sitting outside, jumped to the wheel and managed to control the boat before she could crash gybe. The first reaction, not uncommon when one encounters a problem for the first time, was panic and concern. We needed to do something and fast, before darkness set in.

"Something wrong with the batteries perhaps," I muttered as I started lifting up the navigation station seat to get access to the batteries below. I was worried about a possible short circuit in our main storage batteries. As I got access to the batteries, I realised that the batteries had moved from their position because of the motion of the boat. This had disconnected the terminals, switching off the power supply of the boat. There didn't seem to be any major damage or short circuit anywhere. I connected the terminals and heard Abhilash shout, telling me that things were working. We had detected a small but significant shortcoming in the boat. The batteries had to be secured very well if the boat was to be safe in the big swells she was expected to encounter in the Southern Ocean. We lashed the batteries as best as we could, subsequently making better securing arrangements for them in Mauritius.

As we sailed further in the Southern Hemisphere, our plans of rounding the Chagos Archipelago from the south seemed to have fallen foul with the wind gods. The winds started oscillating between south and west, leaving us with the option of either heading southeast for Australia or northwest to Africa. Both options were unacceptable as they would take us away from our destination. Trying to keep tacking in an effort to take advantage of the wind shifts would take us through the poorly charted archipelago of coral islands that would be nothing short of suicidal. It was frustrating tacking around every few minutes in the incessant rain and big grey seas. Every time I decided to head in one direction, the wind would change direction and I would start wishing I hadn't tacked and changed course. Finally, I lost patience. "Okay, let us try and go west till we are really close to the archipelago and lose our nerve. Let us see if we can hack it somehow," I told Abhilash before tacking and heading in a west north-westerly direction. As we approached the archipelago, the wind started to back slowly, making us head in a more westerly direction till we managed to pass about half a mile north of Lord Nelson Island, a small, sandy, uninhabited island with some vegetation on one edge.

It was tempting to go close and attempt a landing. However, we decided against the idea after seeing a wreck marked on the chart and seeing a part of it protruding out of water close to the beach. Perhaps someone had already tried landing and lost their boat while doing it.

As we crossed the island, a large school of dolphins came to escort us. There must have been hundreds of them, racing with the boat, jumping out of the water and generally showing off as dolphins often do. The wind kept backing slowly as we crossed the island, finally settling from a south-easterly direction and allowing us to head straight for our destination at a clip. We had finally found the reliable south-easterly Trade Winds.

It was a nice and easy sail to Mauritius from then on, barring one day of getting becalmed and drifting around. We finally sighted land on 30 May 2009, 16 days after leaving Goa; by evening, we were close to the northern tip of the Island of Mauritius or Ile Maurice as it is called in French, the common language on the island. We celebrated the last evening at sea with some bhelpuri and orange juice before getting ready to enter the harbour of Port Louis. I was a little apprehensive running the engine with a half uprooted thrust block but things held in place and finally by about 2200 h we were safely inside the harbour.

With over 10 Indian naval and coast guard officers and their families lined up on the jetty to receive us, coming alongside at Mauritius was like coming home! The officers were on deputation with the Mauritius Government and naturally excited about our arrival. As I was to discover the next day, the Indian High Commissioner and the head of the Mauritius Police had been following the boat's progress. They had plenty of questions for us and readily accepted our invitation for a sail once we had got the boat repaired.

I had read about the beauty of Mauritius and it was good to have a look at it firsthand. The island's history is well linked to India with almost 67 per cent of the population being of Indian origin. Their forefathers had arrived on the island 150 years ago as indentured labourers, sailing on tall ships of a different vintage. Having sailed to Mauritius on a boat, it was a little easier to appreciate what they must have gone through. Back then, they had ventured into the unknown and triumphed. We too had been heading into the unknown and had managed to keep our head above water so far, having become the first Indian pair to have sailed shorthanded and non-stop over 2,400 nm. The next big test, however, was around the corner, that of becoming the first Indian to sail solo and non-stop over the same distance. The return trip was never too far from our minds as we went about getting the boat repaired and ready for the next leg.

It was not all work though. As a naval boat in a foreign harbour, *Mhadei* was expected to perform the quasi-diplomatic role of 'flag showing', something all naval ships are expected to do. I think she fared well and attracted a fair share of visitors. We did a bit of sailing off the island with local dignitaries, diplomats and their families. Smitten by the beauty of the island and the excellent weather, we promised ourselves and our hosts that we would return someday.

The nine-day stay got over quickly and it was time to head to sea and finally start sailing solo. I had been preparing for this moment since volunteering for the project over three years ago and suddenly I was there, saying goodbye to everyone on the jetty. While I was interacting with everyone as normally as I could, a part of my mind had detached itself and was going through everything in the boat, trying to tick off a mental checklist. Suddenly, our driver for the past nine days, Mr Vaity, asked me to step out of the boat. He produced a garland of marigold out of nowhere and asked the only lady present, Ms Shuja of the Indian High Commission, to put it around my neck! "This is the proper Indian send off sir, stay safe," boomed Vaity. It was a touching farewell but it was time to leave before anyone could pull any more surprises. I got in the boat, switched on the engine and was off in the next five minutes.

I steered *Mhadei* out of Port Louis harbour and set sail soon after. It was a beautiful day with a clear blue sky and cool winter breeze. There wasn't much swell while we were in the lee of the island but that soon changed as we cleared the island. An hour after setting sail, we were thumping in over 2 m of swell with a stiff 25-kt breeze. These are very normal conditions in the Trade Winds zone and we had enjoyed sailing in the same conditions two weeks ago. The difference was that then we were sailing downwind and enjoying the speed on a relatively stable boat whereas now we were sailing upwind. *Mhadei* was taking the swells on her starboard bow, often letting the water pass over her and making life inside the boat extremely uncomfortable. I seemed to have lost my hard-earned 'sea legs' during the nine-day sojourn at Mauritius and till I earned them back, life was going to be miserable. I was more worried about the boat than the discomfort I was feeling owing to her motion. I had not seen her getting thrashed about like this before and was wondering how well she would fare. I had planned to head straight for Goa, which meant shaping a north-easterly course. With the present wind conditions, sailing close to the wind, we were barely managing a north north-easterly course. There didn't seem any alternative, though, but to continue on this course, the thrashing of the boat and associated discomfort notwithstanding.

A few hours before sunset, Mauritius Coast Guard ship *Guardian* overtook us. They were on patrol and bouncing around as badly as we were. Having commanded a ship of similar size a few years earlier, I could well imagine the misery the crew must have been going through. The Captain, an Indian Naval Lieutenant Commander on deputation, greeted us cheerfully, promised to keep an eye on us and bounced away with his ship, looking almost gleeful! Honestly, I wasn't feeling all that happy.

In the evening, as I logged on to the Internet in order to report my position to the Navy, I found a nice message from Commander Vishal Kanwar, Commandant of the Mauritius Coast Guard.

Dear All,

INSV Mhadei departed for an historic voyage from Mauritius to Goa, India with only Cdr Dilip Donde at the helm. This is the first time an Indian yacht with the only Indian crew is sailing between Mauritius and India. It is interesting to note that ancestors of the Indian Diaspora in Mauritius came from India in the 18th century aboard sailing ships. INSV Mhadei's sailing is creating history and this could be the dawn of sailing/seafaring spirit in India. It makes me wonder as to why many more sailors don't take this historic trip from India to Mauritius! Wish we have many such yachts calling at Port Louis. And I must share that INSV Mhadei flying the Indian flag in the Marina, where you had only seen European flags thus far, was a sight full of pride and satisfaction.

Attached are some more pics of Mhadei taken by the Dornier aircraft. She is about 150 nm north of Mauritius.

Enjoy the pics.

Regards,

Cdr Vishal Kanwar

Vishal is an old friend and was on deputation with the Mauritius Coast Guard. He and his officers had left no stone unturned to make sure our stay was pleasant and that we were ready to head to sea in time. There were also some photographs forwarded by Abhilash, among them a few of me getting garlanded. The state I was in, all I could think about after seeing the photo was that I was looking like a sacrificial lamb being garlanded before being led to the altar! The misery continued for the next four days and I seriously started wondering what I had gotten myself into! I remembered the two stages of sea sickness described by a wise man: "The first stage is when you think you are going to die. The next stage is when you wish you were dead!"

While I wasn't feeling too well, *Mhadei* kept sailing perfectly without any problems, eating up sea miles and making fast progress towards the equator. As we neared the equator, the winds started dying down and the equatorial squalls started reappearing regularly. There had been a real scare about piracy in the area and I had been advised by the Navy to stay as far away from the African coast as possible. A naval ship on her way for a routine antipiracy patrol had been told to keep an eye on us and was being regularly updated about our position. One afternoon as we were passing west of the Chagos Archipelago, I sighted a ship that looked like a large fishing trawler on our port beam. This was the first ship I was seeing after leaving Mauritius, so naturally I kept watching it. After doing a parallel course with us on the port side, the ship crossed in front of us and started doing a parallel course on the starboard side, not too far away. This set the alarm bells ringing on *Mhadei*! There had been enough stories about large fishing trawlers being hijacked by pirates and being used as 'mother ships'. In fact, a few years earlier the Indian Navy had taken the lead in sinking one such mother ship. I picked up the satellite phone and called up the War Room in New Delhi. It was a Sunday and the duty officer answered my call. I explained the situation to him; he was concerned too and informed me that the ship on antipiracy patrol was some 400 nm away and thus of little use in the present situation. I told him to assume that I was kidnapped and to press the panic button if he didn't hear from me in the next two hours. As I sat watching the ship on my starboard beam, keeping a lookout for the 'skiffs' the pirates usually use to board ships, I realised how vulnerable a yacht was when faced with a bunch of pirates. I was sailing at about 6 kts, my best possible speed under the circumstances.

Anyone equipped with a half-decent powerboat and armed with a pea shooter could have jumped in my boat and overpowered me. Luckily, the ship did eventually turn out to be a fishing boat. After a while, I could see her slowing down and large nets being lowered over the stern. I heaved a sigh of relief and called up the War Room to pass on the good news.

A few days later, I accidently discovered a small but significant shortcoming on *Mhadei*. While moving inside the boat, I hit my head and was rewarded with a nasty gash close to my eye. The fresh wound started bleeding profusely making me wonder if it needed to be sutured. Unfortunately, I couldn't see the wound as there were no mirrors onboard. While fitting the boat out a few months back, Ratnakar had asked me if I wanted to fit one on the boat.

"I am going to be alone on the boat and plan to grow a beard at sea, so why bother with a mirror?" had been my rather cocky reply!

I tried using the camera on my laptop to click my own photo to inspect the wound but wasn't too successful. All I managed to do was to splatter a lot of blood over the laptop and the navigation table. I finally gave up on the inspection, pressed a handkerchief tightly on the wound and waited, feeling rather stupid. Fortunately, the bleeding stopped and the wound healed in the next couple of days. Another item was added to the list of jobs to be done on return.

We crossed the equator on 17 Jun 2009 and were back in the Northern Hemisphere, 28 days after leaving it. The south-westerly monsoons greeted us almost as soon as we sailed across the equator, allowing us to head straight for Goa on a broad reach. The winds were lighter than expected, which meant my supposed training for the Southern Ocean would have to wait till I actually reached the Southern Ocean. A naval ship transiting through the area at the end of its patrol came by to check us out. It stayed with us through the forenoon before heading towards Kochi, its home port. The weather was nice and *Mhadei* was sailing peacefully in moderate and steady winds. I had a nice lunch and was having a nicer siesta when I got a call over my VHF.

"Sailboat in position....this is warship calling."

"Why has this guy come back, what's with the accent and why is he being so officious?" I muttered as I got up to answer the call assuming that the naval ship was back for some reason.

"Yes warship, this is *Mhadei*, what happened and where are you?" "Sailboat, this is warship half a mile on your port beam, do you need any assistance?"

I instinctively looked out of the hatch on the port side. There, filling almost the entire porthole, was an aircraft carrier and it definitely didn't look Indian! As I was introducing myself to the carrier a Chinook helicopter flew over briefly. Its markings didn't leave any doubt about its nationality. The OOW of the carrier explained that they had seen light glinting off *Mhadei*, mistaken it for a distress signal and closed in to investigate. They were a formation of US naval ships and had already altered course to keep clear of us. I spent the next hour watching the big hulks sail by and photographing them.

As we moved north and closer to Goa, the winds started getting erratic. On 23 Jun 2009, a couple of miles short of the harbour entrance, the wind died completely. I decided to motor for a while with the sails up, expecting the wind to pick up. It didn't make sense wallowing about in sight of land after such a long trip. I put the boat on auto pilot and came inside to fill up the log. My first solo trip was almost over and I had already started getting into celebratory mode.

It is at times like these that the sea teaches you lessons you won't forget in a hurry! By the time I noticed the big squall building up astern it was already too late. Winds of 40 kts hit us as I came out, almost turning the boat over. The autopilot, totally overpowered, gave up in no time and my best efforts at hand-steering *Mhadei* didn't seem to be of much help. Not too conversant yet in dealing with squalls or reefing in an emergency, I ran forward as soon as I could and let go the main halyard in an effort to bring down the mainsail and get the boat under control. This proved to be a bigger mistake with the mainsail thrashing around and breaking two *battens*. It dumped itself on the deck and became even more unmanageable! By the time the winds subsided a little and I could get some semblance of control on the boat, we were already at the mouth of Mormugao harbour. I was very glad to see Abhilash heading for us in a speedboat.

"Whatever happened to you?" he couldn't help asking as he jumped on *Mhadei*.

"Something really stupid! I will tell you later, for now let us make her as presentable as we can," I replied, feeling far more stupid than Abhilash realised and trying to gather the mainsail on the deck to prevent any more damage.

Luckily, there wasn't any major damage. We motored the boat in the harbour, tied her alongside a naval ship, INS *Bitra*, before jumping off to attend a small reception on the ship. It was good to be back. When we left Goa in May, the predominant colour of the land had been brown. Now, a little over a month later, it was so green that it hurt my eyes. The hot summer had given way to a very pleasant and wet monsoon. The most important change, however, was in my head. For the past three years, in order to make headway on the project, I had listened to whatever people told me, got pushed around, at times allowing myself to be treated like a doormat, because whenever I tried countering an argument or a wrong suggestion, I would be asked: "But what is your experience of solo sailing?" "None sir," I would mutter, feeling very stupid. Never again would I need to feel stupid if someone asked me that. It was time I started showing a bit of attitude and got things moving; I had earned it!

It was a proud moment for all. *Mhadei* had passed her last trial with flying colours. The list of things that needed to be done to her and equipment that needed to be retrofitted had grown but that was manageable. What mattered was that she had proved her seaworthiness, shown that she could be sailed solo over a long distance and was ready to take on the challenge she had been built for. It was time to start focusing on getting her and her skipper ready for the solo circumnavigation! As the mentor of the project, Admiral Awati took it upon himself to fire the first salvo at the powers that be.

Dear Admirals,

I am in Goa to receive Mhadei and her skipper, Dilip, on their return from an historic solo voyage from Mauritius. This was the first ever solo voyage by an Indian across the ocean in an open sailing yacht; reason enough for the Navy to rejoice if it is in a mood to. She will now be readied for the ultimate enterprise by her builder. There is a good deal of work to be done. As usual there are roadblocks, this time set up by Goa Customs who are refusing to release important equipment duty-free despite a certificate from MOD (N). The equipment has to go into Mhadei before she is ready to my satisfaction. Perhaps you will help. Please do try. May I also urge all concerned to recog-

nise the importance and the value of the enterprise to the nation. I have long ago labelled Sagar Parikrama as the Everest of the Seas. Indeed, it is far more daunting and challenging. Those who have been derogating yachts as luxury items for exemption of Customs duty must have a closer look at what she has achieved with her skipper. They are both, the yacht and the man, symbols of a resurgent maritime India.

Warm regards,

Manohar

Chapter 21

Charting My Course

I had planned a circumnavigation with only two stops. I intended to sail solo from Mauritius to Goa, covering about 2,400 nm as part of my final trial and training sortie before undertaking the first leg of the circumnavigation from Mumbai to Fremantle, which, at 5,400 nm, would be about double the training leg. This was to be followed by a long second leg of over 11,000 nm from Fremantle to Cape Town, double that of the first leg. The final leg again would be 5,800 nm from Cape Town to Mumbai. I discussed the plan with Robin, forwarded it to NHQ and got it out of my head for the time being as there were plenty of more pressing commitments. With the boat still months away from floating, sailing seemed a little farfetched. Some time in Sep 2008, almost at the end of the working day, I got a call from the Directorate of Naval Operations who would be responsible for tracking me once I sailed.

"You have proposed a circumnavigation with two stops with a second leg of over 11,000 nm that would take over two months to complete. You are not to have a leg longer than 4,000 nm or six weeks, whichever is less! So please give me names of some more ports where you can stop."

"I don't understand this. I don't think anyone in the country has the sailing experience to issue such a directive!" I responded irreverently, acutely aware of my own lack of sailing experience and making an effort to explain the logic behind my planning.

"You can do the explaining when we call you to Delhi to finalise the plan, but for now give me the names of some more ports to break down the second leg."

"Okay, I will need to go to the Chart Depot to check things out as I don't have any navigation publications in my office. Can I get back to you in a couple of days?" I replied, trying to buy time.

"I will call you in the next 30 minutes, you better have the names of the ports ready else we will put something on our own and you will be stuck with them."

"Can you make it 45 minutes please?" I pleaded, making a tactical retreat and wondering whether to be amused at the situation or be angry.

It would have taken me more than 30 minutes just to reach the Naval Chart Depot which would be ready to shut shop for the day anyway. I could see only one practical solution: Google Earth! I opened the application and started looking for two large ports on the western and eastern edges of the South Pacific without having to take too much of a detour from my original route between Fremantle and Cape Town. The idea of calling in at a reasonably large port was to make the task of repairs and logistics simpler when I stopped. Christchurch on the South Island of New Zealand stood out as the biggest city on the western edge of the Pacific. It was the biggest city on the South Island and not too far from my original route. I didn't realise that it is a landlocked city and the actual port of Christchurch is Lyttelton. The scale of the map I was looking at only displayed the bigger cities and I didn't realise there was a landmass between the city and the sea! Well, no one at NHQ realised it either till I sailed into Fremantle confusing everyone by telling them that I would be heading for Christchurch next.

There didn't seem to be any major port on the west coast of Chile, at least on the scale of the map I was looking at. I also thought that if I had to take a stop after crossing the Pacific, I better plan it after rounding Cape Horn. The biggest port on the south-eastern tip of Argentina was Ushuaia, but I remembered reading about the problems Robin had faced while going there through the Beagle Channel and wanted to avoid a repeat. The next port I saw was Port Stanley in the Falkland Islands. The name was familiar, having followed the Falkland War on radio as a teenager and then studying about it as part of campaign studies after joining the Navy. Most important, it would be familiar to everyone at NHQ, saving me the trouble of giving explanations later. Not much detour was needed to get there nor would there be any language issues, so I selected Port Stanley. It was only when I was heading for Port Stanley that I realised the difficulties of logistics on the island. The ports were finalised for the time being but when I informed Admiral Awati about the incident, he was livid.

"Tell them that there are no floating harbours in the Southern Ocean. What nonsense is this!" he thundered, referring to the conditions that had been put by NHQ.

"Okay, I will," was all I could say, having no intention of doing any such thing for my own good. Admiral Awati, I am sure, figured out what was going on in my mind and called up a few days later, once again booming, "Have you told them what I told you to tell them?"

"Sir, I think it will be best to try and reason with the concerned people when I go to NHQ for the final planning. I don't see much point in locking horns over the phone and jeopardising the project at this stage. We have far more important things to worry about before we start finalising the route."

I did visit Delhi a few weeks later and tried to explain my point of view but soon realised the futility of wasting time over the issue and started planning my trip with four stops.

Apprenticeship on Sir Robin's boat

With Sir Robin at Bilbao

Goddess Mhadei

Uprighting newly built Mhadei

Day after painting

Pouring lead in the keel

Mhadei floating for the first time

Mhadei in her medium

First entry in Mumbai

Mhadei charging to Mauritius

Solo Circumnavigation by Cdr Dilip Donde on INSV Mhadei 2009-2010

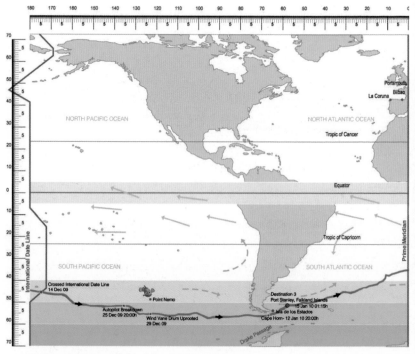

Designed and Compiled by **Mandar Karmarkar**

Doldrums
Roaring 40s
Furious 50s
Screaming 60s

Trade Winds
Westerlies
Ocean Current

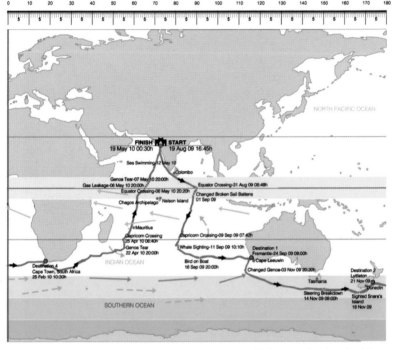

0   10   20   30   40   50   60   70   80   90   100   110   120   130   140   150   160   170   180

NORTH PACIFIC OCEAN

FINISH ◆ **START**
19 May 10 00:30h   19 Aug 09 16:45h

Sea Swimming-12 May 10

Genoa Tear-07 May 10 20:00h   Colombo
Gas Leakage-06 May 10 20:00h   Equator Crossing-31 Aug 09 08:48h
Equator Crossing-06 May 10 20:20h   Changed Broken Sail Battens
                                          01 Sep 09
Chagos Archipelago   Nelson Island

• Mauritius
Capricorn Crossing   Capricorn Crossing-09 Sep 09 07:42h
25 Apr 10 06:40h
Genoa Tear   Whale Sighting-11 Sep 09 10:10h
22 Apr 10 20:00h
INDIAN OCEAN   Bird on Boat   Destination 1
                          16 Sep 09 20:00h   Fremantle-24 Sep 09 08:00h
Destination 4   Cape Leeuwin
Cape Town, South Africa   Changed Genoa-03 Nov 09 20:30h   Destination 2
25 Feb 10 10:30h   Lyttleton
                                                                             21 Nov 09
                                                        Tasmania   •Dunedin
SOUTHERN OCEAN   Steering Breakdown   Sighted Snare's
                                          14 Nov 09 08:00h   Island
                                                                  18 Nov 09

All times mentioned are local times

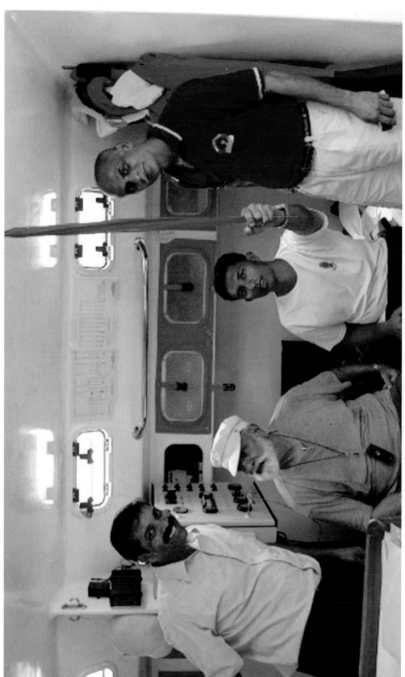

The core team (L-R) Ratnakar Dandekar, Manohar Awati, Abhilash Tomy, Dilip Donde

Equatorial sunrise

Equatorial sunset

Whales ahoy

Visitor aboard

Ratnakar at Cape Leeuwin

Maori welcome at Lyttelton

Leaving Lyttelton

Cape Horn

Royal escort at Falklands

Entering Port Stanley

Sammy, the seal, at Port Stanley

Under Table Mountain at Cape Town

Magellanic penguins

Almost home

Last of the capes

Cape of Good Hope

The finish line

Chapter 22

The Final Checklist

The list of jobs to be done on *Mhadei* had been increasing steadily. This wasn't because she was a badly built boat; far from it, everything fitted onboard had been working perfectly. The increase in the list was almost proportional to the wisdom and experience we gained as we sailed her. We realised the need for fitting extra winches, a generator and a whole lot of other equipment. Most of it again needed to be imported and separate sanctions obtained from the Navy. Time was critical with less than two months to go if we were to meet the 15 Aug 2009 deadline we had set for ourselves two years ago. We had come a long way in the project without missing a single deadline and had no intention of spoiling our record if we could help it.

Getting *Mhadei* ready was important but there were other things that needed attention too. I left the job of getting the boat ready with Ratnakar and Abhilash in Goa and headed for Delhi to sort out the final planning for the trip. As my flight took off from Goa, I was overcome by a strange feeling of loneliness. Since the time we started sailing her, this was the first time I was being away from *Mhadei* for more than a day and it didn't feel good. It took some effort to convince myself that the boat was in good hands and that I needed to concentrate on finishing the work in Delhi. It was a whirlwind trip, working out the tentative schedule, routeing, reporting, SAR arrangements, contingencies, passport, visas. In addition, we had to try and get Ratnakar out of the clutches of the tax authorities, push the Navy to pay his dues at least before the trip started, try to arrange funding for the additional equipment we required and, most important, get some money for provisioning the boat. It may sound strange but such are the ways of the bureaucracy, that with less than a month to go and half a million dollars sanctioned for the project, we still didn't have any ready cash to provision the boat. Everyone I met would keep congratulating me on the Mauritius trip, assure all support for the next one and send me on yet another wild goose chase when I asked them for something real like cash for provisioning, cameras or equipment. It was really amazing!

One day, as I was busy running between various offices in Delhi, I was summoned for a meeting with the Chief of Personnel in his office. I decided to make the best of this opportunity to get many of the bureaucratic obstacles cleared with the blessings of someone so high up in the chain. What actually happened though was totally unexpected.

The Admiral congratulated me on the progress so far, telling me how proud he and the Navy were with all the achievements and then let out a googly!

"Actually, we would have liked to train you better and it is our fault that we haven't been able to do that. You have achieved a lot despite very little training," said the Admiral, all sugar, honey and concern.

I started getting an uneasy feeling in my stomach, wondering where exactly this was leading, but listened with a straight face nevertheless.

"You see, a solo circumnavigation is a difficult task and you need to train some more and be absolutely ready to take it on. I think we should postpone the circumnavigation to next year so you can train better. Just let us know where you want to train and how. You want to train in Europe, do a few trans-Atlantic crossings, spend a year abroad, just let us know and we will send you at the Navy's expense."

"But sir...!" I blurted out, hardly believing what the Admiral was telling me.

"No buts, son. This is for your own good; you don't understand the risks involved. This is the Navy's final decision and you better obey it." The inevitable stick after the carrot of a year-long holiday in Europe.

"Sir, may I say something if you have finished?" I retorted, trying my best to keep my voice even and face smiling.

"Yes, go ahead."

"Sir, I have been working on this project for over three years now. In all this time, the most difficult part has not been the boat building, the confrontations with the bureaucracy or the sailing. The most difficult part has been to keep believing in myself that this project will happen, that I will make it happen despite all odds. Honestly sir, I am fairly close to the limit of my endurance in that respect and am very sure that I will not be able to last till next year. I have so far sailed *Mhadei* safely for some 7,000 nm, out of which about 2,500 nm have been solo. While I cannot guarantee you any results, I have never been more confident about myself. So either I start the circumnavigation next month as planned or you can look for someone else to do the trip." The Admiral seemed rather speechless, not accustomed to being addressed by a Commander in such a manner in his own office!

I had called a bluff, well aware that the Navy didn't have anyone with the amount of experience I had gathered. But the Admiral still had the power to pull the plug and I had no intentions of walking out of the project. I had shown the stick first; it was now time to show the carrot.

"Sir, I fully understand your concerns about safety owing to my lack of training and experience. Let me assure you that if at any point of time I find myself not up to the task, you will be the first person I will call and ask to be taken off the boat. I will not let my ego or pride cloud my judgement." I continued at my conciliatory best while feeling exactly the opposite. "As to the perception of lack of training, I think we need to quantify what we mean by sufficient training or sea experience; either in terms of days at sea or sea miles, or both. If you had done that earlier, I assure you I would have met the target. Making aspersions about my lack of training at this stage does not make any sense. I can undergo all the possible training in the world and still suffer an accident when I start the circumnavigation. There are no guarantees at sea."

Left with little choice, the Admiral grudgingly agreed to let me go the next month. "Is there anything else?" he asked with resignation.

"Yes sir, there is. So far, the Navy has done very little about promoting this project with the media. We are spending good money on this project and if we are not able to get any mileage out of it, it is good money down the drain. Personally, it does not make much difference to me as no one will be able to take away what I will gain from the project. But it will be sad to see the Navy lose out on such a good opportunity."

"Don't you worry about that, you do the sailing and leave the rest to us!" replied the Admiral, getting back to his normal self and keen to get rid of me.

I walked out of the office wondering whose project Sagar Parikrama was! By then I was in so deep it didn't matter anyway. If some people in the Navy weren't interested in making it happen, so be it. There were many more who had contributed to make us reach where we were now and were willing to help us complete the circumnavigation successfully; and to me, they mattered. There was no way I could let them down. I wound up my work in Delhi as fast as I could and headed home for Mumbai.

Meanwhile, Ratnakar and Abhilash had got the boat out of the water for a final inspection and were trying to get as much work done on her as possible. Less than a month to go and we were still far from ready. A note I wrote to Naval Headquarters may perhaps give an idea about how far we were lagging behind in almost all the preparations.

Sir,

1. *There is less than a month to commence Sagar Parikrama and a lot of issues are still pending. I thought it may be a good idea to list them out so that we can follow up on them and sort them out well in time to avoid any last minute chaos and embarrassment. Also, while a look at the calendar tells us that there is a month to go, effectively we have just about 20 days left to do anything worthwhile as the boat will need to be sailed from Goa to Mumbai by 10 Aug 2009. A list of issues that require urgent attention, and there may be more that I have missed out, is given below for your perusal.*

*a) **Visa.** As I understand I will need at least a visa for Australia before*

149

setting out from Mumbai. While a gratis visa usually takes a day or two, it may be better to get this issue over with since as we get closer to the date of departure, I will need to spend more time in Goa looking after the boat.

*b) **Fitting of additional items on the boat.** To the best of my knowledge, the boat builder has given a quotation but is yet to get a firm order for procuring and fitting the generator and other items. He has already intimated that he requires a month to import the items and fit them. As a user, my concern is also the trials after the items are fitted and to ensure that they can be used. Thus we need even more time in hand than the builder to ensure their utility. We need to sort out this issue ASAP if we want to meet the deadline of 19 Aug.*

*c) **Additional winches.** These are still stuck with the Customs at Goa. Fitting them is a time-consuming process as first we need to site them and then do the structural modifications to fit them properly before finally testing them and get used to sailing with them.*

*d) **Refund of excise duty.** We still haven't sorted out the issue thanks to which there is a marked change in the attitude of the builder in getting the boat ready, something that is extremely worrisome especially when I am gearing up to go in uncharted waters. Call me superstitious or call it my mental preparation, something that has been harped about a lot by almost everyone, with suggestions from learning yoga to meeting psychologists, but I would be extremely uncomfortable in setting out for a trip like this with unpaid dues on the boat. I am sure all-out efforts are on in Delhi to resolve the issue but we need to get the desired results.*

*e) **Decorating the boat.** Mhadei's plain white hull and sails can be well used to project the Navy and the country, presumably one of the aims* *of the project. This task is, however, beyond the capabilities of the present team working on the boat, which understandably needs to focus on the core issue of getting the boat ready for sailing.*

f) **Photography.** *The PRO, Navy, did advise as to the requirements of publicity including the type and quality of video footage that the audiences like to see, the stories they like to hear, the inadequacies of the camera held onboard, etc. A lot of these are well known as so far we have been the audience watching others do things. The question, however, is how to deliver what the audience wants and who is going to deliver it! If we need to fit any hi-tech cameras or media equipment onboard, we have very little time in hand as first we would need to give time to the boat builder to fit it and then to me to learn to operate it. Once again, the problem is beyond the capabilities of the team working on the boat and needs action, not advice, by the experts.*

g) **Publicity.** *If the trip to Mauritius is considered to be a test case and the naval community a test audience, it is quite apparent that we managed to generate very little awareness even among our own community, despite establishing two 'firsts' by Indians, of sailing a boat shorthanded and then solo over a distance of more than 2,300 nm. If we continue to follow the same media strategy, the result at the end of Sagar Parikrama may not be any different and we would be losing an excellent opportunity to project the Indian Navy and the country, despite spending over Rs 6 crore. If we indeed want to use this project to its full potential, we need to act now.*

2. *Since commencing over three years back, with absolutely no idea about the requirements for a solo circumnavigation and traversing through uncharted waters at every stage, this project has met all its objectives and schedules while remaining within its budget. It is crucial that we put in concerted*

efforts in this last month to ensure that the project maintains its final schedule and has every possible chance of success.

Regards,

Cdr Dilip Donde

20 Jul 2009

Our date of departure had been revised from 15 Aug to 19 Aug. The Chief of Naval Staff wanted to see us off from Mumbai but was required to be present in Delhi on 15 Aug to attend the functions for the Indian Independence Day. We decided to complete as much work as possible in Goa before sailing *Mhadei* to Mumbai on 10 Aug 2009. Ratnakar would join us in Mumbai to help us with the last minute preparations. It was obvious that we would have to keep working right till the time of my departure. The other alternative was to postpone the departure, but we could not agree on how long. I am a firm believer of the famous Parkinson's Law that states, "Work expands to fill the time available." The moment we hinted at the possibility of delaying the departure, the pressure we had been putting on everyone would have been lifted and slowed the pace of work. That was totally unacceptable.

I got back to the boat in the first week of August. The list of jobs on the boat had reduced considerably but our winches and generator were still stuck in the Customs' warehouse. Both Abhilash and Ratnakar were looking visibly unwell, the long hours of work and stress clearly showing. The local Naval hospital admitted Abhilash for suspected typhoid and threatened to incarcerate him longer if he said a word about going back to the boat! It was time to take it easy for a while.

We were seen off from Goa on 10 Aug 2009 by an enthusiastic

naval crowd and the local press. I had with me a two-man TV crew from a news channel and a journalist from a national daily. Admiral Awati had been enthusiastic about sailing with us but came down with severe backache a day before departure and had to drop out. Abhilash had been packed off home on sick leave to recover and join us in Mumbai. Seeing that I was sailing with absolute rookies, the Flag Officer Commanding, Goa Area, deputed his energetic Flag Lieutenant as crew. He didn't have much experience of sailing but was a qualified naval watch-keeper and, more important, a willing worker, which suited me fine. It was an easy and uneventful sail with a bit of monsoonal swell that introduced the crew to the miseries of sea sickness first hand. By the next evening, we were sitting becalmed outside Mumbai harbour with the city lights beckoning us in. The crew, when asked if they would prefer to motor the last few miles or wait for the wind to pick up, were quick and unanimous in their decision. "Let us get inside and on land. We have enough material to report!" In the next couple of hours, we were alongside at Naval Dockyard in Mumbai.

The last eight days before departure were probably the craziest in the entire project. Everyone seemed to be running around somewhere! Ratnakar and Abhilash were busy sorting out the boat, stocking up spares and tools. At home, my mother was busy sorting out my food. She had been experimenting with her own version of 'ready-to-eat' food for the past two years and was now busy labelling and packing things up. My sister, along with my friend Swati, had taken on the responsibility of stocking the boat with books and music. I was trying to spend as much time as I could arranging the boat and trying to figure out what still needed to be done. We took the boat out for one last trial sail off

Mumbai and decided to start getting ready for departure. We had to draw a line somewhere. We had done whatever best we could. We needed to leave aside what we hadn't been able to do, get it out of our mind and move on with confidence. There were plenty, even at this stage, who doubted the success of the project and my survival. I received a nice mail from Robin a few days before departure, the best among the many I received.

Dilip,

You will be very busy just now I know, so I will keep this short.

I just want to wish you all the best for the forthcoming voyage. It has been a pleasure being involved and watching how the project has developed. It has been a greater pleasure watching your growing confidence. You have reached the point where it is time to go. So go with confidence and the supporting thoughts of all of us who have got to know you.

Remember – You CAN do it.

Jai Hind

RKJ

Chapter 23

Down Under

The day of departure finally dawned. It didn't feel much different than all the hectic days so far! I had been up late the previous night packing my stuff and had to drag myself out of bed when Abhilash called from the Officers' Mess asking for a lift to the boat.

"Sir, our official car will not be available today. The transport pool is telling me that a number of senior officers including the Chief of Naval Staff have landed in town to see off some boat sailing somewhere and there are no cars available! Can you please pick me up from the Mess in your car on your way to the boat?"

"We do need some humour in such busy times," I thought to myself getting ready, fairly certain there was more to come.

The previous evening, just as we were about to leave the boat for the day, Abhilash had remembered the Immigration formalities. It had totally slipped everyone's mind as one never has to go through them while sailing on a naval ship. It had taken us some time to figure out what exactly I was supposed to do and I had planned to start my day with the Immigration office, which turned out to be a police station not too far away. My departure was planned for 1630 h so there wasn't much time left.

"How did you get inside Mumbai harbour without a stamp on your passport? We should be putting you behind bars and impounding the boat," boomed the police officer who was supposed to be stamping my passport as I sat in his office, thoroughly exasperated.

"But the boat was built in Goa and I sailed her to Mumbai. Why would I need to get my passport stamped for sailing between two Indian ports? She is also a naval boat and I have a letter from the Navy asking you to stamp my passport. If you don't want to stamp it, can I have my passport back as I really need to leave this evening? As to impounding the boat she is at Naval Dockyard, go try your luck!"

"You are not getting your passport back nor are you going anywhere!"

The inane and rather colourful conversation went on for over an hour with a break in between, standing outside the office, because it needed to be fumigated with mosquito repellent for a suspected swine flu epidemic in the city! I had seriously started losing patience. Suddenly, the same person who had been arguing with me for so long took one hard look at me.

"Were you on television last night?"

"I must have been."

"So you are the person who is going to be sailing around the world."

"That's exactly what I have been trying to tell you so long and I need to leave this evening. Now, can I please have my passport back?" I replied, trying my best to keep a neutral voice.

"Hey, get his passport quickly, with a stamp, but pass that box of sweets first." he told his deputy.

I was out of the police station in the next five minutes, my passport stamped, mouth stuffed with sweets and the good wishes of the entire police station with me!

I dropped by home one last time, had a quick lunch, put my personal luggage in my car and headed for the boat. It didn't feel any different than going for just another small trip. I wasn't tense or excited as everyone was expecting me to be. It probably had something to do with the 'humour in uniform' that seemed to be cropping up every now and then. Inside Naval Dockyard as I started driving to the boat, I was stopped by the Naval Police.

"Sir, you can't drive any further. The road is closed."

"And why is the road closed?"

"Some boat is sailing somewhere and the CNS and other VIPs are coming to see her off. We have closed the road for security."

"And who is sailing the boat?"

"I don't know sir, but you definitely can't go any further."

"But the boat won't sail unless I put the luggage and myself on her, here let me explain." It took some time and patience to explain to the sentry what exactly was going on till he finally agreed to let me go.

The press descended soon enough and we got busy. It became so chaotic after a while that I couldn't wait to get out. After the brief introductions and speeches, I led the CNS to the boat and showed him around quickly. As he turned towards me to bid goodbye, before getting off the boat, I saluted and, trying to suppress a grin, asked, "Permission to sail around the world, sir!" "Most certainly, all the best!" he replied, smiling. I ran back, switched on the engine and asked Ratnakar and Abhilash to let go the lines.

I had been in a sort of detached state of mind, hardly registering what was happening for the past couple of hours. It was as if I was floating around watching the happenings without actually being involved in them and doing all actions mechanically. There was plenty of noise around with people cheering and the naval band playing on the jetty. Unmindful of all that was happening around me, I was trying to concentrate on getting the boat away from the pontoon without getting anything fouled. In all that, I suddenly heard the voice of a child shouting, "All the best", at the top of her voice. That brought me back to reality instantly. It was my four-year-old niece sitting on her dad's shoulder. She had been very quiet so far, no doubt bewildered by all the noise and chaos around. Now she couldn't contain her excitement anymore and had finally found her voice. I just stopped doing everything, turned around and waved her goodbye.

I motored the boat out of the Naval Dockyard, followed by a few Hobie 16 catamarans from the Naval Sailing Club. In about half an hour, I was sufficiently out of restricted waters to put up the sails. The Western Fleet was entering the harbour so I got a little away from the main channel, turned the boat into the wind, put her on autopilot and got busy cranking up the mainsail. The sail had barely gone up half way when I noticed a big grey hull heading for me, obviously heading for her anchor berth. I left everything, got on to the wheel and swung the boat away with the half up sail flapping. I had another go at setting the sail as soon as I was in the clear, turned the boat on a southerly course and switched off the engine. We were finally under sail and on our way. A dockyard passenger boat passed by, full of cheering friends and family. "Okay girl, the celebrations are over, let us get going now," I said to the boat as I started getting all the banners and decoration off, making her ready for sailing. As I crossed the Prong's Reef Light at the mouth of Mumbai harbour, I offered a coconut to the sea. The CNS had given it to me and someone had told me that it was a tradition to do that. The offering apparently gets you back safely!

The next task was getting out of the maze of fishing nets outside the harbour. There was a nice north-westerly breeze up and we managed to cross the island of Khanderi without having to tack or getting seriously stuck in any of the nets. The plan was to keep heading south southeast almost parallel to the Indian coast till crossing the Indian peninsula. I called up home on my mobile phone before getting out of range. There seemed to be a party on there with everyone back from the send-off and now watching the whole thing on TV. "I think I am going to miss all the fun, but then I would not trade sailing like this for anything," I thought. As I sat outside having some sandwiches and eggs, I heard a very familiar voice on the radio. It was All India Radio airing my interview recorded a while ago.

Three days later, once I had settled down on the boat, I started writing my blog. It had been set up for me by my friend Anshuman Chatterjee more than a year ago but I had been too busy or lazy to write anything on it. There was also the constant uncertainty about the trip not happening. Now, there was no excuse; I was off. And whether I finished the trip successfully or not, people had a right to know what was happening. After all, many of the potential readers, the Indian taxpayers, were actually funding my entire project without even being aware of it. My blog posts follow, in italics, without too many changes as they were the only journal I maintained and may best be able to capture the mood at that time.

SAGAR PARIKRAMA – FIRST TWO DAYS

Wednesday, 19 Aug 2009

Finally left at 1645 h from Mumbai. After all the chaos the media created at the flag-off, frankly I was glad to get off. By 1720 h the sail was up and I was panting like a dog with the effort of putting up the mainsail. Mhadei was sailing nicely on a broad reach with a north-westerly breeze, a bit unusual for this season with the south-westerly monsoon still supposed to be around. The wind kept increasing and for a while we were doing a healthy 10 kts with plans being made to pass Goa in 24 hrs. The wind kept shifting through the night. That and the fishing fleets signalled goodbye to any chance of sleep. By early morning the wind died out completely.

Thursday, 20 Aug 2009

Thanks to almost nonexistent winds, serious sleep deprivation while on land and a painfully stiff neck, 'Sunday routine' was declared after making the mandatory position report at 0800 h. Didn't even need to cook breakfast as Manjiri, wife of my Tarangini shipmate Lt Cdr Atla Mohan, had packed some excellent 'halwa'. A cocktail of brufen and paracetamol took care of the neck. After having slept the whole day, plans of a good night's sleep were again dashed by shifty winds and, most unusually, an attack of large sized moths over 50 nm from the coast. The first one came around sunset and I was wondering about his sense of navigation when slowly more started descending. Obviously attracted by light they were all over, committing 'harakiri' on the chart plotter, navigation equipment, lights, etc. Finally switched off the chart plotter and slept outside as the ones already inside couldn't find a way out. There was not much wind anyway and the boat was hardly moving.

Friday, 21 Aug 2009

Realised it wasn't fair to blame the wind yesterday. It could have been worse as I discovered today! A couple of hours of light north-easterly breeze and then quietness. The sea slowly turned glassy. Nothing you can do but furl up the genoa, get the main fore and aft to reduce its flapping, switch off the autopilot and lock the rudder. In fact I switched off all the navigation equipment as it seemed pointless keeping it on with us drifting around. Made a nice lunch of dal and rice followed by the mandatory siesta. Out of habit and between naps went on deck to find dolphins lounging around. Thanks to absolute stillness around could clearly hear them. It is almost 1900 h as I write. A north-westerly wind seems to be making some efforts at moving Mhadei. In the morning I was 'off Goa', by dusk I am still there. Let us see where I reach tomorrow! Till then celebrating passing off Goa by having some 'Goa sausage pulao', a favourite of my crew Lt Cdr Abhilash Tomy during our past trips, and listening to All India Radio, Panaji.

Friday, 21 Aug 2009 – Late night post from Mhadei

Through the day I was becalmed, since 2100 h cruising at over 9 kts in a 20-kt breeze. There is a huge cloud mass on me almost moving with me and it's pouring buckets outside. The rain screen designed by Abhilash and Ratnakar has already proved its worth keeping me and the insides of Mhadei dry. Looks like another long night ahead but at least we are moving! The sausage pulao was delicious and should keep me going through the night.

Saturday, 22 Aug 2009 – Post from Mhadei

It is around 2130 h, the crew has been well fed on a diet of brown rice and dehydrated spinach while Mhadei is enjoying a cruise on a broad reach in over 20 kts of steady breeze with a following sea. Rain through the day has brought down the temperatures and the radio is still picking up songs. Almost perfect! Makes you wonder if last night actually happened.

Last night soon after I wrote the blog, the wind died out making the sails flap around violently. Furled the headsail and lashed the boom and the wind picked up to 30 kts. Got up and set the sails and the wind decided to vanish again. The cycle of squalls with shifty winds continued through the night making me forget the number of gybes I made just to stay straight. In the middle of one such gybe the Raymarine autopilot decided to strike work. Luckily the Jeffa autopilot held fort and we managed to come through. The extra winches fitted at the last minute came in handy. Looks like the trouble of clearing them from Customs and fitting them was well worth the effort. As if the wind wasn't enough, the moths struck with a vengeance. The constant shifting of sails must have disturbed them, so when I was not struggling with the sails and getting wet outside, I was honing my shooting skills with a can of insect repellent inside the boat. These shifty and light winds can drive one absolutely nuts. They also tend to damage things as I discovered in the morning. The mainsail clew shackle, and it is a real heavy-duty stainless steel shackle, had come off. The seizing wire had broken off and the threads worn out probably due to the constant slating of the mainsail. Luckily a spare was available. One lazy jack was off and entangled with the starboard runner; was lucky to catch it before it was too late. Will see what is wrong with the Raymarine autopilot tomorrow. Morning was absolutely windless with some swell. In a way that was good as I could check out the damage of the night and replace the shackle. Been getting good winds since afternoon. Started with a squall but the wind has continued, from northwest! And I thought it was the season for southwest monsoons. There are regular squalls passing over but they don't seem to go over 30 kts very often, well within the capabilities of my most important crew member, the Jeffa autopilot. Covered over 50 nm in the last 6 hrs, crossed Mangalore about 65 nm away from land and now passing the Kerala coast 67 nm to the east.

That night, a little past midnight, as I was trying to deal with the squally weather, I started hearing calls from a fisherman on my VHF radio. He seemed to have cast very long nets and was trying to warn everyone in the vicinity to stay clear of them. I had just started the engine to charge my batteries and warm up some water for a hot shower. I could see a few lights far away and as the calls on the radio didn't mention any position assumed them to be those of the fisherman and his nets. Suddenly, a search light popped up close to the boat and the fisherman started giving his position on the VHF. There was no doubt that I was almost onto the nets. Not wanting to get stuck in them, I tacked in a hurry and while doing that stumbled on the gear lever of the engine, inadvertently clutching the engine. I was in the middle of tacking the boat and had my hands full. "Never mind, let me first get the boat sailing on the other tack, then I can declutch the engine and feather the propeller," I thought, worried about the nets getting caught in the moving propeller. Suddenly I heard some thumping sounds from inside the boat, the engine shrieked loudly and died. My first thought was that the propeller had taken the nets with it and had tripped the engine. But then the boat was still moving and there wasn't anything visible trailing behind her. Baffled, I went inside to have a look and was confronted with a mini war zone. My rucksack had fallen inside the engine room through one of the panels that I was in the habit of keeping open to provide better ventilation to the engine. The propeller shaft, woken out of its slumber by my stumbling over the gear lever, had shredded the rucksack and all its contents before finally tripping the engine. That explained all the funny noises in the boat. It took me a couple of hours to clear up the mess and assure myself that no permanent damage had occurred to the engine or shaft. By the time I finished with the cleanup, no hot shower was necessary. I was sweating like a pig and waiting for the next squall to have a cool shower 'au naturel'!

Monday, 24 Aug 2009 – No Monday morning blues on Mhadei

One good thing about sailing alone for longer than a week seems to be the total absence of the so common 'Monday morning blues'! Either everyday is a holiday or there are no holidays, whichever way you look at it, though I am inclined to go with the former. A fairly good day after a long night thanks to regular squalls followed by very light winds. We made good progress last night and somehow kept moving through the day. It became unusually cool through the night and I actually had to get my sleeping bag out. We are travelling through a shipping lane so a bit of company of big guys passing us. I would any day prefer them to the unlit fishing boats. Most big ships have the AIS, paint well on the radar and so far seem to respond to a VHF call asking them to keep clear of our erratic course. Not much fishing traffic as we are over 75 nm from land. In fact as I write we are passing Cape Comorin, more commonly known as Kanyakumari, the southernmost point of the Indian peninsula. The last time we passed this route was in May on the way to Colombo with Abhilash for company. Hard to believe that it was just three months back. It was our first trip abroad and I can still remember our apprehensions as the wind started going over 20 kts. The wind is going over 20 kts again but I am comfortably sitting inside writing this. Both Mhadei and I have sailed over 7,000 nm since then and the mutual confidence has grown by leaps and bounds! Today's day, though, truly belonged to the autopilots. The Raymarine autopilot started working after sulking for the last two days. It is steering the boat now and I am keeping my fingers crossed. The wind vane autopilot, probably the least used equipment onboard so far, was put to use for a couple of hours and worked well. Plan to use it through the day tomorrow to reduce my electricity consumption. The day ended with a sail past by INS Bangaram which had come to check us out. The whole ship's company had lined up on deck to wish fair winds to Mhadei! It is almost 2130 h now. After a rather heavy dinner of a large tuna, potato, egg and onion salad washed down with some hot soup it is time to get into the daily cycle of catnaps through the night. Looks like another long night ahead as the wind is picking up intermittently, some squalls are visible and the shipping traffic needs to be watched out for. Started picking up the radio transmission like every night, All India Radio, Goa of all places, which is really nice if one has to stay awake!

The squalls were quite a nuisance and it took me some time to learn to deal with them. It was not until crossing the equator that we finally got rid of them. During the day I could see them approaching but at night the only way to detect them was the radar and I would keep dozing in front of it to keep a watch on them. When they hit there was no option but to be out on the deck trying my best to keep the boat from damaging herself. You keep doing that too often and through the night, tiredness sets in and then you start making mistakes in doing even the simplest of things. Tempers would be running high on the boat in such conditions with plenty of shouting and cursing. There was one golden rule onboard though: "No one answers back to the cursing!"

Tuesday, 25 Aug 2009 – Dosa special on Mhadei
Late last night we crossed the Indian peninsula and by morning had crossed the Gulf of Mannar. That, and the fact that we had covered the maximum distance of 182 nm in 24 hours so far, called for a celebration. The skipper ordered the chef who in turn decided to do away with the usual fare of rice and canned stuff for the day and instead serve hot dosas and kapi (coffee)! So 'pan to plate' piping hot dosas was the menu for breakfast and lunch. Washed down with some fresh coffee brewed in the Italian coffee maker fondly gifted by Ottavio and Pai! Absolutely delicious. Another reason to feel good was that the wind vane autopilot was put to work for over six hours in

the morning and worked without a whimper even with following wind and sea. That is good news because now I can conserve my diesel and also have something to fall back on in the absence of electricity. It is quite a nifty gadget which uses only the force of the wind and water rushing past the boat to keep her at the desired angle to the wind. The day progressed nicely; big ships passing by, rainbows and all, till in the evening saw the first of the equatorial squalls approach. Some sixth sense prevailed and I furled in the genoa. It was too late to put in a reef in the main. The squall hit, strong winds of about 30 to 35 kts first but Mhadei responded to hand steering, then heavy rain, not too bad, I was planning to have a shower anyway! Just when I thought we had weathered this one the strongest of the gusts slammed in. Mhadei almost went over and then turned into the wind and got stuck for good. It was strange, with the mainsail fully out and the rudder hard over, the boat was just standing there facing the wind on an almost even keel. A new experience for me! This was followed by two bone-crunching gybes as the boom slammed into the runner and it was with some difficulty that we managed to get back downwind again. I was soaked and on the edge when I suddenly felt the sun warming my back. Looked back in surprise to see an almost clear sky with the sun shining as if the squall never happened! First thing I did was to put in a reef in the main as that experience is not something you want to go through after dark. Found four dead baby squids washed up on the deck. Took a long time to clear up the mess inside the boat as a lot of things had taken flight during our violent manoeuvres. It is past midnight now and I am sitting in front of the radar keeping an eye on the squalls. Two seem to be closing in so I better stop this and get ready to face them.

Wednesday, 26 Aug 2009 – The perils of sailing a good-looking boat

I have been complimented about Mhadei's good looks and seen her attract crowds in a marina but never thought that this ability will extend to attract-

ing squalls! Saw it firsthand last night when I would see a number of cloud patches on the radar, slowly they would gather together right on top of us, stay there and vent their contents on us with a vengeance. The contents are mainly 30 to 40 kts of gusty winds and tons of water. It is a nightmare to have this happen to you several times on a pitch dark night near a shipping lane. Luckily I had put in a reef in the mainsail and furled the genoa to minimise the damage. Still no choice but to be up on the deck in my raingear trying to control the boat. The entire night was spent like that and by daybreak I was absolutely worn out. The wind had died out almost completely so instead of taxing the autopilot and myself anymore, locked the rudder and went to sleep. Must have slept for a couple of minutes and was woken up by the boat heeling over 30°. Another squall had hit and Mhadei was going all over. Started hand steering to control her when probably due to lack of sleep or poor judgement the boat went into an accidental gybe, the boom crashing on the starboard runner and the boat behaving even more awkwardly. Tried to rectify my mistake and the boom slammed back to its correct position but in doing so the mainsheet got snagged with the boat compass uprooting it. The compass is undamaged but its stainless steel mounting has broken. One job for the next port. Also noticed that the top two battens have broken probably due to the continuous flapping of the sails in nil wind conditions. Though I have spare battens it will be quite a task changing them at sea so will probably do it in port. May affect the efficiency of the sails while going upwind but that is better than messing around with things at sea. Things improved by afternoon and I even managed to get some badly needed sleep. In the afternoon my old friend Cdr Paresh Sawhney came visiting with his ship. We had served together in the Eastern Fleet in 1995 as Lieutenants and it was nice to see him commanding a fleet ship. The axiom that good things have to follow bad ones has been amply demonstrated tonight. As I write, it is a cool, clear night outside with a brilliant half moon, the wind is blowing steadily at about 20 to 25 kts and Mhadei is cruising at 8 kts on a broad reach in a following sea. Absolutely perfect sailing conditions!

The sailing was quite a mixed bag, at times getting buffeted by the equatorial squalls and getting soaked to my gills trying to control the boat, at times finding the mainly westerly monsoonal winds and zipping ahead. The boat had started showing some signs of wear in terms of the broken battens and the uprooted compass but so far there were no serious problems and she seemed to be holding herself well. The breakages had more to do with my inexperience in dealing with the unpredictable equatorial weather and consequent tiredness than the quality of the boat. This was heartening because at that stage there was little I could do to improve the boat but could definitely learn to handle her better as I gained experience. "It can only get better", I told myself. It had been a week since we left Mumbai and the memories of land had already started getting a little blurred. I was trying to make as much progress east as I could before eventually crossing the equator. At times, when the frequency of the squalls increased or the winds became erratic, it was tempting to head south, cross the equator and go searching for the steady and reliable Trade Winds. As I would realise in a few days, it was very good that I avoided the temptation and continued heading east.

Saturday, 29 Aug 2009 – Ten days and 1,500 miles
We have been at sea for 10 days and have covered exactly 1,500 nm. Not too bad considering the slow start. The grand flag-off at Mumbai, the hectic activity before that; all are distant memories as if they happened in a different world! This state of bliss after a few days of sailing is really interesting, because then you stop worrying about the distance to be covered, the speed you are doing and the lack of creature comforts of a land-based life. Suddenly

you are not in a hurry to go anywhere. Today was another perfect day! Just as I was having a cup of coffee, admiring the equatorial sunrise, a school of dolphins dropped by. Decided to use the video camera instead of the still and managed to get some good footage. Starting the day by saying hello to dolphins seems to be becoming a habit. They generally play around for about half an hour or so before going their own way. The sunrises and sunsets close to the equator can be quite spectacular. The visibility is excellent, the sea appears flatter than usual and the sky is coloured with vibrant shades. A steady wind of between 10 and 15 kts through the day with a following sea meant Mhadei cruised along through the day on a beam reach with the wind vane autopilot steering her. Even the squalls let us be today! Two of them did come close but passed us by without disturbing us. A grand breakfast of suji halwa; rice cooked with dried prawns and dal for lunch; soup and curried tuna for dinner all interspersed with helpings of the last of the fresh fruits and siestas after every meal! Can there be a better holiday? It is a beautiful night outside as I write; a bright moon, cool breeze, gentle sea, good music on the national service of All India Radio. I think I will sleep outside tonight, doze off watching the moon. Let us see how long these blissful days last. As we cross the equator and get into the Trade Winds, we will need to do some serious sailing in strong winds and big seas. But till then let us enjoy the moment!

The sunrises and sunsets I saw close to the equator in all my crossings have been nothing short of spectacular. I have not been able to understand the reason but the riot of colours and the typical flatness of the sea one gets to see in that area are something unique. I had really started enjoying the sail now. There was still a long way to go till the next port. All I had to do was look after the boat, look after myself and let the boat keep gobbling up the miles.

Sunday, 30 Aug 2009 – Abbreviated blog from Mhadei

We seem to have sailed into the heartland of squalls and all of them seem to be curious about us and intent on checking us out. Need to be on deck all the time. Looks like tonight is going to be spent in rain gear!

Goodnight.

Monday, 31 Aug 2009 – Greetings from the Southern Hemisphere

On the morning of 31 Aug 2009 at 0848 h, Mhadei crossed into the Southern Hemisphere at longitude 090° 23' East. King Neptune, who resides at the equator, took one look at us and remarked, "You two! Not again!" this being our third crossing since May this year. Slightly north of the equator the wind shifted to south southeast making us head northeast so it was time to tack and head south southwest, a course we will maintain till almost 35° South, then turn east for the home run to Fremantle. Looks like we found the southeast Trade Winds right from the word go as we have been getting a steady breeze since morning. It takes us back west a bit but at least we are moving. What a change from the last 11 days! Both the wind and swell are against us so we are bouncing nicely but that is better than wallowing around in light winds and worrying about squalls. It was good to cross the line finally! Changing tack on a long passage involves certain lifestyle changes. For example, for the last 11 days I was doing everything leaning to the right, now my leanings have shifted a distinct left. Not unlike our politicians I suppose! My galley being to the port and the boat heeling on the same side I could leave one odd cabinet open while cooking, this morning while preparing breakfast the contents tumbled out because the boat had started heeling to starboard! While the Doldrums near the equator drove us nuts with the squalls and shifty winds they also showed us some spectacular sunrises and sunsets. The beauty of the human mind is that the bad memories get erased quickly while the good ones stay on. So the bad weather is already a distant memory while the vividness of the sunrise on 30 Aug will remain with me for a long time.

We were across the equator finally. I would have preferred going further east but the winds had definitely started shifting and there didn't seem much point in struggling for the sake of a few more degrees of longitude.

Wednesday, 02 Sep 2009 – Doldrums still clutching Mhadei
The Doldrums made their presence felt again with a squall last night and then very light winds through the day. I had let down my guard and kept the full mainsail up at night with the wind vane steering the boat. Got up past midnight for a routine check and found a squall almost on top of us! Hectic activity of reefing the main and getting the wind vane off followed and we just about made it through. Need to remember that we are still very much in the ITCZ (Inter Tropical Convergence Zone), commonly known as the Doldrums. Another day or two and we should be out hitting the Trade Winds. Light and shifty winds through the day which died out completely by afternoon. The sea was also fairly calm so made use of the opportunity to change the two broken battens from the mainsail. That involved getting the entire sail down, climbing about 3 m up the mast a number of times to remove the pieces of broken battens, and finally sitting on the boom and mainsail to insert the replacements. I think my horse-riding skills, unused since passing out of the National Defence Academy 21 years back, came in handy in trying to sit on the boom of the rolling boat and working with both hands. It was a task that required to be done before getting into the stronger Trade Winds. The broken pieces have already damaged the sail a bit and in sustained strong winds the damage could only increase. The battery monitor, an instrument that tells me the amount of battery capacity I have and when I need to charge them, seems to have gone off finally. It had become erratic since yesterday so thought of removing its connections and cleaning them. But

having done so it is just refusing to revive itself! Now I don't have any idea how much battery I am left with or when I charge whether they are actually charging. I think I will just run the generator every 12 hrs to ensure they never run out of charge. May increase the diesel consumption marginally but with an efficient generator that should not be a cause for concern. Started the water maker for the first time during the trip as one of the tanks had become half empty. Not bad for 13 days of sailing! Another spectacular sunset in the evening with an already bright moon to the east. Looks like another sleepless night ahead as the wind keeps dying out every now and then. When it dies out you need to get on the deck and tighten the mainsheet to stop the boom from thrashing about and when the wind picks up you need to rush and ease the mainsheet as otherwise the boat starts heeling too much. It's also been a warm and clear day so a lot of moisture must have gone up which will eventually come down as a squall during the night and knowing our penchant for getting under every squall in the area we better keep our guard up.

Being able to change the battens at sea and on my own was quite a confidence builder. Initially, I wasn't sure of success. The big and heavy mainsail tends to become unmanageable when put on deck, especially if there is a breeze blowing. As the top two battens had broken, there was no option but to get the entire sail down. After seeing the broken battens tearing the sail, I had just planned to remove the broken pieces to save the sail. That done, I decided to go a step ahead and put in the spare ones too.

I needed to use both my hands for the work and the only way I could do that was by sitting on the boom, which already had many folds of the mainsail draped over it in a very haphazard manner. There wasn't anything to hold on to and it was somewhat like working with my hands while sitting astride a very large horse that was trying its best to move from side to side to throw me off. More than anything else, I was worried about tumbling over and falling off the boat in the sea. With the sail spread all over the boom and the deck, I couldn't use the harness to tether myself to the boat. Luckily, the wind gods decided to do the vanishing act for a couple of hours and for once I was very grateful! If the wind had decided to pick up, it would have blown away the sail and me sitting on it. It was a timely repair, well worth the effort. The next day we caught on the Trade Winds and it would be over a week before we would get any respite from the strong winds. The mainsail would surely have torn itself to pieces had I not removed the broken battens that evening.

Thursday, 03 Sep 2009 – Out of the Doldrums romping in Trade Winds

Yesterday afternoon, becalmed after going through yet another squall, we drifted across an invisible line and finally stumbled into the Trade Winds! The wind picked up in a matter of minutes and stayed with us. In fact by midnight it became a bit too much for comfort necessitating another reef in the main and replacement of the big genoa with the smaller stay sail. While the Trades make you move they also build up the sea. Also since they are blowing from exactly the same direction we need to go, we have to sail close to them and the resultant swell. The result is that Mhadei has been tossing and slamming around as if possessed! Needless to say everything onboard has to be done slowly, mostly with one hand, the other being busy holding on to the nearest handhold. Often the waves wash over the boat so all portholes need to be closed, making the insides warm and humid, and you get drenched with salt water sitting on the deck. This state is likely to continue for a week at least with the weather forecast promising 26 kts of breeze and 5 m waves in the next two days! We are also getting slowly pushed to the west due to the direction of the wind and the waves, which means once we are south of the

Trade Winds we will need to travel that much more to the east. Well as of now there is nothing much that we can do about it but grin and bear it – or on the tossing Mhadei it should be grip and bear it! Though this is any day better than wallowing around in the Doldrums. The squalls have reduced in their frequency and intensity. Also as we are already moving with reduced sail, when a squall hits it cannot do as much damage as when under full sail. The cook has started serving quick-fix meals of almost ready-to-eat food instead of the elaborate menus of dosas and hot 'dal-chawal'! Tonight, as I write, there is a glorious full moon up in the sky. We left Mumbai on a new moon. It has been 15 days and 2,200 nm so far. Wondering whether we will make it by the next new moon!

Friday, 04 Sep 2009 – Romping turns to battering
Since this afternoon Mhadei is being battered by strong winds and big seas. The winds are blowing at 20-25 kts with regular gusts beyond 35 kts. This has built up a large sea of over 4 m and Mhadei is heading into all this mayhem! The weather forecast is predicting the conditions to last for a couple of days more so we seem to be in it for the long haul. The cook has flatly refused to do anything with fire because while the gimballed gas oven keeps utensils steady against rolling, it does not have any solution to keep them on when the boat thumps itself on a wave and the pots tend to fly off vertically. So the skipper is left to scrounge for himself by nibbling various titbits in the galley. Mhadei bashes on regardless and all the skipper can do is sit and give her that sage, time-tested advice: "This too shall pass!"

It was a miserable week. For the second time in the past three months I was sailing upwind in the Trade Winds and it wasn't any better than before. The winds were steady, blowing from the direction we wanted to go. There wasn't much to do onboard except to keep sailing as close to the wind as practical. The boat would keep slamming in the swells, often taking on sea water, drenching everything outside and making it hot and humid inside. I would often keep lying in my bunk willing the time to pass quickly but at such times it seems to get stuck. I was trying my best to avoid the temptation to check out the distance to go too often or even the course the boat was sailing. Often we would be heading for Africa instead of Australia and it was depressing to see that. Instead it was simpler to tell myself to sail close to the wind on port tack and switch my mind off to everything else. We had been waiting to get into the Trade Winds since we left home and now couldn't wait to get out!

Monday, 07 Sep 2009 – And the battering continues

It has been four days since we headed into the Trade Winds and started thumping south southwest. We are still at it and if the weather forecast is anything to go by, will continue for the next couple of days. The winds have remained a steady southeast about 20 to 30 kts gusting to about 35 kts. Normally we should be able to sail a southerly course with such winds. Unfortunately the winds have also whipped up a swell of over 4 m. Trying to sail closer than about 50° to the wind means heading right into the swell, making the boat stop dead with each wave while making her slam hard, which may cause avoidable damage. So we are heading south southwest, aware that we are actually increasing the distance we will need to travel eastward once we get out of the Trades and into the Westerlies. The cook has finally relented and started doing limited heating so we had hot coffee in the morning and some hot soup and ready-to-eat biryani for dinner. Yesterday was some homemade 'heat & eat' upma with dry fish. Absolutely delicious! I think my mom seriously needs to apply for a patent for her dishes before someone steals her recipes. It has started getting cold after sunset reminding us that it is the winter season in this part of the world. At present course and speed we should be crossing the Tropic of Capricorn (23½° South) by tomorrow night and will remain south of it till next year when we are back in the Indian Ocean heading home. So as much cause for celebration as the equator crossing I suppose! My tracker for the project seems to be busy tonight so giving this morning's updated position. Have a good night.

Tuesday, 08 Sep 2009 – 20 days and 3,000 miles

It has been 20 days since we left Mumbai and we have covered over 3,000 nm so far. Not too bad! More or less what was expected, though we still have over 2,000 nm to cover, before we get in the Westerlies and start making some easting. As I was making my position report in the evening, I realised that despite covering almost 80 nm through the day, the distance to Fremantle had remained constant at 1,900 nm since morning! It may actually start increasing if we don't make any easterly progress soon. Well, such are the ways of sailboats! Covering these 3,000 nm also means that Mhadei has sailed over 10,000 nm in her brief service with the Navy since 12 Feb 2009. That is 10,000 nm in less than 7 months with hardly a whimper! I think the credit entirely goes to her builder Ratnakar and his team at Aquarius Fibreglas, Goa. I hope at least now the Great Indian Bureaucracy will relent and pay up the rest of the money due on the boat. As we near the Tropic of Capricorn, the seas have calmed a bit and the wind has reduced. At the cost of coming down in speed a little, I am still keeping the two reefs and stay sail on through the night just in case the wind decides to change its mind and starts blowing again. While we have done sail changes and reefing at night it is always avoidable and uncomfortable, especially now that it has also started getting cold. I think we are away from the oppressive tropical heat till next year. In fact, henceforth, the sun will be welcome, as I discovered this morning when I saw a cloudy sky and remarked to myself that it would be a cold day and it would have been nicer if it were a clear, sunny day! 20 days back I would have said the exact opposite! The covering of the 3,000 nm passage was duly celebrated with an impromptu recipe of corned mutton garnished with onions and gherkins. When the cook decided to serve the same fare for dinner because he doesn't like wasting food, the skipper had had enough and decided to wash it down with some soup first, followed by the last can of Phoenix Beer from Ile Maurice from the last trip. No more beer onboard till Freo but a good stock of South African wines and cognac for special occasions! The improvement in weather was also celebrated by the screening of the movie Chicago; one of the crew's all-time favourites. Since morning, all that has been watched are promos and behind-the-scenes sections. The actual screening is scheduled on completion of this blog when the battery charging will be over, the engine cut off and there will be silence onboard to enjoy the fabulous soundtrack.

Wednesday, 09 Sep 2009 – Goodbye to the Tropics

Mhadei crossed the Tropic of Capricorn at 0742 h this morning saying goodbye to the tropics and warm weather for the next six months. The sea has calmed down so it was a pleasant day onboard with fairly good progress in light winds. The only worry is that we are still drifting too much to the west and will have to cover all this distance once we get westerly winds, which may still be about two days away. We are also heading for the permanent high pressure system in this area, which would mean light winds till we manage to dodge it. Not complaining much though after the bashing in the Trade Winds. Good to take it easy for a change because the present forecast shows the Westerlies blowing at 35 kts, about 10 kts more than the Trade Winds. Hopefully we will have to negotiate them downwind and downswell so things should not be that bad. We will just have to see as it comes as this is uncharted territory for us. Will need to start taking out cold weather clothing from tomorrow as it is already becoming quite cold as soon as the sun goes down. The comments on the blog indicate a fair amount of curiosity about Mhadei's crew and their metamorphosis over the past three weeks at sea. Posting some photos of the skipper/cook/first mate/publicist/engineer lounging on the deck, satiated with a heavy 'dosa' lunch and enjoying the good life aboard a million-dollar yacht in the middle of the South Indian Ocean.

Had a new type of bird for company in the evening. So far the ones that have been following us were dark brown with a yellowish beak. This one was greyish white with a much longer wingspan. Difficult to click good photos as they keep moving constantly, often a hair's breadth from the water even in the worst of sea conditions. Makes a land-based human mind wonder how they survive as the nearest land is over 1,000 nm away. Posting some photos of sunset which are nowhere close to the spectacular ones we saw at the equator but then it gives an idea why the equatorial ones are so special. My gmail account, which should have received my plotted position by now, is refusing to open so will just have to wait for the next blog. Very roughly we are about 80 nm south of the Tropic of Capricorn and almost exactly below Chennai.

Friday, 11 Sep 2009 – Whales ahoy!

Yesterday was another windless yet busy day. Changed and reset some chafed lines in the morning, cleaned and arranged the boat a bit after the bashing in the Trade Winds. In the afternoon when it looked as if the wind was picking up a bit, went up, and as I was easing the mainsheet saw one of my worst nightmares coming true. The padeye holding the mainsheet block had uprooted itself! This strong fitting basically attaches the boom to the boat and if it gets uprooted there is no way to control the boom which would start thrashing about causing serious damage including a possible dismasting in strong winds. Tried to tighten the padeye only to realise that two of the four bolts attaching it to the boat had sheared off. Immediately shortened the sail and temporarily attached the boom to another padeye on the port side. Consultations with the boat builder over the phone followed, with the conclusion that the only way to carry out repairs was to cut a large hole under the roll bar on which the padeye was attached. Sailing was stopped forthwith;

the shipwright was summoned who spent the next couple of hours drilling a large enough hole in the roll bar to approach the padeye. That done, the broken bolts were removed, new bolts fitted and all bolts secured with nuts to keep them in place. Thanks to Ratnakar's foresight all the necessary tools and spares were available and by midnight we were ready to sail again. The shipwright with bruised fingers and glass fibre all over himself, with the resultant itching, had managed to do a fairly decent job and salvaged an otherwise tight situation for which he was duly awarded an 'On the Spot' commendation and more important a hot shower past midnight! Another sleepless night followed in the shifty and light, often nonexistent, winds. Getting up and easing the main every time the wind picked up and securing the boom to prevent it from thrashing once the bit of wind died out. We are close to a high pressure system and this is expected, the strong Westerlies lie to the south of this area. I have started calling it the 'Coldrums', a colder version of the Doldrums! Thankfully the squalls are missing. The sky has been completely overcast since the last two days and it is getting colder by the day. The warm clothing is out and shoes are being worn at all times except the rare occasion when inside a sleeping bag. As I was having my morning cup of coffee Mhadei was greeted by the local residents. I counted at least four whales who came quite close and I could hear them snorting. Thankfully, they didn't want to play with Mhadei, lost interest after giving her a look over and went their way. Just a courtesy call perhaps.

Uprooting of the padeye was the first major problem on the boat so far and I must admit, it rattled me. While I did manage to detect and rectify the problem in time, the question that kept looming in my mind was, "What if this had happened a few days back when I was sailing through gale force winds for almost a week?" It would have been quite a disaster with the boom and mainsail free to thrash about till they got the rig down. Once I had spoken to Ratnakar and decided that the only option was to make a large hole to access the broken bolts through the roll bar, I started looking for the 'hole saw cutter', a tool that is supposed to be put on the drill machine for making large holes. I remembered Ratnakar showing it to me and instructing me on its use, so initially I wasn't too worried. However, when I actually tried to put the tool in the drill machine, it wouldn't fit. Obviously the tool was of a size suitable for fitting in the large drill machine in the boatyard while I was carrying the smaller and compact drill machine onboard! The only option was to fit the largest drill bit in the machine and keep making holes close to each other, eventually making a hole large enough to allow me to insert a spanner inside the roll bar. To add to my woes, the roll bar had been made extra strong by using additional layers of fibreglass and epoxy. I remembered being at the boatyard and watching the fabrication. It never occurred to me then that I would, in the not so distant future, be trying to drill holes in it and wishing that it wasn't that strong. I knew I had been extremely lucky that the bolts had given way in very light winds, but that could change anytime and I had to finish the job as quickly as I could before the winds decided to pick up. Finally after almost 12 hrs of non-stop work I managed to extract the broken bolts, replace them with new ones and secure them with nuts to prevent a repeat. It was almost 0200 h; I was exhausted and very itchy, covered from head to toe with fibreglass dust with all my fingers bleeding and sore. But I was very relieved; the boat was safe and that is what mattered. I managed to have a long hot shower, covered myself with some prickly heat powder to reduce the itch and crawled in the bunk to get some sleep. It would be a few days before I managed to get all the fibreglass dust out of the boat and my system.

The next morning, as I came out with the first cup of coffee for the day I saw a small plume of water rising about a mile astern. It was an overcast morning with a grey sea and not much swell or wind. Initially I thought my eyes were playing tricks on me, thanks to all the fibreglass dust flying about. But I sighted the plume again and there was no doubt as to what it was. Definitely a whale! I dumped the coffee and ran for the camera inside. The whales came close soon enough, each one bigger than *Mhadei*. I tried clicking as many photos as I could but it was best to leave the camera and watch them in all their glory, especially when they were too close for me to get them in one picture frame. One of them came so close on the starboard quarter that I could virtually look down its nose and got a strong fishy odour every time it exhaled and created the characteristic spout. We were moving sedately with light winds and perhaps the whales, even though moving leisurely through the water, found us too slow. They moved on, heading south. It was an experience that will stay with me for a long time as I never got to see whales that close during the rest of the trip. It won't be an exaggeration to say that I envied them at that moment and wondered about evolution; whether my ancestors had been smarter to come out of the sea and start the human race or theirs to have opted to stay in the ocean with no boundaries and a simple life!

Sunday, 13 Sep 2009 – Out of the 'Coldrums', finally!
The last three days in the high pressure system were probably the worst since we crossed the Equator. The sky used to be completely covered with clouds, no sun in sight, virtually no wind and enough swell to keep the boat rocking and the sails thrashing about. The nights were the darkest I have seen. Despite a half moon somewhere in the sky, its light just wouldn't pass the thick clouds.

Difficult to sleep as either you are going up and tightening the mainsail to prevent it from thrashing about or easing it as soon as you feel a whiff of wind. The autopilot would keep getting confused and start beeping every now and then leaving no option but hand steering. The autopilot needs the boat to move to be able to steer her, once she stops moving it suddenly doesn't know what to do and starts calling your attention. Also in such light winds with swell, the wind vane sensor keeps moving in all directions due to the rolling of the boat, the autopilot tries to follow it for a while and then gives up! These nil wind conditions are definitely more taxing to the boat and the crew than the blustery Trades, as I have started realising from the damage that has been inflicted on the boat in the last three days.

Amongst all the frustrations of the 'Coldrums' something interesting happened late last night. It was drizzling slightly and I had stumbled out in the cockpit yet again, barely awake, to tighten the mainsheet as the boom had started thrashing about. Suddenly it felt as if a live 230 V wire had touched my face and I almost jumped out of my boots. How on earth could I get a shock so strong with the whole boat wired for 24 V. Lightning? But I hadn't seen any lightning since the Equator. Fully awake by now, it slowly dawned on to me that it was static electricity! There is a small strop that keeps hanging from the end of the boom. I keep it there as it comes in handy to hold myself when the boat is owing heeling. The strop was wet with the drizzle and had been swaying due to the thrashing of the boom, developing a large amount of static which it promptly discharged the moment it touched my face. What a jolt!

After the three dull days, today turned out to be an excellent day for sailing. The clouds cleared and the sun came out finally. The sea was calm, light cool westerly breeze just enough to make the boat move in the right direction and the sun just right to warm oneself sitting on the deck. It was an absolute pleasure to shed the woollens, sit in the sun and do some minor repairs. Plenty of birds around, counted at least four different types. It is fun to watch them come and sit on the water. As they are about to land they lower their webbed feet and skid on the water like a water-skier. While taking off they start running on the water till they are airborne. It is a pity that it is almost impossible to capture them on camera from a moving boat.

I recovered quickly from the thrashing we received while sailing upwind in the Trade Winds and had started getting frustrated with the light winds we were experiencing. We were close to 30° South latitude and the weather forecasts indicated strong westerly winds around 40° South, less than 600 nm away. It would have taken us two to three days to get into decent winds if we had continued sailing south. From then on we would have been on the 'Highway' of the 'Roaring Forties' making fast easterly progress. I was tempted to head south, get on the 'Highway' and head straight for New Zealand instead of stopping at Fremantle. I had managed to fix the uprooted padeye and it seemed to be holding. Other than that there were no major problems on the boat and we had plenty of food and water to last till New Zealand. But then we were a naval boat and it would have been a task to get the plans changed.

Monday, 14 Sep 2009 – Surprise visitor!
Another good day with decent progress towards the destination. The 15- to 20-kt south-westerly wind made us head straight for Fremantle at a steady 7 to 8 kts through the day. Unfortunately that seems to be dying as I write. There is a cold front couple of hundred miles to the south causing gale force winds, the swell created is rocking us nicely, unfortunately there is a huge high pressure system advancing on us from the west which will stop all wind. So we are going to have a deadly combo of swell and light winds. Really bad for the boat!

Had a surprise visitor this morning in the form of a large fishing boat. I was on deck repairing some of the blocks that had been deformed owing to the wallowing in the 'Coldrums' when suddenly on the port beam saw this large fishing boat, less than 100 yards away! I had been working on the deck for over an hour, making trips to the mast, etc., but just didn't notice her till she was that close! It is the first ship or boat of any kind sighted for over a week and I had grown complacent about keeping a watch as there was no one to watch for nor did I expect to find anyone over 1,500 nm from the coast away from shipping lanes. Will need to start being more careful again.

With the winds dying out, tonight seems to be another night of frequent trips out to take in or ease the mainsheet. It is quite cold now so every time I go out I need to be dressed in warm clothes with shoes and by the time I get out of them and in the sleeping bag it is time to go up again. What an exciting way to spend a night.

Wednesday, 16 Sep 2009 – Passenger onboard!

Another good day of sailing! With 25 to 30 kts of north-westerly breeze and 2 to 2.5 m of south-westerly swell, Mhadei cruised along through the day clocking almost 100 nm since morning. If only these conditions last for the next couple of days. Though the forecast is for lighter winds for the next two days and already the wind seems to be reducing in strength. It is amazing how much difference sailing downwind makes as opposed to upwind. With similar conditions upwind we would have been slamming around as we did in the Trades, now, going downwind, anything below 20 kts is suddenly a cause for concern!

This evening as I was making dinner, I heard a loud thrashing in the cockpit such as I have never heard before on the boat. After almost a month of solitude it made me jump, so left everything and took a look outside, only to find a passenger onboard! Not sure if the bird is hurt, tired or just missed water and landed onboard. Being a hospitable boat, had to offer him some-

thing so in the absence of fresh fish, which I presume is his only diet, tried some dried prawns but he does not seem to be interested. Doesn't seem to be too scared of me as I discovered when I patted him a little and took snaps. He tries to go out of the cockpit once in a while, needs a bit of help to climb up but then comes back instead of flying away. Not sure if he is unable to fly because he is injured or requires a running start to take off as I have seen them do when they land on water. These type of birds have been following us for days now and we have developed an unspoken companionship so they are always welcome to hitch a ride! I think I will just let him be for the night. Will need to watch my step if I need to go out at night if the wind shifts or dies out lest I step on the poor thing. Maybe Admiral Awati will be able to figure out what bird it is.

There was some speculation from the readers of my blog about the species of the bird. Looking back, I am fairly certain that it was a brown albatross, a smaller cousin of the better known and larger white albatross. Though I hadn't felt lonely so far, it felt nice to have the bird onboard. I suddenly started feeling very responsible and tried my best to make the bird comfortable, mostly by letting him be and not scaring him. That seemed to work as gradually he started walking around, finally getting in the boat just as the wind started picking up and it was time for me to get on the deck and prepare to spend the better part of my night on the deck controlling the boat through a gale.

Thursday, 17 Sep 2009 – Encounter with a cold front
We had our first encounter with a cold front last night. Having lived in the tropics all my life, this was my first experience. Luckily I had read about the various stages of approach of a front in the morning so could understand what exactly was happening. I was watching a movie on the laptop late at

night when suddenly the boat crash gybed with the boom slamming on the windward runner and the autopilot gave up. I realised that the wind had suddenly shifted making the boat gybe on her own. Got the boat under control, setting her on autopilot again, this time on the wind vane option to avoid any more accidental gybes. We were already sailing with one reef in the main and the genoa, enjoying good speeds through the day. My wishful thinking that the wind shift was a one-off occurrence and that we would continue to enjoy steady winds came to naught as the wind kept rising and shifting direction. By around 0300 h the wind was blowing over 35 kts with gusts of 40 kts, while backing slowly, making us head north instead of east with the boat almost out of control! No choice but to reef, furl up the genoa and then gybe to get back to an easterly course. By the time all this was over, dawn was breaking and I was desperate to get in the sleeping bag. The night had just gone by.

My feathered visitor of yesterday had managed to get inside the boat during all this and must have been quite petrified what with me jumping around every now and then and the boat moving around changing her heel making it go skidding from one corner to another. Got the bird out at noon and helped him climb up the cockpit as sitting inside the boat, though safe, he would have starved to death. He spread his wings as if stretching himself in the sun, went to the stern and, when the next wave lurched the boat, was gone! There were other birds around so couldn't make out which one was our visitor. My best guess is that he accidently landed in the boat at night instead of landing on the water and then couldn't take off as he needs space to do that. Or was it a real smart guy who sensed an approaching gale and rode it out in absolute comfort? We will never know!

It was interesting to see how the human mind works with a bit of company even when the company is non-human. As I struggled to keep the boat going through the gale, I realised to my amusement that I was trying to handle the boat more gently and was avoiding violent movements as far as possible so as not to disturb my passenger for the night. While my conscious mind was laughing at this, subconsciously I still kept being careful and feeling very responsible!

Saturday, 19 Sep 2009 – One month at sea

It has been exactly a month since we left Mumbai, which, needless to say, is a distant memory. Feels almost unreal thinking about it. There have been so many changes. For one when we left Mumbai it was so hot I couldn't wait to get my T-shirt off, now I think twice before getting out of my clothes to go to the loo! The Doldrums have been replaced by the 'Coldrums' and the equatorial squalls by the cold fronts. We have covered over 4,600 nm so far and still need to cover about 750 nm. Not really in a hurry, not that it would make any difference if we were, since our progress depends entirely on the winds. Good winds of 25 to 30 kts through the day with a large following sea making us do almost 90 nm in the past twelve hours. Another front passed us couple of hours back. Getting used to them now, which helps in reefing and getting ready to face them so much easier. The day was duly celebrated onboard with a 'bhelpuri brunch'! Looks like another long night ahead with the winds regularly touching 40 kts and a large swell following us. The last time that happened, we were becalmed for the whole of next day! Let us see what tomorrow has in store for us. For now enjoying the fast progress towards destination.

The fronts had started becoming regular now and my ability to deal with them had started improving as each one thumped us and moved on. I remembered a conversation about facing the Southern Ocean with Robin over lunch at my home in Mumbai, a few years back.

"You always seem to understate the severity of the weather

and make it sound so easy dealing with it," I had said, curious to know what he really went through and how he learnt to cope with it.

"What is the point in alarming people ashore when they can do nothing to help you?" he had replied nonchalantly.

"So how long does it take to get used to dealing with that sort of weather?" asked my mother sitting at the table.

"Well, the first time you face a big one, you are convinced that it is the end of the world and you are not going to survive. The second time, you tell yourself that you just might survive as you managed the last time. The third time, you are sure you will come out of it alive as you have survived so far. When you are getting ready to face the tenth one, you are worrying that you may not be able to get hot food for the next few days! But to reach that state, you have to go through the first nine stages. Unfortunately, there are no shortcuts there."

Perfect advice that was! Finally, I was experiencing it.

Wednesday, 23 Sep 2009 – Over 5,000 miles sailed, 225 to go!

Looks like we are close to Fremantle finally! While 225 nm is almost the distance between Mumbai and Goa, after 5,000 nm it does seem close. The wind continues to play its games so still not sure about the time it will take but two more days should be a fair guess. If the wind holds tonight this will be the last quiet night before reaching. By tomorrow we should start encountering some traffic which would mean keeping a watch to avoid collision. Didn't write anything for the last two days. While the main reason was pure laziness, there was also little happening with light and shifty winds, an overcast sky and a feeling of heading nowhere! Kept myself entertained watching old Hollywood movies so thoughtfully stocked by my crew Lt Cdr

*Abhilash Tomy. While I am enjoying my holiday on the boat, the poor chap
is running around from pillar to post in Delhi getting his deputation arranged
for joining me in Fremantle as the support crew. The plan was for him to
be present before we arrived so that things could be tied up better, but looks
like we will beat him to it. The boat builder, Ratnakar, is leaving aside his
business and planning to drop by to get the boat ready for the next leg, which
is when Mhadei and I will have our first brush with the Roaring Forties.
So far it has been smooth sailing but things will get serious once we enter the
Southern Ocean.*

*As I write, the sun would be crossing the equator and entering the Southern
Hemisphere. It is the Autumnal Equinox today, the beginning of summer in
this part of the world. One of the considerations for starting in Aug from
Mumbai was to get maximum summer time in the Southern Hemisphere and
we seem to have achieved it, just a day or two late.*

*Tried clicking snaps of my feathered companions, without much luck!
Difficult to capture their grace on a camera. Looks like there is no substitute
but being at sea to really admire them. When I started writing and uploading
the photos, I was keeping an eye open at the shifty and light wind which was
barely able to hold the boom from thrashing and making us sail almost 40°
away from Fremantle. By the time I finished writing the wind had crossed
25 kts, making me run and put a reef in the main and I am still wondering
if I should have put another reef. Looks like it will not be as quiet a night as
I thought, not complaining though as the wind is making us head straight for
our destination at a healthy 8 kts.*

Facing light and shifty winds for almost 1,000 nm, we were finally close to Fremantle. I needed to give my date of arrival to
the Indian Defence Advisor in Canberra to allow him to reach
Fremantle in time to receive us. By noon on 23 Sep, frustrated
with light winds from the wrong direction, I asked him to catch

a flight on 25 Sep as there was no way we could reach Fremantle before that. The wind gods took offence and decided to prove me and the weather forecast wrong! The wind shifted and kept increasing through the night making us charge towards Fremantle at over 8 kts. By daybreak the following day we were surfing big swells in over 30 kts of winds and were some 50 nm from our destination. By noon we had sighted Rottnest Island outside Fremantle harbour, our first landfall since leaving Mumbai 34 days ago.

As I was rounding the island from the north and getting ready to enter harbour, a big whale suddenly reared up on the port bow, less than 50 m away. It was crossing our path from left to right and for a moment I worried that it may come up under the boat when it surfaced next. What a welcome to the harbour! Not too long after that, with winds blowing at over 35 kts, I got the sails down and switched on the engine to get in the Fremantle Yacht Club Marina.

Two-and-a-half years ago, I had watched Robin start the second leg of his race from the same place and wished that someday I could enter this harbour in my own boat. Building a boat and sailing her around the world had only been a dream then, with some very vague ideas about achieving our aims. Now, here I was sailing my own boat – well, the Indian Navy's actually! – just as I had imagined. It felt great.

Despite the gale force winds and choppy sea, the Fremantle Sailing Club had sent out a boat to guide us in through the narrow entrance of the Marina. We went alongside at about 1630 h, with a couple of knocks but no serious damage. I was pleasantly surprised to find a small crowd waiting on the pier to receive us. There was representation from the Australian Navy,

Customs, Immigration, our hosts, the Fremantle Sailing Club, ISS Shipping (who would be our agents during the stay) and, of course, mandatorily for an Indian, a cousin representing the family! By the end of the trip I was convinced there is no place on earth where you won't find an Indian.

The Indian Defence Advisor had heeded my advice and would land only the next day while my lone shore support crew, Abhilash, was still going around in circles in Delhi trying to sort out the paperwork for his deputation. It is mandatory for Indian government officials to travel by Air India and that included Abhilash. We used to lay bets that *Mhadei* would beat Air India as far as arrival of the shore support crew was concerned. We laughed at it the first time in Fremantle but realised that the joke was on us when the situation repeated itself in the rest of the ports!

One of the first people I met in Fremantle was Jon Sanders, the legendary Australian solo circumnavigator who holds the record for three back-to-back solo circumnavigations. He had come down to receive us and by the time I finished with the Customs and Immigration formalities inside the boat, he had secured all the lines on the deck properly. I was touched. "You didn't have to do that Jon, I would have done it in a while," I told him. He just gave his shy smile and mumbled in his characteristic style that it was not a problem, the boat had to look neat and that I must be tired.

It was nice to be on land and meet people. I think the biggest emotion was a sense of relief on having completed the trip safely – I would experience it whenever I entered a port. I wrote a short message on the blog before locking the boat and switching off my mind from sailing for the night.

Thursday, 24 Sep 2009 – Land ahoy!
Mhadei got alongside safely at Fremantle Yacht Club Marina at 1630 h (GMT + 8). More later, as it is difficult to be 'elbow bending' and blogging at the same time!

'Elbow bending' seemed like a good excuse for wriggling out of writing something long. As the adrenalin rush of completing the leg and arriving at a new place started wearing off, I started realising how tired I was.

Chapter 24

First Taste of the Southern Ocean

Sunday, 04 Oct 2009 – One week in Fremantle

It has been little over a week since Mhadei sailed into the Fremantle Sailing Club Marina escorted by a powerboat twice her size with the wind blowing over 35 kts. She was well received by representatives of the club, the Australian Navy, the boat's agent and the mandatory Customs and quarantine officials who finished off their inspections in no time and made us feel at home. Mr Jon Sanders, with four solo circumnavigations under his belt, dropped by to check us out. Next afternoon we had a little reception at the club with the Hon Consul General of India, the Indian Naval Attaché, Commanding Officer, HMAS Stirling, and a host of retired Indian naval and army officers in attendance. My lone support team Lt Cdr Abhilash Tomy fetched up the next day by air. Mhadei had beaten Air India by a good two days!

We are enjoying the hospitality of the Club and the City of Fremantle with Mhadei at a secure alongside berth and the crew at a serviced apartment not too far away. The Club is planning to have their 'Season Opening' event on 11 Oct and we are invited for the sail past. Probably the first time an Indian boat will be taking part! Started working on the boat, cleaning up, changing chaffed lines, sending sails to the loft for minor repairs, a mast climb to check the fittings on top and a dive to check the bottom. Like the old adage, 'a housewife's work is never done', the work on a boat is never over, you always find something that needs doing.

Apart from working on the boat there are small pleasures to be enjoyed. Like sleeping on a bed for the entire night instead of a bunk or sleeping bag, making a cup of coffee and breakfast in the morning without bracing yourself for the next roll, having a hot water bath daily without having to worry about the water maker, going to a vegetable market and buying fresh fruit, taking a long brisk walk without running out of walking space, the list goes on... Funny how many things we take for granted on land! Staying in a serviced apartment means I can mess around in the kitchen and my crew is the only obvious guinea pig who eats whatever is served to him with a smile, including some juicy kangaroo steaks.

Looking forward to attending a concert by Jagjit Singh in the evening at the invitation of the Hon Consul General.

Once Abhilash arrived in Fremantle we started working, preparing the boat for the next leg. Ratnakar soon followed Abhilash to Fremantle and the team was together again. There was plenty of work, partly repairs, partly improvements. A boat, like any other complex piece of machinery, needs time to settle down, something that we had not been able to give to *Mhadei*. Often equipment that was to be installed and tested by the service engineer of an equipment manufacturer had been installed by us by referring to the installation manuals, in the absence of such service engineers in India. The systems had worked so far with a few hiccups but needed to be installed properly to avoid problems in the future. Fremantle was a nice yacht-friendly port where we could get a lot of such work done, buy good quality tools and spares and generally improve the state of the boat. There were also some doubts about the boat's design especially with regard to her rigging. The near uprooting of the mainsheet padeye had been an unusual accident. While I had managed to deal with the problem in light winds, it could be very serious in the Southern Ocean if it happened again. The best way to prevent a recurrence was to understand why it happened. Was it due to faulty design? Did the boat need a traveller instead of a single padeye to hold the mainsheet block? If so, how could we best fit a traveller, if we could at all? Were the padeye and block of the correct size? Or was it just inexperience resulting in poor sailing skills on my part?

There were opinions, points and counterpoints. Everyone was concerned about the boat's next legs through the Southern Ocean. So far the weather conditions hadn't been too bad. The boat had sailed well across the tropics and through the Trade Winds, proving her mettle. Her biggest test lay ahead, though, that of transiting the Southern Ocean. One can use the best quality equipment on a boat to reduce the chances of breakage or malfunction but if the basic design is not up to the mark, the best of the equipment will fail at some point. Opinions and likely solutions kept increasing the more we discussed the subject, though none could be considered the perfect solution. The final call had to be mine and, yet again, I was acutely reminded of my inexperience on the subject. I wasn't keen on making any major structural modifications to the boat as that would have meant getting in the Southern Ocean with something totally untested. I finally put my foot down against changing the basic arrangements on the boat by trying to fit a traveller instead of the lone padeye. I bought a nice oversized block to replace the mainsheet block and promised to keep checking the padeye bolts daily to detect any potential problem. Still, the discussions on the subject, as well meaning as they were, continued till I left New

Zealand. Fortunately, the problem never occurred again and the boat continued to sail the way she was fixed in Fremantle.

It wasn't a case of all work and no play! As a naval vessel, we were expected to play the role of the country's ambassadors too. We made a lot of new friends, renewed old friendships and generally enjoyed our stay in Fremantle. The weather was perfect; the days had already started getting longer and warmer. The Fremantle Sailing Club offered us all their facilities during our stay and even waived off two weeks of berthing fees. It was great to take part in their season-opening regatta and a few days later take the Indian High Commissioner to Australia, Mrs Sujatha Singh, for a sail in Fremantle Harbour, she having flown down across the continent from Canberra to meet us. Often, people wouldn't believe I was the first Indian attempting such a trip. One question I was often asked was: "How come you are the first person attempting a circumnavigation in a maritime nation of over a billion people?" I didn't have a good answer to it and it touched something inside me – I vowed to ask it to my fellow citizens once I got back. Indeed, why had we not even attempted something like this before?

Realising that I was getting a bit too stressed working on the boat and needed a break in the routine, my old friends Pip Sawyer and John Sharpie practically dragged me for a weekend to their vineyard, which was a few hours' drive from Fremantle. I was understandably a bit apprehensive about leaving *Mhadei* alone but the visit through the South Australian countryside really refreshed me. We managed to visit Cape Leeuwin, the first of the three Great Capes I was to round in a few days. Standing at Cape Leeuwin Lighthouse and looking south, I wondered what it would look like from seaward when I was on my way to entering the Southern Ocean. The sea looked nice from the land, as it always does, the strong wind was refreshing and I was in the midst of my friends having a good time. The thought that all this would change in a few days when I would be alone on a bobbing *Mhadei* was never far from my mind. Eventually, thanks to the wind gods, I didn't catch sight of this landmark from sea as the winds pushed us away from the Australian landmass in the first few days out of Fremantle.

Our very pleasant sojourn in Fremantle came to its end with the month of Oct and it was time to set sail again. Thanks to some creative planning from NHQ, my shore support team had already left. On the morning of 01 Nov 2009, I returned my rented car, picked up some fresh bread from a bakery on the way and walked down to Fremantle Sailing Club to get on *Mhadei* and sail out. As I was walking towards the boat, I met a pair of officers from the Customs and Immigration Department.

"Are you going on that boat, sir?" asked the officer.

"Yes, I am."

"Well, here are your papers, have a good trip." They handed me my papers and drove off, making me wonder about the difference in the working and attitude of their counterparts back home.

It was a beautiful day with clear skies and a nice breeze. It was nice to see a bunch of friends who had dropped by to see me off. The last of the goodbyes said, photographs clicked, I started the engine and *Mhadei* was off on her next leg.

Less than a mile from the entrance to the Marina as I started raising the mainsail, I realised that the reefing lines were hopelessly tangled with the mainsheet block. We had fitted the new mainsail block in a hurry two days ago and I had not bothered to check things out properly. The job could be done in less than 30 minutes alongside with someone to give me a hand. For a moment, I did think about returning and asking Pip and John, who lived nearby, to come down and give me a hand. "No, we are not going back in for something as stupid as this; let us get this thing sorted as best as we can and on our own," ordered my pesky alter ego! It would eventually take me almost two hours to get the lines in order while drifting tantalisingly close to the harbour entrance before we finally sailed out of the harbour under a full mainsail and genoa. It was nice to be back at sea. I had heard and read a lot about the ferocity of the Southern Ocean, which had created excitement as well as apprehension in my mind at various times. The imagining game was finally over and we, *Mhadei* and I, were on our way to experience our biggest challenge firsthand.

We ran straight into some south-easterly winds as we rounded Rottnest Island at the mouth of Fremantle Harbour and headed into the open sea. The winds had built up a good 4-m swell and we were heading into it, slamming into it actually! Not the best situation when you are sailing after a month's sojourn on land. The winds kept increasing as we bore away from the coast, the wind and current pushing us south southwest while we wanted to sail south southeast. The day passed soon, adjusting to the progressively violent motion of the boat and sorting out things inside. As the sun set, we were greeted with a nice moonlit night that, no doubt, could have been better enjoyed without the violent motion of the boat.

At around 2030 h, the boat was slamming through the waves but making good speed. I was lying in my bunk wondering if and when I should take in the genoa and another reef. Suddenly there was a big thrashing noise outside and the boat started vibrating as if something very big were holding the mast and shaking the boat, intent upon uprooting it. I jumped outside, realised that the genoa was thrashing uncontrollably, and started furling it frantically. It must have been just about three seconds from the time I heard the noise and tried to furl the genoa, only to realise moments later that my efforts were futile. My very strong and expensive sail had shredded itself to bits in a matter of seconds. This was not a good way to begin the second leg of the trip. The sail was expected to last me for my entire voyage. I was really distraught. I gathered myself together and tried to figure out the reason for the accident. It hurt to see bits of sail fluttering around from the forestay. The deck fittings seemed alright, which was good news as it meant I could theoretically use the spare genoa I had. The next likely culprit was the genoa sheet, which seemed intact too. I just couldn't figure out the cause of the mishap.

"Never mind what has happened; there will be plenty of time to figure that out," I thought. The more important thing was to plan the course ahead. The boat had slowed down considerably and as the wind dropped, which it eventually would, she would slow down even further. I had a spare genoa in the sail locker but I had never set it up on my own even in harbour. Normally it would take about an hour for the three of us to set it up in windless conditions alongside. Could I possibly do it at sea even when the wind reduced and the sea calmed down? I wasn't all that sure. I also realised that I had a more urgent problem on my hands than the boat's speed. The torn sail every now and then was fluttering violently, threatening to rip apart the mast fittings like the radar and shaking the rig so much that I started getting worried about the mast. I needed to get the torn sail down first if

I didn't want to get dismasted.

The other, easier alternative was to turn back to Fremantle. We were about 80 nm from harbour and could have entered before sunset the next day. The next course of action would be to get a new sail made and sail out again after a few days. The second option sounded like an easier option with fewer chances of failure. As I was weighing my options, the pesky alter ego woke up, causing a virtual mutiny onboard between the skipper and himself!

"How can you think of turning back and heading for the same harbour that bid you farewell a few hours back? No way, you can't turn back. The boat is still sailing, the wind is bound to reduce and the sea will calm down some time. Why not try and change the sail, or at least get the torn one down when that happens?"

"But I have never done it before. It is difficult enough to do it in harbour with a crew; you know it as well as I do."

"Big deal! That is what everyone said when we started the project. That no Indian had done it before because it was too difficult and bound to fail. And here we are about to enter the Southern Ocean with over 10,000 nm behind us. Do you remember how you shut up the naysayers and moved on?"

"Yes, I used to smile and tell them there was always a first time! At worst we would fail, but at least we would not be found wanting for lack of effort."

"And what was that Urdu couplet we used to mutter while dealing with such people?"

"Girte hain sheh sawar hi,
Maidan-e-jung mein.
Woh tifl kya gire,

Jo ghutno ke bal chale."

(Only those who ride in a battlefield can fall; how can cowards who walk on their knees ever fall?)

"So what's so different now? You did all this for the first time and now you are apprehensive about changing one sail? Stop this nonsense. Let the weather improve and then try to get the torn sail off. That will solve one urgent problem. We can then figure out a way of setting up the spare sail. If we can't, we continue sailing slowly till New Zealand. Anyway, if the Southern Ocean shows its true colours, we will be sailing with minimum sails and this big sail won't be needed."

"Okay, deal! Let us continue and keep a lookout for a window of calm weather. We will figure out what to do after that."

"Now, that's a good guy! Can we have something to eat? I am very hungry and tired."

"Bolognese sauce with bread okay? I am too tired to cook anything fresh."

"That will be perfect! Just what the doctor ordered. Let us eat and rest a little, it is not the end of the world, we will manage." So ended one of the many arguments onboard!

We continued slamming south southwest for the next two days before the wind started slackening and the swell reduced. Early morning on 03 Nov I managed to get the torn sail off, well most of it that is – even when I reached New Zealand over two weeks later I was recovering bits and pieces of it from the rigging. I was relieved to see that there wasn't any damage to the furler that takes up the sail. Once the torn sail was off, I started getting a little more ambitious.

"Why not follow the same procedure in reverse sequence and get the spare one up?" I thought. It took much more time and effort to do that. The sail tends to bellow with even a little wind and is big enough to throw you in the water if you are not careful. If a part of it gets out of the boat and in the water, it tends to drag the rest of it in water, including the person who happens to be sitting on it. Eventually I managed to finish the job. It had taken me over four hours of intense work to complete it and I was exhausted but very satisfied. *Mhadei* was almost as good as she was when we left Fremantle and we were ready to take on the Southern Ocean. That evening, I sat and wrote the first blog of the second leg.

Tuesday, 03 Nov 2009 – Goodbye Fremantle

Mhadei left Fremantle as planned on 01 Nov at 1030 h local time on a nice sunny day after a sojourn of five weeks. The stay at Fremantle proved to be an excellent break for both the boat and the crew. However, it was time to move on before the land legs became too strong and the sea legs started fading from memory!

We ran into head seas soon after rounding Rottnest Island north of Fremantle. It was almost a beat for the next two days in winds between 20 and 25 kts. The first night the clew of the genoa parted, making the sail flog uncontrollably. By the time I could furl it the poor thing had shredded itself! The winds finally eased today and I managed to take down the torn sail and replace it with the spare one. Luckily we had bought the sails from New Zealand and the repairs can be carried out at the loft where it was made. Survived on some scrumptious Bolognese sauce, so thoughtfully packed by Pip Sawyer; till today's breakfast. I was supposed to have it with pasta but the boat was bouncing around so much it was much easier to have it with bread instead! Tasted as good.

We seem to be sitting in a high pressure system since morning which means light and shifty winds. For once I am not complaining as otherwise it would not have been possible to change the sail. The weather forecast is predicting backing of the wind in an easterly and then north-easterly direction which should start taking us towards New Zealand, our next destination.

Wednesday, 04 Nov 2009 – Rounding Cape Leeuwin, finally!

As I write this we are crossing the longitude of Cape Leeuwin thus effectively rounding the first of the three 'Great Capes' that make for a circumnavigation. The next will be Cape Horn followed by the Cape of Good Hope. It has been a fairly uneventful day with a decent breeze that has been backing from east northeast to north northeast making us sail in the direction we want to go at a healthy pace. The wind has been picking up for the last couple of hrs and is expected to back further which will allow us to gradually start picking up speed without slamming too much.

The mystery of the broken clew of the genoa and subsequent shredding was finally solved by John Sharpie, our good host at Fremantle and an experienced sailor. He reckons that a big wave must have hit the genoa as we were slamming through the waves making the clew part. We were, when the incident happened, sailing upwind in a fairly large sea and had waves washing over the boat. One wave too big and that was the end of the sail.

On the day I left Fremantle I met an old friend, Timothy Ettridge. We had worked as part of Sir Robin Knox-Johnston's support crew during his Velux 5 Oceans Race in 2006. It was quite a coincidence that he arrived in Fremantle the night before I was leaving and was there to see me off.

Thursday, 05 Nov 2009 – First night in the Roaring Forties

We crossed 40° South latitude today, home of the Roaring Forties! The wind has slowly backed from being easterly last night to northerly through the day and is now blowing from the north northwest at about 20 to 25 kts. That gives us a nice fast reach to sail onto the southern tip of New Zealand. It also means that we are not thumping into the swell any longer but corkscrewing about with an almost quarterly swell. It has been raining on and off since morning with a thick cloud cover making for a cold gloomy day and a colder dark night.

Saw a ship's AIS icon on my chart plotter after lunch at about 3 nm. Couldn't sight him visually and realised that I was yet to fix the VHF MMB set that had stopped functioning the day after leaving Freo. If the ship wanted to call me or warn me there was no way she could, so got down to figuring out the loose wire that was the culprit. Not so easy on a jumping boat and with my terrible skills as an electrician! First managed to shut off the chart plotter by pulling some wire, cause for real concern! Then managed to create enough sparking to panic and switch the mains off only to switch off the auto pilot with them! Ran out to get the boat under control, got the autopilot going, then spent the better part of the day sorting out the connections. Thankfully everything came on line by evening. Just another day onboard!

Friday, 06 November 2009 – A nice calm day in the Southern Ocean

Looks like a cold front coming from the south met a warm front from north not too far from us today. The result was a foggy day with intermittent drizzle, light winds and fairly calm sea. The wind didn't die down completely as I feared it would and we managed to keep moving at a leisurely 6 kts on a beam reach. The preventer rigged at Fremantle proved its utility as now even in light winds with a quartering sea, the boom does not thrash and the boat keeps moving. I had tried rigging it up during the earlier leg but ended up without much success and a mangled snatch block. The flaw in my arrangement was pointed out by Jon Sanders, a veteran at solo circumnavigations, in Fremantle, and looks like he was spot on!

A sedate day, some quick-cook risotto for dinner followed by a movie on the laptop. A far cry from being hosted by Pip and John last Friday to a dinner of gourmet pizza at a fancy place in Perth followed by a nice drive through the King's Park Botanical Garden!

Sunday, 08 Nov 2009 – One week since Freo

Completed one week since leaving Fremantle. I have found the first week to be the hardest to pass, letting go of the land ties; after that the days start passing faster. Unfortunately one needs to go through the first week afresh after every halt!

Another calm day of sailing. Less than 20 kts of following breeze and a following sea making the boat move sedately, sometimes so much that one forgets that she is moving at all! Very glad that the preventer is working otherwise I would have been at my wits' end trying to stop the boom from thrashing about in these conditions.

Watched a movie after dark and got out to see a nice starry sky. The first time in the past week! Can't sit out and admire it for too long though, due to the cold. Nice sunset earlier. Not often that you get to see the sun going down in the sea all the way.

Monday, 09 Nov 2009 – Pumps & pancakes!

The day started with a nice sunny morning, putting the cook in a creative mood after a long gap. A grand menu of hot pancakes & honey, fresh orange and freshly brewed coffee followed. The best part was sitting out in the sun and having it, bare feet and without any woollens! The calm following sea with a light breeze enabled the cook to cook in relative comfort and the skipper to enjoy the breakfast without worrying about spilling things. The catch, and there always has to be one, was that despite buying the smallest of the ready mix bottles, the quantity of batter was enough to last for a couple of breakfasts. So a bit of experimentation followed for lunch, different combinations with cheese, chutneys, pickles, etc! No prizes for guessing tomorrow's menu either, weather permitting of course.

One of my bilge pumps seems to have gone 'whacky' and I mean literally. Realised it was not working in the morning so checked all electrical connections, strainer and everything that could be checked without any luck when finally gave it two good whacks out of sheer frustration, rather than any technical competence, and it came to life! So till the next port the starting procedure includes, in addition to putting the switch on, opening the floor boards and whacking the pump while muttering a silent prayer. Having been somewhat lucky with the bilge pump, the confident electrician decided to tackle the fresh water pump next which had stopped working soon after Freo. Found a blown fuse that needed replacement, but then Murphy started acting up and every fuse except the required 15 amp one could be found. Confidently used a 30 amp one as a substitute, started the pump and saw a wisp of black smoke rising near the pump. The supply to the pump was promptly switched off and the electrician sacked even faster! So no water maker, which isn't a problem really as I have enough fresh water for more than a month, but worse, no hot water showers. Which in this cold effectively means no shower till New Zealand. Looks like the Indian Defence Advisor who has promised to be at Lyttelton before me will be able to sniff me out before I get alongside.

We were sailing along nicely with following seas and winds. I had settled down to the sea routine by now. Checking out things every now and then, repairing equipment that refused to play ball, though nothing serious had malfunctioned so far. Waking up every hour or so to see if everything was all right and then getting back in the sleeping bag for another hour of snooze. Reading a book or watching an odd movie on the laptop when I wasn't too sleepy. The memories of good times spent in Fremantle were getting hazier while I was in no hurry to reach my destination.

It is a blissful state to be in! Your work is cut out for you, all you have to do is look after the boat and keep her sailing. There is no paperwork that needs to be attended to, hardly any responsibilities or stresses that are otherwise part and parcel of daily life on land, no routines, dress codes, appointments to keep. The Southern Ocean had been benign to us so far. The characteristic long swells were around but we didn't have to slam in them and *Mhadei* was sailing well with them. Things were moving smoothly, a bit too smoothly perhaps! This was definitely the proverbial lull before the storm, I said to myself as I sat watching a big front moving from west to east on my weather prediction software. The front was large and seemed to be intensifying. Unfortunately, it was far too large for us to be able to escape it with our average daily advance of about 180 nm a day. There seemed to be no choice but to grin and bear it when it crossed us.

The wind kept increasing as the front approached, whipping up big seas, the crests of the waves full of white foam. The foam would often get whipped off the crests and land on deck as the winds increased. I had read that in the days of sailing ships, one of the tasks for the Officer of the Watch was to stop the helmsman looking over his shoulder for fear of the helmsman bolting from the wheel in fright. We were soon sailing in what I termed 'survival mode'! It didn't matter which direction we were heading as long as we could keep the swells and wind behind us. That seemed to be the best way to handle *Mhadei* in these conditions. There always was the possibility of getting one of those giant waves crashing on the boat from astern, getting pooped in seaman's language, but there didn't seem to be any better alternative. In a situation like this, you are really awed by the raw power of nature and your insignificance in comparison.

On the morning of 14 Nov I was lying fully dressed on my

bunk wondering how much more punishment the boat could take. She seemed to have managed well so far but there had to be a point where things would start breaking down. I was down to the third reef and the boat was clearly getting overpowered. I was wondering if I should take in the fourth reef too. And what next after that? I was quite certain that the boat would lose steerageway if I took off all the sails, so what was I supposed to do if she got overpowered with the fourth reef too? The wind was consistently blowing over 50 kts with frequent gusts of 55 to 60 kts. The swells had started towering to almost 9 m and were relentless. As one of them reared up astern with the boat in the trough of the wave, the horizon astern would be blanked out and all I would see was this huge wall of water coming in to gobble us up. As it got closer, *Mhadei* would raise her stern and start surfing down the wave till the crest overtook her and moved on, now blanking the horizon ahead, while the next wave was already forming astern. This game had been on for almost 24 hours now. It was bitterly cold with plenty of sea spray and a gloomy sky. The washboards used to block the entrance to the boat had to be kept closed at all times, so getting in and out was a bit of a bother. Not doing so and getting pooped by one of the big waves would have been asking for serious trouble with so much electrical equipment inside.

Suddenly the boat gave an unusual lurch and seemed to go out of control. I jumped out of the bunk and was at the wheel in seconds. Obviously the autopilot had given up. "Can't blame the poor thing in this sea," I thought as I disengaged the autopilot and took the wheel. The boat had by now turned broadside to the big swells and the boom had started thrashing uncontrollably. The swells, rearing from her side now, were making her roll violently, threatening to bring the tall rig down. I wasn't so alarmed yet. It wasn't unusual for the autopilot to disengage itself when overpowered. A bit of hand steering and balancing of the boat would usually get it back on line and that is what I tried to do now. I tried to turn the boat downwind, which was how she had been sailing earlier. The boat just wouldn't budge; the wheel seemed to be stuck in the direction I was trying to move it. As I moved the wheel in the other direction, desperate to stop the violent rolling, the boat began to head into the wind and swell.

"Okay, something seems to be working," I thought.

The next thing I knew the boat was heading into the swell and rearing up as if wanting to stand vertically on her stern, her head pointing to the sky. It felt as if she was heading for a perfect back flip with me trapped under her, as if enacting a scene from the movie *The Perfect Storm*! As her head reared up, I realised I was not wearing a harness, having jumped out in a hurry, and could well fall off the stern if she went beyond vertical. There was nothing I could do but cling onto the wheel in front of me for dear life. As the wave passed under the boat, she quickly changed her angle and was now pointing towards the trough of the wave, trying to enact a scene from the movie *Titanic*, threatening to do a somersault. Her motion caught me off guard and I almost went over the wheel and on the deck where there was nothing to stop me from dropping into the sea. All my efforts of getting the boat under control using the wheel seemed to be coming to naught. She just didn't seem to be responding to steering. Clearly, there was more than bad weather to blame for this sort of behaviour. One peek in the stern compartment convinced me we had a serious problem with our steering. Something had broken there, making the steering ineffective, and that explained *Mhadei's* erratic behaviour.

I gave up efforts to control the boat with the wheel, secured the thrashing boom as best as I could and got in the stern compartment to try and understand the problem. I soon saw that the starboard steering gear box had uprooted itself, distorting its linkages, which, in turn, were not allowing the steering to function. The first priority was to free the steering by removing the broken parts that were preventing it from functioning. That way I would be able to get some steerage to point the boat downwind, get her sailing again and stabilise her. I gathered the necessary tools and got down to work while *Mhadei* continued to roll violently as if possessed. In conditions such as these, the tools tend to develop legs and run amok the moment you let go of them, which can be really frustrating! It was tedious work but I was desperate. The job had to be done and done fast to avoid any more damage. Less than an hour later, I had managed to disconnect the starboard steering gear and all its linkages. I got to the wheel and coaxed *Mhadei* into going downwind again. This time she obliged happily and we were sailing downwind again. She was fairly stable and I could now consider the next course of action.

The boat has two steering gears, each with its own autopilot, connected to a single rudder. I couldn't use the starboard gearbox, wheel and autopilot anymore. My wind vane self-steering, which could keep the boat at an angle to the wind without using any electrical power, was connected to the starboard wheel so that was unusable too. The port autopilot, which was the only self-steering I was left with, had never been very reliable. If something were to happen to the port steering gear, I would be left with no alternative but to put on the emergency tiller and steer the boat manually till the next port. The tiller had always looked a bit too small to be able to exert the necessary force to have any meaningful steering in the big seas such as we were facing.

I looked at the chart. I was about 1,000 nm west of Lyttelton, my next planned port of call. The nearest landmass was Tasmania, about 700 nm to my north. Though closer, going to Tasmania would mean making a 90° turn to port and getting the swells on our beam, which would be far worse than having them follow us. There didn't seem much option but to continue sailing to Lyttelton. I called Ratnakar to discuss the problem and possible solutions. The port autopilot was already groaning and threatening to give up any moment. I had to get the uprooted steering gear in place and make it work before I lost steering again. I got down to work, devising a rudimentary arrangement of eyebolts and rope to somehow put the starboard steering gear in place and secure it. Two days of painstaking work and many failed attempts later, I was reasonably confident that the arrangement would hold, albeit for a short while, in the event of an emergency.

To add to the woes, I came across an iceberg warning on my NAVAREA messages. The warning indicated a large iceberg, about 250 nm south of our position, which was predicted to be drifting north towards our path. It is said that if you see an iceberg at sea, you are already too close to it. With the big swells around us we couldn't see too far even in daytime, while at night it was difficult to see the water under the boat. Though worried about bumping into an iceberg, there was very little I could do about it. "To hell with it! We will figure out how to deal with it when we bump into one," I finally decided and tried to put it out of my mind.

Sunday, 15 Nov 2009 – Surviving the first Southern Ocean gale

Since the last three days, winds gusting to 55 kts, swell 8 to 9 m, temp below 10°C. Stay sail came down yesterday probably owing to a broken halyard, waiting for winds to reduce to put it up. Starboard wheel had to be disconnected as the base holding its ram connection to the rudder broke in heavy weather, so one electronic autopilot less and no wind vane autopilot. Port, and the only surviving autopilot, groaning badly and threatening to rip its base out! Doing over 8 kts with just ⅓ of mainsail, three reefs, and still getting overpowered at times. Forecast predicts winds to reduce after tomorrow, keeping my fingers crossed.

Tuesday, 17 Nov 2009 – Heading for the southern tip of New Zealand

The gale that really rattled Mhadei and the crew for the last few days finally subsided. The winds reduced first and it took another day for the swell to come down so by morning it was fairly calm with about 2 m of swell. The winds have started picking up again to about 25 kts and so has the swell, about 4 m. But both are from behind, making us do good speed towards the southern tip of New Zealand. We need to go round Stewart Island off the southern coast and then start heading up the coast in a north-easterly direction for the next two days to reach Lyttelton, the port for Christchurch.

Made use of yesterday's calm weather to open up the broken steering assembly and put it back. While it will require work in harbour, at present it seems to be holding with an ad hoc arrangement of securing with bolts and some good rope. Also managed to have the first hot meal in the last few days with a menu of 'sarson ka saag', steaming hot rice and generous quantities of homemade mango pickle! It is getting increasingly cold by the day. There were reports of sightings of icebergs about 200 nm south while we were going through the gale. Usually I would be very curious to see an iceberg but on a pitch dark night with the boat screaming downwind I would rather stay as far away as possible.

Posting two photos of the different moods of the Southern Ocean taken in a span of less than 24 hours. We were becalmed in glassy seas and then in less than 24 hours struggling with 9-m swell and 50-kt winds!

While the winds and waves were tormenting us, the cold started getting the better of me, chilling my tropicalised bones to the marrow! I had clearly misjudged the amount and type of clothing I should have carried. Every item of warm clothing on the boat and rain gear on top of it wouldn't do much to keep the cold at bay, especially while on deck with the sea spray, drizzle and screaming winds. Lying down in the sleeping bag wasn't a practical option with the boat getting buffeted around constantly and the only working autopilot groaning and threatening to give up all the time. One day, very early in the morning as I was coaxing myself out of the bunk to check things out, I suddenly realised that I was having difficulty in thinking properly. I couldn't remember when I had checked everything out last, how long I had slept or what was it that was compelling me to get out and do something. This cold seems to have frozen my brains, I thought. I managed to crawl out of the bunk and light the stove. My mind was absolutely blank while the water heated and I looked around at the boat vacantly, not registering anything. The water must have been boiling for a while before I noticed it. I poured the hot water in a cup, mixed it with some cold water from the tap and had a long swig of warm water. That thawed the brain, which told me that I should do a routine check of the steering. I looked at my watch and realised that I had taken a 15-min nap since the last check!

Wednesday, 18 Nov 2009 – Land ahoy after 18 days

Sighted Snares Island, a small group of islands and rocks at the southern tip of New Zealand, this morning. Very barren, owing to the harsh weather they are exposed to throughout the year, but teeming with bird life. Small wonder that they have been declared a wildlife reserve. So this is where the albatrosses and petrels that have been following me come to nest! Started heading north-east after crossing the islands, the first time we are heading north on this trip. The next time will be after rounding Cape Horn and all the way home.

Good following breeze and seas today translating into good progress. The winds are expected to start heading and easing from tomorrow which will slow us down so trying to make as much progress as possible while they last. Spent the better part of the day making a list of work that needs to be done during the stopover. Unlike Fremantle, the planned stop is for two weeks so will need to get the work done quickly. The sun came up nicely in the afternoon and it was nice to just sit out and watch the birds putting up magnificent displays of their flying skills. Another 300 nm to go but with a forecast for light and head winds it is difficult to figure out if we will be able to cover the distance in two days and one night or will require two days and two nights.

It was great to sight Snares Island. It was a beautiful day; the sun was shining in a blue sky after what appeared to be a long time. I sat in the sun warming myself, watching the island and the multitude of birds around it, some of whom seemed to have followed us; others seemed to be visiting us from the island to check us out. Just a couple of days ago, I had been wondering if I would ever see land again but that felt like just another bad dream! It is amazing how quickly the human mind recovers from bad situations. In this case, all it took was a bit of calm sea and a sunny day.

I had been mulling over the best route to round the South

Island of New Zealand before heading north for Lyttelton and, for a while, was tempted to go through the Foveaux Strait, which would have taken me close to Bluff, one of the southernmost towns of New Zealand. This option would have reduced the distance I needed to travel but involved negotiating the tidal currents and traffic in the strait and in close proximity of land. With an erratic steering gear, half of it lashed in place with a makeshift arrangement, going close to land didn't seem like a good idea. In the end, I decided to play safe and stay in the open water. That way, we didn't have to worry about grounding or colliding. The weather forecast for the next few days promised light winds and I was looking forward to flatter seas as we rounded South Island and got in its lee.

Friday, 20 Nov 2009 – Mhadei chased by a seal

I was told to look for mermaids before I started and today we were actually chased by a creature that would come closest to being described as a mermaid! A seal kept chasing us for over 15 minutes, coming close, stopping, taking a good look with its head bobbing above the water and, as it fell behind, chasing us again. The sea was calm and we were doing an easy 6 kts. It was quite a sight, seeing it jump out of water and also swimming underwater when it would come close to the transom. A totally different experience from being followed by a dolphin.

Looks like this will be the last post of this leg. As I write we are about 30 nm from Lyttelton Harbour and need to reach there by 0530 h to meet the pilot and our agent for the port. The Defence Advisor has planned some photography as we enter, so will show off a bit around the harbour and then enter by 1000 h.

This will be the end of Leg II, the shortest of the legs. We would have covered over 3,200 nm in 20 days across the Great Australian Bight and the

Tasman Sea. Barring a few days while crossing the Tasman Sea where the Southern Ocean showed a hint of what it can throw up, I must say we have had exceptionally good weather throughout the leg. Trying to remain awake tonight as this is the first time since leaving Mumbai that we are sailing so close to the coast at night. Luckily it is warmer than the last few nights so easy to stay on deck all bundled up, alternating between regular cups of hot soup and coffee.

As we inched our way north, crossing the Port of Dunedin, I recalled an incident in Sir Robin's book about getting grounded there in his boat, *Suhaili*, for a few hours during the 1968-69 Golden Globe Race. I have always found it interesting to cross places that have been mentioned in famous books. In a small way, one gets a sense of sharing the adventure described in the book and becoming a part of it.

Getting chased by the seal was definitely the high point of the last day. With its large expressive eyes and long whiskers, a seal almost looks like a pet dog looking at you. I was tempted to lean down on the transom and try to pet it or give it something to eat. That would have scared it off so I avoided the temptation and kept watching it, making eye contact whenever it got closer, which it held without getting scared.

We reached Lyttelton Harbour shortly after our estimated time of arrival. I had been in touch with our appointed agent Peter Rea on the phone and given him our ETA. As we approached the harbour mouth, he arrived to guide us in a pilot boat. Instead of a land-based manager, as the title 'agent' seemed to convey, Peter turned out to be a veteran master mariner and sailor in his 70s. An old school seaman to boot, he had come up the ranks in the Merchant Navy before settling down at

Lyttelton and doing almost all the appointments in the harbour organisation. Everyone seemed to know Peter and no place was out of bounds for us as long as he was around. He was born in Jabalpur in Central India where his father served in the British Indian Army and was very curious about the country.

We paced around the harbour for a while in very light winds getting photographed from the tall hills surrounding it, before making an approach for our berth inside the protected harbour. Unlike our last port where the surrounding land was flat, here we were entering a passage hemmed in by imposing hills. As we moved past the coal berth, Peter drew my attention to a Shipping Corporation of India bulk carrier close by. "I think they are dipping their ensign to you," said Peter, very excited. I looked up and was really touched by the gesture from the ship. Dipping the ensign is the traditional salute exchanged between merchant ships and naval vessels and I was thrilled to see this ship, many times larger, offering us the honour. What a wonderful way to make someone feel special! I ran and dipped my ensign in return and then got busy getting the mainsail down as Peter took over the wheel. As we were approaching our berth, we were hit by a violent squall and it was with some difficulty and little damage that we finally managed to secure *Mhadei* alongside. The second leg was over and what a fast and furious leg it had been!

Chapter 25

A Little Town with a Large Heart

I was pleasantly surprised to see a fairly large crowd at the pontoon, led by the Indian Defence Advisor Captain Jatinder Singh, Indian Navy. He had come in a day earlier and passed the word around about our arrival. It was a warm welcome, complete with a bottle of champagne to soothe the raw nerves caused by getting knocked about unceremoniously during the final approach by the sudden squall.

Once the welcome was over, we shifted to a jetty close by and had to go through the mandatory Customs formalities. A lady Customs officer boarded the boat and as she started asking the mandatory questions, Peter stepped in, "This guy hasn't seen a woman for the last three weeks. Give him a hug first and then ask him questions!" he said tongue in cheek. Everyone started laughing, the lady obliged and asked the first question, "Sir, I know this may sound odd but I have to ask you this. Are you carrying more than $ 10,000 with you?"

"If I had that sort of money, do you think I would be doing something as silly as this?" I shot back.

"I get the point! Have a good stay in New Zealand!" she said, ending the interview.

I shifted out of the boat by evening and moved into a furnished apartment close by. It was nice to be back on terra firma once again. The apartment was nice and roomy complete with a real tree growing through the drawing room, a pool table and a juke box! The best part was that I could catch a glimpse of *Mhadei* berthed in the harbour while sitting in the house.

Lyttelton is a small, scenic port town that is spread more vertically up the surrounding hills than horizontally. The people are warm and friendly and, by the evening of our arrival, everyone in town seemed to have heard about us and was curious to hear our experiences.

The next day was a Sunday and I was invited for lunch at the local gurdwara in Christchurch. I hadn't shaved since leaving Mumbai three months ago and my beard had grown long enough to compete with most of the members of the congregation there. That probably explained why everyone kept talking to me in Punjabi while I tried figuring out what was being spoken, with a straight face! I do understand bits and pieces of the language but get tongue-tied when I try to speak it. I was presented with a *saropa*, a long piece of cloth presented as a badge of honour, and invited for the *langar*, where you sit cross legged on the floor and are served a basic but delicious meal by the volunteers at the gurdwara. The next few days flew past calling on local dignitaries, including a reception hosted by the Mayor and Indian community at Christchurch, complete with the traditional Maori welcome of *hakka*.

While I was enjoying my stay on land, I was getting nervous about the lack of progress of work on the boat. There was still no sign of my shore support as Abhilash was running around in circles in Delhi getting his deputation approved. The joke about beating Air India yet again didn't seem all that funny any longer.

There was plenty of work to do on the boat and I needed a helping hand who knew the boat. One day, out of sheer frustration, I tried washing off all the salt from the boat. Three hours later, I was half-frozen and exhausted.

"This could have been done in half an hour if there was one more person to help me," I thought, very frustrated.

Finally, a few days later Ratnakar arrived to lend me a hand and we started fixing the major problems. He had designed a new arrangement for securing the steering gear boxes, fabricated the necessary attachments in Goa and brought them along. We also ordered a new genoa to replace the torn one. One day as we were working in the boat, the Defence Advisor, walking around on deck, casually asked if the cobweb-like lines he had noticed on the boom were normal. A closer look revealed that the cobwebs he was mentioning were actually hairline cracks on the boom!

"As if we didn't have enough troubles of our own," I thought, alarmed that none of us had noticed the cracks before and adding another major job to the tasks to be completed. It would have been foolish to venture out on the next leg without fixing them. Eventually, the boom had to be taken off the boat and Ratnakar managed to get them fixed with the help of a local shipyard.

A dose of humour always helps in such stressful times and we got a handful of it with Abhilash's arrival and the insistence of NHQ to audit the boat! It didn't seem all that funny initially, actually it was quite frustrating, but as the farce unfolded we started feeling as if we were part of a big comedy show.

Abhilash arrived at Christchurch on a Friday, over a week late, totally jet lagged, with orders to return after three days as that was the duration his deputation had been approved for. It had taken almost two days for the poor guy to reach us and would take as much time to get back. This was amazing planning indeed! He worked with us on the boat over the weekend and by the time he had started settling down to a routine, it was time for him to leave. My pleas with NHQ to allow him to continue working were brushed off brusquely initially and left unanswered as the weekend started in Delhi. With no other option in sight, Abhilash said his goodbyes to everyone at work on Monday evening and I dropped him off at the airport on Tuesday morning. My lone shore support crew had vanished without achieving much. "What a waste; what am I going to do now?" I wondered as I drove back from the airport. As I was getting ready to go and work on the boat with Ratnakar, I got a call from the Defence Advisor.

"Has Abhilash left? Do you know his routeing?"

"Unfortunately, yes! I don't remember what route he was to take," I replied, wondering about the purpose of the call.

"Was it via Sydney by any chance?"

"Now that you mention it, I think it was via Sydney, Singapore and then on to Delhi. But what happened, why do you need these details, is everything alright?" I had started getting a little apprehensive now.

"All's well, he must be out of Sydney and out of my area by now," murmured the Defence Advisor and cut off the phone.

"Something crazy is about to happen," I told Ratnakar as we drove to the boat and work.

I had guessed correctly. By the end of the day, I got a call from Abhilash asking me if I could pick him up at Christchurch airport the next evening! While we generally figured out what must have happened, we wanted to hear the story from the horse's mouth. The next evening at the airport, we saw Abhilash come out with a spring in his step and a big grin on his tired face. Between guffaws of laughter, we managed to get his story out.

He had travelled smoothly till Singapore. As he was heading to board his flight for Delhi, he was paged on the airport's PA system. Confused and trying to figure out the announcement, a few steps away from the departure gate, he was accosted by two smartly dressed gentlemen who introduced themselves as the Indian Defence Advisor for Singapore and his assistant.

"Lt Cdr Abhilash Tomy, turn about and march straight to the next flight to Auckland and Christchurch," ordered the Defence Advisor, handing him his tickets while promising to extract his luggage from the flight to Delhi!

When Abhilash finally landed back in New Zealand that day, he had been in the air for over 20 hours in one day, causing confusion at the Immigration desk.

"When did you leave New Zealand?" asked the befuddled Immigration officer, looking at the stamps on his passport.

"Yesterday," replied Abhilash, grinning from ear to ear.

"So what brings you back today?" asked the Immigration officer, surely trying to calculate how much productive time a person could get between all this flying around.

"Government of India business!" had been Abhilash's cheeky answer!

It was nice to have the team together again, refreshed by the hilarity of the whole incident. There wasn't much time left for the planned date of departure and we needed to get our act together in time. Meanwhile, we had managed to get a reprieve of four days thanks to – of all reasons – diplomatic protocol.

Admiral Sureesh Mehta, who had seen me off in Mumbai as

the Chief of the Naval Staff, had retired from the Navy while I was making the transit to New Zealand and had been appointed the Indian High Commissioner to New Zealand. It would have been appropriate to have been seen off by him again. However, he had to present his credentials to the Governor General before he could take part in any official function. We thus delayed our departure by four days yet again; the first time had been in Aug 2009, when we had to do so from 15 to 19 Aug. It was a welcome reprieve as we could do our work without resorting to shortcuts. There was also another issue that had started bordering on the ridiculous as it developed, which had to be tackled before departure. The boat audit!

A lot of doubts had been raised about the quality of the boat and our inexperience in repairing her during the previous leg, especially after the problems with the steering gear. A number of emails had been exchanged on the subject, all with genuine concern and the best of intentions. In one such email, Abhilash, in an effort to allay the apprehensions about the quality of the boat, suggested an independent audit of the boat by someone more experienced than us. The idea was to ask someone with more experience to have a look at the boat, suggest improvements and nip any likely problem in the bud; not unlike Sir Robin having a look at the boat when she had been built. Unfortunately, the mandarins at Delhi got stuck on the word 'audit', which for a guy sitting behind a desk has a totally different connotation.

"We need to audit the boat."

"Good idea! But what exactly does that mean?"

"Don't try to act fresh! You have spent enough time in the Navy to know what an audit is. Get an audit done and send us the certificate; you are not sailing out without one!"

"We have had the boat looked over by a reputed boat builder here and prima facie he sees nothing wrong with the boat. He actually complimented Ratnakar for doing such a fine job. That should be good enough."

"But was he an auditor? No! Then we need to get a boat auditor, get the boat audited from him and get a certificate that the boat is seaworthy for the rest of the voyage."

"I have never heard of such a species. Do you mean a surveyor? I can get a survey done if I can tell the surveyor what to survey but I am sure that no surveyor will give a 100 per cent guarantee that a sailboat on a solo voyage will last through the Southern Ocean! In any case, it's my life that will be in danger if something goes wrong and I am confident about the boat."

"We can't rely on your word alone. What do you care if something happens to her? We will be held responsible!"

"But I am the one who will be sailing her! Do you think I would care less than anyone else if something happened to her?"

The game went on for a while, ending in a bit of a standoff. Our planned date of departure was fast approaching and I had started getting a bit edgy. Our agent and self-appointed guardian in Lyttelton, Peter Rea, had been watching the whole game unfold. As an experienced seaman he could see that the boat was in good shape but we were at our wit's end trying to satisfy the bureaucracy. He proposed a safety inspection by Maritime New Zealand, which essentially involved checking the safety equipment like fire extinguishers and life jackets onboard. The inspection was duly carried out and the all important certificate forwarded to NHQ, which was finally satisfied and agreed to let me sail out on the next leg. I don't think anyone really bothered to read the fine print on the certificate!

I had been corresponding with Sir Robin regularly and had kept him in the picture. Some of the mails exchanged during that time make for interesting reading,

Dear Robin,

The deluge of advice and reactions reminds me of the first lines of Rudyard Kipling's famous poem 'If'!

If you can keep your head while all about you
Are losing theirs and blaming it on you,
If you can trust yourself when all men doubt you,
But make allowance for their doubting too...
I feel I am growing by the day in this project! Wonderful feeling!
Regards,
Dilip

You are right. Trust in yourself and only ask when you are not sure from those you trust. The fact is that you now have a lot of solo miles under your belt and don't need advice from those who don't have your experience.

RKJ

Very encouraging words at the beginning of the remotest leg, when everyone else seemed to doubt me and the boat! The evening before departure, I had the customary pre-departure dinner with Peter, Ratnakar and Abhilash. As we were returning home I realised a big cavity had opened up in one of my molars. This was bad news! A toothache at sea with no chance to consult a dentist for the next month or so would be a really innovative form of torture. On the other hand, after all this trouble to leave on time I was reluctant to delay the departure. Taking a dentist's appointment the next day would have meant cancelling the elaborate departure ceremony so meticulously planned by the Defence Advisor. I was in a dilemma and, as I would do while dealing with problems on the boat, asked Ratnakar for a possible solution. He always seems to have one and didn't take too long in this case either! Out came a small bottle of clove oil from his toilet bag.

"Soak some cotton and shove it in the cavity whenever the pain gets unbearable. See if you can consult a dentist at Port Stanley. Don't worry; I am sure you will manage."

The tiny bottle with its fiery contents would prove to be a godsend a number of times during the next month when the toothache got unbearable.

Chapter 26

The Everest of Ocean Sailing

Our departure was planned at noon on 12 Dec 2009, a very special day for *Mhadei*. Exactly a year ago, on this day, she had floated herself in her namesake river at Goa. She had been just a bare hull then without any equipment or mast. Within a year, she had sailed to the other side of the world and was all set to cross the South Pacific Ocean. As we got ready to leave Lyttelton, we were blessed by a priest with the traditional blessings for sailors and seen off by a crowd of friends led by Admiral Sureesh Mehta (Retd), this time in his new avatar as the Indian High Commissioner to New Zealand.

If our arrival alongside had been a bit dodgy, the departure seemed equally bad. A bit of a tug of war between the boat and our unberthing party threatened to knock us about. Luckily we got out of the tight berth without a scratch and were finally underway amid cries of *Bole So Nihal, Sat Sri Akal*, the traditional Sikh call to action or duty, from our friends on the pontoon. That was very inspiring and we were ready to take on the Pacific. As we got out of the protected area, I started getting warnings of a 4-m swell and gusty 40-kt winds outside the harbour on the VHF radio. Ratnakar, Abhilash and Peter had planned to hop in a boat and follow us till the harbour mouth but I was in a hurry to get out and set up my sails.

The boat was moving fast on an ebb tide as I got busy getting her ready to sail. As we came out of the harbour, the gusty winds hit us and so did the swell. I turned the boat into the wind and started winching up the mainsail. Mindful of the strong winds, I had planned to raise it to two reefs and then put on the stay sail, the smaller of the two head sails. I had barely started working on the mainsail when the stay sail opened up in the middle, on its own, flapping violently and shaking the entire rig. The furled portions at its head and foot were getting tightened because of the force exerted from the half-opened centre portion. It was quite a mess and I was worried it would rip apart. It was an important sail for this leg as I was expecting very strong winds and I couldn't afford to damage it. As I worked frantically to untangle the mess, I realised we were closing in on the rocky headland ahead and quickly running out of sea room. This was fast turning into an emergency! Suddenly, tearing a sail looked like a minor issue compared to grounding on the rocks ahead and becoming a monument at the harbour mouth. I was in a state of panic and working so frantically that I couldn't even raise my hand to wave goodbye to the boat that had come to see me off. I just looked in their direction, nodded and got back to work. They too were being battered by the wind and sea and decided to turn back in the harbour leaving me alone to fend for myself. Ratnakar later told me that they had a long rough ride getting into the harbour, almost making him miss his flight in the evening.

I finally managed to untangle the stay sail and bear the boat off towards the safety of the open sea, heaving a mighty sigh of relief. We were off again on what would be the remotest leg of the voyage. There were no safe harbours or anchorages to take refuge in and very little traffic to answer a Mayday call. The vast expanse of the Pacific Ocean lay ahead of us. The next bit of land we were expecting to see was Cape Horn, the southern tip of the South American continent.

It took me a few days to get back to the sea routine that had been disrupted by the good life in Lyttelton. While life ashore had been good, it had also been very hectic, with every waking moment being used to do something. Once at sea, there was plenty of time to do things, no real deadlines to keep and no need to feel guilty about wasting time. Strange as it may sound, it takes time to slow down the pace of life and pull your brain out of the overdrive it has been working in, to the easy pace life at sea demands. I would face this problem at the beginning of every leg, making me wonder if it would have been easier to sail around the world non-stop, instead.

That night as the boat was sailing through 25 kts of wind and I was catching up on my sleep, the wind shifted and started picking up. I sensed the boat's motion but, half asleep, started dreaming that Abhilash was sitting on deck and would look after the boat. I probably even asked aloud if he was okay handling her while I slept and got an affirmative answer! This went on for a while till I decided that Abhilash didn't seem to be handling the boat well and it was time to go out and have a look. As I got out of the bunk, my fuzzy brain slowly realised that I was alone on the boat and the boat needed my attention. I had read stories of solo sailors hallucinating in a boat and realised that I had come fairly close.

The next night as I sat reading late, bundled up in my sleeping bag, I heard a sloshing sound from below the floorboards. The book I was reading was interesting and the comfort of the warm sleeping bag very inviting so I ignored the sound and continued reading. After a while, I got the unmistakable smell of beer and the clinking sound of glass.

"Am I hallucinating with my eyes open now?" I wondered. "I really seem to be missing Lyttelton or the book is so absorbing that I can actually smell things!" I told myself and continued reading till a part of my brain made me aware that there was no mention of beer in the book I was reading and I definitely was wide awake so could not be hallucinating. Reluctantly, I got out of the sleeping bag to get to the bottom of this unusual phenomenon. As I lifted the floorboards I found, to my horror, a couple of litres of beer and a lot of broken bottles sloshing around in the bilges!

"Where did this come from?" I thought in disbelief. "And what a waste!", suddenly feeling a bit like Captain Haddock in the *Tintin* comics I was fond of reading as a child. Slowly, the realisation dawned. A few days before departure, a friend at Lyttelton had gifted me a case of the choicest of assorted beer from his brewery. In a hurry to stow things at the last minute, I had put the case under the floorboards and forgotten all about it. The case had looked well stowed in harbour but as we started getting tossed about, the beer had frothed out of some bottles, dissolving the cardboard case and letting free the rest of the bottles to break themselves. It was an absolute mess under the floorboards with broken glass, cardboard pulp and beer sloshing over it. The place had to be emptied and fast.

"Drink to your fill and share with your subjects," I muttered to Neptune as I poured the first bucket over the side. The next few hours were spent bailing out the contents and cleaning the bilges.

Monday, 14 Dec 2009 – Goodbye Lyttelton – A little town with a large heart

Mhadei sailed out of Lyttelton harbour at noon on 12 Dec 2009, exactly a year after she was floated in her namesake river a year back. She was seen off once again by Adm Sureesh Mehta, this time as the Indian High Commissioner in New Zealand and a number of well-wishers. I am saying a number of well-wishers as there are far too many to name! We couldn't have chosen a better port for a stopover than Lyttelton. This large hearted little town looked after Mhadei and her crew so well and made us feel so much at home that it became a bit difficult to say goodbye. The Indian Navy tried to enlist the services of an agent in the port to look after the boat and the crew; but landed up getting a godfather in Capt Peter Rea. A master mariner and experienced yachtsman who took it upon himself to ensure that both the boat and the crew were well prepared for the journey ahead! The port waived off all the fees, the boat was blessed by a minister, stocked up with fresh fruit and goodies for Christmas; the crew honoured with a traditional Maori welcome at Christchurch...the list goes on! But then all good things have to come to an end and it is the lot of boats and seamen to move on!

Crossed the International Date Line today, 14 Dec, thus making it the longest day! A full 48 hrs as we will continue with 14 Dec tomorrow too. Suddenly from being 13 hrs ahead of GMT we are 11 hours behind. The sea has been kind so far with about 15 to 20 kts of breeze, sunny days and clear nights. In fact we almost got becalmed a few times. We are heading in an east south-easterly direction and should cross Chatham Islands tomorrow, the last bit of land till South America almost 4,000 nm away.

I had been passing my position reports to the Rescue Coordination Centre in New Zealand. On 17 Dec, they informed me that I had company in the remote Southern Ocean. Jessica Watson, a 16-year-old Australian girl attempting a non-stop solo circumnavigation, was about 1,200 nm east northeast of me and heading towards Cape Horn. They suggested that we keep an eye open for each other to provide assistance if necessary. I had read about Jessica while at Fremantle and written to her but my mail must have got lost in the deluge of fan mail she was receiving. We soon started exchanging emails about our positions and weather conditions. Luckily, neither of us would land up in a situation that would require any assistance. But what neither of us realised then was that she would inadvertently give the biggest publicity to my project, attracting a large international readership to my blog.

Saturday, 19 Dec 2009 – Stuck in high pressure!

The last two days have probably been the most sedate so far. Unexpectedly, we are stuck in a high pressure area with very little winds and it feels as if we are just drifting around! Luckily there isn't much swell and the skies have been clear so it is fairly comfortable though we would rather be moving along! The cook is having a field day cooking dosas, bhelpuri, prawn curry, the works, while the skipper spends sleepless nights looking for every whiff of wind and hand-steering often when the autopilot gives up owing to very slow speeds and erratic wind direction.

Finished 'The Glass Palace' by Amitav Ghosh. Excellent book and the second I have read by the same author while sailing on Mhadei. Coincidentally I was wallowing in the Doldrums near the equator on my way back from Mauritius earlier this year while reading the first one! It does help having a good book to read to keep your mind off the frustrations of wallowing around on windless days. Wondering which one to start next, though the wind seems to be picking up slightly. Heading on a more southerly course in an effort to get out of the high pressure system and also reduce the distance to destination by sailing closer to a great circle route.

Wednesday, 23 Dec 2009 – Sailing in the Fearsome Fifties

The unexpected easterly and north-easterly winds in the last couple of days pushed us south earlier than expected but after being becalmed for over two days moving anywhere was welcome! The wind is still oscillating between north and north northwest, making us sail a narrow reach to run the longitudes. Today was an exceptionally good day with a clear sunny sky and 15 kts of northerly breeze propelling us almost dead east at a healthy 7 kts. Let us see how long the good times last and the Fearsome Fifties start showing their true colours!

Finished reading 'A Voyage for Madmen' by Peter Nichols which is an account of the Sunday Times Golden Globe Race of 1968, the first solo round the world race. I think sailing today is a cakewalk compared to what the participants of that race went through. After reading such a spellbinding book almost without a break, it was time for some light entertainment, so watched 'Gentlemen Prefer Blondes', that evergreen musical comedy starring Marilyn Monroe!

Saturday, 26 Dec 2009 – A memorable Christmas!

This year we are bringing up the rear as far as Christmas goes with the rest of the world barring Polynesia, Hawaii and Alaska having already passed on to Boxing Day as I write. One can be a little flexible with dates at sea, especially so close to the date line and alone. Jessica Watson, the youngest solo circumnavigator, sailing 600 nm ahead of me and the closest human being at this moment, confirmed that she was planning to celebrate Christmas on 24 Dec, local date; as it would be 25 Dec at her home in Australia. Deciding to follow suit on Mhadei, some excellent cake, so thoughtfully handed over just before departure by Mrs Fitzgerald of Lyttelton, was cut and devoured for breakfast. A good lunch and dinner should logically have followed but with Mhadei bouncing around in 30-kt winds the cook wasn't really feeling up to something elaborate. He did make up for it today though, serving some

233

excellent Thai curry with dried prawns and hot steaming rice. No prizes for guessing the dessert — Christmas cake naturally! And so shall it be for the next couple of days.

Looking back, it was just two years back on this day that we had a little ceremony at the Aquarius boat yard to start the construction of Mhadei. I had barely made it to the yard having had my car smashed up a few days earlier while attempting to drive down to Goa from Mumbai. The building contract was yet to be signed and Ratnakar flew down the next day to Delhi to sign the contract with the Navy! It may sound strange now but I had never seen a boat being built, Ratnakar had never sailed nor worked with the Navy. I dare say the powers that be at Naval Headquarters who were paying for the construction had no idea either! Warship construction and dinghy sailing yes, but yacht construction and ocean sailing most certainly no. And here we are, two years later, merrily sailing halfway across the world as if it is the most normal thing to do.

Monday, 28 Dec 2009 – Oh, these maddening Easterlies!

For the last two days we have been getting strong easterlies forcing us to head south instead of east. This is something totally unexpected for these latitudes where the normal wind direction is supposed to be westerly! By evening we had almost reached the latitude of Cape Horn, and the end of the skipper's patience! So tacked and now making slow north-easterly progress against a swell. Not the most comfortable way to sail with the boat falling off the swell and hammering in the troughs every now and then, but there didn't seem much choice unless the destination was Antarctica! It has been drizzling throughout making everything damp and cold. Hoping for the wind to shift, well it has to eventually, in any direction but the east!

Since Jessica mentioned my blog on hers, there seems to be a sudden increase in comments and questions. While it may be difficult to answer all from a bouncy boat, here are answers to a few common ones. I do not have any HF communication so all communication is by normal email using Fleet Broadband. I started from Mumbai on 19 Aug and stopped at Fremantle and Lyttelton enroute. Plan to stop at Port Stanley and Cape Town before heading home so one can say I am around the halfway point of my trip. My boat Mhadei was named after the old name of the river she was built on. The river is called Mandovi these days and runs through the State of Goa on the West Coast of India.

Tuesday, 29 Dec 2009 – Murphy strikes!

I tend to get a little wary when things start going too smoothly and, sure enough, just as I was congratulating myself in the morning on finally getting out of the easterlies by slamming northeast through the night, both the electronic autopilots went off in quick succession! Hove to, had a quick breakfast of oats and coffee and got down to finding a remedy. Four bolts holding the starboard autopilot motor have sheared off making the motor rotate around itself instead of steering the boat. By the end of the day managed to lash up the motor as changing the bolts will involve dismantling the entire steering gearbox and make it impossible even to use the wind vane. Not sure how long it will hold especially in stressful conditions, for the autopilot that is, so will keep it for an emergency. Looks like the rest of the leg will have to be done using the wind vane or hand steering. No more comfort of push button steering from inside! The wind played truant through the day so we were more or less drifting around till midnight. Finally started getting a 15-kt north north-westerly breeze and we are back to an easterly course with the wind vane maintaining course.

The problem with the autopilots was very unusual as it takes a lot of force to shear off four 5-mm stainless steel bolts at once. One autopilot malfunctioning could be termed as an accident, but both going off in a span of 30 minutes was weird. I checked the chart. We had left New Zealand about 2,000 nm behind us while Cape Horn and the Chilean coast were about 3,000 nm ahead. A couple of thousand miles to our right were the frigid wastes of Antarctica and there was no point even looking to the left where the entire Pacific Ocean spread out beyond the Equator and into the Northern Hemisphere. In short, we were in the middle of nowhere!

The wind vane proved to be a lifesaver. It was not part of my initial specifications while fitting out the boat but I added it as an afterthought heeding the advice given by Nigel Rowe, an accomplished sailor in his own right. Once we started sailing, I had used it sporadically, just to test it once in a while, relying instead on the electronic autopilots, as they were easier to use. I had two of them and always thought that I had sufficient redundancy in case one broke down. Surely I had underestimated Murphy! It took a while to learn to sail with the wind vane. The boat had to be well balanced and the wind vane adjusted just right. As I started to understand and master the small idiosyncrasies of the gadget, I started getting more and more impressed with its efficiency. It is a wonderful piece of equipment that keeps the boat sailing at the desired angle to the wind without using any electricity. On a sunny day, I would sit out for hours at a time, mesmerised, watching it work, keeping the boat on course. It was fascinating and the best way to describe it would be Black Magic! The wind vane sensor would keep moving as the direction of the wind on it shifted and two lines from it kept moving the starboard wheel, keeping the boat on course. Eventually I got so used to sailing the boat with it that even when the electronic autopilots were repaired, I kept using the wind vane as my primary self-steering, relegating the electronic autopilots to act as secondary self-steering or to be used in very light or shifty winds when the wind vane wasn't very effective.

One night, just when I thought I had mastered the art of using the wind vane and was feeling confident enough to have a snooze in the warm bunk, *Mhadei* went off course and did a bone wrenching crash gybe. I ran on deck and started hand steering, the cold drizzle on top waking me up instantly. The wind was gusting and shifting around, which I thought was the reason for the wind vane giving up.

"Please God! Not another steering breakage!" I thought, very worried.

As I tried to hand-steer the boat in the dark night and get used to the shifty winds, *Mhadei* did another crash gybe, this time entangling the runner in the boom. The runner whipped across the boat, nicking my ear and almost taking my head off in the process. A vision of my skeleton hanging on the stern of the boat with a rope tied around my neck flashed before me as that is exactly how a rescue ship would have found me. I realised I had cheated 'death by hanging' by a whisker!

I settled the boat on a steady course and hand-steered her for a while before trying to engage the wind vane again. It just couldn't keep the boat on course anymore. Something was definitely wrong. Closer inspection revealed that two of the three jubilee clips of the small drum connecting the wind vane lines to the steering wheel had broken, causing the boat to go off course. It would have been simple to take the drum off and replace the clips had the boat not been sailing with the wind vane. But with the electronic autopilots non-functional, that was not an option anymore. Getting the sails down, stopping the boat and doing the repairs would have meant going broadside to the big swells and rolling violently. The memory of the steering gear problems on the previous leg was still fresh in my mind and I was very reluctant to stop the boat. To add to our woes, the rain and gusty winds kept pelting us.

The situation was becoming desperate as I started freezing at the wheel trying to hand-steer the boat. I had to get some form of self-steering going if I didn't want to be glued to the steering wheel forever. The repair would be like trying to replace the pedal of a cycle on a dark wet night while the cyclist continues to pedal on a potholed road! With no other choice, I gathered my tools and started working with my two hands as well as any other part of the body that could be used. Toes, legs, knees, elbows, mouth, head...it is amazing how innovatively one can use one's body when in a desperate situation! Finally, after what seemed like an eternity I managed to fix the drum and raised my head to have a good look around. The pitch dark had given way to a grey dawn. I had been working non-stop through the night and had really earned my morning cup of coffee. It tasted great and so was the pleasure of holding the hot mug in my numb and bruised hands!

Friday, 01 Jan 2010 – A soak in the Southern Ocean

Last night as I was checking up various things on deck I realised that one of the two bolts holding the wind vane together on the transom had fallen off. This was serious especially with the autopilots already on strike! Rushed with a spanner and as I was sitting on the transom putting on a new bolt, a couple of waves washed over me soaking me to the inside of my boots. Exquisite agony is perhaps a good way to describe it! Managed to put on the bolt without losing the spanner as my hands had already started going numb, got inside the boat and it was straight in the sleeping bag for a couple of hours after a quick drying up and change of clothing. Got up grudgingly only when the boat builder, Ratnakar, rang up to wish me a Happy New Year and discuss a solution to the problems onboard. He was celebrating the New Year with friends and family in Goa but by all indications his mind was on the boat in the Southern Ocean!

Midnight of New Year's Eve, just as I was getting out to adjust the wind vane, with the wind dropping, the phone rang. Finding it a bit odd to receive a phone call close to midnight, picked up the phone and what a pleasant surprise: Jessica calling to wish New Year's! So very thoughtful of her. Among all the New Year's wishes I have received in all these years and at various places, I think I will cherish this, from this gutsy girl 350 nm away and the nearest human being to me, as the most special. With wishes like these how can 2010 not be anything but great!

As we sail into 2010, here is wishing all the readers, from Mhadei and her crew, a great year ahead and good times to come!

Monday, 04 Jan 2010 – One gale gone, waiting for the next!
It blew through yesterday and night, building up big seas and keeping Mhadei's crew on tenterhooks with the steering groaning. By morning the wind had come down, the swell reduced marginally and we were moving well again. At the end of my tether with the groaning of the steering, I took a can of WD-40 and sprayed it in every nook and cranny of the steering system, but without any conviction that it would work. An hour later I was so happy to have been proven wrong! Finally no more groaning! Not sure what exactly the problem was but the solution seems to have worked which is all that matters.

The weather forecast is predicting another gale in the next couple of hours so waiting and watching the wind. It is really cold now with the temperature dropping below 4°C at night and not much better in daytime thanks to an overcast sky.

The cold and dampness had really started getting to me. The days had become very long with just about four hours of darkness but the sun wouldn't often be visible, making the days gloomy.

I had bought a good electric heater in Lyttelton for such days but its heavy power consumption meant I couldn't use it with the boat's storage batteries and had to start the generator to operate it. The generator unfortunately had swallowed seawater a while back and stopped working altogether. I used to start the engine and idle it to charge the batteries, which would give me some warm water but no heater. It sounds strange now but shedding my clothes to go to the loo in the morning had started becoming an ordeal. I would put the kettle on the boil in the morning, take a deep breath, take off my clothes and run to the loo to finish with it as soon as I could. That done, run back and gulp down some warm water followed by coffee. Using the wind vane meant going on deck more often to adjust it, unlike the electronic autopilots that I could operate from inside. Every time I went out, I would have to open the washboards and the interior of the boat would lose all the heat. By the time it warmed up a bit, it would be time to go out again!

Wednesday, 06 Jan 2010 – A welcome respite!

The gales of the last 2-3 days subsided today and so did the swell. There was thick fog all around with intermittent drizzle, dropping the temperatures. The absence of wind chill more than compensated for the extra cold! It was good to have three hot and rather heavy meals through the day, shake out a reef or two, go around the boat tightening everything that is not supposed to move and spraying WD-40 on everything that's supposed to! In the morning for a while it looked as if the wind would die out completely but luckily it was just changing direction and started blowing a steady 10 to 15 kts from northwest, as against west southwest of the past three days. That allowed us to do an east north-easterly course at a comfortable 6 kts while keeping the wind vane happy. The forecast for the next few days is not predicting any gale force winds. Keeping my fingers crossed as at sea, especially in remote areas like the one we are in, one tends to take forecasts with a pinch of salt!

On 08 Jan, my coursemates posted in Mumbai were having a grand party at the Naval Sailing Club to celebrate 20 years of commissioned service. It is a landmark in the career of a service officer in India as one becomes eligible for pension after serving for 20 years. I was invited and readily agreed to join the celebrations, albeit briefly, via Skype! My friends set up a laptop with a Skype connection on the Sailing Club terrace while I sat, half-way across the world, on the rocking boat clutching my laptop and holding on to the boat to stop falling off my bench. It was nice chatting with everyone, though I couldn't see their faces too well, and for a few moments I was transported to warm Mumbai surrounded by familiar faces and voices. The ever jealous *Mhadei* shortly broke my reverie, demanding my presence on the deck, making me stow the laptop and quickly jump out in the freezing cold. I think it was one of the most memorable parties I had attended!

Sunday, 10 Jan 2010 – Good wishes work!

Thanks to the good wishes of so many, the sea and the wind seem to have been kind to us for the past few days. The wind has been light and shifty which means frequent visits outside to adjust the wind vane and the sails but we are moving, which is what really matters. The swell is much less and we have been sailing upwind most of the time which puts less stress on the wind vane and the creaky steering. A good current of up to 2 kts has been compensating for the lack of stronger winds to some extent. Jessica seems to have run ahead to meet up with her parents at Cape Horn! As per her last position she was about 90 nm ahead so looks unlikely that we will be able to catch up, with a little over 300 miles to the Horn!

We had clearly started feeling the effect of the Southern Ocean current, which would only get stronger as we approached the relatively narrow Drake Passage, the 600 nm passage between South America and Antarctica. I couldn't have been more grateful for the current as there was a front following us and I wanted to cross the Drake Passage before the front caught up with us. We had survived so far with all the problems in the boat and I was in no mood to test our luck anymore.

As we closed Cape Horn, the leading edge of the front following us started giving us east north-easterly winds again, making us sink further south on an east south-easterly course. I started wondering if we would ever get to see the infamous Cape. It would have been a pity not to sight it after having sailed this far. I finally ran out of patience by the midnight of 11 Jan, decided to tack and head in a north north-easterly direction towards the American continent about 60 nm to the north. On hindsight it turned out to be a good decision. By about 0740 h in the morning, I sighted the tall mountains of Patagonia on my port bow, the first sight of land since leaving New Zealand a month ago. As if on cue, at 0745 h the phone rang with the Chief of the Naval Staff on line calling me to congratulate me on rounding the Horn! It felt good. While the previous night I was worried about not sighting Cape Horn, having sighted it, I was worried about landing on its western shore. The wind had backed west through the night as the front overtook us and we were now sailing a broad reach, fairly close to the Cape, doing short gybes to keep clear of the land. The sky had cleared up a little and I could see patches of blue sky with a slight drizzle. The winds were gusting to about 40 kts and a steep swell of over 6 m had built up behind us. What was different this time was that the crests of the swell had started breaking, which was a cause for alarm. Had any of them decided to break on our stern it would have taken away our only means of self-steering. Luckily, none did!

Cape Horn or Cabo de Hornos was as awe inspiring as I had read in descriptions and seen in pictures. A small rocky, barren and windswept island, not too far from the shore, that has been part of sailors' folklore for centuries. Witness to the worst storms and seas in the world, often regarded as the worst place to sail on the earth or simply as 'the Everest of Ocean Sailing'!

I decided to delay the celebrations till we were well clear of the Cape. As we were passing close to the Cape, I got a call on the VHF from a Chilean Navy patrol boat anchored in a bay east of Cape Horn asking me if I was alright and to let them know if I needed any assistance. It was a touching gesture. Apparently, they had sailed there to stand by for any SAR that may be required as there was a fair amount of traffic in that area. Jessica was a day behind me. I had also read about a few more, including Isabelle Autissier, the famous French solo sailor crossing the Drake Passage on her way to Antarctica with a crew on a research expedition. At that moment I didn't envy the crew of the Chilean patrol boat, sailing in such weather as a matter of routine, offering assistance to people like us.

Once we were well clear of the Cape and on a north-easterly course, it was time for a bit of a celebration. I had managed to save a can of *rasagullas*, a typical Bengali sweet floating in sugar syrup I had found at an Indian store in Christchurch. I opened the can and made the first traditional offering to Neptune, thanking him for keeping us safe so far. The next was to my closest, most trustworthy and only companion at the moment; good old *Mhadei*!

"We made it babe, congratulations!" I muttered, kissing the boat and pouring some sugar syrup from the can on deck. As I was doing this, something very strange happened – I started weeping uncontrollably, something I had never done in my living memory! The last three-and-a-half years it had taken to reach this stage flashed before me as if I were watching a movie. It had been a long, hard grind, full of apprehensions, ups and downs, even humiliation at times. I had used every trick in the book to make this happen and here I was, sitting with my beloved boat on my journey home!

"We did it, sweetheart! We did it! Let us get home safely now!" I told the boat as I tried eating my share of the *rasagullas*. It would be a while before I could swallow one but when I did, it tasted very, very good.

Wednesday, 13 Jan 2010 – Past the Horn!
Mhadei crossed the Horn at about 1500 h GMT on 12 Jan in a howling gale that seems to be going from bad to worse! At present trying to maintain a north-easterly course. More later...

Later in the afternoon of 12 Jan as we were surfing down the steep swells with the Argentine coastline standing tall on our port, I sighted an Argentine icebreaker coming out of the Beagle Channel. They were off to Antarctica for an ice patrol and I had been expecting them. We spoke on the VHF and they invited me to enter Ushuaia in Argentina instead of going to the Malvinas, as they call the Falkland Islands. It was a tempting offer with the weather I was facing, a groaning steering and a wind vane that kept threatening to strike work anytime. I decided against it, thanked the icebreaker for the offer, wished them luck for their voyage and continued on my northeast course.

As it got dark, I started getting an urge to sail through the Le Maire Strait or Estrecho de le Maire to reduce the distance I would need to travel to reach Port Stanley. The strait is a 15 nm wide passage between Tierra del Fuego on the west and the island of Isla de los Estados on the east. I am not sure whether it was the fatigue, uncertainty of the last month and the weather, wanting to get in a harbour quickly or the newfound bravado developed on rounding the Horn, but the route through the strait started looking very inviting. Luckily, better sense prevailed and I decided to consult the *Sailing Directions* for the area before taking any action. These books give detailed navigational information about an area and are a must-read for all navigators. I soon realised how bad my decision would have been as the book described in detail the strong tidal currents, funneling winds and rocks in the area. It would have been too dangerous to try and attempt a passage through the strait on a dark windy night with a fragile steering. "It is just not worth it to save a few miles. I'd rather be in the safety of the open sea," I thought, deciding to continue on the course I was on.

That night, lying on the bunk, having a brief shut-eye, I started feeling a change in the boat's motion. A bit worried, I looked up at the chart plotter and was surprised to see the GPS regularly showing a speed of 14 kts. This was almost 5 kts more than the maximum speed *Mhadei* usually did! We were down to the minimum sail we could use, with the fourth reef in the main and no headsail, sailing a broad reach to keep the steep swell behind us and here she was screaming down faster than ever. Obviously, the Southern Ocean current was helping us in a big way. The wind vane seemed to be doing a good job of keeping the boat on course though.

"Looks like there is nothing more I can do," I thought, as I got back to the bunk, trying my best to stop worrying and get some sleep. Sometimes, one just needs to let things happen!

By around 0915 h on the morning of 14 Jan, I sighted Beauchene Island, the southernmost island of the Falkland Island group. The wind had started reducing and I wasn't sure of covering the 100-odd miles to Port Stanley that day, so I sent an email intimating my arrival for the morning of 15 Jan. The weather forecast was predicting a short lull followed by another blow, which I was very keen to avoid. By the evening, I realised I would be able to reach my destination by midnight so I called John Pollard, our agent at Port Stanley, asking if it would be possible to get in by midnight or whether I should weather out the storm outside and enter at first light. He had been a paratrooper with the Royal Army, as I came to know later, and his reply was typical.

"No question of staying out in this weather if you can avoid it. A boat will be present at the harbour mouth at 2300 h to guide you in."

"But wouldn't it be a problem doing Customs and Immigration formalities at this late hour with such short notice?" I asked, used to the way things work back home.

"Don't you worry about that, just get in. Let me start working on things," was the curt but extremely heartening reply.

As planned, by 2300 h we were close to Port Stanley Harbour and I sighted the small light of the pilot boat bobbing through the big swells. As we entered the sheltered waters of the harbour, the swell that had been my constant companion for a month suddenly disappeared and it felt a bit odd to steer *Mhadei* through calm waters. By 0100 h on 15 Jan we were tied securely alongside and I was filled with a sense of relief. We had managed to sail the better part of the Pacific and round Cape Horn despite all the problems on the boat and the resultant anxieties. I slept like a log that night and had to be woken up around 0900 h the next morning by John and the Customs officer.

Chapter 27

Hop Across the Atlantic

The first day in Port Stanley was spent getting my land legs back and meeting people, including the Indian Defence Advisor, who had flown down all the way from London on a 16-hour flight. The Royal Navy offered free accommodation at their facility and I promptly took up the offer. Staying in naval accommodation and dining in the wardroom somehow made me feel at home. Blame it on spending all my working life in the Navy! Also, as we were to discover in a few days, the wardroom served the best food in town and I had a lot of catching up to do to nourish myself back to shape. The first night as I walked into a local pub with John, he announced that he had with him a guy who had just rounded the Horn singlehanded in a sailboat. Suddenly there was a moment's silence in the pub followed by a flurry of congratulations and offers to buy me a drink. I don't remember buying a single drink that night!

The Royal Navy had planned to escort us ceremoniously in Port Stanley on 16 Jan but thanks to the strong Southern Ocean current we had landed up a day early on a pitch dark night. I had been asked by NHQ, on rounding the Horn, to delay my arrival till 16 Jan and had flatly refused to play ball, having had my share of Southern Ocean thrashing for the time being. So on the morning of 16 Jan we sailed out again to rendezvous with HMS *York*, a Type 42 destroyer on deployment to the Falkland Islands. It was a glorious day with a clear blue sky, calm sea and good breeze. I hadn't seen such a clear day since leaving Lyttelton and felt great sailing *Mhadei* in the harbour. The ship with her helicopter and boats escorted us till the narrow harbour mouth, both of us photographing each other with mutual admiration. Port Stanley boasts a population of less than 3,000 humans and over 750,000 sheep. While the majority of the population preferred to graze on the hills and ignored us, word had gotten around the minority human population about our arrival and I counted at least six sailing boats, two people on horseback and one kayak waving to us as we entered. We were the first Indian sailing boat ever to enter Port Stanley, the weather was perfect and it was time to show off a bit by sailing past the colourful town with full sails. It was an exhilarating experience!

The ceremonials over, it was time to start sorting out the repairs on the boat and get her ready for the next leg. Abhilash arrived shortly with a bag full of spares; the rest had been shipped directly to Port Stanley from the US and Europe. It was only when we started getting our act together in Port Stanley that I realised how remote the place was with a total of one flight a week from Santiago, Chile. That meant that if the necessary spares were not shipped in time, we would get stuck for another week till they arrived by the next flight a week later. Needless to say, there was no one on the islands who would stock items for yachts. With such constraints, it was important to prioritise and plan properly, something I had started doing while still at sea. The first priority was to make the wind vane and steering absolutely reliable.

I had been discussing my wind vane problems with the wind vane designer Ron Geick at Scanmar International, USA, who had supplied the equipment to us. He figured out the problem almost immediately and came up with a solution. Apparently, most boats have a wheel with either six or eight spokes so the standard wind vane drum attachment for the wheel is designed accordingly. For some strange reason, our wheels had seven spokes and, thanks to our inexperience, we had fitted the standard attachment to it, not realising the implications. I couldn't believe how simple the issue had been. Ron agreed to ship a new drum free of cost while adding a pair of better quality blocks to improve the performance of the wind vane. Repairs to the electronic autopilots, however, proved much more difficult and in the end I decided to continue to Cape Town without fully repairing them. The idea was to use the wind vane as the primary self-steering while using the electronic autopilots for short durations when absolutely necessary. The generator proved to be equally difficult and despite the best efforts of local technicians, including a team from the Royal Navy, we could barely get it going.

Friday, 22 Jan 2010 – Greetings from Port Stanley

Looks like many are wondering about our disappearance after rounding the Horn almost a week back! Apologies for not updating the blog earlier but things moved a bit too fast after the Horn and the crew kept getting busier as we entered the port and got on to the most important task of turning around Mhadei for the next leg. We are at present berthed at Port Stanley, getting the steering and generator fixed while also pampering Mhadei by meeting her small little demands which, while not critical, are best attended to when there is a little shore time. She has weathered the Pacific at a trot and deserves all the attention! Meanwhile the crew, Lt Cdr Abhilash Tomy, who landed up a day after I reached to help me with the work, and I, are being looked after by the British Armed Forces and the friendly Falkland islanders. This is perhaps the first time an Indian boat has touched the shores of the islands so we are quite a novelty here. We landed up in time to meet 'Ocean Watch' and her crew. It was great to exchange notes with her skipper Mark Schrader who has two solo circumnavigations under his belt. Taking heed of the old saying that 'a picture is worth a thousand words,' I will stop writing for now and let the viewers see some photos of the trip from rounding the Horn till reaching Stanley. Hopefully this will make up for the silence of the last few days to some extent!

It was good to meet Mark Schrader who was skippering the boat *Ocean Watch* around the American continent. Part of a research project, they had started from Seattle on the west coast of the US, had crossed north of the American continent during the Arctic summer and were getting ready to round the Horn before heading back north again. Mark had been a long-time user of the monitor wind vane, similar to what was fitted on *Mhadei*. He dropped by on the boat, had a look at the steering arrangements and advised me on the best ways to use the equipment, the first time anyone was doing so. The advice helped, improving my handling of the wind vane considerably and making me more confident with it.

Thursday, 28 Jan 2010 – Friends in Falklands
It has been over a week since we reached Port Stanley and time seems to have flown by. The repairs are progressing well and it looks like we will be able to sail out on 01 Feb as planned. A short sortie to test the autopilots this morning went off well except for the tricky coming alongside in gale force

wind, which seems to be a norm here rather than an exception! As mentioned in the last blog, we were in time to meet up with Ocean Watch of 'Around Americas' fame and see them off on their next leg. The local populace here has been really accommodating. Realising that we were extremely short on time and couldn't do much sightseeing, some of them decided to visit us and were captured on camera by my shutterbug crew Abhilash. Talking about friends working in the harbour, my thoughts are often with Jessica, battling the South Atlantic gales and nursing EPL from her knockdowns. In fact every time a gale passes over Stanley, more of a daily occurrence in the past few days, I tend to look up and tell the wind, "Hey! Ease up as you go, there is a brave girl sailing that way!" While Jesse was celebrating Australia Day on 26 Jan talking to Kevin Rudd and screaming up the South Atlantic, my crew and I spent the 60th Republic Day of India putting in a couple of hours of extra work to fix up my steering and the generator. I doubt how many know that the two countries celebrate these days together!

It was extremely windy inside the harbour while tied alongside, often to a point where the boat would be heeling making it difficult to work. One afternoon, with the wind blowing at over 35 kts, we were pondering over the best time to change the navigation light fitted right at the top of the mast. We had waited for a few days but the wind had continued to howl and I had run out of patience. I asked Abhilash to hoist me up on a halyard to enable me to change the light. He was concerned about my safety and wondered if we should wait for another day for the wind to subside.

"I think it is Murphy at work again. If we do this now, I am sure the wind will subside tomorrow but if we don't, it will be stronger tomorrow and we may find it impossible to do the job." I told him, sounding very superstitious. "Just leave the halyard and let me fall in the water if you find me getting blown off by the wind. I would rather fall in the water from a height than get smashed on the mast." Eventually, I managed to go up and replace the light without getting blown off and the wind did subside the next day!

While the work schedule during the stopover remained as busy as the previous stopovers, we did manage to take a few hours off once in a while to have a look at the rugged and windswept island. The landscape reminded me of the Tibetan landscape I had walked through over 10 years ago; stark, treeless and without any sign of human habitation for miles on end. Thanks to the strong winds and extreme cold there are no indigenous trees but the island is teeming with wildlife that survives on the bounty from the sea. Penguins, seals, dolphins, cormorants...the list goes on.

One evening over dinner in the wardroom, Abhilash was pulling my leg, observing that I managed to locate an Indian friend or relative in every port I visited.

"Not in the Falklands! I am sure we are the only two Indians here!" I said with some conviction. Within minutes, however, there were noises of an argument at the door and in walked an Indian-looking man in his 60s with a sentry hot on his heels trying to stop him!

"Hello, I am Dr Bharadwaj. I heard about the Indian boat and I had to come and meet you guys," he said.

For a while, I thought my brain was playing tricks on me while Abhilash started giggling with an 'I told you so!' expression on his face. As it turned out, Dr Bharadwaj, now a British citizen, had not only been born and brought up in India, he had also started his medical career by serving with the Indian Army as a doctor for five years. He was filling in for the local anaesthesi ologist while the latter was away on holiday. I do not argue anymore when someone tells me that there is no place in the world where an Indian cannot be found.

One evening, as we were settling our bills at a restaurant that advertised WiFi connectivity, Abhilash asked the lady at the counter about Internet costs.

"How much does the Internet cost per hour?"

"Ten pounds per hour is the rate here, sir."

"Do you have any other plans?" asked Abhilash innocently, looking for cheaper tariffs, while I started laughing, realising the confusion that was about to take place.

"No, I am free in the evening!" replied the lady, catching poor Abhilash unawares.

"Er, actually I was wondering if you have any other Internet plans," said Abhilash, realising the confusion he had caused and trying to salvage the situation.

"No, we don't. But I am still free in the evening," replied the lady, as all of us burst out laughing.

"I have been on this island for over 10 months and no one has asked me that question before!" sighed the lady.

Time flew by at Port Stanley and we managed to get *Mhadei* ready as best as we could before the planned date of departure of 01 Feb. We had enjoyed our stay at Port Stanley, nursed our wounds and it was time to get to sea again for the hop across the South Atlantic. On the morning of 01 Feb, we were blessed by the local priest who used to be a submariner in his younger days and seen off by the Governor and his wife. As we got out of the harbour, we were joined by our 'Royal Escort', HMS *York*, which escorted us out of the bay.

Wednesday, 03 Feb 2010 – Off again!

We are back at sea after a memorable send-off by the Governor of the Falklands and HMS York, among others, at 1000 h on 01 Feb 2010. Thanks to the hospitality of the Falklanders and the British armed forces, the crew, though busy with repair work onboard, had a great time ashore and are back to the task of finding their rested sea legs. Mhadei is moving along nicely with a much lighter steering post repairs and considerably less swell than experienced during the previous leg. Apart from a couple of hrs of gusty winds touching 40 kts as a front passed over us yesterday it has been good sailing so far with clear skies and moderate winds. In fact as I write there is a beautiful yellow moon rising ahead of us leading the way to Africa, 3,000 nm across the Atlantic. Gales are predicted for the next two days but we will deal with them when we meet them. Now, it is time to enjoy the sail on a calm moonlit night.

Monday, 08 Feb 2010 – Riding a weather system's tail!

Since this morning we seem to have stepped on the tail of an east moving weather system. So big seas, strong winds and a nice following current translating into almost 100 nm through the day! Bit of a wild ride but the boat's holding well and miles are being eaten up, so well worth getting tossed about. Let's see how long we are able to hold on to it! We have finally left the 'Furious Fifties' behind and are trying to cross the 'Roaring Forties' in a hurry before the next system, already forming to our west, catches up with us. It is definitely getting warmer with clearer skies and a sun that actually warms you up.

Since a lot of readers have written that they don't understand much of the sailing jargon, I am attaching a simplified version of the Beaufort wind scale to make things easier. This was given to me by my hosts Pip and John in Fremantle, both experienced sailors themselves. I actually find it more realistic and easy to relate to than the real Beaufort scale!

Thursday, 11 Feb 2010 – Clear sky! After many days!

After over three days of non-stop gales, today was the clearest sky I saw in a long time. The sun was up and warm and it was great working on deck barefoot and without any woollens. Can't remember when I did that last, probably not since leaving Australia in November! The wind has stayed a steady 10 to 15 kts from west-north-west and with a comfortable westerly swell Mhadei has been doing a north-easterly course almost on her own. It is strange how the mind forgets the misery of bad weather days and starts enjoying the good ones. There is a star-studded night outside, as I write, with a gentle 12-kt breeze and a following current making us move at over 7 kts with hardly any bouncing about. I think we bounced around more while tied alongside at Port Stanley. A cold front is expected to pass us later tonight so the winds will pick up and it will be time to shorten sail. Till then enjoying the moment!

I took advantage of the respite in the weather to finish off a few interviews by email. By now the questions had started repeating themselves and it was easy to answer them quickly on a good weather day. It was fun, especially when some of the questions in the interview went like this:

First, about the crew:

1. How many members are sailing with you and are they your friends from before? You also keep referring to a 'skipper' in your blog. Can you tell me more about him? What are their names and experiences?

   We are a crew of three and have known each other for as long as I can remember. Best of friends all, in fact you can't get a more cohesive team than this. Names? I, me, myself! I am sailing alone, I thought you knew that!

2. Also, tell me something about the chef, his name. He sounds like a strong-headed guy, considering he refuses to, as you have stated, cook when the water's choppy as the utensils refuse to stay on the gas.

I think the answer above explains how the cook manages to get away with gross indiscipline!

The voyage:

3. Now for some serious questions; how easy or stressful is it to sail in the ocean?

Depends on the weather and problems in the boat among other things. If the weather is fine with good breeze and everything is working properly in the boat, it is easy and can be a pleasure. The difficulties and stress levels go up if things start going wrong in the boat or as the weather starts going from bad to worse.

4. Can anyone be a sailor? Obviously it takes more than just knowledge and experience to undertake a voyage like this. Your comment.

Of course, anyone can be a sailor! I had never stepped on a sailboat till I was 21 and never sailed solo till less than a year back! There is no substitute to knowledge and experience but that can be built up by anyone willing to make the necessary efforts.

About Mhadei:

5. How do you manage your wardrobe...by that I mean, do you carry loads of clothes so that one doesn't have to do laundry? (Sorry, I know mundane questions, but will add some life to the story.)

The best part of sailing alone is that you can wear what you feel is

comfortable without having to worry about what it looks or smells like! I
carry extra clothes to avoid washing them at sea.

6. It will be nice if, in fact, you guys do your laundry, and have
   some interesting or funny anecdotes to share.

   There is enough to keep one busy onboard than bother about laundry!
   But if one has to do it, probably one of the easiest ways would be to tie
   a pair of clothes with a rope and let them trail behind the boat for a few
   hours. Natural washing machine! The clothes will get sanitised with all
   that salt water. Rinse them in fresh water before drying if you want them
   soft or dry them straight if you like them starched!

About yourself:

7. Obviously the voyage you and your crew members have taken
   is not only amazing but requires as much courage as experience. What kind of mind conditioning did you have to put
   yourself through to actually even think of undertaking something like this?

   When I volunteered for this project, I had no clue what I was getting
   into. It sounded like a nice idea and I volunteered without giving it a
   thought. Once I started reading up on the subject, I realised this was some-
   thing far bigger and more difficult than what I had imagined, which made
   it that much more exciting. As we progressed through the project, things
   kept getting busier and busier till one day it was time to leave! Don't think
   I had the time, inclination or energy for any mind conditioning!

8. Also, it's obvious that as teammates, you guys need a lot of
   understanding and coordination onboard to handle any given
   situation. So, apart from technical talks, what kind of conversations do you have? Any anecdotes you can remember?

Having realised the composition of the team, I am sure you will appreciate that all the conversation onboard happens without opening the mouth and it will be too complicated to make any anecdotes out of it!

9. Tell me what you don't write on your blog...in terms of your fears, some altercation with one of the crew members, highs and lows of sailing for days on end.

There are good days and there are bad days, like on land. You go through a whole spectrum of emotions from raw fear, excitement and elation to being down in the dumps and exuberance! Altercations with my crew? Plenty. Luckily none of them ever shouts back at the other!

By the time I finished answering, I was rolling with laughter! Needless to say, I never saw this particular interview getting published and took the liberty of sharing it with the readers of this book.

Sunday, 14 Feb 2010 – A year and 23,000 miles

Mhadei completed one year of service with the Navy on 12 Feb 10, completing almost 23,000 nm in her brief lifetime. Not too bad for a yacht that is the first of her kind in the country. Had she been a naval ship the crew would have been celebrating her anniversary, maybe cutting a cake. We celebrated doing some smooth and fast sailing, eating up over 170 nm in a day! It has been good sailing the past few days. Not always very smooth, with the winds regularly touching 30 kts, but fairly fast with sunny days and starry nights that you can sit out and enjoy as it is not that cold anymore. The swell is less than what we had been experiencing in the Pacific and that really helps. The forecast for the next few days is predicting winds over 20 kts with the inevitable gales thrown in. We are already at the edge of the Roaring Forties and getting pushed north with a strong south-westerly wind. Would like to remain here a little longer, though, to take advantage of the good winds and avoid slowing down in the high pressure systems further north. Ending this with Valentine's Day greetings from the middle of the South Atlantic! Have a great day!

Wednesday, 17 Feb 2010 – Out of the Roaring Forties

After experiencing a last big roar of almost 36 hrs of gale force winds, we finally seem to be out of the clutches of the Roaring Forties. The roar did push us a little more to the north than expected, though not enough to get into a high pressure system and risk getting becalmed. Sailing at the edge of the system and getting good westerly winds since morning. With a moderate following sea Mhadei is cruising along under clear sunny skies! The forecast looks good for the next couple of days after which the wind is expected to turn southeast which would mean head winds and slamming into the swell till Cape Town. Well, we will see when we reach there! At present, enjoying the sail with the weather getting warmer by the day. No more woollens or boots required during the day and the morning cup of coffee can be had sitting out on the deck rather than standing as close to the stove as possible!

Friday, 19 Feb 2010 – Back to the Eastern Hemisphere

We crossed the Prime Meridian at 2253 h tonight and are back in the Eastern Hemisphere after a little over two months. Another great day of sailing! Not very fast but absolutely peaceful with a flat sea, gentle breeze and clear sky. Little wonder that the cook finally got inspired and whipped up a delicious 'Risotto con Gamberi e Funghi'. A nice lunch under a blue sky without wearing any woollens, washed down with a bottle of Monsoon beer from New Zealand followed by the mandatory siesta. Can life get any better! Tomorrow will be the last of the peaceful days after which the weatherman has fixed up a date with the Cape Town doctor which would mean strong head winds and seas all the way to Cape Town!

The good sailing lasted for another day before we started getting bashed by the strong south-easterly winds, common around the southwest coast of Africa. With the wind and swell coming almost from the direction we wanted to head into and a current against us, it was an uncomfortable leg all the way to Cape Town. The night before reaching Cape Town, as the boat was bashing her way upwind, I got the feeling she was yawing a bit more than normal, though still heading in the general direction I wanted her to go. Usually I would have tried to check out the cause promptly but the last few days of constant bashing against the wind and swell had sapped me and I let her sail the way she wanted to. In the morning, closer to Cape Town as I started doing my usual checks to get her ready to enter harbour, I realised that the wind vane water paddle, a very crucial component of the wind vane, had broken and disappeared! This meant that *Mhadei*, well balanced and sailing upwind, had been sailing on her own and without any self- steering throughout the night. She did gently try to tell her exhausted skipper that something was wrong and she needed his attention by yawing more than normal, but finding no response continued heading for her destination.

By 0600 h on 25 Feb, sipping a hot mug of coffee, I sighted the tall mountains surrounding Cape Town. It was a welcome and familiar sight! The Atlantic crossing was almost over. I had been to Cape Town earlier and found it to be one of the most scenic cities I had visited. Nestled in the lap of the imposing Table Mountain, the city traces its origins to a small outpost created to meet the demands of mariners by the Dutch East India Company, earning itself the befitting sobriquet, 'The Tavern of the Seas'!

"What a welcome sight it must have been over 400 years ago, sighting the Table Mountain from the sea, at the end of a long voyage!" I thought as we started closing in on the coast. As I was getting the boat ready to enter harbour, I noticed a big tear on the stay sail and damage to the main halyard. The former, no doubt a result of the flogging the sail received while getting out of Lyttelton. "Two more items on the repair list", I thought, thankful that the damages hadn't occurred earlier.

We were soon joined by a few boats, including the South African Navy's sailing yacht, and escorted to our berth at the Victoria and Alfred Waterfront. It almost felt like coming home, meeting old sailing buddies from the South African Navy, the Indian Defence Advisor and even an Indian Air Force officer, Wg Cdr Y Y P Rao, on deputation to the UN who had travelled all the way from Congo to meet us. We had been together at the National Defence Academy more than 20 years back and then at Port Blair when I volunteered for the project. Seeing the insignias he was wearing, a journalist couldn't resist the temptation to ask, "What is the United Nations doing here?"

"Oh! He is the special envoy from the United Nations who has been deputed to welcome us," I replied, keeping a straight face.

That night as I made my arrival report to NHQ I wrote that since my shore support crew, Abhilash, was still stuck in Delhi sorting out his paperwork to join me, the UN had decided to help me out by sending a shore support crew. *Mhadei* had crossed the Southern Ocean ahead of her shore support in every port, emphatically proving that it is easier to cross the Southern Ocean than negotiating the South Block! (That's the building that houses the defence and foreign ministries in Delhi.)

Chapter 28

Home Run

We soon settled down to the harbour routine of getting my land legs back and getting the boat ready for the next leg. Unlike other ports, I wasn't too stressed out at Cape Town about the boat's repairs. It is a very 'yacht-friendly' port with most repair facilities readily available. We had bought the mast and rigging from Cape Town and the mast maker, Southern Spars, had promised free servicing while Ratnakar had promised to drop by to help us get back on our feet. The voyage seemed to be over already! I decided to stop bothering about the work schedule for a while and concentrate instead on getting myself in shape. I had dreamt of climbing Table Mountain the first time I had set eyes on it and this was probably the best way to get my legs back in shape.

Thursday, 18 Mar 2010 – Greetings from Cape Town
I suppose the only way I can start this post is by apologising to all the readers for going missing for the past 20 days! Blame it on being busy, lazy and an erratic Internet connection!

Time seems to be flying by in sunny Cape Town with repairs to Mhadei and a bit of R&R keeping us busy. Most of the repairs fall in the 'desirable' rather than 'essential' category which means I could have sailed back home without undertaking them but decided to get them done here due to better availability of spares and skills. Hopefully in times to come the necessary spares and skills for yacht repairs will become readily available in India. Also since we bought the mast and rigging from Cape Town it made sense to get the same serviced at Cape Town. With Ratnakar, the boat builder, dropping by for 10 days we managed to get most of the small repair jobs out of the way. Now awaiting the replacements for furler foils from France, routine repairs to the sails by the local North Sails loft and fitting of the generator post-servicing. Planning to sail out on 29 Mar so as to reach Mumbai around 16 May. Another reason for the longish stay at Cape Town is to avoid the cyclone season in the Southern Indian Ocean which usually lasts till end Apr. Starting in end Mar would ensure that we enter the Trade Winds zone, where the tropical cyclones mostly occur, by end Apr. It will also mean crossing the equator around early May with a hope that the Doldrums will be in a disturbed state due to the onset of the southwest monsoons. If the monsoons set in slightly earlier than usual (last year they were really late), we can have a fast downwind ride all the way home!

Though this is my third visit to Cape Town, I am still in awe of the spectacular beauty of the city and surroundings. The high point of the R&R was a walk up Table Mountain which made me regain my land legs quickly. I think anyone who is reasonably fit and has a day to spare in the city should give it a try!

In addition to the seals in the harbour we also have some more interesting company in the form of Phoenicia, a replica of a Phoenician sailboat trying to recreate the first circumnavigation of Africa by the Phoenicians in 600 BC. You can read about the project on their website, www.phoenicia.org.uk.

It was amazing to see the *Phoenicia* berthed next to us. The fact that she had sailed safely across the Indian Ocean was a tribute to the seamanship skills of her skipper Philip Beale and his crew of volunteers. Compared to her, built the way the Phoenicians built their boats in 600 BC, *Mhadei* definitely looked state of the art.

One of the common questions I was asked was, "How do you manage your sleep as the boat needs to continue sailing at all times?" I would answer that I take cat naps whenever possible but always found it difficult to make people understand how exactly I managed it. One day as I was showing the boat to some visitors from the South African Weather Service, a lady in the group gave me the perfect answer!

"Oh, I understand exactly how you would be doing it," she said, "You see, I have a two-month-old baby. At night, when the baby needs me, I wake up, feed and clean the baby and go to sleep till the baby needs me again. I don't follow any particular routine but have been managing well so far. In your case you have a boat that demands your attention instead of a baby." It was such a simple but perfect explanation!

Time flew by in Cape Town. The whole country was getting ready to host the Soccer World Cup and the spirit was contagious! I was keen to get clear of the southern latitudes before the onset of winter in the Southern Hemisphere. We had managed to fix up everything on the boat except the generator, which kept up its erratic behaviour. I finally decided to just live with the erratic generator for the rest of the trip and leave on 03 Apr. There didn't seem to be much point in delaying the departure anymore.

In the morning, while the city was enjoying a leisurely Easter weekend under a clear sky, we were seen off by a group of friends at the Victoria and Alfred Waterfront. It had been a wonderful stopover and I had every intention of returning to this great city with *Mhadei* in not too distant a future. It wasn't just wishful thinking; a rough plan was already being formed. If things worked to plan, we would be sailing back to Cape Town in less than a year. Eventually, things did work out that way and we were back before the end of the year! But that would be the sequel to this book!

Monday, 05 Apr 2010 – Back to sea: Homeward bound!

We are back at sea again having left Cape Town at 1030 h on 03 Apr. Both Mhadei and her crew thoroughly enjoyed the hospitality and pampering lavished on us by the warm 'Cape Townians'! Both of us would definitely love to come back here some day.

The plan was to head well to the south before turning east to keep clear of the Agulhas Bank which is notorious for its west-flowing Agulhas current and freak waves. As often happens, things didn't go quite as per plan. The southerly winds right after leaving Cape Town pushed us to the southwest for the first day and night, making us move in the direction we came from; that of Port Stanley! By Easter morning, the skipper had had enough of slamming in the wrong direction and decided to head east taking advantage of light south-easterly winds. The winds have remained a comfortable 10 to 15 kts from southeast through the day making slow but steady progress to the east. At this rate, in a couple of hours, we should be crossing Cape Agulhas, the southernmost point of the African continent and saying goodbye to the Atlantic Ocean.

Monday, 12 Apr 2010 – Goodbye to the Southern Ocean

Having crossed the Agulhas Bank and current without getting into the Roaring Forties and seeing a big system moving in from the west, we decided against going any further south and avoid getting into the Southern Ocean. No such luck! The Southern Ocean decided to move up a little and give us a last bit of hiding lest we forget it in a hurry! That meant almost three days of gale force winds with big seas that pushed us well to the northeast. No complaints, of course, as things could have been worse had we stuck to the earlier plan of getting in the Forties. The shackle securing the brand new stay sail to the furler decided to part company, despite all the securing, just as the gales started picking up. It was pointless trying to put in a new one in those conditions so the sail was furled and Mhadei sailed with just the smallest size of mainsail possible. I was surprised how well she managed to hold course at a brisk pace on a broad reach. After sailing her for over 25,000 nm I am still learning to sail her!

The gales got us right under a high pressure system and vanished, leaving us with very light and shifty winds. For a while the calm was good as it allowed things to be put in order both with the boat and the galley but now again we are looking out for some wind!

It wasn't too long before I realised that the light winds and calm seas were a blessing in disguise. One morning as I went about the boat on a routine check, I realised to my horror that the rudder stock had slipped down from its position and was well on its way to getting dislodged from its top bearing. If it had come down any further, especially in big seas when the boat was moving fast, the rudder could have taken away the boat's stern with it! *Mhadei* has a big and heavy rudder and the only way to lift it is using a crane. There was no way I could have lifted the rudder on my own had it come off. Luckily, part of the rudder stock was still held in the top bearing and with the light winds things were manageable. I stopped sailing by getting the sails down, rigged up a tackle from the end of the boom and pulled the rudder stock up in its correct position. One more task was added to the daily checklist!

Thursday, 22 Apr 2010 – Searching for Trade Winds

It has been over 10 days since we said our goodbye to the Southern Ocean and landed under a high pressure system which seemed very reluctant to move in the usual easterly direction and give us some decent wind. A couple of days of light winds were welcomed by the crew after the fury of the Southern Ocean and duly enjoyed lounging on the deck in the cool breeze having good food, doing a bit of maintenance and catching up on 'One Hundred Years of Solitude' by Gabriel Garcia Marquez. The cook got into action serving a wide variety, from the quintessential Mumbai fare of bhelpuri to Thai curries, pasta and risotto! While the crew was having a whale of a time the skipper was wondering about over 4,000 nm of Indian Ocean yet to be covered!

As the high pressure system slowly inched eastward, the wind started picking up, unfortunately from north northeast which is exactly the direction we want to go in. Thanks to the direction of the wind and the resultant swell we have been sailing close-hauled for over a week now, barely managing to do either a north northwest or east southeast course with frequent tacks, sail changes and the boat pitching all the time. While we are still about 300 nm from the Tropic of Capricorn, the weather has already started showing signs of the tropics with day temperatures in the 30s and occasional squalls which give gusty winds from any direction while they are around and take away most of the wind when they move on, leaving us with a nice swell for company! The ever present albatrosses have parted company and we should be entering the territory of dolphins and flying fish soon.

The weather forecast is predicting north-easterly winds for a few more days till we meet up with the steady south-easterly Trade Winds for making a dash to the equator.

Been reading about Jessica and the weather she has been facing. Despite the slow progress we are making I don't envy her much for that. Looks like she is in for a fast run home!

That night as I was about to get into my bunk, we were caught by a freak squall that ripped the genoa, not as badly as the last time but enough to make it unusable. There had been no sign of the squall visually or on the radar till less than 30 minutes back when I had done a routine check. This was bad news, especially as we were expecting lighter winds for the rest of the trip home and needed the large sail to give us some speed. It would be a few days before I could replace the torn sail with the spare I was carrying.

At around 0430 h on the morning of 27 Apr, as the chart showed us nearing the island of Mauritius, I tried to tune in my FM radio and was greeted with a welcome blast of Bollywood songs. It felt like being home! The east south-easterly winds posed a dilemma, whether to go east of the island with stronger winds and bigger swells with a risk of drifting on to the island or to pass in the lee of the island from its west. I finally decided to take it easy and cross the island from its west. I was in no hurry and it was nice to sail past the island sedately as the day broke, listening to Bollywood songs, monitoring port traffic from Port Louis and reliving memories of the last visit less than a year ago.

Saturday, 01 May 2010 – Cruising in the Trade Winds
We crossed the beautiful island of Mauritius on the morning of 27 Apr. Passing less than 5 nm from the island, it was tempting to stop by and meet up with friends from the last visit less than a year back. Last year on 09 Jun I had sailed out of Port Louis, Mauritius, for Mhadei's last trial before the circumnavigation and my first solo sail and here we were back in the same place from the other side of the world. In a way this completed the circumnavigation though we still need to get back home 2,000 nm away.

The elusive southeast Trades finally showed up after crossing the Tropic

of Capricorn and since then Mhadei has been cruising along at a clip head-
ing straight for Mumbai. This blissful state may last for a day or two before
we hit the frustrating Doldrums and start playing cat and mouse with the
shifty and light winds. North of the equator the wind seems to have slowly
started shifting west as the southwest monsoon season approaches. Hoping
that it will set in by the time we cross the equator in a week's time for a nice
downwind leg home.

The tropics are making their presence felt in more ways than one, with the
temperature inside the boat remaining above 30°C almost all the time which
makes life a bit uncomfortable. So a lot of time, especially at night, is spent
sitting out enjoying the cool breeze under a clear moonlit sky!

Worried about the threat of piracy in the waters between
Mauritius and India, the Navy had deputed a naval ship to escort us all the way home. It took some time for the escort to get
used to the erratic ways of a sailboat in tropical waters. When
the winds picked up, we would be charging ahead, not necessarily on a straight course to our destination, making them huff and
puff to keep up with us. When the winds died down we would be
drifting around aimlessly, making the escort wonder if there was
something wrong with us and offering to provide assistance; this
was always declined politely. That would leave him no option
but to keep going around in circles trying to keep us in sight.
Eventually, we learned to live with each other, ignoring the other
most of the time and content with photographing each other
whenever we got close.

Thursday, 06 May 2010 – *Across the equator*
We bid goodbye to the Southern Hemisphere today after spending eight event-
ful months in it and crossed into the Northern Hemisphere at 1639 h local

time. This was our fourth equator crossing in less than a year so Neptune's sentinels let us pass without even giving us a second glance! So far the progress has been better than expected though the Doldrums must have shifted north with the Sun and we may yet encounter them as we move north. Since the last two days, contrary to all weather predictions we have been getting strong westerly winds. If these are an indication of an early south-westerly monsoon setting in, we should be extremely lucky because in that case the Doldrums will be in a disturbed state and we can get out of their clutches easily.

It is getting hotter by the day with the temperature inside the boat refusing to come down below 32°C at any time! All the water that evaporates from the sea during the hot day comes down at night as thundershowers with strong gusty winds and sheets of rain! So we are settling into an interesting routine of staying awake during the night controlling the boat and unable to sleep during the day due to the heat.

The chef suffered a bit of a setback today with the discovery or rather non-discovery of any butane gas in the gas cylinder. That definitely is the end of any cooking onboard and the chef will need to be at his creative best to make unheated canned food taste palatable till we reach home 1,200 nm away!

Running out of cooking gas turned out to be a bigger cause for concern than I had imagined initially. It was unexpected as I had started using a new cylinder a few days before entering Cape Town and judging by the days the previous one had lasted, I saw no reason for the new one to run out. Obviously the cylinder, having stayed in the boat for almost nine months, had developed a leak and the gas had leaked out. While provisioning at Cape Town I had divided my food into two categories: the heat-and-eat type of food for the rough seas south of Africa and proper food that needed cooking for the rest of the trip through the tropics. I had already finished most of the heat-and-eat type of food and so had landed in a peculiar situation where I had plenty of food in the boat but no means to cook it with. The winds had already become very light and shifty, often reducing the boat's speed to less than that required to maintain a steady course. To add to our woes, early morning on 07 May, we were hit by another squall that tore off the genoa yet again! This was the spare sail I had put up with considerable effort a few days ago, and now that was gone too! There was no other replacement available on the boat. I cursed and howled at the sea, the wind, the boat and practically everything under the sun including myself, finally reconciling to even slower progress without the largest head sail.

Thursday, 13 May 2010 – 500 miles from home!

The Doldrums did finally catch up with us with a couple of windless days. One night it became so bad I finally dropped all sails, lashed up the boom and went to sleep letting Mhadei drift around. The next morning turned out to be as windless so had a refreshing swim in the sea, the first time this trip, and started sailing again once a little wind picked up by noon. Been getting light north-westerly winds since then, making slow, but some, progress.

The cooking problem has been sorted out to some extent by using warm water from the water heater which heats up water to about 60°C using the engine coolant. So idling the engine, instead of the generator, to charge the batteries and also for getting warm water once in a few days. A bit of food rationing is being resorted to as the supply of ready-to-eat food, which I usually used to keep for bad weather days, is limited and with the unreliable winds, predicting an ETA even 500 nm away is a bit tricky. The ready-to-eat food is well supplemented by knick-knacks like cereal and chocolate bars, biltong, crackers, canned fruit, etc., so really no cause to worry. In any case the heat really kills one's appetite and what you need is plenty of fluids which are available. The progress in the next few days should give a better idea, at least about the likely day if not the time of crossing the finish line!

The 'sea swim' turned out to be a refreshing break from the monotony of trying to sail on a windless sea under a blazing sun. There was not a whiff of breeze and *Mhadei*, without any sails up, was in no danger of running away without me. I dived under her, did a quick hull inspection and then swam around admiring her. This was the first time I was seeing her from the outside in the middle of the sea and it was difficult to take my eyes off her. She looked gorgeous, the flat sea reflecting on her smooth sides with hardly any sign of the punishment that had been inflicted on her in the past months. I kept going around her in circles, floating on my back in the cool and refreshing sea till I saw our anti-piracy escort closing in to investigate if there was a problem; that's when I realised I was swimming around buck naked!

The monotony of slow progress was broken to some extent with a bit of humour in uniform. The Navy had started planning a grand reception on our arrival. The President of India had agreed to receive us and had been given a date of arrival of 16 May that, thanks to unpredictable winds, we had missed. Having had to tell the President we couldn't make it on time, the Navy had kept some time in hand and invited the Vice President to receive us on 22 May. As luck would have it, we seemed to be on our way to entering earlier than 22 May now. Naval Headquarters, acutely conscious of protocol, didn't want any more changes in the dates and began asking me to slow down and not enter before 22 May.

I was barely moving in the light winds, had my brain fried

with the ever present heat, and was resorting to strict rationing of food onboard in the absence of cooking gas. While I couldn't imagine how the Navy could ask me to stay out for a few days more, just for the sake of protocol, the powers that be couldn't understand how a serving naval officer on a naval boat could question their orders so brazenly. The long and often heated telephone conversations over the satellite phone upset me initially, till I made up my mind that I would enter Mumbai whatever the circumstances. Once my mind was made up, I started seeing the humour in the whole thing! I didn't really have an option. The day I entered, I was surviving on the last of the chocolates and cereal bars. The only other food left onboard was rice and lentils – something I could not cook and thus of little use to me.

Monday, 17 May 2010 – The last 100 miles!

We crossed Goa, Mhadei's birth place, last night and as I write are crossing the port town of Ratnagiri 30 miles to the east, famous for its Alphonso mangoes which will be in season now. A little known fact about the town, which I discovered quite late, is that the last Emperor of Burma was exiled here till his end in the last century. That leaves another 100 miles to Mumbai and the finish line!

It is a clear night outside with a crescent of yellow moon and cool breeze. Enjoying probably the last night of solitude with Mhadei for some time to come, listening to the local radio station. By tomorrow night we will be too close to the coast to relax.

Read about the fabulous and well-deserved welcome for Jessica. I think she has really earned all the accolades being bestowed on her and it will be an honour for us to follow her into the exclusive club of solo circumnavigators!

By the morning of 18 May, we found ourselves some 50 nm

southwest of Mumbai and forced to head towards Africa thanks to a northerly breeze. It was painful not to be able to head home after such a long trip. The debate about our ETA and whether we should stay out till 22 May for the benefit of the Vice President continued! Finally, at around 1330 h, the wind backed to northwest and we tacked on a course that would lead us straight to Mumbai. I passed on an ETA for midnight of 18 May and refused to take any detours or make an attempt to slow down till the next morning. I had been on my feet for the past two nights attempting to dodge the shipping and fishing traffic around the coast and was now tired. There had been two 'near misses' already, with a big merchant ship whizzing past me at less than 50 m and the boat almost landing between a towing ship and its tow.

By 1900 h we got the formal permission to go alongside in Naval Dockyard and, close to midnight, we entered Mumbai harbour with a stiff sea breeze hurrying us in. It didn't feel any different. I don't remember any feeling of excitement. I was probably too busy trying to dodge the port traffic and getting the boat ready to get alongside. At 0030 h on 19 May I motored *Mhadei* inside Naval Dockyard for a subdued but warm reception by close family, friends and all the Admirals present in station standing in uniform! As I passed *Mhadei's* lines to Abhilash, standing on the pontoon, he gave me a triumphant grin and said, "I finally managed to reach a port before you!"

Monday, 31 May 10 – Back home!
This blog is way overdue and my sincere apologies to all the readers for such a long delay. It is amazing how hectic life can become once you finish a trip such as this and just when you badly need a long break!

We reached Mumbai and completed the circumnavigation at 0030 h on 19 May, exactly 09 months after setting out. Till the afternoon of 18 May we were heading for Africa instead of Mumbai, thanks to light northerly winds. Luckily by about 1330 h the wind backed and freshened up allowing us to sail straight towards Mumbai harbour. The uncertainty of the ETA proving once again that 'Sailboats do not have ETAs, they have destinations and that they go towards a destination and not to a destination'. Owing to the uncertainty of the ETA even 12 hrs before arrival, making arrangements for a formal welcome proved difficult. We thus quietly slipped in the Naval Dockyard, from where we had started 09 months back, and were received by close family, friends and the top brass of the Western Naval Command. We slipped out again at first light on 22 May to make a formal entry and were received in right royal style by the Vice President of India Honourable Shri M Hamid Ansari, the Chief of the Naval Staff, the Flag Officer Commanding in Chief, Western Naval Command and a host of other dignitaries. It was good to be back home! The celebrations unfortunately were marred by the news of a horrific air crash of an Air India aircraft that morning at Mangalore.

The week after arrival went in a whirlwind of press briefings, interviews and, most important, making sure Mhadei was well looked after and cared for. She has taken me around the world safely without any major complaints, has been the most forgiving and trusty companion through moments that I cannot share with anyone else and has earned all the TLC I can shower on her and more! Thus, though the trip is over, the work goes on till we manage to put some system in place for her upkeep and utilisation in the future.

I am ending this with some photos and links of our arrival. Also, a big thanks to all the readers of the blog for the support extended by them which came in very handy in keeping up the morale of the crew through-out the trip! And the most important and cherished: a link to Sir Robin Knox-Johnston's website on becoming the 175th member of the exclusive

Solo Circumnavigators' Club! I can't think of a greater honour than being personally welcomed by Sir Robin to this elite club!

Epilogue

Project Sagar Parikrama, as the Navy envisioned it, was completed. A solo unassisted circumnavigation under sail in an Indian built boat was a success. The project, however, was not over for me for a couple of reasons. One of them was a personal goal I had set for myself while planning the project in 2006. Without mentioning it to anyone, I had decided that by the end of the project, I should be able to groom at least one skipper for *Mhadei*. Apart from making sure that the knowledge and experience gained by us during the project were not wasted, it was my way of getting back at the peculiar mindset in the country, where a person after having achieved some experience would be reluctant to share the knowledge with others for the unfounded fear of losing his own importance. I also wanted *Mhadei* to keep sailing, with or without me and on whatever pretext, as that would be the best way to maintain her. At 15 months of service, she was practically a new boat and capable of serving the Navy well for a few decades. I owed it to her and couldn't imagine her falling into disuse and disrepair.

Luckily, once I was past Cape Horn and the success of the project was almost assured, Admiral Awati suggested that we raise the bar and plan the first non-stop solo circumnavigation under sail by an Indian. Our core team, Ratnakar, Abhilash and I, readily agreed. There were no second thoughts about the boat to be used or the skipper; it had to be *Mhadei* skippered by Abhilash. There was no other proven boat in the country nor was there anyone else more experienced than Abhilash. Having had my share of dealing with the bureaucracy, the biggest hurdle I anticipated was that of 'selling' the idea to the Navy.

As luck would have it, during the stopover at Cape Town, our friends from the South African Navy invited us to participate in a race from Cape Town to Rio de Janeiro in Jan 2011. This was a wonderful opportunity to train the new skipper without mentioning the next project. One night, over a nice sushi dinner in Cape Town, we hatched a plan for the future and wrote it down on a scrap of paper. We planned to ask the Navy to let us participate in the Cape to Rio race with a crew, something no Indian boat had done before. Abhilash was to sail the boat back as the new skipper, shorthanded with one crew till Cape Town and then solo till Goa.

The plan worked perfectly! I sailed out to Cape Town with *Mhadei* on 26 Nov 2010, with Abhilash and two volunteers to participate in the Cape to Rio race. On 23 Feb 2011, as I stood at a pier in Rio waving goodbye to a confident Abhilash, watching my beloved *Mhadei* head out into the Atlantic without me, it slowly started sinking in that project Sagar Parikrama, which I volunteered for five years ago out of sheer ignorance, was finally over. All aims had been achieved, all deadlines met and everything had been done within the allocated budget. There was suddenly nothing more to do but to keep track of *Mhadei* and be a good shore support crew for the next project – as Abhilash had been for me.

Glossary

AIS	Automatic Identification System; an automatic tracking system used by ships to identify and locate each other using electronic data exchange
Backing	Anticlockwise shifting of the wind
CNS	Chief of Naval Staff
Corkscrewing	A combination of rolling and pitching
Dinghy	A small boat
Doldrums	Common name for inter-tropical convergence zone that is a band of light variable winds near the equator
EPL	Ella's Pink Lady (Jessica Watson's boat)
ETA	Expected time of arrival
ETD	Expected time of departure
Furious Fifties	Strong westerly winds between 50° and 60° south latitudes
Gennaker	An asymmetrical spinnaker used for sailing downwind in light winds
Genoa	The larger jib
Gybing	Changing the direction of the wind experienced by a boat by moving the stern of

	the boat through the wind; for example, changing from starboard tack to port tack and vice versa
Halyard	A rope used to hoist a sail or flag
Headsail	Sails rigged forward of the mast. Can be a jib (triangular), a spinnaker (a symmetrical sail) or a gennaker (an asymmetrical sail)
Heeling	Leaning of a sailboat to one side owing to external factors like the force of wind on sails, force of waves on the hull or centrifugal force during a turn
Hindustani	A mixture of Hindi and Urdu languages
J 24 boat	A 24 ft long day sailing boat
Jury rig	Improvised rigging made from available tools and material
Keel	Part of the sailboat that helps convert the sideways motion of the boat through the water into forward motion while also acting as a counterweight for the heeling of the boat owing to the force of wind on the sails
Ketch	A sailing boat with two masts where the forward mast (the main mast) is taller than the aft mast (the mizzen mast) and the mizzen mast is forward of the rudder post
Knot (kt)	Unit of speed equal to 1 nautical mile (nm) per hour
Leeward	The direction the wind is blowing towards
Mainsail	The sail on the mainmast of a sailboat located behind the mast

Nautical mile (nm) Unit of distance used at sea; equal to 1.852 km

NBCD Nuclear, Biological, Chemical and Damage Control

NHQ Naval Headquarters

OOW Officer of the Watch

Ocean currents By convention, the direction in which the current is flowing

Open 60 60 ft long, high-performance sailing boat primarily designed for singlehanded ocean races

Pitching Motion of a boat along its beam or transverse axis making the head rise and fall

Port side Left side

Reefing The process of reducing the sail area on a sailboat to prevent the boat from getting overpowered owing to strong winds

Roaring Forties Strong westerly winds between 40° and 50° south latitudes

Rolling The sideways motion of a boat along its fore and aft or longitudinal axis

Screaming Sixties Strong westerly winds between 60° and 70° degree south latitudes

Sheet A rope used to control the movable corners of a sail

Starboard side Right side

Staysail The smaller jib

Tack The relative direction of wind experienced by a boat. If experiencing wind from the starboard side, the boat is said to

	be on starboard tack; if from the port side, then on port tack
Tacking	Changing the direction of wind experienced by a boat by moving the bows of the boat through the wind; for example, changing from starboard tack to port tack and vice versa
Transom	Surface that forms the stern of a boat or ship
Traveller	A mechanical device used to shift the point of attachment of a sheet
VHF	Very high frequency radio
Veering	Clockwise shifting of the wind
Wardroom	Officers' mess on a ship
Wind direction	By convention, the direction from which the wind is blowing
Windward	The direction the wind is coming from

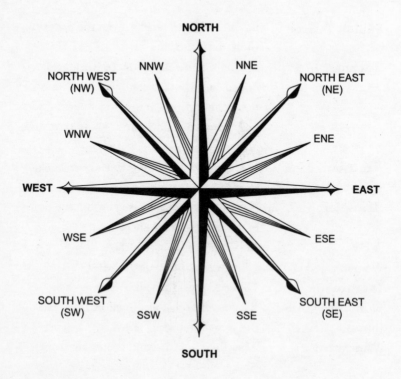

Accepted norms for a circumnavigation under sail

- Should commence and finish in the same port.
- Should cross all the meridians.
- Should cross the equator twice.
- Should not pass through any canals or straits that may require outside assistance or use of engines.
- The distance travelled should be more than 21,600 nm (40,000 km), which is the circumference of the earth.

Sailing Terms

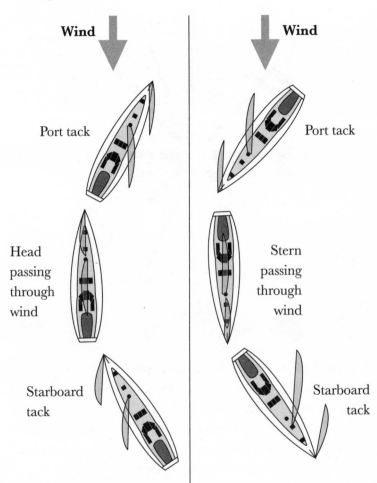

Tacking	Gybing
Changing tack by turning the head through the wind.	Changing tack by turning the stern through the wind.

Points of Sail

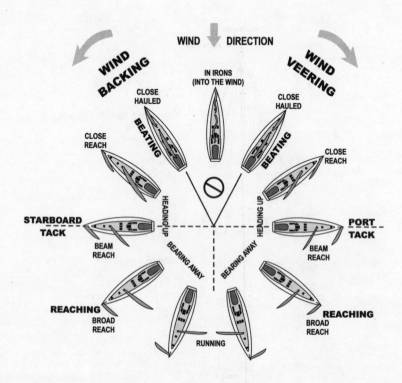

Parts of *Mhadei*

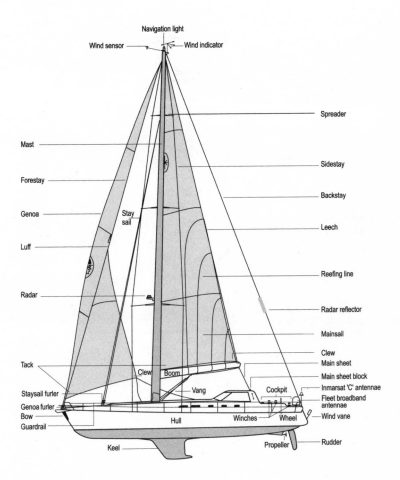

NIGI

As a child, Kiare Ladner wanted to live on a farm, run an orphanage and be on stage. As an adult, she found herself working for academics, with prisoners and on nightshifts. Her short stories have been published in anthologies, broadcast on the radio and shortlisted in competitions, including the BBC National Short Story Award 2018. *Nightshift* is her first novel.

Kiare Ladner

NIGHTSHIFT

PICADOR

First published 2021 by Picador

This paperback edition first published 2022 by Picador
an imprint of Pan Macmillan
The Smithson, 6 Briset Street, London EC1M 5NR
EU representative: Macmillan Publishers Ireland Ltd, 1st Floor,
The Liffey Trust Centre, 117–126 Sheriff Street Upper,
Dublin 1, D01 YC43
Associated companies throughout the world
www.panmacmillan.com

ISBN 978-1-5290-1040-4

1 3 5 7 9 8 6 4 2

A CIP catalogue record for this book is available from the British Library.

Printed and bound by CPI Group (UK) Ltd, Croydon, CR0 4YY

Visit **www.picador.com** to read more about all our books
and to buy them. You will also find features, author interviews and
news of any author events, and you can sign up for e-newsletters
so that you're always first to hear about our new releases.

For Greg

Some are Born to sweet delight,
Some are Born to Endless Night.

WILLIAM BLAKE

PART I

1

At its peak my obsession with her was like a form of self-harm: a private source of pain and comfort.

When I found the ring box in the back of the drawer, I didn't want to open it. Navy and heart-shaped, it has a finely brocaded border and thin silver hook. The lining is pearly satin indented to hold a delicate jewel. A market seller provided it for a sard ring I'd bought, shoving the chunky band determinedly into the slot. I could've saved him the trouble; I'd no need for the box, yet was captivated by its fairytale charm. On leaving the stall, I slid the ring onto my finger and smoothed the satin back into a tight clasp.

For almost two decades, I haven't looked at what's inside the box. Simply having it in the room will hopefully pull me through my task. When doubts hover close, I move it about restlessly. I place it behind my computer as if its reliquary power can channel through the screen, or hide it far away on the windowsill by the mouldy coffee cups. Getting up from my desk, I pace the room with it in my palm.

Since being unable to sleep, I've passed through a shadow curtain. The present has become dark and stagnant; the past circles vividly around me. Sharp memories cut through chronology's thin skin. In the strange energy of these insomniac nights, I have begun to write as consolation. To make a story that will put an end to reliving flash fragments, to remembering only the most troubling details.

Easily, I slip back to the day I first saw her. I had a job in media monitoring; we provided clients in cars and construction with daily updates of press content. The articles were selected by senior analysts; my work was to write the summaries. Given that copying out the opening paragraphs brought no complaints, I wasn't motivated to do much more.

Excused from staff meetings due to client deadlines, I'd twirl about in my office chair. Shutting my eyes, I'd picture the second floor, open plan and strip-lit. The boards separating cubicles decorated with photographs of loved ones, families and pets. One neighbour's neat line-up of sharpened pencils, another's orderly stack of camomile and fennel teas. My desk strewn with tyre-related articles, my board pinned with ideas for me and Graham, my boyfriend. The drawn conference room blinds meant I didn't need to picture my conventionally dressed colleagues. Who were, in turn, spared the sight of me: a woman in a bobbly jumper and jeans with a mid-length tangle of orange hair.

No matter how often I played the game, when I looked again my surroundings would be both as I'd visualized them, and not. The concrete materiality of the objects was identical

4

but the colours, the quality of light, the atmosphere were subtly different. *See*, I'd tell myself, *you don't know it all. Things change. You can't predict how they'll seem in thirty seconds, never mind till the end of time.*

One August morning with sixteen months to the end of the twentieth century, I was more wrong than usual. When I blinked back into the room, a new person was seated opposite me. She didn't appear to have noticed my twirling around in Megan Groenewald's world – but while I'd have noticed her anywhere, in east London suburbia she was like an exotic zebra fish that had swum off course.

She wore a short, black-and-white, Bridget Riley-type number. Her build was lean, long-limbed and coltish; her hair was a shallow sea of inky curls. She had fine, straight features and close-set blue eyes so dark as to glint like pitch. I wanted to introduce myself but the cords that looped from her ears to her Walkman put me off.

Since she was typing like a demon on her keyboard, I flamboyantly increased my own speed. When my document contained more errors than words, I glanced at her. She lifted her head; she had a slight squint.

'I'm Meggie,' I said.

'I'm Sabine.'

'What are you listening to?'

She took her earphones out. Her hands trembled as she passed them over to me; her nails were bitten to such small tabs that her fingers seemed entirely made of skin.

Surprised she didn't mind me sticking her earphones in

my ears, I listened. An expressive male voice sang tenderly to a sweeping accompaniment. Wiping them off with my thumbs before handing them back, I said, 'I like it.'

'It's "La Chanson Des Vieux Amants" by Jacques Brel.'

'Are you French?'

'Belgian. Jacques Brel is Belgian.'

'No,' I said. 'Are *you* French?'

'Belgian,' she said, 'but yes.'

Then she added, 'Also German, Jamaican, Jewish, Egyptian. It's a long story—'

'You don't have to go into it.'

'Thank fuck. I hate this question.'

'People ask me all the time too.'

She frowned. 'If you're French?'

'No, where I'm from. When I say, South Africa, they say, *Don't you miss the weather?* I wish I could press a button to answer them.'

She cocked her head to the side, biting her lip. 'You are how old?'

'Twenty-three.'

'Me too.'

We looked at each other.

'I don't know much about Belgium,' I said.

She shrugged. 'It's flat. How about South Africa?'

'Parts are flat, parts are mountainous. Growing up there in the eighties . . .' I hesitated; she waited. 'I knew things were wrong. I felt it as a child. But I didn't fully understand. Now I do but I'm here.'

What was I getting at? Speaking about this could be awkward. The music from the earphones in Sabine's hand had changed to a tune with a strong beat.

'It's complicated,' she said.

I nodded. Ten minutes later, an apple jelly bean clipped my shoulder. When I looked up Sabine had popped her earphones back in. Her English was almost perfect; the tone of her voice was mesmeric and low. I sucked the tart sweet slowly.

For the rest of the day, I imagined conversations in which I said the things I wished I had and asked the things I wanted to know.

2

Sabine wasn't a big talker and my fantasies of meaningful conversations stayed no more than that: fantasies. If she'd hinted at intimacy in our first chat, she rebounded from it afterwards. Yet had she distanced herself from me consistently, I'd have lost interest. Instead, right from the start, there was a push and pull between us. We had moments of sudden openness, affinity even, and their promise kept me hooked.

Many of our exchanges centred on food. Every day Sabine brought in a cooked dinner. She put it in the fridge in the morning. At lunch, she heated it in a pot on the hotplate. By the time she ate at her desk, the whole floor smelled of her meal.

One day, the MD and the HR director came to our office for a meeting with clients. As they left, the MD wrinkled his nose and looked around. Sniffing suspiciously, he walked down the aisle between the desks.

He stopped when he got to Sabine. 'That smells delicious.'

'It's cuisse de canard confite,' said Sabine.

The HR director said hastily to the MD, 'I sent round an email, and we removed the microwave. She must have used the hotplate—'

'Duck leg?' the MD said.

'Candied,' Sabine said. 'Would you like to try?'

'Don't mind if I do.'

She took a plastic fork from next to her takeaway coffee mug and gave him a taste.

He chewed slowly, swallowed and nodded approvingly. 'Takes me back to a fabulous meal I had at the George Cinq Four Seasons Hotel.'

'I know it,' said Sabine.

'Are you from Paris?'

'No, but I lived there. I worked near the Four Seasons.'

'What work did you do?'

'I was with Crazy Horse. You have heard of them?'

The MD looked goggle-eyed.

I put Crazy Horse into Internet Explorer.

One of the secretaries called the MD to the phone. 'Wonderful to meet you,' he said to Sabine. 'Next time you're at our Victoria offices, drop in for a chat.'

According to the internet, Crazy Horse was an upmarket strip show.

After the MD and the HR director had left, I said to Sabine, 'Wow. You made an impression.'

She shrugged and put some more duck leg in her mouth.

I said, 'Working at Crazy Horse must have been quite something.'

She seemed to be studying me. She took a long, slow sip of water.

Then she said, 'I never worked at Crazy Horse.'

'You didn't?'

'No,' she said. 'But now I get to heat my cuisse.'

Another day, Sabine was late with her meal. When I went into the kitchen, I noticed her shadow on the wall; it was slinky and elongated, like an Aubrey Beardsley sketch. She was wearing a peacock-patterned halterneck dress; all she needed were some feathers in her hair.

While she stirred a rich black ale, onion and beef stew with a wooden spoon, I asked, 'If you weren't at Crazy Horse, where were you before here?'

She stuck a finger in the pot to test it. 'Sunset Strip.'

Sunset Strip in Soho was known for being a more empowering strip joint. For having women-only nights too. I'd read about it in a London listings magazine. I could easily imagine Sabine there but I said, 'You're lying!'

She smiled.

'Seriously, what were you doing?'

'Baking bread.'

'You're just saying that.'

'Why would I just say that? Baking bread is cool. You work through the night. You play loud music. You take drugs. You go for drinks in the morning—'

'So why did you stop?'

'The head baker was hassling me. It was a small town by the sea, the kind of place you can't get away from somebody. One morning I left and didn't go back. In London, it's easy to disappear.'

'Sure,' I said. 'But, why media monitoring?'

She lowered the hob's dial. 'Why did *you* choose it?'

'I was staying with family friends in Telford. Doing a crap job—'

'Like this, then.'

'Crapper. For a company on an industrial estate that bashed out dents in cars. I answered the phones all day. *Dent Mend and Paint Repair 01952 746*—'

'You remember the number?'

'On my deathbed, it'll still be going round my head.'

She laughed.

'Telford wasn't for me,' I said. 'I grew up in a parochial town.'

'Meaning?'

'Narrow, insular. Once, they had a beauty contest in a shopping mall. Anyone could go on the platform, enter themselves. The crowd booed or cheered. If they booed, you came down again. The audience was mostly black people but the winner was a ghostly blonde in a settler's dress. And her prize was . . .'

'Yes . . . ?'

'Two cartons of cigarettes!'

'No wonder you're done with towns,' Sabine said. 'But how did you end up here?'

'The people I was staying with knew someone in media monitoring. They thought it'd be better than temping. How about you?'

She scooped her stew efficiently onto a plate. 'The day I saw the ad in the papers, a psychic told me Ilford was in my stars.' She licked the spoon, then shrugged. 'Who am I to fight destiny?'

Usually I came into the office earlier than Sabine and left before she did. But one afternoon, I hung around. I'd thought of asking her for a drink; if we left together, the conversation might head that way.

As she packed her Tupperware into her lime manga rucksack, I said, 'Your food always smells intriguing.'

'What do you mean?'

'Smells good. What was it today?'

'Moroccan tagine.' She pulled the drawstring closed.

Tossing my small denim handbag over my shoulder, I followed her to the lift. 'I'd love to go to Morocco,' I said.

'I went with my lover once,' she said.

'Lucky you.' I wondered if it was a woman or a man.

The lift arrived, empty.

'And lucky him,' I tested.

'Lucky *her*,' she said, giving me a look as she stepped inside. She pressed the button. 'We went to Fez. It is like in the fourteenth century. We stayed in a palace with an old pool.'

'I'm jealous.'

The lift descended.

'Fez is a sensuous place,' she said. 'You walk in the medina. You go through the dark alleys. You get lost. Around one corner there are perfumes, these perfumed stones the women rub on themselves. Around another corner, you see a tannery, you smell the piss they soak the skins in. And around another corner, you go through a side door into a marble palace.'

I stared at her in wonder.

The lift doors opened.

'I'll send you the recipe for the tagine,' she said.

3

If Sabine's talk was elusive, it seemed to me free; if it was fanciful, it fed my image of her as a brave heroine in a dark fairy tale. I was awed by her ability to be herself – unconventional, uninhibited – where I'd never had the courage to do the same.

Negative space is the lifeblood of obsession. In the late nineties, I felt as if I was mostly negative space. Although I wasn't the daughter my mother wanted, I'd never had the guts to rebel. She said I was like my father: passive, meek, defined more by what I bumped up against than what I chose.

An English lecturer, romantic and dreamer, my father was killed in a car accident when I was two months old. Before his death, my mother was a professional ballroom dancer. The way she told it, she'd had tremendous potential. But finding herself a widow with *an extremely demanding baby*, she gave it up. Taking out a loan, she opened Renata's Roses & Blooms. She hired a trained florist, Thandi, who did most of the work.

My mother's many unquestioning acolytes regarded her as a sparkling force of nature. She could be charming, creative and charismatic. But she also had a deep store of anger within her. In public it occasionally darkened her face, though the thunderclouds only broke when she had me to herself. Unfortunately, with it being just the two of us, this happened often, her fury shaking our tin-roof house as loudly as a pelting of hail.

The outbursts would be followed by tearful apologies. Then by platitudes that made no sense. Then by suggestions of renewed intimacy that I had to comply with if I didn't want the anger to return. Huddled under her sunshine quilt, I'd be asked to tell all, in particular about boys. It took many naive confessions before I realized that our intimacy depended on my being the person she wanted me to be, not the person I was.

After I failed the law degree my mother expected to lead to a solid career, or at least a distinguished lawyer husband, I escaped to the UK. As a child, I'd buried myself in books; the wasted years spent trying to memorize legal cases, I'd had no time to read, but in Telford I began to crave fiction again. I longed to lose myself in other lives, to feel the pulse of other worlds.

Yet the impetus to register for a part-time English literature degree came, unexpectedly, from cocaine. A guy at Dent Mend gave me a tiny 'takeaway' to try at home. I made three dots (there wasn't enough for lines) to share with my hosts' sons. We claimed it had no effect but late that night, sleepless and bursting with bravery, I filled in the registration forms.

I'd assumed that my father's genes would breeze me through the course. But to my surprise, studying a subject I thought I'd love didn't come easy. Getting a grip on theoretical arguments was tough. Nonetheless, I persisted in organizing my life around it.

In a leafy south London suburb, I took a room in a houseshare that was private, professional and quiet. Nights I didn't stay over at my boyfriend's, I got up at four a.m. to work. After scraping through Post-colonialism (just), I moved on to Victorian Gothic. But I was a slow reader, a distracted thinker; when I came across lines I liked, I'd mull them over for hours . . .

Despite my approach leading to flights of fancy rather

than academic completion, I kept thinking I had to seep myself in the spirit of the books. Buying black taper candles on my lunch break, I bumped into Sabine. I told her of what I was trying to do. Later, she burned me a death metal album by Gorguts called *Obscura*.

'This,' she said with authority, 'will definitely help.'

4

One autumn morning, I sat in the light of my black candles attempting to write an essay on *Dr Jekyll and Mr Hyde*. After two hours of getting nowhere with Gorguts in my ears, I decided to go in early to work.

Sabine had been off all week with the flu, and I'd volunteered to write her summaries. 'Don't bother telling the client,' the manager said. 'Just do them as if you were her.' I affected her excellent posture as I typed in her passwords (XaviToujours, lemortlemort87) and signed off her emails *Sabine Dubreil*.

Doing the extra work meant staying late, but with it being Friday I fancied leaving on time. The next inbound train would give me the head start I needed. After brushing my teeth and splashing my face, I hauled on a shirt with a cerise bow chosen by my mother. My make-up, usually minimal, could be nil; without Sabine around, nobody would notice me.

On the train, I buried myself in *Exquisite Corpse* by Poppy

Z. Brite. Though hardly a course book, I allowed it as a public transport treat. By the next stop I was lost in the cannibal killer's New Orleans. The shadow of someone crossed over me, but only when something tickled my ear did I look up.

A white feather was attached to a white wing, which was attached to a lime manga rucksack, which was attached to Sabine. She was head to toe in radiant white: bellbottoms, platform shoes and a crop top. She grinned; with glitter on her cheeks, she didn't look ill at all.

'You're early!' she said.

'Going in early to do *your* work,' I said.

She pulled a shocked face. 'That's terrible.'

'I know. You're bad.'

'Don't go. You can skip it.'

'And do what?'

'Come with me.'

'Thought you had flu?'

She waved her hand in the air. 'What I've got to do matters more than Thomas Telford and Balfour Beatty.'

'Really?' I eyed the wings.

'You have heard of Reclaim the Streets?' she said. 'The global anti-capitalists?' I shook my head. 'They're anti-cars, anti-big corporations. They protest, but in the way of the future. Less of the hairy shirts, more of a celebration.'

I stroked the feathers; they were spikier to the touch than they appeared.

'This week is Toxic Planet by Islington Town Hall. In Africa, they've started GM crops. Farmers get the seeds for free but the plants won't fertilize. So they get stuck in a vicious cycle.'

I smiled. 'Didn't know you were an activist.'

'I'm not.'

I raised my eyebrows.

She tossed her head. 'I'm not dedicated.'

'Skiving off work seems pretty dedicated.'

'You should see what the others do,' she said. 'Me? Sometimes, I do it. Get there before it starts, put out the leaflets, set up the tables—'

'Some of my lecturers at university were activists,' I said. 'I always hoped I'd have been one too. But by the time I was a student, it was our first free election. Then Mandela became president.' I stopped; I wanted to show where my allegiances lay but not sound virtuous.

Sabine was watching me. 'You can be an activist today. If that is what you want?'

The train windows became mirrors as we passed through a tunnel.

'I haven't got any wings,' I said.

'Never mind,' she said. 'My friend is bringing body paint. She is a gifted artist. We can make you brilliant silver. Or – green?'

The train drew into Shadwell station.

Sabine touched my arm. 'Call in sick. Say you caught the bug from me.'

I laughed and got up.

'*À tantôt*,' she called, as I went through the doors.

*

Changing platforms, I could feel the pressure of Sabine's touch. Why was I always such a good girl? It was crazy, going in to do *both* our jobs. *À tantôt* was a Belgian expression for 'see you soon'. I could turn around, go back, make it true.

On the District Line, I kept thinking: get off, switch platforms. But . . . How could I explain? This foreign activism would be wrong for me – laughable, too easy. I'd be an imposter on its high moral ground. I changed trains and changed again until I got to Ilford.

At work, the offices were empty. I thought back to when I was four, my first day at kindergarten. My mother had instructed me never to go anywhere with strangers. When our teacher said we were going for a walk, I told her I couldn't go. She locked me in the classroom. The scent of pine trees blew in through the high windows. I could still see the disintegrated tissue in my hand as I sat in front of my brown cardboard suitcase waiting for everyone to return.

After starting up my computer, I went to Sabine's side of the desk. I sat in her chair. Her workspace was clear: no pens, no coffee mug, no cutlery. Nothing was pinned to her felt board. She wasn't untidy but there were usually a few CDs or pieces of fruit lying about. For a moment, I wondered if she'd come back. What if next week she called in with another illness and then disappeared, like she did with the bakery job?

Staring at her drawers, I recalled my mother snooping among my things. The drama that had followed. *Don't*, I told myself.

In the top drawer was a bottle of Guerlain Shalimar. I breathed in the dusky scent of dry roses, vanilla and some unknown essence. Underneath were a carton of Menthol cigarettes, a couple of keys, a tube of hand cream and a diary we'd been given by Volkswagen. I flipped through the pages. There were lightly pencilled names: the post guy, the team manager, a woman in bookkeeping. Sabine gave birthday cards to colleagues; this was evidently how she kept track of the dates.

About to close the drawer, I noticed a brown envelope at the back. Blank, torn open at the top, it contained three blurred Polaroid photographs of a man or a woman, I couldn't discern which. A Sabine-like figure. Sabine, after a holiday, sunburnt berry-brown. Or Sabine in male fancy dress; the jeans seemed to have a masculine cut, the short-sleeved shirt too. Or perhaps this was the lover who'd stayed with Sabine at a palace in Fez. He or she was moving, or the camera was moving, or both. What was captured was no more than the vaguest impression; a viewer could invent almost anything to fill in the rest.

Footsteps sounded in the stairwell. After they moved on, I opened the lower drawer, which was deeper with folders hung across it. I flipped them back and forth; one felt heavier. Behind copies of news clippings was a square box with Alexander McQueen lettering.

It contained a choker with an oval pendant. On the disc crouched a jewel-encrusted scarab with a tiny skull head. I turned it over in my palm. The back was inscribed: *My Sabine.*

I fastened the choker under the cerise bow at my neck. The scarab had heft where it sat in the hollow of my clavicle. For the rest of the day, I didn't take it off. Again and again, I fingered the engraving.

This was how it felt to wear Alexander McQueen.

I didn't give a fuck what wearing designer jewellery felt like. This was what it felt like to be someone's Sabine.

My Sabine.

5

While my days were spent copying out sentences about tread depth, my boyfriend's were spent organizing courses at a community centre. Graham wasn't crazy about his job but had more tolerance for it than I for mine. Often he recounted funny stories about his colleagues and went for after-work drinks. He fitted them in despite (ironically, but successfully) doing a part-time diploma in law.

Although he'd suggested we try studying together, being at his place distracted me. When he wanted to discuss it, I put the discussion off. With his approaching twenty-five, I worried it might lead to the subject of living together. We'd been going out seven months: we liked and were attracted to each other; sex, talk and intimacy came naturally to us. Obviously, we'd struck lucky – but the topic stuck like a fish bone in my throat.

If I moved in with Graham, I'd surely never leave him or

he me. Which was great, of course it was great. Except, I feared that'd be it. Trapped in a life I hadn't quite intended, I'd never be able to change, to know myself beyond the stencil of my upbringing.

Besides, there were times when a small, unexpressed part of me yearned for another kind of life, to be another person, even. Once, walking home from Telford train station, I passed a pulsing derelict house bathed in ultraviolet light and longed to go inside. Another time, dancing alone in my room to a Lacuna Coil CD I'd bought in imitation of a woman in the queue at Tower Records, I felt as if my fingertips were touching the edge of another world . . .

Yet when I watched classic films with Graham on his worn, leather sofa, my perspective wavered. Much as wilder moments attracted me, the pull they exerted passed. In our different ways, what we both wanted was similar. We shared values and interests but also each had our own dreams. What I ought to do was tell him about lives that intrigued me. If I told him of my longings, he'd tell me his in turn.

So late one November afternoon, naked in bed with a bottle of red wine, I told Graham about my colleague, Sabine.

After I'd described how she looked, how she talked and the places she'd travelled, I said that she'd worked in bread. They'd baked through the night, done drugs and gone to the pub in the morning. Graham didn't look impressed. I recounted the time with Sabine and the MD and the cuisse.

21

He wasn't impressed by that either. Then I told him she was part of a global anti-capitalist movement. If this impressed him marginally more, it was all the encouragement I needed.

'Sabine's the coolest person I've ever met,' I said.

'Ever?'

'Everything about her is strange and beautiful. From her blue-black squinty eyes—'

'She's squint?'

'On her, it looks good.'

'Right,' said Graham.

He strained his face to aim both eyes at my nose.

I swatted him with a pillow.

'We don't talk much,' I said, 'but if I catch her with a far-away look, I pelt her with a jelly bean. Same if she catches me. Sweet start to a friendship, huh?'

He raised an eyebrow. 'A friendship?'

'I hope it becomes a friendship.'

At university I'd slotted into groups I had little in common with. When unable to keep up my cheery image, I'd let connections lapse. In London, I'd hung out with South African acquaintances until they left to teach English in Taiwan. Then I'd piggybacked Graham's social circle. Fearing intrusiveness, with women especially, I ran at the slightest hint of confrontation. In sexual relationships, I felt safer.

Graham tickled his fingers across the freckles on my shoulder. 'Meggie . . . ?'

'Normally I make friends with people who befriend me first,' I said. 'It's time to start choosing.'

Graham slipped on top of me. I liked the feeling of his long lean body pressing into mine. He gave a cheeky smile. 'Like you chose me?'

'*You* chose me.'

'*You* were checking me out at the pool table. My mates were like, *See that cute gingerhead with the brown, puppy-dog eyes—*'

'Sorry, Mr Brown-Haired Dude with brown, puppy-dog eyes yourself. You came on to me, remember?' I rolled us over, so that I was on top of him. '*Would you, um, like to go to the cinema or, um, maybe something else, sometime, if you're free?*'

Graham thwacked my bum.

I grabbed the wine from his bedside table; a single drop fell into my mug.

'More in the cupboard,' he said.

I flung open his wardrobe door: the neat shelves of folded jeans, ironed t-shirts, pants, socks. 'No wine!'

'Kitchen cupboard, Meggie!'

On my way to the kitchen, I stopped off in the bathroom. While I peed I thought: Sabine would pee with the door ajar. I wished I'd left the door ajar. Peeing could be sexy. What else would sexy Sabine do? But in the utilitarian ex-council flat kitchen with its linoleum floor, venetian blinds and Graham's sister's wedding photo on the fridge, I lost her vibe.

Back in the bedroom, filling my mug from a bottle of rum (I hadn't found wine), I tried to explain Sabine again. I described her clothes: a baby-blue shift dress with a sailor collar, a brown-and-yellow circle skirt, black velvet trousers and an oyster-pink jacket. I said how I'd once seen a Vivienne Westwood label sticking out of her shirt. When I asked her about it she'd laughed. She said it was a fake, that all her clothes were. She bought them on Petticoat Lane.

Graham yawned.

'You're bored?' I said.

'We've been on the same subject for hours.'

'One last thing, then. She remembers everyone's birthdays but when I asked about hers, it had been the previous day – and nobody'd noticed!'

'Incredible.'

'It's in my diary so she'll get something from me next year.'

'Very conscientious.'

'I'm not trying to be conscientious.'

Graham yawned again. 'You fancy her.'

'What d'you mean?'

'Seriously, Meggie. If I went on about the bloke at work's enviably squinty eyes and how his birthday was in my diary and there was a sweet jelly-bean game going on between us?'

'Women aren't scared of being fascinated by other women.'

'Sure.' He swirled the rum around in his mug. 'I just don't get it, though. What about her is *that* fascinating?'

I sighed. 'Haven't I been telling you for hours?'

He rolled his eyes. 'Feels like days . . .'

I sipped my rum, moist-eyed and snubbed.

'Hey, come here,' he said. I snuggled up against his chest and he stroked my hair. 'Maybe it would make more sense if I met her?'

'Mm. In the meantime, I could cook you her intriguing tagine.'

'Can't wait.'

'Fine, I won't, then.' I curled away.

'Don't be like that.' He yanked me back.

'I wouldn't mind getting one of those clay pots to cook it in,' I said. 'You know the ones that look like a hat?'

It wasn't the first time I'd spoken of a meal I intended to cook. On the food front, I was both a terrible chef and a dreadful procrastinator. The latter quality was more to Graham's advantage than he knew. He said, 'I could get you one for Christmas.'

'Please! Graham!' I made guttural vomiting noises. 'Don't ever get me cooking shit for Christmas!'

'I was joking, Meggie.'

'Sorry. It's just, I hate Christmas.'

'I know.'

I refilled our mugs. 'Sabine's going clubbing on Christmas Eve. A warehouse rave at a secret location. You phone a number on the day to find out where it is. I overheard her telling someone else.'

Graham took a few contemplative gulps of his rum. Then he put our mugs on the bedside table. As he leaned close, his floppy cow-lick fringe brushed my forehead. 'Talking of Christmas, I'm not doing anything nearly as exciting as

Sabine but . . . I wonder if, um, you maybe, um, fancy coming back to my sister's place in Scotland with me, um, maybe, sometime, if you're free?'

6

If I *had* chosen Graham, I reasoned, then I ought to be able to choose Sabine.

Having turned down her toxic food protest, I needed to make the next move. Other non-cool people at work befriended her easily. I saw the post guy, who peppered every second sentence with 'hey-ho', chatting to her in the kitchen, just her and him there for ages, then her hugging him. Or the placid middle-aged bookkeeping woman who referred to Sabine as her daughter; Sabine didn't mind, they lunched together regularly. One day, she even blew Sabine off. Sloping wearily to our desk, she apologized, saying she'd forgotten a client's meeting.

'No problem,' said Sabine – and my moment had come.

'D'you fancy lunch with me?' I asked.

'OK.'

'Where were you planning to go?'

'Greggs bakery. Then a walk around the Exchange.'

I hated shopping malls. 'Great! We can do that.'

She laughed. 'No, let's go to Valentines Park.'

'I've never been—'

'You've worked here how long?'

'I know.'

'Valentines is the best thing in Ilford,' she said.

Waiting downstairs for Sabine, I put a couple of coins in a call box. I rang Graham at work to tell him about the Valentines walk.

'*Comme c'est romantique!*' he said.

'You go to the park sometimes,' I said.

'Don't call to tell you.'

'Maybe you should.'

'Hn.'

'Should I be worried about your secret days?' I said.

'*Very* worried,' he said.

'What secret thing are you doing now?'

'Reading *Fairer, Faster and Firmer – a modern approach to immigration and asylum.*'

'Are you jealous of me, then?'

'Of your next hour, yes. In general, no.'

'If it were in general yes,' I said, 'I'd take you for supper to make up.'

'You could work on it.'

'I have to work on it *and* take you out?'

'I'll take you,' he said. 'Stockpot at seven?'

Stockpot was a place in Soho that served seventies-style comfort food with a handwritten three-course menu that cost the same as one course anywhere else. I knew already what each of us would have. Graham: three-colour salad starter, me: avocado vinaigrette; Graham: chicken fiorentina and veg, me: poached salmon and veg; Graham: rice pudding, me: golden syrup sponge with custard.

Usually I liked Stockpot, but as Sabine breezed out of the building with her powder-blue scarf wafting behind her, I wished Graham had suggested somewhere sophisticated and French. In (Belgian) French spirit, I said '*à tantôt*', blew a kiss down the line and hung up.

Valentines Park was ten minutes away. Walking there, we listened to Fauré's *Requiem*. It was Sabine's suggestion; she wore one earphone, I the other. I'd not known her to listen to classical music before but she said it was the only thing for Valentines. Perhaps the music was responsible for the serious mood that came over her.

As we strolled through the grounds, past the ponds and canals, the green and coppering shrubberies, she told me that a poor family called Valentine had lived in a cottage here. Then the estate was bought by *quelqu'un* in 1696 after her husband, the Archbishop of Canterbury, died. The mansion was built for her. In the eighteenth century, another *quelqu'un* gave the grounds their features, and thirty years later, Charles Raymond –

'A nice name, no?' she said.

'Nice when you say it.' I pursed my lips for my best French impression.

'Charles Ray*mond*,' she said, mocking my imitation, 'bought the estate and made it more Georgian style. He planted the Black Hamburg vine. It was destroyed but a cutting lives on at Hampton Court. They gave it the name Hampton Court Vine.'

'Original,' I said.

'In the nineteenth century, a Roman stone coffin was found here. Then, the council opened it as a park. It has been public for almost a hundred years. In the First World War, Belgian refugees stayed in the mansion. After the war, it was a convalescent hospital so that's why there are ghosts.'

'Ghosts?'

'Yes, you believe in ghosts?'

'Not sure,' I said. 'My mother who is alive haunts me more than my dead father.'

She took my hand. 'When did your father die?'

'Before I can remember. I was a baby,' I said.

She kissed my hand and let it go.

'How about you?' I said. 'D'you believe in ghosts?'

'Of course. I come here to be near the ones who died.'

'In the hospital?'

'No, my own ghosts. From my own life.'

'Who are they?'

She acted as if she hadn't heard; I was sure that she had losses greater than mine, of people she'd known and loved.

'Why were there Belgian refugees?' I asked, since she seemed more comfortable with her potted history lesson.

'When Germany invaded, they had to flee. A quarter of a million came here. Agatha Christie met one and invented

Poirot.' She turned to me. 'If you write a book, I can be your Belgian.'

'I'm not going to write a book.'

'But you love to read?'

'That's different.'

'I love to read too,' she said.

'What do you love to read?'

'Thomas Mann, Goethe, Shakespeare and Proust.'

'OK,' I said. 'Maybe you will write a book then?'

She laughed.

After nothing more was forthcoming, I asked, 'What happened to the refugees?'

'At the end of the war, Britain sent them back. The government gave free one-way tickets. Their story was forgotten. An old priest told me.'

'A priest?'

'He comes here a lot. He tells me things, then forgets, then tells me again.' She shrugged. 'I feel sad for old men on their own.'

'Not old women?'

'No,' she said.

She took out a joint. I knew what she meant: it was easier to feel sad for people who weren't like you. She lit the joint, had a toke and passed it to me. I had a toke too.

As a layer peeled off the day, I noticed the trees differently. How magnificent they were, how old and dignified. While their leaves chattered high above us, I felt as if I'd slipped into an English storybook from my childhood. I put the flat of my hand on the knobbled bark of what Sabine said was a hornbeam; I ran my palm along it.

Sabine put her hand on the bark too, and then on top of mine.

'Come,' she said. 'We need to go back. But first, the wishing well.'

The wishing well wasn't what I expected. It was a squat dome-shaped concrete structure embedded with flints and quartz. Sabine said fifty years ago children would scratch a wish on a leaf and throw it in. She sat scribbling on her leaf; I tried to see what she was getting down but it was indecipherable. I simply wished for us to be friends.

I thought my wish would come true. But in the days following our walk Sabine was increasingly aloof. She didn't take her earphones out when we talked and responded to my questions with the briefest of answers. When she caught me looking at her, she looked away. I raked through the day at Valentines, trying to work out what I'd done. Finding nothing, I became sure that she saw how hungry I was to know her, to know about her, to be close.

In the local library one rainy lunch break, I came across a leaflet on the park. It contained all the information Sabine had told me. But libraries were often the haunts of old men. The priest had probably come here and read it; he'd passed the information on to Sabine who'd passed it to me. The other possibility was that there was no old priest. But there was no reason for me to choose that explanation.

In early December, I found a book still in its bag on my desk: *The Healing Energies of Trees* by Patrice Bouchardon. When I asked Sabine about it, she said she'd liked it and thought I would too. I wasn't sure what the gift meant. Was it my turn to make another move? Or was it the closing seal on our friendship? Ending relationships, I'd always paid for the last meal, or parted ways after I'd given a gift rather than vice versa. I didn't want any chance that the other person could feel used.

Although this was a friendship, I imagined Sabine was doing similarly. Her gift was about saying no nicely. Hurt, I left the book at the back of my work drawer. Reining in my glances, I tried to look forward to the Christmas holidays in Scotland.

7

The day before Graham and I left for his sister's place in Inverness was the day of the Christmas do. Ordinarily I avoided work drinks, but since the Christmas ones started during office hours, they were pretty much obligatory. I found myself hemmed in at a trestle table with colleagues I hardly knew. Wondering how long I'd have to stay, I heard, 'And Sabine's off to do nightshifts at London Bridge.'

'Sabine *Dubreil*?' I asked.

'Yes,' said the matronly woman to my right.

'She's only been here four months!'

'I know, it's a shame,' said the woman.

'Got to move on for the CV,' said the ex-army head of finance.

'How will nightshifts be good for her CV?'

The hot guy from IT shrugged. 'Different job, innit?'

While he doled out generous refills of Sauvignon from the bottles on the table, I scanned the pub crowd. Sabine's lime rucksack was easy to spot; she was the only woman in a group of men by the bar. After draining my glass, I excused myself.

She was mid-conversation with the best-looking director, the one who with a lot of imagination could look a little like Richard Gere. I tapped her shoulder. The pub was loud. I yelled in her face, 'You're changing to nights?'

'Yes,' she yelled back.

'Why?'

'I'm not a day person.'

I nodded; I could smell her perfume, her smoke and mint breath.

'Are you a day person, Meggie?'

'No,' I said. 'Not at all.'

'So you must do nights, too.'

The director tapped his shiny brogues. He put his pint down heavily; the froth spilled. *I was wrong about* The Healing Energies of Trees. *I interpreted her gift wrongly.*

I considered asking the director for a transfer then and

there, but it didn't seem like quite the right moment. When he started talking as if I was a midge he wanted to bat away, I mouthed '*à tantôt*' to Sabine and left.

Until I heard of Sabine's move, working nights hadn't occurred to me. But over a Christmas break more toddler-centred than I'd anticipated, the idea took hold. On Graham's sister's computer I checked the schedule. Fourteen nights on, followed by fourteen nights and days off. Parents changed their body clocks for the sake of their sprogs. Surely, I said to Graham, I could do it for the sake of my studies?

If the rationale sounded disingenuous, Graham wouldn't question it; he thought my academic efforts were linked to my late father's career. The misconception wasn't my fault, though nor was it easy to correct. I'd told him I didn't miss what I hadn't known. But over the years I'd noticed that people who came from ordinary, stable families didn't believe me.

Usually I was careful not to take advantage but in this case the truth was complex. It wasn't just about working with Sabine; it was about doing what she had done. Inverting the notion of living by day seemed subversive. She'd slipped stream, and invited me to do the same. If I turned it down would I ever get the chance again?

The first weeks of January were greyer, rainier and more drab than usual. The essay I'd been trying to write was stuck.

I hadn't heard about my application for nights. And Graham was pissed off that I wanted to do them so much.

'What about us?' he said. 'Shift work's shit for relationships.'

'Shit work's shit for relationships too,' I said, crabbily.

And shit work it was, shittier than ever. Without Sabine around, my tolerance for the job was shot. My whole life seemed to be a cycle as tedious as my summaries of tyre news.

One morning while my colleagues were in a meeting, I stared despondently at the staff photo board. We'd been asked to bring in pictures of ourselves as children and Sabine's was still there. Above her name tag was a child of eight or nine. She was onstage, dressed in a midriff top, hot-pants and boots. Her mouth was stained bright red as if she'd been eating raspberry sherbet. She was the naughty little girl I'd always wanted to know. The girl I'd been discouraged from inviting home. *A sexualized child*; I could hear the words in my mother's disapproving tone.

I looked at the photograph above my own name: my dorky orange pigtails, my pinafore dress, my shiny brown buckle shoes. Then I took the drawing pins out and, not caring that it didn't make sense, I swapped the photos around.

Of course, it was only after I completely gave up on hearing about nights that a letter came through the internal post. I can't recall where the interview was held. It may have been the Victorian warehouse near London Bridge where the nightshifters worked; by day it would've seemed a different place entirely. All I remember clearly was being sure that I had botched it – but I was wrong. Either that or there weren't as many people clamouring to invert their body clocks as I'd imagined.

By the time I got home, there was already a message on my phone: I was to be at the London Bridge warehouse at ten p.m. the following Monday to start the job.

PART II

8

As instructed, I entered the warehouse building through the cracked glass door. Going up two dirty flights of stairs, I came into a vast workspace with a concrete floor, exposed brick walls, industrial-size bins and glue-stained desks. On some of them were bulky out-of-date computers; on all were stacks of white paper, newspapers, Pritt sticks and scissors.

I scanned the room for Sabine but there were no familiar faces; the unfamiliar ones looked sallow and waxy in the fluorescent light. I was told to trail someone called Earl, a mini Muscle Mary with breath like a firelighter. His hair was in twists dyed gold and he had one gold-capped tooth. He explained that my job would involve reading the papers to find and summarize articles to do with crime. I'd send them out to government clients by six o'clock each morning. He'd show me the ropes but I'd have to figure out the specifics myself.

'Unfortunately, your predecessor's not available,' he said.

'OK,' I said.

'He topped himself,' Earl said.

'God.'

'I know. The shift leader still feels bad.'

'The shift leader?'

Earl put a finger to his lips. 'He was *always* calling in sick. One day, she made a voodoo doll from screwed-up newspaper and stuck pins in it. She did it as a joke but then . . .'

He raised his eyebrows.

'I'll be careful about calling in sick,' I said.

'No, you'll be all right,' said Earl. Then he added, 'So long as you don't take the piss.'

We were by the sink, making coffees. Looking for a sponge to wipe the grubby mugs, I saw maggots at the plughole. Earl called over the shift leader. She wore her fine black hair in plaited buns that she shook hopelessly. 'I keep telling the management.'

Earl filled a quarter of his coffee mug from a clear bottle with a Cyrillic label. 'Vodka. Want some?'

'Vodka and coffee?' I said.

'You don't have to have the coffee,' he said, smiling.

'Maybe later,' I said.

'Won't be a later,' he said.

After I'd stirred the coffees, Earl introduced me to Lizard, a guy in a leather jacket worn scaly at the seams, and then to Coño, the nightshift dog. Lizard told me Coño was actually Earl's.

'Nice name,' I said, patting her. 'I haven't heard it before.'

Earl and Lizard doubled up laughing. 'You've not been to Spain?'

'Not yet,' I said.

They cracked up again.

'It's "cunt" in Spanish,' said Lizard.

'Hey, hey,' said Earl. 'It's not the same thing, it's the language of love.'

'Thought that was Italian,' I said, and they stared at me like I was a square peg.

A woman with breath to rival Earl's put her arm across my shoulders. Her hair was bottle mahogany-red with a short pull of grey at the roots. It gave off an oily scent overlaid by a cloyingly sweet perfume. Her green eyes were clumpily mascaraed and shattered by red veins.

'Ignore them, babes,' she said. 'I'm Sherry. Let's hand out the coffees.'

I don't remember much else from the night other than an overall impression that I'd gone too far, I'd made a mistake. I'd traipsed after Sabine as if she were the Pied Piper. And where was she now? As for me, I seemed to be alone in a land of losers, wasters and misfits.

9

Night after night there was no Sabine.

At the end of another day's struggle to sleep, I'd set off from my houseshare in the dark. Slamming the front door shut, I'd sense my cohabitants' collective flinch. Disregarding it, I'd head down lonely streets past glowing windows. At the station I'd cross over to the empty inbound platform. I'd get a train in that was harshly lit, though scarcely a quarter full.

Disembarking at London Bridge, I'd continue against the flow. Each day had a particular feel to it. Sunday was low with the weight of the week ahead. Monday was simply dogged. Tuesday, a smidgen lighter. By Wednesday, the spirit began to change. Thursday sparkled with the weekend's approach. Friday was carefree, careless, positively ebullient. Saturday sat deep-seatedly in the comfy fat of the weekend. Even being out of sync, the cycle was affecting, reinforced by its effect on my colleagues' moods too; getting buffeted by the day world was unavoidable for any of us.

Leaving the station concourse, I'd pass a taxi rank, then turn off the main drag. The darkness seemed denser here than where I lived. The streetlamps were often broken, the neighbouring buildings abandoned or shut until usual working hours resumed. Except for the one with the cracked glass door.

I'd go in. And up.

Up two flights of stairs to a static buzz and brazen lighting. To grubs and broken chairs and filthy keyboards. A constant supply of farts emitted by who knows who, a blocked-nose-worth of paper dust. Drinking mud-thick coffee to stay awake, I'd scan the newspapers for *murder, accident, assault, crime, prisons, arson, harm, rape, death, die, died.* I'd snip, glue and type. Photocopying summary packs, I'd count the mechanical flashes of light. I did it automatically with my fingers, only keeping track of every tenth flash that passed. Between tens, I'd think of nothing. My sleep-deprived mind would blank; I'd stand.

Around two a.m., I'd eat Pot Noodles at my desk like everyone else. Bombay Bad Boy. Beef and Tomato. Hot 'n' Spicy. Pot Mash. Pot Curry. Chow Mein. If there was a delay due to a late paper, or a problem in the print room, I'd sneak out to the petrol station kiosk. With crisps or a strawberry milkshake or an energy drink for a final boost, I'd go down to the river's edge. Leaning over the cold, concrete barrier, I'd relish the stolen moment off.

Back at the warehouse, the night would burn on. When it finally thinned, I'd feel the end's approach viscerally. Like a sportsperson trained to play to the exact length of a game, I squeezed out the last of my efforts. I emailed my summaries to clients and deposited my press packs in the courier's boxes: HOME OFFICE, PRISONS, CPS, POLICE.

Slinging my denim handbag over my shoulder, I called, 'See you later' to the emptying room.

Whoever was left echoed, 'See you later' back.

10

'Still here,' Lizard noted when I'd passed the mid-shift mark.

'One of us, now,' said Earl.

'Les Misérables,' said Lizard.

'Nah,' said Earl, 'Les Stuck.'

I hoped they were wrong. And also hoped soon to hear a more authentic French accent. Earlier through the stairwell window, I'd seen a woman in a brown raincoat emerging from a yellow convertible. Though her face was obscured by a patterned brown umbrella, I was *sure* it was Sabine.

When by Pot Noodle time she hadn't materialized, I finally approached the shift leader. She shook her plaited buns: she'd never heard of anyone by that name. I checked with Lizard, who said he hadn't either. Earl said she might be a newbie on the opposite team, the ones who did the work during our fortnights off. Maybe I was wrong then, maybe I hadn't seen her. 'Maybe she's *my* opposite?' I said.

'Yours is a twenty-stone bloke,' said Lizard.

'Who's been doing the job for as many years,' added Earl.

I wondered out loud why Mr Twenty-Twenty hadn't shown me the ropes.

'He's in Bangkok,' said Earl.

I gathered then that with this job when you were off, you were off – and I couldn't wait.

Working nights made me feel unexpectedly constrained. You never got to say, *See you tomorrow*; it was always, *See you later*. You never got the blank slate of a fresh, new day. My press packs were shoddy; my clients continually complained. The shift leader said not to worry, that I'd improve with experience. But, since my body was incapable of sleep by day, I hardly intended to give experience a chance.

Instead, I promised myself to look for other work once the

fortnight was up. I promised the same to Graham, whom I'd not seen since starting because it was all I could do to get by. With my autopilot gone AWOL, I expended my energy on instructions to put food in my mouth, smear soap over my body, stand under the shower until it washed off, and then lie pointlessly in bed.

One night, I leaned back against a concrete pillar in the toilets. Doing something I've never managed before or since, standing dead upright I fell asleep.

Sherry shook me awake. 'Babes, are you all right?'

'I'm fine,' I said, embarrassed to be caught off-guard.

'You're sure?'

'Just tired.'

'Come to the pub after work.'

'I don't fancy drinking in the morning.'

'Sorts out the sleep problem,' she said. 'Mother's milk.'

At the basin, I ran the cold tap full volume over my wrists. A teacher at school had said this would cool your blood supply. Perhaps cooler blood would make me more alert.

Instead a bump against my hips jolted me. Winking at my reflection in the mirror, Sherry said, 'We could be sisters! You and I!'

Sherry was the off-grid version of the day-job woman who'd called Sabine her daughter. Had Sherry called me her daughter, it might have been OK. But, sister?

I kept the water running hard while she tra-la-la-ed down the corridor.

11

The last day of shift, I managed a miraculous four and a half hours' sleep. Emerging from survival mode, I blow-dried curls into my hair, depilated the rest of my body, and generally spruced up. My plan was to head to Graham's for some a.m. intimacy after work. But around midnight, in the corridor by the photocopying room, someone grabbed my arm.

'You've changed to nights too?' Sabine's cheeks were flushed.

'Yes!' I said.

We stared at each other.

'I guess we're on different teams,' I said.

She nodded. 'I'm at Energy downstairs.'

'I didn't know there was a downstairs.'

She slanted her eyes at me.

I said, 'I mean, I didn't know anyone was there.'

'You never go to the pub?'

'Not so far. Maybe today.'

'No,' she said. 'Today is . . . on the roof.'

'The roof?' I said.

'A celebration,' she said. 'Exclusive.'

'I forgot, I can't today,' I said.

'It is your last shift?'

'Yes.'

'You have to come, then.' She smiled.

46

I slowly smiled back. 'OK, I'll come.'

She made a zipping sign across her mouth.

Turning to hide my grin, I rushed off to finish my work.

Most of the team had left by the time I was done. A few had asked if I was going for drinks and Earl had replied, 'She never does.' It'd be a surprise for them to see me on the roof – if they'd been invited, that was.

The staircase ended at the sixth floor, which seemed deserted. After going through several double doors I wondered if I'd be able to get back. Ready to retrace my steps, I noticed a shaft of dusty light. A short flight of stairs led to a door jammed open with a brick.

The roof was a flat expanse of black tar. The dawn sky blazed red through oyster frills of grey cloud. Older lower buildings were still in the dark while higher glassier ones flashed beams of sunlight. The railway track was one kind of break in the city's density, the broad shimmering curve of the Thames another.

Sabine was at the far end, smoking a cigarette.

I went over to her. 'Was the celebration called off?'

She inhaled deeply, cheeks hollow.

'I guess obviously it was,' I said.

I put my hands in my bomber jacket pockets.

Sabine was shivering in black leggings, black boots, a black jumper.

'Sorry I'm so late. I'm just unbelievably bad at—'

'Shhhhh.' She put a finger on my lips.

For a moment, I was confused.

Then she leaned in and kissed me.

Her mouth was a toasty combination of toothpaste and cigarettes. I could smell the scent at her neck. I was responding to her almost before I realized. The feel of her kissing, her tongue and mine, was softer than any I'd ever experienced.

But then I pulled away. 'I can't—' I shook my head. 'You know I've got a boyfriend.'

'So?'

'I'm not a lesbian.'

'Me neither.'

I frowned.

She said, 'I like both.' She stepped back. 'You don't like both too?'

'No,' I said. 'I'm sorry, if I . . .'

She flicked her cigarette dismissively. It had burned to the filter. She put it out in a paint tin filled with butts. 'Like the view?'

'Yes. Do you?'

'It makes me feel, how can I say?'

'Alive?'

'Destructible,' she said.

'Destructible?'

'We're so small, Meggie. Just small animals who stay in small buildings, do small jobs, go home on small trains. We fuck, eat, sleep—'

'Can't wait to do more of that,' I said.

'Sleep?'

'Yes.'

She laughed. 'Thought you'd say fuck.'

'That too,' I said, awkwardly. 'Speaking of which, I'd better go. I promised to get to Graham's before he left for work.' I hesitated; I didn't want to seem weird about the kiss. 'Maybe we can swap numbers?'

'I'll give you mine. You give me a missed call.'

After keying her mobile number into my new Nokia, I pressed dial. Her rucksack was just a few yards away but I didn't hear ringing.

'You know the way out?' she asked.

'No,' I said. 'Could you show me?'

'No. But you go down, and right, and left, and left again, and you come to the stairs. Easy peasy.'

Easy peasy, sure. I was lost in the building for three quarters of an hour. By which time it was too late to catch Graham before work anyway.

12

As the reality of having a fortnight off took hold, my perspective on finding another job changed. Of course nights were hard, but hard for a reason. I was turning my life around.

For the first time ever I enjoyed telling people what I did. *On shift I immerse myself in crime. We read the broadsheets and the tabloids too. Murder, rape, abuse, anything to do with prisoners. You see how the same story is told in different papers . . .*

'Isn't it depressing?' asked Graham's cousin over dinner.

'We-ell,' I said, 'the previous guy on the job topped himself.'

She gasped. 'You're happy with your lovely girlfriend doing this, Gray?'

Lovely, friendly and *natural* were descriptors I wanted to leave behind. Giving the cousin a glinting smile like Sabine's, I moved the conversation swiftly on.

Back at Graham's flat that cold February night, we fought.

'What's with the drunken bravado?' he said.

'You've been drinking too,' I said.

'You drink *every* night now.'

'Can't sleep. I need it.'

'You don't.'

'Mother's milk.'

He slammed an armful of law books down on the kitchen counter. 'Where's this going to end, Meggie?'

Still warmed by the dinner's wine, I went over to him. I hitched up my new stripy skirt. His breathing deepened; it turned me on when he was aroused despite himself. He traced a blue zigzag from my mid-thigh upwards. Just before my knickers, he stopped. 'Is Sabine doing nights too?'

I nodded.

He fingered the stretchy material. 'So *that's* what this is about.'

'She's not on my shift, Graham. I've seen her once.'

'But the job was her suggestion?'

'Yes.'

He took his hands from my body.

'What?' I said.

'If she says jump, you'll say how high? If she says run, you'll say how far? If she says dive, you'll say how deep?'

I went to the fridge. Graham sounded drunker than I'd realized.

I remembered my mother's accusing me of a sex life before I had one. Holding a bottle of beer, I turned back to him. 'If she says, *kiss me* . . . ?'

He shrugged resignedly as if the answer were obvious.

I had the urge to hurl the bottle across the room. Very occasionally, I got these violent impulses. I'd read an article that suggested distracting yourself with a strong physical sensation. Touch a kettle, hold ice, drink water quickly.

I drank the beer quickly, so quickly I felt sick.

We stormed off to bed furious with each other. But my body clock was junked and the powers of mother's milk were limited. In the early hours, I woke up and went down on him. Then he woke up too. In the half-light we were at it like prisoners just released. When he fell asleep again, I lay there and thought: *Yup, I guess it's men for me.*

Yet the conclusion was oddly tinged with regret. And so, because I couldn't sleep, I began to play with myself. As I fiddled, my imagination roamed its usual territory of strong, swarthy guys. But the moment before I came, I overlaid their images with Sabine.

Her heart-shaped face, that smile of hers.

13

My last weekend off, I told Graham I'd cook for him. After printing out Sabine's recipe for *Traditional French Moroccan Tagine*, I spent the day hunting down the ingredients. These included three I'd never had: goat meat, harissa paste and argan oil. Argan oil proved the hardest to source. Eventually I found a bottle in the beauty section of a local health food store. The packaging said, *For hair, skin, nails, lips* but the shop assistant said, 'Argan oil's argan oil,' and I went with her view on it.

The recipe was supposed to take three hours and forty minutes. Since I sawed and hacked rather than sliced and chopped, it took me closer to six. At almost ten p.m., done with timing the meal, I laid the table with my phone by the place mat. Then we sat down to eat.

'This is – interesting,' Graham said, his Adam's apple rising and falling.

'Interesting?' I said.

He took another forkful. 'What d'you think of it?'

I chewed thoughtfully, imagining a riad courtyard, blue-and-white tiles, little birds flying overhead. 'It's exotic.'

'Yes,' he said. 'Pretty rich.'

It was exceptionally rich. He selected a few more forkfuls, without the meat. I made myself select forkfuls with meat only. Unexpectedly, my phone lit up. An envelope with *Sabine* appeared on the screen.

'What is it?' he said.

'Nothing,' I said. But, buoyed by the coincidence of the text, I added, 'D'you want to know the tagine's ingredients?'

'Go on.'

I listed the vegetables first, then the harissa paste.

'Harissa!' he said, as if he'd bumped into an old friend. 'Didn't realize there was harissa in it. Harissa's fragrant and delicate.'

My phone's screen had gone dark. 'Maybe it's drowned out by the goat.'

'Goat?'

'You eat meat.'

'Sure, but—'

'It really irritates me,' I said, 'when people think to eat a cow is fine but to eat a goat isn't.'

'Does that mean I have to eat every animal on earth?'

'Yes. Or else become a vegetarian.'

'Maybe I will. I've been thinking about it.'

'Oh, and my meal has turned you?' I picked up my phone.

'It really irritates me,' he said, 'when people can't stop fidgeting with their mobiles.'

'You just wish you had one too.'

'Getting one next week for work.'

'Oh.' I slipped the phone into my pocket. 'D'you want to know the last secret ingredient?'

'Definitely.'

'Argan oil.'

'I've not heard of that.'

'It's got to do with goats too.'

He looked decidedly sick. 'Goat oil? Goat gland oil?'

'No,' I said. 'It comes from argan nuts.'

'Phew.'

'Their shells are hard to crack. But in Morocco, goats climb the argan trees and eat the argan nuts. People fish them out of their poo, which has made them softer. They mash them up. And it goes from there.'

He stared at me, then started laughing. 'You sure know how to sell an *exotic* stew to a meat and two veg kinda guy.'

'You need to broaden out.' I stuffed more goat in my mouth. Then I put my knife and fork together. 'Just nipping to the loo.'

'Your broadening out getting to your guts?' he called after me.

'You're gross,' I called back. 'I need to pee!'

In the bathroom, I opened Sabine's text. It was blank. I closed and opened it again. Same result. I flushed the toilet. If the message was a mistake, I could still send a reply. I turned on the hot tap, then typed: *Looking fwd to seeing you on Mon.* Before I could change my mind, I clicked send.

The mirror above the basin steamed up. I willed my phone

to flash with a return text. But it didn't. Reluctantly, I put it in my pocket and turned the hot tap off.

Graham had cleared the tagine from the living room. In the centre of the table was a pack of deflated-looking éclairs. 'Got dessert.'

'Thanks, Gray.'

'I can bring the goat back if you're not finished?'

'I'm done,' I said. 'It wasn't that great.'

'Wait,' he said, going through to the kitchen.

'I don't want any more goat!'

But he returned with a bottle of cava. 'Not champagne. Though it's good stuff.' He poured it out into the two long-stemmed glasses he called the *poshies*, then raised a toast. 'To meals together.'

As we sipped the fizz, I said, 'I've got a plan. D'you want to hear?'

'Plan for what, Meggie?'

'Managing nights.'

'I've been giving it some thought myself.'

My phone gave a tremor at my hip. 'Hang on.'

I went to Graham's bedroom. But it had only been a phantom vibration. I buried the phone in my denim bag and applied some lip gloss.

He smiled when I came back. 'Glamorized.'

'Glamorized,' I said.

'So what's the plan then?' he said.

'To live by night only.'

His face fell. 'You're doing that already.'

I shook my head. 'From now on, I'm going to be nocturnal in my time off too.'

'Ri-ight . . .' He tapped his glass.

'Switching's the problem, Gray. My body clock's screwed. I can't get into a routine. And like you said, I'm drinking – not too much, I enjoy drinking too much, but – too often.'

I gave him a moment to say something smug.

When he didn't, I added, 'I want to give this job, my studies, everything a chance. This is the only realistic way to do it.'

'Realistic, huh?' he said.

Then, without a single um or uh or hesitation of any play-ful kind, he said, 'The only realistic way to give *us* a chance is if we live together.'

I'd thought I was prepared for Graham's suggestion. But with my mind in a panic, I blurted out that I needed time. I wanted to say yes, I told him, but with such a big decision it seemed disrespectful not to take a bit of time.

'How much time?' he asked, in the tone of someone more narked than respected.

I promised to let him know by the end of the fortnight. To be at his flat by seven a.m. on the morning I was done.

14

Back on shift, I managed somehow to almost forget about the issue of living together. Whenever my bone-tired mind skirted it, daydreams of dykey inclinations took over. Lying in bed at midday, listless, awake, I'd imagine saying to Sabine, *Maybe I was too hasty, maybe I made a mistake, maybe we could try again?*

Meanwhile, my co-workers were doing their best to help with my insomnia. Sherry brought in thick blackout cloth for my bedroom window. Earl gave me industrial earplugs to mute my housemates. Nothing helped: my eyes burned dryly, my lips cracked, my skin was as sensitive as if I'd been everted. After I heard the tulips at the station whispering, Earl told Lizard who provided a blister pack of prescription sleeping pills.

The relief at being able to switch off was immense, though the pills had two disconcerting side effects. One was that I still felt foggy when awake: I forgot half my keywords and made careless mistakes. The other was that in the window between taking the pills and falling asleep, I felt hornier than ever.

As the shift progressed, I used this time to experiment with bringing Sabine from the edge of my fantasies to their centre. Mostly my impulses slipped into their much-worn tracks. But on the last day of shift, Sabine and I were lying naked together in a warm, muddy rockpool from the beginning of my arousal to its end.

Until then, I'd been no closer to finding an answer for Graham. But in the post-orgasm bath of blissful wellbeing, I came up with an idea. If anyone asked me to go for drinks in the pub, I'd say yes. And if Sabine came too, I'd play the decision, my sexuality – stuff it, the rest of my life – by ear from there.

The White Hart had green speckled carpet tiles, a wall-mounted TV, a jukebox, and an imitation antique clock with hands stuck on a quarter to nine. It was a traditional pub in every sense, except for its dawn opening and a plastic pink stag's head festooned with fairy lights above the bar.

'What're you drinking?' said Earl.

'I'll get it,' I said.

'Wine?' he said. 'White?'

'Earl, don't—'

'White wine,' he said to the barman. 'Large.'

'Baby One More Time' by Britney Spears came on the jukebox. Behind me, someone put their hands over my eyes.

'Same for SJ,' Earl said.

I wrestled with strong, cold fingers. '*SJ?*'

'You two know each other?' said Earl.

'Of course,' said Sabine.

Earl paid up.

Sabine gave a boozy half-smile; I grinned back.

'Oi, lovebirds,' said Earl. 'Give us a hand.'

We took the drinks to the table. As we pulled up extra

stools, I made sure to slip in beside Sabine. Everyone clinked glasses.

'*Salud!*' said Lizard.

Sherry caught my eye. 'He's off to Mexico again.'

'*Salud,*' I said.

Prawn, a spotty white-blond teenager from the print room, yelled, '*Na zdrowie!*'

'Poland,' Sherry said for my benefit.

'Where're you off to, Sherry?' I asked.

'Spain,' said Sherry. 'Bor-ing.'

'Spain's cool,' said Earl.

'Yeah, it's cool. He's coming too,' said Sherry.

'Which part of Spain?' I said.

'Fuck knows,' said Earl. 'Wherever.'

'We take our vans,' said Prawn.

Did everyone here have a van? I wanted to ask Sabine if she had a van. And why she'd called herself SJ. I knew so little about her. But the others seemed to think we were close, and I liked them thinking that.

'What're you up to the next weeks?' Earl asked me.

I didn't want to say, *Sleep, see my boyfriend—*

Sabine stepped in. 'We've got plans.'

'Plans, eh?' said Earl.

I glanced at his G-Shock watch. My plans to be at Graham's by seven a.m. were fast messing up. I needed to text him but I'd dumped my bag with my phone on the far windowsill.

Prawn took a crumpled fax from his pocket. 'Seen this?' He flattened it out. DRUGS WILL NO LONGER BE

TOLERATED ON SHIFT. THE MANAGEMENT. With his pale stubby finger, Prawn underlined NO LONGER.

Everybody laughed.

'Bloody management,' said Lizard.

'That fucker who only did one shift sent forty copies of our bet on the Queen Mother's deathday to Inland Revenue,' said Earl. 'The managers had no choice.'

'Don't worry about it, Prawn,' said Sherry.

'Yeah, like I am!'

Earl turned to me. 'Want to have a guess at her deathdate? Costs a pound.'

'Sure.' It was an excuse to fetch my bag.

'Do it next shift rather,' said Sherry. 'I haven't got the list.'

'What if she pegs it before then?' said Earl.

'Is your date before then?' said Sherry.

'Mine's Wednesday,' said Sabine. 'If I win, I'll share.'

I thought, *I should still get my phone.*

But Sabine pulled me down, her lips at my ear. 'I looked forward to seeing you this shift too.'

I could smell the wine on her breath. 'What?'

She wouldn't repeat her belated response to my goat meal text, but I knew what I'd heard. Just like when a phrase I'd read absorbed me to the extent I forgot everything else, so all thoughts of texting Graham flew out of the pub's diamond-gridded windows. Out into the everyday world where men and women were striding purposefully to work. Their dark suits, their shiny shoes, their strained faces, their neat hair . . .

Inside, I looked at Sabine in her schoolgirl lace-ups,

chequered shorts and velvet blazer. Lizard, an old-time rocker in his skinny jeans and leather jacket. Earl, with his sharp rave style and Coño sleeping peacefully at his feet. Prawn, moonfaced but energetically punky. Even Sherry, with her ill-conceived glamour, seemed childishly endearing, like a messy three-year-old.

I'd found the tribe I wanted to join.

We were totally, utterly free.

At almost eleven a.m., the pub was about to shut. It would reopen at five p.m. to mirror its trading hours for dayshifters.

Dayshifters.

Thinking back to the game I used to play with eyes closed in my office chair, I went over to the jukebox. Flipping through the carousel of songs, I found Cyndi Lauper's 'True Colors'. It cost a quid for three tunes. I bought a pack of Menthol Lights at the bar to get change, then pressed the Lauper button three times. Leaving the song to repeat, I went outside.

The streets around the station had quieted. The morning was wintery though bright. After two weeks in the dark, every colour seemed intense. Pink graffiti on the rusty railway bridge. Black branches flecked with lime buds. Overhead, the wide blue expanse of the sky.

Leaning against a bollard, I lit up. I wasn't a real smoker but, inhaling, I rode the headrush.

I didn't notice Sabine until she jostled alongside me. Stretching out her boyish legs, she helped herself to a cigarette from my pack. I offered to light it for her. The wind blew a few stray curls across her face. She had freckles around her nose that I hadn't noticed before. When the cigarette wouldn't catch, I cupped my hand.

She leaned in; I lifted my head.

Her mouth twitched, showed a dimple. A dare.

I took her unlit cigarette out. Then I kissed her.

Her mouth was soft, her lips the undersides of petals. Though her tongue was strong, our tongues were strong. They moved easily together until hers pulled back, darting, teasing. She tickle-kissed my neck. I tasted her dusky perfume and pressed into her. We grabbed at each other; then stopped, lost in the warm darkness of our mouths.

When the pub door swung open, she began to grind against me. As the team came out, I could feel their eyes on us. The guys watching; the way they were watching. I tugged at Sabine's sleeve. But she drew me closer and kissed more showily.

'Can we talk?' I whispered.

She didn't answer.

With my hands on her upper arms, I moved her gently back; we broke apart.

Our colleagues pretended they hadn't been gawking. They scattered; crossed the road, went to queue at a cashpoint.

I took her hand. It was cold like when she'd put it over my eyes. 'Let's go some place we can be alone,' I said.

'What do you mean?'

'D'you live on your own?'

She tilted her head, warily.

'Maybe we could go back to yours,' I said.

She opened her mouth, then closed it.

Her eyes became hard glints.

'It's just a kiss, Meggie.'

'I know.'

'A kiss doesn't mean . . .'

'I know,' I said.

My cheeks were hot, my eyes were hot. Whenever I wanted to cry I distracted myself by spelling words backwards. I looked towards the alley. I spelled snib. I spelled ytpme setarc. I felt her smooth a strand of hair back from my forehead.

In a softer voice, she said, 'You don't usually kiss your girl friends?'

'Not usually.'

'You're cute. My cute friend who I kiss.'

I nodded and swallowed. 'I don't know what nights is doing to me.'

'Come, now. Everything's fine,' she said. 'Let's go find the others.'

15

Sabine and the rest went on to another pub or a park or someone's flat, but I went home. Later I sent Graham a text. When he didn't reply, I called, I apologized. He asked sarcastically if I'd got lost in the building again. Not this time, I said. There was a long silence. Then I asked if I could come round that evening. I said I'd come early, cook a meal. No, he said firmly. We'll skip cooking, get takeaways.

Guilty, grateful and off-kilter, I blew a shitload of cash on a bottle of Pol Roger Cuvée Sir Winston Churchill that came in a special wooden box. To accompany the fancy champagne, I'd *have* to give him good news.

I put the fizz confidently in his fridge when I arrived. But instead of drinking it, we launched straight into unexpectedly affectionate sex.

Afterwards we chatted casually, then ate a greedy number of dishes from Jay's Vindaloo. Towards the end of the meal, the bulb in the table lamp blew. When Graham flicked on the main light, the room seemed smaller.

'So, Meggie,' he asked. 'What's happening?'

I bit at my lip. 'Haven't been able to decide.'

'I thought as much.'

'I'm sorry.' Was not moving in with him true to myself, or was it just selfish?

He studied his empty plate. I put my hand on his. He patted it, then drummed the table. 'Can't do what you can't do.'

Were we breaking up? This easily? This undramatically?

I scraped the bottom of the sag paneer with my fork. A strand of spinach hooked in the prongs. Then I heard myself say, 'Graham, I think I might be a lesbian.'

'It's Sabine, isn't it?'

'No.'

'C'mon,' he said. 'Crazy-Horse Sabine? Jelly-bean Sabine?'

I shook my head. 'She's just a cute friend.'

'She sounded more than *cute* when you went on about her clothes and squinty eyes and candied duck and—'

'Things change.'

'Who're you into now, then?'

'Nobody.'

'Who're you involved with?'

'No one.'

He eyed me sceptically.

'You,' I said. 'That's all.'

We were quiet.

Then he shifted in his chair. 'Have you ever had sex with a woman?'

I frowned. 'That's private.'

'But have you?'

'No.'

He looked amused. 'Really?'

I felt my cheeks redden. 'I think about it, sometimes.'

'Well, then, Megan Groenewald,' he leaned over to plant a kiss on my forehead, 'it's time to do it, huh?'

He started to clear up the empty containers from the meal, putting them back into the takeaway bags.

I thought, *That's it. Over. The end.*

I was tired; the day had been too much. A pathetic snort escaped with a sob.

'Meggie.' Graham came over to my side of the table. He scooped his arms looped with curry bags around my waist. I hugged him tightly back. 'It doesn't have to be *the end.*'

'It doesn't?' I said.

'No.' He let me go, then took the bags to the kitchen.

I stood at the door.

Emptying the bins, he said, 'You just need to try it.'

'And, if I try it? That'll be fine by you?'

'I think so.'

'Will you do stuff of your own too?'

'Maybe,' he said. 'We'll see.'

I helped him clear the rest of the plates. I was impressed by his generosity, though even more by his assuredness, his sense of self-worth.

While Graham did the washing-up, I got the videotape ready in the player. The film he'd hired was *The Truman Show*. At the start, the viewer is told that audiences are tired of seeing actors portray artificial emotions. After rewinding and fast-forwarding, I got the tape to pause at the first frame.

Coming into the room, Graham held up a tub with two spoons.

'You got dessert!' I said.

'Always do.'

We snuggled on the sofa, eating creamy rice kheer, and I told myself: *So. Bloody. Lucky.*

To Graham, I said, 'You know you're sweeter than I deserve?'

16

The following day, Graham left for work experience at a prestigious chambers in Wales. Not having him around made it easier to stick to my intentions. To move away from the everyday, away from the day. To let go of what I knew and push off into the night. Yet pushing off into the night turned out to be harder than I'd thought.

I set a rigid nocturnal schedule with times to get up, run, eat and sleep. But off shift as on, some internal stubbornness resisted. Without sleeping pills, I lay in bed exhausted but mostly awake. Every few days, I'd pass out heavily, though the short, thick slumbers made me feel drugged: more tired, not less.

When I wasn't maintaining functional necessities, I sat at my desk. As deadlines loomed, my calculations for how quickly I needed to read the course books became increasingly desperate. If I could get through X number of pages in Y hours then I'd have Z hours for the essay. Night after night, Z shrank while I stared into the light of my black candles.

The exploration of my lesbian side didn't fare much better. I went to a bisexual women's meeting in a church hall but the atmosphere was earnest, formal and conservative. I felt as uncomfortable as at my all-girls school, as much of an oddity as I'd felt then.

It was hardly a fair way to test my sexuality. London had plenty of gay, lesbian and mixed clubs, pubs and bars. I'd even seen an advert in a listings magazine for a lesbian sauna. Or I could drop in at the First Out cafe by Centre Point for a baked potato. I liked baked potatoes; I gave myself a date – the date slipped by.

I'd long assumed I did relationships better than friendships. With the few lovers I'd had, I hadn't feared boundaries being crossed. A TV psychologist suggested that for people with authoritarian parents, the bedroom could be where they felt most liberated to rescript their lives. What he'd said stuck; I took for granted that the closeness I'd found with boyfriends could theoretically translate into closeness with girlfriends too.

Yet now I wondered if there was more to my ease with men than I'd realized. When I was with a man, I felt as if I could hide behind my form. The differences between us alone were attractive to him. Whereas in close quarters with a woman, I'd be exposed. If she saw in me what I saw, how could it possibly work? Was it transgression more than lesbianism that I was after?

Whatever I called it, with Sabine its current surged; with Graham, it flatlined. *Cute friend* status meant I had to find new ways to hack the circuit. Living nocturnally was not enough, nor was endless contemplation.

What I needed was to push against myself.

17

Southwark was in darkness. With a power cut to London's central areas, our papers were late; our work was stalled. A note on the warehouse door gave instructions to meet on the roof. I followed the emergency lighting up the stairs. The thump of industrial metal guided me to our crew.

They were sitting around candles in a circle. Sabine patted the space next to her but I sat by Earl and Coño instead. Rammstein's 'Du Hast' was playing on the print guys' ghetto blaster. A few people had coffee cups, doubtless half full of spirits, but with it being our first Monday back, the atmosphere was glum.

Sabine wore a blonde faux fur hat and a white appliqué coat decorated with fairytale images. Since her hair was hidden, it could have been platinum. The change of frame around her face made her lips seem fuller, her eyes larger.

When 'Du Hast' began to warp, the shift leader put it off. The gunpowder night was quiet. Last time I'd been up here, I'd felt surrounded by the city; this time, we could have been floating in space.

'Anyone done anything interesting the last two weeks?' asked the shift leader.

When her hair wasn't in plaited buns, it was loosely crinkled. Her body was angular, broad-shouldered: a swimmer's build. I looked at her wide eyes, her high cheekbones. She had an appealing androgyny. If my fascination with Sabine was about looks, or even nonconformism, the shift leader made for a good rival. Why wasn't I fascinated by her?

'I went to the Noche de Brujas in Mexico,' she offered when no one replied.

'Night of the Witches?' said Sabine.

The shift leader smiled; Sabine smiled back.

Fascination was chemical, I thought. But was it my chemicals blending with Sabine's or did she attract everyone as much?

'What d'you get up to?' Earl asked Lizard. 'Wittgenstein, Linear B . . . ?'

'Time before last, he shut himself away to read up on the Serbian-Kosovan crisis,' said Sherry.

'She's a doll,' said Lizard. 'Brought me meals—'

'Oh go on, you couldn't call them meals.'

'The lasagne, the chilli?'

'The Findus Crispy Pancakes?'

A helicopter flew noisily overhead.

'Learn anything that wasn't depressing?' asked a guy from Sabine's Energy team.

'Albania's taking in Kosovan refugees,' said Lizard.

'We are too, aren't we?' said the shift leader.

'If you apply for asylum here,' said Earl, 'it takes nine years to get citizenship.'

'Things are improving, though,' said Sherry. 'Now that Blair's got in—'

'He reminds me of a school prefect,' I said.

'Were you a school prefect?' said the shift leader.

'No!' I said. 'Were you?'

'Dropped out at fifteen,' she said.

'I was expelled,' said Sabine. 'Twice.'

'What for?' I asked, before I could remember to be cool.

'First time, a sex thing. Wasn't my fault but I took the rap. Second time for being a gang leader.'

'Don Sabine!' said Prawn.

'I've never led anything but I was a goth,' said Sherry.

'Me too,' said Lizard.

'I was the darkest goth in town,' said Earl.

Everyone laughed. I wished I'd been a gang leader or a goth. But how would my mother have coped? She got angry if I didn't laugh at the right moments in her anecdotes about the florist shop's regular customers.

The Energy guy turned back to Lizard. 'If Kosovo was the time before last, what did you research this time?'

Lizard screwed up his face. 'Hypnosis.'

'That's – different?'

'When I was a kid, my uncle was into it,' said Earl. 'He'd hypnotize himself, then get me to stick a pin in his hand. Sometimes he stuck one in me too.'

'Did you want him to?' asked the shift leader.

'Not really.'

'Isn't that, like, abusive?'

'It was the pin, not the penis,' said Sabine.

The helicopter flew close again; a candle guttered.

'Can you try the pin thing on me?' said Prawn.

71

'I've only been doing it two weeks,' said Lizard. 'And I don't have a pin.'

Sherry took a needle from a sewing kit in her bulky handbag. 'Ta da!'

Lizard instructed Prawn to raise his hand. Speaking slowly in a monotonous voice, he counted down from ten to one as Prawn's hand dropped. Lizard picked it up, then pressed the needle into his palm.

Prawn screamed. Staring at the bead of blood on his skin, he went whiter than usual.

'Lie down, Prawny,' said Sherry.

Sabine put her hand over her mouth; a hiccup of laughter escaped.

'One of you try it then!' Prawn shouted from where he lay.

The shift leader drew a resolute breath.

Quickly, I said, 'I will.'

Sabine turned to me; they all turned to me.

'You sure?' said Lizard. 'I mean, I don't think I've quite got this.'

'You concentrate on the trance,' Sabine said to Lizard. 'I'll apply the pin.'

In fairness to Prawn, Lizard went to more trouble with me. While I lay there with my eyes closed, he told me to imagine an old weather-beaten staircase leading from a cliff to an empty beach. He described descending it, a single stair at a time. Counting the steps down from twenty, he instructed me to relax more completely. *You feel calm, you feel peaceful. You let go. Surrender.*

Sabine held my hand on her thigh. My heart slowed, my breathing slowed, I began to slip away . . .

Then the needle went in.

It felt like I was being branded by a white-hot torch. Scared I would scream a thousand times louder than Prawn, I imagined myself being welded to Sabine.

At last, Lizard started the talk to bring me back. I heard a train; the world felt noisier. When I opened my eyes, the power cut was over. The buildings around us were lit up. Everyone was congratulating Lizard – but Sabine wasn't there. Clenching my sore hand, I felt cheated.

'Back to work,' said the shift leader.

As the others stampeded to the stairs, Lizard said, 'You'll sleep well tomorrow, Meggie. You went deep.'

'How can you tell?'

He gave a conspiratorial wink.

Alone on the roof, I examined my palm; a bit bloody but I'd live. I distracted myself by naming the sights: Borough Market, Southwark Cathedral, the Thames, London Bridge—

'Meggie, we need to fix you up.'

Sabine stood in the doorway holding a little green first aid box.

From it she took a plaster, cotton wool and Mercurochrome. Swabbing my skin, she gave a low chuckle. 'Lizard's got a way to go with his hypnosis skills, eh?'

'What d'you mean?'

She stuck the plaster on my palm.

Then she looked me in the eye. 'You felt every fucking millimetre of that needle going in.'

18

Bolstered by bravery, my next Saturday night off I caught the train to Charing Cross. Making my way through Covent Garden, I imagined my younger self with me. The thrill she'd have got from being out in London, unaccountable and free. But as I reached the streets near Soho Square, I left her behind. She was too much of her world to understand where I was headed next. Still less, to share my tentative sense of anticipation.

When I found the place, I stood looking at it. I was myself, then I was not myself. Shivering in the early spring cold, I crossed the road to the fat yellow bubble letters above the blacked-out facade. *Honey Bar.*

The women on the door wore biker leathers, had spiky hair and were heavily pierced. As they pointed to an open guest book on a table in the foyer, I realized I needed to write my name. I hesitated.

'Name, name,' one of them repeated, speaking loudly the way people do to foreigners.

I wrote *SJ*, then scribbled indecipherably in the box for signature. Parting a midnight-blue curtain, she let me in.

I appeared to be the only woman on her own. The others, mostly younger than me, were in groups or at least pairs.

Taking a seat at the bar, I ordered a Sol. It was what I'd been drinking the night I met Graham. I thought of him playing pool with his mates, the teasing banter between them. Of his lanky body, his soft brown eyes. He was back from Wales tonight; his train would have just come in. What was I doing here?

With my second beer half drunk, I made myself approach a nearby table of girls. One of them, plump with beaded braids, shoved the others along so I could fit in beside her. She asked if I was alone. I said yes. Was it my first time at Honey Bar? Yes. She gave me a warm hug, then asked my name. I said SJ, and introductions followed all round.

As they chatted, I was impressed by how at ease the group were with their sexuality. The girl next to me had come out to her best friend when she was nine. At nine I'd known the word lesbian only as a fearful aberration from a story of my mother's about a friend who'd been *turned* by a mannish German bassoon player. I told them my mother's story; they laughed. Afterwards the conversation flowed easily, though much of it was buffered in old friends' banter. It was a relief when they suggested that we go downstairs and dance.

We'd been on the dance floor for only a few songs when a new girl joined us. I didn't hear her name properly. Something like Bitte or Britte or Beata. She'd just come back from a year's volunteering in Malawi. She was tall and Swedish and her skin was very tanned. Her eyes were clear, cornflower-blue. Her body was strong; her features were strong. Her hair was peroxided, freshly cut, schoolboy cut, short back and sides. The kind of cut that begs fingers to run up against the grain.

Shyly, I worked my way next to her. Her style was cool and minimal. I reined in my shoulder grooving, my floppy hands. Getting another beer, I got her one too. We shouted back and forth about Malawi. The lake so big you couldn't see the other side, the awesome fish, the hospital where she'd worked. I'd taken a friend to that hospital, I said. I left out that it was because he got alcohol poisoning. She bought the next beers, and we gave up trying to talk. When a slow song came on, we shifted minimally together. I ran my fingers up the back of her hair. And then we were snogging, beer tongues, beer breath. It was different from snogging Sabine; these were straightforward, lustful, warrior-like kisses.

Several beers past midnight, I found myself stepping across the riverbank onto a narrowboat. After unlocking a door at the helm, the Swedish girl lit a gas lamp and let me in.

'My sister's boat,' she said. 'She's away for the summer.'

The interior was lined in wood; it was simple, everything a bit worn, uncluttered but cosily messy. There were a couple of wicker boxes and some wicker drawers. An elephant-print cloth hung like a curtain to demarcate the living from the sleeping area. To one side was a pine trunk with cushions; to the other, a tatty armchair covered in a brown crocheted blanket. Shivering, I wrapped the blanket around me while she set about lighting the stove. It didn't feel so much like being on a boat as in a forest cabin.

Kiare Ladner

Once the fire was burning, she poured some of her sister's bourbon into mugs. The logs smelled amazing. She said they were apple wood. We started kissing again and I felt at ease, content. As I dropped the blanket, she removed my jumper and cami all in one. I took off her t-shirt and bra; beneath it her breasts were luxuriously large. I caressed them, I sucked on the nipples. I yanked my own bra off, grateful then for the chill that made my nipples stand erect. We stroked and kissed and pinched and grappled. Though we didn't speak, my internal monologue wouldn't stop. I kept telling myself she was exactly my type. Hot. Bold. Stunning. But, for all that I tried to talk myself into it, I couldn't seem to get turned on.

Then an idea came to me as clearly as if it were in lights: *Be Sabine.* I changed my posture to Sabine's. I pressed the Swedish girl back against the side of the boat as I imagined Sabine would. Bit and nibbled and teased like Sabine. I enjoyed it; this was fun. But despite losing myself in the performance, I didn't feel the genuine level of arousal needed. When the Swedish girl steered me towards the elephant curtain with the single bed beyond it, I excused myself to go to the loo.

In the tiny bathroom, I fell back on fantasies that usually took me from nought to sixty in two seconds. But they didn't work. I had a pee, flushed, and was about to give up when I saw the dispenser of liquid cucumber melon hand soap. I pumped some out and smeared it around my crotch.

I don't know what I was thinking because as soon as our jeans were off, we went down on each other. Deliberately, I went down on her first. I enjoyed playing with her; I got caught up in what I was doing, but in a voyeuristic, curious way rather than an aroused one. I took my time, was happy to take all the time in the world. But abruptly she swung herself around and it was my turn.

Breathing heavily, I made noises of appreciation. I tried not to think of what cucumber melon liquid soap tasted like or if it made bubbles, if it lathered and bubbled up. The best, I reckoned, would be for me to fake come before she'd licked all the soap off. I did my Lamborghini quickie impression, making gasps louder than I ever normally would.

Fake panting in the fake aftermath, I pulled her head up to mine. The cucumber melon smelled strongly then; I could taste it as she kissed me, surprisingly tenderly. I felt that I had to acknowledge the soap but didn't know how. She spared me by saying, 'You're funny. I like you. But you didn't have to wash down there beforehand.'

'I was sweaty,' I said.

She said, 'I like sweat.'

With more gratitude than she could have guessed, I went down on her again.

She was slower now to rise to where she'd been before. As my fingers began to tire, my jaw to get a little stiff, the situation felt familiar. Not as a sexual experience but as something else. I kept trying to place the familiarity. And then it came to me: it reminded me of exercise. Not of running but of how I used to feel when I went to the gym.

Repeating the same manoeuvre, over and over. Getting a bit of an ache but knowing I'd be glad for it afterwards.

When she came, I kept watching her face. Her glowing cheeks, her fringe damp with sweat; her lips just parted. But even at this, her most magnificent moment, even as I was grateful for the privilege to stare and stare, I didn't feel turned on like when I watched a man. Watching a man brought me close to coming myself – again even, if I already had.

Later, I lay cramped up against the side of the boat while she lightly snored. The alarm clock next to the bed ticked. I counted the ticks wishing I was at Graham's flat where, if I couldn't sleep, I could at least move around. Then I began to wish I was in bed with Graham. The more I thought about it, the more I wanted it; I craved it, restlessly, impatiently.

When the first strain of dawn pressed against the porthole, I snuck out. Closing the door of the boat quietly, I climbed onto the land. I started to walk down the towpath, then accelerated into a run. By the lock I heard someone calling in the distance, '*SJ, SJ.*' I kept going, sprinting up from the canal onto the city's deserted streets. I didn't hesitate or pause or slow down. Only when I reached the station did I realize.

She'd been calling after me.

19

Noisily, I let myself into Graham's flat. The blinds were drawn; the boiler made its reassuring hum. A faint cardboard and pepperoni pizza smell lingered in the air. I put the shower on so the water could heat up.

In Graham's room, I climbed onto his bed. Discarding my clothes, I kissed his stubbly jaw and nuzzled the prickles of his neck. Then I dragged him into the bathroom, under the spray. Kneeling in front of him, I ran my hands up his thighs, following where my fingers had gone with lips, mouth and tongue.

Afterwards, under the warm, steamy rain, I told him, 'I'm not a lesbian after all.'

'You tried?'

'I tried.'

'How many times?'

'I've only had a few weeks!'

'So?' He kissed the freckles on my back.

'Once,' I said, grudgingly. 'But it couldn't have had a better chance.'

'How so?'

'She was totally my type.'

'Your type, huh?'

'My wannabe type,' I corrected.

'And what's your wannabe type?'

I slid my hand onto his crotch. 'You wanna know?'

I gave him a girl-on-girl story for his fantasies but not the one that had been true. I could still hear the call of *SJ* in my ears. To have given him the truth would have betrayed the Swedish girl too far.

While we stood wrapped in towels beneath the blow heater, I asked, 'Is it too early for that Churchill champagne?'

'Meggie,' he said, 'I've got to get back to Cardiff.'

'We'll celebrate another time, then.'

'Thought we just did.'

I circled his nipple with my finger.

'Ye-es?' he said.

'Let's live together, Gray.'

His cheeks were red; I could feel mine were too but we didn't move from the heater's blast.

Then he said, 'Got you a little something in Wales.'

After rummaging in his toilet bag, he gave me a yellow drawstring pouch. Inside was a circular pendant etched with a squiggly little sheep.

'That's cute!' I regretted the 'c' word the moment it came out.

'You like it?' he said. 'There were others, more serious, with Celtic symbols and so on.'

I ran my thumb over the side of the disc that didn't have the sheep. 'You could always get it engraved.'

'With what?'

'*My Meggie.*'

Thinking I was making a joke, he burst out laughing. I pretended it was a joke too.

When the hilarity died down, I said, '*My Meggie* sounds stupid.'

'That's not what I meant—'

'It's got no gravitas.' It didn't compare to *My Sabine.*

'Megan's a beautiful name,' he said seriously. 'Looked it up when I met you. It comes from Margaret, which means pearl.' I thought of how a pearl forms due to a foreign particle in an oyster. 'Pearls have a natural, gentle beauty,' he added.

I tugged the cord to switch the heater off. 'When shall I give notice on my room?'

'Why not move in when I get back?'

'In two weeks' time?'

We stared at each other, hair half dry, eyes wide.

'If I leave now, I'll catch my landlady before she goes to Ireland,' I said.

He pulled me to him; I smoothed his fringe.

'Much as I hate you to go, Mum . . .'

I wriggled away. 'Don't ever, ever call me that, Graham!'

He pecked my forehead. 'You're so easy to wind up.'

PART III

20

Often I am kept awake by guilt. Yet when I truly go back into the past my perspective shifts. As I write the story down, I can see that when I tried to do what I thought I should, my attempts were doomed. How do you treat others decently when you want to become someone else? How do you live well when you yearn to burn with all your spirit in moments of wildness or freedom or excess?

By the April day set for moving in with Graham, I'd been fully nocturnal for almost three months. I'd assumed it would come to feel natural. Instead, the idea of going home to sleep after my last shift began to seem unbearable. Pouring a nip of mezcal by the photocopier machine, Earl asked if I wanted a line of coke.

I thought back to the excitement of the dot I'd tried in Telford. Then I thought of Graham coming round that evening, of the cardboard boxes waiting to be packed.

'Meggie? Yes, no?'

The mezcal burned like a fuse down my throat. 'Yes, please.'

The dust in the warehouse gave me a blocked nose. While

Earl chopped up the coke with a razor blade, I took a squirt of my decongestant. He made two perfectly even lines. Like in the movies, I gave him a fiver. Not like in the movies, he asked for a squirt of decongestant too.

Together we filled our clear nasal cavities with the numbing white dust. I recognized the bitter taste, the widening sense of possibility. Snorting the last traces back, I said, 'I don't come to the pub more often because I'm trying to . . .' *Write an essay on problems of representation.* 'Write.'

'You're a writer.'

'Maybe, one day.'

'If you write, you're a writer,' Earl said.

'I'm not writing,' I said, reining in my lie. 'Just trying.'

'I mix music. The others do stuff too. Sherry designs jewellery—'

'Hang on – you're a DJ?'

'A trier, as you'd put it,' he said. 'We're all triers here.'

The first line of coke was like taking baby steps in high platform boots. The second made me feel as if I could strut my stuff into the daylight. The third, combined with backing out of the building's shadow into the morning sun, gave a hit of euphoria that not even being a *cute friend* in supermarket trainers could dim. On the contrary, when I saw Sabine it seemed crazy that I'd been hurt by . . . what? I'd rejected her, then she'd rejected me. Neither of us wanted a proper relationship. Why not embrace the kissy friendship? Why not have some fun!

Sabine checked my needle-punctured palm then kissed it, though kissy kissing wasn't on the cards. When she leaned in at the pub door it was only to ask, 'Can I get some of what you've had?'

'Coming up!'

Sourcing the dealer's number from Earl, I placed an order that made my overdraft bulge. But when, forty-five minutes later, my delivery arrived with a guy on a bike like a pizza, I felt cool, I felt rich, I felt generous: I felt free.

After our crew left the pub, we went to what might have been a common or a heath. A breezy between-seasons place with tufty grass and a marbled sky. While we sat around drinking spirits from polystyrene cups, Sherry said, 'I hear you're a writer.'

'Nooo.' I scowled at Earl.

'Nooo?' said Earl.

'What're you writing?' Sherry asked.

'If I say, I'll spoil it.'

'You have to keep it in?'

'Yeah.' I took a hefty gulp from my cup.

'Like the multi-orgasmic man,' said Sabine.

'Exactly,' I said, though I didn't know what she was talking about.

'You mean, tantric stuff, SJ?' said Sherry.

'From the Taoists,' said Sabine.

'Taoists,' said Sherry. 'Oh.'

'If a man keeps his ejaculation in when he comes, he can come many times.'

'He comes without cum?' said Prawn.

'It's in his imagination,' said Sabine.

'Who wants to come in his imagination?' said Prawn.

'He has an orgasm for, maybe, ten minutes—'

'But in his imagination!' said Prawn.

'You take the piss,' said Sabine. 'But it's *beautiful*.'

'*Beautiful* for the woman too,' I said, speaking from my imagination.

I borrowed Earl's blade to cut some wonky lines that he refined. We all snorted them back.

Prawn made a bright moue in his pale, spotty face. 'How d'you do it, then?'

'Not easy,' said Sabine. 'You need to learn the technique. I bought a book in Berlin.'

'There's a city I'd go back to in a heartbeat,' said Lizard.

Then Sherry said, 'Meggie, you've got a boyfriend, right?'

I nodded.

'And he does this ten-minute-orgasm stuff?'

'Not this boyfriend.'

'This boyfriend? You have another?'

'No.'

'Only Gra-ham,' said Sabine mockingly.

'There've been others,' I said.

'She likes more than one!' said Prawn.

88

'What's Graham like, then?' said Sherry.

Everyone was watching me.

'He's sweet,' I said.

Prawn said, 'If a girl ever says Prawn's sweet—'

'No danger there,' said Lizard.

Earl pulled a face. 'Sweet, Meggie?'

'I don't know. He's not right for me.' I needed to stop. 'Things just sort of happened.' *STOP, Meggie.* 'And then, they kept happening. And, you know when you're in a relationship that keeps going because you don't get round to ending it?'

I sat there shocked. But wasn't I saying the truth?

'I was married to a guy twelve years for that reason,' said Sherry. 'Lost more than a decade of my life to riding the wrong pony.'

'He wasn't sweet, Sher,' said Earl.

'He was at first.' The cloying scent of Sherry's hair was strong as she leaned close. 'Before the jealousy, and the, you know, abuse.'

'That's hardly Meggie's situation,' said Earl.

'God, no,' I said.

Prawn topped up our cups.

'Graham's a good man,' I said, hoping to compensate for my disloyalty. 'We're not right for each other but there's nothing *wrong* either. He's generous. And mature. And he gives me freedom—'

'An open relationship?' asked Sherry.

I shrugged. 'Sometimes I go with girls.'

Sabine looked up.

'By go with, d'you mean fuck?' said Prawn.

'Yeah,' I said, 'fuck.' This was true too, wasn't it?

'I'll be generous and mature, any day!' said Prawn. 'From now on, I'm only going to be generous and mature.'

'Shut up, Prawn,' said Lizard.

'Why me?'

'You're giving me an earache, that's why. Your voice is a fucking earworm.'

''S true,' said Earl, chortling. 'Before I fall asleep, all I hear is Prawn's voice.'

'Cunts.' Prawn stormed off into the trees to take a leak.

The crew was silent.

Then Earl said, 'Sounds like Graham's not enough for you, Meggie.'

I could feel Sabine's eyes like a hot beam on my cheeks. 'You're right,' I said, 'he's not. The relationship's not. I ought to break up with him. I'm definitely going to—'

'Used to say it all the time,' said Sherry. '*Mañana, mañana, mañana*.'

I shook my head. 'Mark my words: I'm going to do it today.'

Sabine's dimple was flickering. 'Mark my words?'

Then she leaned in and kissed me.

21

Waking up in Graham's bed suggested I hadn't broken up with him. I felt sick in every way: puke-sick, guilt-sick, gutscared-hungover-sick. The white blinds were pulled down to keep out the light. But the sun wasn't even trying to get in; it was already overhead. My phone was on the pillow beside me. 11.07. Tuesday. Twelve missed calls from Graham (yesterday). I tried to curl into a ball but the skin at my knee pulled; a red-black graze glared.

I recalled the nauseating odour of a plastic apple hanging in a taxi, then getting out, falling onto gravel.

At the bedside table was a glass of water on a coaster. A box of paracetamol was balanced on top of it so insects couldn't fall in. If Graham dumped me this was how it would be: kind, considerate and neat.

Had he dumped me?

Unable to find my clothes, I took a faded green t-shirt from his drawer. The scent of his fabric softener stirred me uncomfortably. Usually when he went out he left a note. There was nothing in his bedroom. I went into the study, the front room and then the kitchen.

On the counter by the sink was a pale yellow Post-it; I steeled myself.

Hope you're ok. Speak later.

I looked at his plate, his knife, his coffee mug. I pressed my finger into the singed toast crumbs. When I licked it, there was a trace of marmalade. Did the note mean I could pretend the last thirty-six hours hadn't happened?

The kitchen window faced the terrace of shops across the road: a fried chicken shop, a solicitor's and a launderette. Did I need to stop nights for the sake of me and Graham? Or look for another room to rent? Or was it worse? Did I need to start over in Taiwan? As a child when I'd done wrong, I'd distract myself from the consequences with plans for escape: I'd imagine hitching to Durban, then stowing away on a ship . . .

Awash with fret every option seemed acceptable, except not knowing. I dialled Graham's number.

'How're you feeling?' His voice was as detached as his Post-it.

'Not bad,' I lied. 'And you?'

'Anti-puke pills in the cabinet.'

'Thanks, Gray.'

'Clothes in the wash.'

'Thanks.' Swallowing my shame, I focused on the solicitor's sign. 'I'm sorry about yesterday. I had mezcal on an empty stomach and thought I'd be sociable for a change. Then it escalated—'

'I can't talk now.'

'When I think of you waiting at my place—'

'Got to go, Meggie.'

The solicitor's said *J & B Blac son. Pi king p the piec s.*

'Please, Graham. How can I make up?'

He was quiet.

Then he said, 'It's not your fault you're my weakness.'

'You're my weakness too,' I said.

He groaned. 'Urghhh, bye.'

The phone cut off.

Urghhh, bye? I snorted my diva tears back. I had no diva rights. I had no rights. I didn't even deserve his paracetamol.

Harnessing the energy of my guilt, I put on a pair of large yellow Marigolds and did the washing-up. I didn't stop there. I emptied the kitchen cupboards. Mopped the floors. Scrubbed. Vacuumed.

After defrosting the fridge, I disposed of everything past its expiry date. But for all my efforts, I felt no better. As parts of the previous day seeped back into memory, my relief at Graham's not having broken up with me was replaced by a less comforting cycle of thoughts.

What have I done? I can't move in with him. Can't move in with someone I talk about like that. I've messed this up. I don't want to hurt him. How do I get out of it? What have I done? And why, on the day of my move, did I kiss Sabine?

Once the flat was so spick and span it would have impressed my mother, I lay down shaky and sweaty on the kitchen floor. My phone next to me on the lino tiles vibrated with a text.

Sabine: *you ok*

I didn't want to reply. Didn't want to see her, or anyone else

93

from nights, ever again. Perhaps it *was* time to move, not just home, but country. Give up the booze. Do something good. Sign up with VSO like the real lesbian, the Swedish one, had.

But my renegade thumb typed: *Cool – you?*

Sabine: *cool too*

I turned the Nokia's screen face down. But the six-word conversation revived me enough to topple a Sunny Delight from the fridge shelf. I sucked at the fake juice until the bottle conked in for a gasp. When my phone beeped again, I skimmed it across the tiles, out of reach.

Then I crawled over the floor to fetch it.

Sabine: *want me to come round*

Me (leaving off the punctuation and caps like she did): *im at grahams*

Sabine: *i know we shared a taxi remember*

I didn't remember. Me: *yes ok come*

I reread the sequence of messages. One moment I was full of regret, the next I was being an idiot again.

Yet, humming a Jacques Brel tune while I splashed my armpits with cologne from a dusty bottle in Graham's cupboard, I couldn't deny: the spirit of the day had lifted.

Opening the door to Sabine, my awe of her was for a moment too much. Her skin glowed, her hair was glossy; her limbs, though slim, were curved with muscle. I wondered if us having sex would be an antidote, if it would defuse things as it had with the Swedish woman.

Then I noticed how much she'd girlied up. Under her duffel coat, she wore a skimpy yellow dress and black ankle boots. She had pink pearl polish on her minute nails and a dusting of eyeshadow, lipstick, blush. I interpreted it as a retraction from dykey inclinations. Or could it be to impress my boyfriend, since we were at his flat?

Leading the way to the kitchen, I felt like my teenage self again, bell-shaped and stale. I needed a drink. A couple of beer cans knocked against the fridge door. On the top shelf, the Winston Churchill lay prominent in its box.

'Fan-cy,' said Sabine in her soft, low drawl behind me.

'Need more than fancy on my side later,' I said.

I passed a can to Sabine but she shook her head. 'No beer?' She wrinkled her nose.

I put her can back and tapped the top of mine but didn't open it. 'Graham's upset with me.'

'S'understandable.'

'I know.'

She hitched herself up onto the counter by the sink. '*I'll break up with him! Today! Mark my word!*'

'Sabine. Please don't—'

'And later? He rang and rang. We all said, Meggie, answer! But you didn't want—'

'I'm an arse,' I said. 'Can't stay with someone I treat like that.'

'*He* doesn't know.'

'But *I* know,' I said, my face hot. 'And everybody else knows.'

She swung her legs back and forth. Then leaning over the

sink, she opened the tap and drank. I pictured Graham's slight frown. She wiped her wet lips with the back of her hand. The rim of the tap was smudged with lipstick.

I should offer her a glass, I thought. But I didn't want to be the kind of person who offered glasses, who insisted on doing things the conventional way.

Taking the Winston Churchill from the fridge, I opened its velvet-lined box. I slit the foil, unpeeled it, and popped the cork to release a small genie of vapour. In a tribute to her ways, I took a swig from the neck.

My mouth filled with bubbles; I choked.

Laughing, she whacked my back. 'Can tell you don't have French blood!'

While I continued to cough, she moved efficiently around the kitchen. She found the long-stemmed *poshies* at the back of the Tupperware shelf in no time. She took the champagne from me, stood the glasses side by side, and filled them up.

I'd always liked Graham's front room. Once, when he was at football practice, I spent an entire afternoon lying on his leather sofa watching the breeze in the leaves of a conker tree. But the tree had been hacked back at the start of winter, and as I sat on the sofa with Sabine, the room, rather than feeling peacefully spare, felt sparse.

She leaned over the sofa arm to the console and fingered through Graham's CDs. They were all either jazz or classical. She chose Prokofiev's *Romeo and Juliet*.

'My favourite ballet,' I said.

'You like ballet?'

'When I was a kid I wanted to be a dancer. I was crap at it. But I couldn't stop reading those fifties books: *A Dream of Sadler's Wells, Veronica at the Wells, Masquerade at the Wells, No Castanets at the Wells . . .*'

Sabine bobbed her head to the violins' soaring opening.

Embarrassed, I pressed eject. 'What have you got in your bag?'

From the discs in her flipcase, I selected a CD she'd been handed at a club night called TrailerTrash. As soon as we put it on, the early afternoon atmosphere of the flat changed. We played it loudly while we talked and drank.

Above the TV, a tarnished seventies mirror was screwed into the wall. I kept gazing at our reflections. Then Sabine waved at me.

'It's the tint,' I said. 'Makes it look like we're in a fairy tale.'

'Fairytale friends, no?'

I wanted to secrete myself away with her words, keep playing them over. But forcing my eyes from the mirror, I poured the last of the champagne. 'Why d'you change your name to SJ?'

'If you always do everything the same, your brain gets in a rut.'

'I've heard about brushing your teeth with your other hand. Or altering your route to work.'

My phone beeped.

Graham: *Got a leaving do. Back by eight.*

'Your boyfriend?' said Sabine.

'Yes.'

She ejected the TrailerTrash disc.

'Don't go. It's only two o'clock.'

'Bathroom first,' she said.

The moment Sabine left the room, the mirror emptied itself of the desirable life it had reflected. Alone, my face changed: I saw its asymmetry, its uneven texture. I saw the look of resignation; I was too young for such a look. I didn't want to be this person, or live in this flat, or even wait here until eight.

Taking the empty champagne bottle through to the kitchen, I dumped it in the bin. About to put our glasses in the sink, I noticed the smudge of red at the tap's rim. I listened to make sure Sabine was still at the other end of the flat. Then I put my mouth to the tap. I put my lips around where hers had been. I turned it on and drank as she had.

When I pulled back, her smudge was gone.

I went to fetch my denim bag from Graham's bedroom. I puffed his white pillows and smoothed his white duvet. Glancing at the glass of water on the bedside table, I felt bad. Then I smelled Sabine's scent.

I turned to her. 'Fancy going out somewhere?'

'We can get the bus to Camden.'

'Let's go,' I said.

22

The pub roof garden was gaily decorated with what looked like giant cocktail umbrellas. Silk flowers corkscrewed the iron railing. The concrete tables were decorated with shells and a ragdoll in sunglasses lazed back with her pudgy cloth feet resting on one of them. Otherwise, unsurprisingly for a Tuesday afternoon in spring, we were the rooftop's only occupants.

Screwing up her eyes at the feeble sun, Sabine said, 'So you didn't break up with Graham?'

I chewed the straw of my caipirinha. 'It's more complicated than I made out.'

'You're pregnant?'

'Not as complicated as that.'

'What, then?' She took a cigarette from a crushed pack of Menthols.

'I was supposed to move in with him. Yesterday.'

She laughed. 'Already you fucked up.'

'Thanks, Sabine.'

She fished in her rucksack for her skull lighter. 'But, come. If you change your mind, it's better now, no?'

'You mean for Graham?'

'For both.'

She was right; he'd find someone else. I foresaw a leggy woman in a floral dress: good-natured, pretty. Both successful lawyers, they shared sandwiches in lunch breaks at court.

I put my head in my hands. My own future was less clear. 'I've given notice on my room. I'll need to get another place.'

The cigarette pack shot between my elbows. 'We'll get a place.'

'We?' The pack was empty.

'It makes sense.' She lit up.

I said, 'We're both night owls.'

She gave her cockeyed smile. '*Deux chouettes.*'

Finishing off my caipirinha, I couldn't quite believe it.

I smiled back. 'I'll get us more drinks to celebrate.'

Someone had scrawled on the toilet door: *I'll call you Laurie. When you call me. And you can call me Al.* I took my mobile from my bag. The battery icon on the screen was flashing; it was days since I'd charged it. Before Graham's number could ring, the phone cut out. I pressed down hard on the power button. Dead.

A sign, said my more cautious voice. *You can't end your relationship like this.*

But another voice said, *It's going to be awful however you do it. You might as well get it over with.*

Not wanting to be a *mañana mañana* person, a Sherry type, I slipped out of the pub. A bright red phone box stood like an exclamation mark at the bottom of the block.

I've always been amazed by how quickly things can change. One moment, I was swimming along about to embark on a cohabitation that might have led to a life together. If I'd kept going with the flow, perhaps there'd have been kids, grand-kids, chromosomes forever entwined . . . Except the next I was clutching a bone-shaped piece of plastic in a urine-scented cubicle saying, 'We need to break up.'

'You're pissed again, Meggie?'

'It's not because of that.'

'Where are you?'

'Call box.'

'Look, we'll talk later.'

'Graham, there's no point.' A death rattle of coins went through. 'I'm sorry, this is a crap way to do things.'

'Actually, it's pretty fitting.'

'If it's not going to work, it's better now—'

'Fuck off, Megan.'

The line went so quiet I thought it was dead. 'Graham?'

'I've one last thing to say to you.'

I waited.

'You're obsessed with that woman. I don't know what she's like. But I feel sorry for her. It's terrible to be used like that.'

I was stunned.

'As for you,' he continued. 'With her in your life, nothing's going to work out. No relationships. No literature studies. Nothing.'

A long tone sounded. Then the automated voice: 'The caller has hung up. Please replace the handset. The caller has hung—'

I wanted to howl down the line. He'd got it so wrong.

Failing at law school, I'd expected to die of shame. But after my mother said, *You're no child of mine,* all I felt was relief. Coming to the UK was about escape. But once I was here, I didn't know how to be different. Didn't have the imagination, didn't have the guts. And if we lived together, if it went well, aged fifty I might still feel that way . . .

'The caller has hung up,' repeated the automated voice.

A bleary-eyed woman was banging on the door.

I slammed the handset pointlessly into the bracket and went back to the pub.

Waiting for a pack of Menthols and a couple of gold-flaked tequilas at the bar, I resolved not to mention what I'd done to Sabine. It would be better to keep things separate in my mind. Besides, I didn't want to spoil this day which, while marking the end of me and Graham Willoughby, meant something entirely different for me and Sabine Dubreil.

After we'd knocked our tequilas back, I said, 'Know what, SJ? I'm also going to change my name.'

'What's your middle one?'

'Greta. Yours?'

'Don't have.' She flicked her cigarette into a pot plant. 'MG is magnesium.'

'How d'you know that?'

'I did chemistry at school. Of metals, MG has the lowest melting point.'

'Not cool like SJ, then?'

She lifted her rucksack onto the table. 'If you really want change, it's best to start small.'

I put my paperback-sized bag alongside hers.

'No.' Shaking her head, she opened the drawstring. 'You need a sack like mine. With this one, you can go anywhere, do anything.' She turned the rucksack upside down. 'Look.'

I gazed at the things of her life, freely displayed before me: Guerlain Shalimar perfume, asthma inhaler, skull lighter, make-up, condoms, boxer knickers, frilly knickers, tights, the flipbook of CDs, Walkman, tissues, a hand-knitted chicken, toothpaste, toothbrush, a slim silver wallet, a broken compact mirror, mint gum, a fold-up hairbrush and a passport.

'A passport?' I said.

'I'm portable,' she said. 'We both need to be portable. Let's find you a rucksack too.'

In Camden Market, I withdrew the last of my overdraft from a machine that charged. Egged on by Sabine, I bought a yellow rucksack printed with sunflowers. I transferred the meagre contents of my bag (lip gloss, earphones, Walkman, phone, Jean Rhys novel, clip purse), then splurged on whatever took our fancy. Two lipsticks labelled Toffee Apple that Sabine said were classic Marilyn. Two vintage compact mirrors with Victoriana cases. Giant slices of doughy pizza. Paper cups of overpriced sangria. A yellow silk scarf (for Sabine) and a flowing sea-green dress (Sabine's idea, for me).

At the slightest hesitation in our spree, I'd say, 'What next?' Then she'd suggest something, and we'd do it.

Only when the stalls began to pack up did we stop. I thought we'd reached the end of our adventure. But a few blocks on, Sabine pulled me into a basement lined with plants in glass cases. Specifically, cacti and mushrooms. I'd always envied how people talked of psychedelic trips. Sabine asked the rainbow-haired assistant to see a box of fine shrooms with narrow stems and floaty heads.

'What d'you think?' she said.

'Let's get them,' I said.

'Twenty-five quid a box,' said the assistant.

'One, please,' said Sabine, and I coughed up.

A couple of hours after we'd eaten the shrooms, Camden Town transformed into an early evening parade of storybook characters. People pretending to be shop assistants, bus drivers, metalheads, rock chicks. I hadn't expected the trip to be this palpably material. The sky was a blue so smooth it seemed like we were inside a balloon. Around us, the parade was moving to the thrum of the earth turning. I could hear the thrum, every hollow in my body filled with its vibrations. I was about to ask Sabine if she could feel it too when she said, 'Fuck, I must get to the airport.'

I started to laugh, then couldn't stop. She caught the giggle bug from me and couldn't stop either. We sat on the cracked pavement, cheeks cramping, bellies aching. She kept trying to gain control, to speak again, but the battle on her face was even funnier than her words. Finally, she dragged me to a vendor selling freshly squeezed orange juice. I signalled to him for two cups. We gulped them down.

'Juice neutralizes shrooms,' she said.

I bought two more, which we drank less desperately.

Then she said, 'I must fly to Hong Kong to join Lucian.'

My urge to laugh stalled. I thought, *Who's Lucian?* Then I thought, *I'd better not ask.* She'd probably already told me. Then I asked anyway, 'Who's Lucian?'

'A crime writer,' she said, biting at a nail. 'Nobody here's heard of him but he's big in, I don't know, Japan and the rest of the world. He's got a wife and kids but travels a lot. I travel with him.'

The way she said it, I knew she hadn't told me. I felt my face go dark. I saw myself as a pathetic conquest: her plaything, her paying thing.

'You're going to fly while you're high?' I no longer felt very high myself.

She started to laugh again while waving for a black cab. 'We'll share. I'm going home first.'

In my newfound semi-sobriety, I drew the line. I wouldn't pay for a taxi so she could go back and pack her things. 'I'm not going home.'

The cab pulled up; she opened the door.

'What about getting a flat?' I asked.

She flitted her hand through the air. 'I'll SMS.'

As we hugged goodbye, she whispered, 'Wish I was going to Hong Kong with you.'

Yeah, I thought, *sure you do. Me and my open purse.*
All I said was, 'Ciao, hey. Have fun.'

23

Over the next fortnight, I got no messages from Sabine.

Luckily, my landlady said I could postpone moving out. In anger at my general foolishness, I lived more punitively than ever. The resolve was helped by being broke. I had basic foodstuffs in my cupboard but no money for anything else. I saw no one and, other than my scheduled runs, went nowhere. Days I spent trying to sleep, nights trying to study, but failed dismally at both. The only thing I managed with any success was to block out thoughts about Graham; guilt at how I'd treated him made it easy.

Determined to move on, I took stock of where I was. I'd been in the UK for over two years, in London for over one, doing nights for almost five months. I hadn't found my niche but shift work provided the time to do so. If I stayed nocturnal a bit longer I'd surely get used to it. If I hoped to one day find a job linked to books, I was doing the right degree. Finishing with Graham meant losing his social circle but I'd cope. As an only child, I was used to my own company.

With renewed dedication to my studies, I tried to accept my solitary, marginal life. But it didn't happen. Instead, I began to crave aspects of the ordinary I'd never craved before. Light, noise, colour, people. One night, I blew out my black candles, shut down my computer, and walked four miles to a 24/7 supermarket.

I'd always had an aversion to supermarkets. They epitomized domesticity, suburbia, the life I didn't want to have. But that night! Light, noise, colour, people, life! I wandered up and down the broad aisles, smiling at the packers, making meaningless chitchat, looking in wonder at the jaunty yellow cereal boxes, the cheerful cows on the cheese wedges, the heavy, globular avocados, the smiling bunches of bananas, the little fly that had come in from the outside world to buzz over some spilt blueberry yoghurt on the floor; the marvellous, enviable little fly that tomorrow would return to the sunshiny, bustling, ordinary, everyday outside world.

The experience reminded me of the mushrooms at their most fun with Sabine. I didn't want to leave; I stayed in the supermarket until dawn. When the sun came up over the car park and whited out the night, I stood there on the empty tarmac staring into the bright, brilliant light.

Nocturnality wasn't working. I needed a new plan. But my numbed-out brain couldn't come up with one. Reluctantly I walked home, I ate my pasta, I lay in bed.

Then the next shift began.

24

While my mind shut off every avenue leading to Graham, it was more capricious with Sabine.

At first, I did everything I could not to bump into her. I came in early, left late, and avoided the lavatories on the corridor where I'd first seen her. I didn't talk to anyone more than was absolutely necessary. It was easy since at the start of shift everyone else was in their own world too.

But as the mood of the week lifted, my annoyance diminished. I became curious. Then, I became careless. And then, the pendulum swung the other way. I'd arrive on time, pause by the Energy door, use the lavatory that both teams used and go more than I needed. I'd hang around by the photocopier and loiter on the Energy floor. Once, I even found an excuse to wander into Energy's offices – but there was no sign of her.

Stumped, I couldn't ask anyone where she was because *we* were supposed to be friends. Close friends, even. Lovers, some might have assumed.

What a joke.

Maybe if I got to know her better we could be one or all of those things. As it was I didn't even know what continent she was on. Quite likely, she and Lucian had decided to stay in Hong Kong.

No sooner had I resigned myself to the idea than in my pigeonhole I found a surprise.

Behind my usual hefty stack of newspapers was a blank white envelope, not sealed or even folded closed. It contained a single stalls ticket to *Romeo and Juliet* at the Royal Opera House the next night, Friday night, before work.

The rest of the shift passed in a blur of distracted thinking. Sabine hadn't left the country. She hadn't abandoned the friendship. She hadn't been using me for money. Perhaps she'd lost her phone, or forgotten about messaging me. Or, perhaps I shouldn't make excuses for her. She played games, she was unreliable – but that was her nature. The counterbalance was excitement, spontaneity. As for living together, that had been a bad idea. Had I ever truly wanted it? I needed to stop getting pissed off about things I didn't want. The gifts were special; didn't they show that I was special to her? The thing was not to ever count on Sabine. What was so great about reliability after all? Wasn't it enough that she was special to me too?

At home, I tried on the sea-green dress I'd thought I'd never wear. It looked better than anything I'd have chosen for myself. I needed elegant shoes to match; supermarket trainers would hardly do. In a local charity shop, I found a pair of high silver slingbacks. I spent the afternoon walking around in them. With the house to myself, I played Jacques Brel full blast. I sauntered about my bedroom, then the sitting room, then down the stairs to make a coffee in the kitchen.

Through the ceiling, I heard the high electronic vibration behind Brel's plea. *Ne me quitte pas, Ne me quitte pas, Ne me quitte pas, Ne me quitte pas.*

25

Light reflected off the Royal Opera House's golden curlicue; it shimmered in the crystal chandeliers.

Sabine hadn't said where to meet and I didn't want to spoil the magic of her ticket with a humdrum text. The red carpet was sumptuous beneath my heels as I crossed the foyer scouring the women. Some wore evening gowns and jewels; some were such balletomanes that their outfits resembled ballerina-type garb.

The auditorium bell rang. Presumably, Sabine expected us to meet at our seats. When I found the right entrance, I joined the queue in front of it. I pictured the dancers standing in the wings: clavicles vibrating with their heartbeats, bodies alert. I felt like I was in the wings too. Soon I would be next to Sabine.

A striking couple stood near a recess a little way through the crowd. The woman had a long back exposed in a low-slung silk dress. Her black hair was fixed into some kind of knot with a tortoiseshell comb. The man appeared to be much older: tall, debonair, with notably thick, grey locks. I assumed he was her father until I saw him put his hand on the exposed skin of her lower back. The whole of his hand, the flat of his palm. He slid it down, beneath the draping of the top, to the very base of her spine. It seemed wrong but I couldn't look away. I felt aroused at what he was doing, as if his hand were there on the base of my spine, holding it, cupping it. The woman arched her back into him, then slipped from his hold and turned.

It was Sabine.

The ticket wasn't intended for me. The envelope hadn't had my name on it. What had made me assume it was mine? Sabine had left it in my pigeonhole by mistake. I had to leave; I stepped out of the queue.

Sabine saw me.

Too late.

But her face lit up. Her lips parted; her eyes crinkled. She rushed over and grabbed my hands. 'I *knew* you'd be so beautiful in the dress!'

'I didn't recognize you,' I said. 'Your hair's . . . grown?'

'Trick comb.' She tucked back a loose curl. The tall, grey-haired man had joined us. 'Lucian, meet Meggie.'

He opened his arms. The lining of his jacket was smoky patterned silk; his white shirt was textured with white embroidery. He smelled of frankincense cut with a trace of cigar. He held the hug he gave me for a fraction too long.

Breaking away, I asked, 'How was Hong Kong?'

Lucian raised his eyebrows to Sabine.

'Tokyo,' she said. 'We stayed in a glass hotel with a bar you'd love. Views in every direction. A man played a white piano around the clock.'

'Not the same man, of course,' said Lucian.

'No,' said Sabine, 'in shifts, like us.'

Before anyone could ask about my time off, the highlight of which had been a visit to an around-the-clock supermarket, the auditorium bell sounded its final call.

I was following Sabine towards our row, when Lucian pushed in front of me. On reaching our seats, he sat down between the two of us. I assumed she'd swap places when she noticed. But while the orchestra tuned up, she simply reached across his lap to take my hand.

Lucian leaned back with a closet smile as Sabine drew my fingers to her lips. She'd made this gesture before. But now I saw his hand move between her legs. The tendons rose under his skin as he pressed. Were there expectations for the evening that I hadn't realized? The lights dimmed; the auditorium was quiet. Then Sabine bit the tip of my finger. I cried out.

'Shhhh,' someone said.

A twitch of amusement passed between the two of them.

While Sabine watched the ballet, Lucian watched her. Sometimes she whispered to him; sometimes I caught him glancing at me. In different circumstances, his attention might have made me feel good. But here, everything was related to their sexual dynamic. When the curtains came down after the passionate balcony scene, I told them I had to make a call.

Around the corner in Floral Street, I bummed a cigarette from a sulky teenager in a suit. Then I leaned against the wall by the bins, smoking. My money was on the ballet being Sabine's suggestion but Lucian's funds, Sabine's friend but Lucian's fantasy. What was his fantasy, though?

I didn't need to go back, I told myself, crushing the cigarette under my shoe.

But during the second act, watching the playful carnival dances, my perspective shifted. Perhaps I was being curmudgeonly. If Lucian and Sabine were a bit silly, a bit insensitive, they were also lustily in love. If having a witness to their liaison heightened it, was that so terrible?

When the lights went up for the interval, Sabine hooked her arm through mine, 'so you don't disappear again', and suggested some champagne. She steered us up the carpeted stairs to the newly renovated Floral Hall.

The room was spectacular: glass and ironwork and light and mirrors. It had a barrel-roofed Victorian atrium with tall tables and bar stools shaped like plants.

'Where's Lucian?' I asked.

'Calling his wife.'

'Do you mind that he's married?'

'No,' she said, 'I like it.'

'Why?'

'We don't have the sort of thing that goes with domestic life.'

Waiting at one of the tables, I watched Sabine move towards a bar with sculpted metal leaves. I wondered what kind of thing she and Lucian had, exactly. In my relationships, age had been incidental. But with Sabine and Lucian, the gap of thirty-odd years seemed integral. He was an older man who clearly adored his younger woman; what was it like to be adored like that? Protected, cherished, as a father might cherish his little girl.

Sabine brought back a bottle and two wide-brimmed glasses.

While I poured, she slipped a finger under the neckline of her dress. Hooking a silver choker, she moved its pendant to the front.

I stared. 'That's stunning.'

'I guess it's part of me.' She shrugged. 'My fate.'

The Alexander McQueen scarab glistened against her pale, slender neck.

'Graham once gave me a sheep,' I said. 'I forgot it at his flat. So I guess it wasn't my fate.'

She gave a puzzled smile.

'Lucian's not the kind of guy who'd give you a sheep,' I said.

'No.'

'I mean, a sheep jewel.'

She touched it, frowning. 'Lucian didn't give me the beetle.'

I held a mouthful of champagne against my palate until the bubbles went flat. Then I swallowed. 'Who did?'

She kept rubbing the back of her pendant as if exploring it. I knew the words engraved there.

'Was it . . . another lover?' I prodded.

'That's one way to put it,' she said softly.

I poured more champagne. She drank hers as if it was lemonade, so I did the same. Then I filled our glasses again.

'D'you know,' she said, 'I was going to be a dancer once.'

'Like me?'

'Did the training. Look.'

She shifted her legs at the ankle. She nudged off one black heel then the other and pointed her stockinged feet. I was surprised at the enviably high arches, the deep curves. She slid off her stool and stood on her tiptoes. She lifted one foot to the knee with perfect turnout, perfect balance. Holding the table lightly like a barre, she moved en pointe.

'Stop,' I said, wincing. 'Without shoes you'll hurt yourself.'

'My feet are already fucked.' She rested her weight back against her stool. 'That's why I couldn't go on.' What she'd done would have been painful but it seemed to cheer her up.

'When I was small, I collected ballet programmes,' I said. 'I kept track of the dancers as they rose through the ranks. My mother thought I was peculiar—'

'You were a serious child.' She looked at me with affection.

Then she said, 'My parents didn't have money. We didn't go to the theatre, these sorts of things. But my brother took me to see ballet films in the town hall every Sunday night.'

'Your brother?' She'd never mentioned siblings before. I'd assumed she was an only child like me.

The auditorium bell rang.

I wanted to ask her more but I'd pried too much.

She slipped her feet back into her shoes. We gulped the last of our drinks and returned to our seats.

For the third act, it was a relief not to be next to Sabine. I needed space to think about what she'd said. She was someone who had a brother, who'd loved ballet enough to train to be a dancer, who'd been doing what I dreamed of even before I knew her. But also, there was the thing about the 'lover' who'd given her the scarab. What did she mean by it?

At Juliet's bedside scene, I reimagined Sabine as the ballerina. I watched Juliet trying to wake Romeo, shaking his lifeless body, putting his limp arms around her. Lucian slipped an arm around Sabine. I saw him watching her solicitously in the dark, his cherished little girl. Suddenly, I had a profound ache of confused envy. I didn't want to hold Sabine myself; I wanted to be held like that.

Juliet used her last moment to reach out for Romeo's hand. Then their families came in to find them, fingers entwined.

After the crimson-and-gold house curtains fell, we followed the dazed audience into the street. Lucian summoned a black cab.

He looked at Sabine, and then to me, and then back to Sabine.

She shook her head.

'Shame.' From the cab, he blew us kisses. Lowering the window, he called, 'Thanks, Sabine, for the stupendous treat!'

Sabine's treat? As we headed towards the Thames, I did the maths. Altogether, the tickets would have cost a month's rent. How could Sabine afford that? I'd thought the ballet was her idea. But had she also been the instigator of some sexual fantasy?

It started to rain lightly, rain like damp lace. Then the rain became heavier. We hurried along in melancholic silence with our heads bowed. I was sure it was my fault. Because I hadn't contributed to the intended spirit of the evening. Because I'd pressed her to open up, to speak of things that were hard.

I said, 'Let's find a cashpoint.'

'Now?'

'I owe you, Sabine.'

She was annoyed. 'I don't want your money.'

I kept my eyes focused ahead. She didn't want anything particular from me, nor for me to do anything I didn't want to do. By Southwark Bridge, I spotted a pub with a stained-glass door. Friday night glowed promisingly through it. I hooked my arm in hers, as she had mine earlier. 'I'm getting you a drink at least.'

Several tequilas later, the rain had subsided. Although we hadn't spoken of anything much, our mood had shifted to become dreamy and close. As we crossed over to the other side of the river, I thought of how I'd almost left the theatre, almost ended everything before it had even begun. I resolved not to let it happen again. I wanted whatever we had, whatever we might have, at any cost.

The lights beside the water plated the Thames silver and gold. With lemon and salt still tanging my lips, I felt exhilarated. What Sabine had said at Graham's when she saw us in the tarnished mirror was coming true. *Fairytale friends.*

PART IV

26

From the moment I gave in to my craving for her, everything changed. Sabine was no longer a catalyst for what I wanted, she was it. I longed to know her, to know about her – but more than that, to *be* her. Tired of the rooms in my own dreary house, done with measly alterations, I let go, the house burned down . . . and it felt good.

Though Sabine set the terms of our togetherness, I accepted them. In part, her unreliable ways were the flipside to her playful qualities. In part her talk, especially at the ballet and in Valentines, had hinted at a past that deserved allowances. But mostly, her influence gave me permission to explore a freer version of myself.

I lost touch with old friends; what we used to discuss came to seem dull, our bonds circumstantial. Phone calls to my mother, never regular, became rare. I took to using inter-national cards in call boxes. It was easier to steer away from her despair in a public place, on a handset greasy with others' fingerprints.

Since Sabine wasn't solely nocturnal, I stopped trying to be that too. Shifts on, I was; shifts off, I wasn't. My brain felt constantly woolly but it no longer seemed necessary to be sharp. Mainly this was because I'd quit my literature studies. If I did it with some regret, I reassured myself the decision was temporary. The longer I stayed away from my books, the surer I felt.

As an outsider, I'd always found refuge in reading. But as Sabine and I grew closer, I didn't need it. My outsider's life began to feel extraordinary. I didn't want to read about characters, I wanted to be them. I didn't want to read about adventures, I wanted to have them.

Sabine made our lives feel like enough of a story in itself.

After the night at the Royal Opera House, nine months since Sabine and I had first met, our friendship accelerated. No longer stuck in the house of the self, I felt as if I was on a long journey in a sleeper train with a changeling companion. A train that sped through unknown territory, not stopping at timetabled stations but arbitrarily here and there.

With late spring as good a time for change as any, I moved into the small flat in New Cross that Earl shared with his dog, Coño. It was an easy-going environment: relaxed and sociable with a regular flux of guests when Earl was around. Although Sabine and I never spoke of living together again, she enjoyed rocking up there with her rucksack full of food. She'd cook for us, and whoever else, a meal that was hearty and homely.

'Meatballs in fruit sauce served on mash, Meggie, Earl?'

'Soupe à l'oignon with fat slices of crusty bread?'

'Boozy mussels fresh today from Borough Market? *Quatre, cinq, six?*'

She prepared the food conscientiously like a *maman* but ate voraciously, greedily, like a teenage boy.

The few times she stayed over, she slept on my mattress in a vest and panties. After falling asleep, she'd kick the duvet off. By day she tended to be cold, particularly her hands and feet; by night she was always hot. Occasionally I'd lie like a succubus with my gaze fixed on whatever part of her was in view: an elbow with the shadow of a bruise on it or the oval soap curve of a breast pressed into a pillow. More often, though, I kept my eyes screwed closed since it was in bed I felt most estranged from her. We never cuddled or held hands or let so much as a foot touch a foot. It was as if she regarded the bed solely for sleep, and sleep a solemnly private matter.

Being so close to her yet so far, I would get a strange sensation in my belly. She was there, she wasn't there; she was by my side but I couldn't reach her.

Obsession is about not wanting to be the self. Wanting to be *other*. Next to her, I must have known, at some level, the ultimate impossibility of that.

When it came to kissing, Sabine and I did it only drunk and in public. Sometimes, I enjoyed the performance; surfing her wave of exhibitionism could be fun. Other times, it irritated me, though not entirely without contrariety . . .

Coming from a starchy, puritanical environment, I rejected pointless sexual boundaries. The more I knew of Sabine, the more I wanted to know. And I wanted to be wanted, of course. But I was also ambivalent about us getting more physical. Sex involves expression; fascination allows negation. My confused feelings were tossed about by our pushes and pulls, by frustration, curiosity and pride.

The closest we came to discussing it was at the Ladies' Pond in Hampstead. I recall the texture of the day clearly. Trying to lick the Smarties off before the soft-serve melted as we crossed the road to the Heath. My mouth filled with the sickly mix of chocolate, strawberry and caramel as we wandered along the paths through the trees. My fingers still sticky when we sat on the cement at the edge of the cold, broad pool.

Spontaneously, Sabine had suggested we go swimming. We were wearing lost property bathing suits that the lifeguard, charmed by her, had found us. For hygiene's sake, we'd put them on inside out; they were too big and slightly damp. Sabine's was tan with crisscross straps. Mine was pink with white dots and had a residual scent of coconut oil.

When the sun shone the afternoon felt almost summery, but it kept disappearing. As the cement flickered from cream to grey, I traced a crack with a long stick of grass. The water under my feet was clean but not clear; almost golden at the surface, though smoky mustard deeper down. The air was so quiet I could hear the crackle of a dragonfly's wings.

Then Sabine said, 'I leave every person I fuck.'

'You've never been left?'

'Not once.'

'You're too proud, Sabine!'

She swung her pale muscled legs back and forth, toes skimming the water without splashing. 'Do you ever imagine us having sex?'

'Sometimes,' I said. 'Do you?'

'Sometimes.'

I flung the trembling stick of grass away.

'An Austrian director told me actors often want to do it with each other,' she said. 'They want to do it badly. And it's great for the film. It keeps the, what d'you call . . .'

'Tension?'

'No, electricity. It keeps the electricity between them strong. But sometimes, the actors get weak. They give in. And then,' she blew the air out between her lips, '*pfff.*'

'*Pfff?*' I said.

'If you watch, you can see the exact moment. This scene, this scene: exciting. Then, *pfff.*'

I had a deflated moment of my own. 'You agree with him?'

She shrugged.

'You think fucking is weak?' I said.

'What if it is?'

'What are you, a nun?' I hugged my knees tight to my chest.

Her back straightened, eyes cut. 'What if I like it weak? What if I like it dirty, fucked up? What if I like it pushed to where you don't even exist—'

'I like that too.'

'But, Meggie, if we went there, you and I, we'd never come back. We'd skid off the piste, lose everything. We'd eat each other alive, cannibalize each other.'

I gazed at the silky gusset of my loaned costume. 'After we were done, I'd dump you so as not to be like all the others you've left.'

She gave a hurt laugh.

Was this our moment that I'd ruined?

I put an arm across her narrow shoulders. She picked at my costume straps. She flicked them against my skin. Her cold hand pressed below my shoulder blades. I felt her cold palm on the other side of my heart.

She pushed.

I fell forwards, headlong into the pond.

Surfacing from the icy water, I gasped, choking. Sabine pin-dropped in beside me and pulled me under. We wrestled. I couldn't see a thing but I had her in my grasp. I held on to her. In the privacy of the murk, I didn't disguise my obvious determination. Then abruptly her face appeared in front of mine, so close it almost touched. I rearranged my features; she didn't. I held her longer than I should have.

Above the water, she spat a stream into my eyes. We raced to the other side and I let her beat me to it. After circling the pond a few times, we floated together into the middle. The sun was a dazzling pom-pom that whitened out the sky. I wanted to store what I saw as a bright mental photograph.

But what has stayed with me instead is the image of Sabine when she appeared up close. Her expression as I held on to her was not spirited, as I might have expected, or determined, or even angry. Her eyes were blank, her jaw was slack; her face was vacant.

27

Just as in company Sabine and I kissed whereas on our own we didn't, in company we talked a lot about sex. *Yes, you can be a feminist and a sex worker. Yes, being a dominatrix is a bit like being a therapist. Yes, exploring destructive fantasies in sexual play can be empowering.* We did it with the other nightshifters, as well as with complete strangers: people we met in pubs, on buses, in markets and at clubs. They bought us drinks, gave us drugs; invitations fell like winnings into our laps.

One time in Camden Market we found a stall selling fetish furniture. I was in a green skirt with a tight purple dragon t-shirt. She was in a knitted minidress, navy with black stars. We wandered among heavily carved beds with ornate hook-and-eye headboards. Sabine ran her hand down a chair that looked like a throne with a hole in the seat. We made silly faces in the shadows cast by a spiky wrought-iron lamp. As we passed a bench contraption that resembled an inclined leg press, I slapped my palm on the cushion.

'Do you like my work?' A gaunt man with an emerald goatee and a double-angled nose emerged from a door at the back.

'Very cool,' said Sabine.

'Looking for something special?'

'Just looking.'

'How about this?' He showed us what appeared to be a collection of intricately decorated leather straps and silver buckles.

Sabine ran her fingers over them.

'My own design. You won't find it anywhere else.' He spoke with a slight Polish accent. 'You want to feel the weight?'

I held out my arms; it weighed more than I'd expected. 'Hea-vy.'

He quickly took it back. 'But very comfortable. Want to try it on?'

Once he'd fastened the buckles to my wrists, torso and ankles, I was wearing a swing. He yelled to a woman at the back who hurried over with a stepladder. He lifted me up and attached the harness to a scaffolding bar above our heads. A small crowd had gathered below us. He called to his assistant again and Górecki's *Symphony of Sorrowful Songs* swelled through the stall's speakers. He gave me a little push; I curved back and began to fly.

Though I knew the affecting music was based on words

etched into a wall by a Gestapo prisoner, I couldn't help being moved as I flew through the air in the erotic harness. Was it really less than a year since I'd been wearing a top with a cerise bow that my mother had chosen for me?

When I came down from the heights, the emerald-goateed man invited us to a castle in Germany. He organized a festival there every full moon. He said he'd be honoured if we'd attend as his guests.

We never made it there; our only trip away together was to Eastbourne. But after listening in on the conversation, a woman with a diamanté mohawk told us about a club in east London called Studio X. She raved about the circus freaks theme so much that we decided to give it a go . . .

At the next blowout with our crew, Sabine was away with Lucian. The rest of us sat around a low table in a basement flat with the blinds pulled down. Candles in an assortment of stalagmited bottles were scattered here and there. Missing Sabine, I longed to conjure up the spirit of our times together. After a few snorts of crushed-up MDMA crystals, I told the crew of our find.

'Imagine a seedy, intimate club under a railway bridge,' I said. 'It's open every night of the week. Imagine cheap, generous drinks. Drugs available on request from the doorman too. Imagine comfy sofas, a space-age dance floor and an ancient harem with a dungeon touch. A black club cat called Slinky making eyes at you.'

'Sounds like a dream,' Sherry sighed.

Encouraged, I carried on, 'Imagine no look required, all looks accepted. Being as comfortable to chat the night away as to spend it in a dark room. Imagine a secret dock where the underworld of the city can wash up against anyone else. A true democracy of race, age and gender—'

Prawn's pale, spotty face shone bright pink in the flickering light. 'Dudess, you've got to fucking take us there!'

'When SJ's back,' I said. 'Promise.'

28

Every time Sabine was away, she was incommunicado. It wasn't unusual; most of the crew had separate off-shift lives. Since she hardly touched her phone anyway, I supposed she got caught up in being wherever she was. Sometimes she forgot to say she was leaving but I accepted that too. She and Lucian often headed off at the last minute. Her disappearances didn't always correspond with her shifts but her opposite number seemed obliging. I assumed that he, a whippet-thin man with earnestly combed hair, was in love with her. It was easy to assume.

Although Sabine and I were more than merely work friends, I was proud that I didn't question her. That I didn't try to pin her down or make her conform to hackneyed etiquette. But I also had a more covert reason for my unpossessive attitude.

When we were together, I kept my obsession in check –
but apart, I indulged it. Not that anybody would have
guessed. I didn't talk about Sabine incessantly; I didn't talk
about her at all. Instead, I discreetly tried to be as much like
her as I could. The changes were subtle, hidden behind my
skin. She was there in the way I held myself, the way my
muscles arranged my face, the relaxation of my vocal cords
into their softest, lowest drawl.

My external self, with what others had called its *teardrop*
shape, *apricot-vanilla* colouring and *friendly* accent, was contrary enough to Sabine's for the imitation to go unnoticed.
But from the inside – unless I caught a glimpse of Meggie in
a mirror, I could almost forget who I was.

The sensation was expansive; I felt newly wired, freshly
connected to life. It happened with the crew, at Earl's parties
and with people Sabine didn't know. It happened with one-
night stands before, during and after sex. But it was the most
intense when I indulged it alone.

Since I couldn't find clothes like Sabine's on Petticoat
Lane, from charity shops I made up outfits similar in style. I
hid them at the back of my wardrobe behind my jeans, jump-
ers and camisoles. (Once I saw an astronomically priced
designer jacket identical to hers; she told me she'd got her
fake in Japan with Lucian for twenty quid. Japan was especially good for fakes, she said. The next time she went, she
got me fake Vivienne Westwood gloves and I had to agree:
indistinguishable from the real thing.)

Preparing to go out, I'd talk to myself using Sabine's

cadences. I'd wash, dress and apply make-up her way. Then I'd walk along the road with her gait. What I liked best, though, was to take on the version of Sabine that I'd never seen: the person I imagined she was by herself, for herself, when she was alone. I noticed what I thought she'd notice, went where I thought she'd go. I reacted in the way I thought she'd react when nobody was watching.

One weekday afternoon, I attended an exhibition of photographs by Francesca Woodman. Having selected it while channelling Sabine, I wandered around in the same vein. I paused at the self-portraits where she'd pause: the blur of a woman behind creased paper or the faceless woman curled towards a coiled eel in a bowl. I passed by the pictures whose titles alone would have made her yawn: *I'm Trying My Hand At Fashion Photography* or *It Must Be Time For Lunch, Now.*

Leaving the exhibition, I strolled on from the bars and buzz of the West End to the industrial buildings and new loft conversions of Clerkenwell. Segueing off to a lonely stretch of Regent's Canal, I saw a swan floating upside down on the water. Staring pensively, it took a while before I realized the bird was dead.

Hurrying away through the back streets of Islington, I came upon a French cafe. After taking a table under a kitsch mural of the Sacré-Coeur, I ordered a pastis, which I'd never ordered, or seen Sabine order, but could picture her doing in the circumstances. Sipping it slowly, I let my ears flood with the Marilyn Manson *Sweet Dreams* album she'd burned for me.

29

Convinced that Sabine's sexual past was aligned with our wilder leanings, it bothered me that mine wasn't. To catch up, I decided to treat my body as something to be used, to use it to gain access to what was outside my usual realm.

Early on, I made the mistake of trying to explain this to Earl. On a walk with Coño to Peckham Common, I told him how sex gave you a shortcut into other people's lives. You got to meet a range of individuals more varied than you would by ordinary socializing.

'You mean sex with women?' Earl said.

I shrugged. 'Mostly with men.'

Earl grimaced. 'Men are animals, Meggie.'

'Women are animals too, Earl.'

He shook his head. 'It's not the same thing.'

We waited for a van to reverse out in front of us.

'A guy might be getting what he wants,' I said. 'But I get what I want too.'

'Which is?'

'Connection. After fucking, people tell you things you'd hear no other way. They open up to you. Like that, you're in their home, their bedroom, their fantasies—'

'You want to be careful whose fantasies you're in.'

'But I don't! That's the whole point, Earl. I don't want to *curate* people according to what I think I like. Or *standards*. Or the need for mutual attraction even.'

Earl was dismayed.

'I want to use my body to access all of it,' I said. 'Uncensored.'

As we crossed over onto the Common, he said with real concern, 'That's not *respecting* yourself, Meggie.'

I was deeply annoyed with him then. Unhooking Coño's leash, I ran off with her across the grass. Why was it such a great thing to respect yourself? If you let go of vapid ideas like that, of that kind of preciousness, you could explore so much else. If you swept your precious self out of the way a bit.

After the conversation with Earl, I refrained from telling anybody quite how much I swept my own precious self aside. Often, I had to do it with a steel broom because it didn't come naturally. I'd research edgy encounters in clunky forums online; then, fuelled with wine, I'd force myself into the field. Yet, years later, it's the incongruous intimacy with strangers that sticks in my mind more than the actual sex. Small, personal details . . . A smell like boiled sausages on the neck of a wealthy, well-groomed man. The to-do list on a young woman's fridge that ended with 'BE KIND!' Erotic art books placed backwards on cluttered bookshelves. A dusty box of tampons in a man's otherwise meticulous bathroom.

For casual lovers, I had only four rules, though I treated them as gospel: I'd have sex drunk, but never on drugs; I'd have sex privately in public places (bathrooms or locked parks at night), but never publicly in clubs; I refused to have sex without condoms; and I never invited anyone back to Earl's. The last was important, not because of what Earl might think but because being away meant I could escape. I don't recall ever not wanting to escape as soon as the sun came up.

One morning I crept out of a Soho apartment before the guy I'd slept with was awake. Aside from a foam mattress, the place had been bare. He'd said it belonged to an old friend of his who was an artist. The luminous sign saying 'MODEL' flashed above the building's open doorway as I left.

Sashaying through the streets of Covent Garden, I felt fine and carefree in my short yellow dress and black ankle boots. Soon I became aware of a man with a large camera behind me taking snaps. I kept walking but secretly I courted it. I flirted, he followed me; I paused outside a high-end lingerie shop that was just opening. He stopped a few paces back. In the plate glass, his hair was thick and white; his tanned cheeks had deep vertical creases.

Wandering around the shop's interior, I fingered a salmon lace negligee.

'You like it?' he said in a European accent I couldn't place.

I nodded.

He took it to the counter and paid for it, then asked if I wanted a bag.

I said, 'No.'

He gave me the parcel wrapped in black tissue paper and tied with golden string. We walked outside together. 'Are you Austrian, or maybe German?' he said.

'French, Belgian, Jewish, Jamaican . . .' I said.

Placing two fingers on my waist, he signalled the coffee bar over the road.

Demurely, I smiled.

No sooner had we sat down than I made the excuse of needing the bathroom. Picking up my parcel, I said, 'I might try it on.'

'Good idea,' he said, X-ray eyes flickering.

In the kitchen area at the back, I told a waitress I was being harassed. Could she let me leave by the staff exit? Out on the street, I ran to the Underground. I just made it through the doors of a waiting train, the tissue paper of the parcel damp in my hands.

Back home, I felt bad. Not about the man, or my deception, but about the crudeness of the exchange. Though a minor thing, it ripped the performance that only hours before I'd affected with brio. I felt sullied by what I'd done. It made me wonder about Sabine, if she'd have acted like that. For the first time, when I brought her to mind nothing lit up.

I hid the negligee in my cupboard. But I didn't want it in my room; I didn't want it in the flat. After a few hours, I threw it away in a public bin. I dismissed the incident, and the odd shadow it briefly cast, as an unimportant blip.

Now, it reminds me of when, as a child, I saw a strikingly pretty shell on a rock at the beach. I tried to pick it up, to add it to the collection in my bucket, but it was stuck. I knew I wasn't meant to take shells stuck to rocks, but using my spade I smashed it loose. A week later there was a terrible stink in my room. It came from the shell, the rotten creature inside. My neighbour scooped it out and washed the shell – but when he gave it back to me, I couldn't keep it. I threw it into the dam near where we lived and it sank out of sight.

30

After the negligee incident, I sought clarity. What was I doing? Why was I doing it? And what exactly did I want from Sabine? Despite his disapproval of my promiscuity, I ended up talking to Earl again. He'd asked my opinion on some tracks he was mixing.

His bedroom was like an intricate 3D puzzle perfectly constructed. Though filled with records, turntables and computer equipment, it didn't feel crammed. Each object had its place and he kept it immaculate. There was a mild citrus scent from his shower gel. If it hadn't been for the majestic dog bed you'd never have guessed Coño slept there too.

Yet while Earl's room was a safe, ordered space, the sounds he filled it with were unrestrainedly creative. From his computer, he'd play me different versions of the same tune. Sitting on a three-legged stool across the room, I'd tell him which I preferred. He said he rated my musicality; it felt like a fun, random thing. Since there were no expectations, it was easy to go on instinct. That day, I shifted topics in the same spirit.

'Did you always know you were bisexual?' I asked.

'No,' he said. 'Some gay men try to be straight, then realize they aren't. With me, it was the opposite. Once I came out, I found I liked women too.'

'How come?'

'A friend's sister asked me to be her date as a favour. And then we fell in love.'

'So it was about one specific woman?'

'As opposed to . . . ?'

'What if you're actually gay? And she was the exception?'

He toyed with one of his twists; they were dyed purple this week. 'Why choose an illogical explanation over bisexual?'

'If it's honest?'

'But you're bi, Meggie?'

'Not sure.'

He slotted a new disc into the hard drive. 'All those one-nighters with men put you off?'

'No, it's women I'm not sure about.'

'But you and SJ are crazy for each other!'

'You reckon she's crazy for me?'

'Definitely.'

I wanted to scamper off to my room. It had been like that since I was a child. Whenever someone said something nice I wanted to get away so as to preserve it.

'You're into Sabine too, though?' Earl asked.

I pressed my palms against the stool. 'That's what I've been trying to work out. Am I gay, or straight, or bi? But maybe I've been asking the wrong question.'

'What's the right one?'

'Is it possible in life to want to fuck just one person of the same sex?'

He frowned as the disc ejected itself; he wiped it. 'Unlikely.'

I said nothing.

'*Are* you into Sabine?' he asked.

'I love to watch her.' I chose my words carefully. 'And I want to touch her.' He put the disc back in the slot. 'To touch her while watching her. And I think about her constantly—'

The disc began to play but he paused it. 'You want my advice?'

I nodded.

'You like men. You're into Sabine now. So you're bi.'

'Mm.'

'Or else a psychosexual obsessive.'

'*What?*'

'Someone who's so fixated on a person or thing that their sexuality focuses on it too.'

I stared at him.

He stared back, exaggeratedly. 'Meggie, for fuck's sake!'

'But what if I am that?'

'You're way too sensitive. Now help me out here. Apply your sensitivity to listening for the reverb on these tracks.'

He played three versions of an electronic piece recorded in a studio, a bathroom and under a bridge.

Listening, I felt like Eve after eating the apple. My fixation with Sabine extended into every area of my life. Was that what my sexual interest in her was about? Earl was just too sunny a person to truly believe what he'd uncovered.

Then again, I wasn't driven by desire for her. More, by insatiable curiosity about her. And some impossible fantasy of being her. *It* didn't make sense – but *she* made me feel alive.

As the third track finished, Earl waited for my response.

Instinctively, I liked the version with the imperfections, the one under the bridge. But I felt wary of my openness. 'The studio's best,' I said.

'Really, Meggie?'

I shrugged a shoulder. 'It's polished.'

Earl looked disappointed. 'I was *sure* you'd say the bridge. But I guess I was wrong.'

31

Sabine and I made our single trip away together the week after the summer solstice. It happened swiftly, unexpectedly. In the morning, we were looking in the window of a travel agent at Victoria station; by midday, we were checking into a Georgian hotel in Eastbourne. The manager upgraded us to a top-floor suite with a clawfoot bathtub in the bedroom and a bay window filled with sea and sky.

Attracted to the shimmering town by its sweepingly grand facades, we hadn't realized we'd be a quarter of the average age. Then that became part of the adventure too. After a blustery walk along the promenade, Sabine ran us a deep bubble bath. Stripping off our clothes, we kept on the long strings of plastic granny beads we'd got in a local store.

As we climbed into the tub, steaming water rose towards the brim.

'Let's make a pact,' Sabine said. 'To come back here when we're eighty.'

I felt pastel-mooded, light-hearted. 'OK.'

I didn't think she meant it. She had this way of being sincere and careless, both. 'How will we seal the pact?'

'Tattoos,' she said. 'Seahorses.'

'Where would you like yours?'

Languidly, she arched her slender foot against the rim of the bath. I traced a seahorse figure on the side of her sole. 'Here?' I said. Rivulets of water trickled from her muscled calf into the tuck of her knee. 'Or here . . . ?' I followed them down the back of her thigh.

At the bubbles that hid the rest of her, I stopped. The skin of her shoulders, her neck, her cheeks was radiant and dewy. Her eyes were half closed but she was watching me through her lashes.

I tossed my hair, feeling damp burnished spirals framing my face. Our beads floated on the water: mine green, hers white. Two flappers from the nineteen twenties. Chorus girls on a clandestine break.

I turned the taps off behind me. If she wanted something to happen between us, it was her turn to make a move.

Water ran into the overflow pipe.

Then she said, 'You hardly ever talk about your mother.'

'No.'

'You don't get on?'

'We're different,' I said. 'We think differently.'

'What's she like?'

Narcissistic was the word that came to mind. But I wanted to keep things light. I told her how my surname, Groenewald, was common in South Africa but my mother didn't pronounce it the usual way. Depending on her audience, sometimes she anglicized it, claiming she was Mrs Greenfields; other times, with foreigners, she preceded it with 'von' for an aristocratic spin.

'Meggie Greenfields?'

'Meggie von Groenewald to you, Sabine.'

'What does your mother do for a living?' she asked.

'Florist,' I said. 'Or rather, she owns a flower shop.'

'What's the difference?'

'Thandi, who works for her, does the arranging. She makes beautiful understated bouquets. My mother gives them *flair*. So if Thandi ties up a bunch of baby's breath and pink rosebuds, my mother will add a *striking strelitzia*. Or if Thandi fills a basket with Namaqualand daisies, my mother will poke in a *swizzy grasshopper* on a stick.'

'She sounds like a character.'

'You could put it that way.'

Thandi was the reason the shop survived. And yet my mother treated her as its weakest link. If the flowers weren't properly stored or the orders were incorrect, Thandi got the blame. As a teenager, the only times I'd crossed my mother were to defend Thandi but whenever I did, she'd get annoyed and defend my mother in turn. My mother's superpower was to make allies of those who by right should have been her enemies.

Sabine slanted her eyes at me. 'It's hard not to have a father.'

Ordinarily, I'd correct people, saying it wasn't hard, or sad, or whatever they'd assumed because I'd never known him. But the way Sabine said it made me ask, hesitantly, 'Is your father . . . ?'

'Does your mother have other servants?' she said.

'Thandi isn't her servant,' I said. 'But she has a cleaner twice a week.' I left out that she also had a weekly gardener.

'My mother is a cleaner,' said Sabine.

'Of houses?'

'Offices. My father was a bricklayer.'

Was?

'He left when I was eight.'

'*That's* tough,' I said.

'My mother made his life hell. But she knows how to make the other person believe they are the bad one. She can make someone feel so shit they want to die.'

My mother could do that too, though I'd never told anybody.

'Living in a different country to your family has advantages,' I said.

'Does your mother beg you to visit?' Sabine asked.

'No,' I said. 'Does yours?'

'She says I owe her. But I hate to do it. She calls me a Jezebel, blames me for everything. When I'm not with her, I feel sorry for her. But when I'm there . . .'

'I know what you mean,' I said. 'My mother and I are not estranged, but almost. On the phone I feel guilty. But when I'm with her, I feel trapped. I don't think she likes the real me very much.'

'Do you like the real her?'

I took a shaky breath, shrugged. Even with it being six years since I'd first left home for university, I still felt my mother's monitoring presence.

The hot tap was dripping; I tried to screw it tighter. It was like we were in a bad mother competition. When I turned back to Sabine, I flicked some bubbles at her.

'Sometimes I can see you as a child,' she said.

'What sort of child?'

'Fiercely loyal, a dreamer. Eager to please.' Her eyes shone; she looked like she was about to say more, then shook her head.

'What sort of child were you?' I asked.

'Guess.'

What came to mind was *sexy*. But I couldn't say that. 'Not eager to please.'

She looked hurt. 'I *was* eager to please my brother.'

She bit one of her tiny fingernails. Then she said, 'My mother chased him away too. Said he was a bad influence.'

'Was he?'

She didn't answer at once. Then she held up two fingers,

crossed. 'We were like this. Xavier loved me more than life itself. He told me, *I love you more than life itself.*'

'How old was he when he left?'

'Seventeen. I was twelve.'

'Does Xavier look like you?'

'He looked . . . like Jacques Brel.'

I reached for her hand and held it.

'After my mother kicked him out, Xavier didn't care about living. He started to free climb, high up, without ropes.'

'I've seen it on TV,' I said.

'Then he did base jumping. I thought he'd die base jumping. But he didn't.'

I gripped her hand tightly.

'He dived off a high rock into a pool,' she said. 'His friends did it, everybody did it. It was a place known for this. You won't die unless you fall sideways and hit the rock. Or aim for the rock. People say, it's safe, you'd have to be aiming for the rock.'

Bath water splashed over the sides as I put my arms around Sabine. I stroked her silky black hair. I held her, and she held me. Our bellies touched, our breasts, our cheeks. I wanted to kiss her then, but recalled times with men when they'd converted an emotional moment into an opportunity for sex. How even when it was tender, I'd had this sense of rewarding their empathy, that they'd been hoping for the reward. It made me feel detached, slightly more alone. Not a big thing – forgivable even. But I didn't want Sabine to feel like that. I didn't want her to feel alone at all.

When Sabine let go of me, the way she did it was solicitous. As if she was the comforter, the one comforting me. She smoothed my forehead and kissed my cheek: a dry, maternal kiss.

Then she heaved herself out of the tub with both arms. 'Water's cold.'

I stared at the hole in the bubbles as she traipsed across the carpet, confused.

After she closed the bathroom door, I sat on the bed wrapped in a thick, white towel. From the bathroom came the roar of the hairdryer. I went to the door and pressed my ear to it, sure I'd hear Sabine's crying behind the dryer's noise. But I heard only the dryer, then silence, then the dryer again.

With dinner in the hotel's smart restaurant included in our deal, we'd packed clothes to match. Waiting for Sabine, I put on the sea-green dress I'd worn to the ballet with my silver slingback heels.

When she finally emerged, she was in a diaphanous lilac gown that trailed to her ankles. I didn't understand why she'd needed to dress privately. As she sat at the mirror, trying to fasten her scarab pendant, her fingers were trembling.

'Hungry?' I asked, going over to her.

She shook her head.

After I'd fastened the clasp, she said she felt ill. When I asked what was wrong, her expression was disconsolate. With my hands on her shoulders, I told her we didn't have to go down to eat. We could do whatever she wanted to do. Her muscles relaxed, her relief palpable. She said she wanted to take a sleeping pill and go to bed.

Since I didn't fancy lying awake beside her, or eating downstairs on my own, I took the pill she offered me too. Side by side, we stretched out on the ivory covers of the enormous divan in our long dinner dresses. I went from staring at the stucco patterns on the ceiling to feeling the sharp glare of sunlight pressing at my eyelids.

The phone was ringing; it was reception. The pills, stronger than any I'd had before, must have hit instantly. We'd overslept and it was already two p.m. The staff needed us to check out so that they could clean the room.

Afterwards, I wasn't sure how to think of the trip. Certainly I knew more about Sabine and she about me. But I was also unsettled by it. At the age of five, I'd had a friend who got too homesick to cope with sleepovers. Normally a confident child, she would tremble and sob until she threw up. Sabine's need for the sleeping pills reminded me of that.

32

Back in London, Eastbourne got stored in the miscellaneous section of my memory. The chest for arbitrarily recalled dreams, unjustified predictions. Meanwhile things between Sabine and me returned to normal. Better than normal: closer, warmer. As the last summer of the century progressed, our uneven journey continued – but now with a soundtrack to match.

We both had similarly eclectic taste; I was always either listening to an album she'd burned for me or finding one to burn for her. But recently she'd started a little game by slipping PJ Harvey's 'Is This Desire?' in among the tracks of a Tricky album. It was typical Sabine: surprises, contradictions. One moment I was listening to a complex low-tempo groove, the next to a lone female voice with guitar and drum.

In response, I slotted 'Kiss Me' by Sixpence None the Richer in among Bach's *Cello Suites*. She put 'Kiss You All Over' by Exile into an album by Kate Bush. I put James Brown's 'Please, Please, Please' onto a Debussy album. She put 'I'm Your Man' by Leonard Cohen into Missy Elliott's *Supa Dupa Fly* . . .

Applying myself fully to our project, I used music shops as lending libraries when my money ran out. I assumed Sabine did the same, though she never said. Money wasn't a topic that came up, nor did I want it to; financial complaints sat cheek by jowl with materialistic aspirations in my mother's world. Her chief bugbear was that my father had died before insuring his life. *We could have been like Mrs Esterhuizen, with her new BMW every year and her overseas trips. And her husband wasn't even a lecturer.*

Alternating extravagance with extreme frugality, I got by – until one day, I didn't. I was a hundred pounds short on my August rent. It wasn't a huge amount but I had no way of raising it. That night at work, *money money money* was all that was on my mind. I hoped to get through the shift without having to talk to anyone. But in the early hours, I got stuck in a lift with Sherry, Lizard, the shift leader and Sabine. Huddling to myself, I shut my eyes.

'Love your outfit, SJ,' the shift leader said.

Today it was a black net vest under a grungy slip dress.

'Everything looks good on you,' Sherry added. 'D'you ever do modelling?'

I opened one eye; Sabine was shaking her head.

'You and her, both,' Sherry said, referring to the shift leader, 'could be models. Whereas me and Meggie are girl-next-door types.'

I opened my other girl-next-door eye. What Sherry had said was true. The shift leader's hair was loose; crimped, it rippled onto her shoulders. She had a smudge of maroon shadow on her eyelids. Sabine wore no make-up but her lips were as red as if tinted, her lashes as black as if kohled.

'Girl-next-door types are the best,' said Lizard.

'Yeah, and my favourite bird's a pigeon,' I said.

'Is it?' said Sherry.

'No,' I said.

Sabine laughed. 'Pigeons are pretty, pearly at the neck.'

'I prefer blue tits,' said Lizard.

'Did I hear tits?' Prawn shouted from the other side of the lift.

'You are so missing out, Prawny,' Sherry said.

Wedging a large screwdriver between the lift doors, Prawn prised them open a centimetre. His white-fringed eye appeared in the gap. Lizard joked that it was like we were in a peep show. Prawn latched on to the idea as *da bomb*.

While the others laughed it off, I cleared my throat.

'What d'you want to peep at?' I asked Prawn.

'You and Sabine. Kissing.'

'OK,' I said.

'OK?' Sabine raised her eyebrows.

'For money,' I said.

'You didn't charge before,' Prawn said.

'Wasn't a peep show before,' I said.

Sabine was studying me.

'How much?' said Prawn.

'Twenty to start,' I said. 'Rolled tight, and slotted through the gap.'

'*Twenty quid?* I haven't got twenty pee!'

'No twenty, no peep,' I said.

'Aw . . .' said Prawn.

'I've got an idea,' Sabine said. 'We'll do the kissy peep show for you, if you do one for us first.'

'No, I veto that,' I said.

Why . . . ? mouthed Sabine.

'Hang on,' said the shift leader. 'This is getting interesting.'

'Beg, borrow or steal, but cough up,' I said firmly.

'*I'll* do it with Sabine,' the shift leader said to Prawn, 'if you do it for us first.'

Inside a tune twisted; since the hypnosis night some months back, I'd suspected she wanted this.

'Do – what?' said Prawn.

'Kiss a bloke,' said the shift leader.

'I've never done that.'

'First time for everything,' said Sherry.

'But who can I ask?' said Prawn, his eye blinking. 'Lizard?'

'I'm in here, mate. Can't do it through the peep.'

In the silence, we heard footsteps in the corridor.

Prawn's eye left the hole, then came back. 'Göker?'

Göker was a hairy, butch guy from Energy. Though he never came out drinking with us, from the marinade of his eyes and skin I'd assumed he took alcoholism to a level that made us seem like children.

'Don't even go there,' I warned Prawn.

But the shift leader seemed to have lost her head at the prospect of kissing Sabine.

'Ask Göker, Prawn,' she instructed.

We heard Prawn walk off.

Sherry's lips stretched with anxiety.

Next thing, big, butch Göker came over. His bullish eye roamed across us. He tried to prise open the lift doors.

I smiled; Prawn had bottled it, Göker had come to rescue us.

The gap between the doors widened a few more centimetres before the screwdriver snapped. Göker tossed the two pieces aside.

'Now you can all see,' he said, beaming.

Göker and Prawn faced each other. Göker stood as upright as a guard. Prawn moved in, pulling a constipated face. At first, it was like bad porn; then Göker put his hands on either side of Prawn's pale head and kissed him, hard. Prawn seemed momentarily almost swept away. Göker broke the kiss off with a laugh.

'Good enough?' he asked us.

'Thanks, mate,' said Prawn, moving his hand to wipe his mouth, then thinking better of it.

Göker thumped his shoulder, and left.

'Is he gay?' said the shift leader.

'Maybe gay, maybe bi,' said Lizard.

'Whatever,' said Sabine. 'He's cool.'

'So's Prawny,' said Sherry. 'The nineties aren't exactly the swinging sixties!'

Sabine winked at me; grudgingly, I winked back.

Prawn filled the gap between the lift doors with his shiny pink face. 'Swinging or not, I'm getting a fucking *deckchair*. You girls owe me big time.'

'*Pas de problème,*' said the shift leader. She turned to Sabine. 'Is that the right expression?'

'*Oui,*' said Sabine.

Pas de problème. Oui.

The shift leader draped one slim arm around Sabine, then the other. Sabine glanced at me. She mouthed, *Shall I say no?*

I shook my head, surprised. She kept looking at me while the shift leader did flitty kisses up her neck. I didn't know what face to make; I wanted to watch, I didn't want to watch. *Close your eyes*, I mouthed to her.

Prawn's chair squeaked as he opened it out.

'Start again!' he shouted. 'I'm back!'

Sabine closed her eyes and they kissed. A long, sensuous, aesthetically pleasing kiss. I pretended they were models on a photo shoot.

But I didn't need to pretend. When they broke apart, I didn't feel jealous. Sabine's eyes were on me, her lips asking, *You OK?*

I knew then I was her girl at work if I wanted it.

Yet when I tried to smile back, to reassure her, *Yes, of course*, I was overwhelmed by a sense I didn't deserve her. I wasn't beautiful like a model. I didn't do my job well, wasn't able to get a degree, couldn't even be counted on to have the money for rent. Not to mention maybe being a psychosexual obsessive . . .

Feeling like an altogether inferior species, the moment we were released from the lift I sought the solitude of the lavatories. Locked into the far cubicle, I cried. Then I kicked the wall. I shoved a toilet roll into my mouth and screamed.

Sabine's white face appeared at the top of the cubicle divider.

Over a mug of horrible French herb tea on a back staircase, I gave the most straightforward explanation for my behaviour. I told Sabine I'd been overspending. Things had spiralled out of control. The bank sent a letter. I didn't open it for two days. Then I did. The more I spoke, the more my words hit home. I had penalty charges for overdrawing. My credit card was maxed. But that wasn't the worst of it.

'What's the worst?' she asked.

'Tomorrow's rent day. I'm a hundred quid short.'

'Earl will understand, Meggie.'

'It's not up to *Earl*. He doesn't own the flat.'

'Is this really just about money?'

'Yes!'

'You weren't making a hundred-pound noise in there. You were bankrupted.'

I frowned at her.

She touched my arm. 'Don't worry, it's not the end of the world.'

'Just the end of my rent. Next week I'll be on the streets.'

She shook her head. 'Something will work out.'

The rest of that night, I didn't listen to music. Wherever I went, Sabine was chatting away. Relieved she didn't attempt to include me in her gaiety, I kept my head down.

At last, the interminable shift came to an end. But as I was leaving the warehouse, she ran up to me. She pressed a paper bag into my hand.

I unfolded the top; it was filled with notes.

'We had a little whip round—'

'Sabine, I can't accept this!'

'Pay the rent,' she turned back to the building, 'then buy us a drink.'

After work the next morning, I went to the White Hart. Sabine wasn't there. I tried to buy everyone else a drink, but they wouldn't hear of it. While there'd been over a hundred pounds in the bag, they insisted they'd contributed no more than a couple of pounds each. Maybe they had.

And maybe they hadn't.

33

After Sabine's kiss with the shift leader, I wondered if anything would develop between them. She'd been reassuring in the lift, though that was before she saw me in the loos. But, miraculously, neither drama nor irresponsibility appeared to have put her off. On the contrary, she embedded *two* rogue tracks into a metalcore album: 'Déshabillez-Moi' by Juliette Gréco and 'I'll Make Love To You' by Boyz II Men. I'd chosen Schubert's 'Liebesbotschaft' as my first reply; the other I planned to select following the solar eclipse.

Sabine and I had made arrangements to watch it together. We had the protective sunglasses provided free with the daily papers, and a bucket of water to reflect the phenomenon too. Earl had gone off to Cornwall so we had his balcony to ourselves. I'd read that the earth would go dark, cold and quiet. Birds would return to their nests; bats would flit across the sky.

Despite the New Cross sky being solidly overcast, as Sabine and I held hands, I felt the build-up of something momentous. The muggy August air began to cool, the mid-morning light to dim . . . We looked from the clouds to the water in the bucket, to the clouds again. Through the orange tint of the cardboard glasses, Sabine resembled a nerdy person caught on old film negatives. Seeing her like that gave me courage for my secret plan: to kiss her at the moment the earth went dark.

With the handicap of being sober, I should've gone through my moves. Would I slide a hand around her waist, then draw her to me and kiss her neck? Or would I take her cheeks in my palms and brush her lips with mine? Instead, I thought of how she always seemed like someone slightly different; I could never get to the bottom of her. She was perceptive, intuitive and compassionate. The sort of person who did things without fussing. I admired her streetwise savvy and how she was also kind.

So my paean to Sabine continued until the sky began to get lighter. I hauled the glasses off and stared brazenly into the sun. 'Was that *it*?'

'*Oui, mon chouchou.*'

I couldn't believe it. In place of the thick cover of darkness I'd been counting on, the experience felt like no more than driving in and out of the shadow of a mountain.

Unceremoniously, I tried to take Sabine's glasses off too.

'Wait,' she said, stopping me. 'I'm still looking.'

'Nothing's there. Look at me, rather.'

Amused, she held the boxy glasses back from her face.

I leaned in, intending one of our deep, intimate kisses. But then I saw she wasn't expecting it. Her lips were closed. I was too late to make my lips do a peck. So I sort of breathed on her with my open mouth, then ran away, embarrassed, into the flat.

She came running after me, giggling. 'Poor Meggie!'

'Poor Sabine!'

'But you had *Great Expectations*, no?'

In my room, we both collapsed onto my mattress. My side was by the street; hers by the door. She opened a bag of chewy sweets and threw me one. I threw it back. Her eyes teased; I felt silly. Everything seemed like a tease that I took too seriously: our kisses, the tracks we swapped, 'Déshabillez-Moi'.

While she busied herself with her phone, I reached behind the blackout curtain to open the window. As the cloth flapped against the glass the room was never dark, just more shadowy or less.

A truck below blasted out rap lyrics to the tune of 'Jesus Loves Me'. *Wha's yo mutherfukkin game? Wha's yo mutherfukkin game? Don mess wit me . . .*

When she put her phone away, I asked, 'Where's Louche today? Lucian?'

'Fuck knows.'

'Is that what you call him for short?'

'No.'

'D'you call him *mon chouchou*?'

She tossed her head. 'I call him Papa.'

'He likes that?'

'*I* do.'

The truck hadn't moved; it was caught in a traffic jam. *Wha's yo mutherfukkin game? Don mess wit me, yo JHC . . .*

'What does he call you?' I asked.

'My girl.'

My girl was different to *My Sabine.* It could be innocent, like the soul song. Or it could be dark. I stared hard at Sabine in the dimness. Then I looked down at the childish feet sticking out of my jeans; at moments my own body could seem equally foreign. *Who is she, this woman in my bed?*

'Tell me a fact from your teenage years,' I said.

'You go first,' she said.

'I was a Christian,' I said. 'It was everything to me.'

'And then – it just stopped?'

'At university, I met people from other religions. When I saw how strongly they believed in their gods, Christianity didn't make sense any more. It's the same with relationships, I guess. If I realize it's not happening, I shut the door.'

The truck had moved on. Sitar music was coming from a colourful campervan. I expected Sabine might offer up something spiritual.

But she said, 'One summer I had to go to hospital by the sea.'

I thought of her dancing. 'For your feet?'

'Don't like to say.'

'In Belgium?'

'No. *En Suède.* Sweden, the islands.'

The campervan was stuck in the traffic jam now.

'They made us do tiring things,' she continued. 'Though we also swam in the lakes. Sat around a big fire. Talked, told stories. Sometimes what we said was true, sometimes not. But lies can be . . . more true than the truth.'

I held the blackout cloth back.

'What are you thinking now?' I asked.

'I like the music.'

'Me too. I wonder what it is?'

'But, Meggie. What matters isn't the facts. It's how our lives cross when we're together. This changes us, makes us unstable—'

'Unstable?'

'It's good,' she said. 'Exciting.'

The sitar music moved on; the conversation felt harder to continue without the soundtrack. I wished the campervan would come back.

'Impermanence is life,' I said, letting the blackout cloth drop.

'Sleep is life too.' Sabine yawned.

A few minutes later, I could hear the soft rhythm of her breath. In the shifting greys of the room, I watched her: the line of her back, her neck, her hair. The wonder of another person. I felt something retract. It was pointless to try to push the physical boundary between us. I promised myself not to initiate anything again. What I had was enough.

34

Around this time, Sabine appeared to have moved. Where she'd lived previously was grim: a run-down terrace in Peckham with a flaking green door. I'd glimpsed an empty hallway and a stack of unopened post. She'd said the house belonged to an elderly woman and her rented room was shabby, that I'd be shocked by how shabby it was. She didn't say much else about her landlady other than that having friends over would be an invasion of her space. Not interested in invading anyone's space, I'd text Sabine when I got there and wait for her in the street.

I never saw another person enter or leave the building. Though I do recall a grey, blustery day and the metallic, sickly smell of the butcher's shop opposite. How it troubled me to watch men unloading the milky-white carcasses from behind the plastic fronds of their frosty van.

Shortly after the eclipse, Sabine began texting me to swing by a smart Georgian mansion block in Mayfair instead. A black wrought-iron fence framed a couple of steps that led up to a studded double door. Antique lanterns were mounted either side of it. In the arch between them hung the building number: 29. To the left was a brass intercom system that I never used. As with the place in Peckham, I'd send a message when I arrived and she'd come down.

Apparently the place was Lucian's. Sabine pointed to a window at the right corner; his studio flat was up there on the second floor. He required a bolt-hole away from the family home to work on his latest novel. As soon as she left he had to get on; he hardly needed the distraction of her bringing me upstairs with her. 'He likes you, though,' she said. 'He thinks you're lovely.'

I grimaced at the word. 'Are you and he getting more serious, then?'

'Not really.'

'You're always there nowadays.'

'We used to go to hotels. Now it's not necessary.'

'I didn't pick you up from hotels.'

'Obviously not, Meggie.'

Then she said that the mansion block was an odd place. She hadn't met any of their neighbours. The whole building seemed to be owned by rich people from other countries who were never around. 'Most of the time it's dead quiet inside,' she said.

'Suits Papa,' she added.

After I ran out of money, I'd give Earl my rent in advance, the day I got paid. The rest of the month I'd leave to balance itself, prioritizing times with Sabine. For each adventure we had, whoever made the suggestion funded it. Mostly we alternated, though sometimes I'd do a few in a row or vice versa. Since I didn't feel used and wasn't using Sabine, I assumed it worked out reciprocally.

Occasionally, before she went back to the Mayfair flat,

Sabine suggested ending the night at Claridge's. We'd be warmly greeted by staff as we went in. She'd waltz up to the bar and ask for two glasses of Cristal. Because of its silly spelling, I assumed it was cheap. She'd insist it was her treat and I'd let her enjoy being generous. We'd take our favourite table; then she'd repeat the order and we'd Cristal the night away.

Once, I suggested ending an evening with a date similarly. I finished my glass of Cristal in no time, though he seemed to be taking inordinately long with his. When the waiter came round and I asked for another, my date said, 'How about a cocktail this time?'

'OK,' I said.

'Two mojitos,' he said.

When the waiter had disappeared, I said, 'Don't you like Cristal?'

He looked a bit sheepish. 'I'm thinking of the bill.'

'I'll get it—'

'No, no.'

'Of course I will,' I said. 'But why d'you order cocktails if you're worried?'

'They're cheaper than Cristal.'

'No way,' I said.

'Bet you the next round of cocktails!'

'You mean the next round of Cristal!'

He opened the drinks menu. On the third page, he showed me – cocktails, mojito: twelve pounds. I smiled while he carried on flipping the pages. When he reached the last page, he turned the menu around. He pointed at Cristal: fifty pounds. That was way more than I'd expected. But at fifty a bottle, a glass would still probably be cheaper than a cocktail.

'No,' he said, 'it's per glass.'

I checked; he was right.

Astonished, I paged through the menu again, trying to find a different way to interpret it. When the waiter returned with our mojitos, to my date's embarrassment I asked, 'Is this the price?'

'Yes,' the waiter said.

'Has it always cost that much?'

'It's Cristal,' he said. 'And, darling, you *are* in Claridge's.'

After he'd gone, I said, 'My friend buys us rounds and rounds of the stuff every time we're here.'

'Your friend must really want to impress you,' he said.

35

Cal Janssen was someone I'd had a crush on for half my life. He was tanned, rangy and blond with lake-blue eyes. At school I'd gone out with his softer-featured younger brother. We'd both worshipped Cal and he'd been consistently kind to us.

On holiday in Gordon's Bay when I was twenty, I'd bumped into Cal at a beach party. Skinny dipping in the sea, he'd said he fancied me. I'd said I fancied him too. Our sex was briefly intoxicating. But he called the next day to say what we'd done was, *Not cool, Meggie.* Although I didn't think it was that terrible, I pretended to agree.

I'd assumed that'd be the last I'd see of Cal, but we seemed destined to bump into each other randomly. On a hot September night when Sabine and I were in a Chinatown dive bar it happened again. He left his group of blokeish guys to drink with us. When they moved on elsewhere, he stayed. He said they were colleagues from the architects' firm where he worked. He was involved in a project on social housing: eco, sustainable stuff. He asked what we did for a living. Sabine excelled herself in making our jobs sound important and us indispensable. We drank more shots together, made silly toasts, laughed, told stories and smoked.

Shortly before the bar closed, Sabine followed me to the bathroom. Adding a coat of mascara, she said, 'He's hot.'

'You fancy him?'

'You do too.'

'No way.'

'I know you do!' Turning from her reflection, she put her arms around me. 'Let's have a threesome.'

Despite the undercurrent at the Opera House, Sabine hadn't suggested anything like this before. *She must like him a lot*, I thought.

Back in our candlelit corner, I weighed it up. On the one hand, it'd be fun. On the other, I didn't want Sabine to have sex with me just because she wanted it with him. I didn't want pity sex from her; if it happened between us, it needed to be completion sex. But there was also an invisible third hand to the problem: I didn't want Cal to say again, and in front of Sabine, *Not cool, Meggie.*

I considered telling Sabine about Gordon's Bay. I trusted that she'd prioritize our friendship. That she'd change the direction of the evening to one of tease-not-touch revenge.

Yet, as I waited at the bar watching the pair of them take such obvious pleasure in each other, I thought maybe Papa wasn't good for Sabine. Maybe she needed someone like Cal. Maybe with him she'd be happier than she could ever imagine. After all, who wouldn't be?

When Cal went outside to take a call, I told Sabine I was tired, exhausted; I had a cold coming on. I didn't fancy him but, definitely, she should—

'Meggie, you're lying.'

'No. He's a great guy—'

'But?'

I sighed. 'I'm not doing it, Sabine. But you want to. And I want you to.'

When Cal came back downstairs I slipped off the bench. Planting kisses on each of their cheeks, I left.

The night bus home was noisy with drunken teenagers and stinky with stale farts. When I tried to look out the window, the reflection of the interior blocked the city beyond. At my feet the floor was sticky; an orange can rolled to and fro.

I'd given Sabine a long-term boyfriend, a fiancé, a husband. Already I could see her simple white dress, her slender hands holding frangipanis. She and Cal would be as infatu-ated with each other as I'd been with each of them. They'd have kids together, rangy and beautiful, a boy and a girl. Emi-grating to Canada, they'd live by a lake in a wooden eco house, designed and built by themselves. I'd visit, bearing gifts for the little Janssens. Meggie, the London godmother. No more than the character in their fairy tale who'd brought them together.

When I didn't hear from Sabine the next morning, I went for a run to Crystal Palace. Then I took a bracingly cold shower. Afterwards I played Bill Evans' *Conversations With Myself*, which I hadn't listened to in a long while.

I imagined a room with a black futon bed beneath a window shaded by a bamboo blind. Sabine wouldn't be curled into herself like she was with me. Her and Cal's bodies would be shadow-striped in the early light, their limbs tan-gled together.

I switched Bill off, then tidied my room. I tried to read a few pages of the Jean Rhys novel I'd had in my rucksack for months. Nothing from Sabine.

Twelve o'clock, one o'clock, two o'clock, nothing. I left the flat and walked two hours to Hyde Park. In the cafe by the Serpentine, I allowed myself to be chatted up by a greasy, lank-haired man. I let him have my number with no digits altered. Five minutes later, I got a text. *PrT, Brighton, 2nite. Driving down. Wn2 come?* I walked home, checking my phone. Every ten minutes, every five. But it was always only more texts from the Serpentine man. *U SxC gal. PrT b orsum! I cn pik u up? Gud tyms :) :)*

Back at my flat, I finally texted Sabine. *how're things*

ok, she texted back. Then, *i could come round now ish*

lets go out rather. I wanted the armour of public surroundings. *pig and hen at 9*

ok

I dressed in black jeans and a lace cami. I blow-dried my hair to make it sleek and took time over my make-up. When I saw her, I was glad of the effort I'd made because it seemed she'd done the same. She was all in black too, eyelashes curled, lips glossed.

I set a glass of red wine in front of her with my hands trembling a little, like hers sometimes did. I was so sure of what I was about to hear.

So sure that I made her repeat what she'd said twice.

She claimed it had been fine, all right. Cal wasn't really her type either. 'Like you said, Meggie, he's a nice enough guy.'

36

The Pig and Hen was out of cigarettes so I nipped to a mini supermarket a couple of doors down. As I joined the queue by the cigs and booze counter, I looked, and looked again. Graham, my ex-boyfriend, was standing there in fruit and veg, dressed in a charcoal suit. I'd not seen him in a suit before but he filled it out; he looked amazingly good in it.

Since, thanks to my earlier efforts, I felt okayish too, I dared myself to go up to him. Maybe he'd say get lost – but probably he wouldn't. Our disastrous end had been such a small part of the relationship as a whole. Besides, even if Sabine's night with Cal hadn't worked out, some day she'd meet a single guy with whom it would. I wanted that for her, and I wanted it for myself too. Then again, quite possibly I'd *already* met my guy. In hindsight, what I'd had with Graham was pretty rare. We'd been intimate, able to talk about anything, even shared a sense of humour.

I'd just left my place in the queue when Graham tossed a bunch of flowers into his basket. A large unambiguous bouquet of oxblood roses. For a moment, I stood stuck between cigs and booze, and fruit and veg. Then, he saw me. Unquestionably, he saw me. But his eyes kept moving. They moved on as evenly as if I were no more significant than the 2-for-1 toilet roll promotion by the cleaning materials aisle, which was where he headed next.

Cheeks flaming, I abandoned the cigarettes along with my temporary delusion. I tried to walk in as nonchalant a manner as possible back to the pub.

A few drinks later, seeking distraction from the fading supermarket scene, I asked Sabine if she fancied partying with the Serpentine guy. Showing her his messages, I told her he was safely neither of our types. I expected the texts to put her off but to my surprise she was up for it. So I sent him a reply: *I'd like 2 brng sum1. Cn U pik us both up?*

Immediately my phone beeped. *SxC gal like u?*

I groaned. 'He's a creep. Let's leave it.'

Sabine flipped the phone around.

With a half-smile, she texted him back: *SxCR*

Forty minutes later a two-tone army-green car with a turbo exhaust roared past us. At the bottom of the road, it reversed and came back. It screeched to a halt where we stood outside the Pig and Hen. The stereo was thudding with drum and bass; when the Serpentine guy opened the doors, the night pounded with it. I felt a wave of affection for his exuberance. He'd spruced up by ponytailing his hair and dousing himself in acrylic cologne. *'Laydeez!'*

We squeezed in together on the front seat. The dashboard was flecked with what could have been dandruff but a couple of blocks on was confirmed as coke. He pulled into a deserted alley under a graffitied archway behind a building site. By the white light of a security lamp, we snorted lines as thick as pupae. The pungency of Serp Guy's cologne in the station-ary car almost made us sneeze them right out. Holding our noses closed, we waved to the security cameras.

As we hit the outskirts of the city, the streets became wider and darker and quieter. The night sky was shifting black; the moon and stars were smothered by roiling cloud. At the last traffic lights before the highway, Serp Guy took three acid tabs from the glove compartment. He gave us one each.

Sabine ejected his drum and bass CD and flung it into the back.

In the silence, I had a plunging moment of misgiving. Driving on coke was one thing but driving on LSD? I remembered an anti-drugs film we'd been shown at high school. With an eye on the red traffic light, I lifted the door-knob. Sabine and I could get out here, we could run; if we went in the opposite direction to the traffic he couldn't follow us.

As 'The Sunshine Underground' came onto the car stereo, Sabine took my hand away from the door. She put my fingers, clutching the tab of LSD, into her mouth. The traffic light turned orange; it flashed and I released the tab. She kissed my fingers, then put her tab into my mouth. The light went green. I thought, *I have chosen.* I thought, *I have seen the future and I have chosen this.* And then, as if I were following something already scripted over which I had no control, I was no longer afraid. I helped Sabine open the sunroof wide as the car accelerated off onto the open river of black tar.

While the journey continued, we played trippy electronic themes full blast. Tricky, Chemical Brothers, Kraftwerk . . . Once the tabs kicked in, we stayed mostly in the slow lane, though it didn't feel slow. The speedometer said thirty, forty, but it felt like we were flying; the world was rushing at us in party streamers of brightness. When we stopped on the hard shoulder to snort more coke, the car lights diffused into magical patterns. I could have gazed at them forever. But

Sabine and Serp Guy insisted that we move back through the portal into the traffic flow that led to the sea.

Somewhere in what really did seem like a euphoric channel of floating lights between cities, Sabine stood up on the front seat. Her legs were underwater roots while her body reached through the sunroof like a translucent white water lily. When I stood and made myself a flower too, wedged alongside her with my pincushion protea-orange hair tailing out, a scene from the anti-drugs film came back to me. Two teenagers high on acid were driving a car through the mountains. As they rounded a cliff bend, instead of slowing down, they accelerated and the car took off from the road. It flew into the air in slow motion while they held hands high above their heads, shouting, *WEEEeeeeee.*

For a reason I'd never fathomed, I'd always envied them that moment. Now, although there were no mountains let alone cliffs around, I yelled into the night at the top of my lungs, 'WEEEeeeeee.'

When Sabine joined me, I took her hand and held it tight above our heads.

Together, the two of us yelled as loud as we could, 'WEEEeeeeee, WEEEeeeeee, WEEEeeeeee . . .'

The night didn't end as we'd expected. We drove for hours but got nowhere. Or rather, we got to Mornington Crescent. When I saw the Tube station sign, I realized we either hadn't left London or else had somehow returned. Serp Guy painstakingly negotiated the back streets of Camden but something in his driving style must have seemed off. Next thing we knew, a police car was careering towards us, sirens, lights, everything. To Serp Guy's credit, his reaction was extremely generous. He skidded around a corner, flung open the passenger door, and said, '*Laydeez, run!*'

Sabine and I didn't need any convincing; we left him to take the rap and skadoodled. Terrified of being caught, instead of running, we marched through the streets like soldiers – Sabine said soldiers were the people least likely to be arrested – until we got to Primrose Hill. It was a welcome swathe of darkness, with a path lit up by what appeared to be a line of small moons.

'Shall we leave earth, Sabine?' I said. 'Shall we venture into the beyond?'

'I will do it with you, Meggie.' Sabine took a couple of steps towards the first moon. She looked back and reached out her hand. 'Will you do it with me?'

'*Where you go I will go, and where you stay I will stay,*' I said. '*Your people will be my people and your God my God.*'

I took Sabine's hand and we began to follow the moons dot-to-dot up the hill. At moon three or four, Sabine said, 'Say it again, what you just said.'

I did, adding, '*Where you die I will die, and there I will be buried.*'

'That's the most beautiful thing I ever heard,' she said.

'It just came to me,' I said.

'You are a poet,' said Sabine.

'No, it's the Bible.'

'Oh.'

We had reached the top of Primrose Hill. Below us lay the spread of its dark pelt, spotted green where the moons lit it. Beyond lay all of London.

'You must remember this,' said Sabine.

'My mind's a sieve,' I said.

'No, Meggie. You have a beautiful mind.'

'You have a beautiful everything.'

'What's an *everything*?'

I pointed mock seriously into the distance. 'The BT Tower. And Canary Wharf. And that big hoop they just put up—'

'London's Eye,' she said.

'Everything's the stars,' I said, 'the sun, and the moon.'

In the distance, a lion roared.

We stared at each other, confused.

'Everything is London Zoo,' she said, triumphantly.

We started to giggle.

I knelt down on the grass; she knelt opposite me.

I lifted her tank top. 'Your beautiful everything is your belly button.' I lifted the top higher. 'And your ribs.' I pulled it over her head and flung it aside. 'It's your breasts.' I unhooked her bra. 'And your shoulders.' I tossed the bra into the dark too.

She was an ancient sculpture, a carved goddess. Totemic against the skyline, but breathing, alive. I ran my fingers wonderingly over her.

She popped the buttons of my jeans open slowly, one by

one. 'Yours is your hips.' She kissed my panty line. 'And your bum.' She gave it a pinch, then slipped her fingers into my pants. 'And your . . .'

I slid my hands down the front of her skirt. She wasn't wearing knickers.

'Your ruby,' I said.

'Your pearl,' she said.

We were solemn. She shut her eyes, I mine. While we began to feel each other's secret folds and ripples, my lives near and far, internal and external, present and past came together in a moment that felt holy.

Then we both froze.

Footsteps were clacking up the path. Too scared to look, I listened. They became muffled as they went across the grass. I tried to will them away. But they strode determinedly closer.

'Come on, girls,' said a stern voice. 'What's happening here? What are you two up to? This is a public place, you know?'

'Is she real?' I asked Sabine.

'Unfortunately, yes,' said the policewoman.

She handed Sabine her top and her bra. Then firmly, though with a crinkle of compassion at her eyes, she gave us a talk about the wrongs of doing what we were doing in the place we were doing it.

Sabine dressed with insouciance; I tried to do the same.

But after that, the magic of the night disintegrated. Like when they switch on the lights in a club and suddenly everybody is worn out and overdressed and smells of acrid drug sweat. And your energy is so low that getting home feels like the last leg of an ill-advised expedition that you'd be better off doing alone.

As we left Primrose Hill, neither Sabine nor I spoke. It wasn't even six o'clock but we'd somehow missed the dawn. The September morning didn't have the poignancy of autumn; it felt overexposed and hot. I reminded myself that this reality was no more valid than the previous one. Daylight doesn't bring more clarity than night. Sober isn't necessarily the truer perspective.

Twenty years on, I still believe that. But immersion in the mundane can be overpowering. Our Cinderella coach had turned into a pumpkin. Sabine would be ever divine whereas I was just Megan again; I couldn't get beyond the body, the mood, the self. There was a walk, a wait, a train, a bus. As we tenderly parted ways, I tried to think, *This is only the beginning –*

But I knew, even then, it wasn't true.

On shift the following week, things were OK between us but not intimate. It was as if Primrose Hill and all that led up to it hadn't happened. Scanning the papers, I was reminded of what could have gone wrong by the headlines of articles for clients. *Joyrider Kills Passengers. Female Hitchhiker Found Dead. Drugs Death at Party.*

In the photocopying room, casting hurt gloom on our night, I showed Sabine.

Her blue-black eyes flashed. 'This makes me angry, how they write. A whole person's life is, what d'you call it?'

'Eclipsed?'

'Yes, eclipsed, by how it ends. A tragic death doesn't mean a tragic life. You might have a beautiful life with ten minutes of tragedy in it. But if you die like that, it's a beautiful life forgotten. Everyone thinks only of the end.'

She was agitated; her English was halting, her hands trembling as she lit a cigarette. 'The ending is not the whole story.'

I didn't know what to say.

I imagined she was thinking of her brother, Xavier.

Then she said, 'If I die in some horrible way, Meggie, please tell people: it's not the whole story.'

PART V

37

Now in middle age, I wonder about the weight of endings. Why should the way a person dies colour the memory of their life? Or does the finality of death alone do it? Sometimes to put aside the disquiet of a night's writing, I stroll along the disused railway line near where I live. My thoughts turn to the amputation of dreams, of potential – a life seen minus anything that might have been.

After my mother died a few years ago, peacefully but without resolution between us, the figure in my mind shifted from threatening to intermittently sympathetic. And then when Thandi died of a heart attack three days later, the image I'd had of *her* one day running the flower shop drew to an equally abrupt end. Just as a sentence comes to a close with a full stop, death fulfils the final requirement of a story, completes it. A life looks different when the ending makes it an entire life.

Yet as autumns past and present converge, I am aware of how temporary endings affect perspective too. On my walks, I come across tiny spiders floating mid-air. Apparently they travel hundreds of miles by ballooning. At a high point, exposing their abdomens, they release a fan of silk strands; their flight is propelled less by wind than by electric fields. And so I imagine an artist's impression of me and Sabine at the highest point in Camden, more intimate than ever, little realizing that gossamer strands were already spooling out, about to whisk us apart . . .

The last time I bumped into Calvin Janssen was at a Halloween barbecue given by a Jo'burg acquaintance. His trendily shaven head revealed a slightly conical skull. Focusing on the fire, we spoke about his latest design project, his involvement with a local school in Kenya and his plans to cycle around Vietnam.

While we turned the meat, I realized that Sabine's dismissive words made him seem far less desirable. I felt better about the time he'd said, *Not cool, Meggie*, as if her rejection had balanced us karmically.

Given how their night had panned out, I didn't think he'd mention her. But at the first lull in conversation, Cal said, 'Your friend's very beautiful.'

'She is.' I waited for the self-deprecating follow-up line. *I was punching above my weight.* Or, *I guess she doesn't usually go for guys like me.*

'I felt bad about it,' he continued. 'She kept texting me. *Let's go for a drink. How about lunch.* But there was no point replying.'

'Didn't you fancy Sabine?' I asked, hiding my surprise.

'You're *ve*-ry fond of her.'

'Of course I am. She's my friend.'

'She's really attractive . . .'

'*Ja*. Enough already, Cal.'

'But fucked up, hey?' he said.

I took an empty foil platter from the table, then handed one to him. 'What d'you mean?'

The meat didn't look done but, platter in hand, he began to load it.

'She's not natural like you, Meggie. She has to play a situation. I'm not saying it's her fault.' He rested the tongs a moment on the grill. 'Actually, she reminds me of this pretty girl I knew who'd been abused. A person gets screwed up like that, they can't connect properly. Everything's sexual, everything's about attention.'

'That's one hell of a conflation—'

'How?'

'Pretty girls, all fucked up?'

'Look, I didn't mean to offend you. Probably I'm making the wrong connections.'

He went back to methodically transferring the chops, marking them with soot. Then he said, 'This other girl, though, it was sad. She overdosed every few months. I felt sorry for her. But sorrier for the husband. He was always rushing her to hospital. One day he came home too late.'

The meat was all on Cal's platter. Mine was empty; I felt foolish holding it.

'Did she die?'

'*Jys*, it shattered him.'

As we walked across the garden to the kitchen, I said, 'Sabine doesn't do stuff like that, Cal. Overdosing, or whatever.'

He said that wasn't what he'd meant. Then he said the other reason he hadn't replied was that he'd started seeing someone else. Also an architect but from another firm. I wondered if he'd gone out to phone her when we were in the dive bar, if he'd been involved with her already then. The two of them were having people for dinner the following Friday. In the kitchen, he perked up. 'Meggie, why don't you come along?'

'I suppose you don't want me to bring my fucked-up friend?' I said.

He looked momentarily taken aback. Then he said, 'Sabine monopolized you last time. It'd be nicer to see you without her.'

I didn't go to Cal and his new girlfriend's dinner party. Nor did I stay much longer at the barbecue. Without bothering to say goodbye to anyone, Sabine-style I simply left.

Back at Earl's, I ran a bath with lavender salts. That Sabine had lied about Cal didn't bother me. I was flattered at her wanting someone I'd recommended that badly – and that she'd felt the need, afterwards, to save face. I hadn't told her about bumping into Graham; my style wasn't to lie, it was to keep quiet. But that wasn't any better.

Stirring the salts around, I couldn't get them to bubble. I always wanted them to, though they don't. After I poured in the entire box, they wouldn't even dissolve. As I climbed into the tub, the crystals crunched under my feet.

What *did* bother me was the way Cal had spoken about Sabine. Not just what he'd said but hearing it in his South African accent. I tried to think why.

Relationships between people from different countries involve translation. And this I found liberating. But it could also obscure things. One acquaintance's macho South African ways were given the kind of tolerance his feminist girlfriend would never accord a fellow Brit. Another's impressive small-town nonconformism was lost in Soho's mainstream.

Grinding the salts pointlessly against the enamel of the tub, I wondered: if I were Belgian, how would Sabine feel about me? Would we hang out, or would I not be her type? Would she see me as *natural* like Cal did?

And would Sabine still enchant me if I knew the specifics of her life? Not just the town where she'd grown up or the schools she'd attended – but the way her accent sounded to other Belgians, the clues about herself she gave away subconsciously?

The question that troubled me more, though I struggled to fathom why, was how I'd feel about Sabine if she were South African. When I remembered girls at school with similar personalities, I knew we'd never have been close. But perhaps I needed to look at it from another angle.

Letting some of the oversaturated water out, I added more hot and tried mixing again. The girls who'd fascinated me back then had been beautiful, kind, tough and restrained. Sabine had all of those qualities.

I lay back and tried to pretend the gritty bathtub was a beach.

It wasn't my problem if Cal couldn't see beyond Sabine being *fucked up*. When I'd been with his brother, Cal had brought home only dark, moody, gothy, fucked-up-seeming girls.

But from the dismissive way he'd said *fucked up* at the barbecue, Cal hadn't seen Sabine in the light he'd seen them. He hadn't found her alluring or captivating; he appeared to feel sorry for her while wary of involvement, mindful of protecting himself. With my toes I pulled out the plug.

So Cal had become old and conservative: stuff him.

38

Yet despite my initial reaction, I added Cal's sense of *fucked up* to my understanding of Sabine. When frustration at being myself became too painful, I'd recall it. When I felt I was acquiescing too far, I'd use it to dilute her effect. The words became my first amulet against her, the first time another person had managed to dull her sheen.

The next amulet didn't come through anyone else's perspective.

We'd been drinking since morning with the rest of our crew. I'd taken things slowly for once whereas Sabine had been at it full tilt. By the time we hit the Black Cap in Camden, she was all over the place: stumbling, slurring, bellowing out wrong answers to a pub quiz we weren't playing. *Disneyland Florida! The Queen of Hearts! Seventeen-fifty-fuckish!*

I'd never seen Sabine drunk other than when I was too, and the distance it created between us hurt. It reminded me of when she was asleep, but whereas asleep she was beautiful, this was different. When the pub quiz teams complained, like a mother embarrassed by her usually impressive kid I said I'd take Sabine out, take her home, put her to bed.

As we went down the stairs, she slammed into a bloke coming up. His pints drenched us. He yelled at her and she yelled back. Then she crashed through the doors onto the street.

She wove ahead of me through the early evening crowd. Catching up with her at the bus stop, I said, 'Come, Sabine. We're going home.'

'Don' wanna go home.'

'Back to my place, then.'

''M huuuungry,' she brayed.

'Fine.' Gripping her arm, I pulled her into a caff.

Under a flickering neon sign that read *No Signs On This Wall*, I ordered two builder's teas and a large portion of chips. I hoped it would bring her down, help equalize us again. But when the chips arrived, she wasn't interested in eating them. Her eyebrow twitched.

'Let's have liver,' she said.

'No,' I said.

'I like liver in blood.'

I felt scared. 'Stop being such a fucking pain.'

'Whaaayouwanmetodo?' That twitching eyebrow.

'Eat what's on your plate, Sabine.'

She stuffed her fist with chips and squashed them into her mouth. As she chewed, bits of potato leaked out, dribbling down her chin. Appalled, my eyes filled.

'Don't, Meggie.' She pressed a fat red napkin into my face. Prising it from her, I tried to wipe her chin.

She flicked her head away and gazed at her reflection in the window. 'You must be careful of Sabine Dubreil,' she said in her low voice. 'She is a bad influence.'

I thought of how her mother could make someone feel so shit they wanted to die, of the scarab pendant, of our time in Eastbourne. I thought of her brother's death. I felt out of my depth. Sabine was in a place I couldn't reach.

The sign flickered; her eyebrow twitched.

'Eat your chips,' I said. '*Please.*'

Perhaps the fear in my voice got through where nothing else would. Abruptly, obediently, she gobbled all the chips up.

But then things went beyond her control. On the pavement just outside the door, she puked for Belgium. As the staff began to shout, I dragged her away. Took her hand and ran.

We kept running until the fork to Euston or King's Cross. Then we bent to catch our breath. If the chips didn't do Sabine any good, the puking seemed to. When she stood up, the odd twitching had stopped. She looked exhausted but beautiful again. 'I need a shower, Meggie.'

'Me too,' I said, getting a whiff of puke and beer.

'Let's do it at the station.'

'Sabine?' I called wearily as she went ahead of me again. 'What are you talking about?'

But at King's Cross she led me down some stairs to a corridor beneath the train platforms. Turned out, you could rent a towel and buy sample-size soap and shampoo. She asked for two sets of toiletries and one cubicle key.

In our rucksacks combined we had all we needed. We washed our hair, brushed our teeth, soaped each other's backs and stood under icy water to finish off. Then we creamed ourselves head to toe with her *fleurs blanches sauvages*.

We surfaced onto the street with damp hair blowing in a late autumn wind that was oddly warm. Sabine seemed normal, back to her usual self. The things that would later concern me – the dramatic talk, the twitching brow, the fear then coldness I'd felt towards her, the mark I'd left on her arm from where I'd gripped her too hard – were momentarily forgotten in the crushed scent of the night. *Wild white flowers.*

We were twenty-four and everything seemed possible.

'Studio X?' she said.

'Great minds,' I said.

Then I said, 'You were telling the others about it earlier. D'you remember?'

She shrugged. 'So, ask them along. If that's what you want.'

39

'Imagine a harem, imagine cheap drinks. A dark room, a symbolic womb. Drugs from the doorman. Imagine, dsh-dsh . . .'

Prawn's improvised rap on the Studio X pitch I'd given several months back was embarrassing. The people queuing under the bridge with us looked more suited to a Kenny G concert than what I'd hyped as the world's edgiest club.

Sabine stood a bit apart. Her mood had changed after I'd called the crew; she'd become subdued, sulky, as if here against her will. Was she getting bored of them? Maybe she was also getting bored of me. I tried not to think, too tired to trust my view on it.

When we reached the front of the line, a man I'd not seen before was on the door. He wore a dirty black t-shirt and low-slung grey tracksuit pants.

Prawn nudged me, mouthing, *Drugs*.

The man glared at Prawn, scratching his eczemaed eyebrows. Then he saw Coño. 'No entry with that.'

'He's well trained,' I said.

'Goes everywhere with us,' said Sabine.

'Not here,' said the man.

'Could we leave him quietly by the door?' I said.

The man shook his head. 'I don't want the dog in sight.'

'It's cool,' said Earl. 'I'll go home.'

'You're not going—'

'Next,' said the man.

'I need to set off at four for Spain anyway,' said Earl.

'If you go, we all go,' said Sabine.

'Not me,' said Prawn. 'I'm going in the symbolic womb!'

I felt myself redden. 'Let's just leave this whole thing—'

But Earl had yanked Coño over the road before we could stop him. As they climbed on a number forty-eight bus, he waved the dog's paw from the window. She turned her head to watch us as the bus drove off. Once they were out of sight, the night seemed to drop several degrees.

A cross-dresser in transparent heels came over. 'You lot in the queue?'

I glanced at Prawn's eager pink cheeks. 'Yes.'

'Twenty-five quid,' said the doorman, holding out his palm.

'How about a Christmas special?' said Sherry.

'Christmas is a month away,' said the doorman.

Lizard said, 'How 'bout a hundred for the lot?'

'Hundred and twenty-five for the lot,' said the doorman.

'Deal,' said Sherry.

'That's twenty-five each, Sherry,' groaned Lizard.

Sabine slipped out her silver purse, handed the doorman a fat fold of notes, then strode into the club.

As I reached for my money, the man said, 'Your friend paid.'

'For me too?' said Prawn.

'Chancer,' said Sherry.

'For you all,' said the man.

'SJ!' called Sherry, running after her into the club.

'Imagine, dsh-dsh, free entry,' rapped Prawn, as he followed.

But I hung back. Sabine had sorted this; I'd fix the rest. I spoke to the doorman.

'What d'you want?' he said.

'Charlie,' I said.

'Wait here.'

I waited. After some time, the owner of the club appeared. He was about seventy, skinny, unshaven, hoary. I'd seen him around before. I repeated what I wanted. He rubbed his bristles. 'Might be able to get it for you later.'

'OK,' I said. 'Shall I come find you?'

'I'll let you know,' he said.

'So—' But he'd started talking to someone else in the queue.

Our crew were at the bar. Sabine was there too, though with her back to them. She was talking to a girl who looked distinctly out of place. First, because she was clean-cut in blue jeans and a white t-shirt; second, because she was a dead ringer for Kate Moss.

Sherry handed me a large white wine.

I drank half of it, then asked the barman, 'Have you got tequila?'

'Nope.'

'I can see it.' I pointed at a bottle.

'Belongs to someone else.' He pointed to the name label on it.

'Relax, Meggie,' said Sherry. 'Get the next round.'

'No,' I said. 'I want to get something now. How about vodka?'

The barman reached for a bottle under the counter. 'Eighty quid.'

I handed over the cash. 'Five shot glasses too, please.'

The club didn't have shot glasses so I distributed heavy-handed pourings into plastic tumblers. Four tumblers, because Sabine was still busy with Kate. I waved in her direction but she didn't see. So I said to the others, 'Tour time!'

By the side of the bar was the dance floor. It looked like a wedding disco set-up. I gulped my vodka. 'Pretty ordinary, huh?'

They nodded.

'But come downstairs.'

As soon as we were in the basement I was aware of the rasp of damp. 'Normally it smells gorgeous,' I said.

'Not tonight,' said Prawn.

'They burn this special incense—'

'To hide the toilet smell,' said Prawn.

'Oh, stop it, you,' said Sherry.

The lighting downstairs was glaring. I recalled candles or at least lamps but there were only bare bulbs. A few of the rooms had double beds with plastic-covered mattresses. One had, in addition to a bed, a jumble of sadomasochistic equipment. It looked like a half-assembled home gym. A metal contraption had a piece of paper with *Broken* scrawled across it. The place was seedy, as I had promised, but not in an interesting way. Rather in a threadbare, depressing way.

'And the dark room?' said Prawn.

'Yes,' I said. 'I nearly forgot.'

I led them to what looked like the door to a broom cupboard. I pushed it open. At least the dark room was dark, but nobody was in it. We hadn't yet seen the club cat, though she attested to her existence with a strong smell of cat piss. 'This may seem a bit crap . . .'

'Cat piss, dsh-dsh,' said Prawn.

'But it's the people who make it,' I insisted. 'They're not here yet.'

'We're here, though,' said Sherry.

'You said there were sofas upstairs?' said Lizard.

At the top of the spiral staircase, a ruggedly handsome man with a large nose was kissing a striking brunette. A bald man with bold eyebrows was simultaneously occupied with Handsome's tackle. When the brunette squeezed Lizard's butt, I thought the night was stoking up. But Lizard just said, 'Pity Earl's not here.'

Studio X had been a mistake. Our crew clearly weren't into

this stuff. You had to be into it to see it as I'd done. Aware of how it appeared to them, I could barely remember its appeal myself.

Afterwards, I'd think this was the point where I should have said, *Guys, let's cut our losses and leave.* Instead, I tried to force the evening to slipstream. I poured more vodka and led the way to the chillout area. The sofas were as wide as I'd promised but also tatty and sunken. Prawn stretched out on the nearest one. As Sherry flopped down beside him, the springs made a loud crack. She put a hand to her back, grimacing dramatically.

'Ooooeee,' yelped Prawn, 'my back, my back.'

But Sherry's face stayed contorted.

'You're not joking?' said Lizard.

'No!' said Sherry. 'You bloody noodles.'

We helped her up, then laid her flat on the floor. She said she got spasms sometimes, then they passed. 'Poor you, huh,' said Lizard.

'I get spasms too but in my dick,' said Prawn.

'I get hernias,' said Lizard. 'Got two that need to be removed.'

'Hernias play up something awful,' said Sherry from where she lay.

What was this conversation we were having? And where was Sabine?

Gathered on the floor around Sherry, we were like mourners at a wake. Clubbers coming upstairs began to make their way over to check out the action. Lizard's duty became to chase them away. Mine was to keep the vodka topped up. Then it struck me: we hadn't slept in almost thirty hours. I handed vodka duty over to Prawn and reassigned mine to finding us some Charlie.

After looking in the basement, I wandered up to the dance area. Sabine wasn't at the bar. But I wouldn't ask after her yet. In clubs, we often separated, then came back together again. Maybe we'd just missed each other and she'd already rejoined the crew. Quite likely, she was by the sofas waiting for me. If I just got something good, the night could still perk up.

Making a pest of myself in the toilets, I was befriended by a woman called Katiana. About my age, height and build, she had toffee skin and frizzy peroxided hair. She was wearing a bum-skimming pink lycra dress. Yanking me into a cubicle, she offered a bottle lid of GHB. Touched by a response to my drugs quest, even if not the one I'd sought, I swallowed it. At once I felt weirdly spinny . . .

If I passed out it was only briefly. When I came to I was sitting on the cubicle floor. Through the door, I could hear Katiana talking to someone else. I wished Sabine would appear; she could look after me now. Or not look after exactly; I didn't feel bad – I felt pretty good but ve-ry out of it. It'd be nice to leave the club and go back to Earl's, for us to go back together. I took my phone from my bag to text her – but she'd got there first.

tired sorry gone home

Neither of us had ever left the other in a club. Staring at

her message, I tried to put the words in a different order. But the meaning was always the same. Clumsily, I opened the toilet door. I hung on to it.

'More, please,' I said to Katiana's pink dress.

'I don't have more.'

'Not this,' I said. 'Charlie.'

'Can get but I don't have money.'

'Don't worry. I have money.'

She pulled me to her and I let her kiss me with a madly probing tongue.

Then, arm in arm, we set off. We joined the growing crowd on the dance floor. They were jigging to some repetitive mechanical beat.

'I love this song!' she shrieked.

She grabbed me by the elbows and we whirled about until we fell down. I looked at the legs dancing around me. Silver, bare, leather, satin. A high chant had been added to the beat. It was cycling up, gathering momentum. I shifted my bum back and leaned against the warmly spinning wall. Closing my eyes, I let the music wash over me in great blossoming waves.

Sabine and I were kissing in a wild field out in the sunshine. I felt our mouths, soft and deep and dark and wet on each other. Our tongues were two snails mating. We were biologists who had been there twenty years. Flowers were growing out of our palms. Except . . . the dance music was so loud. Where were we? I couldn't remember. It didn't matter.

I put my arms around her and pulled her close. But she felt odd, different, wrong.

'What's your name again?' I said.

'KATIANA!'

Sabine had left. Flaky Sabine. Fuck Sabine.

'The beautiful Katiana!' I yelled as I stroked her brittle candy-floss hair.

She pointed towards the corner. 'Those guys will get you stuff.'

Several groups of men were hanging round in the dark. I couldn't see which of them she meant. 'Let's go find my friends,' I said. 'Tell them the good news.'

'Soon we'll be getting stuff,' I rehearsed as we climbed the spiral metal stairs. 'Soon, yeah, soon.'

The chillout area was deserted. Or almost: Lizard and Sherry were the only people left. Sherry wasn't lying flat on the floor any more. She and Lizard were leaning by the banister, waiting.

'Prawn was looking for you earlier,' said Sherry.

'We wanted to go,' said Lizard, 'but didn't want to leave you.'

'Though I see you've found a friend,' said Sherry.

Katiana shook her head. 'Not friends. We're in love!'

'IN LOVE,' I cried at the top of my voice.

Sherry's face pressed into a closed-mouth yawn. Her tired green eyes watered at the corners. *She doesn't believe me*, I thought. So I snogged Katiana fully in front of them.

'You're staying, I guess?' said Sherry.

'Yes,' I said. Then, I thought maybe they were sad because I had a new lover. I gave them each a snog to make up. 'LOVE you guys TOO!'

Afterwards . . . I remember dancing in strobe lights with Katiana. Then going to some guys in the corner. And then being with them in a small room.

The room has a torn orange curtain and a beige filing cabinet. A dirty piece of Sellotape stuck to it is coming off. The guys are saying, We can get what you want. They are laughing. I am saying, I want Charlie. But I think I've said it before. Because they say, We can get you Charlie, Mikey, Ben. They laugh like it's the answer to a joke. They carry on saying things I don't understand but I keep laughing to show I do. Some are smoking, putting ash in beer cans. When I ask for a cigarette, they give me one of theirs half smoked.

They put on a screen with a hospital show. The patient has her hair in bunches and flutter-doe eyes. She is on an operating table but it's all a big gangbang. Do it to me, she says to the doctors. Do it to me hard. She is looking sideways from under the poking-out dicks like she's trying to give me a message. I keep staring at her to see what it is.

A guy with muscles so huge it's like he's a blow-up man says, D'you dig that? I say, Yeah, I dig it. A guy with a thin moustache says, D'you want some? I say to the blow-up man, Do it to me, like in the show. He laughs. Everybody looks impressed. I say, Do it to me, again. Can I join in? says a guy with hairy hands and a gold ring. Yeah, you too, I say. And me? says another one. And me? Only four, I say. God-damn, says an older Rasta guy. I feel sorry for him so I say, Stuff it, everybody can take part. You want K first? says the thin-moustache guy. I mistake K for the blow-up man. Yeah, I say. But they stick a key with white powder up my nose. I taste its bitterness at the back of my throat.

I am lying on my belly on a plastic-covered mattress. A man is inside me. A trouser zip grates: another man. I am lying there not moving. Like a thing, not like a person. Then a man presses at the base of my neck. His hand holds around it. He is rough while he thrusts. I can't move but I can feel him. I can feel my body being pounded like it's something being pounded into something else. I use the pounding feeling. I think, Fuck you to lovely and friendly and natural. To every way I've been misunderstood. To every situation I've hated. To everything I've tried and failed. I am in the dark, I am in a hole. I let go, I give up. I am the dark, I am the hole. I am nothing. I let go, I give up. I lose myself.

Footsteps are coming down the stairs. Stomping along, loud, fast, strong. Voices too: a woman's, a man's, another man's, excited, agitated. I recognize the voice of that girl I kissed. Then of the old man who owns the club. Get out, he is saying low and tight. I know he is disgusted, but I can't make my legs walk. Get the fuck out of my club right now, he says. My heart gets the message. It starts to race. Will he lift me up? Will he dump me in the street? Will he dump me in a tip?

Nobody is inside me any more. I hear a thud like a body hitting the other side of the room. Feet are stomping again, up the stairs, down the stairs. The noise hurts my head. I cover my ears with my hands. Then I realize I can move again. I lift my head and look around. People are staring at me. I am the centre of a big fuss. My jeans are down. The girl I kissed pulls them up. The old man says, What're you all looking at? Get out. Out, out.

When they've left, I say to him, I'm sorry, I'll go. He says, You're not going on your own. I say, I have a friend. We always stick together, like in the song. Where is she? he says. I don't know, I say. He says, Can you phone her? I get my phone out but the screen reminds me: *tired sorry gone home.* Oh, I say, I forgot, she has gone.

Then I am in an old car with the old man. He is driving and the radio is on. Where are we going? I say. He says, I'm taking you home. He says my address, the flat number and the street. Yes, I say, that's my address. It's the address you gave me, he says. His face looks tired and crumpled and sad. You look like Samuel Beckett, I say. I am seeing you to your door, he says. I tell him, Thank you. Then I tell him, I'm sorry about what happened. I tell him, You have an amazing club. I tell him, Don't worry, nobody will know about this. I try to remember the words I've used to describe his club to others. I tell him, Studio X is a true democracy of race and age and gender.

I don't know if he says anything. I don't remember anything else except the smooth late-night radio voices and the old man's profile in the flickering sulphur of the streetlamps and me trying hard to make up to him. Sorry. Thank you.

Don't worry. Please. Yes, sorry. It's here. Thank you. I'll keep schtum.

40

The next morning, I told Earl.

He rang from Calais to remind me to water his orchid. When he asked how the night had been, I heard myself say, 'Oh, gangbangish . . .'

'*What?*' I told him more; I said too much. And then he said, 'I'm coming back.'

'Don't, Earl. Please.'

'Where was Sabine?'

I stuck my finger in the orchid's soil. 'She left.'

'But you two look after each other?'

'We do things alone too.'

'I'm turning around *right* now.'

'Seriously, Earl, please don't.'

The soil was dry but it hadn't affected the plant yet. Nine white flowers went up the stem; I counted.

'Will you go to the police?' he said.

'How can I? I asked for it.'

'You didn't ask for rape—'

'It wasn't, exactly.'

He gave a long sigh.

'This is between us, Earl.'

He was quiet. Then he said, 'You need to go to the hospital. Get some antiretrovirals.'

I turned on the kitchen tap, cupping water in my hand.

'They might ask questions, Meggie. Do you remember the guys?'

'Only bits and pieces.'

'Did you hook up with anyone else? Swap numbers?'

I trickled water around the orchid's stem. 'I'll go to the hospital, Earl. I promise.'

After we'd finished speaking, I felt ashamed. Earl had never approved of my gung-ho attitude and now this. I shouldn't have told him. Everything seemed worse than before; the words made it seem shocking. Had I used the wrong ones? Had I used the right ones?

I fished about in my sunflower rucksack. As usual, there were scraps of paper with phone numbers from *new friends*, people I'd have chatted to briefly while high. *Call me, definitely, we must go out sometime, there's this other club . . .*

To appease Earl's voice in my head, I began to call around. Every person I spoke to wanted to get off the line as fast as if my words were burning them. I left Katiana until last. Her voice when I got through was disturbingly high-pitched, childish, out of it. 'I dunno what the fuck you on about. You expect me to know? Dahling, I don't even know who you are. You the one with the pink hair?'

'I'm the one fucked by a million guys,' I said.

'Ooooo,' she said. 'That one.'

'D'you remember anything about them?'

'Two were North African.'

'That's a start,' I said.

'From Cambodia, dahling.'

'Cambodia's not—'

She hung up and wouldn't answer when I called back.

I put my clothes and bedsheets in the wash on a ninety-degree cycle. Then I took a long, scorching-hot shower. Using a worn nailbrush, I scrubbed every part of me.

When I was done, I felt brittle. I needed to be with someone outside the judgement zone. I needed Sabine. Arriving at the Mayfair flat uninvited, I buzzed the intercom. She didn't respond. I waited. Though she dropped round Earl's whenever she felt like it, I'd never done the same.

I looked up at where she'd pointed. Second floor, right corner: a light went off, another went on. For a moment I thought I had the wrong window. But then I saw Sabine's silhouette against a red lampshade. She was in there. I waited longer.

Perhaps the buzzer was broken. I didn't bother with texting; I called. Her mobile rang and rang. I tried a second time, a third. After that it was engaged. When I finally got through, she didn't pick up. I buzzed a rat-a-tat-tat on the intercom. Then I pressed my thumb on the button and held.

A concierge in a maroon-and-gold uniform appeared. He asked if he could help. I told him I was trying to get hold of Sabine Dubreil. He buzzed her using his own intercom system with the same result.

'Never mind,' I said. 'I'll wait.'

'Sorry, you can't do that,' he said. 'You have to leave now. The residents don't like people hanging around.'

Although he'd spoken apologetically, as I strode from stupid up-its-own-arse Mayfair, tears squished out of my eyes. Brushing them away with my fists, I spelled everything I saw backwards. I walked quickly but aimlessly until I found myself spelling latipsoh. I went in and got a ticket at noitpecer.

Being in a place where out-of-the-norm was the norm grounded me. The plastic chairs, the silent subtitled TV, the crisp and soda can machine. When my turn came to see the nurse, I explained the situation. I kept to the facts, then got to the point. 'I'd like some antiretrovirals.'

'Did they ejaculate inside you?'

'Don't think so.'

'Have you showered or washed since?'

'Yes.'

'And your clothes?'

'In the machine. Ninety degrees.'

She shook her head in disbelief. 'You should have gone straight to the police. We can't do anything until you've reported it.'

As I stood, my chair fell over.

'You can do it from here,' she said.

Pretending I hadn't heard, I strode off along the corridor, then exited through the wrong door. I found myself in a yard filled with hospital bins. The nearest had a label that said *For Incineration.* From my rucksack, I took the phone-numbered slips of paper and disposed of them. I looked at what else was in the bag. Keys, purse and phone fitted in my coat pockets; the Jean Rhys novel too.

'Yo, what're you doing?' a porter hollered.

I dumped the rucksack with the rest of its contents into the bin. I pictured the Marilyn lipstick, the compact mirror and the cheap skull lighter that I'd bought in imitation of Sabine's, all melting.

The porter started across the yard but I slammed the lid down – and ran.

Parking lot, street, pavement, tar. Fleeing through the city, I dodged people and vehicles as if I were in a computer game. By a designer boutique, I almost collided with a stiletto-heeled woman laden with packages.

'Watch your step,' she rasped.

To prevent the leakage of any more tears, I pushed myself to run faster, to go as fast as I could.

I was sprinting, I was numb.

41

When Sabine rang that evening, I let it go to voicemail. She left a message which, admittedly, was more than I'd done. *Sorry to miss your calls. I'm in Belgium. My mother needed me to go home. Speak soon.*

She'd never spoken of Belgium as home or of her mother other than disparagingly. If Sabine was away now, she hadn't been earlier. But I suspected the reason behind her excuse, and the cause of her anxious tone, was my pursuit of her.

It was understandable that she'd been alarmed by my behaviour at the Mayfair flat. How could she guess at what had happened in the club? I'd never gone to her place uninvited before; I didn't phone her, didn't even initiate conversations by text. Had I left a message explaining, we'd have drunk horrible French tea together and she'd have been kind.

But what sort of message should I have left? I replayed hers. *Speak soon* meant, I don't give a fuck why you rang. It meant, I'm not going to risk a conversation with you by asking. It meant *back off*.

I was upset. Why did I always have to see things from her side? This was the only time I'd ever needed her. Why didn't she trust me enough to know that?

After Studio X, I shut the door to all thoughts of Sabine, self-pity and dwelling on the past. Though Earl knew what had happened, I didn't tell anyone else. Yet while shame strengthened my inner resolve, my body began its own quiet rebellion. At first it wasn't with any serious illness but a chain of minor physical failures: a couple of colds, then infections that wouldn't heal. Whatever went wrong, I never missed work. When my GP said, *Rest up, slow down, take it easy*, I laughed. What could happen to a twenty-four-year-old with an infection in London? A day later I was hospitalized with cellulitis. It knocked the laughter right out of me.

At the time, I'd just finished three weeks of nights, the extra one Sabine's idea. After my display of neediness, we were continually on different shifts. Then one night she sent a text: *lets work 3 weeks in a row lets go to brazil.* I replied: *yes lets.* Despite knowing what she was like I persisted in building *castelos* in the air. But halfway through the gruelling stint, she jetted off to Guadeloupe.

When I got ill, I didn't even consider telling Sabine. Earl made a deal with his opposite to extend his time in Spain by two months, so I didn't tell him. Given that calls to my mother were minimal, I hardly needed to reintroduce drama there. Because I wasn't in touch with the rest of the crew except through Earl, I didn't tell them. Since it was ages to go before my next shift, I didn't need to tell anyone. And I didn't.

Lying in the hospital bed, I couldn't be bothered to read or listen to music or watch TV. Mostly, I stared out of the window at a yellow brick wall. If I died, nobody would notice until January when I was due back at work. Even then, they'd probably assume that I'd found another job. I wouldn't be the first nightshifter to disappear without warning. The shift leader might make a screwed-up newspaper voodoo doll and stick pins in it.

Discharged on the day of the winter solstice, I went home alone. I got in touch with nobody, and nobody got in touch with me. The blackout cloth still covered my bedroom window and I left the curtains in the other rooms drawn. Half the light bulbs in Earl's flat blew but I hadn't the energy or inclination to replace them. I lit candles until my lighter fluid ran out.

Although there was no fresh food, going to the corner shop seemed too much effort. Christmas passed while I huddled under a red blanket on the fake zebra-skin rug in the front room. I boiled rice and ate it with UHT boxed milk. My days went by watching shadows edging each other across the walls.

At midnight on the eve of the New Millennium, my phone beeped with texts. Everybody was out having a good time with someone else. Sherry was in Grimsby clubbing with her nieces. Lizard and the shift leader were watching fireworks on Arthur's Seat. Earl and Coño were somewhere on the Costa Brava. Prawn sent a text too incoherent to begin to decipher where he was. And Sabine, typically, sent a text that was blank. I imagined her under a palm tree in Guadeloupe. Or who knows, maybe she was with Lucian at the Ritz.

I ignored all the messages.

Curled up on the rug, I tried to ignore the voices in my head too. I needed to drown them out, to replace them with new ones. Since we didn't have a radio or TV, I fetched my computer to get on the internet. The dial tone sounded and the modem screeched but the server wouldn't connect. Switching it off and on, I unplugged, re-plugged and tried again. Rumours were rife about a computer virus triggered by the numerical shift to 2000. But in the early hours of the morning my internet connection came through.

The first radio station I found was in Canada. Listeners were calling in with resolutions for the new year, the new century. I turned the sound down low and opened another tab. Searching for cheap holiday deals, I looked at photos of crowded beaches, built-up resorts and waterslides. A caller from Winnipeg said she wanted to learn Cantonese. I switched from the Canadian radio station to a Cantonese one. What was the cost of a flight to Hong Kong? Expensive. I looked up learning Cantonese, and browsed other adult education courses. The idea of returning to English literature seemed like a backwards step. Then I came across an introductory writing workshop. But it ran on Thursday afternoons; I couldn't attend day classes while doing nights. Closing all the tabs, I quit the browser.

In my bedroom, I pulled down my blackout curtain. Dawn hadn't yet come but a faint blue light was pressing at the horizon. After putting paper in my printer, I opened a blank document in Word. It seemed like a long time since I'd sat before an empty white screen. I typed my address at the top of the page. Then the press agency's address beneath it.

Then: **Letter of Resignation for Megan Groenewald**

42

I scarcely saw Sabine at work in January. By the start of February, I had a new job in a second-hand bookshop. Since it was in north London, I got lodgings in a retired artist's house nearby. The creative writing workshop I'd found online was full but I joined the local gym. I lifted heavy weights in a series of slow, controlled repetitions. My body didn't change but the workouts helped me feel like I was developing stability and strength.

I didn't hear from Sabine for the whole of February. By the time March slid into April, I assumed the friendship had fallen apart of its own accord. After I left a few texts unanswered, I lost contact with the rest of the crew too. Sometimes I felt a well of sadness that I hid shelving books in the stockroom. More often, I was overcome by a sort of mental exhaustion; Studio X and Sabine and nightshifts were all linked together in my mind.

That spring, I gave my Sabine-style clothes away to charity. I took to wearing cheap combat trousers and tank tops. My sole accessory was the sard ring that I'd bought on Portobello Road. Apparently sard came from volcanic rock and was used to deflect bad spells. As for my more abstract amulets against Sabine, I was almost disconcerted at how little I needed them.

A major contributing factor was the retired artist. She was nonconformist, empathetic and politicized. I wasn't sexually attracted to her, but I respected her. I didn't want to be her; I wanted to learn from her. Observing how she lived in the day-to-day, I saw, close up, the workings of an intellectual life. In our conversations, I hung on to what she said. I wanted to be someone she'd respect too.

The only regression of those first months was a dream I had in which Sabine was drowning. We were out on open water. I was on a raft but a powerful current was separating us. Though I had an oar, I wasn't using it; I was watching her but somehow not moving. When I awoke, I was overcome by cold waves of sorrow and guilt. But as consciousness returned, I became angry with myself. Why was I feeling bad? In life, *I*'d been the one drowning.

When the artist noticed my blues the next day, I gave her an account of Sabine so reduced as to be barely true – though her response was profoundly useful. She described an experiment where rats were given a pedal to press for a reward. Half were rewarded logically, the other half randomly. Over time, the logical group continued to be logical whereas the random group lost all control; crazed, they pressed the pedal increasingly feverishly in hope of reward.

While the rat aspect was only one part of my relationship with Sabine, it helped with my resolve. I needed a clean break; any leniency would suck me back into our game. Over Christmas I'd sunk as low as I could go. For survival's sake, I couldn't afford to be drawn into Sabine's orbit again.

*

In mid-April, the magnolia tree outside the second-hand bookshop was coming into bloom. The leaves were light green furls, the yellow flowers startling against the charcoal branches. One afternoon as I arranged a couple of cuttings in a flame-red vase, my phone buzzed with a text. It was written in Sabine's usual style, as if nothing had changed: *want to meet at the pig and hen tomorrow at six*. Compulsively, my fingers itched to type *yes* – but I resisted.

Getting more messages from Sabine over the next few days, I felt bad, as if I'd turned into one of the rat controllers. Then I thought of what Cal Janssen had said about replying when there was no future in it: what's the point? Sabine had so much pride; she was bound to give up sooner or later. But when, instead, she rang and left a voicemail in an urgent tone, I couldn't ignore her any more. I returned the call. She said she needed to speak to me. She asked if we could meet. I agreed.

Sabine had suggested a loud pub at King's Cross station. My plan was to drink sparkling water, but when I arrived she was in front of two large white wines. Earl's dog, Coño, was at her feet, but that wasn't what caught me off-guard. It was her appearance.

She'd never had an ounce of fat to spare but now she was skeletal. Her collarbones protruded from the top of her black shoestring dress. Her chest seemed to cave inwards, her lips were tinged blue and her skin was chalky. Despite it being late spring, she hugged a thick duffel coat around her.

'Sabine, what's wrong?' I said.

'Nothing.'

'You're too thin.'

'I lose my appetite,' she said irritably. 'It happens. Then it comes right again.'

'A few months ago, you were fine—'

'That's what you think.'

I considered my time in the hospital, then in the flat. 'Are you ill?'

She pushed one of the glasses over to me; her nails were bitten to bleeding.

Coño barked.

'Are you looking after her for Earl?' I asked.

She narrowed her eyes. 'He said, *Why not take Coño for a bit, now that Meggie's never around?*'

'That's not fair.'

'No?' She took out her phone, glancing at the screen. 'Can you walk with me to St Pancras? I need to get the 19.39 to Paris.'

'Sure,' I said.

She downed her wine, then said, 'Drink.'

I shook my head.

'C'mon, Meggie . . .' She smiled.

After downing my wine too, I followed her across the concourse to a back exit. Behind the building, I felt disoriented. The streets between King's Cross and St Pancras were deserted. The Channel Tunnel was being extended, both stations refurbished and connected. The blocks around us had become demolition or construction sites. Cranes, gaping holes, rows of metal rods and scaffolding.

Sabine stopped under the sulphurous light of a streetlamp.

I gave Coño a scratch between the ears and she growled at me. *Yeah, I deserve it*, I thought. I hadn't been in touch with Earl for months either.

When I looked back at Sabine, her eyes were wet. She'd never cried in front of me before. Reaching out, I touched her sleeve. I felt the coarse material of her coat, her arm buried like a twig inside.

Clumsily, I grabbed the bulky black folds. I pulled her to me and held her. She was so insubstantial that it felt like holding someone else. But when she gave me that look, her dimpled half-smile . . .

Despite my intentions, we started to kiss.

Immediately it felt wrong. Our movements were the same but her breath had the sharpness of fasting. Her saliva was bitter and metallic; her boniness was disturbing. We'd never kissed without an audience, and I wanted to lose myself in it. But I couldn't.

Sabine broke away, tossing her head. Flecks of yellow light reflected in her eyes. Her face became closed, distant. 'Goodbye, Meggie.'

I stared at her.

Then she said, 'That's it. We're done.'

Everything was over.

And in that moment, I saw her again as I had in the office when I opened my eyes and she was *there*. Fascinating, free, unreachable . . . and way beyond anything I'd ever be.

I was just somebody who'd followed her for a short while. Somebody whose hand now reached out and slapped her face. Hard.

Her cheeks coloured. 'What was that for?'

She slapped me back but a play slap, a kitten slap.

My cheek didn't sting but my eyes did.

'Why d'you leave me in the club?' I heard myself say. 'These guys—'

'It's always *these guys*—'

I stared at her. 'What?'

'You get out of it, and then you're absolutely—'

'And you can talk, Sabine?'

'With you, it's different. Like Earl says, you don't respect yourself.'

'Really?' The night slowed down. 'What else has Earl said?'

'Nothing, Meggie.' She looked confused, then concerned.

'Don't pretend to care, Sabine. Where were you that day?'

'What day?'

'After the club—'

'I told you, I left a message. My mother asked me to go home.'

I shook my head. 'I saw you in the Mayfair flat.'

'So you were spying?'

'I needed you!'

'Why couldn't you just say?'

'Like you *just say* things? *Let's work three weeks in a row, let's go to Brazil?* And then you disappear.'

'You didn't want me, Meggie. Already by then you had decided.'

I clenched my fists. 'For a year and a half, *I* have fitted in with *your* life, Sabine. With how you led it. With what you wanted.'

'Is that true?'

'Yes.'

'What do you know about me after your *year and a half*?'

My breath was uneven; my head throbbed.

'You used me,' she continued. 'Used, then dropped. Like you dropped Graham—'

My arm went back intending another slap. But my fist was tight, my body was tight. I swung at her full force.

She turned but into the punch. My ring hit bone. Her head kept moving with the impact but she didn't stumble or fall.

There was a pause. Stillness.

What have I done?

Slowly, she looked back at me.

Blood was coming from her mouth. She swallowed several times. She put her hand to her jaw, stroking it. Then she laughed.

Coño began to bark, straining at her lead. She whined until Sabine gave in to her. Together they headed away, towards a footpath through the construction site.

I watched them go with my heart thrashing.

Then Sabine stopped and turned back.

She threw something, calling, 'To remember me by.'

After she was gone, I bent down and picked up what had hit me.

It was a tooth.

PART VI

43

For two decades I've kept her tooth in the heart-shaped box.

Glancing up at where I've put it, I take a sip of cold coffee and carry on. Typing has become the sound that soothes me most on the nights I can't sleep. It's like I'm trying to crack a code; the light taps are the different combinations. I don't know what I'm doing. But a few moves forward, a few back, I keep on.

King's Cross was the last time Sabine and I were together. Though I was also never again free of her. She became part of the fabric of my mind; a line of the music in my head; a colour, the colour blue, whenever I saw it. Because of her, I learned French, even lived with a French partner near the border of Belgium in the Ardennes. When the misconceived relationship ended, I stumbled into a job as a freelance translator; over the years, it turned into a career.

Yet Sabine was more than in the language, the subtle tonalities, the pulse of what I was, what I had become. Ideas of her life continued to influence me long after we lost contact. The nature of the influence shifted according to the

various endings, like ledges, which I assumed she'd scaled or
fallen to.

Once, I thought I saw her at Piccadilly Circus. I was thirty-
two, so she would have been the same. Standing by a bin, she
was eating a greasy pastry. Her appearance had changed. She
was thick-waisted and heavy-limbed, her hair dyed a prematurely middle-aged burgundy; even her elfin features seemed
broader, coarsened. She wore a fake fur coat and make-up
that looked gaudy in the daylight. Discarding the wrapper,
she slurped from a paper cup and belched. When she tried
to squash the cup in the bin, it wouldn't fit. She checked to
see if a woman a few paces away had noticed.

Her companion had red trainers, splayed legs, and a
jumper with a giant yellow M&M on it. She watched sullenly
as Sabine licked the grease from her fingers. Thick flakes of
pastry caught in the faux fur of her coat's collar. As she
turned her head, slowly, like an injured animal, I withdrew
into the doorway of a sports shop. I allowed myself to be
pushed past several rails of luminous polyester t-shirts
before elbowing my way out.

By then, Sabine had left. Gone.

Just as in nightmares I start by whispering 'help' then
escalate to a shout, I called, quietly at first, 'Sabine,' then
louder, 'SABINE, *SABINE!*'

Amidst the honking of buses and cars, I ran across the
intersection. Shoving through a crowd mesmerized by a
beatbusker, I climbed the steps of the Shaftesbury Memorial
Fountain. From the top, I scanned the streets for a black

coat alongside a giant yellow M&M jumper. Both had disappeared.

Later, I felt guilty about what Sabine appeared to have become. Had my violence towards her been the start of it? Yet along with guilt, I nursed a shameful sense of schadenfreude. I went home grateful, so, so grateful, that my new partner was a neat, normal man rather than a giant yellow M&M jumper person. Though we'd been on the verge of splitting up, I stayed with him for another five years. Or to be more accurate, I stayed until I came across the next temporary ending to Sabine's story.

Although I'd googled her on and off plenty of times and found nothing, one night I located her name in an interview on a personal travel blog. She was a diving instructor on the Cayman Islands. Her girlfriend owned a bar on the beach. In a photograph, the two of them clasped hands. Sabine's eyes were covered by bug-eye dark glasses but she looked no different from when she was twenty-three. Her tooth was fixed and they were grinning into the camera like mischievous kids. The sun was going down behind them over a clear stretch of aquamarine.

My tired eyes hurt; my heart limped with great thuds. So, I'd got it wrong about Piccadilly Circus. So, she hadn't been sexually complex; she'd just not fancied me enough. So, she'd left anything fucked up with men far behind. She'd found herself a fairytale ending after all.

I don't believe it was mere coincidence that shortly afterwards my neat, normal partner and I split up. The idea that

Sabine had grabbed at something out of the ordinary made me long to have the courage to do the same.

Except, I didn't. We had to sell the flat we'd bought together. Then a significant translation project came through. In a stroke of luck, I managed to rent the newly converted loft above the artist's place where I'd lived before. Now eighty-seven, she was as inspirational as ever. But though for a time my guilt about Sabine subsided, I still somehow couldn't find the energy to truly change my life.

44

Last January, I enrolled on a creative writing course called *Release Your Creativity*. Classes were held in a local church crypt and the tutor was enthusiastically dippy. Since I hadn't ever released a sentence that wasn't a modification of someone else's, I reckoned there was nothing to lose.

At the fourth or fifth class, we were given newspapers to scan. The idea was to tear out anything that snagged us without bothering to question why. We were supposed to do the exercise through the eyes of a character we'd invented. Determined to keep things impersonal, my character was a cyborg sex worker called Capucine's mechanical cat called Tom. But what stopped me halfway through my stack had nothing to do with either of them.

It was a short article about a woman found dead in her home in Peckham. Police estimated that she had been dead for seven months. She was only discovered because new neighbours wanted to ask about an adjoining roof leak. The woman was believed to have been forty-four at the time of her death. Given the body's state of decomposition, it was impossible to determine what had killed her. The condition of the house indicated that she might have been a hoarder. Originally from Belgium, she'd lived in London since the late nineties. The online retailer thought to have been her last employer was unavailable for comment. A colleague from a previous place she'd worked at, Denton Ink Cartridges, said of her, 'She was a smashing girl. Pretty, funny, caring, popular. She remembered our birthdays. She made us these great cards. I can't believe this happened to her.'

I excused myself to go to the toilet. In the cubicle, I looked up the story on my phone. It had broken a week ago and was repeated in several online sources. One showed a photograph of the staff at Denton Ink with a circle around a pale woman with short black hair. Another had an obituary-type last line: *She is survived by her brother, Xavier Dubreil.*

Sabine was dead. Her brother was not. Never had been.

As I left the church the afternoon turned dark, blustery and cold. Bare trees lined the pavement like bony hands grasping for the sky. Segueing off into the privacy of an empty common, I listened to the swish of damp grass.

I wondered about Sabine's beach bar girlfriend. What had happened to being a diving instructor in the Caymans? I thought of an idea I'd had more recently, perhaps not an idea so much as a dare, to get in touch with her. Of the wasted hours I'd spent swinging indecisively between whether to or not, thinking about what I'd say to her – when all the while she'd been dead. Lying dead, with nobody even aware of it, in a house in Peckham.

Despite having been teetotal for years, when I got home I cracked open a bottle of whiskey. Then I trawled the internet again. There was no additional news on Sabine's death, nor anything regarding the Cayman Islands. Though I did find a photograph of her in a black swimsuit, hair streaming, bare-faced, pulling herself out of a lido.

She looked like a little girl; I desperately wanted to hug her. Remembering her lie about her brother, I felt stupid for trying to be like her. I thought of her being a hoarder, of her not wanting me to visit her place, of the fear it must have evoked in her. More than ever, I wanted to befriend her again, to do better by her. Of course she'd made birthday cards for people at work. That was what she was like. I missed her in a way I'd never allowed myself to before. She looked so alive.

Folding my arms on the desk, I buried my head in them.

When grey daylight woke me I remembered why I'd stopped overdoing it with the booze. Not the headache or the nausea but the anxiety. Huge, as if I'd accidentally killed someone. I plugged the charger into my phone. A client wanted a video conference at eleven about an art catalogue. There was also a missed call from a number I didn't

recognize. The caller had left a voicemail. 'Meggie, this is Earl
from back in the day. Found you through your translation
site. Don't know if you've heard, and sorry to break the news
if not, but SJ died. There's a funeral tomorrow. Her bro from
Japan asked me to tell those she used to work with. I'll text
the address. Hope you can be there.'

45

If Sabine had been taller, about forty and tanned berry-
brown, if Sabine had been male with brown-black eyes and
no squint – then she might have looked something like the
man who stood alone in the front row of the crematorium.

I'd arrived late. Somehow I'd managed to get lost. To think
I had the wrong crematorium and cycle to another one, only
to have to cycle back. The small hall was overheated and
stuffy. None of the people there looked like those I'd have
imagined in Sabine's life. Most were middle-aged and older,
conventionally dressed. I vaguely recognized a handful from
the Energy office, a few more from even further back when
we'd worked days.

The speaker at the lectern was scrawny and balding, with
a grey beard. He was reading an obscure text which, having
missed the first part, I couldn't make sense of. I didn't think
it was religious; there was no mention of God, although it
addressed the listener as 'Brother', and had a religious tone.

I slunk into the back row next to Sherry and Earl. Sherry's

hair was still grey at the roots but the rest was ivy-green and shaped in a pompadour style. She didn't look that different in her sixties to how she'd looked twenty years ago: still like an old child, pretty much. Earl's hair was grown out into a statement Afro and he was wearing an olive pin-striped suit that comprised trousers with a sort of straitjacket. It wouldn't have been right for everyone but he pulled it off. He passed me a hipflask. Assuming it contained vodka, I took a hefty gulp. It was so strong that I almost spat it out. He patted my back, more as if to say 'well done' than to stop me choking. The afterburn spread through my body; I felt as if I were being illuminated. Sherry smiled while dabbing her puffy eyes with an embroidered hanky.

I stared at the dark wooden casket. Mauve lilies lay on top of it. I could almost hear Sabine say, *The colour of the old ladies' hair.* Her soft, low drawl. I thought of the satin inside the casket. Sabine laid out on the satin. Like a jewel. Not like a jewel: she'd been dead seven months. Like something unbearable to think of, that had nothing to do with her.

When the service was over, a few phrases of piano music tinkled through the air. Then it stopped. I realized it wasn't a recording; there was an upright piano in the crematorium. I shifted to get a better view. The man who had been at the front adjusted the stool and started again. He played with a light, effortless touch.

The red velvet curtains at the foot of the casket parted.

The music was almost sentimental but not quite. Simple, repetitive, sweet, it seemed distantly familiar to me, though

I couldn't place it. I was sure I'd never heard it from Sabine. It wasn't her type of music. I thought of my embarrassment when she'd bobbed her head to the start of Prokofiev's *Romeo and Juliet.*

The casket slid towards the curtains. The idea of Sabine being inside it felt forced. The ideas of Sabine being a hoarder, of Sabine having a brother who was alive, those were foreign enough. But Sabine dead? And dead for seven months? The words, the place, the music, the coffin: I struggled to connect them with the person I thought I'd known.

The coffin slowly slid through the curtains.

When the music ended, the crematorium was quiet. I'd asked Sabine once, *What music would you like in the afterlife?* She'd said, *Silence.* I wondered if she'd told the man at the piano something different. He smoothed a piece of navy felt over the piano keys and, gently, put the lid of the piano down. I felt strangely moved by his delicate tribute.

The red velvet curtains closed and the coffin disappeared.

The pub closest to the crematorium had green carpet tiles, a wall-mounted TV, and an imitation antique clock with hands stuck on a quarter past three. Unlike the White Hart, it didn't have a plastic pink stag's head festooned with fairy lights above the bar. Nor did it have a jukebox. But it had a fruit machine: two apples in a row next to a number seven.

'Have a go?'

I turned to see the pianist next to me at the bar. He had

something of Sabine's drawl, though his voice was deeper and louder. 'I was wondering who'd come here in the mood to play,' I said.

He cocked an eyebrow. 'Sabine would. She could never resist fruit machines.'

'You're her brother?'

'Yes, my name's Xavier. And you are?'

'Meggie.'

'Nice to meet you, Meggie.' After getting a large red wine, he moved off.

With three of the same, I headed back to Sherry and Earl.

We clinked our glasses. 'SJ.'

There was a silence.

Then Sherry said, 'Can you believe nobody missed her in seven months?'

'I hadn't seen her in about twenty years,' I said.

'Ditto,' said Earl. 'Big city. People move on.'

'Still,' said Sherry. 'Nobody.'

'It's easy to fall off the grid,' said Earl. 'She obviously had mental health issues.'

'Maybe she got involved with an abusive guy,' said Sherry. 'He isolated her until he was all she had. Then . . .' She slit her hand across her neck.

'She might have been murdered?' I said.

'Murder, suicide. We'll never know,' said Earl.

We were all quiet, chastened.

Eventually, I said to Earl, 'It's strange to see you without Coño.'

'She died seven years ago in February.' Earl rubbed a knuckle in the corner of his eye.

'How?' I said.

'Canine bloat.'

'I'm sorry, Earl. She was a great dog.'

'Her greatness lives on in her daughter,' said Sherry.

'What's the daughter called?'

'Also Coño,' said Earl.

'Why d'you call every dog Coño?'

''S a beautiful name,' said Earl. 'The best.'

I drank some more wine. Then I said, 'I thought some of the others might be here. Like Lizard—'

'He's gone Mexican,' said Sherry.

'Remember the shift leader? She's with him in Mexico City,' said Earl.

'Otherwise they'd have come,' said Sherry.

'And Prawn?' I said. 'Where's he gone to?'

Sherry and Earl exchanged a look.

I said, 'Mexico? Thailand? India?'

'The Scrubs,' said Earl. 'Got three years for dealing.'

'Shit,' I said.

'It was fucking unlucky,' said Earl. 'The pigs were chasing someone else. They broke into his flat by mistake. Then their dogs went mad—'

'It's not all bad, though,' said Sherry. 'He's made some good friends.'

'Yeah, we'll see,' said Earl. 'Good friends can be a problem.'

'That's true,' I said.

I wished I hadn't said it. I gulped my wine.

Then Sherry said, 'Anyway, he'll be staying with us when he gets out.'

I said, 'Us?'

Earl looked sheepish.

Sherry planted a purple rose of lipstick on Earl's cheek.

'Guess who got lucky,' she said.

After Earl and Sherry had left, I sought out Xavier. He was by the window talking to an elderly man. I got myself another red wine and waited at the bar. There were plenty of people milling around but they seemed to belong to another group; most of those who'd been at Sabine's service had gone.

Xavier wore leather brogue boots, charcoal jeans, and a sandy shirt under a brown plaid blazer. Stylish, as Sabine had been. I couldn't hear what he and the elderly man were saying although it didn't seem particularly intense; they looked like spectators commenting on a distant cricket match. Xavier fiddled from time to time with a leather thong around his wrist. Neither seemed in a hurry to end the conversation.

After I finished the wine, I went to the bathroom. I touched up my make-up, refreshed my perfume and smoothed my hair.

When I came out, Xavier and the elderly man had gone. Looking up and down the road in front of the pub, I couldn't see either of them. How could they have disappeared? Perhaps they'd visited the Gents while I was in the Ladies. Returning to the pub, I scanned it methodically. A back exit led out into the car park.

There were plenty of cars but no pedestrians.

'Shit,' I said loudly. 'Shit, shit.'

'Need a lift?' said a man's voice.

Xavier was in an old yellow convertible parked by the fence, smoking a cigarette.

'No,' I said. 'Though I wouldn't mind one of those.'

He waved an empty carton for me to see. 'The pub has a vending machine.'

'OK, thanks.'

I turned, then turned back. 'I liked what you played. The tune seemed familiar but I can't place it.'

'It's a ballet tune,' he said. 'Ta ta tada tada, ta ta tada tada . . . Often used for warm-ups at the bar.'

'You play for ballet classes?'

'Not any more. I did when Sabine and I were at school.'

'She could've been a brilliant dancer.'

'Could've been many brilliant things if she'd stuck at them,' he said.

'She was forced to stop dancing, though,' I said. 'Because of her fucked-up feet.'

'Yeah. Her fucked-up feet wanted to take her to – now, where was it that time? Goa, I think.'

I frowned at him. 'Then why the ballet music?'

'To annoy her.' He stubbed his cigarette out in the car's ashtray. 'She'd have appreciated the irony.'

'Could I – ask you some things about Sabine?'

He swung open the passenger door. 'Feel free.'

I climbed into his car. The interior was beautiful, soft saddle leather. Close up, Xavier appeared to be nearer fifty than forty. There were fine lines on his face, silver at his hairline. I wished I'd caught him in the pub. I felt the distinct absence of props. Wine glass. Cigarette. Loo escape. General buzz.

The silence between us lengthened.

He said, 'You're wondering how I didn't notice . . . ?'

'No,' I said. 'I—'

'Sabine went out of contact intermittently. I used to chase her, harass her, but it never really worked. When she wanted to go AWOL, it was best to let her be. She always rang eventually. Except this time she didn't.'

I shifted in my seat. 'Actually I wanted to ask something else.'

'Go ahead.'

'Did she ever mention me to you?'

'Might help if you tell me your name.'

'I told you in the pub. It's Meggie.'

He shook his head slowly. I looked out through the windshield at the wooden fence. A sign read, *Car Park. Patrons Only.* There was a weeping willow on the other side of the fence. An empty children's playground beyond the willow. I heard myself say, 'Sabine mentioned you to me.'

'Did she?'

'Yes.'

'What did she say?'

'That you were dead.'

Xavier burst out laughing. 'Typical Sabine! What death did she give me?'

I shook my head.

'You can't back out now, Meggie,' he said.

'Sorry. I shouldn't have told you.'

'It's OK,' he said.

'I'm trying to understand things—'

'Maybe I can help,' he said. 'But you need to tell me the rest.'

In a splurge of words, I told him everything I could remember. About his mother kicking him out, about the base jumping, and free climbing, and finally about him diving to his death off a high rock into a deep pool.

When I finished, he was silent.

Spots of scarlet appeared at his temples.

'I'm sorry.' I tried to open the door.

But he grabbed my arm. 'Sabine needed attention, Meggie. She didn't care what she did to get it. She had these crazy destructive stunts. Everybody gave up on her. They had to because she screwed them over. One, by one, by one. I was the only person in our family who still spoke to her.'

'She was very popular at work,' I said, shaking off his grasp. 'I did nightshifts with her many years back. But I also read about a guy at Denton Ink—'

'Denton Ink? She didn't need to do these menial jobs.'

'Menial?'

'The family has properties in London. She was in one when she died. She had everything going for her. She could do anything she wanted. What did she choose? Cartridges? Cutting up newspapers all night? Gluing them back together again?'

'That was pretty much it.'

'You said you worked with her?'

'Yeah, if work's what you'd call it.'

He gave a deep laugh, unexpectedly warm.

Suddenly I felt as if I could ask him anything. I thought of the photograph of Sabine as a child. The one I'd swapped with mine on the board when I did days. I said, 'What made her like that? What happened to her?'

Xavier sighed. 'You want to know?'

'Yes.'

'This is the saddest part.'

'I want to know.'

He kept staring in front of him for so long I thought he'd decided not to tell me. Then he said, 'Nothing.'

'What do you mean, *nothing*?'

'She had a nice childhood. We had a good, stable home.'

'Didn't your father leave?'

'When I was seventeen, so she was twelve, our father died. This was a tragedy, it hit her hard. But Sabine's problems started before then. My mother did everything a parent can do for us. Everything and more. Nothing made Sabine like that. Nothing happened to her. Nothing.'

Beyond the willow tree, a scrawny little girl with a nest of fuzzy hair ran across the playground and hid in a green metal barrel. 'Arabella?' a woman called after her.

Xavier said, 'You know what else?'

'What?'

'I am angry with her. *But* – whatever trouble she caused, and Sabine caused massive trouble – I've never had more fun with anybody.'

'Me too,' I said.

He turned to me as if a thought had occurred. 'Were you her girlfriend?'

'No.'

He smiled as if he didn't quite believe me. I was glad he didn't.

'Arabella!' called the woman. 'Where are you? Answer me immediately!'

'I need to get to a class,' I said.

'I'll give you a lift.'

'It's fine, I've got my bike.' I opened the door.

He took a business card from his glove compartment. 'Meggie, many people were taken in by Sabine. I'm in town for another week. If it helps, I can answer your questions. I can tell you everything you want to know. I can even show you some photographs.'

'Thanks,' I said. 'I appreciate it.'

He scribbled a number on the back of the card and handed it to me. 'Give me a call.'

46

We met up the day after the funeral in a large department store coffee shop. Xavier seemed reserved. Then we got lost in the kitchen section coming out, and the mood between us changed. He bought a red-and-white picnic basket on the spur of the moment. Leaving the till, he stared at the purchase as if it had magically appeared in his hand. 'Your fault, this,' he said.

'My fault?' I said.

'So now, tomorrow, we have a picnic,' he said.

It was still very much winter, but the next day I sat on a tartan blanket in the middle of Hyde Park and listened to him until an icy cloudburst soaked us. To make up, the date after that, only four hours later, was in a swanky Knightsbridge restaurant. He talked and talked and wanted to talk more. Despite my ability to speak his language, English suited us both, played to our fantasies perhaps. After the meal, we went to a hotel bar. Then we went to his hotel bar. When it closed, we went up to his suite. And so our affair began.

From the start, all the time that we spent together was punctuated by conversations about Sabine. He needed to talk about her, and I allowed him to think I did too. In truth, his accounts of her bore almost no relation to the person I had known. His stories meandered contradictorily; some recollections seemed fantastical, others surprisingly dour. Once, he put me on the phone to the elderly Irish au pair who had looked after them as children; her descriptions of Sabine as 'timid, sensitive, soft-hearted and prone to fits of crying' were no more illuminating.

Everybody had their own version of Sabine. With this in mind, I let Xavier's stories wash over me. They were compensated for by the instances when glimpses of Sabine slipped through. His presence could be almost as visceral as hers, as compelling. His gestures had her unpredictable quickness. When he was tired, his brown-black eyes developed a slight squint. I kept him up late deliberately; I plied him with espresso martinis strong on caffeine. And then there was his voice; from the beginning I thought I recognized beneath the boyish boldness something of her timbre. Soon I discovered that if I spoke softly to him, he spoke softly back. Her low, soft tones emerged behind his; soft, low words pulsed back and forth between us.

At night in bed his skin was hot, just as hers had been. Like her, he tossed around and threw the duvet off. Like her, when he slept he seemed sufficient unto himself: solemn, untouchable. Unlike her, when he awoke he drew me to him. He held me so tightly I could scarcely breathe, though I stayed in his embrace for as long as he would allow.

Everything during those weeks we spent together seemed poignantly heightened. I turned down translation jobs. He postponed his flight back to Japan. We often stayed up until the dawn chorus sang us to sleep. We ate dark chocolate for breakfast. We watched films in empty cinemas at midday. We fed the ducks and geese in St James's Park. We did all the things that lovers do when the city is their playground. Though I knew that it couldn't last, when he asked if I'd move to Kyoto, I said yes.

Only hours later, as I returned to my flat, I got a call from a woman with a Japanese accent. Could I please stop chasing her husband? Could I please leave her Xavier alone? He had promised to be at Akihiko's birthday. Who's Akihiko? I asked. She said, Our eldest son. If Xavi didn't leave soon, he would miss the occasion. Could I please just let him come home?

I rang Xavier the moment I got off the phone but he didn't pick up. When I hadn't heard from him by evening, I blocked his number. Then I blocked his address from my emails and activated a vacation auto-response on my account:

Away for some time. Will reply to messages only intermittently.

I couldn't block my postal address, and it was through the post that Xavier sent his single addendum to our affair. A rectangular package covered in postmarks from Japan. It contained the scarab pendant with *My Sabine* engraved on the back. His note provided no apology, no explanation – just, *I gave this to Sabine. She'd want you to have it. X*

*

After the affair ended, I began battling with insomnia. I started out doing everything you're supposed to do. The things I'd done when I worked nights, updated with contemporary extras. A strict sleep schedule with minimal time in bed. Rigorous daily exercise with no naps. No tea or coffee after midday. Plus sleep stories, hygiene checklists, and soothing meditations on smartphone apps.

None of it helped. The moment I lay down in the dark, I saw Sabine as painfully thin as she had been at the station. The way she had turned her face into my punch. At Piccadilly Circus licking her fingers by the bin. I heard myself ask if a lover had given her the pendant, and her say that was one way to put it. I remembered her face underwater in the Hampstead Pond. I got stuck on morbid last scenes in a way that would have made her angry. But when they weren't at the forefront of my mind, it was worse.

Eventually, I consulted my doctor. She spoke about counselling or antidepressants, or sleeping pills as a last resort. Given my lack of enthusiasm for these options, she suggested focusing on something pragmatic. Insomnia could be your body's way of rousing you to get on with a task. An activity you had previously been blind to, or neglectful of, in your waking hours.

I cleared my desk of French–English dictionaries, soup bowls and coffee mugs. What I had to do, the shadow thing that had been waiting its turn, was write. I thought of returning to the course in the crypt but sleep deprivation made me a snail needful of my shell; the idea of heading into the city's bustle was about as appealing as a sprinkling of salt.

Instead, when the night withdrew into its quietest hours, I put on my lamp. I sat down in front of my computer. I didn't feel drawn to exploring the cyborg sex worker with her mechanical cat. I needed to write about something that burns in me like phosphorus. Someone I can't extinguish from my mind.

Who else could I ever write about?

I have almost made a story of what happened. Most of what I remember is here, though the memories are continuously shifting. I have my theories about Sabine but that's all they are; she's no longer my Sabine any more than she is yours. As I gaze at a streak of crimson in the slate sky, for a moment I don't know whether it is dawn or dusk. But no matter.

When the thickest part of the night comes around again, I'll sit on the blue silk throw that covers the sofa. After lighting five white tealight candles, I'll smoke a cigarette. Playing some of our favourite tracks, I'll drink tequila toasts. To what can never be resolved: to endings, to Sabine. I will open the heart-shaped box.

And then, when I am ready, I will write the final sentence.

ACKNOWLEDGEMENTS

Thanks to Matthew Francis for sage advice throughout.

Thanks to Howard Lester, Rachel Mendel and Melanie Newman for insightful feedback.

Thanks to Evan James for open generosity and valued judgement.

Thanks to Greg Keen for trenchant critique, time and again.

And thank you to my father, Glen Ladner, the storyteller I was so lucky to have as a child.

Also, thanks to Cathryn Summerhayes, my extra-mile agent at Curtis Brown, and to Anna Davis at CBC for introducing us. Thanks to Ravi Mirchandani for his intuition and vision. Charlotte Greig for her all-round editorial wisdom. Emma Bravo, Grace Harrison, Chloe May, Roshani Moorjani and all the team at Picador for their generous enthusiasm for the book. Emilie Fauré for specific and timely input.

Finally thanks to Aberystwyth University for the PhD funding that gave me the time to write *Nightshift*.